JOURNAL FOR THE STUDY OF THE NEW TESTAMENT SUPPLEMENT SERIES

220

Executive Editor
Stanley E. Porter

Sheffield Academic Press
A Continuum imprint

The Temple of Jesus' Body

The Temple Theme in the Gospel of John

Alan R. Kerr

Journal for the Study of the New Testament
Supplement Series 220

Copyright © 2002 Sheffield Academic Press
A Continuum imprint

Published by Sheffield Academic Press Ltd
The Tower Building, 11 York Road, London SE1 7NX
370 Lexington Avenue, New York NY 10017-6550

www.SheffieldAcademicPress.com
www.continuumbooks.com

British Library Cataloguing-in-Publication Data

A catalogue record for this book is available from the British Library

Typeset by Sheffield Academic Press
Printed on acid-free paper in Great Britain by Bookcraft Ltd, Midsomer Norton, Bath

ISBN 1-84127-262-0

In loving memory of my father and mother,
Dick and Barbara

CONTENTS

PREFACE

This study is an exploration of the Temple theme in the Gospel of John. Numerous scholars have detected Temple allusion in John, but when I embarked on this study there had been no systematic and sustained treatment of the topic. Dr Paul Trebilco encouraged me to pursue this line of enquiry and so over the past eight years I have worked on this study. I am conscious that it is an unfinished task—that there are more Temple references in John to be uncovered and analysed. However, I am confident that what is offered here points in the direction of Jesus being the fulfilment and replacement of the Temple and its associated festivals.

Throughout my study I have been supported and encouraged by a number of people and organizations. I am indebted to the Presbyterian Church of Aotearoa New Zealand, who financially contributed towards my travel to the United Kingdom in 1995 through the Bill and Margaret Best Travel Fund; to the trustees of the Helmut Rex Trust for a grant to offset costs incurred with the 1995 study leave; and to the congregation and Session of the then Andersons Bay Presbyterian Church, whose generous provision of study leave made my overseas research possible and whose encouragement and support throughout the project has been much appreciated. I also record my warm thanks to the Revd John Proctor, Director of New Testament Studies, Westminster College, Cambridge, who supervised my three and half months' study leave in the United Kingdom. He read everything I wrote during that period, raised useful points for discussion and offered helpful suggestions. I am very grateful for his interest and kindness. My thanks also to the Warden and staff of Tyndale House, Cambridge, for making their accommodation and library facilities available during my stay in Cambridge.

Here in Dunedin I have been accorded long-term lending privileges from both the Hewitson Library of Knox College and the Central Library of the University of Otago. I am thankful for the patience of the staff in both libraries and their diligent persistence in tracking down elusive titles.

During the summer holidays of 1997 and 1998 I was able to spend time studying at Waihola, just south of Dunedin. Thank you to the Council of Christian Youth Camps, who allowed me the use of their accommodation, and also to the Manager, Grant Bullin and his wife Joanne, for their kind hospitality during both periods of study.

While Dr Paul Trebilco was away during 1994, Dr Gregory Dawes of the Department of Theology and Religious Studies of the University of Otago, guided me in my research and I thank him for his help.

On the academic front my main thanks goes to Dr Paul Trebilco. He has been unfailingly supportive and encouraging throughout my eight years of study. His meticulous attention to detail, his gentle nudging to consider an alternative view, his wide knowledge of the field of New Testament Studies alerting me to possible academic 'land mines', his generosity with his time, his sympathy for the project, and his kindness and patience all leave me profoundly in debt. It has been a privilege to have worked with him. I am also grateful to Dr Derek Tovey, Dr Judith McKinlay and Dr Robert Hayward who read my work in full and made many useful comments for improvement.

I am also thankful for many friends and colleagues who have given me incidental encouragement along the way. In particular I mention my friend Dr Steuart Henderson who has followed my study with interest and raised questions to stimulate further thought.

I am grateful to Sheffield Academic Press who accepted my manuscript and have carefully prepared it for publication. Although the editorial staff have been meticulously thorough in eliminating errors I accept responsibility for any that remain.

My chief thanks goes to my dear wife, Marion, and my children who have had to put up with me spending long hours in the study. Their support and love, throughout this project, means most to me.

Alan R. Kerr
Dunedin, New Zealand

ABBREVIATIONS

AB	Anchor Bible
ABR	*Australian Biblical Review*
Anbib	Analecta biblica
ATR	*Anglican Theological Review*
AUSS	*Andrews University Seminary Studies*
BDB	Francis Brown, S.R. Driver and Charles A. Briggs, *A Hebrew and English Lexicon of the Old Testament* (Oxford: Clarendon Press, 1907)
BDF	Friedrich Blass, A. Debrunner and Robert W. Funk, *A Greek Grammar of the New Testament and Other Early Christian Literature* (Cambridge: Cambridge University Press, 1961)
BETL	Bibliotheca ephemeridum theologicarum lovaniensium
BHS	*Biblia hebraica stuttgartensia*
Bib	*Biblica*
BJS	Brown Judaic Studies
BTB	*Biblical Theology Bulletin*
CBQ	*Catholic Biblical Quarterly*
CBQMS	Catholic Biblical Quarterly Monograph Series
ConBNT	Coniectanea biblica, New Testament
Ebib	Etudes bibliques
ETL	*Ephemerides theologicae lovanienses*
EvQ	*Evangelical Quarterly*
ExpTim	*Expository Times*
HTCNT	Herder's Theological Commentary on the New Testament
HTR	*Harvard Theological Review*
ICC	International Critical Commentaries
Int	*Interpretation*
JBL	*Journal of Biblical Literature*
JPH	Jewish Passover Haggadah
JSNT	*Journal for the Study of the New Testament*
JSNTSup	*Journal for the Study of the New Testament*, Supplement Series
JSOT	*Journal for the Study of the Old Testament*
JSOTSup	*Journal for the Study of the Old Testament*, Supplement Series
JTS	*Journal of Theological Studies*

LAE	Life of Adam and Eve
LAS	Libreria Ateneo Salesiano
LCL	Loeb Classical Library
LXX	The Septuagint
MT	Massoretic Text
NCB	New Century Bible
NEB	*New English Bible*
Neot	*Neotestamentica*
NICNT	New International Commentary on the New Testament
NRSV	New Revised Standard Version
NovT	*Novum Testamentum*
NTS	New Testament Studies
NovTSup	Novum Testamentum Supplement
OTP	James Charlesworth (ed.), *Old Testament Pseudepigrapha*
P. Oxy.	Oxyrhyncus Papyri
RB	*Revue Biblique*
RSR	*Recherches de science religieuse*
RSV	Revised Standard Version
SBLASP	Society of Biblical Literature Annual Seminar Papers
SBLDS	Society of Biblical Literature Dissertation Series
SBLMS	Society of Biblical Literature Monograph Series
SBLSP	Society of Biblical Literature Seminar Papers
SBLSS	SBL Semeia Studies
SBT	Studies in Biblical Theology
SCM	Student Christian Movement
SJT	*Scottish Journal of Theology*
SNTSMS	Society for New Testament Studies Monograph Series
TB	*Tyndale Bulletin*
TDNT	Gerhard Kittel and Gerhard Friedrich (eds.), *Theological Dictionary of the New Testament* (trans. Geoffrey W. Bromiley; 10 vols.; Grand Rapids: Eerdmans, 1964–)
TDOT	G.J. Botterweck and H. Ringgren (eds.), *Theological Dictionary of the Old Testament*
TGUOS	*Transactions of the Glasgow University Oriental Society*
TLZ	*Theologische Literaturzeitung*
TPI	Trinity Press International
VT	*Vetus Testamentum*
WBC	Word Biblical Commentary
WTJ	*Westminster Theological Journal*
WUNT	Wissenschaftliche Untersuchungen zum Neuen Testament
ZNW	*Zeitschrift für neutestamentliche Wissenschaft*

Chapter 1

INTRODUCTION

1.1 *The Aim of the Study*

R.E. Brown, in the introduction to his commentary on the Gospel of John, mentions 'the importance given to the theme of Jesus' replacement of Jewish institutions like ritual purification, the Temple, and worship in Jerusalem (chs. ii–iv) and Jewish feasts like the Sabbath, Passover, Tabernacles and Dedication (chs. v–x)'.[1] Other scholars have similarly pointed out this theme.[2] Most have been content to mention the theme without allowing it to impact significantly on their exegesis. For example, Carson, in commenting on the Feast of Dedication (10.22) remarks: '…as with other feasts, this one, too is understood to be fulfilled in Jesus the Son of God.'[3] But the feast is only relevant in his comments on 10.36 where he speaks of Jesus' sanctification echoing the Feast of Dedication, which commemorates the sanctification of the Temple after it was desecrated. It has even less relevance for Barrett, who, in commenting on 10.22-42, says that 'it does not seem possible to detect any symbolical correspondence

---

1. R.E. Brown, *The Gospel According to John* (AB, 29–29a; 2 vols.; Garden City, NY: Doubleday, 1966, 1970), I, p. lxx.
2. D.A. Carson (*The Gospel According to John* [Grand Rapids: Eerdmans, 1991], p. 182) in commenting on 2.21 says: '…the human body of Jesus…[is] the living abode of God on earth, *the fulfilment of all the temple meant*, and the centre of all true worship (over against all other claims of "holy space", 4.20-24)' (my italics). C.K. Barrett (*The Gospel According to St John* [London: SPCK, 2nd edn, 1978], p. 201), remarks on 2.21: 'the human body of Jesus was the place where a unique manifestation of God took place and consequently became the only true Temple, the only centre of true worship…' Further he maintains that John was in 'opposition to the Jerusalem Temple.' B. Lindars (*The Gospel of John* [NCB; London: Oliphants, 1972], p. 144) is more sceptical about allowing 2.21 to have any relevance beyond the pericope of 2.13-22. He offers no suggestion that Jesus might be the fulfilment and/or replacement of the Temple.
3. Carson, *John*, p. 391.

between the conduct of the feast and the ensuing discussion'.[4]

On the other hand, Moloney allows the replacement theme, with regard to the Dedication Festival, to pervade his exegesis more extensively. Not only is it pertinent for his discussion of Jesus' sanctification in 10.36,[5] but it is also relevant in his comments on the hostility of the Jews towards Jesus:

> Israel had lost its Temple because leading Jews betrayed YHWH and his people. Will 'the Jews' stand by their resolve never again to betray their God? 'The Jews' take up stones against Jesus (v. 31), repeating the profanations of Antiochus IV and his representatives. They are attempting to rid Israel of the visible presence of God in their midst... 'The Jews' continue to pay no heed to Jesus' claims, as they celebrate the feast of the Dedication, remembering the reconsecration of a temple built in stone by human beings. They betray their God as they attempt to eliminate the one who now dwells among them in the flesh of his only begotten Son (see 1.14; 8.30).[6]

The Feast of Dedication, which Moloney sees as relevant to Jesus' encounter with the Jews in Jn 10.22-39, is part of what I term the complex of Temple life—the Temple itself as the place of the presence of God and its associated festivals, priestly rituals and sacrifices.

The object of this study is to explore the theme of this complex of Temple life in the Gospel of John and demonstrate that it is a significant strand of thought in the Gospel. It is my contention that the Johannine Jesus replaces and fulfils the Jerusalem Temple and its cultic activity.

1.2 *Contemporary Scholarship*

1.2.1 *'Broad Brush' Studies*
Some intimation of possible Johannine Temple allusions was made in a section of R.J. McKelvey's book, *The New Temple*, published in 1969.[7]

---

4.   Barrett, *St John*, p. 379.

5.   F.J. Moloney, *Signs and Shadows: Reading John 5–12* (Philadelphia: Fortress Press, 1996), pp. 149-50.

6.   Moloney, *Signs and Shadows*, pp. 148-49.

7.   J. McKelvey, *The New Temple: The Church in the New Testament* (Oxford Theological Monographs; Oxford: Oxford University Press, 1969), pp. 75-84. McKelvey's book focuses on the image of the church as God's new Temple throughout the New Testament. He describes this as a 'neglected image' (p. vii) and states, 'Apart from Père Congar's book [Y. Congar, *The Mystery of the Temple: The Manner of God's Presence to His Creatures from Genesis to the Apocalypse* (trans. R. Trevett;

There he refers to 1.14; 2.13-22; 1.51; 4.20-26; 10.16;11.52 and 12.20-23. as having Temple connections.[8] He also drew into his discussion the festivals of Passover[9] and Tabernacles,[10] thereby indicating that they are relevant for the Temple theme in John. Understandably in so few pages, McKelvey's treatment is cursory, but even so it provides some useful hints in terms of texts and associated concepts for my exploration of the Temple complex theme in John.

Peter Walker's publication on Jesus and the Holy City presents a clear appraisal of the theological significance of the Temple in the New Testament.[11] He devotes a chapter to the Temple in the Fourth Gospel and concludes that the Tabernacle and Temple imagery (1.14; 2.21) point to a deeper truth concerning Jesus being the new 'place' where God dwells.[12] He explores the scene at Jacob's well and the festivals of Tabernacles and Dedication to show the way Jesus appropriates the symbolism of these Temple festivals. But he goes further, and in commenting on 'Jesus' explosive revelation that "before Abraham was, I am" (8.58)' he concludes:

> If this divine Name ('I am') was recited as part of the Tabernacles' liturgy, then Jesus was again using the Temple's ritual as a pointer to his identity. In this case however, what Jesus was appropriating to himself was not just some particular ritual within the Temple, but the whole essence of the Temple as being the dwelling place of the divine Name.[13]

Walker also sees the reference to 'my Father's house' (14.2) as an allusion to the Temple. For Walker this Temple is the heavenly Temple, where the disciples will dwell in the future. However, in the interim, the disciples themselves are to be the Temple, the place where God dwells through the agency of the Spirit.[14]

London: Burns & Oates, 1962)], which is a more general study, I know of no treatment of the subject' (p. vii; book title interpolated). Certainly that was almost 30 years ago, but even so, it points to the comparative neglect of the Temple theme in relation to the New Testament generally.

8. The last three texts deal with the gathering of *people* as the new Temple.

9. McKelvey, *The New Temple*, pp. 76-77.

10. McKelvey, *The New Temple*, pp. 75-76, 80, 81. McKelvey associates mention of water in John with Tabernacles and in turn connects the water pouring ceremony with the outpouring of the Spirit (p. 81).

11. P. Walker, *Jesus and the Holy City: New Testament Perspectives on Jerusalem* (Grand Rapids: Eerdmans, 1996).

12. Walker, *Jesus and the Holy City*, p. 164.

13. Walker, *Jesus and the Holy City*, p. 168.

14. Walker, *Jesus and the Holy City*, p. 171.

While Walker's chapter breaks some new ground and makes useful suggestions, as a 'broad-brush' New Testament survey, it understandably lacks detailed exegetical support.

1.2.2 *Detailed Exegetical Studies*

There have, however, been three detailed exegetical studies of Johannine texts where a Temple motif has been discerned. The first of these is *Destroy This Temple* by Lucius Nereparampil, published in 1978. The author describes this work as 'an exegetico-theological study on the meaning of Jesus' temple-logion in Jn 2.19'. After a thorough investigation of the text, Nereparampil draws two conclusions that are helpful for our study. He makes a distinction between the Temple-cleansing (2.14-16) and the Temple-Logion (2.19) and then says, 'Jesus' Temple-cleansing symbolically expresses the cessation of the old Temple and old economy of salvation, while his Temple-Logion symbolically proclaims the beginning of the new Temple and the new economy of salvation in his own person.'[15] This points to a shift from the old to the new that I believe undergirds Johannine thought on the Temple complex. The second conclusion I wish to highlight is that 'the Temple-Logion is a pointer to the *Sitz im Leben* of the Fourth Gospel'.[16] This sentence provides some justification for looking outside the text to ascertain strands of Jewish thinking about the Temple following its destruction. I will argue that the urgent question of the time was, What is to replace the Temple? And I will endeavour to demonstrate that the Johannine answer is Jesus.

The second study is James McCaffrey's *The House with Many Rooms: The Temple Theme of Jn 14, 2-3*, published in 1988. This thesis broke new ground by suggesting that there are Temple implications in Jn 14.2-3, part of one of the farewell discourses. Prior to this, Temple allusions had been detected almost exclusively in John 1–12. McCaffrey argued that Jn 14.2-3 had links with 2.13-22, which is obviously concerned with the Temple and where the new Temple is stated to be Jesus' resurrection body (2.21).[17] McCaffrey emphasized the word τόπος, which occurs twice in Jn 14.2-3 and interpreted it to mean 'temple' or 'sanctuary'.[18] He also made a con-

---

15. L. Nereparampil, *Destroy This Temple: An Exegetico-Theological Study on the Meaning of Jesus' Temple-Logion in Jn 2.19* (Bangalore: Dharmaram College, 1978), p. 90.

16. Nereparampil, *Temple-Logion*, p. 91.

17. J. McCaffrey, *The House with Many Rooms: The Temple Theme of Jn 14, 2-3* (Rome: Biblical Institute Press, 1988), pp. 185-91.

18. McCaffrey, *The House with Many Rooms*, p. 21.

nection between Jn 14.2-3 and 8.35 (a verse concerned with membership of the family) by means of the common phrase ἐν τῇ οἰκίᾳ, thus suggesting that the new Temple is the family of God.[19] In his seventh chapter McCaffrey made a brief study of what he called 'complementary texts' where he discerned the Johannine Temple theme, albeit through the lens of his interpretation of Jn 14.2-3.[20] These texts are useful suggestions for my research, some of which I will take up in the course of the study.

In her recent article[21] Judith Lieu highlights the importance of the Temple for John. She says that 'for John, the Temple is the supreme centre of "the Jews". If Paul thinks of "the Law", John thinks of "the Temple".'[22] She takes Jn 18.20 as a 'key to the pattern of [Jesus'] ministry'[23] and points out that all his teaching is 'in synagogue and in the temple'.[24] The Temple (and the synagogue) is the place of divine manifestation.

Lieu argues that the Johannine Jesus does not place the Temple under judgment and that Jesus does not replace and fulfil the Temple and its institutions.[25] On the other hand she emphasizes that while the Temple is the place of revelation, it is also the place where Jesus is rejected.[26] Jesus' glory, which is closely connected with the glory of the Father (1.14; 17.22), is never experienced in the Temple. It is only ever manifested[27] to

---

19. McCaffrey, *The House with Many Rooms*, pp. 179-83.

20. McCaffrey, *The House with Many Rooms*, pp. 222-44. The texts are as follows: The New Temple of Truth (Jn 1.14); The New Temple as the Meeting-Place between God and Man (Jn 1.51); The New Temple of Worship (Jn 4.20-24); The New Temple as the Source of the Spirit (Jn 7.37-39); The Sanctification of the New Temple (Jn 10.36); The Goal of the New Temple (Jn 11.47-53); The Glory of the New Temple (Jn 12.41); The 'Sign' of the New Temple (Jn 20.19-29).

21. Judith Lieu, 'Temple and Synagogue in John', *NTS* 45 (1999), pp. 51-69.

22. Lieu, 'Temple and Synagogue', p. 69.

23. Lieu, 'Temple and Synagogue', p. 51.

24. Lieu, 'Temple and Synagogue', pp. 64-65.

25. Lieu, 'Temple and Synagogue', pp. 66, 67. It is true, as Lieu says, that Jesus speaks no words of judgment against the Temple, but his actions in the Temple and the narrative structure of John, imply judgment.

26. Lieu, 'Temple and Synagogue', p. 69. She takes the 'his own' of Jn 1.11 to refer to the Temple. He was rejected by his own people in his own place.

27. It seems that Lieu (p. 68) is making a subtle distinction between manifesting and experiencing the glory. In the Temple the glory is manifested, but not experienced because the Jews are blind. For the disciples the glory is manifested *and* experienced. Whether ἐφανέρωσεν τὴν δόξαν αὐτοῦ of 2.11 will bear that sort of meaning is a question Lieu does not explore in her article.

his disciples, first in 2.11 and not again until ch. 17.[28] And those who respond to Jesus in faith do so outside of the Temple.[29]

The Temple is never the place of faith in Jesus and never the place of the experience of his (and/or his Father's) glory. It seems to me then that Lieu's conclusions, at least by implication, point towards the Temple being under judgment and that Jesus replaces the Temple as the locus of Father's glory.

The significance of this recent article is that it interacts with some contemporary scholarship on the Temple in John, and, while it super-ficially does not favour my argument, yet it highlights the importance of the Temple in John and I believe its conclusions tend to confirm, rather than nullify, the direction of this study.

1.2.3 *Mary Coloe's Dissertation*

As the research for this study was coming to an end I obtained an un-published Doctor of Theology thesis by Mary Coloe, submitted at the Melbourne College of Divinity in 1998, entitled 'The Dwelling of God among Us: The Symbolic Function of the Temple in the Fourth Gospel'. This dissertation is similar to the present work, with many of the Gospel passages discussed being the same (Jn 1.1-18; 2.13-22; 4.1-45; 7.1-8.59; 10.22-42; 14.1-31). Coloe's conclusion is similar: '...the human flesh of Jesus fulfils and replaces Israel's Temple traditions... In Jesus God dwells and achieves a communion of life with us which Israel had sought through cultic rituals.'[30] As with my study Coloe's emphasis is theological and thematic with some exegetical underpinning. Coloe tends to treat the text as a whole, and there is, for example, little or no discussion of theories of

---

28. Lieu (p. 68) comments on the manifestation of glory: '"[Isaiah] saw his glory" (12.41); the reference is to Isaiah's vision of God in the Temple (Isa. 6), now interpreted as a vision of Jesus. In 1.14 this was already proclaimed as the theme of the Gospel and of Jesus' coming: "We beheld his glory." Where else, not just from Isaiah but within the whole biblical tradition, should his glory be manifested but in the Temple?' But the point is surely that although the glory was manifested in the Temple it was only seen outside the Temple by the disciples. Indeed 1.14 contains hints that the glory of God dwells in the Word made flesh and so the Word functions as a Temple (cf. 2.21). I will develop this in Chapter 4 on the Prologue.

29. Lieu, 'Temple and Synagogue', pp. 68, 69.

30. M. Coloe, 'The Dwelling of God among Us: The Symbolic Function of the Temple in the Fourth Gospel' (unpublished Dr Theol. thesis, Melbourne College of Divinity, Australia, 1998), p. 308. See also M. Kinzer, 'Temple Christology in the Gospel of John' (SBLSP, 37.1; Atlanta: Scholars Press, 1998), pp. 447-64.

composition or redaction criticism. As with my study there is some inter-action with extra-biblical texts.

Nevertheless there are differences: whereas Coloe tends to focus on literary analysis of the text with little or no attention to historical issues, such as the authorship of John,[31] possible audience of John and limited discussion of first-century Jewish responses to the fall of the Jerusalem Temple, the present study has a greater mixture of diachronic and syn-chronic approaches. There is a further difference on the ordering of the chapters. Coloe has ordered her chapters according to the flow of the Johannine narrative, but I have chosen to order my argument beginning with the most evident presence of a Temple replacement theme in John (2.13-22) and working towards those passages where it is less clear (e.g. 13.1–14.3)—in effect my argument is cumulative. In the third place Coloe has devoted an entire chapter to 1.14 whereas I have incorporated my discussion of that verse in the treatment of the Prologue. Fourthly, while Coloe has no substantial discussion of 1.51, I have devoted a whole chapter, probing it for possible Temple allusions. Fifthly, although Coloe has some helpful observations on Jn 17, she has no extensive exegetical engagement with it as the present work has in Chapter 9. On the other hand, Coloe has an excellent chapter on the Passion narrative that is not present in this work. Coloe argues that the Temple in John finds fulfilment in the Christian community,[32] whereas my study argues that Jesus is the primary fulfilment and replacement of the Temple and only in a secondary and derivatory sense is the Christian community the new Temple. Al-though Coloe has much to say about the festivals of the Tabernacles (Jn 7–8) and Dedication (10.22-42), her treatment of the Passover lacks any systematic engagement with John 6, and her discussion of the Sabbath has no substantial linkage with Jn 5.1-18, whereas in this work both 5.1-18 and 6.1-71 of John are important in the discussion of Passover and Sabbath respectively. Finally Coloe does not mention John 13 as a possible

---

31. Throughout this study I will refer to the Gospel of John as 'John' and the author as 'John'.

32. Coloe, 'The Dwelling of God', p. 310. Coloe does not deny that Jesus is the fulfilment and replacement of the Temple, but in my view she places unwarranted emphasis on the Temple as the community of disciples. For example, her punctuation of Jn 7.37, 39 favours the rivers of water flowing out from the believer, whereas my punctuation makes Jesus the source of the waters in keeping with the powerful christological emphasis of the Gospel as a whole.

purificatory entry to the 'Father's house' (the new Temple) of 14.2, 3,[33] whereas this study takes up that theme.

Despite these differences Mary Coloe's thesis with its many similar insights is a remarkable independent corroboration of the present work and I am grateful to her. There are other works of tangential significance,[34] but Coloe's dissertation stands out as the most relevant for this thesis.

I turn now to issues of authorship, date and readership/audience of John. These are relevant for my study because in arguing for a Temple theme in John the case is strengthened if I can find (a) the possibility that the author had Temple and/or priestly connections; (b) the likely date of the final composition of John is post-70 CE; and (c) the audience would have some sympathy with and concern for Jewish Temple worship.

1.3 *Authorship*

This study is not the place to survey the considerable literature on the authorship of the Fourth Gospel and come to any definitive conclusion about the personal identity of the author.[35] However, I wish to discuss this issue because it opens the possibility that the author had priestly and therefore Temple connections that strengthens the case for finding a

33. Interestingly Walker (*Jesus and the Holy City*, p. 172) makes brief mention of this: 'All those who entered the Jerusalem Temple had first to make themselves ritually clean; now Jesus [in Jn 13.1-10] offers that cleansing to his disciples.'

34. Of tangential significance is Craig R. Koester's *The Dwelling of God—The Tabernacle in the Old Testament, Intertestamental Jewish Literature, and the New Testament* (CBQMS, 22; Washington: Catholic Biblical Association of America, 1989). As the title indicates, this is a wide ranging survey and the section on John is confined to 15 pages (pp. 100-115) and focuses almost exclusively on Jn 1.14, the only passage in John where it is reasonably likely that the tabernacle is referred to. So it has minimal relevance for my topic. On the other hand, the discussion of the tabernacle in inter-testamental Jewish literature has general value as background to the theme of the Temple complex in John. Also of general relevance is R.E. Clements, *God and Temple* (Philadelphia: Fortress Press, 1965); J. Daniélou, *The Presence of God* (trans. W. Roberts; London: A.R. Mowbray & Co., 1958); Y. Congar, *The Mystery of the Temple*; M. Barker, *The Gate of Heaven: The History and Symbolism of the Temple in Jerusalem* (London: SPCK, 1991).

35. In the third chapter of his recent book (*The Beloved Disciple: Whose Witness Validates the Gospel of John?* [Valley Forge, PA: Trinity Press International, 1995], pp. 127-224), James H. Charlesworth has a good summary of scholars' suggestions as to the identity of the Beloved Disciple, a question I believe is related to authorship (but see n. 37 below).

Temple theme in the Gospel. The purpose of this section, then, will be to argue for priestly/Temple connections for the author of the Fourth Gospel.

1.3.1 *Internal Evidence*

The clearest internal statement on the authorship of John is 21.24: οὗτός ἐστιν ὁ μαθητὴς ὁ μαρτυρῶν περὶ τούτων καὶ ὁ γράψας ταῦτα.[36] It is possible that γράψας could imply 'had it written by a secretary' and the secretary could have been given some freedom by the author. But an author employing a secretary is still an author.[37]

1.3.1.1 *Internal Evidence: the Pronouns.* The question is, Who is οὗτός ὁ μαθητής? Tracing the reference back through the chapter we come to v. 20 where the disciple in question is clearly identified as the disciple beloved of Jesus. Ἐπιστραφεὶς ὁ Πέτρος βλέπει τὸν μαθητὴν ὃν ἠγάπα ὁ Ἰησοῦς ἀκολουθοῦντα, ὃς καὶ ἀνέπεσεν ἐν τῷ δείπνῳ ἐπὶ τὸ στῆθος αὐτοῦ καὶ εἶπεν, Κύριε, τίς ἐστιν ὁ παραδιδούς σε;[38]

This disciple, then, who is beloved by Jesus and close to Jesus, is the stated author of John.[39] As indicated in 21.24 this author is a witness and

---

36. Dodd proposes that ταῦτα refers to vv. 20-23, but allows for the possibility that it refers to the whole of ch. 21 (C.H. Dodd, *Historical Tradition in the Fourth Gospel* [Cambridge: Cambridge University Press, 1963], p. 12). But if ch. 21 belongs to the Gospel as an integral part of it (cf. n. 46 below), then why not permit ταῦτα to refer to the whole Gospel? Brown (*John*, II, p. 1124) says, 'A...widely held view is that vs. 24 is a type of colophon indicating the writer's outlook upon the authorship (in the broad sense) of the entire Gospel.'

37. Cf. Rom. 16.22; 2 Thess. 3.17; Gal. 6.11. There is no justification for inferring from 21.24, 25 that there were a number of redactors. The natural way of reading the verses is to see them as the work of a single editor who speaks for himself in the first person singular of v. 25 and possibly on behalf of the Johannine author(s) in the first person plural of v. 24. However v. 23 is doubtless to be included as the work of a redactor. It is most unlikely that the author would have concluded the Gospel with v. 23; on the other hand v. 22 would have been an effective ending: Ἐὰν αὐτὸν θέλω μένειν ἕως ἔρχομαι, τί πρὸς σέ; σύ μοι ἀκολούθει.

38. The reference is to Jn 13.23-25. This is the first reference in John to the Beloved Disciple. Richard Bauckham ('The Beloved Disciple as Ideal Disciple', *JSNT* 49 [1993], pp. 21-44 [28]) suggests 21.20 forms a deliberate *inclusio* with 13.23-25, indicating that the double story of Peter and the Beloved Disciple that began there ends with 21.20-23.

39. Here the author is identified with the Beloved Disciple. This is by no means universally accepted. One recent writer who distinguishes the evangelist from the Beloved Disciple is Sandra M. Schneiders ('"Because of the Woman's Testimony...":

his witness is true (ἀληθὴς αὐτοῦ ἡ μαρτυρία ἐστίν). This is emphasized in 19.35 where the author testifies concerning the flow of blood and water from the pierced side of the crucified Jesus: καὶ ὁ ἑωρακὼς μεμαρτύρηκεν, καὶ ἀληθινὴ αὐτοῦ ἐστιν ἡ μαρτυρία, καὶ ἐκεῖνος οἶδεν ὅτι ἀληθῆ λέγει, ἵνα καὶ ὑμεῖς πιστεύ[σ]ητε. There is a double forward reference in 19.35. On the one hand καὶ ἐκεῖνος,[40] οἶδεν ὅτι ἀληθῆ λέγει, is taken up in 21.24 where the same idea is expressed in the first person plural: καὶ οἴδαμεν ὅτι ἀληθὴς αὐτοῦ ἡ μαρτυρία ἐστίν. This suggests that the witness in both cases is the same, namely, the Beloved Disciple. We know that the Beloved Disciple was present at the cross (19.26) and therefore in a position to be an eyewitness of the outflow of blood and water and that the soldiers did not break Jesus' legs. Whereas in 19.35 the witness himself vouches for the truthfulness of his testimony, in 21.24 a plurality of witnesses[41] (via an editor) endorses the veracity of his witness. The second of course is much stronger. On the other hand, the phrase ἵνα καὶ ὑμεῖς πιστεύ[σ]ητε in 19.35 anticipates 20.31 even down to the textual variant.[42] ταῦτα δὲ γέγραπται ἵνα πιστεύ[σ]ητε. Jn 20.30-31 speaks of the written narrative of chs. 2–20, a narrative of signs that Jesus did. The seventh sign, the climatic and pre-eminently important one, is the death and resurrection of Jesus. I believe this is the sign that Jesus speaks of to

Reexamining the Issue of Authorship in the Fourth Gospel', *NTS* 44.4 [1998], pp. 513-35). She suggests that the Beloved Disciple is '*a textual paradigm* derived from and realized in the leading figures in the Johannine School in the text through such characters as Nathanael, the Samaritan Woman, the Royal Official, the Man Born Blind, Martha and Mary and Lazarus of Bethany, Mary Magdalene, and Thomas the Twin' (p. 534). The evangelist on the other hand is the single individual who actually wrote the text. Schneiders also suggests that the '*textual alter ego* of the evangelist, whatever her or his actual identity and gender might have been, is the figure of the Samaritan Woman' (p. 535, author's emphasis). I think this is overly subtle and therefore unlikely.

40. I take the demonstrative pronoun to refer to the eyewitness himself. Cf. Josephus, *War* 3.202 as an example of how an author can oscillate between first person singular and third person singular in referring to himself. Cf. also the discussion in Carson (*John*, pp. 625-26). The emphatic use of this pronoun underlines the importance and veracity of the eyewitness's testimony.

41. Bauckham ('Beloved Disciple', pp. 28-29) suggests the 'we' refers to the Johannine community. But in the light of his persuasive arguments in 'For Whom Were the Gospels Written?', in *The Gospels for All Christians: Rethinking Gospel Audiences* (Grand Rapids: Eerdmans, 1998), it is perhaps unwise to assume that the 'we' does, in fact, refer to 'the Johannine community'.

42. The presence of the same variant in both 19.35 and 20.31 (πιστεύ[σ]ητε) suggests that some interpreters saw these two verses as being tied closely together.

the Jews in Jn 2.18-21. He speaks of his body as a Temple that shall be destroyed and then he will raise it up. It is this sign that is witnessed in 19.35. It will be argued later that the outflow of the blood signifies death and the stream of water speaks of life and Spirit (4.14; 7.37-39).[43] On the one hand 19.35 refers to the climatic sign, whereas 20.30-31 refers to all seven signs. We are told that Jesus did many other non-recorded signs 'in the presence of his disciples' (ἐνώπιον τῶν μαθητῶν). This implies that those that are recorded were also done in the presence of his disciples, including the climatic seventh sign. We know that only the Beloved Disciple and women disciples were at the cross (19.25-26). Thus in the light of the connection of 19.35 with 20.30-31, as well as in the light of the editor's comment in 21.24, I believe that the witness of 19.35 is indeed the Beloved Disciple.

1.3.1.2 *Internal Evidence: the Beloved Disciple.* It is popular to see the Beloved Disciple as the ideal of discipleship.[44] It is true that in some respects the Beloved Disciple functions as a model for others. He is portrayed in 19.26-27 as the only one of Jesus' male disciples who is faithful enough to be with him at the cross. And in this respect he contrasts with Peter who denies Jesus three times (Jn 18.16-18; 25-27). The Beloved Disciple may also be a disciple representative of the new relationships established by Jesus' death and resurrection (19.26-27; 20.17).[45] But he is not consistently presented as a model and representative disciple. This is especially the case at the conclusion of the Gospel when Peter and the hearers are emphatically and deliberately told that what Jesus has in store

---

43. See below 7.2.5.1.

44. See, for example, Raymond F. Collins, 'From John to the Beloved Disciple: An Essay in Johannine Characters', *Int* 49.4 (1995), pp. 359-69 (367): 'In his anonymity and stylization, the Beloved is the epitome of discipleship; he is the disciple par excellence…the Beloved is the consummate disciple and authentic witness…' See also K. Quast (*Peter and the Beloved Disciple: Figures for a Community in Crisis* [JSNTSup, 32; Sheffield: JSOT Press, 1989]), who combines this idea with the notion that the Beloved Disciple represents the Johannine community.

45. For example, it is sometimes suggested that the mother of Jesus is in some sense the mother of all believers (of whom the Beloved Disciple is representative). R.E. Brown (*John*, II, p. 926) offers the possibility that Jesus' mother is the New Eve. Earlier he says that she 'is symbolically evocative of Lady Zion who after the birth pangs, brings forth a new people in joy (Jn xvi 21; Isa. xlix 20 -22, liv 1, lxvi 7-11)' (*John*, II, p. 925). The reference to the new family in 20.17 is a realization of 1.12.

for the Beloved Disciple is none of their business (21.20-22).[46] They are commanded to follow Jesus, not the Beloved Disciple.

Further, while it is true that Peter sometimes is adversely contrasted with the Beloved Disciple, it is not always the case. Bauckham[47] makes the point that Peter and the Beloved Disciple represent two different kinds of discipleship: active service and perceptive witness. Peter is presented as the disciple who is eager to follow and to serve Jesus (13.6-9, 36-37; 18.10-11, 15). While it is true that Peter could act as a perceptive spokes-man for the disciples (6.68-69), on the other hand he is more often portrayed as lacking understanding and perception. He does not see that he cannot be a disciple unless Jesus washes his feet (13.6-9); he does not understand that Jesus the good shepherd must lay down his life for him (cf. 13.37 with 10.11, 15); he does not grasp that Jesus' arrest and death is the Father's will for him (18.10, 11); he fails to comprehend and believe the significance of the empty tomb and the arrangement of the grave clothes (20.6-9);[48] and he does not recognize that the man on the beach after the catch of fish is Jesus (21.7). But on the other hand, Peter is the disciple who loves Jesus (21.15-17) and who is active in service (21.11) and is commissioned as Jesus' chief under-shepherd (21.15-17). Despite his threefold denial (18.15-18; 25–27), Peter will follow Jesus faithfully even to death (13.36; 21.18-19), and, like Jesus' death, his death will also glorify God (cf. 12.32, 33).

The Beloved Disciple, however, is portrayed as the perceptive witness, with spiritual insight into the meaning of the events in the narrative. This disciple is represented as having an intimate relationship with Jesus. At the supper he is the disciple who was reclining ἐν τῷ κόλπῳ τοῦ Ἰησοῦ (13.23) and conveyed Peter's message to Jesus.[49] This echoes 1.18 where

46. This argument presupposes that Jn 21 is an integral part of the Gospel. Paul S. Minear has argued this with some cogency in 'The Original Functions of John 21', (*JBL* 102.1 [1983], pp. 85-98). Cf. also S.S. Smalley, 'The Sign in John XXI', *NTS* 20 (1974), pp. 275-88.

47. Bauckham, 'Beloved Disciple', p. 35.

48. Specific mention of the Beloved Disciple's faith (20.8) suggests that Peter's response was possibly not a comparable faith response. At the beginning when Peter and the Beloved Disciple set out for the tomb, they are together, but thereafter they seem to undertake slightly different journeys. I believe this is a deliberate contrast. Moreover, Jn 20.9 emphasizes that the Beloved Disciple's faith is not grounded on the fulfilment of Scripture, but on what he saw. It was only later that the disciples under-stood from Scripture that Jesus must rise from the dead.

49. Jn 21.20, which acts as an inclusio, has ἐπὶ τὸ στῆθος αὐτοῦ.

Jesus the μονογενὴς θεὸς ὁ ὢν εἰς τὸν κόλπον τοῦ πατρὸς ἐκεῖνος ἐξηγήσατο. The intimate relationship between Father and Son makes it possible for the Son to make the Father known. Likewise, the intimate relationship between Jesus and the Beloved Disciple makes it possible for him to be a true witness for Jesus.[50]

It is 'traditional'[51] to identify the unnamed disciple of 1.35-40 as the Beloved Disciple. Bauckham ('The Beloved Disciple', p. 36) says it is 'almost certainly the Beloved Disciple'.[52] He argues that the specific time references indicate an eyewitness account and that this is the only case in the first chapter of the Gospel where there is anonymity. If Bauckham is right about the anonymous disciple being the Beloved Disciple, then, in the course of the narrative in John 1, he was one of the first disciples—indeed, a disciple of John the Baptist, the forerunner, and heard his significant testimony to Jesus as the sacrificial lamb of God (1.35; cf. v. 29). As a result of that, and of Andrew and him spending time with Jesus (1.39), he was in an ideal position to be a witness. In terms of the Gospel narrative he had been in the company of Jesus from the beginning.

John the Baptist's testimony (1.29, 35) is realized in the Beloved Disciple's witness at the cross—a witness specifically highlighted by the author's intrusion into the narrative (19.35). The author, the Beloved Disciple, sees the flow of blood and water and sees that Jesus' legs are not broken—signs that this is the Passover Lamb of God. This disciple is the

---

50. Bauckham ('Beloved Disciple', p. 38) brings out the point of Jesus' love for the Beloved Disciple in contrast to Peter's love for Jesus: '...whereas in Peter's case the Gospel emphasizes his love for Jesus, in the Beloved Disciple's case it emphasizes Jesus' love for him. The former emphasis is appropriate for the active role of discipleship as participation in Jesus' activity of serving and sacrificing: it corresponds to Jesus' love for his disciples. The latter emphasis is appropriate for the more receptive role of discipleship as witness and corresponds to Jesus' enjoyment of his Father's love.'

51. Carson, *John*, p. 154.

52. This is contrary to Schneiders ('Because of the Woman's Testimony...') who suggests the 'other disciple' 'is the evangelist's creation of an "empty set" into which the reader, who is called to become a Beloved Disciple, is intended to insert him or herself' (pp. 519-20). But if the 'other disciple' = 'reader' as Schneiders suggests then what is one to make of the details of Jn 18.15, 17, for example? One can perhaps understand that the reader is admitted to the courtyard of the high priest so as to see and hear what happened, but why should the reader then be instrumental in gaining access for Peter? It is difficult to see how the reader can fully insert him or herself into the 'other disciple' in Jn 18.15, 16.

only male disciple at the cross and therefore he is the only one who can, as a male disciple, testify to Jesus' hour of exaltation.

Not only is the Beloved Disciple a witness, he is a *perceptive* witness. While it is clear that he does not understand any better than any of the other disciples what is going on at the supper (13.25-30; cf. esp. 13.28), nevertheless his breakthrough to understanding comes sooner than the others. When he came to the tomb and saw, he believed (20.8-9). Further, he recognized that it was the LORD on the beach before any of the others (21.7).

These considerations mark out the Beloved Disciple to be the author of the Gospel. He was in a position to witness key events in the ministry of Jesus. He was beloved of Jesus and knew him intimately. He was spiritually perceptive. The Johannine community trusted him as their witness. They said οἴδαμεν ὅτι ἀληθὴς αὐτοῦ ἡ μαρτυρία ἐστίν.

1.3.1.3 *Internal Evidence: the 'Other Disciple' of John 18.15.* Is the ἄλλος μαθητής of 18.15 the Beloved Disciple? Schnackenburg advances three 'weighty objections' against a positive answer. First, he says: '[T]he lack of an article forbids our supposing a reference back to 13.23.' However, I am not convinced. In 21.2 we have the words καὶ ἄλλοι ἐκ τῶν μαθητῶν αὐτοῦ δύο—and it is almost certain that one of these disciples is the Beloved Disciple yet there is no indication of one of these being special. The Beloved Disciple is on a level with his anonymous other. He is not marked out from the others in any way. I see no reason why the author should not maintain the same lack of precision in 18.15. Secondly, Schnackenburg says: '[T]here is no reason why the anonymous one who was already introduced as "the disciple, whom Jesus loved" should not be described in the same way here.' However, it seems that the designation 'whom Jesus loved' is reserved for instances where the disciple is functioning as an intimate of Jesus and therefore a perceptive and reliable witness. The reason why the disciple is not called the beloved of Jesus in 1.35-40 is because that incident depicts the beginning of the establishment of intimacy. In 18.15-16 the ἄλλος μαθητής is not concerned with his relationship with Jesus or with being a perceptive and reliable witness. The important relationship is with the high priest (ὁ μαθητὴς ἐκεῖνος ἦν γνωστὸς τῷ ἀρχιερεῖ) and it is that relationship that provides the key for Peter's entry to the high priest's αὐλή. There is therefore no reason why the disciple should be designated as the one whom Jesus loved. Finally, Schnackenburg says: '[H]is [the disciple's] acquaintance with the high priest not only rules out, with some certainty, his identification with John, the fisherman's son from the lake of Gennesaret, but would also be astonishing for a close intimate of Jesus.' The first part of this reason applies only if the Beloved Disciple is John the son of Zebedee. I shall argue below that the Beloved Disciple is not the son of Zebedee. The second part of Schnackenburg's reason is answered by himself: 'This last, is, admittedly, no serious argument against the disciple whom Jesus loved, because John's gospel knows of still more "disciples" of Jesus in Judea (7.3), describes Joseph of Arimathaea as a "secret disciple" (19.38), and reports much else about Jesus' connections with Judea-Jerusalem (cf. Nicodemus, Bethany and Ephraim [11.54]).'[53]

An argument in favour of identifying the ἄλλος μαθητής of 18.15 as the Beloved Disciple depends on comparing 18.15-16 with 20.3-10. F. Neirynck has addressed this comparison in terms of source analysis and redaction criticism and reached the following conclusion:

> In the hypothesis that 'the other disciple' in 20,3-10 is the evangelist's insertion in the Peter story of Lk 24,12 (or the pre-Johannine source), there is no reason for dividing over two stages of composition 'the other disciple' and 'whom Jesus loved'. The composite phrase of 20,2 can include the evangelist's own double reference to 18,15-16 and 13,23; 19,26. On the other hand it is a reasonable assumption that the '(an)other disciple' passage of 18,15-16 should be assigned to no other than the evangelist who is held responsible for the insertion of the Beloved Disciple texts. This conclusion can be drawn, it seems to me, from the close similarity with 20,3-10.[54]

There is then the possibility that the Beloved Disciple, the author of the Gospel, was known to the high priest. If this was true, then it would not be a surprise to find 'priestly' concerns in the Gospel—namely, the complex of Temple life—the Temple itself, as the place of the presence of God, and its associated festivals, priestly rituals and sacrifices.[55]

However, if the Beloved Disciple was John the son of Zebedee, then, as Schnackenburg argues, it would be unlikely for the Beloved Disciple to

---

53. R. Schnackenburg, *The Gospel According to St John* (trans. K. Smyth *et al.*; HTCNT; 3 vols.; London: Burns & Oates, 1968–82), III, p. 235.

54. F. Neirynck, 'The "Other Disciple" in Jn 18, 15-16', *ETL* 51 (1975), pp. 113-41 (140).

55. Given the widespread importance of the Temple, a non-priestly author may also show these concerns, but it is likely they were more significant for an author with priestly connections.

have priestly connections. What can be said about this? Bauckham (24–26) makes a convincing case from internal considerations that the Beloved Disciple is not John, the son of Zebedee. The only time John the son of Zebedee is referred to in the Gospel is in 21.2 where he is linked to his brother James in the phrase οἱ τοῦ Ζεβεδαίου. We know that the Beloved Disciple is present somewhere in the list in 21.2. Could he be named as one of the two sons of Zebedee? Bauckham thinks not. He argues that:

> The convention that the Beloved Disciple appears only anonymously in the Gospel is well enough established by this point [21.2] for the reader not to expect it to be breached here, especially without any indication that it is and when there are no less than two genuinely anonymous disciples[56] to cover the presence of the Beloved Disciple.[57]

1.3.2 *External Evidence*

I have looked at the internal evidence and seen some signs that the author of the Gospel may have had priestly connections. Now I turn to external considerations. There is one reference that deserves careful evaluation. This is from Polycrates, bishop of Ephesus, in a letter written in the last decade of the second century to Victor of Rome during the paschal controversy.

It is as follows: ἔτι δὲ καὶ Ἰωάννης, ὁ ἐπὶ τὸ στῆθος τοῦ κυρίου ἀναπεσών, ὃς ἐγενήθη ἱερεὺς τὸ πέταλον πεφορεκὼς καὶ μάρτυς καὶ διδάσκαλος, οὗτος ἐν Ἐφέσῳ κεκοίμηται.

The words ὁ ἐπὶ τὸ στῆθος τοῦ κυρίου ἀναπεσών are virtually identical with Jn 21.20 ὃς καὶ ἀνέπεσεν...ἐπὶ τὸ στῆθος αὐτοῦ, suggesting that the John referred to is in fact the Beloved Disciple of the Fourth Gospel. It is this very verse that identifies that the Beloved Disciple is the author of the Gospel. Interestingly Irenaeus uses precisely the same words to indicate that John is the author of the Gospel in *Haer.* 3.1.1: 'John, the disciple of the LORD, who also had leaned upon his breast.'[58]

John, in Polycrates, is described as ἱερεὺς...καὶ μάρτυς καὶ διδάσκαλος. The positioning of the μάρτυς between ἱερεὺς and διδάσκαλος

---

56. One could hardly say that οἱ τοῦ Ζεβεδαίου were anonymous. James and John were well known and needed no further identification beyond οἱ τοῦ Ζεβεδαίου.

57. Bauckham, 'Beloved Disciple', p. 25.

58. Eusebius, *Hist. Eccl.* 5.8.4 has the Greek ὁ καὶ ἐπὶ τὸ στῆθος αὐτοῦ ἀναπεσών. Did Polycrates copy Irenaeus? Richard Bauckham emphasizes the independence of Polycrates' testimony in 'Papias and Polycrates on the Origin of the Fourth Gospel', *JTS* 44.1 (1993), pp. 24-68 (31 but esp. n. 26).

suggests that the word does not refer to the manner of his death (martyr-dom), but rather to his function as a witness and therefore both Jn 19.35 and 21.24 could be in view as Polycrates describes John as μάρτυς, in which case the term could well designate John as the author of the Gospel. Polycrates' final statement about John dying in Ephesus accords well with the tradition that John 'did himself publish a Gospel during his residence at Ephesus in Asia' (*Haer.* 3.1.1).

However, what are we to make of the words ὃς ἐγενήθη ἱερεὺς τὸ πέταλον πεφορεκὼς? Bauckham argues convincingly that these words refer to John exercising the high priest's office in the Temple.[59] He insists that they are to be taken literally. Bauckham's conclusion is that according to Polycrates the John who was the Beloved Disciple, who wrote the Gospel, also exercised the office of the high priest in the Temple.[60] Bauckham suggests that because there is no corroborative evidence that the author of the Fourth Gospel was a high priest, then it is very unlikely that he was actually a high priest. How then did Polycrates decide that the John who leant on Jesus' breast was a high priest? Bauckham suggests:

> The simplest explanation…is that Polycrates (or the Ephesian Church tradition which he followed) identified John the Beloved Disciple, who had died in Ephesus, with the John of Acts 4.6, not because he had any his-torical information to this effect, but as a piece of scriptural exegesis. The tradition that John the Beloved Disciple was a high priest is neither meta-phorical nor historical, but *exegetical*.[61]

But is this likely? I think not. The John of Acts 4.6 is one of a high priestly party who sit in judgment on the two apostles, Peter and John. Is it likely that the author of the Fourth Gospel, one whom Polycrates describes

59. Bauckham, 'Papias', pp. 34-40.
60. Bauckham, 'Papias', p. 44.
61. Bauckham, 'Papias', p. 42. Bauckham supports this mistaken (in his view) identification of the John of Acts 4.6 with the author of the Gospel by highlighting Polycrates' confusion of Philip the apostle with Philip the evangelist (p. 42; cf. p. 30). He gives other examples of how different people of the same name were mistakenly perceived as one and the same person. The significant conclusion Bauckham draws from the hypothesis that Polycrates' 'John' is identified with the John of Acts 4.6 is that it is therefore impossible for identification to be made with John the son of Zebedee, for it is this John who appears in the narrative, along with Peter, as one of the two disciples who are there interrogated before Annas, Caiaphas, John and Alexander. Another possibility explored in detail by M. Hengel (*The Johannine Question* [trans. John Bowden; London: SCM Press, 1989]) is that the John referred to by Irenaeus is John the Elder.

as μάρτυς καὶ διδάσκαλος, a disciple of Jesus, would sit in judgment on fellow disciples, indeed apostles? The incongruity of the situation would surely have struck Polycrates so sharply as to make the possibility of identifying his 'John' with the John of the high priestly opposition very remote indeed.

We therefore have to look elsewhere to justify Polycrates' description of John as one ὃς ἐγενήθη ἱερεὺς τὸ πέταλον πεφορεκώς. Bauckham says that Delff supposed that John was not actually the high priest but stood in for the high priest on one occasion. However, this, according to Bauckham, is contradicted by all the evidence.[62] Ordinary Jewish priests in New Testament times did not hold the office of the high priest, even temporarily.

1.3.3 Conclusion

Was the author of the Fourth Gospel a high priest? The evidence seems inconclusive. What Polycrates' statement tends to do is to corroborate the internal evidence of the Gospel that the author, the Beloved Disciple, had priestly connections. This evidence is well summarized by Burney:

> He [the author] (on the assumption that he is the unnamed disciple) was known to the high priest and gained ready admission to his house, which was denied to Peter until he intervened (18.15, 16). He alone of the Evangelists mentions the name of the high priest's servant, Malchus, whose ear Peter cut off (18.10), and also the fact that one of those who questioned Peter was a kinsman of Malchus (18.26). He has special knowledge of people like Nicodemus and Joseph of Arimathaea, who were both members of the Sanhedrin (3.1ff.; 7.50; 19.38ff.), and seems to have gained inside information as to what went on at meetings of the Sanhedrin (7.15-52; 11.47-53; 12.10), which may have come to him through Nicodemus.[63] The fact that, when our LORD commended His Mother to his care, he took her εἰς τὰ ἴδια 'from that hour' suggests that he had a house at or near Jerusalem (19.27).[64]

Further, given Polycrates strong external indication of the author's priestly connections, it strengthens the case for finding 'priestly' concerns in the

---

62. Bauckham, 'Papias', p. 41.

63. The point here is not whether the author of the Gospel of John reported what actually happened at the Sanhedrin meetings, but that he had sufficient knowledge of the tradition and what went on at such meetings to construct a plausible narrative.

64. C.F. Burney, *The Aramaic Origin of the Fourth Gospel* (Oxford: Clarendon Press, 1922), p. 134. Cf. also Kinzer ('Temple Christology', p. 461), who argues the Johannine witness 'was himself a priest'.

Gospel—namely, the complex of Temple life—the Temple itself, as the place of the presence of God, and its associated festivals, priestly rituals and sacrifices.

1.4 *Is John Post-70 CE?*

I turn now to the dating of John. Since I wish to argue that the Johannine Jesus replaces the Temple and that such a replacement is one response (among others) to the Fall of the Temple, then it requires that John be dated post-70 CE. I will endeavour to argue that this is the case.

1.4.1 *The Argument from* ἀποσυνάγωγος

The Gospel of John is notoriously difficult to date because there are so few unambiguous historical allusions that tie the Gospel to a particular historical period. However, the word ἀποσυνάγωγος, which appears three times in John (9.22; 12.42; 16.2), provides a possible clue for dating it post-70 CE. The first point to note is that John's is the only occurrence of ἀποσυνάγωγος in the New Testament. Indeed, there are no subsequent examples outside the Christian use, all of which evidently depend on Johannine usage.[65] The word then appears to be original to John.[66] Secondly, the contexts of the occurrences in Jn 9.22, 12.42 and 16.2 suggest that ἀποσυνάγωγος was a fearful and severe measure. In fact death is mentioned in 16.2, but whether as a consequence of being expelled from the synagogue (i.e. ἀποσυνάγωγος), or for some other reason, is not clear. Thirdly, 9.22 indicates a definite policy of excommunication based on a confessional test, a Jewish agreement: ἤδη γὰρ συνετέθειντο οἱ Ἰουδαῖοι ἵνα ἐάν τις αὐτὸν ὁμολογήσῃ Χριστόν, ἀποσυνάγωγος γένηται. What is the significance of ἤδη? The emphasis seems to be on 'now' or 'at this time' rather than the meaning 'already'

---

65. W. Schrage, 'Ἀποσυνάγωγος', *TDNT*, VII, pp. 848-52 (848). Pierre Grelot ('Problèmes Critiques du IVe Évangile', *RB* 94.4 [1987], pp. 519-73 [533]) says: '...on ne trouve nulle part ailleurs, indépendamment de Jean: tous les emplois patristiques proviennent de lui.' He mentions in n. 24 that in Lampe's *A Patristic Greek Lexicon*, the first citation mentioned comes from a homily of St John Chrysostom on John.

66. Grelot ('Problèmes Critiques du IVe Évangile', p. 533), however, comments, 'Le mot *aposynagogos* n'a peut-être pas été créé par l'évangéliste lui-même, car celui-ci a pu reprendre un terme que s'appliquaient, dans la *Diaspora*, les chrétiens exclus du Judaïsme, à moins que sa création ne soit due aux Juifs de langue grecque.' But he offers no evidence for this.

(which would denote rapidity of development).[67] It seems, then, that ἤδη allows a substantial lapse of time for this development from initial animosity towards Christians to the full-fledged ἀποσυνάγωγος to take place. So there is a clear possibility that expulsion from the synagogue happened post-70 CE.

Elsewhere the New Testament envisages the punishment of Christians in the synagogue (e.g. 2 Cor. 11.24;[68] Mk 13.9; Acts 22.19) and their exclusion from it (Lk. 6.22).[69] But there is nothing that corresponds to the settled and definite policy of excommunication that appears to be implied in Jn 9.22 by (a) the original and specific Johannine term (ἀποσυνάγωγος); (b) the Jewish agreement (γὰρ συνετέθειντο οἱ Ἰουδαῖοι); and (c) the fear associated with it. It seems then that the situation envisaged in Jn 9.22 and 12.42 is a later development of the sporadic Jewish opposition reflected in Paul's relationship with the synagogues in 2 Cor. 11.24 and possibly Acts. It is also a further development of the punishment mentioned in Mk 13.9 where Christians are warned they 'will be beaten in synagogues', implying that they are still members of the synagogues and subject to their discipline. But in John no punishment is mentioned. The time for correction is finished: it is the season of excommunication according to an agreed policy where the test for exclusion centres on the name of Christ.[70]

67. W. Bauer, W. Arndt and F.W. Gingrich, *A Greek–English Lexicon of the New Testament and Other Early Christian Literature* (Chicago: Chicago University Press, 1957), p. 345), under 1c has 'now at length' for ἤδη ποτέ (cf. Rom. 1.10), which is rather different from the connotations of English 'already'.

68. Some doubt the historical reliability of the Acts' references that indicate that Paul went to synagogues. However 2 Cor. 11.24 is Paul's own testimony that he was subject to synagogue discipline five times.

69. According to Acts, in a number of cases Paul leaves the synagogue of his own violition (Acts 18.7; 19.9), but there were occasions when for his own safety he was sent away by the believers (Acts 17.10, 14), and there is one occasion when he, along with Barnabas, was driven from a town (Acts 13.50). This represents sporadic Jewish hostility, but not a settled policy.

70. The breach between Jews and Christians in John is also reflected in the way Jesus speaks of the law in relation to the Jews: 'your law' (8.17); 'your law' (10.34); 'their law' (15.25). Jesus seemingly distances himself from the Jewish law suggesting that there has been a rift between Jews and Christians—they are no longer in the same camp. Indeed Christians are ἀποσυνάγωγος. Grelot ('Problèmes Critiques du IVe Évangile', pp. 534-36) goes further with this evidence and indicates that it is a sign of 'la restauration juive sous la direction rabbinique' that 'a été réalisée par des Pharisiens du courant hillélite. A défaut du Temple disparu, du culte arrêté, du sacerdoce qui a

J.L. Martyn has searched for an historical event that reflects the situation envisaged in the usage of ἀποσυνάγωγος in Jn 9.22, 12.42 and 16.2.[71] His conclusion is that it seems probable that the *Birkat ha-Minim* issued under Gamaliel II is such an historical event which is in some way reflected in Jn 9.22.[72] However, Martyn has a struggle to sustain such a conclusion. He argues[73] that a 'very early form of the whole prayer' has the following words in the Twelfth Benediction: '…and let them [Nazarenes (= Christians) and Minim (= heretics)] be blotted out of the Book of Life and not be inscribed with the righteous.' However, Martyn does not say how early this form of the prayer is. Horbury maintains[74] that 'no surviving text can be assumed to reproduce a specimen form of the Jamnian prayer' so we do not know whether or not the prayer asked for Minim to be blotted out of the Book of Life. Further it is notable that even Martyn falls short of actually saying that the prayer means practical excommunication. Nevertheless he comes very close to it: he says, 'Whoever utters this prayer asks for Jewish heretics a destiny wholly unthinkable for any member of the people of Israel.'[75]

Scholarly reassessment of the *Birkat ha-Minim*[76] has cast doubt on a

---

perdu sa fonction culturelle et son crédit, elle a mis la Tôrah au premier plan des préoccupations, et les "docteurs de la Loi" ont pris la direction de l'institution rénovée.' Consequently Grelot dates John towards the end of the first century, when the law was being established as *the* cohesive force of Judaism. J.L. Martyn (*History and Theology in the Fourth Gospel, Revised and Enlarged* [Nashville: Abingdon Press, 2nd edn, 1979], p. 52) has a useful, but generalized comment: 'It is often remarked that the Judaism of Jesus' day was an ellipse, the two foci of which were the Temple and the Law. After CE 70, the saying continues, the ellipse became a circle whose centre was the Law.'

71. Martyn, *History and Theology*, pp. 42-62.

72. Martyn, *History and Theology*, p. 55 n. 69.

73. Martyn, *History and Theology*, pp. 58-59.

74. W. Horbury, 'The Benediction of the *Minim* and Early Jewish–Christian Controversy', *JTS* 33.1 (1982), pp. 19-61 (59).

75. Martyn, *History and Theology*, p. 59.

76. R. Kimelman, 'Birkat ha-minim and the Lack of Evidence for an Anti-Christian Prayer in Late Antiquity', in E.P. Saunders *et al.* (eds.), *Jewish and Christian Self-Definition. II. Aspects of Judaism in the Graeco-Roman World* (London: SCM Press, 1981), pp. 226-44. Kimelman's fifth conclusion (p. 244) is that '*birkat ha-minim* does not reflect a watershed in the history of the relationship between Jews and Christians in the first centuries of our era', and he further remarks, '[T]here never was a single edict which caused the so-called irreparable separation between Judaism and Christianity. The separation was rather the result of a long process dependent on local conditions

definite link between the excommunication of Jn 9.22 and the *Birkat ha-Minim*. James Dunn steers a middle course through the controversial issue of whether Christians were in view when the pronouncement against the *Minim* was included in the *Birkat ha-Minim*. He says 'that this emenda-tion, to include a curse against the heretics, had the Christians specifically in mind is not certain'. On the other hand, he says: '[I]t is equally probable that the *minim included* the Christians; since the boundary was beginning to be drawn more tightly round rabbinic Judaism to exclude some other Judaisms of the pre-70 period, (Jewish) Christianity would almost cer-tainly be numbered among the other Judaisms thus targeted.'[77] In the light of these remarks Dunn's conclusion about the connection of the *Birkat ha-Minim* and Jn 9.22 seems balanced and reasonable:

> the best explanation of John 9.22 is that it refers directly to something like the *birkat ha-minim*, if only a local equivalent. Either way, 9.22 would seem to provide sufficient confirmation that *by the time the Fourth Gospel was written, there was a form of official Judaism which no longer regarded it as acceptable for Jews to confess Jesus as Messiah, and which could enforce its ruling on the subject among the local synagogues.*[78]

The two measures, the *Birkat ha-Minim*, and the excommunication of Jn 9.22, seem to belong to approximately the same time, which many put at 85 CE plus or minus ten years. Even within this tolerance the dating for the writing of John would still be post-70 CE.[79] This would tally with the time

---

and ultimately upon the political power of the church.' This conclusion would preclude a link between the *Birkat ha-Minim* and Jn 9.22. However, William Horbury ('Benediction of the *Minim*', p. 52) advocates different conclusions when he argues that the *Birkat ha-Minim* was approved at Jamnia under Gamaliel II and further that 'the impression of Jewish opposition given by Christian sources from Paul to Justin, confirmed by the scattered but hostile references in early rabbinic literature, suggests that Christians were prominently in view at the time of the benediction's approval' (p. 60). Horbury therefore leaves open the possibility of a link with Jn 9.22, but in fact favours Lindar's suggestion that Jn 9.22 reflects an earlier, regional and more drastic exclusion of Christians from the synagogue (p. 52). For overviews of the recent scholarship see S.J. Joubert, 'A Bone of Contention in Recent Scholarship: The "Birkat Ha-Minim" and the Separation of Church and Synagogue in the First Century AD', *Neot* 27 (1993), pp. 351-63, and Pieter van der Horst, 'The Birkat ha-minim in Recent Research', *ExpTim* 105.12 (1994), pp. 363-68.

77. J.D.G. Dunn, *The Partings of the Ways between Christianity and Judaism and their Significance for the Character of Christianity* (London: SCM Press, 1981), p. 222.

78. Dunn, *Partings*, p. 222 (author's emphasis).

79. Horbury ('Benediction', p. 60) remarks, 'The Jamnian ordinance...probably

needed for the hostility between Jews and Christians to evolve beyond synagogue discipline to actual formal excommunication.

1.4.2 *Consideration of John A.T. Robinson's Arguments*

John A.T. Robinson is one scholar who has challenged the prevailing scholarly consensus that the Gospel of John is post-70 CE.[80] In the beginning of the second chapter of his *Redating the New Testament*, he says:

> One of the oddest facts about the New Testament is that what on any showing would appear to be the single most datable and climactic event of the period—the fall of Jerusalem in AD 70, and with it the collapse of institutional Judaism based on the temple—is never once mentioned as past fact.[81]

Robinson makes this point with regard to John:

> there is nothing [in John] that suggests or presupposes that the temple is already destroyed or that Jerusalem is in ruins...[82]

But he goes on to say:

> Of all the writings in the New Testament, with the exception of the epistle to the Hebrews and the book of Revelation, the gospel of John is that in which we might expect an allusion (however indirect, subtle or symbolic) to the doom of Jerusalem, if it had in fact already been accomplished. For the focus of the gospel is on the rejection by metropolitan Judaism of the one who comes to his own people (1.11) as the Christ and King and Shepherd of Israel. This coming and this rejection must inevitably mean the judgement and supersession of the old religion, represented by the law (1.17), the water-pots of purification (2.6), the localized worship of Gerizim and Jerusalem (4.21), the sabbath (5.10-18), the manna that perishes (6.31f.), and much else. Above all it means the replacement of the temple by the person of Christ himself (2.21).[83]

This cuts both ways. Robinson's argument is that, given the concerns of John, we should expect some reference to the fall of the Temple, if it had already happened. That there is no specific reference is possible evidence,

reinforces an earlier exclusion attested in John, although uncertainties of dating leave open the possibility that these two measures may be contemporaneous.'

80. J.A.T. Robinson (*Redating the New Testament* [London: SCM Press, 1979], p. 261) has a discussion of the prevailing consensus that John was written c. 90–100.

81. Robinson, *Redating*, p. 13.

82. Robinson, *Redating*, p. 275.

83. Robinson, *Redating*, p. 276.

according to Robinson, that John is to be dated pre-70 CE. On the other hand, an argument from silence can never be conclusive. Indeed, if John is to be dated post-70 CE, the fall of the Temple may, from John's perspective, be a given that is universally known and within the post-70 CE historical milieu, it would make admirable sense for John to present Jesus as the answer to the catastrophe of 70 CE. Jesus is the new Temple raised on the ashes of Judaism. This is Robinson's argument turned on its head.

But if this is the case, why does John not mention the fall of the Temple? Possibly Robinson provides us with a clue when he says: '...for all the capacity of this evangelist for overtones and double meaning and irony, it is hard to find any reference which unquestionably reflects the events of 70.'[84] The very capacities Robinson lists for John, in my view, provide a possible reason why he does not make a specific reference to the fall of the Temple. The nature of irony and double meaning is to make one's points with subtlety, not baldly. John could very well be working with the unexpressed, but universally known, presupposition that the Temple had fallen, in the interests of shrewdly presenting Jesus as the new Temple complex of Judaism.

Such an approach could well strengthen John's case for Jesus being the replacement of the Temple. No doubt the catastrophe of the fall of the Temple had been the cause of a great grief for the Jews and others associated with Jewish worship. To labour it could be construed as 'rubbing salt into the wound'.[85] We could understand if John thought it would serve no useful purpose. Better to assume it and offer a new way forward.

Robinson draws attention to what he calls the 'explicit prophecy' of Roman intervention placed on the lips of Jewish leaders in 11.47-48: 'This man is performing many signs. If we let him go on like this, everyone will believe in him and the Romans will come and destroy our holy place and our nation.' He claims 'this is an unfulfilled prophecy. They did not leave him alone, and the Romans still came.'[86] However Robinson has missed the point. The Council was concerned that if Jesus continued performing signs, then the Romans would come. Jesus did perform one more sign. In fact, the Jewish leaders, together with the Romans, actually aided Jesus in the enactment of the greatest sign of all, the crucifixion and resurrection

---

84. Robinson, *Redating*, p. 276.

85. Below (see 1.5.2) I will take up the issue of the intended audience of John. I believe that the intended readership of the Gospel could be *both* Jews and Gentiles.

86. Robinson, *Redating*, p. 276. I believe that John sees 11.47-48 as fulfilled. He is writing with hindsight.

(cf. 2.19).[87] And the Romans did come and destroy the Temple and the nation. We shall see when I examine 2.17-21[88] that the death of Jesus and the destruction of the Temple are juxtaposed. Something of the same juxtaposition is present in 11.47-52, where the destruction of the Temple is linked with the death of Jesus. Further Caiaphas prophesies 'that Jesus was about to die for the nation, and not for the nation only, but to gather into one the dispersed children of God'.[89] Certainly amid the subtle and richly layered irony of Jn 11.47-48 there is no compelling evidence to date John pre-70 CE.

While it is not possible to enter into a comprehensive discussion of the evidence both for and against a post-70 CE date for John, I have put forward an argument for a date around 85 CE and countered a number of arguments proposed by Robinson for a pre-70 CE dating. In the light of the discussion above I would favour the consensus of a post-70 CE dating of John. This means that John would be writing in a situation where the Temple and its associated rituals would be gone.

1.5 *Purpose and Audience of John*

Why did John write his Gospel and what was the intended audience? This question is relevant for this study. I wish to argue that with the demise of the Temple and its associated rituals John presents Jesus as the replacement and fulfilment of the Jewish Temple complex. In effect Jesus is

---

87. See below 3.7.2 for the discussion of 2.19.

88. See below 3.7 and 3.8.

89. Robinson (*Redating*, pp. 277-78) advances an argument for a pre-70 CE dating based on Jn 5.2: ἔστιν δὲ ἐν τοῖς Ἱεροσολύμοις ἐπὶ τῇ προβατικῇ κολυμβήθρα ἡ ἐπιλεγομένη Ἑβραϊστὶ Βηθζαθά πέντε στοὰς ἔχουσα. He mentions the present tense (ἔστιν), presumably to indicate that the building is still standing and has not been destroyed by the war of 66–70 CE because it has not yet happened. He concedes: '[T]oo much weight must not be put on this [namely, the present tense].' Nevertheless if one is to opt for a post-70 CE dating for John then some explanation of Jn 5.2 is required. Daniel B Wallace ('John 5,2 and the Date of the Fourth Gospel', *Bib* 71.2 [1990], pp. 177-205) has examined the explanations offered for 5.2 and subjected them to close scrutiny, especially the explanation that ἔστιν should be read as an historical present. He concludes: '[A]lthough it has been rather popular to describe the ἔστιν of John 5,2 in the same manner in which grammarians describe the historical present, there is no sound linguistic basis for doing so' (p. 205). Although he argues against it, Wallace believes that the best explanation is that the pool survived the Jewish War intact and was still standing at the time of writing Jn 5 (p. 185).

John's answer to the urgent question following the fall of the Temple in 70 CE, What now? This question presupposes some degree of understanding of, and sympathy with Jewish Temple worship. Would this have been true of the intended audience of the Gospel?

1.5.1 *Purpose*

I look first at the issue of purpose, which is addressed directly in the text: ταῦτα δὲ γέγραπψαι ἵνα πιστευ[σ]ητε ὅτι Ἰησοῦς ἐστιν ὁ Χριστὸς ὁ υἱὸς τοῦ θεου, καὶ ἵνα πιστεύοντες ζωὴν ἔχητε ἐν τῷ ὀνόματι αὐτοῦ (20.31).[90] The textual variant (πιστεύσητε, aorist subjunctive, or πιστεύητε, present subjunctive) does not amount to a clear variation in purpose since it can be shown that 'both expressions can be used for initial faith and continuing faith'.[91]

Syntactical evidence suggests that the first purpose clause should be rendered 'that you may believe that the Christ, the Son of God, is Jesus'.[92] This suggests, then, that the purpose of the Gospel was to persuade hearers to believe that the Christ, the Son of God, is Jesus.[93]

---

90. John Painter (*The Quest for the Messiah: The History, Literature and Theology of the Johannine Community* [Edinburgh: T. & T. Clark, 2nd edn, 1993], pp. 119-31) writes of 'purposes of the Gospel'. He says, 'While [20.30-31] is the most comprehensive statement of the purpose of John at the stage at which 20.30-31 was made the conclusion, account needs to be taken of the process of composition prior to that point which reflects a variety of purposes in the completed work.' Consequently he discerns purposes in relation to the Baptist sect, to the Samaritans and to the Jews. While one may discern possible purposes other than the stated purpose of 20.30-31, it is difficult to tie them to varying stages in composition, especially when those stages are not at all certain. In this study I will tend to accept the Gospel of John as it has come down to us and not speculate on stages of composition.

91. Carson, *John*, p. 90. Cf. D.A. Carson, 'The Purpose of the Fourth Gospel: John 20.30-31 Reconsidered', *JBL* 106.4 (1987) pp. 639-51(640-41). For example, Jn 11.15 has the aorist subjunctive πιστεύσητε with the sense of having faith corroborated; 1.7 has the aorist subjunctive πιστεύσωσιν signifying a coming to faith (cf. also 4.48). On the other hand, the present subjunctive πιστεύητε occurs in the best reading of 6.29 to refer to the entire process of coming to faith and continuing to believe: this is the work of God ἵνα πιστεύητε εἰς ὃν ἀπέστειλεν ἐκεῖνος.

92. Carson ('Purpose', p. 642), building on McGaughy's conclusion that where εἶναι is used as a linking verb, the word or word cluster determined by an article is the subject, suggests the rendering: 'The Messiah, the Son of God is Jesus.' This parallels Acts 18.5, 28 and perhaps 5.42.

93. A number of scholars argue that the Gospel was written exclusively to confirm Christians in their faith (e.g. W.G. Kümmel, *Introduction to the New Testament* [Lon-

But what sort of hearers? Christian or non-Christian or both? Jewish or Gentile or both? Taking the Christian/non-Christian issue first, it is difficult to avoid the impression in John that disciples of Jesus are being addressed and encouraged to continue in his word (8.31). Even D.A Carson, who argues that John is an 'evangelistic'[94] document says that much of the Johannine Gospel material presupposes that hearers are at different stages on their faith journey. For example, he cites John 14–17 and says that these chapters emphasize the need to grow, persevere and develop as disciples.[95] There may well be an intention to persuade non-Christians to become Christians, but John is certainly not a purely 'evangelistic' document and it seems fair to allow its message to be directed to those who are already disciples as well as those who are potential disciples. It is worth observing that the usual and obvious way non-Christians could become knowledgeable about John would be through those who were already disciples.

1.5.2 *Audience*

What of the second issue—is John for Gentiles or Jews or both? Certainly the question, Who is the Messiah? would be of utmost interest to Jews.

---

don: SCM Press, 1966], p. 162). This seems to be the purpose of Jn 1 (cf. 5.13), but the stated purpose of the Gospel is wider and could include persuading non-Christians to become Christians. Barrett (*St John*, p. 135) seems to allow for both. He comments: '…John, though doubtless aware of the necessity of strengthening Christians and converting the heathen, wrote primarily to satisfy himself. His gospel must be written: it was no concern of his whether it was also read.' This is extremely unlikely given the stated purpose and the rhetorical power of John.

94. Carson ('Purpose', p. 649) uses this term in the narrow sense of persuading people to become converts to Jesus. But it is almost certain that John had a much broader understanding of the related term εὐαγγελίον. Used as a heading for each of the Gospels (including John) it seems to indicate the announcement of the good news of Jesus Christ according to each of the evangelists and that good news is relevant for everyone, both Christians and non-Christians, Jews and Gentiles. C.H. Dodd (*The Interpretation of the Fourth Gospel* [Cambridge: Cambridge University Press, 1953], p. 9) who tends to favour the view that John is primarily directed to non-Christians 'who are concerned about eternal life and the way to it', nevertheless, in commenting on the possibility of πιστεύητε as a continuous present, says, 'Yet the continuous present could be justified, even as addressed to those who were not yet Christians, if the writer were thinking not so much of the moment of conversion, as of the continuing union with Christ, the condition of which is faith, and which means the possession of eternal life.'

95. Carson, 'Purpose', p. 649-50.

And the many biblical allusions[96] virtually rule out a biblically illiterate readership.

On the other hand, Teresa Okure has argued with some persuasion that there is a missionary motif in John that is universal in scope.[97] The cosmic setting in the opening verses of the Prologue (cf. esp. 1.9, 10a), the universality of God's love (3.16-17), the striking declaration of the evangelized Samaritans: οἴδαμεν ὅτι οὗτός ἐστιν ἀληθῶς ὁ σωτὴρ τοῦ κόσμου (4.42), and the desire of the Greeks (Ἕλληνές)[98] to see Jesus

---

96. 'The Son of Man' for which no explanation is offered, 'the prophet' (1.21, 25; 6.14), the devil (13.2), Satan (13.27) and ἐν ἀρχῇ (1.1) are only a few of the terms that are significant to those steeped in the Old Testament. Further Jesus presents himself in line with or in fulfilment of such figures as Jacob (1.51) and Moses (3.14; 5.46), both key figures in Jewish history. A number of scholars have examined the Old Testament quotations in John (e.g. E. Freed, *Old Testament Quotations in the Gospel of John* [Leiden: E.J.Brill, 1965]; Bruce G. Schuchard, *Scripture within Scripture: The Interrelationship of Form and Function in the Explicit Old Testament Citations in the Gospel of John* [SBLDS, 133; Atlanta: Scholars Press, 1992]). The following are listed by Freed with his favoured Old Testament (and occasionally New Testament) source for the quotation: Jn 1.23 (Isa. 40.3); 2.17 (Ps. 69.10); 6.31 (Exod. 16.4, 15; Ps. 78.24); 6.45 (Isa. 54.13); 7.37, 38. Here Freed lists 26 texts that 'may have influenced the thought and language of the author': Deut. 8.15-16; Ps. 36.9-10; 46.5; Joel 3.18; Zech. 13.1; Prov. 5.15-16; 18.4 (LXX); Sir. 15.3; 24.28-32; Song 4.15; Isa. 32.1-2; 35.5-7; 41.18; 43.19-21; 49.10; Jer. 2.13; 17.13; Ezek. 36.25-27; 47.1-12; Jub. 8.19; 1 En. 17.4; 22.9; 96.6; Rev. 7.16-17; 21.6; 22.1, 17); 7.42 (Mt. 2.6 or Lk. 2.4); 10.34 (Ps. 82.6); 12.13-15 (Zech. 9.9 with some dependence on Mt. 21.5, 9); 12.38-40 (Isa. 6.9-10); 13.18 (Ps. 41.10); 15.25 (Ps. 69.5); 17.12 (Prov. 24.22a); 19.24 (Ps. 22.19); 19.28 (Ps. 69.22, although Freed suggests John used Mk 15.36 and changed it to suit his own theological purpose [p. 107]); and 19.36, 37 (Exod. 12.10, 46 and Zech. 12.10). This list gives some indication of the way the Old Testament permeates the text of John.

97. T. Okure, *The Johannine Approach to Mission: A Contextual Study of John 4.1-42* (Tübingen: J.C.B. Mohr, 1988), pp. 198-204.

98. J.A.T. Robinson ('The Destination and Purpose of St John's Gospel', in *Twelve New Testament Studies* [London: SCM Press, 1962], pp. 107-25) has argued that the Greeks of 12.20 are Greek-speaking Jews, but this flies in the face of the evidence in the New Testament and elsewhere (e.g. Josephus, *War* 7.45), which consistently distinguishes between Jews (regardless of their Palestinian or Diaspora origin) and Greeks. The further attempt by Robinson ('Destination', p. 112 n. 7) to refer τὴν διασποραν τῶν Ἑλλήνων to Jews is wholly unconvincing. See Okure, *Mission*, p. 202 n. 27. H.B. Kossen ('Who Were the Greeks of John XII 20?', in A. Geyser *et al.* (eds.), *Studies in John Presented to Professor Dr J.N. Sevenster on the Occasion of his Seventieth Birthday* [NovTSup, 24; Leiden: E.J. Brill, 1970], pp. 97-110) argues that the Greeks were representatives of the Gentiles (p. 104). He believes that Isa. 49.6 lies behind much of Jn 12.20-32.

(12.20-21) favour a universal audience, both Jewish and Gentile.[99]

Recently Richard Bauckham has edited a book entitled *The Gospels for All Christians: Rethinking the Gospel Audiences*,[100] in which he argues that 'the Gospels were written for all Christians, not specific churches'.[101] He and his colleagues have argued their case with cogency.[102] In particular Stephen Barton has exposed some cracks in W.A. Meeks's thesis that John 'is a book for insiders'[103] and exposed the possibility that the Gospel is an open text intended not only for audiences of believers, but for audiences of unbelievers as well.[104] This purports well with what I have argued above: namely, that John's audience is a general audience made up of Jews and Gentiles, some of whom are unbelievers whom John seeks to persuade that 'the Christ, the Son of God is Jesus' (Jn 20.31).

Presumably a non-Christian Jew might find his or her way through the dense thickets of Johannine Jewish allusion and in particular feel the force of Jewish Temple allusions, but how would a non-Christian Gentile cope? For an answer I use the Epistle to the Romans as an analogy. It seems almost certain from Rom. 11.13-32 and 15.7-12, and strongly implied in

99. Cf. also the 'all flesh' of 17.2, the 'all' of 12.32, and the use of 'world' in 10.36; 12.47b; 17.18a. Further, universality seems to be implied in Pilate's inscription (19.20) and the Gentiles seem to be in view in 10.16.

100. R. Bauckham (ed.), *The Gospels for All Christians: Rethinking Gospel Audiences* (Grand Rapids: Eerdmans, 1998).

101. Bauckham, *Rethinking Gospel Audiences*, p. 2.

102. Certainly Francis Watson thinks Bauckham has succeeded: 'In my view, Bauckham's attack on the consensus that the Gospels presuppose an initial setting within a specific community is entirely successful' (Bauckham, *Rethinking Gospel Audiences*, p. 195). On the other hand Philip Esler ('Community and Gospel in Early Christianity: A Response to Richard Bauckham's *Gospels for All Christians*', *SJT* 51.2 (1998), pp. 235-48) maintains that Bauckham's book's 'primary assertion fails to convince' (p. 248). Bauckham in his 'Response to Philip Esler' (*SJT* 51.2 [1998], pp. 249-53), believes Esler 'actually concedes our case'. Esler, to some extent, misses Bauckham's point. He criticizes Bauckham for not paying attention to the influence of the evangelist's local context on his writing, but Bauckham never denies that influence; his concern (and that of his fellow authors) is the issue of the expected audience of the Gospels, which is a different matter.

103. Bauckham, *Rethinking Gospel Audiences*, p. 190.

104. Bauckham, *Rethinking Gospel Audiences*, p. 194. Dodd (*Interpretation*, p. 9) would concur with this: 'It seems therefore that we are to think of the work as addressed to a wide public consisting primarily of devout and thoughtful persons... in the varied and cosmopolitan society of a great Hellenistic city such as Ephesus under the Roman Empire.'

1.6, 13 and 15.15-16, that the Roman church included some Gentiles.[105] Clearly 2.17 is addressed to Jews and it seems that all of the argument through chs. 2–4 applies primarily to Jews. Further, if we allow that ch. 16 was addressed to Rome, then we may conclude that the church included Jews because among the people greeted, Aquila (cf. Acts 18.2) and Andronicus, Junia and Herodion, whom Paul describes as his συγγενεῖς, were Jewish. So Paul's letter was in all likelihood directed to a church made up of both Jews and Gentiles.

The argument of Romans presupposes considerable familiarity with the Jewish Torah[106] even though some of his audience is Gentile. This strengthens the likelihood that at least some of the Gentile converts had previously been closely associated with Jewish synagogues and had considerable knowledge of, and sympathy with, Jewish thought and worship. Indeed Dunn says:

> The pattern of early Christian evangelism was most probably focused, at least initially, within synagogues… This again is what we would expect in a movement which saw itself as a form of Judaism; where else should they share their beliefs?…such a strategy would be an excellent way of reaching out to Gentiles as well, since most synagogues seem to have had a number of interested or sympathetic Gentiles who linked themselves with the synagogue.[107]

Even though, as argued above (see 1.4), a breach had opened between synagogue and Church by the time John came to be written, Gentiles sympathetic to, and well-informed about, Jewish worship would not have disappeared. It is very likely that John was addressed to the thoughtful and wondering Jew as well as the knowledgeable and enquiring Gentile.

It is therefore fair to conclude that the audience of John could well have been both Jews and Gentiles, both Christian and non-Christian, who were concerned, along with other matters, about Jewish questions regarding

---

105. Rom. 5–8 also seems to be addressed primarily to Gentiles.

106. For example, 7.1, γινώσκουσιν γὰρ νόμον λαλῶ.

107. James D.G. Dunn, *Romans 1–8* (WBC, 38A; Dallas, TX: Word Books, 1988), p. xlvii. Teresa Okure (*Mission*, p. 202 n. 27) observes that 'concerning Gentiles going to Jerusalem to worship, one needs only recall that "the court of the Gentiles" in Herod's Temple was not a mere decoration. Besides, Josephus (*Ant.* 11, 329-39, esp. 336) narrates how Alexander the Great sacrificed in the Temple guided by the priests (the understanding being that the Macedonian performed the sacrifice himself); he states further that "all peoples" were allowed to worship together with the Jews (*Ant.* 11, 87).'

worship, namely, the relevance of the festivals and place of worship, especially in the light of the demise of the Jerusalem Temple.

1.6 *Summary*

So far in this introduction I have considered the authorship, dating, purpose and intended audience of the Gospel of John. The conclusions on the intended audience of John leaves open the possibility of a Temple theme in the Gospel. Whether Jews or Gentiles, Christians or non-Christians, the intended audience would have some understanding and appreciation of Jewish worship and the centrality of the Jerusalem Temple. It is possible the intended audience had participated in Temple worship. Further, the conclusion of a post-70 CE date for John means that the Gospel is addressed to a situation where the Jerusalem Temple and its cultic life are finished, at least for the present. This represents a cultic vacuum for all who participated in the worship at the Temple and the associated festivals. The question for those participants would be, What now? And I suggest that John addresses that question and provides the answer, Jesus is the new Temple. He replaces and fulfils the former Jerusalem Temple and its cultic institutions. Finally, whoever the author of John might be, both the internal and external evidence of the Gospel suggests that he had priestly links, which suggests, in turn, he may have had a special interest in the Jerusalem Temple. Given a possible affinity with the Temple and its institutions some encouragement is offered for searching for a Temple theme in John.

1.7 *Development of the Study*

My second chapter will highlight the importance of the Temple for Jews and Jewish proselytes. The fall of the Temple in 70 CE was an enormous catastrophe and I will illustrate that with reference to a number of first-century writings in the Old Testament Pseudepigrapha, Philo and Josephus. There were a number of responses to the catastrophe and I will consider some of these briefly, indicating that the Christian response was one among a number. In this study I am concerned with the particular Johannine Christian response and the remainder of the study will be taken up with arguing for and expounding this response through engaging with the Johannine text.

The clearest passage for a Temple theme in John is 2.13-22, and my third chapter will be an analysis of this passage. I will argue that this scene goes far beyond a 'cleansing' of Israel's cultic practices; rather, Jesus' actions and words declare the Jerusalem Temple as void and in v. 21 we will discover a hermeneutical key: 'But he spoke of the temple of his body.' Jesus therefore is the new Temple, the new dwelling place of God, and we will find there are hints that this newness will be accomplished through Jesus' death and resurrection.

Having established a bridgehead for my argument, I will turn in Chapter 4 to the Prologue where I will argue that Jesus is introduced in cultic terms as the tabernacling presence of God's glory now visible in human flesh (1.14). This is the new beginning representing a decisive break from the Jewish torah and cultic institutions.

Jn 1.51, coming at the end of Jn 1, seems to function as something of a climax for the chapter and offers a programmatic vision for the future. I will argue in the fifth chapter that Bethel imagery (cf. Gen. 28.12-22) is present in this verse and that it tilts towards a Temple allusion even though this kaleidoscopic and elusive verse makes it difficult to come to a definite conclusion.

The dialogue with the Samaritan Woman (4.1-26) raises issues of place and manner of worship. While the Temple is not explicitly named, the discussion of a sacred τόπος (4.21) and of future worship in Spirit and truth (4.23) is relevant to this study and I will develop my argument in relation to this passage and these issues in the sixth chapter entitled, 'The New Worship'.

In Chapter 7 I will examine four Jewish festivals: Passover (6.1-71), which permeates the Gospel and to which I will devote the first part of the chapter; then in the second part I will explore the Festivals of Tabernacles (7.1-10.21); the third part, Dedication (10.22-40); and finally in the fourth part I will consider the Sabbath, which is significant in 5.1-18, but is also referred to in 7.19-24, 9.14 and 19.31. As a result of these investigations the conclusion will be reached that Jesus replaces and fulfils the symbolic character of each of these festivals: he becomes the Passover Lamb (1.29; 35; 19.14, 29, 31-36); he proclaims himself the light of the world (8.12) who enlightens those who are blind (9.3-7); he offers living water to the thirsty, which is identified editorially as the gift of the Spirit (7.37-39); in revealing his intimate identity with the Father (10.30, 38), Jesus confirms that he is the consecrated dwelling place of God (10.36); and, although it is not so clear, there are hints that Jesus' death brings in the cessation of the Sabbath (19.30) and the beginning of a new day (20.1, 19, 26).

In the eighth chapter I will examine the image of 'My Father's House'

(14.2) and suggest that this refers to the new Temple of Jesus himself. While this Temple is Jesus' Father's house, there are hints that the disciples can have a share in it. This is first intimated in 13.8 where I will argue that purificatory washing precedes entry into the Father's house. I will also pay attention to the 'many dwelling places' (14.2) and the striking reference to the mutually indwelling Father and Son coming and making their home with those who love Jesus and keep his word (14.23). These texts suggest that the Temple-as-building has been replaced by Temple-as-community.

In the ninth chapter I will offer some preliminary reflections on finding Temple allusions in John 17. This Johannine prayer has sometimes been called 'The High Priestly Prayer', and I will revisit this possibility and will argue that Jesus is praying as the 'High Priest' of the new Temple into which his disciples are incorporated. In this Temple-as-community they are protected, loved, bound together in unity and sent out in mission to the world.

This chapter is followed by a concluding overview of the study, a summary of the major findings and some suggestions for further research on this topic.

Chapter 2

OUTSIDE THE JOHANNINE TEXT: SOME JEWISH RESPONSES
TO THE FALL OF THE TEMPLE IN 70 CE

The Fall of the Temple in 70 CE was a calamitous event likely to occupy the minds and hearts of thoughtful Jews towards the end of the first century. The purpose of this chapter is to look at some of the responses from such Jews so as to gain an appreciation of the ferment of thought surrounding the Temple towards the close of the first century. This is not a comprehensive survey of such thought; however, a few soundings will be made in the ocean of literature with a view to appreciating something of the ethos in which the Gospel of John came to birth. In particular it is hoped to show that the Fall of the Temple was a huge loss to the Jewish people of the first century. They struggled with the questions Why? and What now? and offered different answers. The thesis of this study is that the Gospel of John offers a distinctive answer to these questions, especially the second, What now? John offers a Christian (more precisely 'christo-logical') response to the Fall of the Temple in 70 CE. He presents Jesus as the one who fulfils and replaces the Temple and its associated festivals.

But first it is necessary to look back and see how important the Temple was for the Jewish people so we can understand what a huge loss its demise in 70 CE represented.

2.1 *The Temple in Jewish History*

2.1.1 *Consecration of the First Temple*

For centuries the heart of Israelite religious practice was the Temple cult in Jerusalem. For example, the fundamental significance of the Temple can be discerned in the response of YHWH to Solomon's prayer of consecration in 2 Chron. 7.12-16:

> Then the LORD appeared to Solomon in the night and said to him: 'I have heard your prayer, and have chosen this place for myself as a house of sacrifice. When I shut up the heavens so that there is no rain, or command

the locust to devour the land, or send pestilence among my people, if my people who are called by my name humble themselves, pray, seek my face, then I will hear from heaven, and will forgive their sin and heal their land. Now my eyes will be open and my ears attentive to the prayer that is made in this place. For now I have chosen and consecrated this house so that my name may be there forever; my eyes and my heart will be there for all time.'

The Temple, then, is the place where YHWH's name dwells, sins are forgiven, prayer is made and heard, diseases are healed and agricultural prosperity is assured. The Temple decisively touched every inhabitant of the land.[1]

The Temple was set on a mountain—Mt Zion. J.M. Lundquist suggests that this is typical of all temples in the ancient Near East. He maintains that the Temple is the architectural embodiment of the cosmic mountain and is often associated with epiphany. The expression 'before the LORD', signifying the presence of the LORD, indicates a temple site.[2] Mt Sinai was where the LORD appeared to Moses, but because the people were on the move in the wilderness the presence of YHWH had to be transportable— hence the tabernacle.[3] But once settled in the land, Mt Zion became the

---

1. McCaffrey (*The House with Many Rooms*, p. 59) lists the blessings that flow from the Temple and summarizes them with: 'In a word, the temple was the source of salvation.' He goes on to say: '…to attain to the goal of the temple is to be-with-God, and so to share in the blessings of salvation, as a member of the worshipping community' (p. 60).

2. J.M. Lundquist, 'What Is a Temple? A Preliminary Typology', in H.B. Huffmon *et al.* (eds.), *The Quest for the Kingdom of God: Studies in Honor of George E. Mendenhall* (Winona Lake, IN: Eisenbrauns, 1983), pp. 205-19 (207).

3. Mary Coloe ('The Dwelling of God') has a discussion on early Sinai traditions and how they were differently interpreted by the Yahwist, the Elohist and Deuteronomist (pp. 52-56). Coloe suggests the Yahwist sees the Ark 'as an extension of YHWH's presence' (p. 54) and that 'in the D and E traditions, the Tent of Meeting was not a cultic institution housing a deity; the interior of the Tent was empty and was simply a place where Moses went to prepare himself for a moment of revelation, a fleeting prophetic glimpse of God' (p. 55). She further suggests there are probably two tents in these traditions, 'one in the midst of the people to shelter the Ark when they are at rest, and a second tent, called the Tent of Meeting, pitched outside the camp as a place of prophetic revelation' (p. 58). In both cases God was free to come and go. God's sovereign transcendence was maintained. However, with the Ark being installed in the newly built Temple in Jerusalem (1 Kgs 8) YHWH comes to *dwell* there (Ps. 132.11-15). Something more permanent is envisaged, although God's transcendence is still not compromised (1 Kgs 8.27). YHWH's dwelling in Jerusalem is justified in terms of

place for the Temple and the presence of YHWH.[4]

The regular Temple cult's central activity was sacrifice. The priests were, among other things, butchers. Their task was to slay animals efficiently and commit parts or all of them to the flames of the altar. Wine and bread were also offered on the altar. The offering of a sin offering resulted in the forgiveness of sin (Lev. 4.26, 31, 35; 5.10, 13, 16, 18). Guilt was removed, the proper relationship with God restored, and the cosmic balance re-established.[5] The fundamental and far-reaching significance of the loss of Temple sacrifice in an earlier era is well illustrated by Grabbe: '…loss of the daily offering of flesh and blood to God was an event that shook heaven and earth to their foundations and heralded the eschaton itself, according to a contemporary witness (Daniel 7–12).'[6]

I therefore turn now to consider some attacks on the Temple prior to its eventual fall in 70 CE and note how alarming these were to some Jews.

2.2 *Desecration of the Temple*

The desecration and attempted desecration of the Temple provoked a reaction from the Jewish people, and it is in their reaction that we can gauge

election: as YHWH chose David to be king of his people, so YHWH chose Zion as his dwelling.

4.   In the Gospel of John the only mention of mountains is to discount them (Jn 4.19-21). Unlike the Synoptics John has no mention of a mountain of transfiguration. This is possibly because John wants us to see Jesus as the epiphany of God. The epiphany is not isolated to a single event on a mountain, but is constantly happening in the person of Jesus.

5.   J.Z. Smith (*Map Is Not Territory: Studies in the History of Religions* [Leiden: E.J. Brill, 1978], p. 118), referring to *m. 'Abot* 1.2, says that 'on three things the world stands: on the law, on the Temple service, and on piety', and adds the comment: 'The Temple and its ritual serve as the cosmic pillars or the "sacred pole" supporting the world. If its service is interrupted or broken, if an error is made, then the world, the blessing, the fertility, indeed all of creation which flows from the Center, will likewise be disrupted.' The Temple is associated with abundance and prosperity, indeed it is perceived as the giver of these. On the other hand, the destruction or loss of the Temple is seen as calamitous and fatal to the community in which the Temple stood. The cosmic character of the Temple is also extensively discussed in Clements, *God and Temple*, pp. 65-72, and in C.T.R. Hayward, *The Jewish Temple: A Non-Biblical Sourcebook* (London: Routledge, 1996). Cf. pp. 8-10 for a summary of the Hayward's findings in the writings of Jesus ben Sirah, Josephus and Philo.

6.   L.L. Grabbe, *Judaism from Cyrus to Hadrian* (London: SCM Press, 1994), p. 540.

something of the high esteem in which they held the Second Temple. Therefore I will look at three cases, one of desecration and two of attempted desecration. While the factuality of features of the various accounts is questionable, they at least indicate that such views were held by the authors and that some Jews were ready to die for the sake of the holiness of the Temple.

2.2.1 *Attempted Desecration by Ptolemy IV*[7]

3 Maccabees takes up the story of Ptolemy IV. Having defeated Antiochus III the Great of Syria at Raphia, Ptolemy IV visits Jerusalem where he is so impressed by the Temple that he longs to enter the sanctuary. His request sparks an outrage in the city:

> Even the young women who had been confined to their chamber rushed out with their mothers, and they took dust and covered their hair with it and filled the streets with cries of grief and moans. Those recently married left the chambers where the marriage bed had been prepared and, heedless of the modesty appropriate to their station, ran about in disorder in the city. The mothers and nurses in charge of the youngest children left them here and there, in houses or in the streets, and, abandoning all caution, thronged to the most glorious Temple. Many and varied were the prayers of those who gathered there because of the king's sacreligious designs (*3 Macc.* 1.18-21).

Bolder citizens prepared to take up arms, but they were dissuaded by the elders and instead took up the posture of prayer. However:

> The combined shouts of the crowd, ceaseless and vehement, caused an indescribable uproar. It seemed as if not only the people but the very walls and the whole pavement cried out, so much at that moment did they all prefer death to the profanation of the Temple (*3 Macc.* 1.27-29).

Anderson says: '[T]he story of his [the King's] encounter with the Jews at the Jerusalem Temple is told in such highly legendary terms as to cast grave suspicion on the factuality of the whole episode.'[8] Nevertheless, the author of *3 Maccabees*, probably writing far from Jerusalem at the beginning of the first century BCE,[9] certainly held the Jerusalem Temple in very high reverence. The suggested entry by the king was enough in the author's mind, to cause a great and extensive uproar in the city with people ready to die to defend the holiness of the Temple.

---

7. Ptolemy IV Philopator, was king of Egypt 221–204 BCE.
8. H. Anderson, *OTP*, II (1985), p. 513.
9. Anderson (*OTP*, II, p. 512) suggests Alexandria.

2.2.2 *Desecration under Antiochus IV*

The causes of the Maccabaean Revolt in 168–65 BCE are debated,[10] but
certainly the abuse of the Jerusalem Temple was a contributing factor.
Daniel speaks of an 'abomination of desolation' (Dan. 11.31; 12.11). Josephus (*Ant.* 12.253) is more specific when he says: '[T]he king had built an
idol altar upon God's altar, [and] he slew swine upon it...' 1 Maccabees is
more reticent. Something was erected on the altar of burnt offering (1.54;
4.43-47) that included a pagan altar on top of the original altar in the
Temple courtyard (1.59). This sacrilege and pollution cut deeply into the
heart of Jewish people.[11] The lament in 1 Macc. 1.39-40 indicates the
profound sorrow caused by the desecration of the Temple during the
persecution by Antiochus:

> Her [Jerusalem's] sanctuary became desolate as a desert;
> her feasts were turned into mourning,
> her sabbath's into a reproach
> her honour into contempt.
> Her dishonour now grew as great as her glory;
> her exaltation was turned into mourning.

Similar sentiments occur on the lips of Mattathias in 1 Macc. 2.7-9:

> Alas! Why was I born to see this,
> the ruin of my people, the ruin of the holy city,
> and to dwell there when it was given over to the enemy,
> the sanctuary given over to aliens?
> Her temple has become like a man without honour;
> her glorious vessels have been carried into captivity.

2.2.3 *Attempted Desecration by Caligula*

Grabbe says, 'The emperor Caligula's (Gaius's) attempt to place his statue
into the Temple at Jerusalem is a monumental event in the religious history of Judah.'[12] Had he succeeded it would have been at the cost of much

---

10.   Grabbe (*Judaism*, pp. 247-56) has an extended discussion of this in which he
reviews the theses of Bickerman, Tcherikover, Goldstein and Bringmann and offers
some conclusions of his own.

11.   While it is acknowledged that 1 and 2 Maccabees reflects a Hasmonaean point
of view (cf. H. Attridge, 'Historiography', in M.E. Stone [ed.], *Jewish Writings in the
Second Temple Period* [Assen: Van Gorum; Philadelphia: Fortress Press, 1984], pp.
157-84) they become part of the heritage of the Jewish people that informs the attitudes
towards the Temple that were current in the first century CE.

12.   Grabbe, *Judaism*, p. 401.

bloodshed. Josephus indicates the powerful Jewish resistance to the Emperor's plan. Petronius, the Syrian legate, was charged with making the statue and getting it installed in the Temple:

> but there came many tens of thousands of the Jews to Petronius, to Ptolemais, to offer their petitions to him, that he would not compel them to transgress and violate the law of their forefathers; but if, said they, you are entirely resolved to bring this statue, and erect it, first kill us, and then do what you have resolved to do; for, while we are alive, we cannot permit such things as are forbidden to us to be done by the authority of our legislator.[13]

Such was the honour in which the Temple was held that Josephus tells us that the Jews would have resisted to the death. His account in *War* 2.197 is much the same, with the Jews saying to Petronius 'that if he would place the images among them, he must first sacrifice the whole Jewish nation; and that they were ready to expose themselves together with their wives and children, to be slain'.

These three examples suffice to demonstrate the high honour in which the Temple was held.[14]

---

13. Josephus, *Ant.* 18.264. Whether the events are as Josephus tells them in *Ant.* 18.257-308 and *War* 2.184-203 is an open question. Philo's account (*Leg. Gai.* 184-338) also indicates strong resistance. It seems, according to Grabbe (*Judaism*, p. 405), that Caligula planned to set up the statue in the Jerusalem Temple as a punishment for what he saw as an anti-Roman political act, the Jewish destruction of a Roman altar (in honour of himself) in Jamnia. Judaism was tolerated on condition that it was not politically disruptive. If it was seen to be otherwise then in Caligula's view the Temple would have to be Romanized or destroyed.

14. There is a further case. On 12 March 4 BCE Matthias and Judas and some of their students were burned alive for having torn down an eagle from a gate in the Temple. Herod had placed it above the 'great Gate' and at midday, in clear view of both people and guards, the students got up on the roof, let themselves down by ropes, hacked off the golden eagle, and were promptly arrested by the Temple guard with a band of soldiers. The crowds fled, but 40 students were seized along with Matthias and Judas. They were taken to Herod and defended their actions on the basis of the Torah, 'the laws that Moses wrote as God prompted and taught him', and happily accepted punishment for their piety. Herod sent them to Jericho where the main perpetrators were burned alive and the others executed. Herod's grounds for punishment was that they had committed sacrilege against God (Josephus, *Ant.* 17.149-67; *War* 1.648-55). Once again the incident illustrates the tensions that surrounded the Temple and how individuals were prepared to sacrifice themselves for the sake of its purity.

2.3 Temple Practice

It is impressive to see the struggle for the purity of the Temple in the past, but was this passion for the Temple shared by the general populace or was it something that burned in a few heroic individuals? It is unlikely that the rank and file of the Jews saw the Temple with the single mindedness of some of the Maccabaeans, but how important was it for them? It is to this question that we turn now.

2.3.1 Passover Attendance

Josephus says the priests counted 255,600 Passover Lambs being slain at the time of the revolt. He estimates that ten people shared each lamb and concludes that there were 2,700,000 people present at the Passover festival (*War* 6.420-27). According to Josephus, therefore, the crowd at the festival in 67 CE could have been 3,000,000 (*War* 2.280). Sanders says that 'no one believes the largest of these figures'.[15] He therefore turns to other sources to estimate the Passover attendance. Tacitus put the number besieged in Jerusalem at 600,000 (*The Histories* 5.13).[16] Sanders, tending to be conservative, suggests that perhaps the Jewish population of Palestine was about half a million, depending on the estimate of the non-Jewish population.[17] If there is any truth at all in the figures Josephus supplies, then it would seem fair to say that the Passover attendances could have been of the order of some hundreds of thousands. This would tally with the figure Tacitus gives for those besieged in the city. With numbers of this order in mind, Sanders assumes that about half the Jewish population

15. E.P. Sanders, *Judaism: Practice and Belief 63 BCE–66 CE* (London: SCM Press; Valley Forge, PA: Trinity Press International, 1992), p. 126.

16. C. Tacitus, *The Histories IV–V: Annals I–III* (ed. T.E. Page *et al.*; trans. C.H. Moore and J. Jackson; LCL; London: Heinemann; New York: G.P. Putman's Sons, 1931), pp. 198-99 v. 13. Joachim Jeremias (*Jerusalem in the Time of Jesus: An Investigation into Economic and Social Conditions During the New Testament Period* [London: SCM Press, 1969], p. 78) says that Tacitus probably got this figure from Josephus in *War* 5.569, where we are told that deserters reported that the number of corpses of poor people thrown out through the gates amounted to 600,000 and that it was impossible to determine the number of the rest. It appears that Jeremias's reason for this suggestion is that the figure of 600,000 is common to both sources. If in fact Jeremias is correct then Sanders is back with Josephus whom he has already claimed is an unreliable source as far as the numbers at the Passover festival in 67 CE is concerned.

17. Sanders, *Practice and Belief*, p. 127 nn. 26, 27, 28.

of Palestine made the pilgrimage to the Passover and comes up with a number around 250,000. In addition to these Palestinian Jews there would have been some from the Diaspora. There is no way of knowing how many may have come from this group of Jews. According to Sanders a realistic guess at the total Passover attendance could be 300,000, requiring the slaughter of 30,000 Passover Lambs. Given this number Temple space would have been a problem. Sanders suggests that pilgrims were arranged in lines in the court, and in a more or less continuous flow, filed past as priest,[18] who caught the blood of the slaughtered lamb in a basin and handed it on to be splashed against the altar. Then the carcase would be hung either on a hook or wooden staves resting on the shoulders, possibly of the owner, while the priest skinned the animal and cut out the the fatty portions to be burned on the altar. The remaining carcase and skin would be returned to the owner. The priests would do this work in shifts.[19] In this way the slaughter of the 30,000 lambs could have been accomplished.

There is, however, considerable guesswork in estimating Passover atten dance in Jerusalem. Is there any other evidence that the Passover was well supported? One possible source is the attitude of the Diaspora Jews. Aristobulus, for example, writing about 150 BCE, possibly from Alexandria, discusses the dating of the Passover and gives every indication that it is central for his religion.[20] Ezekiel the Tragedian has the Passover featuring prominently in his play as 'the beginning of months and years'.[21] The Passover was certainly well enough known in Rome for Tacitus to comment on it (*Hist.* 5.4).[22] Given its centrality for Aristobulus and Ezekiel and the acknowledgment by Tacitus, we should expect it to be well supported.

While it is very likely that Diaspora Jews actually killed animals in their

---

18. Jeremias (*Jerusalem*, pp. 79-84) adopts a static model for his calculation and understandably comes up with a figure considerably smaller than Sanders, namely 180,000. Sanders is a little closer to Josephus's figure, but not much. Either way the number at the Passover would be in the order of some hundreds of thousands.

19. Sanders, *Practice and Belief*, p. 137.

20. Fragment 1.16-18. A. Yarbo Collins (*OTP*, II, p. 833) dates the fragments of Aristobulus in the latter part of the reign of Philometor (155–145 BCE) and suggests the most likely provenance for the work is Alexandria.

21. *OTP*, II, p. 816, line 192. R. G. Robertson (*OTP*, II, p. 804) dates Ezekiel's work at the beginning of the second century BCE and maintains that his characterization as 'the Jewish poet of Alexandria' has not been seriously challenged.

22. Tacitus, *The Histories*, pp. 272-73.

homes at Passover,[23] it is certain that many thousands travelled to Jerusalem to celebrate the Passover. It is impossible to say how many pilgrims journeyed to the Temple or how frequently. Philo indicates in passing that he has been there (*Prov.* 2.64).[24]

It seems therefore that the Temple and its festivals (including, and especially, the Passover) established a powerful and extensive magnetic field, drawing Jews from all points of the compass. Given the widespread, knowledge of, and support for, the Passover, it is not unlikely that, whatever the precise numbers at the festival and the exact organizational details, the Passover was evidently well supported, involving possibly 50 per cent of the Jewish population of Palestine plus Diaspora pilgrims, and giving an attendance of about 300,000.

2.3.2 *Temple Tax*

By the time of the first century, the two Temple tax texts (Exod. 30.13-16; Neh. 10.32) were interpreted as requiring an annual tax of one half-shekel (i.e. two drachmas) from every Jewish male, including freed slaves and proselytes, between the ages of 20 and 50. The tax was intended to support public sacrifices and the city's municipal needs. In the case of Diaspora Jews the tax was transported to Jerusalem. Sanders comments 'that it was paid is one of the things about first-century Judaism that is most certain'.[25]

Josephus and Philo agree that the sum was paid by Jews all over the world,[26] and Josephus claims that convoys brought the tax from the Jews

---

23. Philo, *Spec. Leg.* 2.145; *Vit. Mos.* 2.232; Josephus, *Ant.* 14.260.

24. Joachim Jeremias (*Jerusalem*, pp. 62-71) has a collection of evidence relating to both pilgrimage and long-term residence in Jerusalem by Diaspora Jews.

25. Sanders, *Practice and Belief*, p. 156.

26. Philo mentions the envoys who took money from every city to the Temple (*Spec. Leg.* 1.77-78). Sanders argues (*Practice and Belief*, pp. 156-57) that this is the Temple tax. He mentions that Philo uses the word ἀπαρχαί and says they are payable by every male beginning at age 20 and to be for 'ransom' (λύτρα), as in LXX Exod. 30.12. This word, Sanders says, almost certainly refers to the Temple tax. Cf. also *Leg. Gai.* 156-57, 291, 311-16 where Philo refers to Augustus's permission to Jews to collect money, and in 312 the purpose of the money is specified as paying for the daily public sacrifices that was one of the purposes of the Temple tax. There the same word, ἀπαρχαί, is used. In *Ant.* 16.163, 166, 169 Josephus mentions τὰ ἱερὰ χρήματα which Augustus allowed Diaspora Jews to send to Jerusalem. Again Sanders maintains that this sacred money sent to Jerusalem is almost certainly Temple tax. He maintains this follows from the fact that this money is sent with the official permission of the Emperor. Subsequent history shows that that money which was covered by Rome's

of Babylonia.[27] Successive Roman emperors permitted the money to be exported from other provinces to Jerusalem. It seems that the people complied with the Temple tax requirement wherever they may have been in the Empire. Indeed, where the permission to export silver and gold was in jeopardy the Jewish communities took active steps to ensure that permission was continued. Paul Trebilco documents this evidence and concludes, 'We see, then, that some Jewish communities in Asia Minor (and elsewhere) felt sufficiently committed to the Temple tax to take active measures to ensure they could pay it.'[28]

That the Temple tax generated a vast amount of money can be gauged by a story Cicero cites about the confiscation of some of the tax by Roman administrators: 100 Roman pounds of gold at Apamaea, 20 pounds at Laodecia, an unknown amount at Adramyttium and a small amount at Pergamum.[29] Trebilco points out that, because of disturbed conditions in Jerusalem prior to 62 BCE, the tax may have not been sent for a number of years. Further, the four cities mentioned by Cicero were centres of a regional conventus that would draw in many Jews. We also know that occasionally gifts of gold were forwarded with the tax.[30] Nevertheless it is still a large amount of money, and, even allowing for the special circumstances that Trebilco highlights, it indicates that the Temple was well-supported financially by the Jews from this region. This is not an isolated case. We hear of King Ptolemy sending 'one hundred talents of silver for

decree was indeed the Temple tax. After the fall of the Temple Vespasian diverted the tax of what is described as 'two drachmas' to Rome itself. There is little doubt this refers to the Temple tax since it was two drachmas. This then was the tax that Rome officially knew about and sanctioned but later diverted into its own coffers. Josephus also refers to the delivery of the two drachma coin from Babylon in *Ant.* 18.312-13 (see below in n. 27).

27. *Ant.* 18.312. Neerda and Nisibis were Babylonian cities with natural and human-made defences in which the Jews were willing to deposit their half shekel 'for they made use of these cities as a treasury whence, at a proper time, they [the offerings] were transmitted to Jerusalem; and many ten thousand men undertook the carriage of those donations...'

28. P. Trebilco, *Jewish Communities in Asia Minor* (SNTSMS, 69; Cambridge: Cambridge University Press, 1991), p. 16.

29. Cicero, 'Pro flacco', in *Cicero in Twenty-Eight Volumes* (ed. G.P. Gould; trans. C. MacDonald; LCL, 10; Cambridge, MA: Harvard University Press; London: Heineman, 1977), pp. 434-574 (28.66-69).

30. Trebilco, *Jewish Communities*, p. 13.

sacrifices and the other requirements'.[31] We also hear of donations from the Adiabene royal family (Josephus, *Ant.* 20.49-50; cf. *War* 4.567; 5.55).

These, however, were additional to the Temple tax, which every adult male was expected to pay. And as I have indicated above, not only did they pay, but many Diaspora Jews lobbied for the continued right to pay. Trebilco concludes:

> The Temple tax was connected with the notion that the daily sacrifices were to be provided by the entire community of Israel. The payment of the tax by the Jews of the Diaspora was a way for them to be a tangible part of the worship offered in Jerusalem. In the concern of the Jews of Asia Minor in this period to pay the tax, we see a strong attachment...to the centrality of the Temple and its worship.[32]

2.3.2 *Summary*

With respect to the Temple Sanders concludes: '...the temple was the visible, functioning symbol of God's presence with his people, and it was also the basic rallying point of Jewish loyalties. To it came the temple tax and other offerings from Jews throughout the world, as well as thousands of pilgrims.'[33] Given this widespread and popular support of the Temple, it is not surprising that any desecration of the Temple would be met with outrage and any attack on the Temple would provoke a strong defence. Indeed, Philo threatened world-wide revolt should the Temple be desecrated: 'Everyone everywhere, even if he was not naturally well disposed to the Jews, was afraid to engage in destroying any of our institutions.' And later he says, 'Heaven forbid indeed that the Jews in every quarter should come by common agreement to the defence. The result would be something too stupendous to be combated.'[34]

---

31. *Arist.* 40. Cf. Josephus, *Ant.* 12.50. Sanders argues that this is Temple tax. He says: 'Its purpose is the same as that of the temple tax: the official or public offerings and general expenses. My guess is that the author intended this to be a precedent which would allow Egyptian Jews of his own time to send the temple tax. Ancient governments controlled the export of money, and during the Roman period it was a point of Jewish privilege that Diaspora Jews could pay the tax. There is, as far as I know, no direct information about the rights of Jews in Ptolemaic Egypt to pay the tax' (*Jewish Law from Jesus to Mishnah: Five Studies* [London: SCM Press; Valley Forge, PA: Trinity Press International], p. 293). Whether or not it was Temple tax it was certainly sent to support the Temple and its worship.

32. Trebilco, *Jewish Communities*, p. 16.

33. Sanders, *Practice and Belief*, p. 144.

34. *Leg. Gai.* 159, 215.

The result was indeed stupendous, but not sufficient to repulse the Roman attack and preserve the Temple as we shall see in the following section.

2.4 *The Fall of the Temple*

Josephus (*War* 2.647–7.455; *Life* 407-23) is the only source we have for most of the war that culminated in the burning of the Temple and the sack of Jerusalem. At times his account is confused and often exaggerated[35] so that it is difficult to know precisely what happened. It is clear that the causes of the war were various, but one factor that stands out above others is the inflammatory action of Eleazar b. Ananias, the captain of the Temple. He halted all sacrifices by foreigners, which meant that the daily offerings for Caesar were stopped. Agrippa sent troops to get the sacrifices restarted. They occupied the upper city, but the lower city and Temple were in the hands of Eleazar and his 'war party'. So the stage was set for war with Rome.

2.4.1 *Jewish Factionalism*

I do not wish to traverse the course of the war as narrated by Josephus except to point out that when Jerusalem (Rome's ultimate target) was eventually isolated and surrounded there was much Jewish infighting centred around the Temple. John of Gischala allied himself initially with a group known as the Zealots. They originated in 68 CE (cf. *War* 4.138-61) and began a programme of arrest and execution of those deemed to be traitors. They elected their own high priest. The official high priest Ananus and some of the leaders (including Simon b. Gamaliel) attemped to dislodge the Zealots from the inner court of the Temple (which was their base) but without success. The Zealots sent to the Idumaeans for help, and they eventually combined together and attacked the followers of Ananus

---

35. Grabbe (*Judaism*, p. 458) points out that in *War* 4.566-70, Josephus says that the Idumaeans mutinied against John of Gischala even though they were all said to have left Jerusalem some time earlier. And as an instance of exaggeration Grabbe (*Judaism*, p. 460) says, 'If Josephus is to be believed, they [innocent victims] must all have perished several times over: on several occasions his narrative describes things so that no one among the citizenry could have been left alive, yet the next episode reports more victims. That Josephus's father lived through the siege without harm indicates that the insurgents were perhaps not the out-and-out monsters he makes them out to be (*War* 5.533). Enough horrific things happened without the need of recourse to exaggeration.'

who had taken over the outer court of the Temple. They were annihilated and Ananus was caught and killed.

It appears that some Idumaeans went home at this stage. The Sicarii, who had taken over Masada, used it as a base for raids on the countryside. Simon b. Gioras attacked and overran much of Idumaea. The Zealots feared that he might attack them and so they made a strike against him but were defeated. Eventually Simon took over all Idumaea and came to Jerusalem and set up his camp before the gate.

Some of the Idumaeans (who were left) mutinied against John of Gischala and he and the surviving Zealots fled into the Temple. It seems from *War* 5.1-26 that Eleazar b. Simon, one of the original Zealots, led the split from John and occupied the inner court of the Temple. There was now a three-way split in different sections of the Temple and city: Eleazar and his group were in the inner court; John and his group were in the outer court; and Simon and his group held the rest of the city. All three were fighting each other, with considerable loss of life on all sides.

2.4.2 *The Fall of the Temple*

This was the state of affairs when Titus marched on Jerusalem in the spring of 70 CE. It continued until Passover time. Then, when Eleazar was allowing worshippers into the inner court, John was able to slip some of his men in secretly. They attacked Eleazar's faction and eventually won, uniting the two groups into one with John now in charge and Eleazar retaining a position of command. They maintained control of the Temple, Ophla and the Kedron valley. Simon's force occupied the upper city and part of the lower city. They continued to fight each other despite the progress of the Roman siege. Eventually the Roman army gained the city, breached the Temple walls and set fire to the Temple. There is no doubt that Titus was determined to reduce the Temple to ruins. Gedalyahu Alon has a convincing discussion of this. In *War* 6.228, 241-265 Josephus makes the point that the Temple was burned down against the wish of Titus. But Alon argues conclusively from a wide range of sources (the tradition of the Sages—Tannaim and Amoraim), from the events that immediately preceded and followed the destruction of the Temple, and from other passages in Josephus in which he writes without ulterior motives, that the Temple was put to the torch at Titus's behest.[36] It is very

---

36. G. Alon, 'The Burning of the Temple', in *Jews, Judaism and the Classical World: Studies in Jewish History in the Times of the Second Temple and Talmud* (Jerusalem: Magnes Press, 1977), pp. 252-68.

likely that the Romans saw the Temple as a source of political rebellion. Their very determination to destroy the Temple underlined the strategic place it occupied for the Jewish people.

2.4.3 *Summary*

The foregoing account reveals two things: the strategic place of the Temple in the war and the bitter infighting among the Jews. It is evident that the Temple played a large part in the war. The various Jewish factions were determined to occupy its courts and to fight from that vantage point. I suggest that this determination was driven by not only the Temple's strategic location, but also by the Jewish factions' zealousness for the Temple's sanctity and profound awareness of its symbolic significance. The Romans on the other hand saw the Temple as the root of their troubles with the Jews and were determined to destroy it.

The causes of the war were various, but there is a strong Temple component amongst them. It seems that Eleazar's zeal in excluding sacrifices to Caesar was a major factor. Indeed zeal for the Temple seems to be writ large across this war. Admittedly there is lust for power and greed, but zeal for the Temple seems to be a constant factor and it was this zeal that consumed the nation, the city of Jerusalem and ultimately the Temple itself.[37]

2.5 *The Trauma of the Destruction of the Temple*[38]

The destruction of the Temple in 70 CE was without doubt a cataclysmic event. Neusner describes it like this:

> When the Temple was destroyed, it is clear, the foundations of the country's religious–cultural life were destroyed. The reason is that the Temple had constituted one of the primary unifying elements in that common life. The

---

37. The Gospel of John, after Jesus 'cleansed' the Temple, remarks, 'His disciples remembered that it was written, "Zeal for your house will consume me"' (2.17). It certainly consumed many Jews. Their blood was spilt in the courts of the Temple, but their sacrifice meant only death. From a Johannine perspective the Temple was finished. But the zeal that issued in the sacrifice of Jesus (the Johannine Temple, cf. 2.21) ultimately brought life (10.10; 20.31).

38. For some of the headings and the line of thought for the remainder of this chapter I am indebted to S. Motyer ('John 8.31-59 and the Rhetoric of Persuasion in the Fourth Gospel' [unpublished PhD thesis, Kings' College, University of London, 1993], pp. 92-123) and J. Neusner ('Emergent Rabbinic Judaism in a Time of Crisis: Four Responses to the Destruction of the Second Temple', *Judaism* 21 [1972], pp. 313-27).

structure not only of political life and of society, but also of the imaginative life of the country, depended on the Temple and its worship and cult. It was there that people believed they served God. On the Temple the lines of structure—both cosmic and social—converged. The Temple, moreover, served as the basis for those many elements of autonomous self-government and political life left in the Jews' hands by the Romans. Consequently the destruction of the Temple meant not merely a significant alteration in the cultic or ritual life of the Jewish people but also a profound and far-reaching crisis in their inner and spiritual existence.[39]

The impact of what Neusner says is revealed in the heart cry of 'Why?' that pours out in the writings of *4 Ezra*:

> Why have I been endowed with the power of understanding? For I did not wish to enquire about the ways above, but about which those we daily experience: why Israel has been given over to the Gentiles as a reproach; why the people whom you love have been given to godless tribes, and the Law of our fathers has been made of no effect and the written covenants no longer exist; and why we must pass from the world like locusts and our life is like a mist, and we are not worthy to obtain mercy...[40]

Similar powerful feelings are unleashed by the author of *4 Ezra* as he speaks to the sorrowing woman whose son died when he entered his wedding chamber (*4 Ezra* 21–23). He rehearses the profound loss movingly and eloquently:

> For you see that our sanctuary has been laid waste, our altar thrown down, our Temple destroyed; our harp has been laid low, our song has been silenced, and our rejoicing has ended; the light of our lampstand has been put out, the ark of our covenant has been plundered, our holy things have been polluted, and the name by which we are called has been profaned; our free men have suffered abuse, our priests have been burned to death, our Levites

---

39. J. Neusner, 'The Formation of Rabbinic Judaism: Methodological Issues and Substantive Theses', in *Formative Judaism: Religious, Historical and Literary Studies, Third Series: Torah, Pharisees and Rabbis* (BJS, 46; Chico: Scholars Press, 1983), pp. 99-144 (122). Others have also pointed out that the Temple provided a point of cohesion for the many diverse groups in Judaism, for example, Martyn (*History and Theology*, p. 52) and S.J.D. Cohen (*Yavneh Revisited: Pharisees, Rabbis, and the End of Jewish Sectarianism* [SBLASP; Chico, CA: Scholars Press, 1982], pp. 45-61 [57]). Bruce Longenecker (*2 Esdras* [Sheffield: Sheffield Academic Press, 1995], p. 14) links the loss of the first and Second Temples in terms of exile: 'To be removed from the temple is to be in exile, whether the exile is brought about by forceful removal of the people from the land or by the forceful removal of the temple from the land.'

40. *4 Ezra* 4.22-24.

have gone into captivity, our virgins have been defiled, and our wives have been ravished; our righteous men have been carried off, our little ones have been cast out, our young men have been enslaved and our strong men made powerless. And, what is more than all, the seal of Zion—for she has now lost the seal of her glory, and has been given over into the hands of those who hate us.

The trauma is also evident in the vision the Eternal One gives to Abraham in the *Apocalypse of Abraham*:

> And I looked and I saw, and behold the picture swayed. And from its left side a crowd of heathens ran out and they captured the men, women and children who were on its right side. And some they slaughtered and others they kept with them. Behold, I saw (them) running to them by way of four ascents and they burned the Temple with fire, and they plundered the holy things that were in it. And I said, 'Eternal One, the people you received from me are being robbed by the hordes of the heathen. They are killing some and holding others as aliens, and they burned the Temple with fire and they are stealing and destroying the beautiful things which are in it. Eternal, Mighty One! If this is so, why now have you afflicted my heart and why will it be so?[41]

2.6 *Explanations for the Destruction*

I turn now to consider the explanations offered by our sources for the destruction of the Temple. I will argue in Chapter 3 where I analyse Jn 2.13-22 (the so-called episode of the cleansing of the Temple), that the destruction and resurrection of the body of Jesus as the new Temple (cf. 2.21) is in view. Therefore the crucifixion of Jesus amounts to the destruction of the new Temple (his body). We will see that there is an overlap between the explanations offered for the destruction of the Jerusalem

---

41. *Apoc. Abr.* 27.1-6. *2 Bar.* also laments the fall of the Temple (10.6-19) and asks questions: 'What have they profited who have knowledge before you, and who did not walk in vanity like the rest of the nations, and who did not say to the dead: "Give life to us," but always feared you and did not leave your ways? And, behold, they have been diligent and, nevertheless, you had no mercy on Zion on their account. And if there are others who did evil, Zion should have been forgiven on account of the works of those who did good works and should not have been overwhelmed because of the works of those who acted unrighteously. O LORD, my LORD, who can understand your judgement? Or who can explore the depth of your incomprehensible counsel? Or who of those who are born has ever discovered the beginning and end of your wisdom?' (14.5-9).

Temple and the explanations implicitly offered in John for the destruction of Jesus' body.

What then were the explanations for the demise of the Jerusalem Temple?

2.6.1 *Chastisement for Sin*

Neusner in commenting on Yohanan ben Zakkai's response to the fall of the Temple says, 'Yohanan shared the common sense of grief, and taught, like others, that the sins of the nation had brought the disaster...'[42] For some the sin was especially associated with the Temple. In the *Apocalypse of Abraham*, for example, there is a vivid description of the idolatry in the Temple. There is mention of 'the likeness of the idol of jealousy...and its body was of glittering copper, and before it a man, and he was worshipping it. And there was an altar opposite it and boys being slaughtered on the face of the idol.'[43] It is this idolatry that prompts the destruction of the Temple dramatically presented in ch. 27 only a few verses later.

Sib. Or. 4, well known for its strong polemic against the Temple, says:

> An evil storm of war will also come upon Jerusalem from Italy, and it will sack the great Temple of God, whenever they put their trust in folly and cast off piety and commit repulsive murders in front of the Temple.[44]

Trusting in folly and casting off piety may well be the author's way of describing Temple worship of which he clearly disapproves (cf. *Sib. Or.* 4.6-9, 25-27); committing 'repulsive murders in front of the Temple' is certainly beyond the bounds of Temple worship, but did happen when the various Jewish factions fought and killed one another in the Temple precincts prior to the Roman invasion of the city and Temple. However, we understand the precise designation of the words 'trust in folly', 'cast off piety' and 'commit repulsive murders', the author lays the blame for the Temple's demise on the sins of the people.[45] In 2 *Bar.* 10.18 (cf. 4 *Bar.*

---

42. J. Neusner, *A Life of Rabban Yohanan ben Zakkai Ca. 1–80 C.E.* (Leiden: E.J. Brill, 1962), p. 145.

43. *Apoc. Abr.* 25.1, 2. Idolatry is also mentioned in *T. Mos.* 2.8-9; cf. 5.3-4; 6.1.

44. *Sib. Or.* 4.115-18. J.J. Collins (*OTP*, I, p. 387) suggests that the murders are probably done by the Romans. The pronoun 'they' more likely refers to the people of Jerusalem who 'put their trust in folly and cast off piety...' Collins allows for the possibility that the 'repulsive murders' are done by the Zealots, and I think this is more likely than the Romans.

45. This contrasts with *Sib. Or.* 5.154, 398-409 where the Jewish people are exonerated as 'righteous' and the blame falls squarely on the Romans.

4.4-6) the author pinpoints the false stewardship of the priests: 'You, priests, take the keys of the sanctuary, and cast them to the highest heaven, and give them to the LORD and say, "Guard your house yourself, because, behold, we have been found to be false stewards."' [46]

We conclude that some writers saw the sin in terms of the Temple: idolatry, false stewardship, murder in the Temple precincts and even Temple worship as such (*Sib. Or.* 4). Others saw it in more general terms,[47] including failure to submit to Rome.

2.6.2 *The Plan and Will of God*

We have seen how some texts support the view that chastisement of sin was the cause of the overthrow of the Temple. Another cause suggested is the plan and will of God. Indeed many contemporary authors saw this as the primary cause.

This line of thought is particularly clear in *4 Baruch*, where emphasis is laid on the fact that *God* destroyed the city before the Chaldeans (that is the Romans) did (1.6-8; 3.4; 4.1-3). The reason for this emerges in 4.8-9: 'Do not let the outlaws boast and say, "We were strong enough to take the city of God by our power"; but because of our sins it was delivered to you.'[48]

This is further developed in *2 Baruch* where the disaster of the fall of the Temple was more than was required as a judgment for those who sinned:

46. In addition Josephus targets the Zealots and other warring factions in Jerusalem and adds the sin of not submitting to Rome. Cf. *War* 5.376-78.

47. *4 Ezra* 7.(72); 9.36-37, are texts that highlight the peoples' failure to keep the law, even though the law is good and does not perish (cf. Rom 8.3). There is an interesting later rabbinic text that lays the cause specifically on love of money and hatred namely (*t. Menaḥot* 13.22): 'A. Said R. Yohanan b. Torta, "On what account was Shiloh destroyed? Because of the disgraceful disposition of the Holy Things which were there…" C. "But [as to] the latter [building] we know that they devoted themselves to Torah and were meticulous about tithes". D. "On what account did they go into exile? Because they love money and hate one another". E. "This teaches you that hatred for another is evil before the Omnipresent,…"' (J. Neusner [trans. and ed.], *The Tosefta: Quodoshim* [New York: Ktav, 1979], p. 162). Jesus' concern in Jn 2.16 is that the Jews were making the Temple a marketplace. Whether this constitutes a love of money is a moot point. Sanders argues (*Jesus and Judaism* [London: SCM Press, 1985], pp. 61-71) that commercial activity was necessary in order to fulfil cultic requirements.

48. The fall of the first Temple is immediately in view in *4 Bar.*, but the author probably reflects the fall of the second Temple in the first four chapters (S.E. Robinson, *OTP*, II, p. 414) and so it is possibly legitimate to make the equation Chaldeans = Romans. It is also interesting to note the divine passive—'was delivered to you'.

And if there are others who did evil, Zion should have been forgiven on account of the works of those who did good works and should not have been overwhelmed because of the works of those who acted unrighteously (14.7).[49]

But this did not happen. Why then was the Temple destroyed? It seems in *2 Baruch* that God has a larger purpose: 'I now took away Zion to visit the world in its own time more speedily' (20.2). With this in mind the author can say that the suffering was actually 'for your good' (78.6), and it is possible to rejoice in the present suffering (52.6) because of the certainty of future hope.

What is this future hope? It is that Zion 'will be renewed in glory and that it will be perfected into eternity' (32.4).

This involves an interesting reinterpretation of the status of the Temple:

Do you think that this is the city of which I said, 'On the palms of my hands I have carved you?' It is not this building that is in your midst now; it is that which will be revealed, with me, that was already prepared from the moment that I decided to create Paradise (4.2-3).

Here Isa. 49.16 is applied not to the physical Temple, but to the heavenly Temple that will be 'revealed' in the age to come. While the physical Temple is presented positively in *2 Bar.* 68.5-8, when it comes under the judgment of God that judgement is perceived to be a sign of the heavenly Temple to come. 'The destruction, and not the building, of the Temple is what points forward to the age to come.'[50] This is a radical reinterpretation of Isa. 49.14-26.[51]

---

49. *2 Bar.* struggles with the fact that the righteous and the unrighteous are lumped together under God's judgment. The author reasons that the good deeds of the righteous should have mitigated the severity of God's judgment, but this is not what has happened. Cf. 77.8-10; 78.5; 79.1-4.

50. Motyer, 'Persuasion', p. 106.

51. While the author of *2 Bar.* stops short of saying that the physical Temple was a mistake (cf. 68.5-8), there is no hesitation in *Sib. Or.* 4: 'Happy will be those of mankind on earth who will love the great God... They will reject all temples when they see them; altars too, useless foundations of dumb stones...defiled with blood of animate creatures, and sacrifices of four-footed animals. They will look to the great glory of the one God and commit no wicked murder' (4.24-25, 27-31). Here we see Old Testament polemic against idols as 'dumb' now being applied to the Jerusalem Temple and altar. This represents a radical abandonment of the whole cultic heritage which is rare in early Judaism. Acts 7.48-50 may be a further example.

While *2 Baruch* offers some hope,[52] things are less clear in *4 Ezra*. It seems that the author attributes the fall of the Temple to the action of God,[53] but the inscrutability of God's purpose is a profound problem for him:

> He said to me, 'You cannot understand the things with which you have grown up; how then can your mind comprehend the way of the Most High? And how can one who is already worn out by the corrupt world understand incorruption?' (4.10-11).[54]

Motyer believes that the author of *4 Ezra* cannot understand the disasters of earth because the will of God is inscrutable. He maintains:

> The fundamental dualism between heaven and earth is never overcome: 'Who is able to know these things except he whose dwelling is not with men?' (5.38). In spite of the fact that visions are given to Ezra, there is a fundamental lack of revelation.[55]

It is true that Ezra struggles with lack of insight into the the mind of the Most High and admits 'neither did I ever ascend into heaven' (4.8), but the climatic fourth vision (9.38–10.59) does supply an answer of hope. The Most High shows him Zion as she really is, in 'the brightness of her glory and the loveliness of her beauty' (10.50), in spite of the fact that the woman is mourning the loss of her son.

I conclude that a number of first-century (CE) writers believed that the Jerusalem Temple was destroyed according to the plan and will of God. Josephus is among these when he says, 'But as for that house [the Temple], God had, for certain, long ago doomed it to the fire.'[56]

---

52. 'Israel should rejoice in her sufferings (52.6). After the destruction of the city, Israel has nothing left other than God and his Law (85.3), which will last for ever and ever (77.5 sic) [should be 77.15]... Those who live according to the Law will be gathered together (78.7), and will take part in the resurrection of the dead, and will enjoy life on a new earth (30.1-2)' (A.J.F. Klijn, *OTP*, I, p. 618).

53. Cf. 4.30 where the author challenges the justice of God's judgment against Zion.

54. This section of *4 Ezra* parallels the thought of Jn 3.12, 13: 'If I have told you about earthly things and you do not believe, how can you believe if I tell you about heavenly things? No one has ascended into heaven except the one who descended from heaven, the Son of Man.'

55. Motyer, 'Persuasion', p. 103.

56. Josephus, *War* 6.250.

2.7 *Responses to the Destruction*

I now turn to responses to the destruction, the main one being a renewed emphasis on the Torah, but there was development of other strands of thought that I will note as I proceed.[57]

2.7.1 *A Renewed Emphasis on Torah Piety*

The replacement of the Temple cult with an emphasis on Torah piety is highlighted by the famous exchange between Yohanan ben Zakkai and his disciple Joshua ben Hananaiah:

> Once as Rabban ben Zakkai was coming out of Jerusalem, Rabbi Joshua followed after him, and beheld the Temple in ruins. Woe unto us, Rabbi Joshua cried, that this place, the place where the iniquities of Israel were atoned for, is laid waste. My son, Rabban Yohanan said to him, be not grieved. We have another atonement as effective as this, and what is it? It is acts of lovingkindness, as it is said, "For I desire mercy and not sacrifice" (Hos. 6.6).[58]

Neusner's comment on this is worth quoting:

> To Yohanan ben Zakkai, preserving the Temple was not an end in itself. He taught that there was another means of reconciliation between God and Israel, so that the Temple and its cult were not decisive. What really counted in the life of the Jewish people? Torah, piety… What was the will of God? It was doing deeds of lovingkindness: 'I desire mercy, not sacrifice' (Hos 6.6) meant to Yohanan, 'We have a means of atonement as effective as the Temple, and it is doing deeds of lovingkindness.' Just as willingly as men could contribute bricks and mortar for the rebuilding of a sanctuary, so they ought to contribute renunciation, self-sacrifice, love, *for the building of a sacred community*.[59]

---

57.   One I do not consider in detail is the rejection of the cult per se. This is clear in the text, *Sib. Or.* 4. The author describes a temple as 'a bane which brings many woes to men' (*Sib. Or.* 4.9; *OTP*, I). God does not have a Temple of stone, but one which is not made by mortal hands (8-11). Indeed the pious reject all temples and sacrificial cults (27-30). While these passages are not specifically an attack on the Jerusalem Temple (which was no longer standing [*OTP*, I, pp. 125-26]), they undermine the Temple worship and make the very idea of a Temple unacceptable. While piety is a strong theme in *Sib. Or.* 4 it is not linked specifically to the Torah. Indeed there is no mention of the Torah anywhere in *Sib. Or.* 4. I do not think this response was widespread and therefore does not warrant much emphasis.

58.   *The Fathers According to Rabbi Nathan* (trans. J. Goldin; Yale Judaica Series, 10; New Haven: Yale University Press, 1995), p. 34.

59.   Neusner, 'Four Responses', p. 324. The emphasis is mine, although elsewhere

Some preparation for understanding the community as the Temple had been provided by Qumran. The founders of Qumran were Temple priests who saw themselves continuing the true priestly line as the sons of Zadok.[60] For them the Temple was desecrated not in 70 CE, but in the times of the Maccabees by the rise of a high priest from the Hasmonaean family whom they rejected. Moreover they rejected the calendar followed in Jerusalem. They therefore set out to create a new Temple, until God would come and, through the Messiah in the line of Aaron, establish the Temple once again. The Qumranians believed that the presence of God had left the Jerusalem Temple and come to the Dead Sea Community. The corollary of this would seem to be that the community of Qumran now constituted the Temple. There is some evidence for this in their writings. For example in 4Q174 there is a commentary on 2 Sam. 7.10 where there is promise of the LORD appointing a place for his people Israel where they will no more be troubled by enemies or afflcited by a son of iniquity:

> This (refers to) the house which [they will establish] for [him] in the last days, as it is written in the book of ₃ [Moses: Exod 15.17-18 'A temple of the LORD] will you establish with your hands. YHWH shall reign for ever and ever'. This (refers to) the house into which shall never enter ₄ […] either the Ammonite, or the Moabite, or the Bastard, or the foreigner, or the proselyte, never, because there [he will reveal] to the holy ones; ₅ eternal [glory] will appear over it for ever… And he commanded to build for himself a temple of man, to offer him in it, before him, the works of the law (4Q174. 2-7).[61]

There appears to be some conflation here. On the one hand there is the house that the LORD will build in the last days, the eschatological Temple,

---

Neusner makes the same point with emphasis when he is commenting on leprosy and bodily discharges keeping people out of the community. 'What kept people out of the sanctuary in olden times therefore is going even now to exclude them from the life of the community…*because the community of Israel now is regarded as the temple*' (J. Neusner, 'Judaism after the Destruction of the Temple: An Overview', in *Formative Judaism: Religious, Historical and Literary Studies, Third Series: Torah, Pharisees, and Rabbis* [BJS, 46; Chico, CA: Scholars Press, 1983], pp. 83-98 [97]).

60. Brief summaries of the probable origins of the Qumran community can be found in F.M. Cross, *Canaanite Myth and Hebrew Epic: Essays in the History of the Religion of Israel* (Cambridge, MA: Harvard University Press, 1973), pp. 326-42; and James VanderKam, *The Dead Sea Scrolls Today* (Grand Rapids: Eerdmans, 1994), pp. 99-108.

61. Florentino García Martínez, *The Dead Sea Scrolls Translated* (trans. W.G.E. Watson [Leiden: E.J. Brill, 1992]), p. 136.

which will be completely pure and will endure forever. On the other hand, the LORD has commanded 'to build for himself a temple of man', which may possibily be an interim measure until the eschatological Temple is built. But at least the notion of a 'temple of man' is clearly in view and furthermore, in the absence of an altar, the acceptable offering is 'the works of the Law'. This is an adumbration of what Yohanan ben Zakkai later advocated: 'We have a means of atonement as effective as the Temple, and it is doing deeds of lovingkindness.' What is not clear from this text is whether the 'temple of man' is made up of the Qumran community. Nowhere in 4Q174 does it say unequivocally that the community itself is the Temple. However in 1QS 8.8-9 it is clear that the Council of the Community is described as the House of Israel in obvious Temple imagery:

> the Community council shall be founded on truth, *Blank* like an everlasting plantation, a holy house for Israel and the foundation of the holy of 6 holies for Aaron, true witnesses for the judgement and chosen by the will (of God) to atone for the earth and to render the wicked their retribution. *Blank* It (the Community) will *be the tested rampart, the precious cornerstone that does not Blank / whose foundations do not/ shake or tremble in their place. Blank* It will be *the most holy dwelling* for Aaron with total knowledge of the covenant of justice and in order to offer a pleasant /aroma/; and it will be a *house* of perfection and truth in Israel (emphasis is mine).[62]

The italicized words constitute a strong reference to the Temple. The Council are said to be the rampart and the cornerstone of the Temple. The thought is surely that the Council is the foundation on which the Community is built as a Temple with the cultic function of offering up a 'pleasant aroma', which, as I noted above, are 'the works of the Law'.

Atonement in Qumran is effected not with the flesh of holocausts, but with prayer and perfect living:

> [So] in order to atone for the fault of the transgression and for the guilt of sin and for approval for the earth, without the flesh of burnt offerings and without the fat of sacrifice—the offering of 5 the lips in compliance with the decree will be like the pleasant aroma of justice and the correctness of behaviour will be acceptable like a feewill offering...(1QS9.4-5).[63]

For Qumran, then, the cultic function of the Temple was expressed in doing the works of the Law and offering up prayer. The Temple became

---

62. García Martínez, *The Dead Sea Scrolls*, p. 12.
63. García Martínez, *The Dead Sea Scrolls*, p. 13.

the community itself with the Council as the foundation.[64]

Qumran's response then to the desecration of the Temple (for them the Temple had been desecrated through introducing priests who were not sons of Zadok) was to retreat to the Dead Sea and constitute the community as a Temple. The sacrifices offered in this 'new Temple' were deeds of obedience to the Law. This is, of course, strikingly similar to the rabbinic response mentioned above.

2.7.2 Merkabah *Mysticism and Apocalypticism*

With the Fall of the Temple the presence and revelation of God became an issue: Where was God to be found? How could one get 'in touch' with God now that the tangible Temple had gone? It is not surprising then that some Jews sought God through *merkabah* (מֶרְכָּבָה = chariot) mysticism[65] so that by means of a mystical ascent they could gain the revelation of the throne of God.[66]

While there was nervousness about *merkabah* mysticism among some Jews, there is evidence that there was a growing interest in it following the demise of the Jerusalem Temple. Neusner, in discussing Yohanan's interest

---

64. B. Gärtner (*The Temple and Community in Qumran and the New Testament* [SNTSMS, 1; Cambridge: Cambridge University Press, 1965], pp. 20-21) says, 'But when the cultus of the Jerusalem Temple could no longer be accepted, a substitute was found in the community itself: the temple, its worship [עבדה], and its sacrifices were made to apply to the community per se, its life of obedience to the Law and its liturgy. This process may have been further facilitated by the idea, found elsewhere in late Judaism, that the works of the Law were sufficient to make atonement for sins.' Coloe ('The Dwelling of God', p. 88 n. 102) usefully comments, 'In an unpublished thesis, Brendan Byrne modified Gärtner's claims by showing that it was a core group and not the whole community, who were designated as the Temple. See B. Byrne, " 'Building' and 'Temple' Imagery in the Qumran Texts" (MA; Middle Eastern Studies; Melbourne, 1971), pp. 146, 170-71.' My conclusion, indicated above, is that the 'core group' is the Council and is the *foundation* of the Temple.

65. J.D.G. Dunn ('Let John Be John: A Gospel for its Time', in Stuhlmacher [ed.], *Das Evangelium und die Evangelien: Vortäge vom Tübinger Symposium 1982* [Tübingen: J.C.B. Mohr, 1983], pp. 293-322 [307]) has a helpful explanation of *merkabah* mysticism: '...the means in which one sought by meditation, particularly on the chariot vision of Ezekiel 1 (but also passages like Isa. 6 and Dan. 7.9-10, as well as the story of creation in Gen. 1), to experience for oneself a mystical ascent to the revelation of the throne of God...'

66. The language of ascent/descent is evident in Jn 1.51 and 3.13. The thrust of these verses taken together is to emphasize the uniqueness of Jesus, the Son of Man, in gaining access to the revelation of God.

in *merkabah* speculation, suggests as one reason for it the parallel between Yohannan's experience and Ezekiel's: just as the departure of the chariot from Jerusalem signalled the destruction of the Temple for Ezekiel, so the destruction of the Temple in Yohanan's day prompted a similar interest in the chariot now located in heaven.[67] Neusner remarks:

> Yohanan apparently succeeded in using the ancient images of prophecy once again to embody religious experience, for he found in the visions of Ezekiel viable and appropriate forms for his own vision…when Jerusalem lay in ruins, he [Yohanan] and his disciples found the faith to continue their study [of Torah].[68]

While it is possible to distinguish between *merkabah* mysticism found among some rabbis and the visionary emphasis of the apocalypses of the first century, there is nevertheless considerable overlap, as Dunn emphasizes when he says, 'Both apocalyptic and *merkabah* mysticism are characterised precisely by their claim to a direct knowledge of heavenly mysteries, either by means of a vision, or, more frequently, by means of an ascent to heaven.'[69]

While it seems likely that *merkabah* speculation provides the imagery of the vision in *Apoc. Abr.* 18 where there is a clear reference to the vision of Ezek. 1,[70] it is more common in apocalyptic literature for visions to be attained by ascents to heaven. For example, the archangel Michael takes Abraham on a chariot of cherubim and lifts him up into the air of heaven from where he can see the whole inhabited world (*T. Abr.* 10.1, 2).[71]

---

67. Neusner, *Yohanan*, p. 101.

68. Neusner, *Yohanan*, p. 103.

69. Dunn, 'Let John Be John', p. 306. Dunn makes the interesting observation that 'this overlap has been obscured by identifying apocalyptic too closely with eschatology' (p. 306 n. 39).

70. '…under the throne four fiery living creatures, singing. And the appearance of each of them was the same, each having four faces. And this (was) the aspect of their faces: of a lion, of a man, of an ox, and of an eagle… And while I was still standing and watching, I saw behind the living creatures a chariot with fiery wheels. Each wheel was full of eyes round about. And above the wheels was the throne I had seen' (18.3-5, 12, 13).There is also *merkabah* mysticism based on Ezek. 1 in the Qumran Songs of the Sabbath Sacrifice (4Q405.21-22).

71. *4 Ezra* 3.14 speaks of God making a revelation to Abraham of the end of the times secretly by night. Cf. also *2 Bar.* 4.4, which says the same thing. Is there a link here with Jn 3.2 where Nicodemus comes to Jesus by night seeking knowledge of heavenly things (cf. Jn 3.12) and is told: 'No one has ascended into heaven except the one who descended from heaven, the Son of Man' (3.13)?

Similarly Levi is granted a heavenly vision after entering the heavens from a high mountain (*T. Levi* 2.5-10).[72] Isaiah also is taken by an angel's hand on a journey through the seven heavens (*Mart. Isa.* 7.1–9.18). So too the account of Moses' ascent of Mt Sinai (Exod. 19.3; 24.18) is extended within some circles of Judaism to an ascent to God marked with special revelations (Philo, *Vit. Mos.* 1.158; *Quest. in Exod.* 2.29, 40, 46; Josephus, *Ant.* 3.96; cf. *4 Ezra* 14.5). In particular he received a vision of 'the likeness of Zion with its measurements which was to be made after the likeness of the present sanctuary' (*2 Bar.* 59.3, 4; cf. 4.5.).[73]

In some of these visions there is the appearance of a glorious being closely related in appearance to God (Ezek. 8.2; Dan. 7.13 (LXX); 10.5-6; *Apoc. Abr.* 10.1-17), and in some cases there is a transformation into an angel-like form of the one who ascends, notably Moses and Isaiah (see references above) and interestingly Enoch (*1 En.* 71.11; *2 En.* 22.8;[74] *Mart. Isa.* 9.9), who is called 'son of man' in the Similitudes of Enoch (*1 En.* 71.14).[75]

There was mention above that Yohanan ben Zakkai was interested in Ezekiel 1 and probably practised meditation on it (*t. Ḥag.* 2.1 and parallels). But more striking is the tradition about the four sages who 'entered the garden (*parades*)' (*t. Ḥag.* 2.3-4 and parallels). Dunn comments: '…as most agree, the tradition probably refers in a veiled way to a vision of the chariot of the throne of God. This is confirmed by such fuller information as we have about these rabbis.'[76]

There was however a cautionary reaction against *merkabah* mysticism

72. Other examples include Enoch (*1 En.* 14.8-25; 39.3-8; 70–71; *2 En.* 3–22), Baruch (*2 Bar.* 76) and Adam (*LAE* 25-29).

73. W.A. Meeks has an extensive coverage of the ascents of Moses in *The Prophet-King: Moses Traditions and the Johannine Christology* (NovTSup, 14; Leiden: E.J. Brill, 1967), pp. 110-11, 117, 122-25, 141, 147-49, 156-59, 205-209, 232-36, 241-44.

74. 'The LORD said to Michael, "Take Enoch, and extract (him) from the earthly clothing. And anoint him with the delightful oil, and put (him) into the clothes of glory."'

75. Charlesworth offers a cautionary note (*OTP*, I, p. 50 n. s) when he says that the expression 'son of man' should not be identified as 'the Son of Man'. He suggests the term means 'human being'. However, the context and other exalted terms used to describe Enoch (e.g. 'the righteousness of the Antecedent of Time will not forsake you') suggest that the expression may be closer to 'the Son of Man' than Charlesworth allows.

76. Dunn, 'Let John Be John', p. 308. In n. 50 he cites the references to the fuller information on the rabbis.

and apocalyptic visions. This is noticeable in Sir. 3.18-25 where the son is advised:

> Do not try to understand things that are too difficult for you, or try to discover what is beyond your powers. Concentrate on what has been assigned you, you have no need to worry over mysteries. Do not meddle with matters that are beyond you... (21, 22).[77]

And *4 Ezra* 8.20-21 seems to be directed against claims to be able to see and describe God's throne. This seems to be so even in the apocalyptic literature itself (e.g. *4 Ezra* 14.47).

By way of conclusion we can say that there evidently was considerable interest in the possibility of gaining heavenly knowledge through visions and heavenly ascents following the fall of the Temple. There was some interest prior to 70 CE, but it certainly continued after the destruction of the Temple and possibly gained ground. The misgivings and even hostility against *merkabah* mysticism and apocalyptic visions suggest that they formed a sizable current of thought in first-century Judaism and an understandable response to the catastrophe of the fall of the Temple in 70 CE. As Motyer says, 'It attests *a longing for heavenly knowledge, at a time when the ways of God seemed past comprehension.*'[78]

2.7.3 *Quietist Eschatology*

Motyer makes the helpful distinction between 'quietist' and 'activist' eschatologies. By 'quietist eschatology' he means that the solution to the problem is left entirely in the hands of God and does not envisage any kind of 'holy war' to solve it. By 'activist eschatology' he means a response to the calamity that looked for a future restoration in which the people of God themselves played an active role—often a military role.[79]

The clearest example of quietist eschatology is found in *2 Baruch*. The author emphasizes that God (not Titus) was responsible for the destruction of the Temple (6.3–7.1). In fact the Romans only enter the Temple after the angels have breached the wall, the vessels have been removed and God has left it:

77. Even though Ben Sirach was cautious he mentions Ezekiel's vision without disapproval (Sir. 49.8) and searches the law and prays for 'the spirit of understanding'. 'He will ponder the LORD's hidden mysteries' (Sir. 39.1-8). This too attests a longing for heavenly knowledge—only rather than coming through visions, it comes through careful research of the law.

78. Motyer, 'Persuasion', p. 115 (his emphasis).

79. Motyer, 'Persuasion', p. 116.

> Now the angels did as he [God] commanded them; and when they had broken up the corners of the wall, a voice was heard from the midst of the temple after the wall had fallen, saying: Enter, enemies, and come, adversaries, because he who guarded the house has left it (8.1, 2; cf. 80.1-4).

The purpose of this calamity is so God can come in judgment more speedily (20.2) and scatter his people among the nations that they may do good to the nations (1.4). There will be vengeance for what has been done to Jerusalem (13.5; 82.2), but this rests entirely in the hands of God. 'The Most High will cause all these things to come' (85.12). Furthermore there is no reference to a reconstruction of the Temple in the restoration after the judgment.[80]

The same quietist tenor is found in Yohanan ben Zakkai. He links messianic activism to the desire to rebuild the Temple and he is sceptical of both:

> If you are in the process of planting a sapling, and they say to you—'Behold, there is the Messiah'—go on with your planting, and after go out and make him welcome. And if the youths say to you: 'Let us go and build the Temple (בית המקדש)', do not listen to them. But if the elders say to you: 'Come let us destroy the Temple', listen to them, for the building of youth is destruction (מפני שבנין ילדים סתירה), and destruction of elders is building—proof of the matter (ראיה לדבר) is Rehoboam, son of Solomon.[81]

Revolutionary fervour and a desire to rebuild the Temple are countered with the judgment that the destruction of the Temple was actually a good thing. Yohanan tells us to listen to the elders who advocate the destruction of the Temple for the 'destruction of elders is building', that is, the gentle,

---

80. Frederick Murphy ('The Temple in the Syriac *Apocalypse of Baruch*', *JBL* 106.4 [1987], pp. 671-83 [682]) considers the possibility that 32.2-4 ('For after a short time, the building of Zion will be shaken in order that it will be rebuilt. That building will not remain; but it will again be uprooted after some time and will remain desolate for a time.') may envisage a third building of the Temple and concludes: '…32.2-4 is a slender thread upon which to hang the conviction that our author expects a rebuilt Temple. This conclusion is strengthened by the observation that there is no restoration of the Temple in the messianic passages…or in the world to come… It is likely that although the author did not care to deny *explicitly* the possibility of a third Temple, it was of no ultimate significance to him. If built, its value would be as relative as was that of the first and Second Temples.'

81. S. Schechter (ed.), *Aboth de Rabbi Nathan* (Text B; Vienna: Ch.D. Lippe, 1887; reprinted New York: Georg Olms Verlag, 1979), ch. 31, pp. 66-67. Cf. Neusner, *Yohanan*, p. 134.

quietist approach recommended to Rehoboam by the elders, is building. On the other hand, the so-called 'building' of youth, that is, the oppressive, militant advice given to Rehoboam by the young men, brought destruction. Rehoboam's harsh regime sparked revolt and division of the kingdom (2 Kgs 12.6-19).

This was not the only form 'quietist eschatology' took. *Sib. Or.* 5 also leaves the restoration entirely to God, but it will be brought about by the Messiah ('the best of the Hebrews', 5.258), who will destroy all evildoers (418-19), and rebuild the city with 'a holy temple, exceedingly beautiful in its fair shrine' (422-23).

4 Ezra is somewhere in between the hope of the heavenly Temple (only in *2 Baruch*) and the thoroughly earthly construction envisaged in *Sib. Or.* 5. Here too the Messiah conducts a judgment of the nations (12.31-33; 13.37-38) and at this time 'the city which now is not seen shall appear' (7.26). 'And Zion will come and be made manifest to all people, prepared and built, as you saw the mountain carved out without hands' (13.36). The new Temple will not be built with human hands; it will simply appears as it did to Ezra in his vision (10.25-27). So while the Messiah acts to judge the nations, only God, it seems in *4 Ezra*, acts to build the Temple. To this extent it is quietist in its eschatology.

The Johannine Jesus shares the same quietist perspective. In Jn 18.36 Jesus insists that the kingdom of God is not something for which people should fight. But this saying is set in the context of a realized eschatology to which there is no parallel in contemporary literature. John's message is that God had already acted to rebuild the Temple and bring in the messianic age. And John is emphatic that this has come about through God alone and only incidentally through human agency.

2.7.4 *Activist Eschatology*
The Temple cult is clearly in focus in the *Apocalypse of Abraham*. Activity in the Temple is seen to be the cause of both its demise and its restoration. On the one hand, idolatry and murder in the Temple precipitated its demise (25.1-4; 27.1-7); on the other, Temple sacrifices will 'affirm' those who act for God in taking vengeance on their enemies (29.18, 19). Indeed, the focus on the Temple cult is so strong in the *Apocalypse of Abraham* that there is scarcely any mention of the law as a feature of both problem and solution.[82] This is strikingly different from the emphasis in *2 Baruch*

---

82. Motyer ('Persuasion', p. 119, esp. n. 79) draws attention to this.

and Yohanan ben Zakkai where the Torah plays a large part in the analysis of the cause and in the solution. In fact Yohanan saw the study and practice of the law as the proper response to the fall of the Temple.

But the *Apocalypse of Abraham* sees the solution in terms of a tribulation of ten plagues brought upon all earthly creation (29.15; 30.2-8):

> And then I [The Eternal, Mighty One] will sound the trumpet out of the air, and I will send my chosen one, having in him one measure of all my power, and he will summon my people, humiliated by the heathen. And I will burn with fire those who mocked them and ruled over them in this age and I will deliver those who have covered me with mockery over to the scorn of the coming age. Because I have prepared them (to be) food for the fire of Hades, and (to be) ceaseless soaring in the air of underworld (regions) of the uttermost depths, (to be) the contents of a wormy belly. For the makers will see in them[83] justice, (the makers) who have chosen my desire and manifestly kept my commandments and they will rejoice with merrymaking over the downfall of the men who remain and followed after the idols and after their murders (31.1-4).

Clearly 'the makers' are those who are, as it were, on God's side. They are defined as those 'who have chosen my [God's] desire and manifestly kept my commandments'. These will rejoice with merrymaking over the downfall of the remnant of those who indulged in idolatry in the Temple and who committed murder there. But what is it that they 'make' or 'do'? It is certainly not clear from the immediate context, but if we look back to 29.17-19 we get a possible answer:

> And then from your [Abraham's] seed will be left the righteous men in their number, protected by me, who strive in the glory of my name toward the place prepared beforehand for them which you saw deserted in the picture. And they will live, being affirmed by the sacrifices and the gifts of justice and truth in the age of justice. And they will rejoice forever in me, *and they will destroy those who have destroyed them, they will rebuke them who have rebuked them through their mockery, and they will spit on their faces* (29.17-19, emphasis mine).

The 'righteous' here are clearly God's agents of vengeance against those who destroyed and mocked them. They are 'affirmed' by 'sacrifices'

---

83. Rubinkiewicz (*OTP*, I, p. 705 n.j) says the reference of this pronoun is unclear, but ventures no opinion as to its meaning. The interpretation that seems to make sense is as follows: 'the makers' or 'doers' are those who act for God—they 'have chosen God's desire and manifestly kept his commandments'. The pronoun 'them' refers, I believe, to the judgments that fall on the mockers and oppressors of God's people in 'this age'. God's agents will see these judgments and see 'justice'.

among other things. These sacrifices may well be Temple sacrifices offered in a restored Temple. It is not certain what is referred to by 'the place prepared beforehand for them [the righteous] which you [Abraham] saw deserted in the picture', but given the vivid description of the demise of the Temple, the mention of the righteous striving 'in the glory of my [God's] name toward' this place, it seems likely that the restored Temple is in view. Furthermore they are summoned by God's chosen one (31.1). Given this larger context, then, I believe that it is likely that those referred to as 'the makers' in 31.4 are God's agents of vengeance. And not only do they make vengeance against 'the heathen', they rejoice and make merry as they do so. This is activist eschatology. It is possible to see how this kind of writing could inspire the sort of revolt that occured under Bar Kokba in 135 CE.

Pseudo-Philo, probably writing before 70 CE,[84] illustrates the extent of popular interest in a prophetic deliverer, an interest that evidently survived the fall of the Temple and erupted in the Bar Kokba revolt. There is a strong emphasis in Pseudo-Philo on the importance of a leader to guide and intercede for the people. Joshua reminds God of his promise, when he himself is about to die:

> Now let the fullness of your mercy sustain your people and choose for your heritage a man so that he and his offspring will rule your people. Did not our father Jacob speak about him, saying 'A ruler will not be lacking from Judah...' (*Ps.-Philo* 21.4-5).

And for Pseudo-Philo this leader is to be a prophet rather than a king. This emerges when Saul is anointed king and the people say:

> We are your servants; but we have a king, because we are not worthy to be governed by a prophet... And all the people and the king wept with a great lamentation and said, 'Long live Samuel the prophet!' (*Ps.-Philo* 57.4)

Motyer observes:

> the leaders who are also prophets (Moses, Joshua, Kenaz, Deborah, Samuel) are shown in a very good light, while those who are not prophets (Gideon, Abimelech, Jair, Jephthah, Samson, Saul) all fall into sin and lead the people astray, even though they are appointed as deliverers.[85]

---

84. D.J. Harrington (*OTP*, II, p. 299) after careful consideration of the evidence dates the composition of the original Hebrew version of Pseudo-Philo as most likely 'around the time of Jesus'.

85. Motyer, 'Persuasion', p. 120.

At the time of Pseudo-Philo's writing, probably before 70 CE, the Jerusalem priesthood did provide much of the leadership along with other bodies, but what was lacking was a single prophetic leader and this seems to be what people longed for. Popular messianism at the time desired such leadership as would deliver Israel from the enemies surrounding her. This longing is confirmed by Josephus, who writes of political disturbances during Felix's rule in the early sixties in *War* 2.259:

> These were such men as deceived and deluded the people under pretence of divine inspiration, but were for procuring innovations and changes of the government; and these prevailed with the multitude to act like madmen, and went before them into the wilderness, as pretending that God would there show them the signals of liberty.

Obviously Josephus thinks the people were deluded, but the fact that they were apparently so easily deluded attests the willingness of the people to entrust themselves to one who promised to lead them to freedom. In a further story Josephus tells of the Egyptian referred to in Acts 21.38 and he describes him as a 'false prophet' and a 'cheat' (*War* 2.261). In Acts it says he led 4,000 men but in Josephus the number is 30,000. Even if the smaller number is accepted, this incident also reveals the popular readiness not just to believe a prophetic leader might appear, but also to follow such a figure to almost certain death. This suggests that there was a strong hunger for freedom and people were willing to risk their lives in revolt.

2.8 *Relevance for John*

Where does John fit in the range of these responses to the Temple's destruction? As noted the response of an activist eschatology has been ruled out by Jesus' instruction to Peter to put his sword back in its sheath (Jn 18.11) and by his reply to Pilate:

> My kingdom is not from this world. If my kingdom were from this world, my followers would be fighting to keep me from being handed over to the Jews. But, as it is, my kingdom is not from here (19.36).

As we will see in the next chapter,[86] there is a clear eschatological dimension in John, but it is quietist, not active. God is at work through Jesus' death and resurrection to bring in a new family of God (1.12; 20.17) through faith in Jesus Christ. As we will see, this new family, in a derivatory sense, constitutes the new Temple.[87]

---

86. See below 3.3 and 3.4.
87. See below 8.9.2.

Neither is John Torah-directed. The law given through Moses is acknowledged, but the coming of Jesus Christ, the Word made flesh represents a new beginning (1.14, 17). No longer is the law the focus of obedience and study; rather the law (often designated as the *scriptures*), witnesses to Jesus (5.39): Moses wrote about Jesus (5.46) and Isaiah saw Jesus' glory and spoke about him (12.41). The goal of the Torah is Jesus. John is not Torah-directed, but christologically directed.

Further, in John there is no hint of *merkabah* or apocalyptic mysticism. If anything it is given a definitive christological focus in Jn 3.13: 'No one has ascended into heaven, except the one who descended from heaven, the Son of Man.' The only one to ascend and gain the revelation of the throne of God is Jesus himself, who has come from heaven.

Finally, the Qumran emphasis on the Council as the foundation of the Temple finds an echo in John where Jesus is the Temple and in a derivatory sense the community of faith, his disciples, are also the Temple, as I shall demonstrate in Chapter 8.

I conclude therefore that the Johannine response to the demise of the Jerusalem Temple is neither Torah-directed, nor advocating *merkabah* or apocalyptic mysticism; rather (as I will argue) the response is to present Jesus as the fulfilment and replacement of the Temple and its associated rituals within the ethos of a quietist eschatology. And as we shall see, there are also some hints that Jesus' disciples share in this new Temple.

Chapter 3

THE NEW TEMPLE: JOHN 2.13-22

John 2.13-22 is the crucial passage to examine in this study on the Temple theme in the Gospel of John. First, the Temple is central to the narrative and to the exchange between Jesus and the Jews. Secondly, the explanatory remark in 2.21, ἐκεῖνος δὲ ἔλεγεν περὶ τοῦ ναοῦ τοῦ σώματος αὐτοῦ, makes an explicit link between Jesus and the Temple. This will be pivotal to the development of my argument. Thirdly, this episode in the Temple occurs early in the Gospel; it is the second of Jesus' public acts. I will argue that it heralds the eschatological 'hour', the hour that comes to dominate the Gospel as Jesus moves towards the cross and the resurrection.

3.1 *Overview of this Chapter*

After acknowledging the extensive debate over what happened in the Temple I examine the Johannine context to see what clues there are for understanding Jn 2.13-22 as an eschatological event. Further, I explore possible Old Testament allusions to see if there is any support from that quarter for such an eschatological ethos. I conclude that there *is* a cleansing of the Temple in 2.13-22, but it is a cleansing that signals that the day of the LORD has come or is very near. Judgment will begin at the house of the LORD and a new Temple will be raised. It is indeed an eschatological event.

I then turn to the text itself and note that, in the narrative, the disciples also engage in inner biblical exegesis and apply Ps. 69.9 both to the immediate situation and to the 'sacrificial consumption' of the body of Jesus on the cross. I argue that 2.17 brings the death of Jesus into view and that his death is the death of God's Paschal Lamb.

The exchange between the Jews and Jesus (2.18-20) is overlaid with subtle double meanings which only become clear when the narrator lets us into the secret in v. 21 and declares that Jesus is speaking of the Temple of his body.

By way of summary, use is made of narrative analysis of the two partial stories in 2.13-22 and then of the overall story.

3.2 *What Happened in the Temple?*

What did Jesus do in the Temple and why did he do it? I am aware of an extensive debate over this,[1] but to go into it at length would detract from

---

1.   For a useful comparison of John with Mark's version of the Temple incident, see Mark A. Matson, *The Contribution to the Temple Cleansing by the Fourth Gospel* (ed. E.H. Lovering; SBLSP; Atlanta: Scholars Press, 1992), pp. 489-506. B.D. Chilton ('[ὡς] φραγέλλιον ἐκ σξοινίων [John 2.15]', in W. Horbury [ed.], *Templum Amicitiae: Essays on the Second Temple Presented to Ernst Bammel* [JSNTSup, 48; Sheffield: JSOT Press, 1991], pp. 330-44), argues that different sources of the Temple incident are conflated in John's pericope.

As for the motives for Jesus' action (whatever it precisely was) Peter Richardson (*Why Turn the Tables? Jesus' Protest in the Temple Precincts* [ed. E.H. Lovering; SBLSP; Atlanta: Scholars Press, 1992], pp. 507-23) argues that the Tyrian coinage was offensive to Jesus and he objected to the Temple tax being levied annually, whereas it should have been paid once in a lifetime; Craig Evans (*Jesus' Action in the Temple and Evidence of Corruption in the First-Century Temple* [ed. David J. Lull; SBLSP, 28; Atlanta: Scholars Press, 1989], pp. 522-39) marshals impressive evidence to show that Jesus objected to a corrupt priesthood, whereas Haim Cohn (*The Trial and Death of Jesus* [New York: Harper, 1971], pp. 54-59) argues that it was the corrupt traders that roused Jesus' ire; R.H. Lightfoot (*The Gospel Message of Mark* [Oxford: Oxford University Press, 1950], pp. 60-65) presents the view that Jesus' action was because of the exclusion of the Gentiles from God's house. Others who express this view are J. Jeremias, *Jesus' Promise to the Nations* (Philadelphia: Fortress Press, 1982) and T. W. Manson, *Only to the House of Israel?* (Philadelphia: Fortress Press, 1964). Richard A. Horsley in *Jesus and the Spiral of Violence* (San Francisco: HarperSanFrancisco, 1987), pp. 285-300, 130-32, and also in his *Sociology and the Jesus Movement* (New York: Crossroad, 1989), argues that Jesus was rejecting all Jewish institutions, including the Temple, by his actions. E.P. Sanders (*Jesus and Judaism* [London: SCM Press, 1985], pp. 61-71) argues strenuously that there was nothing amiss in the Temple and that what Jesus did was a symbolic demonstration of what would befall the Temple. Richard Bauckham ('Jesus' Demonstration in the Temple', in B. Lindars [ed.], *Law and Religion: Essays on the Place of the Law in Israel and Early Christianity* [Cambridge: James Clarke, 1988], pp. 72-89) argues against Sanders and says that 'our interpretation of Jesus' demonstration amounts to a symbolic denunciation of the activities he attacked' (p. 86). Bauckham finds evidence of commercial activity in the Temple in the name of God that could have provoked Jesus to do what he did (pp. 78-85). Finally Craig A. Evans ('Jesus' Action in the Temple: Cleansing or Portent of Destruction?', *CBQ* 51 [1989], pp. 237-70, and also *Jesus' Action*) endeavours to my main purpose of inquiring about the Temple theme in John.

In brief, according to John, Jesus drove out the sheep and oxen (possibly also the sellers) and overturned the tables of the money changers, pouring the coins (κέρμα) on to the ground. He spoke to the sellers of pigeons saying, 'Take these (the pigeons) out of here!' And then he said, μὴ ποιεῖτε τὸν οἶκον τοῦ πατρός μου οἶκον εμπορίου.[2] This is the stated reason for Jesus' action.

3.3 *Eschatological Context of John 2.13-22*

3.3.1 *Eschatological Shalom*

What of the Johannine context for this action of Jesus? The first half of John 2 tells of Jesus turning water into wine. There are eschatological overtones here. First, this happens on the third day. C.H. Dodd remarks: '[I]t is surely not without significance that this manifestation (cf. Jn 2.11) takes place τῇ ἡμέρᾳ τῇ τρίτῃ... The "third day" was in Christian tradition from earliest times the day when Christ manifested his glory in resurrection from the dead.'[3] This formula signals the resurrection of Jesus.

Secondly, the sheer abundance of wine (120–180 gallons!) intimates a fulfilment of Amos 9.13. Here is shalom 'gone crazy'. With the superabundance of wine from the hand of Jesus, the day of which Amos spoke seems to have been intimated in a dramatic way.

Thirdly, the setting is a wedding. The wedding theme is also found in Jn 3.29 where the bridegroom is Jesus himself. This is a clue that the story of the wedding celebration means more than meets the eye. The placement of this miracle story here alerts us to the great eschatological marriage spoken of in Isa. 54.4-8 and the banquet of Isa. 25.6, 7 where v. 6 speaks of the abundance of wine and v. 7 of 'swallowing up death for ever'. This brings together the feast of wine and the theme of the resurrection.

---

refute Sander's claim that nothing was amiss in the Temple and argues that Jesus did effect a cleansing of the Temple.

2.   'Stop making (μή + pres. imper. has the effect of stopping something that is already in existence. Cf. Blass, Debrunner and Funk, § 336, 172) my Father's house a house of trade.' There is an emphasis on οἶκος. I believe this is a deliberate emphasis which will be picked up later in 8.9.

3.   Dodd, *Interpretation*, p. 300. Nereparampil (*Temple-Logion*, pp. 50-54) has an extended discussion of the 'three day' formulae: τῇ ἡμέρᾳ τῇ τρίτῃ (Hos. 6.2; 1 Cor. 15.4); διὰ τριῶν ἡμερῶν (Mt. 26.61); ἐν τρισὶν ἡμέραις (Mt. 27.40); and μετὰ τρεῖς ἡμέρας (Mt. 27.63). He concludes there are no substantial differences in meaning.

3.3.2 *The New Creation*

Finally, there may be a hint of realized eschatology in the chronology. The words τῇ ἐπαύριον crop up three times in John 1 (vv. 29, 35, 43). If we count these days we get a total of four days. Then if we take the phrase from Jn 2.1 and credit it with some chronological significance in the narrative, then it must mean something like 'on the third day after the last mentioned day'.[4] So counting three days out from number four we come to a total of seven days.[5] The scheme of days therefore looks like this:

1st day	1.19-28	The Baptist's testimony about himself.
2nd day	1.29-34	The Baptist's testimony about Jesus.
3rd day	1.35-42	Andrew and another follow Jesus and Simon Peter becomes a disciple.
4th day	1.43-50	Philip and Nathanael.
5th day[6]	(none)	
6th day	(none)	
7th day	2.1-11	The wedding at Cana.

Jesus then celebrates the wedding on the seventh day. He turns the water into wine on this day. The seventh day is the sabbath day and later in the Gospel we see Jesus working with his Father on the sabbath day to heal the man at Beth-zatha (5.17), to make his whole body healthy (7.23). Again it is on the sabbath that Jesus gives sight to the man born blind (9.14). These seventh day works are signs of new life.

The message seems to be that with the coming of Jesus the Messiah, there is a New Creation. The new age, intimated in the Prologue, has

4.   I am suggesting that the phrase has both chronological and symbolic significance.

5.   The notion that a new eschatological era will commence after a period of seven world days or weeks of years was known in Judaism: Dan. 9.24-7; *1 En.* 93.1-10; 91.12-17; *4 Ezra* 7.31; *T. Levi.* 16.1-5; *2 En.* 33.1-2.

6.   Some interpreters (e.g. Carson, *John*, p. 168) can muster only six days from the text of John. Carson uses inclusive reckoning for 'on the third day', which means two days later rather than three. He finds another day (No. 4) for Andrew's introduction of Peter to Jesus, since four o'clock in the afternoon would presumably be too late in the day to effect the introduction. This involves an over subtle 'reading between the lines' to find the extra day to make up the number 7. Mark Stibbe also seems to accept this suggestion in *John: Readings: A New Bible Commentary* (Sheffield: JSOT Press, 1993), p. 46. I believe it is much simpler to follow the reading I have outlined above. See also Harold Saxby's article 'The Time-Scheme in the Gospel of John', *ExpTim* 104 (1992), pp. 9-13, which has a helpful summary of suggestions offered by scholars on time-scales covering the narrative of Jn 1.19-2.11.

dawned.[7] Thus we are provided with a perspective from which to read 2.13-22. We are to see its significance not only heralding the demise of the old Temple, but also looking forward to the raising up of the new Temple, the body of Jesus. The old gives way to the new.

3.3.3 *The New Beginning*

So much for the passage that precedes Jn 2.13-22. What of the passage that follows it—the story of Jesus' encounter with Nicodemus? Again there are eschatological elements here. Nicodemus is a Pharisee, a leader of the Jews. He represents the old order. He comes to Jesus by night, and, while this may indicate secrecy, the darkness of the night also in John signifies ignorance[8] and unbelief. But if Nicodemus is to see what God is doing ('see the kingdom of God', as 3.3 puts it), then he must be born ἄνωθεν—that is, he must be reborn from above.[9] This means a radical new beginning. More of the old—the Mosaic law—is not enough. It is not enough to be a child of Moses. Nicodemus must become a child of God, and the way to become τέκνος θεοῦ is to receive Jesus and believe on his name (1.12). The law was given through Moses; grace and truth came through Jesus Christ (1.17).

This new beginning is further defined in 3.5: ἐὰν μή τις γεννηθῇ ἐξ ὕδατος καὶ πνεύματος, οὐ δύναται εἰσελθεῖν εἰς τὴν βασιλείαν τοῦ θεοῦ. Leaving aside the contentious interpretation of ἐξ ὕδατος, it is almost universally accepted that Spirit here refers to the Spirit of God. But at this stage in the Gospel there was no Spirit (7.39), because Jesus was not yet glorified. It is not until Jesus is risen and appears to the disciples and breathes on them and says, 'Receive the Holy Spirit' that the Spirit is given (20.22). So from the point of view of Johannine timing what Jesus says to Nicodemus should only be realized in a post-resurrection setting. Properly speaking he can only be reborn from above when Jesus is glorified.[10]

---

7. Cf. Stibbe, *John*, p. 46.

8. Nicodemus's ignorance is exposed with a clever play on the words 'we know'. In v. 2 Nicodemus says 'we know…' Later Jesus says 'we speak what *we know*…yet you do not receive our testimony' (v. 11). Nicodemus does not know!

9. This catches up both meanings of this important word—being born again and being born from above. I believe both are intended.

10. However the Johannine Spirit's work cannot be confined by the time constraints that seem to be implied in Johannine passages, such as Jn 7.39. The spiritual harvest in Samaria evidently shows signs of the Spirit. This is a case of 'tomorrow's

This brief look at the Nicodemus passage makes the point that there are elements of the new order here—there is the need for a break from the old and a radical new beginning. The thought is of entering into what God is doing in Jesus Christ. This is God's kingdom. This is the new age—the age of resurrection life, of the Holy Spirit.

Looking beyond the pericopae immediately on either side of Jn 2.13-22 there is further evidence in chs. 1 and 5 that with Jesus comes the eschatological era and the newness that is part of it.

For example, in 1.23 John the Baptist takes for himself the words of Isaiah the prophet (Isa. 40.3):

Ἐγὼ φωνὴ βοῶντος ἐν τῇ ἐρήμῳ,
Εὐθύνατε τὴν ὁδὸν κυρίου...

Just as YHWH came to deliver his people from exile in the day of the prophet so now a new Liberator is being announced. Later John proclaims this One to be the new Lamb of God who will take away the sin of the world (1.29). Further, Jesus is declared by Nathanael to be the Son of God, the king of Israel (1.49) and the words of Jesus himself (1.51) imply that he is the new Jacob/Israel by evoking Jacob's dream in Gen. 28.12 when the angels ascend and descend on the ladder set on the earth and reaching to heaven. Jesus claims that his disciples will see the angels ascending and descending on him—that is, he is the new Jacob.

Turning now to John 5 I note Jesus' defence against the Jews in 5.19-25 centres on the realization of Jewish eschatological hopes in his own words and works. In 5.26-30, however, Jesus' second defence is that these eschatological hopes will finally be fulfilled by him in the future. These

bread' coming today! Cf. J. Jeremias, *New Testament Theology: Part I, The Proclamation of Jesus* (trans. John Bowden; London: SCM Press, 1971), p. 199. The incarnate Christ already brings the resurrection life to the world of needy humanity. Stibbe (*John*, p. 177) has some helpful comments on this issue: 'Throughout John, there is a powerful sense of the presence of the eschatological future. Though the last day is still anticipated as a future event, many of the characteristics of that future day (resurrection of the dead, judgment, the giving of eternal life) are dispensed to a needy humanity in and through the ministry of Jesus. The realities of God's tomorrow are present in the today of Jesus' life.' Cf., e.g., Jn 5.25-29. However, in general terms the rebirth by the Holy Spirit is grounded in a post-resurrection event—the giving and receiving of the Spirit (20.22). This event is intimated by the narrator at the moment of Jesus' death in 19.30c: 'Then he bowed his head and gave up his spirit' (παρέδωκεν τὸ πνεῦμα). A more literal translation is 'he gave over the Spirit'. This has overtones of succession—Jesus passes the mantle of the Spirit on to his disciples.

two passages parallel one another even though the first is generally seen to be realized eschatology and the second is mostly future eschatology:

9//30	The Son can only do what he sees the Father doing.
20//28	The amazement of the Jews at the Son's works.
21//26	The power to give life is given by the Father to the Son.
22//27	The right to judge is given by the Father to the Son.
25//28	A time is coming when the dead will hear the voice of the Son
25//29	Those who will rise to life.

The overall defence of Jesus in vv. 19-30 is as follows: 'The Father and the Son are one. The Father has given the Son power and authority in the world's today and in God's tomorrow.' Stibbe says:

> What the narrator creates is a reader whose response is a matter of *realized eschatology*—that is, a matter of living in the end-time of the story even while it is still in progress. As such, form matches content, for in the content of the story Jesus Christ is depicted as the *eschaton* in person, the one who brings the end of history into the middle of time.[11]

As an illustration of this Stibbe mentions the apparent analepsis in 11.2 which is really a prolepsis of 12.3.

3.4 *Eschatological Perspective in John 2.13-22?*

The foregoing discussion has argued for an eschatological context for the Temple episode of 2.13-22. In both the immediate and wider context there seems to be a strong eschatological ethos and it would be surprising if this did not flow into the Temple episode also.

Is there, however, any allusive evidence in the Temple narrative itself that an eschatological perspective is present?

3.4.1 *Allusion to Malachi 3.1, 3*
A number of commentators[12] see in Jesus' action in the Temple an allusion to Malachi 3.1, 3:

> See, I am sending my messenger to prepare the way before me, and the LORD whom you seek will suddenly come to his temple...and he will purify the descendants of Levi and refine them like gold and silver, until they present offerings to the LORD in righteousness.

---

11. Stibbe, *John*, pp. 78-79, 128.

12. E.g. Carson, *John*, p. 179; F.F. Bruce, *The Gospel of John* (Basingstoke: Pickering & Inglis, 1983), p. 74; E.C. Hoskyns, *The Fourth Gospel* (ed. F.N. Davey; London: Faber & Faber, 1947), p. 202.

Bruce Schuchard supports his case for this allusion by pointing out that the LXX (Mal. 3.3) uses the verb χέω, which finds some affinity with ἐξέχεεν in Jn 2.15.[13] If there is an allusion to Mal 3.1, 3 then the eschatological character of that passage would very likely be transported into the narrative of Jn 2.13-22.

Another possibility is that Jn 2.16 echoes Zech. 14.21 and I now turn to discuss this in some detail.

3.4.2 *Canaanites or Traders?*

According to John Jesus believes his Father has been supplanted in his own house by traders. Many commentators[14] mention Zech. 14.21 (καὶ οὐκ ἔσται χαναναῖος ἔτι ἐν τῷ οἴκῳ Κυρίου παντοκράτορος ἐν τῇ ἡμέρᾳ ἐκείνῃ) in connection with Jn 2.16. However, in most cases they feel the link is tentative. None offer any substantial evidence for their judgment. Beasley-Murray[15] who is among the more positive advocates, sees Zech. 14.21 as a good support for his eschatological interpretation of what Jesus is doing.

The Hebrew word for trader/Canaanite is כְּנַעֲנִי for which the LXX has Χαναναῖος. In Zech. 11.7, 11 there is לָכֵן עֲנִיֵּי הַצֹּאן, but the editor of *Biblia Hebraica Stuttgartensia* suggests that the first two words be run

---

13. Schuchard, *Scripture within Scripture*, pp. 24, 25 n. 40. However, B. Lindars in his commentary (*The Gospel of John* [NCB; London: Oliphants], p. 140) remarks: 'There may be something in this speculation…but there is no verbal allusion to this obvious passage. It is hazardous to build any theory on this basis.' Presumably he would not accept Schuchard's argument.

14. Brown (*John*, I, p. 121) says that Zech. 14.21 seems to be implied in Jn 2.16; Barrett (*St John*, p. 198) says: '[T]here may well be a reference here to Zech. 14.21'; Carson (*John*, p. 179) allows the allusion, but also includes reference to Mal. 3.1, 3; R. Bultmann (*The Gospel of John: A Commentary* [trans. G.R. Beasley-Murray *et al.*; Oxford: Blackwell, 1971], p. 124 n.1) says it is customary to find an allusion to Zech. 14.21, but that the text does not suggest it; Bruce (*John*, p. 74) favours a reference to Mal 3.1-3, but says there may be an echo of Zech. 14.21 in Jn 2.16; G.R. Beasley-Murray (*John* [WBC, 36; Waco, TX: Word Books, 1987], p. 39) says: '[T]here is probably an allusion here to the final words of Zechariah's vision of the kingdom of God'; R. Schnackenburg (*The Gospel According to St John: The Greek Text with Introduction and Notes* [trans. K. Smyth *et al.*; HTCNT; 3 vols.; London: Burns & Oates, 1968-82], I, p. 347) says there could be a reference to a messianic text like Zech. 14.21, but he favours Jn 2.16 as arising out of Jesus' consciousness of his Sonship with the Father (cf. Dodd, *Interpretation*, p. 300).

15. Beasley-Murray, *John*, p. 39.

together and repointed to make לְכְנַעֲנֵי הַצֹּאן, following the LXX, which has εἰς τὴν Χαναανῖτιν. Hence the NRSV translates the phrase as 'on behalf of the sheep merchants'. Prov. 31.24 also has לַכְּנַעֲנִי and the context of the capable wife distributing her wares makes clear that it should be rendered 'to the merchant'.[16] On the other hand, Gen. 12.6 has כְּנַעֲנִי, and from the context this should be translated 'Canaanite'. So the one Hebrew word has the two meanings—trader/merchant or Canaanite.[17] This word is found in the LXX as Χαναναῖος irrespective of whether it means trader or Canaanite and the two meanings are attested in Liddell and Scott.[18]

It is possible to take Zech. 14.21 as referring to Canaanites and thereby foster a spirit of exclusive nationalism,[19] but this would be foreign to the tenor of Zechariah 14, which seems to look forward to the nations, particularly Egypt, coming up to Jerusalem to keep the Festival of Booths.

16. R.N. Whybray (*Proverbs: New Century Bible Commentary* [Grand Rapids: Eerdmans; London: Marshall Pickering, 1994], p. 429) makes the point that 'merchant' for כנעני is probably a late usage and refers the reader to Job 41.6 (Heb. 40.30) for a similar translation of the same word.

17. *BDB*, pp. 488-89, has the predominant meaning 'Canaanite' but also 'merchant' for the usage in Zech. 14.21 and Prov. 31.24 (but cf. Ezek. 16.29 and Zeph. 1.11 where כנען is rendered 'merchant'). W.L. Holladay (*A Concise Hebrew and Aramaic Lexicon of the Old Testament* [Leiden: E.J. Brill, 1971], p. 160) has both meanings: Canaanite (Gen. 12.6) and tradesman. He indicates that the latter meaning is found only in Zech. 14.21 and Prov. 31.24; however, he translates כנעניה in Isa. 23.8 as 'tradesman'.

18. Interestingly Liddell and Scott (H.R. Liddell and R. Scott, *A Greek–English Lexicon: A New Edition Revised and Augmented Throughout by H.S. Jones with assistance of R. McKenzie* [Oxford: Clarendon Press, 1925–40], p. 1976) have 'merchant (of Tyre and Sidon)'. No evidence for the bracketed words is cited, but if this word did have associations with Tyre and Sidon and it was well known in Jesus' time, then the use of Tyrian coinage in the Temple would have made the allusion to Zech. 14.21 all the more fitting. However, this is speculative.

19. This interpretation is reflected in Josephus, *War* 5.194; 6.124-26; *Ant.* 15.417; and Qumran (4Q174: 1.1-7). It is discussed in C. Roth's article, 'The Cleansing of the Temple and Zechariah 14.21', *NovT* 4 (1960), pp. 174-81 (178). On the other hand, some recent commentators on Zechariah suggest that Zech. 14.21 reflects *inclusive* nationalism: 'The all-pervasive holiness of the future age will pertain to all in the land, Canaanites (if they are still there) and Israelites alike. And because the holiness is that of Yahweh and not of the gods of Canaan, it is the identity of Yahweh's people that will prevail in the land and that will be filled with God's sanctity' (Carol M. and Eric M. Meyers, *Zechariah 9–14* [AB, 25C; Garden City, NY: Doubleday, 1993], pp. 506-507). Eugene H. Merril (*An Exegetical Commentary: Haggai, Zechariah, Malachi* [Chicago: Moody Press, 1994], p. 366) expresses the same view.

Indeed they will be punished if they do not do so.[20] Therefore the context of Zech. 14 possibly counts against the nationalistic interpretation.

The other interpretation is to take Zech. 14.21 as referring to traders or merchants. This is what Roth calls the more broad-minded interpretation, and he finds support for it in rabbinic tradition, in the Targum and Talmud (*b. Pesaḥim* 50a) and Aquila, who was followed by Jerome ('mercator').[21]

Allusions to Zechariah are not uncommon in the Gospel of John. For example: Jn 12.15 is clearly a citation of Zech. 9.9; Jn 19.37 is an editorial reference to Zech. 12.10; Jn 16.32 may well recall Zech. 13.7 with the scattering of the sheep, which is more explicitly remembered in Mt. 26.31, 56 and Mk 14.27, 50; and below in Chapter 7 on the festival of tabernacles I will argue that the living waters of Zech. 14.8 are possibly in view in Jn 7.38.[22] Given this ethos of Zechariah allusions in John, I believe it is not unlikely that as John's readers, who read and re-read the Gospel, came to Jn 2.16 they would hear an echo of Zech. 14.21 and that the use of this word from the lips of Jesus in the Temple (Jn 2.16) could possibly form a link back to this Old Testament passage of Zech. 14.21.

3.4.3 *The Day of the* LORD

If Zech. 14.21 is in view what then is the basic message of the latter chapters of Zechariah? The clear thrust of Zech. 12-14 is what will happen on the day of the LORD. The phrase 'on that day' occurs no less than 15 times in these three chapters and once there is mention of a 'coming day'. This future eschatological tone reaches a climax in the last two verses where 'in that day' forms an inclusio in a suggested chiastic structure proposed by Merrill:[23]

---

20. Zech. 14.17: 'If any of the families of the earth do not go up to worship the King, the LORD of hosts, there will be no rain upon them.' While it seems there is a still a strong nationalistic spirit in the text (e.g. 'we are the centre of the earth—come to us or else…!') nevertheless the Gentiles will come to worship the LORD and that will presumably mean entry to the Temple.

21. C. Roth, 'Cleansing and Zech. 14.21', p. 180. Roth notes that the Talmud and Jerome indicate knowledge of the previous interpretation. However all this evidence postdates the New Testament era. Cf. Schuchard (*Scripture within Scripture*, p. 25 n. 44), who cites the same evidence sometimes with more specific detail.

22. This may also be the case with the living waters of Jn 4.10.

23. Merrill, *An Exegetical Commentary*, p. 366. Merrill, as indicated previously, prefers to retain the reference to Canaanite in 14.21. However, as I have argued above, he is out of step with later exegesis in the Targum and Talmud.

A In that day

   B There will be on the bells of the horses 'Holy to YHWH'

      C The pots in the house of YHWH will be like bowls before the altar.

         D Every pot in Jerusalem and Judah will be holy to YHWH of hosts.

      C' All who sacrifice will come and take some of them to boil in them.

   B' There will no longer be a Canaanite in the house of YHWH.

A' In that day.

The context is clearly 'in that day'. This day refers to the 'day of the LORD', which is the pervasive eschatological context of Zech. 14.21.

This eschatological thrust thus fits the picture of Jn 2.13-22 and the neighbouring pericopae.

3.4.4 *Summary: the New Temple*

The preceding passage of Jn 2.1-11 has an evident eschatological thrust, heralding a new creation; the subsequent story of Nicodemus has eschatological overtones emphasizing the need for a new beginning. It would be no surprise then to find the same eschatological theme running through the Temple episode in Jn 2.13-22. And if we allow the allusions to Zech. 14.21 and Mal. 3.1, 3, this would confirm an eschatological character to the narrative. That is to say, the dismissal of the traders from the Temple would signal the eschatological day of the LORD. With Jesus' action there are no longer any traders in the house of the LORD, the Father's house.[24] The day of the LORD has come.[25]

24. John has 'the Father's house' rather than 'house of the LORD'. Given the marked emphasis on the Son's relationship to the Father in the Gospel this should occasion no surprise. It also makes the relationship between Jesus and the Temple, and what happens in it, more intimate. To dishonour the Temple is to dishonour Jesus' Father. It is no wonder that Jesus is consumed with zeal for his Father's house. The Father's honour is at stake.

25. John does not put it this way. He has Jesus speak of 'the hour'. The first mention of 'the hour' is 2.4 and the last 19.27. The earlier references sometimes speak of it in the future (4.21), sometimes ambivalently as 'the hour is coming and now is' (4.23) or as 'not yet' (2.4). Nevertheless the clear impression is that it is imminent. From 12.23 onwards there is a clear tendency to say 'the hour has come'. This is the hour of Jesus' passion, crucifixion and resurrection. The goal of this hour is the glory of God (cf. 12.28). This hour will usher in the new age. Interestingly the last reference to 'hour' is 19.27, 'And from that hour (the Beloved Disciple) took (the mother of Jesus) into his own home.' This marks the return of Jesus to the Father, leaving the Beloved Disciple as his successor in caring for his mother.

3.5 The Structure of the Text: John 2.13-22

1. The Temple Cleansing (Verses 13-17)

Introduction

A   2.13   Καὶ ἐγγὺς ἦν τὸ πάσχα τῶν Ἰουδαίων, καὶ ἀνέβη εἰς Ἱεροσόλυμα ὁ Ἰησοῦς.

The Temple Action and Words

B   2.14   καὶ εὗρεν ἐν τῷ ἱερῷ τοὺς πωλοῦντας βόας καὶ πρόβατα καί περιστερὰς καὶ τοὺς κερματιστὰς καθημένους,

    2.15   καὶ ποιήσας φραγέλλιον ἐκ σχοινίων πάντας ἐξέβαλεν ἐκ τοῦ ἱεροῦ τά τε πρόβατα καὶ τοὺς βόας, καὶ τῶν κολλυβιστῶν ἐξέχεεν τὸ κέρμα καὶ τὰς τραπέζας ἀνέτρεψεν,

    2.16   καὶ τοῖς τὰς περιστερὰς πωλοῦσιν εἶπεν, Ἄρατε ταῦτα ἐντεῦθεν, μὴ ποιεῖτε τὸν οἶκον ἐμπορίου.

The Disciples Remember

C   2.17   Ἐμνήσθησαν οἱ μαθηταὶ αὐτοῦ ὅτι γεγραμμένον ἐστίν, Ὁ ζῆλος τοῦ οἴκου σου καταφάγεταί με.

2. The Temple-Logion

Introduction

A'   2.18   ἀπεκρίθησαν οὖν οἱ Ἰουδαῖοι καὶ εἶπαν αὐτῷ, Τί σημεῖον δεικνύεις ἡμῖν ὅτι ταῦτα ποιεῖς;

The Temple-Logion

B'   2.19   ἀπεκρίθη Ἰησοῦς καὶ εἶπεν αὐτοῖς, Λύσατε τὸν ναὸν τοῦτον καὶ ἐν τρισὶν ἡμέραις ἐγερῶ αὐτόν.

    2.20   εἶπαν οὖν οἱ Ἰουδαῖοι, Τεσσεράκοντα καὶ ἓξ ἔτεσιν οἰκοδομήθη ὁ ναὸς οὗτος, καὶ σὺ ἐν τρισὶν ἡμέραις ἐγερεῖς αὐτόν;

The Disciples Remember

C'   2.21   ἐκεῖνος δὲ ἔλεγεν περὶ τοῦ ναοῦ τοῦ σώματος αὐτοῦ.

    2.22   ὅτε οὖν ἠγέρθη ἐκ νεκρῶν, ἐμνήσθησαν οἱ μαθηταὶ αὐτου ὅτι τοῦτο ἔλεγεν, καὶ ἐπίστευσαν τῇ γραφῇ καὶ τῷ λόγῳ ὅν εἶπεν ὁ Ἰησοῦς.

A and A' are parallel as each introduces the two parts of the passage. The mention of 'the Jews' in A is repeated in A'. The remembering of the disciples (ἐμνήσθησαν οἱ μαθηταὶ αὐτοῦ) of C is repeated in C'. The expression γεγραμμένον ἐστίν in C is paralleled by τῇ γραφῇ in C'. If one allows an inclusio, then it could be that mention of the Jewish Passover in v. 13 is mirrored in v. 22 with mention of Jesus' death and resurrection—the fulfilment of the Jewish Passover. This is perhaps possible, but that it would represent a powerful structural message to the reader of the Fourth Gospel seems unlikely.[26]

3.6 *Analysis of the Temple 'Cleaning' (2.13-17)*

3.6.1 *My Father's House*

In Jesus' statement μὴ ποιεῖτε τὸν οἶκον τοῦ πατρός μου οἶκον ἐμπορίου (2.16), the word οἶκος seems to bear a deeper meaning. In Bauer, Arndt and Gingrich οἶκος is used for YHWH's house[27]—the Temple, as for example, in Isa. 56.7 where YHWH calls the Temple 'my house of prayer'. The other term, οἰκία, is never used to designate the Temple. The phrase οἶκος τοῦ πατρός μου as a designation of the Temple is found only in John and only twice, once in 2.16 and once in 14.2.[28]

In commenting on this Nereparampil says:

> this idea [i.e. the Temple being the house of Jesus' Father] is in perfect harmony with the general trend of the Johannine theology, according to which the Father and the Son have such a deep unity that they may be said to be one (Jn 10.30). Everything that the Father has is the Son's and everything that the Son has is the Father's (Jn 17.10; 16.15). Jesus, therefore, appears in the Temple as the Son in the house. He conducts himself as the LORD of the Temple. By the Temple cleansing therefore, Jesus was manifesting himself as the Son of God who came to defend the honour of his Father.[29]

3.6.2 *The House of Trade*

Of the four Gospel writers John is the only one to offer the commercial activity in the Temple as the reason for Jesus' action. Why?

There is a fierce polemic against commercial activity in holy places and holy times in the Old Testament. In Neh. 13.15-22, Nehemiah would not even allow the merchants to enter the city during the sabbath. And in Ezek. 22.26 the prophet brings the word of YHWH's judgment against the priests who have profaned holy things and made no distinction between

26. Nereparampil (*Temple-Logion*, p. 14) advances this suggestion with seeming confidence.

27. W. Bauer, W. Arndt and F.W. Gingrich, *A Greek–English Lexicon of the New Testament and Other Early Christian Literature* (Chicago: University of Chicago Press, 1957), p. 536, under 1aβ.

28. The closest parallel is Lk. 2.49.

29. Nereparampil, *Temple-Logion*, p. 20.

the holy and the common, and this presumably would include the distinction between market activity and the holy offerings made to God. Further, there is in Ezek. 27-28 an overwhelming judgment pronounced against the merchant city of Tyre.

In the New Testament Babylon and her merchants come under judgment. Four times in Rev. 18 the ἔμπορος is specifically mentioned (in vv. 3, 11, 15, 23) as coming under God's judgment. Furthermore there is a negative view of wealth in Lk.16.9, 11, 13 and Mt. 6.24 where it is characterized as mammon. This sort of ethos is not particularly favourable to any commercial activity, let alone in the holy place of the Temple.

What of commercial activity in John? There are two references to money. The first is in the narrative of the feeding of the five thousand. Seeing the crowd Jesus asked Philip, 'Where are we to buy bread for these people to eat?' (6.5). Philip's answer focuses not on the remoteness of a baker's shop, but on the lack of financial resources: 'Two hundred denarii would not buy enough bread for each of them to get a little' (6.7). The implication seems to be that even if there was a shop nearby they would not be able to buy enough bread for all the people.

What is the point of this exchange between Philip and Jesus? Barrett suggests that it is to point to the disciples' inadequacy to deal with the problem of feeding so many.[30] Be that as it may it also points to the inability of the disciples to buy food for such a crowd. Here is a problem that the disciples' money will not solve.

The second mention of money in John occurrs in John 12 where Judas suggests that the expensive perfume with which Mary anointed the feet of Jesus could have been sold for three hundred denarii and the money given to the poor. The interpolation into the narrative (12.6) makes clear what Judas really had in mind. He did not care about the poor. He kept the common purse and he wanted the money for himself because he was a thief.

Neither of these references to money in John is favourable. On the other hand it is reading too much into the text to say that John is mounting a polemic against commercial activity. There is too little evidence to go on.[31]

---

30. Barrett, *St John*, p. 271.

31. Jn 2.21 identifies Jesus' body with the Temple—that is, the person of Jesus is the Temple, which is equivalent to 'the house of my Father'. The Synoptic tradition has it that Judas sold Jesus to his enemies, which implies that the person of Jesus became an object of trade—'a house of trade'. The weakness of this suggestion is that

Without exception in the Synoptics the accusation is that the Jews have made the Temple a σπήλαιον ληστῶν. This echoes Jer. 7.11, the famous chapter where the prophet warns the people that there will be no safety from YHWH's judgment in the Temple.[32] So why does the Johannine Jesus say μὴ ποιεῖτε τὸν οἶκον τοῦ πατρός μου οἶκον ἐμπορίου? Given the presence of the moneychangers (Jn 2.15) in the Temple, there was commercial activity so within the flow of the narrative that it is reasonable to call it a οἶκον ἐμπορίου. But why not use the phrase of the Synoptics: σπήλαιον ληστῶν?[33] I suggest that John used οἶκον εμποριου deliberately to echo Zech. 14.21 and thereby evoke and reinforce the eschatological ethos that is so much part of Jn 2 and the chapters around it.

3.6.3 *The Disciples Remember*

We have mentioned above the eschatological character of the context of the Temple episode. Verses 17-22 are in keeping with this tenor. The disciples' remembering and the dialogue between Jesus and the Jews intimates that there is a lot more involved in Jesus' action in the Temple than a mere (and no doubt temporary) cleansing.[34] There is that, but there is also a portent that the day of the YHWH has come. Judgment has come to the house of the YHWH and the Temple is about to be destroyed and with it the sacrifices will end.

nowhere in the passion narrative does John mention that Judas sold Jesus for 30 pieces of silver. John says that Judas betrayed Jesus.

32. Bauckham ('Jesus' Demonstration', pp. 81-85) has a good discussion of Jer. 7.11 as it occurs in Mk 11.17.

33. Did John know the Synoptics? Here I follow D. Moody Smith, who, in *John among the Gospels: The Relationship in Twentieth-Century Research* (Philadelphia: Fortress Press, 1992), p. 179, remarks: 'The nature of the agreements of wording and order has led eminent and careful scholars such as Barrett and Kümmel to the conclusion that John knew the Synoptics, certainly Mark, probably Luke, and possibly Matthew. This is, on the face of it, a reasonable conclusion.' R. Bauckham ('John for Readers of Mark', in *The Gospels for All Christians: Rethinking the Gospel Audiences* [Grand Rapids: Eerdmans, 1998], pp. 147-71) argues that John not only knew Mark but wrote his gospel on the assumption that some of his readers would also have read Mark, and he maintains that Jn 3.24 and 11.2 were 'intended specifically for readers/hearers who also knew Mark's Gospel' (p. 151).

34. There *is* a cleansing as I will argue below. Sanders, *Jesus and Judaism*, pp. 61-71, argues that there was nothing amiss in the Temple. I believe he is not correct as far as John is concerned. If the cleansing is disallowed, then Jesus' words, 'Stop making my Father's house a house of trade', would not make any sense. On the other hand, more is involved. It is not a case of 'either or' but of 'both and'.

This is where the subtlety of John's narrative comes into its own. I will argue that John's narrative contains intimations that Jesus himself, as the new Temple, will be destroyed and raised again. There is therefore no future for the old Temple and its sacrifices. God no more dwells within its walls, and its sacrifices have been replaced by Jesus, the Passover sacrifice. Jesus is now the house of the Father. God dwells in Jesus.

Jn 2.17 reads, 'His disciples remembered that it was written, "Zeal for your house will consume me."' When did they remember? It is not at all clear.[35] I think this is deliberately vague. The text, like many other texts in John, can be read on two levels. On the one hand, it can be read as though the disciples remembered at the time Jesus drove the traders out of the Temple. They remembered that it was written in the Psalms that a jealous concern for the welfare of God's house will take over the person, which is what happened with Jesus. He evidently saw what was happening in the Temple and, consumed with zeal for the house of his Father, drove out the

---

35. Schuchard, in his study *Scripture within Scripture* (p. 18 n. 5), favours the view that the disciples recollected this passage from the Old Testament immediately at the scene and he cites a number of scholars who support this, namely J.H. Bernard, *The Gospel According to St John* (ICC; 2 vols.; Edinburgh: T. & T. Clark, 1928), I, pp. 91-92); Dodd, *Fourth Gospel*, p. 158; Schnackenburg, *St John*, I, p. 347; Barrett, *St John*, p. 198; E. Haenchen, *A Commentary on the Gospel of John* (Hermeneia Commentary; 2 vols.; Philadelphia: Fortress Press, 1984), I, p. 184; and R.T. Fortna, *The Fourth Gospel and its Predecessor: From Narrative Source to Present Gospel* (Edinburgh: T. & T. Clark, 1989), pp. 125-26. A number of scholars are indecisive; for example, Bruce (*John*, p. 75) and Carson (*John*, p. 180), while others favour a post-resurrection recollection: Bultmann (*John*, p. 124) and Lindars (*John*, p. 140). But as Schuchard says, the flow of the narrative suggests that the disciples remembered at the time of the Temple episode (*Scripture within Scripture*, pp. 29-31). This is also supported by v. 22: 'After he was raised from the dead, his disciples remembered that he had said this [presumably v. 19]; and they believed the scripture [v. 17—although a number of scholars favour the view that it is that body of scripture that testifies to Jesus' passion and resurrection] and the word that Jesus had spoken.' The suggestion here is that the disciples remembered and heard at the time, but did not believe or understand. On the other hand the notion of remembering in John is rather strongly emphasized and it is often post-resurrection remembering (2.22; 14.26; 12.16; cf. 13.19; 14.29; 16.1, 4). There seems in 2.17 that there is a present and a future remembering. This is a hint of what comes in the farewell discourses. As Gail O'Day puts it, the 'future and present [come] together in one narrative moment in ways that challenge conventional notions of time' (G. O'Day, '"I Have Overcome the World" [John 16.33]: Narrative Time in John 13–17', *Semeia* 53 [1991], pp. 153-66 [156]).

traders.[36] On this reading the future tense for 'consume' (καταφάγεται) suggests that the Old Testament text finds fulfilment in Jesus' Temple action.

On the other hand, 2.17 can be read as though the disciples remembered the Old Testament text later, after the resurrection, and saw it as a prophecy that came to fulfilment with Jesus' *crucifixion*. I will now investigate this in more detail.

3.6.4 *Zeal for the House of the Lord*
The Old Testament passage to which John refers in 2.17 is Ps. 69.9a (10a in the MT and 68.9 in the LXX):[37] 'It is zeal for your house that has consumed me...' (ὅτι ὁ ζῆλος τοῦ οἴκου σου κατέφαγέ[38] με...). What was the nature of this zeal in Ps 69? It is almost impossible to say. The term is unfocused. Was it rebuilding the Temple and re-establishing its worship in the postexilic restoration? Was it directed more to the people of Israel—the house of the LORD—so that love for the people took over his life?

If we transfer these thoughts into the Johannine context of 2.13-22, the quotation of 2.17 produces a number of possible meanings depending on the interpetation given to the three words in the verse: 'zeal', 'your house', 'consume'. Possible meanings are: 'zeal' means 'love' or 'jealous passion'; 'your house' means 'the Temple of Jerusalem' or 'the people of Israel' (which in the Johannine context may refer to the New Israel);[39] 'consume' means 'an engulfing passion' or 'being devoured in death—that is, a

---

36. F.J. Moloney ('Reading John 2.13-22: The Purification of the Temple', *RB* 97 [1990], pp. 443-44 [443]) speaks of recognizing in Jesus 'a passionate figure committed to the honour of God unto death, like Phineas, Elijah or Mattathias (see Num. 25.11; 1 Kgs 19.10, 14; Sir. 48.2; 1 Macc. 2.24-26).'

37. Schuchard (*Scripture within Scipture*, p. 20 n. 17) offers evidence that Ps. 69 is quoted elsewhere in the New Testament, notably in Rom. 15.3 (69.10b in the MT). Allusions to parts of the psalm are seen in Jn 15.25; Mt. 27.34; Mk 15.36; Jn 19.28; Acts 1.20. B. Lindars (*New Testament Apologetic: The Doctrinal Significance of the Old Testament Quotations* [Philadelphia: Westminster Press, 1961], p. 105) claims that almost every line of Ps. 69.23-29 is quoted or alluded to in the New Testament. E.D. Freed (*Old Testament Quotations in the Gospel of John* [Leiden: E.J. Brill, 1965], p. 9) is not convinced.

38. Codex Vaticanus has κατέφαγε and Codex Sinaiticus has κατέφαγεν, reflecting the perfect tense of the MT: כִּי קִנְאַת בֵּיתְךָ אֲכָלָתְנִי

39. Cf. on 1.47 in 5.3.3 where Nathanael seems to be representative of the New Israel.

sacrificial death'. This results in eight possible interpretations: (1) love for
the Temple will engulf me (the future being in relation to Ps. 69); (2) love
for the Father's people will engulf me; (3) love for the Temple will
swallow me up in death; (4) love for the Father's people will swallow me
up in death; (5) jealous passion for the Temple will engulf me (again the
future being in relation to Ps. 69); (6) jealous passion for the Father's
people will engulf me; (7) jealous passion for the Temple will precipitate
my death (swallow me up in death); and (8) jealous passion for the
Father's people will swallow me up in death. Suggestions (2), (4), (6) and
(8) are perhaps less likely than the other four because it is the love of the
Father for the world that is the Johannine driving force that sends the Son
into the world (3.16), not Jesus' love for the Father's house (family). But
there are hints that Jesus' love for others is a motive for his death (see
15.13, 14). Obviously the merits of various interpretations can be debated.
However, what is clear from this brief exercise is that 2.17 is multivalent
in meaning—deliberately so I believe.

What we *do* know is that the psalmist suffered for his zeal. He was
ostracized and insulted (Ps. 69.10b). Drunkards made songs about him (v.
12). He was alienated from his own family (v. 8; cf. Jn 7.5 and the
mention of Jesus' family just prior to the Temple episode in Jn 2.12).

In whatever way the psalmist's zeal for the LORD's house manifested
itself, it triggered a hostile reaction, a reaction that devoured (perf. of
אכל/κατέφαγέν in the LXX) him. This is in the perfect tense in Ps. 69 but
it is in the future in Jn 2.17.[40] As I mentioned above this future can be read
either in relation to the psalm (in which case the disciples witnessed the
consuming zeal in what Jesus did in the Temple) or in relation to the
Temple episode itself which would mean that the 'consuming' is yet to
happen.

---

40. Schuchard (*Scripture within Scripture*, pp. 21-22) demonstrates that the LXX
κατέφαγε (aorist) for MT אכלתני (perf.) is well attested. It is true that a Hebrew
perfect is sometimes rendered in the LXX with the future, but not this time. It may be,
of course, that John was working from the MT and translated the Hebrew perfect into a
Greek future. On the other hand, he may have deliberately translated the perf./aorist
into a future so as to prophesy Jesus' crucifixion. Schuchard certainly favours the view
that John uses the LXX (or Old Greek as he prefers to call it), but he is not rigid in
this conclusion and allows for the possibility that John was familiar with a Hebrew/
Aramaic version of Old Testament texts.

3.6.5 *A Sacrificial Consumption*

There are indications in the Synoptics that whatever Jesus did and said in the Temple precipitated his death.[41] It certainly spurred the authorities to seek his death. And I think it is significant that Caiaphas in Jn 11.48 is ready to destroy Jesus so as to preserve the Temple (τὸν τόπον ὑμῶν) (and the nation).[42] Indeed his pronouncement is an intimation that Jesus will be sacrificed for the Temple and the nation.

I use the word sacrifice advisedly. Jesus will be consumed. The Hebrew word lying behind 'consume' commonly means 'to eat', but it (and also its LXX counterpart) can be used of the fire that consumes the sacrifice offered to God.[43] Given then that καταφάγεται is used to describe Jesus' death[44] and that notions of sacrifice lie in the Hebrew and LXX Greek of this word, it is possible that here too there is an allusion to Jesus' death being a sacrifice. Already John the Baptist has announced Jesus as the Lamb of God who will take away the sins of the world (1.29; cf. 1.34). Now within this pericope dealing with the expulsion of the sacrificial animals from the Temple here is an intimation that Jesus himself will become a sacrifice. Furthermore, Caiaphas's prophecy as noted above has a clear sacrificial nuance. Hoskyns[45] puts it succinctly when he says: '[T]he purification of which His action is a sign depends on the sacrifice of his body (19.30, cf. 13.4-11,17.19).' And with his sacrifice Temple sacrifices will end.

---

41. Mk 11.18: 'The chief priests and teachers of the law heard it [what Jesus did and said in the Temple] they kept looking for a way to kill him...' Cf. Lk. 19.47. Consider also the accusation at the trial in Mk 14.57, 58.

42. In John, what seems to precipitate the death of Jesus is not the Temple episode but the raising of Lazarus. It was the report of this that prompted the gathering of the Sanhedrin and Caiaphas's prophecy that Jesus would die for the nation (11.45-53).

43. Cf., e.g., Lev. 6.3; 9.24 in MT; 1 Kgs 18.38; 2 Chron. 7.1.

44. Many commentators read Jn 2.17 as an omen of Jesus' death: Lindars (*John*, p. 140): 'Verse 2.17 connects the Cleansing with the Passion'; Bruce (*John*, p. 75); Moloney: 'Reading John 2.13-22', pp. 443-44, esp. n. 41; Hoskyns (*The Fourth Gospel*, p. 204): 'The zeal of Jesus must be consummated in his own death...'; Schnackenburg (*St John*, I, p. 347): zeal for the house of God 'will cost him his life'. There are other scholars who see no allusion to Jesus' death or make no mention of it: B.F. Westcott, *The Gospel According to St John: The Greek Text with Introduction and Notes* (2 vols.; London: John Murray, 1908 [1880]), I, p. 92: 'The reference is not to the future Passion of the LORD, but to the overpowering energy and fearlessness of His present action.' Barrett (*St John*, p. 199) seems unclear on this point, but later (p. 201) he says καταφάγεται referring to the destruction of Christ's body in death is 'a strained interpretation.' Cf., finally, Bernard (*St John*, I, p. 92).

45. Hoskyns, *The Fourth Gospel*, p. 204.

In commenting on the structure of 2.13-22 I mentioned the possibility of an inclusio with reference to the Passover in v. 13 being mirrored by a reference to the death of Jesus as the Paschal Lamb (v. 17). The Passover and Jesus' fulfilment of it is a prominent theme in John and I will take this up in Chapter 7.

3.6.6 *Two-Level Reading*

To sum up, Jn 2.17 has a two-level meaning. It can be read at the basic narrative level where the disciples remember a text from the psalms that epitomises what they see happening in front of them. Jesus is consumed with zeal for his Father's house and drives out the traders and the sacrificial animals. But on a post-resurrection reading the text takes a deeper meaning. Zeal for Jesus' Father's house will precipitate the consumption of his life as a sacrifice. Indeed I will argue that he will become the Passover Lamb to take away the sin of the world (cf. 1.29).

3.7 *Analysis of the Temple-Logion (2.18-22)*

3.7.1 *The Johannine Sign*

Now to v. 18. The Jews[46] waste no time in challenging Jesus' authority: Τί σημεῖον δεικνύεις ἡμῖν ὅτι ταῦτα ποιεῖς; (2.18).

But what is meant by σημεῖον? The word occurs frequently in John; I will look at its usage.

Miracles are σημεῖα (2.11; 5.54)—they seem to take the role of the 'mighty works' (δυνάμεις) described in the Synoptics (e.g. Mt. 7.22; 11.20-21, 23; 13.54, 58; Lk. 10.13; 19.37). But the Johannine σημεῖον is more than a miracle. It has symbolic character. The σημεῖον carries a deeper meaning than the actual happenings. Jesus in John is the exclusive author of σημεῖα; nobody else, not even John the Baptist performs a σημεῖον (10.41). If the ἔργα are done by both the Father and by the Son (5.17), the σημεῖα are performed only by the Son. The understanding of the σημεῖον, however, is reserved for the believer (6.26; 12.37). These σημεῖα therefore are always connected with faith (e.g. 2.11). The purpose of the σημεῖα is to reveal the glory of Jesus and bring people to believe (4.48; 2.11, 23; 6.30; 12.37) that he is the Son of God and Messiah, so that they may be saved by him (1.12; 3.16, 18; 20.30-31). This is the Johannine

---

46. Schuchard, *Scripture within Scripture*, p. 27 n. 52, says '"the Jews" probably refers to the Jewish leadership functioning in a representative fashion'.

σημεῖον and the Jews ask Jesus to give such a sign to validate his action in the Temple.

3.7.2 *Jesus' Response (2.19)*

Jesus' response is not what they expect: Λύσατε τὸν ναὸν τοῦτον καὶ ἐν τρισὶν ἡμεραις ἐγερῶ αὐτόν. Almost every word here is worthy of discussion:

3.7.2.1 Λύσατε. Λύσατε is an aorist imperative of λυεῖν. In the LXX it is used with diverse meanings. It can refer to untying one's shoes (Exod. 3.5; Josh. 5.15) and to setting prisoners free (Ps. 102.20; 146.7; Isa. 14.17). Sometimes it is used in a moral sense to mean pardoning sins (Sir. 28.2; Isa. 40.2; 58.6).[47]

Interestingly Liddell and Scott cite instances (p. 1068) where λύειν, used with βίον or αἰῶν, can mean death. However, I can find no such citations in Bauer, Arndt and Gingrich and therefore there is need to tread cautiously in suggesting that λύσατε here in Jn 2.19 could refer to Jesus' death at the hands of the Jews.

In John λυεῖν has been used in both the material and moral sense.[48] It appears in the material sense when John the Baptist says that he is unworthy to untie (λυεῖν) the thong of Jesus' sandals (1.27), and when Jesus tells the people to unbind the resuscitated Lazarus (11.44, Λύσατε αὐτόν). In all other contexts outside 2.19, John has used this word in the moral sense of 'breaking' the sabbath (e.g. 5.18).

It is unlikely that the Jews to whom Jesus speaks will destroy the Temple by tearing it down stone by stone. Rather, as Nereparampil suggests, they will destroy its 'templeness'.[49] Instead of it being the 'house of my Father', the house of God, it will increasingly be a mere 'house of trade'. So the force of λύσατε is, as Bultmann proposes, an ironic

---

47. See Bauer, Arndt and Gingrich (*Greek–English Lexicon*, p. 485, §3) for λύειν, destroying a building. Schnackenberg (*St John*, I, p. 349) draws attention to an interesting use of λυεῖν in a variant reading of 1 Jn 4.3.

48. I am indebted to Lucius Nereparampil (*Temple-Logion*, p. 37) for these categories.

49. Nereparampil (*Temple-Logion*, p. 37) exploits the moral category he has invoked to get at the idea of 'templeness'. But as I note below (3.7.2.5) this is an abstraction that would very likely have been foreign to John's audience. Still there is perhaps something in it when the Johannine Jesus says the house of his Father is being made into a house of trade.

prophetic imperative similar to those verbs in Amos 4.4 ('Go to Bethel and transgress!...') and Isa. 8.9-10 ('Band together, you peoples, and be dismayed!...') and Mt. 23.32 ('Go on then, finish off what your fathers began!').[50] The meaning in Jn 2.19 then will be, 'Carry on the way you are going and destroy this Temple!'

In Jn 11.48 Caiaphas says that if they let Jesus carry on, everyone will believe in him (i.e. acknowledge his messianic claim) and so the Romans will come and destroy (ἀροῦσιν = wipe out) 'our holy place' (which is almost certainly the Temple). It is interesting that Caiaphas postulates the Romans as the immediate cause of the fall of the Temple, but that Jesus and the size of his following will be the true cause of the destruction of the Temple. But in 2.19 Jesus says the Jews themselves will be the cause of the Temple's dissolution by his use of the ironic prophetic imperative, Λύσατε. However, the very ambiguity of the expression possibly allows for each of these to have a share in the downfall of the Temple.

3.7.2.2 ναός.[51] Nereparampil argues for a distinction between ναός and ἱερόν. He maintains that ναός in the LXX 'could be used as a synonym for οἶκος θεοῦ, while ἱερόν could not'.[52] The latter, according to Nereparampil, was often used of pagan Temples. He mentions that in Josephus 'ἱερόν represents the whole Temple-complex, while ναός stands for the Temple proper'.[53] He goes on to say, 'John takes the LXX distinction [and for that matter Josephus's distinction] and applies them differently when he speaks of the Jerusalem Temple and of Jesus.' John always refers to the Jerusalem Temple by ἱερόν, never ναός, except for this enigmatic saying of 2.19.[54]

50. Bultmann, *John*, p. 125 and n. 4. In passing he makes the point that 'one can hardly say that the imperative here is equal to a concessive clause.' Schuchard, *Scripture within Scripture*, p. 27 n. 54, also recommends that this construction be taken as a prophetic imperative and given its full force. Barrett (*St John*, p. 199), Brown (*John*, I, p. 115) and Beasley-Murray (*John*, p. 40) all, in varying degrees, concur with this opinion.

51. ναός can refer to the whole of the Temple area (Bauer, Arndt and Gingrich, *Greek–English Lexicon*, p. 535, 1a) and often to the inner sanctuary of the Temple, but also it can refer to the human body as a sanctuary of the soul or, in Christian language, of the Holy Spirit. Cf. 1 Cor. 6.19; 2 Cor. 5.1; 6.16.

52. Nereparampil, *Temple-Logion*, p. 45.

53. Nereparampil, *Temple-Logion*, p. 45.

54. ἱερόν, Jn 2.14, 15; 5.14; 7.14; 7.28; 8.2, 20, 59; 10.23; 11.56; 18.20. ναός, Jn 2.19, 20, 21. In 2.20 it is the Jews who refer to the Jerusalem Temple as ναός and that

Why? Because, according to Nereparampil, ναός is no longer applicable to the Jerusalem Temple—it is only a ἱερόν. The real Temple (ναός) is now the σῶμα of Jesus (2.21). Jesus is the true ναός. Nereparampil finds support for this from Revelation where ἱερόν is never used. The Jewish Temple is completely ignored, while ναός has been identified with God and the Lamb (Rev. 21.22).[55]

A point against Nereparampil is that if, as he suggests, John uses ἱερόν to refer to the Jerusalem Temple, indicating that it is a mere shell of what it was meant to be—desolate of the presence of God—why does Jesus refer to it as 'my Father's house'?[56]

Therefore, while I tentatively agree with Nereparampil, I would be careful about reading too much into the use of ναός in 2.19.

3.7.2.3 ἐν τρισὶν ἡμέραις.[57] I have already mentioned that variation in the initial preposition of this formula does not substantially alter the meaning. Beasley-Murray summarizes the significance well:

> The expression 'within three days' points to a meaning of the words closely in harmony with the unique ministry of Jesus. 'After three days' or 'on the third day' and the like denotes in Jewish tradition the time when God may be counted on to deliver his people from their troubles.[58]

He goes on to say that the tradition in Israel was so explicit that the third day was not just a short time, but a time with special significance:

> The third day brings the turning to something new and better. God's mercy and righteousness creates a 'new' time of salvation, of life, of victory; the third day brings a difficult circumstance from decision, through God's saving action, to a final solution which is creative of history.[59]

is manifestly (cf. 2.21) a misunderstanding. Jesus is not talking about the Jerusalem Temple, but about the ναός of his body.

55. Nereparampil, *Temple-Logion*, pp. 46-49.

56. Coloe ('The Dwelling of God', p. 120) suggests that the phrase 'my Father's house' refers to 'the enfleshed *logos*, [where] God and humanity meet. A building is no longer required for there is in creation a new sacred place where God dwells among us (1.14).' This amounts to saying that 'my Father's house' is the incarnate Word, namely Jesus. What, then, is the significance of the word of Jesus (2.16): 'Stop making my Father's house a house of trade'? In the Matthean and Lukan betrayals Jesus' body is traded (Mt. 26.15; Lk. 22.5), but John makes no mention of it (cf. above 3.6.2 n. 31). I think Coloe's suggestion is unlikely and that 'my Father's house' refers to the Jerusalem Temple.

57. See 3.3.1 n. 3.

58. Beasley-Murray, *John*, p. 40.

59. Beasley-Murray, *John*, pp. 40, 41.

In the light of this tradition it is appropriate that, according to the Synoptics, Jesus used such an expression to prophesy his resurrection (cf. Mk 8.31, Mt. 17.23; Lk. 9.22). It also confirms that in 2.19 the Johannine Jesus is speaking of a great intervention of God that in the Johannine context probably refers to the resurrection.

3.7.2.4 ἐγερῶ. The meaning is simply 'I will raise.' Apparently it is only rarely used of erecting a building (e.g. Sir. 49.13). There are a few cases where it is used of the Temple (e.g. Josephus, *Ant.* 15.391; 20.228). It can be used of waking someone from sleep and figuratively of helping someone, restoring them to health. In the passive it is the verb for raising the dead.[60] The passive is used because the dead do not raise themselves—that is the work of God.

If then the resurrection of Jesus is in view why does he use ἐγερῶ, the active future first person singular? I suggest two reasons: first, Jesus is answering a challenge from the Jews. They have asked him for a sign to validate his action in the Temple. If he had used the passive of ἐγείρειν that would not have been sufficient to convince the Jews that he was authorized to do what he had done. Lazarus had been raised from the dead. That did not give him the right to cleanse the Temple. But if Jesus raised himself that would indeed be a sign that he was LORD of the Temple of his body and therefore LORD of the Jewish Temple as well. Secondly, John indicates that Jesus is able to raise himself. In 10.17, 18 Jesus speaks of having power to lay down his life and to take it back of his own accord. The active voice for ἐγείρειν with reference to Jesus' resurrection is therefore in harmony with Johannine theology.

3.7.2.5 αὐτόν. Bultmann says 'the object of λύειν and ἐγείρειν must be one and the same'.[61] Obviously τὸν ναὸν τοῦτον must refer to the Jewish Temple in which the action of Jesus has taken place. That has been in view from the beginning of the pericope and there has been nothing to indicate a change. But it also seems clear that Jesus does not raise up this Temple. Indeed, if the explanatory interpolation of 2.21 is allowed to impact on the interpretation of αὐτόν, then it seems to refer to the raising up of the body of Jesus, not to the Jewish Temple.

How can this problem be resolved? The suggestion that at the word τοῦτον Jesus pointed to his own body to indicate a change of reference is

60. Bauer, Arndt and Gingrich, *Greek–English Lexicon*, pp. 213, 214.
61. Bultmann, *John*, p. 127 n. 6.

nowhere supported by the text. The attempt to show that τοῦτον is a word that has strayed from another context, and thus omit it, does not solve the problem because αὐτον still refers back to τὸν ναὸν. The αὐτον would have to be replaced by ἄλλον for this solution to work.[62]

Nereparampil endeavours to overcome the problem by saying that τὸν ναὸν τοῦτον refers to 'templeness' (i.e. where God is truly present and worshipped 'in Spirit and truth'). This is what the Jews are destroying and will destroy, and this is what Jesus will raise up (re-establish).

> In the first part of the Temple-Logion, Jesus speaks of the *templeness* that had materialized in the then existing Jerusalem Temple. In the second part he speaks of the same *templeness* which would materialize in his own resurrected 'body'.[63]

This proposed solution is unlikely. It involves an abstraction ('templeness') that does not do justice to the bodily resurrection of Jesus intimated in 2.21, 22. It is true that John speaks of worship 'in Spirit and truth'. But Jesus does not raise up an abstraction called 'templeness'; he raises his body.

I think it is best not to press this text too strongly. Léon-Dufour says that at this point the author is playing on two keyboards at the same time. On the one hand, he plays on the keyboard of the Jews and their Temple; on the other hand, he plays on the keyboard of Jesus and the Temple of his body.[64] There seems to be a crossing over from the Jewish Temple to the Temple of Jesus' body and it is not easy to pinpoint when this happens.

3.7.3 *The Jews Misunderstand*
After presenting the Temple-Logion, John describes the immediate reaction of Jesus' audience: εἶπαν οὖν οἱ Ἰουδαῖοι, Τεσσεράκοντα καὶ ἓξ ἔτεσιν οἰκοδοδομήθη ὁ ναός οὗτος, καὶ σὺ ἐν τρισὶν ἡμέρας ἐγερεῖς αὐτόν; (2.20). This reply of the Jews shows they have understood the Temple-Logion as referring to the then existing Jerusalem Temple. They have misunderstood Jesus.[65] They say, 'Forty six years[66] were spent[67] in building this Temple.'

62. Bultmann, *John*, p. 126 n. 2.

63. Nereparampil, *Temple-Logion*, p. 58.

64. X. Léon-Dufour, 'Le Signe du Temple selon saint Jean', *RSR* 39 (1951), pp. 155-75 (156-57).

65. These misunderstandings are frequent in John. Those to whom Jesus is speaking think one thing, but he is actually speaking about something else. For example, Nicodemus thinks Jesus is speaking about physical rebirth (3.4), whereas

The Jews, by their reply, understood that the words of Jesus contained a comparison between the then existing Temple and the future Temple that he had promised to raise up. The emphasis of this comparison is centred on the time element 'three days' and 'forty-six years'.

Furthermore the Jews are not concerned about the destruction of the Temple but the rebuilding. The phrase οἰκοδομήθη ὁ ναός οὗτος refers to the then existing Temple of Jerusalem and the verb has the sense of 'being constructed'. However, in speaking of the Temple Jesus would build, the Jews use Jesus' own word—ἐγερεῖς αὐτόν. Do the Jews acknowledge that the action of Jesus in 'building' the Temple will be entirely different from the way in which it was previously built? Or are they merely mocking Jesus?

Jesus is speaking about a new birth from above by the Spirit (3.5). The Samaritan woman at the well thinks Jesus is talking about physical water (4.11), whereas he is offering her the water of eternal life (4.14). When Jesus tells the Jews that he is going away and they will look for him and not find him, they understand him to be speaking of a physical geographical departure (7.35), but in fact he is speaking of his departure to the Father (16.28). Cf. also 4.32-33; 6.32-35; 14.4-5; 14.7-11. Literally, these misunderstandings function as foils to expose 'deeper' layers of meaning regarding the person and teaching of Jesus.

66.   There are problems associated with the chronology suggested here but they are not germane to the meaning of the Temple-Logion itself. Brown (*John*, I, p. 115) has some interesting points to make on the 'forty six years'. 'Jos. *Ant*. XV. 380, says that the Temple reconstruction was begun in the 18th year of Herod the Great (20/19 BC…). Reckoning from this we reach a date of A.D. 27/28, or more exactly the Passover of 28. The hazards of establishing an exact chronology for the ministry of Jesus are well known, but this date agrees with that of Lk. iii.1, which fixes the ministry of John the Baptist in the 15th year of Tiberias (October 27 to 28 according to the Syrian calendar with antedating). The number in John obviously refers to the Temple; however, because John says that the Temple is Jesus' body and because of viii. 57 ("You're not even fifty years old") Loisy and others accept 46 as the age of Jesus, suggesting that he died at the Jubilee age of 50. The fact that the Greek letters in the name Adam have the value of 46 was the basis of the interpretation of many Fathers, especially Augustine, who saw this number as reference to Jesus' human nature… While we do not regard "forty six years" as a reference to Jesus' age, we by no means exclude the possibility that Jesus was considerably older than Luke's approximation of "about thirty years of age" (3.23) might indicate.'

67.   The verb is in the aorist, but the building was not completed until 63 AD, some 35 years later. Brown (*John*, I, p. 116) suggests that the aorist be taken as a complexive, summing up the whole process of building that is not yet completed. The translation, 'this temple has been under construction…', in the NRSV catches the situation well. Nereparampil, *Temple-Logion*, p. 68.

Given the Johannine perspective on the Jews the latter is more likely. The Jews' obtuseness is underlined at the conclusion of Jesus' public ministry in 12.37-40 where he quotes from Isa. 53.1 and 6.10 and applies them to the unbelieving Jews.

3.7.4 *The Temple of Jesus' Body*

All through this exchange with the Jews one has the feeling that they and Jesus have been talking past each other. And now in v. 21 the narrator brings it out into the open: 'But he (Jesus) was speaking of the Temple of his body' (ἐκεῖνος δὲ ἔλεγεν περὶ τοῦ ναοῦ σώματος αὐτοῦ). The Jews think he has been speaking of the Temple made of stone, but, in fact, he has been speaking about another Temple—his own body.

There are only four instances where σῶμα is used in John. There is the present case here in 2.21 and then the word does not occur until 19.31 when the soldiers inspect the bodies on the cross to break the legs to hasten death. Then Joseph of Arimathea and Nicodemus come and take the body of Jesus, anoint it and lay it in the tomb (19.38, 40). Finally there is the absent body at the tomb (20.12). What is the significance, if any, of this reference to the dead σῶμα of Jesus?

Nereparampil suggests, in view of the above texts, that Jesus' body only becomes the Temple from the moment of his death onwards. It is this body of Jesus in the tomb that is raised from the dead. It is the resurrection *body* that is the new Temple.[68]

There is a certain plausibility in this. In John the crucifixion of the body of Jesus is consistently presented as a glorification, an ascension.[69] The dead body of Jesus is therefore the *beginning* of the great eschatological victory. From a Johannine theological point of view, then, it is appropriate for John to focus on the dead body of Jesus, and it does not seem out of place for Nereparampil to say that this also is the beginning of the new Temple of God.

However, how shall we speak of Jesus prior to his death? Is his body the Temple before his crucifixion? Nereparampil also discusses this question, drawing attention to Jn 1.14, which speaks of the Word becoming flesh

---

68. Nereparampil, *Temple-Logion*, p. 68.

69. See, for example, 12.31-33: ' "Now is the judgement of this world; now the ruler of this world will be driven out. And I, when I am lifted up from the earth, will draw all people ('things' if the alternative reading is allowed) to myself." He said this to indicate the kind of death he was to die.'

(σάρξ).[70] Σάρξ is used in Jn 6 when Jesus speaks of eating his flesh (σάρξ) and drinking blood (6.52-56). But then he says that the 'flesh is useless' (6.63), which seems to confirm 1.13 in the Prologue, namely, that no-one can be born a child of God by the flesh. The σάρξ is powerless to generate the life of the Spirit.[71] This seems to be in accord with the view that the σάρξ, while not sinful, is nevertheless weak and frail.[72] This may be why John does not speak of the Temple of Jesus' flesh, but the Temple of his body. The strength of this proposal is that it meshes in with the overwhelming emphasis in John on the cross and the resurrection of Jesus. Everything hinges on this climatic event[73] and it makes sense that Jesus is constituted as a Temple in that event.[74]

70. Nereparampil, *Temple-Logion*, p. 68, acknowledges the tent-sancturay imagery in 1.14 and comments, 'From the vocabulary of σάρξ and ἐσκήνωσεν, the most we can infer is that perhaps, John might have conceived of the σάρξ as a Tent-Sanctuary, which had a sort of temporary character, but not as a "Temple" (ναός) which is permanent.'

71. If the Eucharist is in view in 6.52-56, then it is interesting that John speaks of eating Jesus' σάρξ, whereas the Synoptics have Jesus saying: 'Take, eat; this is my body (σῶμα)' (Mt. 26.26 and parallels). Is John combating an overemphasis on the Eucharist in this Gospel by speaking of σάρξ rather than σῶμα? While good in itself the σάρξ of Jesus has no power to give life (see my Chapter 7, where I discuss 6.63 in relation to the Passover), whereas the σῶμα of Jesus is a living Temple from which will flow the waters of life (Jn 7.37-39; 19.34). See also the substantial discussion in Chapter 7 on the Tabernacles.

72. Nereparampil, *Temple-Logion*, pp. 68-72, has an extended discussion on the difference between σάρξ and σῶμα. He says that Hebrew had only one word to represent the two—בשׂר. However consultation of E. Hatch's and H. Redpath's, *A Concordance to the Septuagint and Other Greek Versions of the Old Testament* (2 vols.; Leiden: E.J. Brill, 1897), II, p. 1330, reveals a more complex situation. Overwhelmingly σάρξ is a translation for Hebrew בשׂר. Exceptions are Mic. 3.2, 3 where σάρξ translates שׁאר, which, according to *BDB*, pp. 142, 984-85, is really indistinguishable from בשׂר. On the other hand, while σῶμα is used for בשׂר 20 times, there are a number of other contenders: נבלה (9x) e.g. 1 Kgs 13.22, 24; פגר, e.g. Gen. 15.11; שׁאר, e.g. Prov. 5.11; 11.17; גּוה, e.g. Gen. 36.6; טף, e.g. Gen. 47.12; etc. Despite this more complex evidence, Nereparampil is basically correct. One could say that *generally* Hebrew has only one word to represent σάρξ and σῶμα—בשׂר. Σάρξ therefore may well refer to the weakness and frailty of the human body.

73. As a second example, the giving of the Holy Spirit hinges on this event. The Spirit was given only after the glorification of Jesus—namely his death and resurrection (cf. Jn 7.39).

74. N.T. Wright says, '[Jesus] and the city were both making claims to be the place where the living God, Israel's God, was at work to heal, restore and regroup his people.

3.7.5 *The Gospel of the Resurrection*

It remains to look at v. 22: 'When he was raised from the dead, his disciples remembered that he had said this; and they believed the scripture [γραφῇ][75] and the word that Jesus had spoken.' As I have indicated above,[76] this post-resurrection-remembering is important in the Gospel of John. It is only after the resurrection that the events begin to fall into place. With the help of the Paraclete-Spirit the disciples remember (14.26; 16.14) and as they remember in the light of the resurrection they are led to faith. In fact the perspective of the Gospel of John is dominated by the resurrection.[77]

Lindars gathers up the thrust of v. 22 when he remarks that it is the memory of the word of Jesus (v. 19),[78] plus the scripture of Ps. 69.9 (cited in verse 17),[79] viewed in the light of the resurrection, that brings faith. The

Though many people still say that Israel had no idea of the incarnation, this is clearly a mistake: the temple itself…was seen as a dwelling place of the living God. Thus it was the Temple that Jesus took as his model, and against whose claim he advanced his own' ('Jerusalem in the New Testament', in P.W.L.Walker [ed.], *Jerusalem Past and Present in the Purposes of God* [Cambridge: Cambridge University Press, 1992], pp. 53-77 [62]). I note that Wright equates the incarnation with Jesus as Temple, but if Nereparampil is correct, the Johannine picture may be more complex. That is, Jesus may only become the Temple after the death of his body.

75. According to Brown (*John*, I, p. 116) and Carson (*John*, p. 183) John uses the dative after πιστεύειν for things.

76. See 3.6.3.

77. The narrative events and dialogues are undergirded and directed by the resurrection. John has often been called the Spiritual Gospel (after Clement of Alexandria in the early third century), but perhaps a better name would be 'The Gospel of the Resurrection'.

78. Lindars (*John*, p. 144) says the 'word of Jesus' is v. 19. Beasley-Murray (*John*, p. 41) concurs. Enigmatic as 2.19 was initially to the disciples it became clear after the resurrection and they were able to understand that Jesus, in speaking of raising up the Temple within three days was, in fact, speaking about himself. He was speaking of the Temple of his body (2.21).

79. There is a variety of opinion about this. Barrett (*St John*, p. 201) does not believe the word 'scripture' refers back to 2.17 and Ps. 69.9, which lies behind it. He correctly says that the quotation in v. 17 can only be intended if καταφάγεταί refers to the destruction of Christ's body in death, which, in his view, would involve straining the word. Lindars' (*John*, p. 144) response to Barrett's 'complaint' is to say that 2.17 refers, in fact, to the whole of Ps. 69, which, according to Lindars, is 'known to be a Passion proof text in the thought of the primitive Church'. Schnackenburg (*St John*, I, p. 353) sees a possible reference to 2.17 as does Beasley-Murray (*John*, p. 41). Carson (*John*, p. 183) thinks it refers to a number of passages like Ps. 16.8-11 cited by Peter in

disciples believed the scripture and the word that Jesus had spoken. The scripture, in the given context here in ch. 2, and viewed from the post-resurrection perspective, speaks of the passion of Jesus as the Lamb of God who takes away the sins of the world. The word of Jesus in v. 19b speaks of his resurrection. These two things, then, the significance of his death and the reality of his resurrection, form, in part, the post-resurrection faith of the disciples.

3.8 *The Sign*

What was the sign? There are various answers to this question. C.H. Dodd confines the sign to Jesus' action in the Temple. He insists that for John a 'sign' is something that actually happens, but carries a meaning deeper than the actual happening. Since, according to Dodd, John the evangelist does not view the destruction of the Temple and its subsequent rebuilding as actually happening, they cannot therefore be the sign. His conclusion is:

> In the words 'Destroy this temple and three days I will raise it up', Jesus is not promising a significant event yet to come, but inviting His questioners to see the actual occurrence of the Cleansing of the Temple as the σημεῖον they desire.[80]

Dodd's condition for a Johannine sign to be an actual event seems reasonable. But how can he be so confident that John knows nothing of the destruction of the Temple and Jesus rebuilding it? That the Temple was destroyed is a matter of history, and the Gospel was almost certainly

Acts 2.25-28. Brown (*John*, I, p. 116) feels that it is not clear what the term 'scripture' refers to. It could be the Old Testament in general or Ps. 16.10 or perhaps Ps. 69.9 cited in 2.17. He mentions 1 Cor. 15.4: '...he was raised on the third day in accordance with the Scriptures'. Other commentators who think it refers to the Old Testament in general are Bernard (*St John*, I, pp. 97-98), Haenchen (*John*, I, p. 185) and Hoskyns (*The Fourth Gospel*, p. 196). One who thinks it definitely refers to Ps. 16.10 is Westcott (*St John*, I, p. 95). I have argued above (3.6.5) that 2.17 has clear overtones of the death of Jesus. Not only is the passion in view, but Jesus is presented, albeit subtly, as the Passover Lamb. I conclude that 'the scripture' refers to 2.17, which in turn is a quotation from Ps. 69.9.

80. Dodd, *Interpretation*, pp. 300-301. He cites Origen in support of his interpretation: 'I believe He wrought a deeper sign, so that we understand that these things are a symbol that the service of that temple is no longer to be carried on by way of material sacrifices' (*Comm. in Joann.* 10.24). This points to the end of Temple sacrifice, but fails to point to what replaces it, namely the Temple of the resurrection body of Jesus.

written after that event (cf. above 1.4). As for Jesus rebuilding the Temple, he is, in the light of 2.21, speaking of his resurrection. This also is an actual event, pivotal for John's Gospel.

It is true that no one may have witnessed the actual resurrection but that does not discount it as a sign any more than changing the water into wine is discounted from being a sign (2.11) because no one saw the actual change take place. In both cases people experienced the results of the signs.

Nereparampil[81] argues strenuously that the resurrection should be seen as the sign, but does not allow the destruction of the Temple to be part of it because it is not something Jesus does and is not miraculous. I think this is overly restrictive. Does Jesus have to be involved in every part of a σημεῖον for it to be authentic? His mother and the servants were involved in changing the water into wine and its authenticity as a sign is verified in 2.11. Even though Jesus destroys neither the Jewish Temple nor himself those who do these things are the servants of the composite sign.[82]

I believe Bultmann[83] is right to take the compound of destruction and rebuilding, of death and resurrection, as the sign. These two are in-separable—there is no rebuilding without destruction, no resurrection without death. John takes both the crucifixion and resurrection together as the glorification and exaltation of Jesus. Bultmann sees the sign in eschatological terms: judgment and salvation and these are two sides of the one sign that the YHWH has come![84]

---

81. Nereparampil, *Temple-Logion*, pp. 92-98.

82. Is permission implicit in the prophetic ironic imperative, Λύσατε, of 2.19? Certainly the Jews are unable to take Jesus' life from him without his permission: 'No one takes it (my life) from me, but I lay it down of my own accord, and I have power to take it up again' (10.18).

83. Bultmann, *John*, p. 125.

84. This is similar to what Matthias Rissi says ('Die Hochzeit in Kana Jon. 2, 1-11', in Felix Christ [ed.], *Oikonomia: Heilsgeschichte als Thema der Theologie. Oscar Cullmann zum 65. Geburtstag gewidmet* [Hamburg: Reich, 1967], pp. 76-92 [90]): 'Das Wesentliche am Semeiabegriff tritt nicht ins licht (*sic*), wenn man die unmittel-bare Beziehung der Zeichen zu Leiden, Kreuz und Auferstehung Jesu nicht erkennt (in Joh 12,33; 18,32 wird auch das Verbum σημαίνειν auf den Tod Jesus bezogen (damit wird auch zusammenhängen 21,19, wo das Verbum auf den Tod des Petrus anspielt, der ein "Verherrlichen" Gottes genannt wird!). Es geht im Zeichen, das eine Wirk-lichkeit zur Erscheinung bringt, die grösser ist als das Zeichen selbst, die sich in ihm anzeigt, aber in ihm nicht aufgeht, nicht nure um die Offenbarung des "Sohn-seins" oder "Gott-seins", überhaupt nicht um ein Sein, sondern um ein Werk, nämlich das im Tode Jesu vollzogene Erlösungswerk Gottes.'

3.9 *Summary via Narrative Analysis*

3.9.1 *The Model*

It is helpful by way of a summary to use A.J. Greimas's actantial approach to the analysis of the narrative in Jn 2.13-22. Greimas suggests the following model[85] which he regards as the permanent structure behind all narratives:

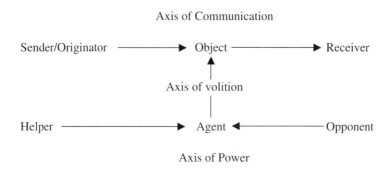

The diagram reveals six different character poles of narrative (sender, agent, object, receiver, helper and opponent) and three functional axes (communication, power and volition). A story often begins when a sender tells (communication) an agent to undertake some task for the benefit of a receiver. The volitional axis represents this quest (object) and the power axis, the struggle involved in its execution.

There are two stories in Jn 2.13-22. The first (2.14-16) is Jesus driving out the animals and sellers and overturning the tables of the money-changers. The structure of that story looks like this:

---

85. See Mark Stibbe, *John as Storyteller: Narrative Criticism and the Fourth Gospel* (Cambridge: Cambridge University Press, 1992), pp. 35, 36. Greimas's model is presented in his *Semantique Structurale* (Paris: Larousse, 1966), and *Du Sens* (Paris: Seuil, 1970). Stibbe has 'subject' designating the person or people who undertake the quest or seek to achieve the object. It is true that the 'subject' is subject to a power struggle between the 'helper' and 'opponent' and from that point of view it is appropriate. But it also has almost the opposite meaning as one who does something—he/she/it/ or they is/are the subject of the verb. 'Subject' has both passive and active connotations. The term is ambiguous so I have chosen N.T. Wright's 'Agent' (*The New Testament and the People of God* [London: SPCK, 1992], p. 71), which seems to capture the active function of that particular character pole in the actantial scheme. Wright has also put arrowheads to his axes, indicating the flow of action in the story.

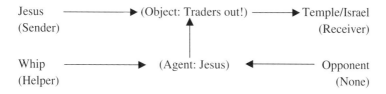

3.9.2 *The First Story*

According to this structural analysis Jesus tells the traders in his Father's house (the Temple) not to make it a house of trade. Consequently as the one who seeks to put this message into effect, he uses an improvised whip to drive out animals and sellers, pours out the coins of the money changers and overturns their tables and orders the pigeon sellers to take the birds out. Hands, voice and improvised whip are all employed by Jesus to execute his object and no one opposes him—at this stage. The receiver (beneficiary) of this action is initially the 'Temple', but through the Temple, all Israel.

3.9.3 *The Second Story*

The second story of the dialogue between Jesus and the Jews (2.17-20) when submitted to this structural analysis appears as follows:

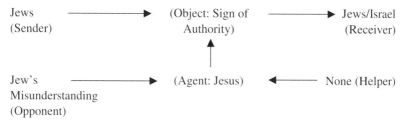

The Jews ask Jesus for a sign of authority for what he has done in the Temple. The message to Jesus (the agent) is reflexive. The Jews want a sign that will communicate back to them as those who supposedly represent the interests of the Temple and the nation. Jesus offers the sign of raising the destroyed Temple in three days. The executor of this sign is ambiguous. We know from the narrator's comment in v. 21 that Jesus is speaking of the Temple of his body, so the sign he offers is his own resurrection—his lordship over death. In a sense the Jews help to bring this about by destroying Jesus, but, possibly in the light of Jn 10.18, it is Jesus who raises himself and, if so, he is properly the one who achieves the sign of his authority and he does this independently with no helper. The Jews are unable to receive this sign because they are thinking not of the Temple of Jesus' body, but of the Temple of stone. What this analysis highlights is the vast gulf between what Jesus says and what the Jews understand. The Jews are defeated in their quest by their misunderstanding, and at a deeper level by their unbelief.

3.9.4 *The Whole Story*

Now the two stories can be combined into a single story and subjected to actantial analysis:

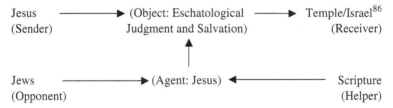

This kind of analysis highlights the overall thrust of what John is saying in 2.13-22. The object of the story is the sign. There is one sign with two sides: first, Jesus' action in the Temple is a sign that the eschatological day of the LORD has come and that the Temple and its sacrificial cult is to be destroyed and, secondly, Jesus will raise a new Temple—his own body. These are two sides of the one sign that heralds both judgment and hope. The Jews understand neither side of the sign. Their lack of understanding and unbelief (implied in their rhetorical question in 2.20) oppose what Jesus is saying and doing. However, the disciples are enabled to understand with the help of faith, scripture (Ps. 69.9) and the logion of Jesus in retrospect after the resurrection. Scripture and the word of Jesus act as a kind of lens that helps the disciples to see and understand.[87]

3.10 *Conclusion*

At the beginning of this chapter I said that Jn 2.13-22 is the crucial passage for a discussion of the Temple theme in the Gospel of John.

Jesus' action in the Temple sparks a discussion between the Jews and himself about his relationship to the Temple.

---

86. The traders receive the initial message: 'Get out!' But the significant message is really delivered to Israel as a whole in relation to the cleansing of the Temple and also in the destruction and raising of the Temple (the body of Jesus) in three days.

87. This structural analysis functions as a summary of the previous linguistic and intertextual analysis I have carried out in this chapter. I would not have been in a position to make this analysis at the beginning.

I have argued that Jesus comes as LORD of the Temple. Indeed his action is an intimation that the eschatological day of the YHWH has come and the 'hour' is near.[88]

The Temple is no longer 'my Father's house'; it has become a 'house of trade'. Its inner life has already been destroyed by the Jews. Jesus with bitter irony urges them: Λύσατε τὸν ναὸν τοῦτον! That is: 'Finish what you have begun!' And in the course of time the stones were torn down and the timber fired. The destruction was completed. This was the judgment intimated by the Temple cleansing and confirmed by Jesus word: Λύσατε!

But the remembering of Ps. 69.9 in Jn 2.17 brings a further dimension to the narrative. On the surface it provides a motive for Jesus' action in the Temple. However, read on a deeper level it intimates that Jesus himself will be sacrificed (consumed). So his passion for the honour of his Father not only spurs his action in the Temple, but also triggers the hostility that will end in his death, a sacrificial consumption.

But it is not all judgment—there is hope. Jesus will raise up the Temple in three days. This is not a Temple of wood and stone, but the Temple of his body, as 2.21 makes clear. This is a key statement in the Gospel via the narrator's comment.[89] This simple statement acts as a lens, albeit one among many, through which we can view the Gospel of John. I have already made use of it to interpret Jn 2.13-22, but it can also be used to discern other references to the Temple that we might not otherwise see. This verse then provides the rationale for turning to other texts in John and exploring them for Temple allusions with respect to Jesus. This will be done in subsequent chapters.

---

88. Earlier (3.3.2–3) I suggested that Jn 1 introduces a new week, paralleling the week of creation (cf. the opening words of the Gospel, ἐν ἀρχῇ). The seventh day of that week is announced in Jn 2.1 as 'the third day'. This is the day of the beginning of the signs Jesus performs (2.11). I have argued that this is the Johannine version of the eschatological day of the LORD (3.4.3–4). Within this day there is the 'hour' when the eschatological work of the LORD reaches its climax in the crucifixion, resurrection and ascension of Jesus (3.4.4 n. 25).

89 This is the narrator's comment. The narrator assumes a certain omniscient perspective with respect to the words of Jesus. Not only has the narrator/author seen what has happened (19.35), he also knows the inner meaning of what he hears and sees (cf. 2.24b, 25; 6.6, 64, 71; 7.5, 39; 9.7; 11.13, 51-52; 12.6, 33; 20.9).

Chapter 4

THE NEW BEGINNING: THE PROLOGUE

The thesis of this study is that John is writing to demonstrate that Jesus is the answer for a Judaism that has lost its central institution. The Temple has gone with its associated ritual and festivals and they have been fulfilled in Jesus the new Temple. With Jesus a new beginning has come and the purpose of this chapter is to see how this theme of the new beginning emerges in the Prologue of John.

4.1 *The Relation of the Prologue to the Rest of the Gospel*

Brown reflects on the debate on the relation of the Prologue to the Gospel in his commentary. He points to the stylistic and thematic differences between the Prologue and what follows in the Gospel, yet at the same time acknowledges the similarities. In the light of these observations he considers the possibility that the Prologue was originally an independent poem that has been adapted to the Gospel. However, he concedes that the Johannine character of the Prologue is such that 'it seems reasonable to posit that the Prologue was composed in Johannine circles'.[1]

On the other hand, Carson is much more positive. He regards the Prologue as the foyer to the rest of the Gospel. He cites Robinson's findings about common themes in the Prologue and Gospel and mentions a number of words that are first introduced in the Prologue and which subsequently become central for the Gospel.[2]

---

1. Brown, *John*, I, pp. 18-21.
2. Carson, *John*, p. 111. The words he mentions are: life, light (1.4), witness (1.7), true (1.9), world (1.10), glory, truth (1.14). These words do not merely crop up in the later Gospel; rather they are pivotal to the development of Johannine themes. It is true that Λόγος/Word occurs only in the Prologue, but the idea that Jesus is God's messenger, that he speaks for God, dominates the pages of the gospel. The term χάρις/covenant love (according to Brown, *John*, I, p. 19) is also absent. However, the theme of

C.H. Dodd sees the Prologue as 'an account of the life of Jesus under the form of a description of the eternal Logos in its relations with the world and with man, and the rest of the gospel an account of the Logos under the form of a record of the life of Jesus; and the proposition ὁ λόγος σάρξ ἐγένετο binds the two together'.[3] Thus while the Prologue for Dodd functions on a broader scale than simply introducing the rest of the Gospel, it nevertheless does introduce the Gospel.

Whatever the overall function of the Prologue may be, part of its function is to introduce what follows in the Gospel. The similarities between the Prologue and the Gospel are too great to conclude otherwise. If this is so, then I believe it is legitimate and even desirable to search the Prologue for clues of a Temple theme in the Gospel.[4]

In the previous chapter I conducted an analysis of the pericope that deals most obviously with the Temple theme in John, namely, 2.13-22. I drew a number of conclusions from that investigation, the most notable being that Jesus is now the Temple—he replaces the Temple of Jerusalem. Are there in the Prologue any intimations that Jesus may replace the Jewish Temple? The purpose of this chapter then is to answer this question.

In the course of the investigation of the Prologue I will pay special attention to vv. 14-16 where Moses (representative of Judaism) and Jesus Christ (representative of the new creation) are mentioned. I will argue that the word ἐσκήνωσεν in v. 14 echoes the Tent of Meeting where YHWH met with Moses. At that time the glory of YHWH filled the Tent (Exod. 40.34, 35) as a sign of his presence. However, in John the presence of God is no longer found in the Tent/Temple, but in the incarnate Word, Jesus Christ, who manifests his glory (2.11), the glory of God, his Father. This incarnate Word is full of grace and truth (cf. 1.14). Thus the old gives way to the new in Jesus Christ. With Jesus, the Word made flesh, there is a new

God's love is powerfully present throughout the Gospel. C.K. Barrett (*New Testament Essays* [London: SPCK, 1971], p. 48) says the Prologue is 'one piece of solid theological writing…necessary to the Gospel as the Gospel is necessary to the Prologue.'

3.   Dodd, *Interpretation*, p. 285.

4.   Udo Schnelle (*Antidocetic Christology in the Gospel of John* [ET; Philadelphia: Fortress Press, 1992], p. 212) approaches it this way: 'If the prologue represents the opening of the Gospel in both time and content, it has an introductory function. It leads us into the theme of the Gospel by treating central features of what is to come, and thus prepares us to understand the Gospel and gives substantial direction and understanding. This is clear from the terminological and material agreements between the prologue and the rest of the Gospel.' And he goes on to list these in detail in much the same way as Carson (and before him Robinson) has done.

beginning—in particular a new beginning for the locus of the presence of God. His presence is no longer found in the Tent of Meeting/Temple, but in Jesus Christ.

4.2 A Possible Prologue Structural Pattern

I will begin by looking at the structure of the Prologue because the structure of a pericope can often provide helpful clues for the interpretation of the smaller units within that pericope.[5]

4.2.1 Past Structural Proposals for the Prologue

Alan Culpepper[6] has summarized chiastic structural proposals for the Prologue going back as far as N.W. Lund's suggestion in 1931. This historical survey demonstrates basic agreement about the general chiastic structure, but diversity of opinion about the pivot of the suggested chiasm.[7] How does one assess the validity of structural proposals? Culpepper cites David

---

5.   Peter F. Ellis (*The Genius of John: A Composition-Critical Commentary on the Fourth Gospel* [Collegeville, MN: Liturgical Press, 1984], pp. 16, 17) mentions some of the rewards of chiastic analysis of John. Leaving aside aesthetic rewards he mentions: confirmation of the substantial unity of the Gospel; some appreciation of the positioning of various sections (e.g. why the cleansing of the Temple comes relatively early in the second chapter—it balances the passion narrative and both speak of the destruction of the body of Jesus); and leads to a proper appreciation of what has been called the 'spiral' movement in John's thought. In addition I believe the chiastic structure can help to illuminate the smaller units within a pericope, but this should be handled with care and not be pressed too far.

6.   A. Culpepper, 'The Pivot of John's Prologue', *NTS* 27 (1981), pp. 1-31.

7.   N. Lund ('The Influence of the Chiasmus upon the Structure of the Gospels', *ATR* 13 [1931], pp. 42-46) finds the centre of the Prologue in v. 13; M.E. Boismard (*St John's Prologue* [trans. Carisbrooke Dominicans; London: Blackfriars Publications, 1957], pp. 79-80) in vv. 12-13; P. Lamarche ('Le Prologue de Jean', *RSR* 52 [1964], pp. 529-32) in vv. 10-13; A. Feuillet (*Le Prologue de Quatrième Evangile* [Paris: Desclée de Brouwer, 1968], p. 160) finds no pivot because vv. 10-11 balance vv. 12-13; Morna Hooker ('John the Baptist and the Johannine Prologue', *NTS* 16 [1969-70], pp. 354-58 [357]) sees the Prologue consisting of two parts, vv. 1-13 and vv. 14-18, with the respective pivots being vv. 6-8 (the testimony of the Baptist) and v. 15 (the testimony of the Baptist). Interestingly, Morna Hooker is arguing against those who want to see the Baptist's testimony in vv. 6-8 and v. 15 as secondary additions. Her proposed structure suggests that, far from being secondary, they are *central* for both sections of the Prologue. This might be too good for her case to be true!

Clark's work[8] and, using a modified version of his criteria, puts forward his proposal for a chiastic structure for the Prologue. He divides the Prologue into 15 sections, 14 of which are balanced in parallel pairs with the fifteenth being the pivot that he finds in v. 12b: ἔδωκεν αὐτοῖς ἐξουσίαν τέκνα θεοῦ γενέσθαι. For the purpose of the discussion here, I will follow a simplified version[9] of Culpepper's structure, taking note of George Mlakuzhyil's recognition of the spiral development within the Prologue's thought.[10] While this structural proposal perhaps lacks the detail of, for example, Culpepper's, and the form-critical rigour of Giblin's proposals, it is sufficient to give some kind of feel for the flow of thought in the Prologue, which is all that is necessary here.

8. Culpepper, 'Pivot', p. 7 n. 30. D. Clark, 'Criteria for Identifying Chiasm', *Linguistica Biblica* V (1975), pp. 63-72. The criteria Clark suggests are: (a) content—the theme or themes of each pericope; (b) form or structure—the type of narrative and/or dialogue of which the pericope is composed; (c) language—primarily the occurrence of catchwords; (d) setting; and (e) theology. Clark makes the observation that each of the criteria involves abstraction and will be weighed differently by different scholars and so the acceptability of the proposed structure has to be gauged by the cumulative impact of the criteria. Culpepper makes use of criteria (a) and (c) and a third that he calls 'conceptual parallels', which seems to be unnecessary since it is subsumed under (a), namely content. To make the assessment of the validity of chiastic structure proposals extremely difficult, Culpepper mentions two other considerations: (1) imperfections of form are the rule in antiquity, and he warns that we should not expect perfect symmetry or complete adherence to an identifiable pattern and; (2) that a given passage may give evidence of two or even three structures. This makes evaluating chiastic structures exceedingly complicated.

9. J.L. Staley, *The Print's First Kiss: A Rhetorical Investigation of the Implied Reader in the Fourth Gospel* (SBLDS, 82; Atlanta: Scholars Press, 1988), pp. 52-57. There have been proposals that the Prologue of John is a hymn that the author has modified, and there are numerous suggestions about which parts of the Prologue are secondary additions. For example, C. Homer Giblin ('Two Complementary Literary Structures in John 1.1-18', *JBL* 104 [1985], pp. 87-103) classes vv. 6-8, 15 and 13 as 'patent additions' (p. 88) and believes that attempting, as Culpepper does, to find a structure of the Prologue as it now stands is to engage in an enterprise that should be 'based on more objective textual data'(p. 87 n. 3). While it is true that the meaning of the Prologue is sometimes elusive and the connecting links are not always obvious, I do not believe that is sufficient reason to rule certain verses as secondary. But overall my aim is to endeavour to make sense of the text as it stands, taking account of variant textual readings.

10. G. Mlakuzhyil, *The Christocentric Literary Structure of the Fourth Gospel* (AnBib, 117; Rome: Pontifical Biblical Institute, 1987), p. 132.

4.2.2 A Chiastic Structure of the Prologue

A (1-5)

1 Ἐν ἀρχῇ ἦν ὁ λόγος,
κὰι ὁ λόγος ἦν πρὸς τὸν θεόν,
καὶ θεὸς ἦν ὁ λόγος.
οὗτος ἦν ἐν ἀρχῇ πρὸς τὸν θεόν.

2 πάντα δι᾽ αὐτοῦ ἐγένετο,
καὶ χωρὶς αὐτοῦ ἐγένετο οὐδὲ ἕν.

3 ὃ γέγονεν[11] ἐν αὐτῷ ζωὴ ἦν,
καὶ ἡ ζωὴ ἦν τὸ φῶς τῶν ἀνθρώπων·
καὶ τὸ φῶς ἐν τῇ σκοτίᾳ φαίνει,
καὶ ἡ σκοτία αὐτὸ οὐ κατέλαβεν.

B (6-8)

1 Ἐγένετο ἄνθρωπος
ἀπεσταλμένος παρὰ θεοῦ,
ὄνομα αὐτῷ Ἰωάννης:

2 οὗτος ἦλθεν εἰς μαρτυρίαν,
ἵνα μαρτυρήσῃ περὶ τοῦ φωτός,

11. I accept this as the better of the two readings even though it is clumsy and difficult. Metzger (B. Metzger, *A Textual Commentary on the Greek New Testament* [London: United Bible Societies, 1971], pp. 195-96) just tips the balance in favour of taking ὃ γέγονεν with ἐν αὐτῷ ζωὴ ἦν. E.L. Miller (*Salvation-History in the Prologue of John: The Significance of John 1.3/4* [NovTSup, 40; Leiden: E.J. Brill, 1989]) argues strongly for this reading (pp. 17-44) *and* an incarnational interpretation (pp. 45-89). He points out that while the verb γίνομαι bears a kind of ontological-existential signification ('to be', 'to become', 'to come into being', as, e.g., in 1.3: 'All things came into being [ἐγένετο] through him...'), it also bears a historical-temporal meaning ('to come to pass', 'come on the scene', 'appear', 'happen', 'occur', 'arise',) (as, e.g., in 1.6: 'There appeared [ἐγένετο] a man sent from God...'). For this and other reasons Miller translates 1.3/4 as 'What appeared in him was life and the life was the light of men.' In view of Miller's arguments and the fact that the Prologue functions as an introduction to the ministry and work of the incarnate Word in the Gospel, I am inclined to think that it is indeed the incarnate Word that is referred to as early as v. 4a. The remainder of v. 4, and v. 5, find extensive development in the gospel as a whole. The life in the incarnate Word is portrayed as the light of humankind (cf. esp. Jn 8.12) and that light does shine into the darkness of unbelief, especially as it is represented by the unbelief of the Jews (3.18-19; 16.9) and the treachery of Judas (13.30c). That darkness does try to master the light (11.50) but does not suceed. Indeed, in trying to master (suppress/overcome) the light, Jesus' opponents cause it to shine ever more brightly (11.51, 52). There are of course alternative explanations of ὃ γένονεν. For example, see Peter Cohee ('John 1.3-4', *NTS* 41 [1995], pp. 470-77), who reads ὃ γένονεν as an intrusive gloss.

ἵνα πάντες πιστεύσωσιν δι' αὐτοῦ.
3 οὐκ ἦν ἐκεῖνος τὸ φῶς,
ἀλλ' ἵνα μαρτυρήσῃ περὶ τοῦ φωτός.

C (9-11)
1 Ἦν τὸ φῶς τὸ ἀληθινόν,[12]
ὃ φωτίζει πάντα ἄνθρωπον,
ἐρχόμενον εἰς τὸν κόσμον.
2 ἐν τῷ κόσμῳ ἦν,
καὶ ὁ κόσμος δι' αὐτοῦ ἐγένετο,
καὶ ὁ κόσμος αὐτὸν οὐκ ἔγνω.
3 εἰς τὰ ἴδια ἦλθεν,
καὶ οἱ ἴδιοι αὐτὸν οὐ παρέλαβον.

D (12-13)
1 ὅσοι δὲ ἔλαβον αὐτόν,
ἔδωκεν αὐτοῖς ἐξουσίαν
τέκνα θεοῦ γενέσθαι,
τοῖς πιστεύουσιν εἰς τὸ ὄνομα αὐτοῦ,
2 οἳ οὐκ ἐξ αἱμάτων
οὐδὲ ἐκ θελήματος σαρκὸς
οὐδὲ ἐκ θελήματος ἀνδρὸς
ἀλλ' ἐκ θεοῦ ἐγεννήθησαν.

C' (14)
1 Καὶ ὁ λόγος σὰρξ ἐγένετο
καὶ ἐσκήνωσεν ἐν ἡμῖν,
καὶ ἐθεασάμεθα τὴν δόξαν αὐτοῦ,
δόξαν ὡς μονογενοῦς παρὰ πατρός,
πλήρης χάριτος καὶ ἀληθείας.

B' (15)
1 Ἰωάννης μαρτυρεῖ περὶ αὐτοῦ

12. Verse 9 is ambiguous. It could be translated as 'He was the true light who enlightens every one who comes into the world…' or 'That was the true light which enlightens…' I believe this is speaking of Jesus the light of the world (8.12) who shines on all people. Cf. also 3.20 where the shining light of Jesus judges people. In relation to Jn 1.9 Lesslie Newbigin has said that it is possible to read the early verses as implying Hindu thought behind the Prologue, but John is not wanting to go down that track and it is the particularity of the incarnation that forms the lens through which these early verses of the Prologue are to be read. I am indebted to Revd John Proctor, Director of New Testament Studies, Westminster College, Cambridge, for this comment of Newbigin.

καὶ κέκραγεν λέγων,
Οὗτος ἦν ὃν εἶπον,
2 Ὁ ὀπίσω μου ἐρχόμενος
ἔμπροσθέν μου γέγονεν,
ὅτι πρῶτός μου ἦν.

A' (16-18)
1 ὅτι ἐκ τοῦ πληρώματος αὐτοῦ
ἡμεῖς πάντες ἐλάβομεν
καὶ χάριν ἀντὶ χάριτος·
2 ὅτι ὁ νόμος διὰ Μωϋσέως ἐδόθη,
ἡ χάρις καὶ ἡ ἀλήθεια διὰ Ἰησοῦ Χριστοῦ ἐγένετο.
3 θεὸν οὐδεὶς ἑώρακεν πώποτε·
μονογενὴς θεὸς ὁ ὢν εἰς τὸν κόλπον τοῦ πατρός,
ἐκεῖνος ἐξηγήσατο.

4.2.3 *A Chiastic Spiral*

This chiastic pattern can be set out under the following headings so as to highlight the parallel and antithetic elements:

A The relationship of the Logos to[13]   vv. 1-5
  1 God
  2 Creation
  3 Humankind
    B The witness of John   vv. 6-8
      C The journey of the Light/Logos (negative)[14]   vv. 9-11

---

13. The first five verses strongly echo Gen. 1, having the following words in common: ἀρχή , λόγος (for ויאמר אלהים), φῶς, θεός, σκότος (LXX)/σκοτία (John), ἐγένετο. The Prologue echoes the beginning not only of Israel's book (the Old Testament) but the beginning of all things. The evangelist wants to announce a new beginning with the coming of the incarnate Word, but at the same time this new beginning has some continuity with the first beginning. Hence the words ἐν ἀρχῇ at the commencement of the gospel.

14. This journey of the Logos is parallel to the obviously incarnational journey of the Logos in v. 14. There has long been a debate whether the journey of vv. 9-11 is incarnational. Käsemann believes the Word enters history as early as v. 5 and it will be seen from the above footnote (n. 12) that Miller believes the incarnation is in view as early as vv. 3, 4. Culpepper's argument in favour of a reference to the incarnate Word in vv. 9-11 is set out in 'Pivot', pp. 13, 14, cf. n. 54. He reasons: '[T]he chiastic structure demands that there be two references [to the incarnate Word], just as there are two references to John the Baptist.' It is surprising that Culpepper says 'demands' when he has already conceded that 'one should not generally expect perfect symmetry or complete adherence to the identifiable pattern.' I think the chiastic parallel can be a

D The gift to become God's children   vv. 12-13
C' The journey of the Logos (positive)   v. 14
B' The witness of John   v. 15
A' The relationship of the Logos to   vv. 16-18
    3 Humankind
    2 Re-creation
    1 God

In addition to this parallelism there are signs of a spiral development. For example, in v. 5, where the light shines in the darkness and the darkness seeks to master it,[15] it is clear that the life-giving, revelatory Word is being opposed. This thought undergoes development in v. 11 where the Word is not merely opposed, but in fact rejected. There is also a movement from a cosmic perspective to a focus on the incarnate Word as early as 1.3/4 and the historical presence of John the Baptist in vv. 6-8. Progression is also evident in vv. 9-12. The racial pattern of membership of God's family (v. 11) is replaced by a faith membership that depends on God (vv. 12-13). Further, the theme of revelation progresses through the Prologue and reaches a climax in v. 18: θεὸν οὐδεὶς ἑώρακεν πώποτε· μονογενὴς θεὸς ὁ ὢν εἰς τὸν κόλπον τοῦ πατρὸς, ἐκεῖνος ἐξηγήσατο.[16]

useful aid in making an exegetical judgment, but I do not think it can bear the entire weight of such a judgment. For my part I think the referent of vv. 9-11 is to the coming of the incarnate Logos, who comes into his own world and to his own people, namely the Jews, who reject him. The rejection of the incarnate Christ in John is comprehensively narrated throughout: Jn 5, 7, 8, 9 (esp. vv. 40, 41); 10.31-39; 11.45-57; 12.37-43; and also in the passion narrative of chs. 18 and 19. On the other hand, reference to the incarnate Word in vv. 9-11 is certainly not as clear as v. 14. There is in vv. 9-11 a distinct echo back to v. 3 with the words 'the world was made by him', and so there are traces of the cosmic perspective in these verses as well as the particular prospect of the incarnate Word. But given that the incarnate Word has already appeared as early as v. 4, a reference to his coming in vv. 9-11 should come as no surprise.

15. κατέλαβεν, aorist of καταλαμβάνω for which Bauer, Arndt and Gingrich (*Greek–English Lexicon*, pp. 413-14) suggest grasp (in the sense of comprehending) or overcome. They allow that John may have intended both meanings, in which case some such translation as 'master' would encompass both. Stibbe (*John*, p. 27) makes the point that the failure to master the light involves a failure to master it both intellectually and physically.

16. Coloe ('The Dwelling of God', p. 28) argues against this structure, insisting that A is not strictly parallel to A'. This is true; they are not strictly parallel. However, there is development within the chiastic structure, as I have demonstrated above, which

I now come to vv. 16-18. How does John understand the coming of Jesus Christ in relation to Moses and the institutions of Israel, including the Temple? This was (and still is) a fundamental question for a faith that grew out of the Old Testament and Early Judaism. These verses in the Prologue, I believe, herald how John sees the past and therefore we must turn to them now and seek to understand them.

At this point I want to make use of the structural analysis developed above to see if it offers any hints for interpreting these verses.

4.2.4 *Some Chiastic Consequences*

Using the structural notation, A3 (vv. 4, 5) parallels A'1 (v. 16). There are no verbal parallels, but the concepts may be parallel: ἐν αὐτῷ ζωὴ ἦν (v. 4) parallels ἐκ τοῦ πληρώματος αὐτοῦ...χάριν (v. 16). In both cases the incarnate Word is the source. In v. 4 the incarnate Word is the source of life; in v. 16 the fullness of the incarnate Word is the source of χάριν ἀντὶ χάριτος. The word for life (v. 4) in John or the Johannine Epistles (ζωή) never means natural life, but always eternal life.[17] It is a gift that God gives through Jesus Christ (cf. 4.10; 3.15, 16, 36). If this is so, then χάρις in v. 16 could perhaps result in the gift of eternal life. What strengthens this suggestion of a parallel is a quote from the *Odes* 18.4-6, which shows a striking affinity with Jn 1.4, 5 and the πλήρωμα of 1.16:

> O LORD, for the sake of those who are in need,
> Do not expel your Word from me.
> Nor, for the sake of their works,
> Withhold your perfection (πλήρωμα) from me.
> Let not light be conquered by darkness,
> Nor let truth flee from falsehood.[18]

allows for differences. My structure is not static as she suggests (p. 30). Her own structural analysis based on parallels with Gen. 1 (p. 42) is implausible. While it may be true, as Evans observes (C.A. Evans, *Word and Glory: On the Exegetical and Theological Background of John's Prologue* [JSNTSup, 89; Sheffield: JSOT Press, 1993], pp. 77-78), that the conceptual parallels between Genesis and the Prologue are 'obvious and quite significant', it is quite another matter to go beyond Evans and postulate structural parallels, as Coloe does.

17. Brown (*John*, I, p. 7). Brown says that in 1 Jn 1.2 'life' is specified as 'eternal life'. ζωή is used 36 times in the Johannine literature in contrast to the 16 occasions in the Synoptics. The word for natural life in John is ψυχή (see 13.37; 15.13), whereas ζωή means the life of the age to come.

18. On the appropriateness of the translating πλήρωμα with 'perfection', see J.H. Charlesworth and R.A. Culpepper ('The Odes of Solomon and the Gospel of John',

The use of πλήρωμα in this quotation together with light, darkness and truth (all words to be found in Jn 1.4, 5, 16) offers further evidence for the proposal of parallel concepts between vv. 4 and 5 and v. 16.

While I do not want to push the parallelism too hard for the purpose of interpreting v. 16, it has offered some hints about how we might view this verse. Verse 4 says that what appeared in the incarnate Word was life; and in v. 16 what we have received from the incarnate Word is πλήρωμα and χάριν ἀντὶ χάριτος. Is it possible that this complex of words in v. 16 represents the ζωὴ that is found in Jesus Christ?

I now come to v. 17: is there a parallel between A'2 (v. 17) and A2 (v. 3), and, if there is, does it offer any assistance in interpreting v. 17? There is first of all a verbal equivalent to the phrase δι' αὐτοῦ ἐγένετο in v. 3 with διὰ Ἰησοῦ Χριστοῦ ἐγένετο in v. 17. Both verses emphasize 'what came to be' through the Word in v. 3 and through Jesus Christ, the Word made flesh, in v. 17. In v. 3 it was creation that came into being, whereas in v. 17 it is grace and truth that has come on to the scene.[19] There does seem to be a parallel between these two verses, but it remains to be seen in the subsequent exegesis whether it will help in the interpretation.

Verse 18 of the Prologue contains a dogmatic statement: θεὸν οὐδεὶς ἑώρακεν πώποτε. Verses 1 and 2 speak of the Word being with (πρὸς) God. This idea is expressed more vividly and personally in v. 18: μονογενὴς θεὸς[20] ὁ ὢν εἰς τὸν κόλπον τοῦ πατρός. If anything it is v.

CBQ 35 [1973], pp. 298-322). There is no evidence that John used this reference as a source. I quote it as an example of where the same concepts come together. Cf. J.H. Charlesworth, 'Odes of Solomon: A New Translation and Introduction', in *OTP*, II, pp. 725-71 (727).

19. Culpepper ('Pivot', p. 10) says the parallelism is antithetical. I think this is going too far; creation and grace/truth need not be antithetical. There could well be grace/truth in creation, especially since it has come into being through the Word. What I believe is in view is a new beginning, and for this reason we would translate ἐγένετο in v. 17 as 'appeared', 'came onto the scene', rather than as 'came into being' because it allows some continuity with the first beginning.

20. Metzger (*A Textual Commentary*, p. 198) has μονογενὴς θεός as the preferred reading for the majority of the Committee. P[66] and P[75], both of which read θεός, strengthen the external attestation and the preferred reading is certainly the more difficult. μονογενὴς υἱός could be the result of scribal assimilation to Jn 3.16, 18; 1 Jn 4.9. The shorter reading, ὁ μονογενής, while attractive for internal reasons has weak external attestation. Translation has posed problems for commentators. Carson (*John*, p. 135) has 'the unique one, [himself] God' and Beasley-Murray 'the only Son, by nature God' (*John*, pp. 15-16) both of which are clumsy. Brown (*John*, I, p. 17) has the simple 'God the only Son', which is adequate.

18 that fills out the πρός in vv. 1-2 rather than vv. 1-2 shedding light on v. 18. Perhaps one could say that vv. 1-2 in direct, spare language sketches out the relationship between the Word and God, and v. 18 spells this out in more intimate terms and how 'God the only Son' functions as the Word in exegeting (ἐξηγήσατο) the Father. In both cases the uniqueness of the central character is emphasized. Jesus-the-Word is both separate from God and the same as God ('the Word was with God, and the Word was God'), and in v. 18 he is God the only Son (μονογενὴς θεός) from the κόλπον of the Father.[21]

While the creational beginning is in view in 1.1, the movement in the Prologue is towards a new beginning with Jesus Christ as the Word made flesh. It is through this new beginning with Jesus Christ, God the only Son made flesh, that we are to assess the former ways in which God dealt with his people. Moses gave the law; grace and truth came through Jesus Christ. Moses never saw God's face, only the 'afterglow of his glory' (Exod. 33.17-23); God the only Son is in the Father and the Father is in him (14.11)—or, as 1.18 puts it, εἰς τὸν κόλπον τοῦ πατρός. Moses met with God in the Tent of Meeting, the place of his glory; now the dwelling of God is in the Word made flesh—it is through Jesus Christ we meet with God and behold his glory. This last point is especially important for the development of this study. The place of God's glory where his people met with him became, in time, the Temple. What is true of the Tent of Meeting is true also of the Temple. Both are supplanted by Jesus Christ. He is now the 'place' where God's people meet with him.

4.2.5 *John the Baptist Testifies to the New Beginning*

Why introduce John the Baptist in vv. 6-8 and again in v. 15? The theme of the Prologue is the new beginning. A new order is about to dawn with the coming of the incarnate Word. The herald for this new order is John the Baptist. He is not the light, but is to bear witness to the light. He is the friend of the bridegroom who is to usher in the bridegroom for the eschatological wedding banquet (3.28-30). John's work is to point to the incarnate Word, to herald the new beginning.

John the Baptist's opening utterance is therefore a powerful testimony to the incarnate Word: 'The one who comes after me ranks ahead of me

---

21. Cf. Jn 13.23 where the Beloved Disciple rests in the κόλπον of Jesus and becomes the expositor of Jesus for the other disciples. This could be saying that the Beloved Disciple is the one who makes Jesus known. It is the Beloved Disciple who is the witness who tells the truth (19.35) and has written what he has testified (21.24).

for he existed before me.'²² This is a testimony to the pre-existence of the incarnate Word. It is closely akin to the striking words of Jesus himself in 8.58: 'Very truly I tell you before Abraham was, I am' (Ἀμὴν, ἀμὴν λέγω ὑμῖν, πρὶν Ἀβρααμ γενέσθαι ἐγὼ εἰμί)—a statement that was interpreted by the Jews as blasphemy because they immediately (8.59) took up stones to throw at him.²³

The depth of the Baptist's testimony is in harmony with the powerful statements about Jesus elsewhere in the Prologue: namely, that he is the Word who was in the beginning with God and was God (1.1) and that all things came into being through him (1.3) and that he is God the only Son who is in the κόλπον of the Father (1.18). Given the Baptist's profound testimony to Jesus' pre-existence, it is fitting that the next verse (v. 16) should begin by reference to Jesus' πληρώμα,²⁴ even though there is a natural word link with the πλήρης of v. 14.

---

22.   This verse is substantially repeated in v. 30. Brown (*John*, I, p. 15) says, 'It is agreed today that this verse is an addition to the original hymn, an addition of the same type as vv. 6-8 (9), awkwardly breaking up vss. 14 and 16.' This may be so. However, it is possible to argue that v. 16 follows from v. 15. The other difficulty that Brown mentions is how John the Baptist could have said such a thing. Presumably, how could he have known about the pre-existence of the incarnate Word? The same question, of course, can be asked of John the Baptist's utterance in 1.29: 'Behold the Lamb of God who takes away the sin of the world.' How could John have known this at the beginning of Jesus' ministry? If one adopts the view that John has written his gospel from a post-resurrectional perspective on the ministry, crucifixion, resurrection and ascension of Jesus of Nazareth, then the problem of what John the Baptist knew or did not know does not arise. In the hands of John, John the Baptist functions as witness to Jesus the incarnate Word. He testifies to all the fullness of that Word.

23.   Analysis of 8.58 reveals that more than pre-existence is suggested. The contrast between the two Greek verbs is startlingly vivid. γενέσθαι is the aorist infin. of γίνομαι, which expresses the coming into existence of Abraham, maybe even his birth. The aorist expresses an event usually in the past—a point on the time-scale (see BDF, §318 [1]). ἐγὼ εἰμι is in stark contrast. There is a tense change—we are now in the present and it is a 'timeless present', if we can use that expression. There is a contrast between the created and the uncreated, the temporal and the eternal. The construction of Jesus' statement itself shows that his claim is not simply to pre-existence; for that Jesus could have claimed that he was (ἤμην, imperfect of εἰμι, cf. 1.1), or even came into existence (ἐγενόμην) before Abraham. But he does not do that—he says, 'Before Abraham was, I am.' So they picked up stones to throw at him! That is, they judged that he had committed the capital crime of blasphemy.

24.   Elizabeth Harris argues that John's witness includes all of vv. 15-18 (and not just v. 15) (*Prologue and Gospel: The Theology of the Fourth Evangelist* [JSNTSup, 107; Sheffield: JSOT Press, 1994], pp. 35-38). In brief her arguments are: (a) The verb

4.3 *Analysis of John 1.16-17*

This brings me then to 1.16, 17:

ὅτι ἐκ τοῦ πληρώματος αὐτοῦ
ἡμεῖς πάντες ἐλάβομεν
καὶ χάριν ἀντὶ χάριτος·

ὅτι ὁ νόμος διὰ Μωϋσέως ἐδόθη,
ἡ χάρις καὶ ἡ ἀλήθεια διὰ Ἰησοῦ Χριστοῦ ἐγένετο.

πλήρωμα is used in Col. 1.19, 'In him (the Beloved Son) all the fullness [πλήρωμα] of God was pleased to dwell...' I believe this Pauline sentence illuminates what John is saying in 1.14, 16; however, the fullness of God in 1.14, 16 is in relation to the fullness of divine grace and truth. Interestingly, in commenting on this word, Delling[25] cites Ps. 67.17 (LXX): εὐδόκησεν ὁ θεὸς κατοικεῖν ἐν αὐτῷ to indicate God's dwelling in Zion. He goes on to say, 'In Col. Christ replaces the Jewish Temple.' But this replacement is greater and fuller than what prevailed with regard to the Temple. Christ is greater than the Temple (Mt. 12.6). 'The word πλήρωμα emphasises the fact that the divine fulness of love and power acts and rules in all its perfection through Christ.'[26] This is also true for the

κέκραγεν is used by John to introduce solemn, oracular utterances of Jesus at some length (7.28, 37; 12.44), and inspired speech is one of its meanings. It would be disappointing and unusual if such a word was used to introduce an utterance as brief as v. 15b and have vv. 16-18 tacked on without introduction. (b) If vv. 15-16 are taken as all belonging to John's witness then ὅτι, which introduces both v. 16 and v. 17 could be taken as ὅτι recitative, ὅτι continuing the speech of v. 15. This would overcome the interpretative difficulties of a causal ὅτι and what this might mean in linking v. 15 with v. 16 and v. 16 with v. 17. (c) Verse 19a καὶ αὕτη ἐστὶν ἡ μαρτυρία τοῦ Ἰωάννου...is taken to refer back to the Prologue, not just to v. 15 (Bultmann), but more naturally to vv. 15-18. The ὅτε then commences the next section.

I believe Harris's argument falters on point (c). The most natural way to read v. 19 is as an introduction to the further witness of John the Baptist. The καὶ at the beginning of v. 19 tells against Harris's interpretation. Indeed, if it is translated as 'also', then it clearly favours v. 19 functioning as an introduction rather than a recapitulation. Despite rejecting Harris's proposal, it is still possible to make sense out of the text. If v. 15 is taken as parenthetic and the ὅτι of v. 16 as referring back to v. 14, then the ὅτι of v. 17 makes good sense in flowing through from v. 16 given the emphasis on the newness of what has come through Jesus Christ.

25. G. Delling, *TDNT*, VI, pp. 302-303.
26. G. Delling, *TDNT*, VI, pp. 302-303 and n. 42.

Gospel of John. The fullness of God by way of grace and truth in Jesus Christ is greater than what was given through Moses.

I now want to look carefully at v. 17, and particularly at the meaning of ἀντί in χάριν ἀντὶ χάριτος and the meaning of νόμος.

4.3.1 *The Meaning of* ἀντί

4.3.1.1 *Ruth Edward's Proposal.* Ruth Edwards has surveyed the various meanings that have been given to ἀντί in an article entitled 'XARIN ANTI ΧΑΡΙΤΟΣ (JOHN 1.16): Grace and Law in the Johannine Prologue'.[27] She favours the translation of ἀντί as 'instead of' or 'in the place of'. She says this is by far the most common usage at all periods and by far the most frequent meaning in the LXX, corresponding to Hebrew תחת. She discusses a number of improbable interpretations of this translation (namely, 'in the place of') of ἀντί and points out that v. 17 has no adversative—no ἀλλά or δέ in the Greek—to justify what many commentators claim; that there is a case of antithetic parallelism in v. 17. She sets out the verse thus:

Noun Phrase	Prepositional Phrase	Verb
ὅτι ὁ νόμος	διὰ Μωϋσέως	ἐδόθη,
ἡ χάρις καὶ ἡ ἀλήθεια	διὰ Ἰησοῦ	ἐγένετο

Grammatically and structurally the two halves of the verse are exactly balanced. Edwards argues that this is not to suggest, however, that the two halves of the verse are equal, that law is equivalent to grace and truth or that Moses is as important as Christ or even that ἐδόθη has the same meaning as ἐγένετο.[28] On the contrary, she believes there is a progression of thought and rather than classifying this verse as synonymous or antithetic, it would be better to describe it as 'synthetic' or 'progressive'. The new grace is 'fuller' than the old (but not of a different kind) as the Church Fathers emphasized in their comments on this verse.[29] Such is Edward's case.

4.3.1.2 *The Fatal Flaw.* There is, however, one serious consideration that she has left out of account. If ἀντί means 'in place of', as Edwards insists,

27. R. Edwards, 'XARIN ANTI ΧΑΡΙΤΟΣ (John 1.16): Grace and Law in the Johannine Prologue', *JSNT* 32 (1988), pp. 3-15.

28. Edwards has the interesting suggestion that ἐγένετο may have been deliberately chosen so as to refer back to v. 14 where the Logos is said to become (ἐγένετο) flesh.

29. See Edwards, 'XARIN ANTI ΧΑΡΙΤΟΣ', p. 7 nn. 17-22.

then it follows that the grace and truth that come by Jesus Christ have replaced other grace, presumably the grace that was given by Moses, namely the law. But there is nothing in v. 17 that indicates that grace and truth have come via the law. On the other hand, it does say very clearly that grace and truth have come through Jesus Christ. Edwards has failed to give this matter the weight that it deserves, and I believe that on this point alone her argument falters. I do not say that there is not some force in her case, but I believe we cannot interpret this text as saying that grace and truth also come through the law, as they do through Jesus Christ. The reading of the text simply does not allow for that possibility.

It is this issue that has led many commentators to abandon the meaning of ἀντί that Edwards presents (namely 'in place of') and opt for something like 'upon'.[30] This allows for grace and truth to come through Jesus Christ, but says nothing about the possibility of grace and truth coming via Moses and the law. It does not mean that the law and Jesus Christ are *necessarily* in conflict.

What then does ἀντί in v. 16 mean? In order to answer this question I will need to investigate the phrase 'grace and truth' and see how the reader of John might understand the phrase. The words first crop up in the Prologue in v. 14: 'And the Word became flesh and dwelt amongst us and we beheld his glory, the glory of the Father's only Son, full of grace and truth.' I will argue that lying behind these words is the theophany of Exod. 34.6 and that they should be understood in the context of the Sinai narrative of the second half of Exodus.

In the light of that background I wish to establish that, while it is acknowledged that the law was given through Moses, nevertheless grace and truth have come by Jesus Christ (v. 17) and from his fullness the community have received one blessing *after* another (χάριν ἀντί χάριτος) (v. 16).

---

30. This translation has been adopted by many modern translations (RSV, NEB, GNB, NIV, NRSV). The weakness is that there are few parallels to this usage in Greek Literature. Edwards ('XARIN ANTI XAPITOΣ', p. 5) mentions that a number of scholars (F.F. Bruce, Barrett, Hoskyns, Bultmann, Lagrange) quote Philo, *Poster. C.* 145, to support their claim that ἀντί can mean 'upon'. διὸ τὰς πρώτας αἰεὶ χάριτας, πρὶν κορεσθέντας εὐβρίσαι τούς λαχόντας, ἐπισχὼν καὶ ταμιευσάμενος εἰσῦθις ἑτέρας ἀντ' ἐκείνων καὶ τρίτας ἀντί τῶν δευτέρων καὶ αἰεὶ νέας ἀντὶ παλαιοτέρων...ἐπιδίδωσι. The literal meaning of ἀντί in this text is 'instead of', but it is the overall sense of the passage that points in the direction that ἀντί could mean 'upon'. Bultmann (*John*, p. 78 n. 2) draws attention to Sir. 26.15 and Phil. 2.27 where ἐπί means much the same as ἀντί does in Jn 1.17.

4.4 *Hearing Exodus Echoes in John 1.14-18*

4.4.1 *Preliminary Remarks*

I believe a good case can be made for John's reader hearing Exodus echoes in the last five verses of the Prologue and particularly in the words 'grace and truth'. Craig Evans[31] cites an impressive number of scholars who support this view.[32] A.T.Hanson also says, '[s]ince at least the beginning of this century the suggestion has been made by Johannine scholars that behind the important passage in John's prologue 1.14-18 there lies the whole narrative of the theophany in Exodus 33–34.'[33]

He also cites scholars who see a reference to Exod. 34 in the passage, some of whom are mentioned by Craig Evans.[34] There are a few scholars (Hanson cites at least four)[35] who have doubts about a reference to Exod. 34 but allow that χάρις καὶ ἀλήθεια in 1.14 and 17 does reproduce the familiar Hebrew phrase חסד ואמת. The third group (what Hanson calls 'a

31. Evans, *Word and Glory*, p. 79 n. 2.

32. Boismard, *St John's Prologue*, pp. 135-45; M.D. Hooker, 'The Johannine Prologue and the Messianic Secret', *NTS* 21 (1975), pp. 40-58; A.T. Hanson, 'Jn 1.14-18 and Exodus 34', *NTS* 23 (1976), pp. 90-101; M. Rissi, 'Jn 1.1-18 (The Eternal Word)', *Int* 31 (1977), pp. 395-401; C.R. Koester, *The Dwelling of God*, p. 104. In recent years commentators have heard echoes of Exod. 33-34 in Jn 1.14-18; e.g., Beasley-Murray (*John*, pp. 14-15), Brown (*John*, I, p. 36), Carson (*John*, pp. 129, 134), Hoskyns (*The Fourth Gospel*, pp. 144, 150) and Lindars (*John*, pp. 95, 98). On σκηνοῦν Bultmann (*John*, p. 67, n. 1) says that it is 'in the Wisdom myth that we find actual parallels' and he mentions *1 En.* 42.2; Sir. 24.4, 8.

33. A.T. Hanson, *The New Testament Interpretation of Scripture* (London: SPCK, 1980), p. 97.

34. Namely, Westcott, Hoskyns, Barrett, Boismard, Brown, Sanders, Lindars. In his more recent book (A.T. Hanson, *The Prophetic Gospel* [Edinburgh: T. & T. Clark, 1991], p. 25) Hanson finds other scholars to support the connection between Jn 1.14d and Exod. 34.6, namely Glasson (T.F. Glasson, *Moses in the Fourth Gospel* [SBT, 40; London: SCM Press, 1963], p. 97), who says ' "full of grace and truth" may reflect Exodus 34.6'; Borgen (P. Borgen, *Bread from Heaven* [NovTSup, 10; Leiden: E.J. Brill, 1965], p. 150), who writes that 'recent scholarship has shown convincingly that John 1,14-18 interprets the theophany at Sinai...' Later (p. 151) he says that '...the Evangelist wants to show clearly that there is no vision of God apart from the Son, not even in the theophany at Sinai. John 6, 46 probably indicates that God's "form" (εἶδος 5.37) was the Son of God'; and Meeks in a footnote says χάρις καὶ ἀλήθεια is equivalent to חסד ואמת (W.A. Meeks, *The Prophet-King*, p. 288 n. 2).

35. That is, Bernard, Dodd, R. H. Lightfoot, Strachan.

very select group indeed') are those that deny any connection with Exod. 33–34 and it consists of Loisy, Bultmann, Marsh[36] and especially de la Potterie. I say 'especially de la Potterie' because Hanson goes on to analyse de la Potterie's article and refute that part of it which denies a connection of Jn 1.14-18 with Exod. 33–34. In doing so Hanson amasses much evidence to support his claim that Exod. 33–34 lies behind Jn. 1.14-18 and I will look at this below.

4.4.2 *Are There Echoes of Exodus 33–34?*

In 1984 Henry Mowvley wrote an article for the *Expository Times*[37] in which he found echoes of seven different themes in Exodus 33.7–34.35.

They are as follows: (a) 'And the Word became flesh'. Mowvley sees an echo here with Exod. 33.7-11 where God *speaks* with Moses at the Tent of Meeting. However, a voice in a cloud is not quite the same as a voice coming from a visible body. (b) 'And dwelt among us'. Mowvley prefers to see a connection here with Exod. 33.7 (ἡ σκήνη μαρτύριου [LXX]) rather than with Exod. 25.8. I will say more about this later. (c) 'And we beheld his glory'. Mowvley sees in Exod. 33–34 three sections dealing with glory: (1) 33.9, where the cloud covers the glory; (2) 33.18-23 where Moses sees what follows or comes after the passing of the glory of God; and (3) 34.29, where the skin of Moses' face shone ὅτι δεδόξασται ἡ ὄψις τοῦ χρώματος τοῦ προσώπου αὐτοῦ (LXX). (d) 'Full of grace and truth'. Most link this with Exod. 34.6, but Mowvley finds it echoes with the LXX of Exod. 33.16 (καὶ πῶς γνωστὸν ἔσται ἀληθῶς ὅτι εὕρηκα χάριν παρὰ σοί), and to make the connection he opts for a translation of the Johannine phrase πλήρης χάριτος καὶ ἀληθείας as 'truly full of grace', but it is unlikely. It is possible, as Schnackenburg proposes,[38] that ἀλήθεια is subordinate to χάρις, and that ἀλήθεια qualifies χάρις,[39] but Mowvley has gone a step further and made ἀλήθεια an adverbial qualifier of πλήρης (which is not in the LXX of Exod. 33.16) to obtain the

---

36. Marsh (J. Marsh, *Saint John* [Pelican New Testament Commentaries; Harmondsworth: Penguin Books, 1968], pp. 108-109) does not mention Exodus or any other Old Testament passage in his exposition of the phrase 'grace and truth'. However, he allows Old Testament allusions for some of the other phrases in Jn 1.14-18.

37. 'John 1.14-18 in the Light of Exodus 33.7-34.35', *ExpTim* (1984), pp. 135-37.

38. Schnackenburg, *St John*, I, p. 273.

39. See also Edwards ('XARIN ANTI XAPITOΣ', p. 11) where she suggests that 'grace and truth' should be translated as 'the true χάρις', just as Christ is the true vine, or the true bread from heaven.

translation 'truly full of grace'. Only then is it possible to make a connection with ἀληθῶς in the LXX rendering of Exod. 33.16. And it is worth
noting that the adverb is really introduced in the LXX of Exod. 33.16; there
is no notion of it in the MT.[40] Mowvley's proposal is too tenuous to be
convincing. (e) 'And grace instead of grace'. Here Mowvley takes ἀντί to
mean 'instead of', and says 'believers received the grace of God, allowing
them to see the δόξα of Jesus instead of the grace which Moses experienced, allowing him to see only τά ὀπίσω μου while the δόξα passed
by'. (f) 'Because the law was given by Moses'. Exod. 34.1-28 tells of how
Moses received the 'two tables of stone'. (g) 'No one has seen God at any
time.' Exod. 33.20 speaks of the impossibility of seeing God's *face* and
living; Moses saw only the back of God's glory.

It seems then that a number of themes come together in Jn 1.14-18 that
are also contained in Exod. 33–34. The most obvious is Moses himself. He
is the central figure in Exod. 33–34, and in Jn 1.14-18 his centrality gives
way to the centrality of Jesus Christ. Then there is mention of the glory of
God in Jn 1.14-18, which is a prominent theme in Exod. 33–34, and in the
third place there is the invisibility of God in Jn 1.18, which reflects something of Exod. 33.20. So it is possible to discover obvious links between
Jn 1.14-18 and Exod. 33–34. But I am not convinced that πλήρης
χάριτος καὶ ἀληθείας echoes Exod. 33.16 as Mowvley suggests.

4.4.3 *Focusing on Exodus 34.6*
More likely is the proposal that πλήρης χάριτος καὶ ἀληθείας reflects
the Hebrew of Exod. 34.6. The context of this verse is where YHWH
descends in a cloud and stands with Moses and declares the name 'YHWH'
and passes before him proclaiming, 'YHWH, YHWH, a God merciful and
gracious, slow to anger, and abounding in steadfast love and faithfulness...' The Hebrew of this last phrase is רב חסד ואמת. It is true that
there is only one clear example in the canonical books of the LXX, where
χάρις translates חסד, namely, Est. 2.9, where the context suggests
'favour' and does not give full weight to the covenantal overtones usually
associated with חסד. However, Hanson marshalls considerable evidence to
show that חסד has often been translated as χάρις in such writings as Ben
Sirach, and observes:

---

40. ובמה יודע אפוא כי מצאתי חן בעיניך translates to 'How then shall it be known
that I have found grace in your sight...'

[W]hen we turn to the remains of the other Greek translations, we find much less restraint in using χάρις for חסד: Symmachus uses it in 2 Sam 2.6;[41] 10.2; and in Symmachus' version of Ps. 89.25 [24 in LXX] he renders חסד אמונה with βεβαίωσις καὶ χάρις, a translation for חסד in a context where חסד and אמונה come together. Four other examples can be quoted: Theodotion's rendering of Proverbs 31.26; Quinta's of Ps. 32(33).5; and Sexta's of Pss. 30(31).7; 32(33).18.[42]

He also mentions that J.A. Montgomery has drawn attention to the fact that χάρις in the New Testament is regularly translated by *heseda* in the Syriac. This is the case with the Syriac translation of χάρις in Jn 1.14, where he says the Syriac text is 'reproducing the Hebrew of Exod. 34.6'.[43]

Finally, Hanson makes an interesting and, I think, telling point, when he says:

[I]f it is correct to say the πλήρης χάριτος καὶ ἀληθείας in John 1.14 renders רב חסד ואמת in Exod. 34.6, then רב is translated by πλήρης. For such a translation I can find no parallel anywhere else. From this, however, I would conclude, not that the equivalence is mistaken but that the author of the Fourth Gospel has translated the phrase for himself direct from the Hebrew.[44] It is, all the same, a perfectly reasonable translation of the Hebrew phrase. As Lindars points out, it is a more literal rendering than that which the LXX offers, πολυέλεος καὶ ἀληθινὸς.[45]

In the light of this evidence (and the other links mentioned above) it seems reasonable to conclude that πλήρης χάριτος καὶ ἀληθείας is a

41. The Hebrew has חֶסֶד וֶאֱמֶת, which is exactly the combination we find in Exod. 34.6.

42. Hanson, *Interpretation of Scripture*, p. 100. See also Dodd (*Interpretation*, p. 175) and Schnackenburg (*St John*, I, p. 272).

43. Hanson, *Interpretation of Scripture*, p. 100 n. 4.

44. While it seems clear that John generally worked from the LXX when making quotations, it is also likely that John was familiar with textual traditions other than the LXX. Schuchard says 'there is much about the language of John's Gospel which seems to suggest…a Semitic background for John… There is, in John's language, evidence that seems to suggest that John thought in Aramaic but wrote in Greek. That he knew Hebrew as well is also suggested. These observations, in turn, suggest that John knew of the Aramaic and Hebrew Scriptures of the Jews' (*Scripture within Scripture*, pp. 153-54). See Chapter 3, p. 84 n. 40, for a similar discussion. It is possible then that John would have been familiar with the Hebrew words of the theophany of Exod. 34 and deliberately translated so as to make it apparent that Jesus' incarnation was the fulfilment of the Sinai theophany.

45. Hanson, *Interpretation of Scripture*, p. 100.

translation (possibly direct from the Hebrew) of the phrase in Exod. 34.6. If this is so, then it is also reasonable to conclude that the whole context of 34.6 lies behind Jn 1.14-18, and in particular, the use of ἐσκήνωσεν and δόξαν in 1.14.

4.4.4 *The Significance of* ἐσκήνωσεν

Barrett says 'σκηνόω properly means "to live in a tent" '.[46] He thinks there is probably no more in the use of the word than that the Logos took up temporary residence among humankind. But why should the Evangelist use this picturesque term unless it has special significance? If he wants to say that the Logos lived among humankind for a while, there are other Greek words that would express the idea. Why did he not use the word that the LXX translators used for God's dwelling in the tabernacle, namely, ὀφθήσομαι? On the contrary, he did not follow the LXX, but he followed the Hebrew text, evoking the imagery of the tabernacle and all that was associated with it.

But which text? Mowvley thought the most likely text was Exod. 33.7. It does mention the אהל מועד and that[47] כל מבקש יהוה יצא אל אהל מועד but there is no reference at all to God's dwelling amongst the people.[48] A

---

46. Barrett, *St John*, p. 165.

47. In the LXX the tent is called τὴν σκηνὴν αὐτοῦ, but in the MT it is simply called 'the tent' (האהל). The other interesting change is that MT אהל מועד becomes in the LXX σκηνὴ μαρτυρίου. There is some similarity between the Hebrew for meeting (מועד) and witness (מעיד hiphil pt. of עוד) but not sufficient to justify a translation of אהל מועד as σκηνὴ μαρτυρίου. There is a hint here that the LXX has deliberately distanced itself from the notion of a real meeting with YHWH and opted for some sort of witness to the presence of God, but not a real presence. Coloe ('Dwelling of God', pp. 68-80) charts what she calls the development of spiritualization with regard to the presence of God. She mentions there was a concern to preserve God's transcendence, and she comments on how this was expressed in Deuteronomic theology: 'As Kingship was reinterpreted in the light of a conditional covenant, so to (*sic*), the Temple was described, not as a dwelling place for GOD, but as a house for the *name* of God (1 Kgs 5.5). Central to Deuteronomic theology was the notion that God could not be contained, for God's true dwelling was in the heavens (1 Kgs 8.27, 30, 39, 43)... The literal and theophanic mode of presence was refuted in the reinterpretation of the Temple as a house of prayer rather than God's dwelling place' (p. 69).

48. As the previous note indicates, אהל מועד (tent of meeting) in the MT is translated in the LXX by ἡ σκηνὴ μαρτυρίου. Mowvley accepts this link and points out that it would help to make sense of Jn 1.15, which has often been seen to interrupt the flow between vv. 14 and 16. Verse 15 speaks of John the Baptist bearing witness (μαρτυρεῖ) to the Word, which fits in well with the possible previous mention of the

more likely text is Exod. 25.8 where YHWH commands Moses: וְעָשׂוּ לִי
מִקְדָּשׁ וְשָׁכַנְתִּי בְּתוֹכָם (Now make for me a sanctuary and I will dwell
among them). Clearly it is the tabernacle that is in view when Exod. 25.9
speaks of 'making this מִשְׁכָּן (dwelling) and all its furnishings exactly like
the pattern I will show you'. Further, the LXX translates מִשְׁכָּן with
σκηνῆς.[49]

I now turn to Jn 1.14: 'And the Word became flesh καὶ ἐσκήνωσεν ἐν
ἡμῖν…' Here the verb is from σκηνόω, which is related to σκῆνος and
σκήνωμα, both of which can mean 'tent' though 'dwelling, lodging' are
also cited meanings.[50] Interestingly, σκήνωμα is used in the LXX of the
Temple in Ps. 131(132).5 where David swears he will not rest ἕως οὖ
εὕρω τόπον τῷ Κυρίῳ, σκήνωμα τῷ Θεῷ Ἰακωβ.[51] The cluster of
words: σκηνόω, σκῆνος and σκήνωμα have the notion of tent/dwelling in
common, and it seems that the Hebrew verb/noun (מִשְׁכָּן/שָׁכַן), can be in
the background, as the LXX version of Ps. 132.5 and Exod. 25.9 testify.

What strengthens the appeal to Exod. 25.9 are the connections between
Jn 1.14 and Exod. 32–40. First of all, 'we have seen his glory'. The glory
of YHWH filled the tabernacle (וּכְבוֹד יְהוָה מָלֵא אֶת הַמִּשְׁכָּן) (Exod. 40.34,
35), the Tent of Meeting. Although it seems the Tent of Meeting was
covered by a cloud that hid the glory (Exod. 33.9, 10; cf. 24.16), neither
Moses nor the people actually saw God's glory. It is true that Moses was
granted a sight of the back of YHWH's goodness (that is, glory) after it had
passed by and that Moses' face shone (δεδόξασται [having been
glorified], as the LXX has it) presumably because of the reflection of
YHWH's glory that he had seen. But he did not actually see the glory of

---

Tent of Witness through the use of σκηνόω in v. 14. Witness (μαρτυρία) is a
prominent theme in the first chapter of the gospel and is especially mentioned in the
Prologue in connection with the Baptist on both occasions, vv. 6-8 and 15. This is an
attractive suggestion and some recent commentators, such as Carson (*John*, p. 127),
have taken it up, but it is somewhat speculative.

49. What may count against this connection is that the LXX has ὀφθήσομαι for
שָׁכַנְתִּי in Exod. 25.8. If the LXX translators had rendered the Hebrew verb with
σκηνώσσω, the connection with Jn 1.14 would have been strengthened. However, I am
not concerned with the LXX but with John, who, I have argued above, is making links
with the Hebrew text at this point, perhaps in the interests of going back to the stronger
expression of the presence of God, namely, God dwelling among the people, rather
than simply appearing from time to time.

50. Bauer, Arndt and Gindrich, *Greek–English Lexicon*, p. 762.

51. Hebrew: עַד אֶמְצָא מָקוֹם לַיהוָה מִשְׁכָּנוֹת לַאֲבִיר יַעֲקֹב

God.[52] Yet those whom John represents say 'we have seen his glory'.

Secondly, Jn 1.14 tells us what kind of glory it was that they saw. It was δόξαν ὡς μονογενοῦς παρὰ πατρός. This falls short of saying that it was God's glory, but when links are made with other parts of the Prologue, namely Jesus = Word = God (1.1) = God the only Son (1.18), then John is very close to saying that the glory of 1.14 is really the glory of YHWH and this is what the Gospel will develop. Jesus says 'I and the Father are one' (10.30; cf. 14.9), and Thomas worships the resurrected Jesus with the words, 'My LORD and my God' (20.28). So those who have seen the glory of the Word-made-flesh have really seen the glory of YHWH, which neither the people nor Moses were able to see in the Exodus.

Finally, the glory that filled the Old Testament tabernacle (40.34, 35) was the LORD's, a God abounding in steadfast love and faithfulness (רַב חֶסֶד וֶאֱמֶת), which, as I have earlier argued, is probably equivalent to πλήρης χάριτος καὶ αληθείας. This then makes a further link with Jn 1.14 and Exodus.

I believe then that the use of the word ἐσκήνωσεν in Jn 1.14 does connote special significance. Indeed, it seems likely that John had Exodus themes in mind in Jn 1.14-18. This should therefore alert the reader that these will be developed in relation to Jesus in the course of the Gospel and further, that with the coming of Jesus, the Word-made-flesh, the events of the Exodus will be greatly surpassed, including the presence of the glory of YHWH in the Tent of Meeting. A new Tent of Meeting will be established in the person of Jesus whose glory will be manifest to all who have eyes to see it (2.11).

4.4.5 *Two Questions*

4.4.5.1 *Is the Shekinah in View in John 1.17?* Two questions remain before I return to consider Jn 1.17. First, is the Shekinah in view? To say the שְׁכִינָה is in view because there is a link back to the root שָׁכַן may appear reckless, except there are two points in favour of it. First, the שְׁכִינָה was the place of glory and the theme of glory is very much present in the

---

52. Cf. Exod. 33.14, 15 where 'my presence' is equivalent to 'my face'. Moses could not see the face of God (Exod. 33.23b), which was closely associated with God's glory. I wonder whether the equivalence between 'face' and 'presence' needs some exploration especially in relation to Moses not being allowed to see the face of YHWH (Exod. 33.20, 23). Does this mean that Moses did not actually see God because he did not see his face/presence? There is some ambiguity here that may be deliberate.

text of 1.14, and, secondly, שכינה became a substitute for the sacred name of YHWH, which is heavily emphasized in the key verse of Exod. 34.6 and which I have argued is a possible source for the words 'full of grace and truth': ויעבר יהוה על פניו ויקרא יהוה יהוה...רב חסד ואמת (And YHWH passed by before him, and proclaimed, 'YHWH, YHWH God…full of grace and truth'. Cf. also 34.5, which says the name of YHWH will be proclaimed). Given the convergence of these two themes it is not impossible that the Shekinah is in view, but I would not want to press it.

4.4.5.2 *Did Moses See God in Exodus 34?* The second question is simply stated but not easy to answer: Did Moses see God? This concerns Jn 1.18: 'no one has seen God at any time'. However, Moses was evidently allowed to see something of YHWH from the cleft of the rock. Most commentators are content to say that Moses did not really see YHWH. What he saw was so partial, visionary and evanescent that it does not count.[53] However, Hanson maintains that in Exod. 33–34 Moses really did see YHWH. But how can that be when Jn 1.18 says 'no one has seen God at any time'? Hanson suggests: '[A]ccording to John, on those occasions in Israel's history when God is described as being seen, it was not in fact God who was seen, but the Logos.' He asks us to consider Jn 12.41: John is commenting on the obduracy of the Jews and says this is a fulfilment of the word spoken by the prophet Isaiah and goes on to quote first of all from Isaiah 53 and then Isaiah 6, the chapter where the prophet says, 'I have seen the King, the LORD of hosts!' Then the narrator in John says, 'Isaiah said this [that is, "He has blinded their eyes and hardened their heart…"] because[54] he saw [Jesus'] glory and spoke about him.' According to Hanson, then, what Isaiah saw was not the LORD of hosts as he supposed, but the glory of the Logos.[55] Arguing from this striking passage

53. See Westcott (*St John*, I, p. 28), Morris (*John*, p. 113), Schnackenburg (*St John*, I, p. 278), Lindars (*John*, p. 98) and also Carson (*John*, p. 134), who quotes Bruce (*John*, p. 44), who speaks of Moses seeing the 'afterglow of divine glory'.

54. ὅτι is the preferred reading by the Editors of the United Bible Societies' Fourth Edition of the Greek New Testament chiefly because of the age and weight of the supporting manuscript evidence, but also because, on the surface, ὅτι would seem to be the more difficult reading and thus provoke scribal alteration (see Metzger, *Textual Commentary*, p. 238).

55. C.A. Evans ('Obduracy and the LORD's Servant: Some Observations on the Use of the Old Testament in the Fourth Gospel', in C.A. Evans and William F. Stinespring [eds.], *Early Jewish and Christian Exegesis: Studies in Memory of William Hugh Brownlee* [Atlanta: Scholars Press, 1987], p. 232) says that Jesus *is* God's glory. There

Hanson says, 'It therefore follows that in John's theology the Word is the visibility (as well as the audibility) of God; whenever God has been described as appearing in Israel's history, it has always been the Word who appears.'[56] However, this may be reading a Patristic understanding of the presence of Christ in the Old Testament[57] back into the New Testament. There does seem to be definite ambiguity in the Old Testament about 'seeing God'. With reference to the passage in question, namely, Exod. 33.17-23, I have already mentioned how Moses does not actually see the face of the LORD, but only his back. And it seems that the face of God (פְנֵי אֱלֹהִים) denoted his presence. Could one have been said to have seen God if one had only seen his back and not his face? If not the question arises then as to what Moses did see. It seems that the best we can do is to say with F.F. Bruce that Moses saw the afterglow of God's glory.[58] That is to say he was far from actually seeing God.[59]

is the possibility that John may have in mind the Targum of Isaiah where in 6.1 Isaiah sees not the LORD, but 'the glory of the LORD' and in 6.5 not the LORD of hosts, but 'the glory of the *shekinah* of the LORD'. W.G. Macdonald ('Christology and "The Angel of the LORD"', in G.F. Hawthorne [ed.], *Current Issues in Biblical and Patristic Interpretation* [Grand Rapids: Eerdmans, 1975], pp. 324-35 [334-35]) makes the theological point that 'true Christology necessitates the doctrine of the Trinity. Only by a false separation within God, isolating one "person", does the angel–Christ equation take its form… Again and again its advocates have written, "Christ was seen, but not the Father who is invisible." But in the incarnation Jesus said that if one had seen him, he had seen the Father (Jn 12.45; 14.8-11). If the invisibility of the Logos, like that of God (Jn 1.18; 1 Tim. 1.17), is not maintained in the Old Testament, *then neither can we maintain his true and full deity there* (Exod. 33.20; Jn 1.18; 1 Jn 4.12, 20)' (author's emphasis).

56. Hanson, *Interpretation of Scripture*, p. 104. John Calvin has a similar view in his comment on Jn 1.18: 'God was known to the patriarchs of old only in Christ' (*The Gospel According to St John 1–10* [trans. T.H.L. Parker; Calvin's Commentaries; Edinburgh: Oliver & Boyd, 1959], p. 25).

57. Macdonald ('Christology', pp. 325-26) says, 'Justin Martyr, who wrote in the middle of the second century, pioneered the way for succeeding apologists to find "a second God" in the Old Testament under the title of "an angel" as well as under other names, e.g. the glory of the LORD, firstborn, power, Logos, Son, man. Justin elaborated four instances (i.e. with Abraham, Gen. 18; with Jacob, Gen. 28; with Moses, Exod. 3; with Joshua, Josh. 5) that he interpreted as pre-incarnate appearances of Christ under the guise of an angel.' (Cf. Justin, *Dial.* 56-61, 126-29.)

58. Bruce, *John*, p. 44.

59. In fact John is careful to maintain not only that God (the Father) is invisible but also inaudible in terms of speech. Cf. Jn 5.37, which speaks of neither hearing the

As for the perplexing passage of Jn 12.41 where it says that Isaiah saw Jesus' glory, it is possible to interpret this with Brown[60] and say that Isaiah looked into the future and saw the life and glory of Jesus. This is certainly the thought found in the vision section (6–11) of the *Martyrdom and Ascension of Isaiah.*[61] Furthermore Sir. 48.24-25 says that through his powerful spirit (πνεύματι μεγάλῳ) Isaiah foresaw the future and foretold what should be until the end of time. This future vision would tend to concur with what Jesus says elsewhere in John about Abraham rejoicing that he would see Jesus' day and he did see it and was glad (8.56). This purports even more than 12.41 does to be a vision of the future. It is not necessary to interpret 12.41 as saying that Isaiah saw the glory of the pre-incarnate Word as Hanson does. It may quite properly be understood as a vision of a future event that has come to pass in and through the incarnation of the Word.

4.5 *Returning to John 1.17 and the* νόμος

4.5.1 *Preliminary Remarks*
With all this background in mind I return to Jn. 1.17. The law was given through Moses, but who gave the law to Moses? We are not told, but, seeing that there are echoes of Exod. 20–40 throughout vv. 14-18 of the Prologue, it seems appropriate to take Exod. 34.27 at face value: 'The LORD said to Moses: Write these words; in accordance with these words I have made a covenant with you and with Israel. He was there with YHWH … And he wrote on the tablets the words of the covenant, the ten words.' So according to Exod. 34 the law was given to Moses by YHWH.[62]

But John does not say grace and truth came by this law; rather he says

---

Father's voice (see also 12.29 where the crowd think the Father's voice is thunder) nor of seeing his form.

60. Brown, *John*, I, p. 487.

61. Specifically, 9.37-42: 'And I [Isaiah] saw the Great Glory while the eyes of my spirit were open, but I could not thereafter see… But I saw the righteous as they beheld with great power the glory of that one. And my LORD approached me and the angel of the Spirit, and said, "See how it has been given to you to see the LORD…"' A subsequent verse (10.7) suggests that the 'LORD' is Jesus: 'And I heard the voice of the most High, the Father of my LORD, as he said to my LORD Christ, who will be called Jesus…' Knibb (*OTP*, II, p. 150) dates the vision section of the *Martyrdom of Isaiah* about the second century CE.

62. There are other traditions about the giving of the law—e.g., Heb. 2.2 suggests it was mediated by angels.

grace and truth came by Jesus Christ. This seems to be borne out by what follows the Prologue in the body of the Gospel where I examined the second question that was raised earlier in my treatment of this passage. What is the meaning of νόμος in John? S. Pancaro has considered all the texts in which νόμος occurs and he says:

> The conclusion which can be drawn from a survey of all the Johannine texts where the term νόμος appears is that νόμος always retains the specific meaning given in the Jewish tradition to the word תורה which is probably why it is always used with the article.[63] Moreover, even when John refers to a particular aspect or text of the Law, it is always the Law as a whole,[64] as the body of divine revelation given to Moses, passed on from generation to generation and constituting the foundation of Judaism, which lurks in the background.[65]

4.5.2 *The Johannine Approach to the Law*

Nevertheless John often indicates a certain 'distance' from the law as far as Jesus is concerned.[66] Often he refers to it as 'the Law of the Jews' (ὁ νόμος ὑμῶν, ὑμετέρος, αὐτῶν, 8.17; 10.34; 15.25). Nicodemus, one of the Pharisees, refers to the law as ὁ νόμος ὑμῶν (7.51) and at 19.7 the Jews say ἡμεῖς νόμον ἔχομεν καὶ κατὰ τὸν νόμον (i.e. our law)...

On the other hand, there are occasions when Moses and the law are referred to in an affirmative manner. Nathanael says in 1.45, 'We have found him of whom Moses wrote in the law and of whom the prophets also wrote.' In 5.45-47 Jesus reproaches unbelieving Jews: 'If you believed in Moses, you would believe in me; for he wrote of me.' In 7.19 the Jews are actually reproached for not believing Moses and in 10.34 Jesus refers to the law as the word of God, saying that scripture cannot be broken.

There is therefore something of an ambivalent attitude towards the law in John. On the one hand there is a kind of aloofness of Jesus towards the

---

63. Jn. 19.7a has no article, but immediately in v. 7b the law is specified by the definite article τόν.

64. This invariable comprehensive usage of νόμος in John is debatable. What I think Pancaro is suggesting is that John does tend to equate Moses and the Law with Judaism.

65. S. Pancaro, *The Law in the Fourth Gospel: The Torah and the Gospel, Moses and Jesus, Judaism and Christianity According to John* (NovTSup, 42; Leiden: E.J. Brill, 1975), p. 517.

66. The hint of polemic here is not endorsed by Edwards ('XARIN ANTI XAPITOΣ', p. 8): 'John invariably alludes to Moses and the Law in a neutral or clearly affirmative manner.'

law. He seems to dissociate himself from it, to say to the Jews, in effect, 'The law is your law, not mine.' On the other hand it clearly bears witness to Jesus (e.g. 5.39-40).

4.5.3 *The Johannine Approach to the Scriptures*

This last reference brings us to the Scriptures (γραφαί). Pancaro maintains that 'insofar as νόμος stands for the Scriptures or a part thereof, γραφή, γραφαί and νόμος are synonymous. To this extent it is clear that, by fulfilling the Scripture(s), Jesus fulfills the Law.'[67] The Scriptures are universally referred to positively. Nowhere are the Scriptures said to be the property of the Jews. Jesus always claims the Scriptures for himself and John sees Jesus as the fulfilment of the Scriptures. The Gospel is saturated with Old Testament scriptural allusions to Jesus.[68]

The question arises, Why this distinction between the Law and the

---

67. Pancaro, *Law*, p. 327.

68. There are the quotations: 1.23; 2.17; 6.31; 6.45; 7.38-39; 7.42; 10.34; 12.14-15; 12.38; 12.39; 13.18; 15.25; 17.12; 19.24; 19.28; 19.36; 19.37. From 12.38 onwards all the introductory formulae (except 19.28) use the expression ἵνα πληρωθῇ or associate with it through the use of πάλιν (as in 12.39-40 and 19.37). Is there a link here with 1.14, 16 where πλήρωμα is used in reference to Jesus? In addition to these John makes use of Old Testament themes and motifs, such as the vine and the branches (15.1-8, 15); the sheep and the shepherd (10.1-18); the serpent in the wilderness (3.14); the lamb of God (1.29); such Jewish feasts as the Passover (2.13; 2.23; 6.4; 11.55; 12.1; 13.1; 18.28; 18.39; 19.14), the Tabernacles (7.2), the Festival of the Dedication (10.22) and the Sabbath (5.9; 5.10; 5.16; 5.18; 7.22-23; 9.14; 9.16; 19.31); Abraham and his sons (8.33-58); Moses and the law (1.17; 1.45; 7.23; [8.5]); the law of the Jews (8.17; 10.34; 12.34; 15.25; 18.31; 19.7); wisdom (Σοφία/Λόγος) 1.1, 14; the Temple (ἱερον) 2.14-15; 5.14; 7.14; 7.28; 8.2; 8.20; 8.59; 10.23; 11.56; 18.20; (ναός) 2.19-21; (οἰκία/οἰκός) 2.16-17; 14.2; (τόπος) 11.48; the Messiah (1.41; 4.25) = the Christ (1.20; 1.25; 1.41; 3.28; 4.25; 4.29; 4.42; 6.69; 7.26-27; 7.31; 7.41-42; 9.22; 10.24; 11.27; 12.34; 20.31); Elijah (1.21, 25); Son of Man (1.51; 3.13-14; 5.27; 6.27; 6.53; 6.62; 8.28; 12.23; 12.34; 13.31); king of Israel (1.49; 12.13-15); king (6.15); king of the Jews (18.33-39; 19.3, 12-21); kingdom (3.3-5; 18.36); salvation/Saviour (4.22; 4.42); and David (7.42).

As with the direct quotations these Old Testament themes overwhelmingly focus on Christ. He is the true vine (15.1), the good shepherd (10.11), the Lamb of God (1.29), the true manna (6.35), the brazen serpent lifted up (3.15), the Logos/Wisdom become flesh (1.14), the true Temple (2.20), the Messiah (1.41; 4.25), king of Israel (1.49) and the Saviour of the world (4.42). Jesus also is presented as the light of the world (8.12) and the water of life (4.14; 7.38-39) thus outstripping the symbolic lighting of the candelabra and water-pouring ceremony in the Feast of Tabernacles.

Scriptures? Pancaro suggests that the νόμος, as understood by Christians and referred to as the Scriptures, speaks in favour of Jesus and against the 'Jews'; but the νόμος, as (mis)understood by the Jews themselves receives, at times, a 'negative' qualification in John and is considered with detachment. This explains (a) the distinction between νόμος and γραφή; (b) the use of the qualification of the law as 'the Law of the Jews'.[69]

Furthermore Pancaro says: '[T]he misunderstanding of the Law by the Jews, whereby the Law is considered opposed to Christ (viz., Christ to the Law), is viewed negatively by John, but not the Law as such.'[70] Later, leaning on an article by J.A.T. Robinson,[71] Pancaro asks the question, 'How can one believe on Jesus without ceasing to be a Jew?' and he says, 'John answers this question by saying that it is the one who believes on Jesus who is the true Jew.'[72] The overwhelming thrust of the Gospel of John is that the law leads to Jesus; its fulfilment is found in him.

4.5.4 *Grace and Truth in the Gospel*
4.5.4.1 *Grace in the Gospel.* 'Grace and truth came by Jesus Christ...' How are grace and truth understood in the body of the Gospel? The term χάρις is found only in the Prologue, so looking at the body of the Gospel is not much help. There has been a hint from structural considerations that it might refer to the blessing of eternal life. If it is conceded that חסד underlies χάρις, then some notion of covenantal love and faithfulness may be attributed to the term and perhaps may approximate to ἀγάπη.[73] However, with only three occurrences of χάρις in the Prologue, these are really only guesses as to what John might mean. It is better to focus on ἀλήθεια.

4.5.4.2 *Truth in the Gospel.* All through the Gospel John insists that Jesus is 'the way, the truth and the life' (14.6), that salvation is impossible unless one accepts Jesus and finds the truth in him. Jesus is the one who is 'truthful', who speaks the 'truth' he has heard from the Father. By becoming his disciple, one discovers the 'truth' that sets one free from the slavery of sin. Eternal life is to come to know the one and only God and

---

69. Pancaro, *Law*, p. 522.

70. Pancaro, *Law*, p. 528.

71. Robinson, 'Destination', pp. 117-31.

72. Pancaro, *Law*, pp. 531-32.

73. Brown (*John*, I, pp. 14, 16) favours this suggestion. Indeed he translates χάρις καὶ ἀλήθεια as 'enduring love'.

the One whom he has sent, Jesus Christ (17.3), to be sanctified in the 'truth' that is the 'word of God', which comes to humankind through the incarnate Word. Because Jesus does not seek his own glory but the glory of the one who sent him, he is true and there is nothing false in him (7.18). The 'truth' Jesus proclaims is not opposed to that of Moses, not subordinated to it, but something new. Unlike Moses Jesus is taught directly from God and proclaims the 'truth' he has heard from the Father of the One and Only Son who is in the κόλπον of the Father.

In contrast, the law, including the scriptures, does not contain truth or life in itself. Jesus says to the Jews: 'You search the scriptures because you think that in them you have eternal life; and it is they that testify on my behalf. Yet you refuse to come to me to have life' (5.39). The scriptures of themselves do not have life, or for that matter, truth. One may only speak of the law and the scriptures containing 'truth' and 'life' in a derivatory sense: in so far as they lead to Jesus, who is the truth and the life.

In this way, then, the law that is given through Moses finds its proper fulfilment. The law's function is to lead to Jesus and testify of him. This is the whole thrust of the Gospel of John: to focus everything on Jesus,[74] and this includes the law and the scriptures. They have no proper function apart from testifying of Jesus.

4.5.5 *The Law before and after the Incarnation*

Pancaro[75] makes a distinction between the way the law should be understood both before and after the incarnation. Before the incarnation the law was a divine revelation, an expression of God's חסד ואמת, but once Christ came then the law was no longer a vehicle for grace and truth; they now came through the incarnate Logos. Pancaro goes on to say:

> Once this is affirmed two consequences necessarily follow: 1) The value of the Law is simply prophetic. Whatever may have been its salvific power in the past (John does not reflect upon this explicitly), in the light of the Christ-event it appears as a pedagogical tool used by God to prepare his people to accept Christ as his Son and Revealer. In this sense the Law retains all its meaning and value. 2) To wish to consider the Law as the revelation of God

---

74. This is the ministry of John the Baptist; the ministry of the Spirit (16.8-11, 14); the work of God is to believe on Jesus whom the Father has sent (6.29); and even sin is defined in terms of not believing in Jesus (16.9). There is an extraordinary concentration on Jesus throughout the whole of the Gospel.

75. Pancaro, *Law*, pp. 525-26.

and the way to life *after*[76] Christ's coming means to have misunderstood it, to have never understood it in the first place. It means to reject God's revelation, to remain in sin and to refuse the gift of life.[77]

4.5.6 *Conclusion for John 1.17*

The question has been posed: But if the law is fulfilled in Jesus there must be something of Jesus in the law? The answer to this is to appeal to the distinction between a sign and the thing signified. A road sign pointing towards a city is not the city itself, but it points towards the city and its purpose is fulfilled when the traveller follows the sign and reaches the city. Once the city is reached there is a sense in which the road sign is redundant. So it is, it seems, with the law in John. The law points towards Jesus (the prophetic function that Pancaro highlights) and finds its fulfilment when it leads to Jesus. Once Jesus is 'reached' the law effectively becomes redundant,[78] or putting it in terms of the flow of history, it is superseded.

76. 'To ask whether John believed that the Law *once was* the revelation of God (but can no longer be considered as such), whether the Law *once gave* life (but can no longer do so), is to go beyond the horizon of the evangelist' (Pancaro, *Law*, p. 526). This is true in the context of Jn 1.17, but John does have a view on the Jews' place in God's purposes. This is clearly stated in 4.22: 'Salvation is from the Jews.'

77. Pancaro comments (*Law*, p. 540) on John's view of history by quoting from N. Dahl: 'The consistent Christocentricity of the Fourth Gospel does not exclude a sense of historical continuity, going backwards from the Church Universal to the first disciples...and farther back to those who believed and bore witness to him before his incarnation. In this sense, even John is aware of a "history of salvation"... John is not a historian telling about the past and trying to find cause and effects. Neither is he a theologian of *Heilsgeschichte*, seeing a series of redemptive acts of God in history... All his (historical) material the author interprets in order to make it serve his own purposes, to bear witness to Christ... The question may remain as to whether the Old Testament is not, factually, deprived of a historical meaning of its own, when Moses and the prophets (we [i.e. Pancaro] would say: "and the Law") are simply made supporters of John's own testimony to Christ. But basically John shares the Old Testament faith in God, the Creator, who acts in history and is, accordingly, not an unknown God to be reached by a mystical escape from history. The continuity between Israel and the church is understood in a peculiar way, but it is not dissolved' (N. Dahl, 'The Johannine Church and History', in W. Klassen and G.F. Snyder [eds.], *Current Issues in N.T. Interpretation: Essays in Honour of O.A. Piper* [New York: Harper, 1962], pp. 124-42).

78. Irenaeus speaks of Jerusalem in this way (*Irenaeus against Heresies* 4.4.1 in A. Roberts and J. Donaldson [eds.], *The Ante-Nicene Fathers* [Edinburgh: T. & T. Clark, 1872; repr. Grand Rapids: Eerdmans, 1981], pp. 465-66). He speaks of straw (a

4.6 *Overall Conclusion: Drawing Some Threads Together*

Early on in this chapter I argued that the incarnation was in view from vv. 3/4 of the Prologue. This is in keeping with the overall tenor of the Prologue. The emphasis is not on what God has done in the past, but on what God is doing through the incarnate Word. To introduce this Word John the Baptist is sent, but, in introducing the Word, John bears witness that this one ranks before him because he existed before him. This is a striking testimony to the pre-existence of the Word of God. The Evangelist then draws on Sinai imagery and especially the occasion when Moses saw the back of God's glory from the cleft in the rock and God spoke to Moses: 'YHWH, YHWH, a God merciful and gracious, slow to anger and full of steadfast love and faithfulness [רב חסד ואמת]...' I have argued that the Prologue uses a Greek translation of these Hebrew words (רב חסד ואמת), which describe not God's glory, but the glory of the Word made flesh (v. 14)—he is the one whose glory is full of steadfast love and faithfulness, or, as the Gospel puts it, 'of grace and truth'. Further, while it is acknowledged that the law was given through Moses, nevertheless grace and truth have come by Jesus Christ (v. 17) and from his fullness the Christian community has received one blessing after another (χάριν ἀντὶ χάριτος) (v. 16). While John draws from the Exodus imagery, and especially Moses' sight of the glory of God, he does not say that Moses saw God. He denies this when he says, 'No one has seen God at any time,' and then he goes on to say, 'It is God the only Son, who is close to the Father's heart, who has made him known.' As Jesus says to Philip later in the Gospel, 'Whoever has seen me has seen the Father' (14.9).

4.7 *Setting the Stage for a New Beginning—Including a New Temple*

There has been a prior beginning and the Prologue refers to that with the opening words of v. 1, ἐν ἀρχῇ. This was the beginning when the Word was, and was with God and was God and all things came into being through the Word. But now there is a new beginning. This pre-existent Creator-

creation of God) that has served its purpose once the wheat has come. Similarly the vine twigs—once they have produced the grapes they are lopped off. This is an analogy for Jerusalem: '...which had in herself borne the yoke of bondage...when the fruit of liberty had come, and reached maturity, and been reaped and stored in the barn, and when those that had the power to produce fruit had been carried away from her, and scattered throughout the world...she was deservedly forsaken...'

Word becomes the incarnate Word. He comes as the light shining in the darkness of unbelief and ignorance. He is heralded by John the Baptist and his glory of grace and truth is made manifest in the works/signs he does (2.11).[79]

Effectively what John is doing is offering a new hermeneutic for the whole of Judaism—its institutions, its Temple, its ritual and its membership. He is saying, 'How shall we interpret the Torah?' And he answers, 'As a signpost pointing towards Jesus.' And this is true of every aspect of Judaism, including the Temple and its associated ritual and festivals which is the special focus of this study.

We have had some intimation of how this works in the consideration of ἐσκήνωσεν in 1.14. Jesus 'tabernacled amongst us' in his flesh and so became a new Tent of Meeting with God. And in the previous chapter I indicated how Jn 2.13-22 presented the resurrected Jesus as the new Temple, replacing the Jerusalem Temple. This chapter confirms those conclusions. They are in harmony with the intimation of tabernacle fulfilment in 1.14 and with the new hermeneutic I have uncovered in the Prologue— Judaism is a signpost pointing to Jesus and finds fulfilment[80] when it leads

---

79. For example, consider the first miracle called the ἀρχὴν τῶν σημείων. This echoes the ἀρχῇ of 1.1. This is the beginning of the new creation. The ἐγένετο of 2.1 echoes the six occurrences of ἐγένετο in the Prologue (vv. 3 (2x), 6, 10, 14, 17), three of which perhaps speak of the first beginning (v. 3 [2x], 10) and the other three of the new beginning through the incarnation of the Word (6, 14, 17). The sign that Jesus does on this the first of the days of the new age (see Chapter 3 on 'The New Temple') is to turn water into wine. He uses the six stone water jars for the Jewish rites of purification. This signifies that with the coming of Jesus the Jewish rites are transformed into the wine of the new age. With the coming of Christ, as Paul says, 'There is a new creation: everything old has passed away; see, everything has become new!' (2 Cor. 5.17).

80. It is an open question whether one should speak of Jesus as the fulfilment of Israel's institutions or their replacement. Replacement carries with it the idea that there has been a radical disjunction. One thing has been removed and another put in its place. This is in effect what happened with the Temple. It was removed in 70 CE and Jesus became the Temple in its place. On the other hand, John speaks often of the scriptures finding fulfilment in Jesus and the events of his life, and this suggests that the proper outworking of Judaism was the Christian faith. As I say above, the true Jew is the one who believes in Jesus. I think it depends on emphasis. Where John wants to stress the radicality of the new beginning in the Word made flesh, replacement is the better word. However, where the accent falls on the outworking of the purpose of the Torah, fulfilment is the better word. This affirms some continuity with the past, though the nature of that continuity is problematical (see above, n. 77).

to Jesus. That is, the true Jew, is one who has faith in Jesus.

This is also in harmony with the eschatological thrust of 2.13-22 that I argued for in the previous chapter. The climax of Israel's history is not in the Temple or its institutions but in Jesus Christ. Nevertheless the overall purpose of this eschatological event is so that people may find life in God. The chiastic focus of the Prologue tells us how people can become members of God's family. Membership does not come through the old institutions of Israel, but now it is 'to those who received him (the incarnate Word), who believed in his name, he gave power to become children of God.' This is congruent with the purpose of the Gospel stated in 20.31: 'But these are written so that you may come to believe that Jesus is the Messiah, the Son of God, and that through believing you might have life in his name.'

4.8 *Appendix*
The Possible Relevance of Wisdom Motifs in the Prologue

That there are Wisdom motifs to be found in John has long been recognized. J.R. Harris was one of the earlier scholars to draw attention to to Wisdom motifs in the Prologue[81] and a little later R. Bultmann had substantial discussion on the same subject in a well-known essay.[82]

My hesitation in entering into the world of Wisdom antecedents in John is that I am unable to find a firm linkage with the Temple theme. On first sight one of the most promising is Sir. 24.8-12. A superficial reading of this text reveals some conceptual and verbal links with the Prologue:

Sirach 24.8-12	*John 1.1-18*
Creator of all things (v. 8)	All things came into being through him (v. 3)
Before eternity from the beginning he created me (Wisdom) (v. 9)	In the beginning was the Word (Wisdom) (v. 1)
In the holy tabernacle I (Wisdom) served before him (v. 10).[83]	And the Word (Wisdom) became flesh and tabernacled amongst us (v. 14).

---

81. J.R. Harris, *The Origin of the Prologue to St John's Gospel* (Cambridge: Cambridge University Press, 1917).

82. R. Bultmann, 'Der religionsgeschichtliche Hintergrund des Prologs zum Johannes-Evangelium', in *Eucharisterion*, II (Festschrift H. Gunkel; Göttingen: Vandenhoeck & Ruprecht, 1923), pp. 3-26.

83. 'In v. 10a, Wisdom is said to minister before the Creator "in the holy Tent"— an allusion to Wisdom (= the Law) stipulating the religious and liturgical rules to be

There are also some important differences. In John the creation of all things came into being through the Logos, whereas in Sirach there is only one Creator; Wisdom is not a Creator (but cf. the ambiguous Prov. 3.19). This is similar to Prov. 8 except for the puzzling word about Wisdom in v. 30 where Wisdom says, ἤμην παρ αὐτῷ [YHWH] ἁρμόζουσα, that is, 'I was with him meshing in[84] with him.' What exactly this means is uncertain, but it is not sufficient to suggest that Wisdom is a Co-Creator with the LORD.[85]

So there are similarities and also substantial differences. The use of the term 'tabernacle' suggests a link with Jn 1.14, but it is not clear what the nature of the link might be.[86] I think the Exodus echoes are more substantial, but Wisdom could also be making her voice heard through the use of the term Logos and the clear connection with the Torah (cf. Jn 1.17). But it is uncertain how the Wisdom motif ties in with the theme of the Temple.

---

followed in the worship of the LORD. The "Tent" is the Tabernacle or Dwelling that Yahweh commanded Moses to build; cf. Exod. 25.8-9; 26.1-37' (P.W. Skehan and A.A. Di Lella, *The Wisdom of Ben Sira* [AB, 39; Garden City, NY: Doubleday, 1987], p. 333).

84. It is difficult to know what this could mean. The English translation of the LXX has 'suiting myself to him' and suggests an alternative 'arranging all things'.

85. This is the conclusion of Whybray (*Proverbs*, pp. 134-36). He repoints אמון according to the versions LXX, S and V and obtains אָמָן, a noun meaning artisan or creator. So his translation is: 'Then I [Wisdom] was beside him, [that is] the Creator.' This noun is taken in apposition to the pronominal sufix.

86. John Ashton ('The Transformation of Wisdom: A Study of the Prologue of John's Gospel, *NTS* 32 [1986], pp. 161-86 [178]) confidently asserts: '[I]t is hard to deny that the second half of the verse [Jn 1.14] rounds off the Wisdom theme with a deliberate allusion (in the use of σκηνοῦν) to Sir. 24.' The basis of the confidence about the 'deliberate allusion' is not clear.

Chapter 5

THE PROGRAMMATIC VISION OF JOHN 1.51

In 1974 W.D. Davies published a thought-provoking book, *The Gospel and the Land*. It included a chapter on land in the Fourth Gospel and special comment on Jn 1.51 under the heading 'Bethel'. After his analysis of this enigmatic verse he concluded:

> It would be arbitrary to fix on any single interpretation of 1.51 as the right one: the verse is kaleidoscopic. But at least among its many connotations we may legitimately find a contrast drawn between the holy *place* of Jacob's vision which was for him 'the house of God and the gate of heaven' and, therefore, in Jewish tradition associated with the Temple and the *person* of Nathanael's vision, the Son of Man.[1]

The purpose of this chapter is to examine Davies's claim in respect of Jn 1.51 and see if indeed there is an allusion to the Temple in this verse, and, if there is, what its significance might be in the overall purpose of the Gospel.

5.1 *A Puzzling Pericope*

The Johannine account of the call of the disciples concludes with the encounter between Nathanael and Jesus (1.45-51). Even a superficial reading of this passage raises questions. Why does Jesus focus on Nathanael's national identity and describe him as an Israelite in whom there is no deceit? One can understand why Nathanael asks, 'Where did you get to know me?' But what kind of answer does Jesus offer when he says, 'Before Philip called you I saw you under the fig tree'? How is that an answer? How does one evaluate a man's character by watching him sitting

---

1. W.D. Davies, *The Gospel and the Land: Early Christianity and Jewish Territorial Doctrine* (Berkeley, LA: University of California Press, 1994), pp. 296-97 (author's emphasis).

under a fig tree? And then the response to what seems to be a non-answer is astonishing. Nathanael says, 'Rabbi, you are the Son of God, the King of Israel.' How does Nathanael come to that insight? It seems to drop out of nowhere. Jesus then says Nathanael will see greater things. Greater than what? What are these greater things? When will he see them? And then, as a climax to the dialogue (and seemingly to the entire call to discipleship in ch. 1), there is this enigmatic saying of Jesus, no longer addressed just to Nathanael, but to a wider audience, indicated by the plural ὑμῖν followed by a second person plural verb:[2] λέγω ὑμῖν, ὄψεσθε τὸν οὐρανὸν ἀνεῳγότα καὶ τοὺς ἀγγέλους τοῦ θεοῦ ἀναβαίνοντας καὶ καταβαίνοντας ἐπὶ τὸν υἱὸν τοῦ ἀνθρώπου. What does this mean? When will Nathanael and others see it? Why does Jesus call himself the Son of Man? And what does John mean by this title? This pericope bristles with questions, and it will be the aim of this chapter to endeavour to find some answers to them.

5.2 *Chapter Guide*

In exploring the possibility of Temple allusion in 1.51 I begin by getting some 'feel' for the allusive character of the first chapter of John by looking at the adverb πόθεν. This adverb occurs in 1.48 and signals the possibility of a deeper meaning, but it is by no means an isolated instance of the subtleties that abound in John 1. Nevertheless it is enough to indicate that there is more in the text than appears on the surface. In keeping with the flow of 'deeper meaning' in John 1, I then look at what the fig tree of 1.50 may mean. Discerning some allusion to Israel in the fig tree, this then leads on to a discussion of how Nathanael is representative of the new Israel/the new Jacob, who, empty of deceit, is open to the truth of Jesus. The significance of Nathanael's confession of faith is examined, and this is succeeded by Jesus saying, 'You will see greater things than these…' Obviously 'seeing' in these closing verses of John 1 means more than physical sight and the strong emphasis on 'seeing' echoes a popular (though erroneous) etymology of Jacob's new name, Israel.

Given the dense thicket of allusions to Jacob in Jn 1.45-51, it is no surprise to discover in 1.51 an echo of Jacob's dream in Gen. 28.12-18. In relation to this dream I probe the possible relevance of rabbinic readings

---

2.   This may signal that Nathanael is the representative Israelite as Nicodemus is the representative teacher in Israel and the royal official of 4.46-54 the representative Galilaean. I owe this suggestion to Revd John Proctor, Director of New Testament Studies, Westminster College, Cambridge.

of Gen. 28.12-18 and pre-Christian Jewish writings for a link with the Temple. The dating of the former, and the tenuous nature of the latter, make the likelihood of a strong Temple allusion to Gen. 28.12-18 towards the end of the first century, rather slim. Furthermore, the idea of the 'opened heaven' of Jn 1.51 having some reference to the torn Temple veil is unlikely.

The strong focus of Jn 1.51 is on the Son of Man. The final section of the chapter surveys all the occurrences of this title in John to see if a comprehensive meaning can be found. This is then applied to Jn 1.51 and some conclusions are drawn as to how 1.51 functions in the Gospel as a whole. Finally I return to Davies's comment on 1.51.

5.3 *Analysis of John 1.47-51*

5.3.1 Πόθεν, *a Sign of Deeper Meaning*
Before moving into the flow of the text I want to focus on one small word in v. 48 that is often overlooked. I refer to the 'where' at the beginning of Nathanael's question, 'Where did you get to know me?' (Πόθεν με γινώσκεις;). This could be translated, 'How do you know me?' (cf. Mk 6.2); on the other hand, the Evangelist may intend that we give the full weight to πόθεν and translate, '*From where* do you know me?' And lurking behind that question is another: 'Who are you to have access to this sort of knowledge? Where do you come from? Πόθεν ἐστίν;' This may not seem very significant in isolation, but if we look at the use of this word throughout the Gospel the cumulative effect is that John signalling to us: 'Be on the alert! Look for deeper meaning.'

For example, in the the second instance of πόθεν in 2.9, the master of the banquet did not know from where (πόθεν) the wine came, but the servants who had drawn the water knew. The immediate level of meaning is that the wine had come from the water, but it is Jesus who is the source of the water-made-into-wine, and near at hand is the pressing question regarding him: 'πόθεν ἐστίν;'

The source and destination of the wind in 3.8 is a mystery too. Jesus says, τὸ πνεῦμα ὅπου θέλει πνεῖ...ἀλλ' οὐκ οἶδας <u>πόθεν</u> ἔρχεται καὶ <u>ποῦ</u> ὑπάγει. So too with everyone born of the Spirit (3.9) and so with Jesus himself (cf. 8.14, 'But you do not know from where [πόθεν] I came and where I am going.')[3]

_____

3. Continuing through the Gospel we read in 4.11 how the Samaritan woman enquires where Jesus would get the living water from, and in 6.7 how Philip asks

So with πόθεν in 1.48 we are placed on the alert. We are not to make do with a superficial reading of this pericope, but are to look deeper and see subtle references to Jesus himself, always highlighting him and urging the reader to trust in him according to the stated design of the author (20.31).

5.3.2 *The Fig Tree*
Jesus displays his supernatural knowledge concerning the true Israelite Nathanael when he says, 'Before Philip called you, when you were under [ὑπὸ] the fig tree, I saw you' (1.48).

The reference to the fig tree is curious. Does it mean any more than that Nathanael happened to be sitting under that particular tree when Jesus saw him? Is there some significance in the fact that Jesus saw him sitting under the fig tree rather than some other tree or in some other place? Some commentators have suggested that there is and have looked hard for it, while others have found no recoverable significance in the fig tree.[4]

---

where Jesus will get bread for so many. As the teaching of the chapter unfolds, we see that the bread the multitude needs is the living bread from Jesus. Then there is the question of the origin of Jesus himself, highlighted by the presence of 'πόθεν εἶ σύ;', which can be interpreted either as a legal loophole or as a question as to whether Jesus is from heaven or earth. The use of this little word throughout the Gospel turns the spotlight on Jesus and underlines the issue of his origin—is he of the earth or from Heaven? I am indebted to Rene Kieffer for these insights (R. Kieffer, 'L'espace et le temps dans l'evangile de Jean', *NTS* 31 [1985], pp. 394-409). Another sign that a more than superficial narrative reading is at stake occurs in the exchange between Jesus and the disciples in 1.38-39. They ask where he is staying (ποῦ μένεις;) and Jesus says, 'Come and see'—an invitation not only to the disciples but also to the reader to come and see where Jesus does indeed dwell, and to discover in ch. 14 that Jesus has his home (μονή) with the Father and the disciples will be taken into that home (14.23). Bultmann (*John*, p. 100) acknowledges the deeper meaning and makes a connection with 14.2.

    4.   Schnackenburg (*St John*, I, p. 317) follows rabbinic phrases about doctors of the law sitting under the fig tree to study Scripture, and then remarks, 'Nathanael then, hidden from the eyes of others under a sheltering fig-tree, would have been studying Scripture, especially the Messianic prophecies.' This conclusion is based on late and sparse rabbinic evidence and speculation about what Nathanael might have been reading. Admittedly Schnackenburg advances this scenario somewhat tentatively. He concludes: '[T]he words are so brief that it is impossible to explain with certainty what they refer to'. Barrett (*St John*, p. 185) suggests that 'to be under the fig tree may be a sign of peace and prosperity (e.g. 1 Kgs 5.5), or to the study of the Law (e.g. *Ecclesiastes R* 5.15).' Barrett says that R. Aqiba is mentioned in this rabbinic text, a rabbi of *Ecclesiastes R.* Barrett's conclusion seems to be that 'the supernatural

Burkett,[5] following some clues offered by Michaels[6] (who takes Hos. 9.10 as his point of departure) suggests from consideration of Jer. 24.1-8; 29.17; 8.13; Lk.13.6-9; Mk 11.12-14, 20-21; and Mt. 21.18-20 that Israel is symbolized by the figs on a fig tree and that the vision showing Nathanael 'under the fig tree' pictures him as a member of the Jewish nation and Israelite by natural descent.

Hosea 9.10 does compare Israel to the fruit of the fig tree: 'Like grapes in the wilderness I found Israel.[7] Like the first fruit on the *fig tree*, in its season, I saw your fathers.' A similar comparison is made in the Jeremiah texts, but the tone is predominately negative. In Jer. 8.13 the fig tree is barren; the figs in Jer. 24.1-8 are divided into baskets of good and bad figs; and Jer. 29.17 speaks of figs that are so rotten they cannot be eaten. All three texts speak of Israel under the judgment of God. The same imagery is continued in the Gospels. In the parable of the barren fig tree (Lk.13.6-

knowledge of Jesus could not be brought out without reference to some landmark', suggesting that a fig tree was as good as any other tree, or any hill, or rock or whatever. Bernard (*St John*, I, p. 63) draws on 1 Kgs. 4.25, Mic. 4.4 and 1 Macc. 14.12 to support his claim that 'national tranquillity is often pictured by the image of every man sitting "under his vine and his fig tree"'. He suggests that when Jesus saw Nathanael under the fig tree (probably at his home) he is alluding to some incident of which the evangelist gives no explanation. The virtue of this remark is that it acknowledges something is missing in the narrative! Hoskyns (*The Fourth Gospel*, p. 189) cites the same texts as Bernard (except that for 1 Macc. 14.12 he has Zech. 3.10), and he also reflects rabbinic opinions gleaned from Strack-Billerbeck. Lindars (*John*, p. 118) also thinks the reference to Nathanael under the fig tree indicates that he is a pious Jew, again citing Strack-Billerbeck as evidence. He tends to concur with Barrett when he says that 'this apparently gratuitous detail of the story thus has symbolical significance, which must clearly affect our estimate of the historical value in it'. Brown (*John*, I, p. 183) has half a page of views on what the fig tree might mean and he concludes: 'We are far from exhausting the suggestions, all of which are pure speculation.'

5.   D. Burkett, *The Son of Man in the Gospel of John* (JSNTSup, 56; Sheffield: JSOT Press, 1991), pp. 113-14.

6.   J.R. Michaels, 'Nathanael under the Fig Tree', *ExpTim* 78 (1966–67), pp. 182-83. Michaels maintains that inasmuch as some have argued that the woman of Samaria of Jn 4 is not just an individual but a representative of the people of Samaria and of their religion, so Nathanael could be considered a representative of the true Israel and, as I mention in the text, finds the key to this mysterious saying of Jesus in Hos. 9.10.

7.   C.R. Koester, 'Messianic Exegenesis and the Call of Nathaniael (John 1.45-51)', *JSNT* 39 (1990), pp. 23-34 (23), objects that Nathanael was 'found' by Philip (1.45), not Jesus. However, one could say that Philip is Jesus' agent (1.43-45; cf. 12.21) and, further, Hos. 9.10 suggests that 'being found' is parallel to 'being seen' ('I saw your fathers'), and Jesus is certainly the subject of the verb 'saw' in 1.48.

9), the owner of a vineyard threatens to cut down a fig tree from which he has sought fruit for three years and found none. The fig tree apparently represents the Jewish nation, which has not responded to Jesus' ministry. The threat of the parable is carried out symbolically in Jesus' cursing of the fig tree during the week of the passion in Jerusalem (Mk 11.12-14, 20-21; Mt. 21.18-20). These Synoptic Gospel references strengthen the link of the fig tree with Israel—indeed Israel under judgment.

5.3.3 A New Israel

There is some difficulty with Jesus' expression of Nathanael being 'under [ὑπὸ] the fig tree'. If, as Burkett suggests (and it seems plausible), Israel is symbolized *by* the figs on the fig tree (cf. Hos. 9.10), what is to be made of saying that Nathanael is *under* the fig tree? We would expect him to be part of the fig tree or the fig tree.[8] Burkett counters this objection by explaining that the word 'ὑπὸ' defines Nathanael's identity in terms of membership in natural Israel. Nathanael belonged to the Israelite community, a member of the Jewish nation by natural descent. This was where Nathanael belonged until Philip came and called him away from old Israel to follow Jesus. As Burkett says: '[T]he implication is that Nathanael has now been called out from "under the fig tree" into a new community centred around Jesus.'[9] The inadequacy of 'natural descent' (membership of the old Israel) is emphasized in the Gospel, but especially in 1.12, 13 where we learn that the way into God's family is not by natural birth but by receiving Jesus and believing in his name, that is, being born of God (cf. also 3.3, 5).

How plausible is this explanation of the fig tree? First, there is a high density of 'Israel/Jacob' allusions in Jn. 1.47-51. Jesus calls Nathanael 'a genuine *Israelite* in whom there is no deceit';[10] Nathanael's confession of

---

8.   On the other hand, it would destroy the narrative to say that Nathanael was part of the fig tree or the fig tree.

9.   Burkett, *The Son of the Man*, p. 114.

10.   An obvious comparison with Jacob (later named Israel in Gen. 35.10), who deceived his father Isaac (Gen. 27.35: 'Your brother came deceitfully [LXX has μετὰ δόλου], and he has taken away your blessing'). However, what does it mean to call Nathanael 'a genuine Israelite in whom there is no deceit'? Brown (*John*, I, p. 87) translates the phrase as 'a genuine Israelite without guile', and I think this emphasizes Nathanael's commitment to the truth *as an Israelite*. Some scholars focus on the words ἐν ᾧ δόλος οὐκ ἔστιν and find there is an allusion to the Suffering Servant of Isa. 53.9, which speaks of one 'in whose mouth there was no guile'. Brown's own suggestion arises from 1.31: 'The very reason why I came and baptized with water was

Jesus is 'King of *Israel*'; and we shall see soon that the angels ascending and descending on the Son of Man is almost certainly an allusion to Jacob's (*Israel's*) dream at Bethel. Given such a thicket of allusions it is not unlikely that Burkett is right when he also refers the fig tree to *Israel*. It would certainly be in keeping with the tenor of the pericope.

If the fig tree of 1.48 is a metaphor for Israel (and a rather negative view of Israel if the connotations of the Old Testament and synoptic references are allowed to have their say), then 'under the fig tree' must refer to some association with Israel, probably membership in Israel, and very likely this membership would be by natural descent. Nathanael is distinguished from the old Israel (Jacob) by being without deceit (see n. 10 below). As such he, and the other disciples with him, are open to the truth about Jesus as the Son of Man, whereas some Jews (e.g. Pharisees) are not (cf. 9.35-41 where the man-born-blind is open to the light, but the Pharisees are blind). Indeed, not only are Nathanael and the other disciples open to Jesus, they are already in the new community—they are followers of the new king of Israel, the Son of God (1.49).

In the light of these considerations there is much to be said for Burkett's proposal—it fits the allusive character of the immediate pericope and it also fits the radical call to discipleship that characterizes the Gospel as a whole.[11]

5.3.4 *Son of God—King of Israel*
Nathanael's response to the words of Jesus seems like a confession of faith:[12] 'Rabbi, you are the Son of God. You are the King of Israel.'[13] Both

that he [Jesus] might be revealed to *Israel*.' Although Brown is rather enigmatic here, we take it that he considers the Baptist's words are (at least partly) fulfilled in the revelation that comes to Nathanael, the representative to Israel. My view is that Nathanael is a genuine Israelite, because, according to the Fourth Gospel, he represents the fulfilment of Israelite religion, namely, faith in Jesus, the one 'whom Moses in the law and also the prophets wrote' (1.45). The entire focus of Israelite faith is Jesus. And those that are not turned aside by the 'father of lies' (8.44) will follow Jesus, who is the truth. Nathanael is one who does this. He responds to Philip's call and follows the one to whom the prophets testify, namely, Jesus son of Joseph from Nazareth (cf. 5.39-47).

   11. I have intimated this by referring to Jn 1.13, but it is corroborated by the dialogue with Nicodemus where Jesus speaks emphatically about the need to be reborn from above. The disjunction between the old and new Israel in John is radical. See Chapter 4 where I discuss continuity/discontinuity in relation to Jn 1.17 and come out in favour of a *new* beginning.

   12. Schnackenburg (*St John*, I, p. 317) says 'in the style of a confession of faith'.

   13. I suggest the impetus for this confession from Nathanael is a *combination* of

these titles have their roots in the history of Israel. Much has been written about them in the past,[14] but it would be inappropriate for me to go into an extensive survey of scholarly discussion in this study. It is enough to indicate briefly some of the links in the history of Israel and then mention what significance these titles might come to have later in the Gospel.

Both titles, Son of God and King of Israel, have their roots in the history of Israel, especially in the person of King David in the Nathan oracle of 2 Samuel 7.[15] David wanted to build a house for YHWH, but the word of YHWH came to Nathan and he told David:

καὶ ἔσται ἐὰν πληρωθῶσιν αἱ ἡμέραι σου καὶ κοιμηθήσῃ μετὰ τῶν πατέρων σου, καὶ ἀναστήσω τὸ σπέρμα σου μετὰ σέ, ὃς ἔσται ἐκ τῆς κοιλίας σου, καὶ ἑτοιμάσω τὴν βασιλείαν αὐτοῦ · αὐτὸς οἰκοδομήσει μοι οἶκον τῷ ὀνόματί μου, καὶ ἀνορθώσω τὸν θρόνον αὐτοῦ ἕως εἰς

two things: first, Philip's words 'we have found him about whom Moses in the law and also the prophets wrote', and, second, Jesus' miraculous knowledge of him (cf. below, 5.3.5 and n. 17, where the importance of Jesus' supernatural knowledge in John is highlighted). Philip's news could well have raised awareness of messianic expectations and Jesus' words of supernatural knowledge confirmed them. There have been other suggestions that a coded message passed between Jesus and Nathanael when he uttered: 'I saw you under the fig tree before Philip called you.' See, for example, Koester, 'Messianic Exegesis', who focuses on Zech. 3.10, which speaks of the time when a man would call his neighbour under a vine and fig tree. According to Koester, Jesus made reference to this text when he said to Nathanael: 'Before Philip called you, when you were under the fig tree, I saw you.' Through the link with Zech. 3.10 the immediate context is also gathered in, including Zech. 3.8, which speaks of the advent of the messianic Branch: 'Being called by a friend under a fig tree marked the advent of a messianic Branch who would reign as king according to Zech. 3.10 and 6.12, and be a Davidic figure according to Jer. 23.5 and 33.15.' I think Koester's coded message is overly subtle.

14. See V. Taylor, *The Names of Jesus* (London: Macmillan, 1953), pp. 53-54; J. Howton, 'The Son of God in the Fourth Gospel', *NTS* 10 (1963–64), pp. 227-37.

15. Other references include Ps. 2.7 (where sonship is linked with Davidic royalty); *4 Ezra* 7.28-29; 13.52 and 14.9. Marié Boismard ('Le titre de "fils de Dieu" dans les évangiles', *Bib* 72.3 [1991], pp. 442-50 [448]) confirms the suggested Old Testament connections when he says, 'Ce titre de "fils de Dieu" est...mis ici en parallèle avec celui de "roi de Dieu" en tant que "roi d'Israël", dans la perspective ouverte par l'oracle de Nathan et reprise dans le psaume deuxième.' Boismard maintains that 'Son of God' does not have a transcendent connotation (such as the Jews' action suggests in 10.31); rather it has an adoptive significance and God the Father comes to protect and save such children. He did this for Jesus when he raised him from the dead, and Boismard suggests that he will do the same for Jesus' disciples who are incorporated into the family (Jn 20.17).

τὸν αἰῶνα. ἐγὼ ἔσομαι αὐτῷ εἰς πατέρα, καὶ αὐτὸς ἔσται μοι εἰς υἱόν· καὶ...τὸ δὲ ἔλεός μου οὐκ ἀποστήσω ἀπ' αὐτοῦ...(LXX 2 Sam 7.12-15a).

Here David the king of Israel is addressed and YHWH says, ἐγὼ ἔσομαι αὐτῷ εἰς πατέρα, καὶ αὐτὸς ἔσται μοι εἰς υἱόν. That is, the offspring of David will be a son of God.

For my purposes, however, it is highly significant that both these titles come together in the matter of building a house for YHWH. The texts are ambivalent. The LXX of 2 Sam 7.11c has David (presumably through his offspring) building a house for YHWH: καὶ ἀπαγγελεῖ σοι κύριος ὅτι οἶκον οἰκοδομήσεις αὐτῷ. On the other hand, the MT has YHWH building a house for David: והגיד לך יהוה כי בית יעשה לך יהוה. 'House' can mean building or family. The house that came to be built under Solomon was the Temple—a building for YHWH. On the other hand, YHWH established the family (house) of David. As we shall see in Chapter 8, this second point becomes important for this study. I will argue that through Jesus YHWH builds a new 'house' for his people and that this 'house/Temple' is Jesus and his disciples, and it looks very much like a family (cf. Jn 1.12).

Another connection suggested by Boismard[16] is Ps. 89.26, 27. These verses bring together not only the concept of the Davidic king of Israel (the Psalm is about God's love and faithfulness towards David [89.2, 14, 24, 28, 33]), but also the concept of 'son of God': 'He shall cry to me, "You are my *Father*, my God, and the Rock of my salvation!" I will make of him the *firstborn*, the highest of the kings of the earth' (89.26, 27). Boismard believes there is an echo with this text when the risen Jesus said to Mary, 'Go to my brothers and tell them "I am ascending to my Father and to your Father, to my God and to your God"' (Jn 20.17). He also believes the ascension of Jesus connotes the consummation of the title 'King of Israel' and that the incorporation of disciples into his family points to the extension of his title, Son of God, to his followers, who are children of God (1.12; 11.52). This is difficult to prove but it is aiming in what I believe is the Johannine direction.

5.3.5 *The Greater Things*

Now I want to focus on Jn 1.50: ἀπεκρίθη Ἰησοῦς καὶ εἶπεν αὐτῷ, "Ότι εἶπόν σοι ὅτι εἶδόν σε ὑποκάτω τῆς συκῆς, πιστεύεις; μείζω τούτων ὄψῃ.

---

16. Boismard, 'Le titre', pp. 449, 450.

As mentioned above, Nathanael came to believe in Jesus as the Son of God and the king of Israel on the expectation aroused by Philip's witness and confirmed by the experience of Jesus' supernatural knowledge of him. This special knowledge is apparent throughout the Gospel, especially in 2.25: 'But Jesus…knew all people and needed no one to testify about anyone; for he himself knew what was in everyone.' And then there is 4.18 where Jesus tells the Samaritan woman she has five husbands and the present man she is living with is not her husband. In v. 29 we hear how her testimony to her townsfolk is marked by wonder at Jesus' knowledge of her: 'Come and see a man who told me everything I have ever done! Could this not be the Messiah?'[17] Peter too comes to this realization when interrogated by the risen LORD. He exclaims, 'LORD, you know all things!' (21.17). Other references, such as 6.6; 9.2; 11.4, 11-14; 13.1, 26-27, 38 and 21.6, 18, 19, indicate that Jesus knows what is going to happen in the future. Not only has Jesus insight into people, but he also has prophetic insight that sees into the future and assesses the outcome of events. Given that this is such a prominent theme in the Fourth Gospel, it is not surprising that Nathanael should have been profoundly impressed with Jesus' knowledge of him, and so on that basis he believed.[18]

In the second half of 1.50 Jesus says to Nathanael, μείζω τούτων ὄψῃ. A key question is, What does the demonstrative pronoun 'τούτων' refer to? As it stands it could refer to people (masc. or fem.) or things. So it could be read as, 'You will see greater people than you have already seen,' or, 'You will see greater things than you have already seen.' It is of course almost universally taken in the neuter, 'greater things', and usually commentators suggest that the sense is that Nathanael has already 'seen' Jesus' supernatural knowledge at work in his life and obviously been impressed. Jesus therefore says, 'You will see greater things.' That seems to be the straightforward interpretation in keeping with the surface flow of the narrative.

---

17. See also 6.26, 64, 70, which all indicate Jesus' ability to see into people and discern their motives and in Judas's case to pronouce him a devil.

18. I see no reason to read Jesus' question to Nathanael in v. 50 as a criticism of his faith. I realize that elsewhere in the Gospel miracle-based faith is criticized (e.g. 2.23-25) and portrayed negatively (e.g. 4.48; 6.14-15). Barrett (*St John*, p. 186) makes the point that the words at the beginning of v. 50 might be better read as a statement than as a question. This would lessen the tendency some have felt to take the words as a criticism of Nathanael's confession of faith. Paul Duke (*Irony in the Fourth Gospel* [Atlanta: John Knox Press, 1993], p. 59) puts it well when he says: '[T]he acclamations of chapter 1 [including Nathanael's] will be enlarged and never negated.'

5.3.6 *What It Means to See*

There is, however, another more subtle way of reading the sentence. In this Nathanael pericope the narrator has made much of seeing. Philip's invitation to Nathanael is toˮΕρχου καὶ ἴδε (v. 46). Jesus *sees* (εἶδεν) Nathanael coming to him and invites people to *see* (ʼ Ἴδε) a genuine Israelite in whom there is no deceit (v. 47). In answer to Nathanael's question Jesus says how he *saw* (εἶδόν) him under the fig tree before Philip called him (v. 48). Then, in response to Nathanael's acclamation of faith, Jesus says, 'Because I said I *saw* [εἶδόν] you under the fig tree do you believe?' And then, 'You will *see* [ὄψῃ] greater things,' followed by 'you will *see* [ὄψεσθε] heaven opened...' Within these few verses the verb 'to see' occurs seven times. Given that Nathanael is one who represents the fulfilment of Israel (see above), then it is well within the bounds of possibility that here there is an echo of Gen. 32.30, where, after receiving a new name (Israel),[19] Jacob calls the name of the place of his night-wrestle with 'a man', 'Vision of God' (Εἶδος θεοῦ)[20] (following the LXX rather than MT). This memorable expression in the life of Israel would have been well known (and also Jacob's vision at Bethel, which I will argue is in view in Jn 1.51), and it is not at all unlikely that Jesus is saying to Nathanael, 'Israel had experiences of seeing "God"[21] at Peniel and seeing angels at Bethel. You will see greater things than he did.'

The Jacob allusions and emphasis on 'seeing' in the verses preceeding v. 51 need to be kept in mind as we approach this verse. I believe the μείζω τούτων of v. 50 are developed in v. 51: Ἀμὴν ἀμὴν λέγω ὑμῖν, ὄψεσθε[22] τὸν οὐρανόν ἀνεῳγότα καὶ τοὺς ἀγγέλους τοῦ θεοῦ

---

19. The etymology of Israel given in Gen. 32.28 is that Jacob has striven with God (שׂרית עם אלהים) (and men) and prevailed. Therefore his name is ישׂראל. However, a tradition developed, perhaps under the influence of the LXX rendering of the name of the place, that the etymology of Israel's name had to do with seeing God. Bernard (*St John*, I, p. 65) documents this and says: '[T]he ancient (although erroneous) interpretation of his new name equated it with אישׁ ראה אל *vir videns Deum*. This etymology was adopted by Philo (*Somn.* 1.21).'

20. The NRSV follows the Hebrew (פניאל) with 'Peniel'.

21. The Genesis narrator does not say that Jacob saw God face to face; it is Jacob who says that. What the narrator says is that Jacob wrestled with 'a man' (ἄνθρωπος; אישׁ). It is unlikely that John concedes that Jacob actually saw God because of the emphatic statement in the Jn 1.18: 'No-one has ever seen God.'

22. The pronoun and verb change to the plural: ὑμῖν ὄψεσθε... Whereas Jesus was speaking to Nathanael in v. 50, he is now talking to a wider audience and so the translation should be: 'Truly, truly, I say to *all* of you, you shall see...' Some scholars

ἀναβαίνοντας καὶ καταβαίνοντας ἐπὶ τὸν υἱὸν τοῦ ἀνθρώπου. 'Very truly,[23] I tell you,[24] you will see heaven opened and the angels ascending and descending upon the Son of Man.' I now turn to this verse.

see this as a pointer to considering 1.51 as a detached saying. However, there is a shift from singular to plural in 3.7, and few scholars think that what follows there is detached from what precedes it. Further, the use of the typical Johannine ἀμὴν ἀμὴν λέγω ὑμῖν signifies that what is introduced is not unrelated to what precedes. The formula always functions in this way. Brown's point is well taken: '...we are faced with the problem of what it [the verse] means in its present sequence...' (*John*, I, p. 89). It may be as Margaret Pamment suggests in her article 'The Son of Man in the Fourth Gospel', *JTS* 36 (1985), pp. 56-66 (59), that v. 51 is Jesus' response to all seven confessions/christological titles in ch. 1:

The Lamb of God who takes away the sin of the world (v. 29)
The one who ranks ahead of me (the Baptist) because he was before me (v. 30)
The one who baptizes with the Holy Spirit (v. 33)
The Son [Elect] of God (v. 34)
The Messiah (v. 41)
The one about whom Moses in the law and also the prophets wrote (v. 45)
The Son of God; the king of Israel (v. 49).

Within the flow of the narrative this is a good justification for the change to plural. W.O. Walker, Jr ('John 1.43-51 and "The Son of Man" in the Fourth Gospel', *JSNT* 56 [1994], pp. 31-42) suggests that 'Son of Joseph' should be a title too.

23. This is the first occasion in John when Jesus' pronouncement begins with 'Ἀμὴν, ἀμὴν... John is the only Gospel to use this double ἀμὴν and he does so 25 times. Brown has a good discussion of this (*John*, I, p. 84), outlining some of the approximating usages, but it is only in John that we find utterances prefaced by the double ἀμὴν. The Hebrew verb underlying it is אמן, denoting covenant faithfulness. As Brown points out, Jesus has heard from the Father all that he says (8.26, 28), and the double ἀμὴν with which he introduces the message from the Father makes it a faithful and sure word. The Son speaking on behalf of the Father is not going to lead the children (cf. τέκνα of 1.12) astray. Of this they can be sure.

24. Some MSS. have ἀπ' ἄρτι inserted at this point in the Greek text. The editors of the United Bible Societies' *The Greek New Testament* (4th edn, 1994) have not mentioned it, so it is not likely to have been part of the original text. The question arises as to why it should have been added. Many commentators (e.g. Bruce, *John*, p. 67 n. 69) think that it was added under the influence of Mt. 26.64, where Jesus appears before the high priest and quotes from Dan. 7.13, combining it with Ps. 110.1 but prefaced with the words ἀπ' ἄρτι ὄψεσθε... It is thought that later scribes of John were endeavouring to make a link with the Synoptic Son of Man sayings and thereby offering their clues for understanding the Johannine saying.

5.4 *Analysis of John 1.51*

5.4.1 *Heaven Opened*

I want to begin by looking in 1.51 at the phrase 'you will see heaven opened'. Few writers comment on this phrase in terms of what it might mean; rather they focus on the purpose of the opened heaven: namely, to enable a descent[25] or to represent a permanently open heaven symbolizing Jesus' ministry of revelation on earth[26] or simply to enable the disciples to see into heaven.[27] One scholar who has looked at this phrase more intensively is Michele Morgen, who believes the concept of heaven in the Gospel of John is the place of God.[28]

He says that the open heaven enables communication to take place between heaven and earth. In the Synoptic Gospels the open heaven allows the descent of the Spirit; in John the open heaven permits the disciples to see Jesus, the Son of Man.[29]

Does the opened heaven have any link with the Temple? One writer who endeavours to make this connection is Margaret Barker, who, in her book *The Gate of Heaven*[30] links the veil of the Temple with the heavens.

She points out that Isa. 40.22 describes the place of God as a tent and a curtain: 'It is he who sits above the circle of the earth, and its inhabitants are like grasshoppers; who stretches out the heavens like a curtain, and spreads them like a tent to dwell in.'

While there is nothing here to link the tent with the tabernacle sanctuary of the Exodus, other texts do suggest that this was imagery associated with the *form* of the sanctuary. Ps. 104.2-4 describes the LORD's tent and his palace established over the waters, his chariots of clouds and his host of

---

25. So C.C. Rowland, 'John 1.51. Jewish Apocalyptic and Targumic Tradition', *NTS* 30 (1984), pp. 498-507 (504).

26. Schnackenburg, *St John*, I, p. 321.

27. William Loader, 'John 1.50-51 and the "Greater Things" of Johannine Christology', in C. Breytenbach und H. Paulsen (eds.), *Sonderdruck aus Anfänge der Christologie für Feredinand Hahn zum 65 Geburtstag* (Göttingen: Vandenhoeck & Ruprecht), pp. 255-74 (260).

28. 'ἐκ τοῦ οὐρανοῦ ou ἐξ οὐρανοῦ représent une expression favorite de Jean. Elle traduit l'intérêt johannique a parler de ce "lieu" du divin comme le lieu d'origine et du retour en fin de la mission de Jésus: ἐκ οὐρανοῦ équivaut à ἐκ θεοῦ.' M. Morgen, 'La promesse de Jésus à Nathanaël (Jn 1.51) eclairée par la Hagaddah de Jacob-Israël', *RSR* 67 (1993), pp. 3-21 (6).

29. Morgen, 'La promesse', p. 9.

30. Barker, *The Gate of Heaven*, esp. pp. 104-32.

heavenly messengers, creatures of flame and fire. Barker also mentions the dramatic poem in 2 Sam. 22, which describes the LORD riding upon his cherub, enveloped in a canopy of clouds (2 Sam. 22.12). Barker remarks:

> In these three texts are the roots of several later ideas associated with the curtain, but whether the texts represented the ideas in an earlier form, or whether they were the basis of later speculation about the curtain, we cannot know. Later tradition certainly did associate the tabernacle curtain with the high place from which the LORD (or his prophet) could look down and see the earth...[31]

In the first century Josephus believed that the veil represented the created world:

> Before these [doors] hung a veil of equal length, of Babylonian tapestry, with embroidery and fine linen, of scarlet also and purple, wrought with marvellous skill. Nor was this mixture of materials without its mystic meaning: it typified the universe. For the scarlet seemed emblematical of fire, the fine linen of the earth, the blue of the air and the purple of the sea; the comparison in two cases being suggested by their colour and in that of the fine linen and the purple by their origin as the one is produced by the earth and the other by the sea. On this tapestry was portrayed a panorama of the heavens, the signs of the Zodiac excepted (*War* 5.212-13).

In fact it was believed the whole tabernacle represented the universe in all its different aspects. Philo mentions this:

> The highest, and in the truest sense the holy temple of God is, as we must believe, the whole universe, having for its sanctuary the most sacred part of all existence, even heaven, for its votive ornaments the stars, for its priests the angels (*Spec. Leg.* 1.66).

Each of the Synoptic Gospels mentions the tearing of the Temple veil immediately upon Jesus' death (Mt. 27.51; Mk 15.38; Lk. 23.45).

The only New Testament author who appears to offer any explanation of this event is Mark in 15.39, who, through the words of the centurion (a Gentile: 'Truly this man was God's Son!')[32] points possibly to the uni-

---

31. Barker, *The Gate of Heaven*, p. 108.

32. In Mark it is possible to see four moments of opening: baptism (1.10—revelation to Israel); transfiguration (9.2-8—revelation to disciples); high priest's robes (14.62—revelation of the Son of Man); curtain (15.39—revelation to the Gentiles). The tearing of the curtain has been interpreted variously as (a) judgment on the Temple and Israel by extension; (b) access to the presence of God through Jesus; (c) a prefiguring of Pentecost—the opened Temple releasing the Spirit as Jesus 'gave up his Spirit' when he died.

versal accessibility of God, and the writer to the Hebrews in 10.19, 20, who points in the same direction: 'Therefore, my friends, since we have confidence to enter the sanctuary by the blood of Jesus, by the new and living way that he opened for us through the curtain (that is, through his flesh)...' In commenting on this idea J.A.T. Robinson says that 'the whole argument of chapters 9 and 10 [of the Epistle to the Hebrews] leads to the climax that Jesus has now "opened" the new sanctuary in the temple of his body'.[33]

The question is whether the torn Temple veil in Mk 15.38 and Heb. 10.20 and the open heaven in John refer to the same reality. The torn Temple veil in Hebrews and Mark evidently provides universal access to the throne of God in the holy of holies. But how current were the ideas of Philo and Josephus at the time of the New Testament? Was the Temple indeed seen as a microcosm of the universe with the heavens being the veil that separated the creation from the holy presence of God? If so then the 'open heaven' of Jn 1.51 could well speak of access to the divine presence—this access being gained through Jesus, the Son of Man, who himself is Bethel, the house of God, the Temple being his body (cf. Jn 2.21). This is attractive (albeit tenuous), but what makes it unlikely is the fact that John does not speak of a 'torn heaven', but an *open* heaven. It is Mark who speaks of a torn heaven when he says, 'εἶδεν σχιζομένους τοὺς οὐρανοὺς... (Mk 1.10), which would be in keeping with the idea of the ripped veil. But σχιζομένους is absent in John. Surely, if an allusion to the torn veil was intended, he would have used this word to forge some kind of link. As it is, there is no suggestion that the open heaven has any reference to the ripped veil of the Temple. It remains then to pursue Morgen's suggestion that it signifies divine communication.

5.4.2 *Jacob's Dream*

5.4.2.1 *Allusion to Jacob's Dream.* As far as modern interpreters of Jn 1.51 are concerned, 'almost universally scholars recognise an allusion to Jacob's dream at Bethel'.[34] First, I have drawn attention to Jacob allusions

33. J.A.T. Robinson, *Twelve New Testament Studies* (London: SCM Press, 1962), p. 172.

34. Loader, 'John 1.50-51', p. 257. Loader mentions one exception: W. Michaelis, 'Joh 1.51, Gen. 28.12 und das Menschensohn-Problem', *TLZ* 85 (1960), pp. 561-78. However, Bernard casts some doubt on the antiquity of the connection with Gen. 28.12-18 when he says: 'No commentator before Augustine suggests any connexion between Gen. 28.13 and Jn 1.51' (*St John*, I, p. 70). While it is true that of the Church

in the previous verses, and there is an obvious Jacob allusion in 4.12 where the Samaritan woman asks Jesus, 'Are you greater than our ancestor, Jacob…?' and the answer is clearly 'Yes!' Given both the immediate and wider Gospel context of Jacob allusions, it is in keeping with the flow of the narrative to make the link between v. 51 and Jacob's dream in Gen. 28.12-18. Secondly, the order of words, ἀναβαίνοντας καὶ καταβαίνοντας, in v. 51 is the same as in the LXX of Gen. 28.12.[35] Given the Johannine Logos Christology, one could well expect the order to be reversed, namely, descent precedes ascent (cf. 3.13); that this is not the case tends to confirm dependence on the order of verbs in Gen. 28.12. Thirdly, angels are not frequent in John. Throughout the Gospel Jesus' sovereignty and independence are emphasized over and over again. For example, no one puts him to death. He says, 'No one takes my life from me, but I lay it down of my own accord' (10.18). And it appears in a number of references that he is not raised from the dead; he raises himself (cf. 2.20; 10.18b). Consequently it is not surprising that Jesus feels no need of the assistance and mediation of angels (cf. Mt. 4.11; Mk 1.13). Apart from 1.51 the only other mention of angels is in 20.12 when Mary sees 'two angels in white, sitting where the body of Jesus had been lying, one at the head and the other at the feet.' Traditionally angels were associated with the empty tomb and John's reference to them here may reflect that tradition. In fact Lindars says that 'John only refers to angels when he is reproducing a source.'[36] That could well apply to the presence of angels in 1.51. The ascending and descending angels are part of Jacob's vision that Jesus evokes in his promise to the disciples. Finally, I mention a suggestion put forward by A.T. Hanson.[37] He believes the repeated words of John the Baptist in 1.31, 33, κἀγὼ οὐκ ᾔδειν αὐτόν, act as a

Fathers Bernard quotes, none makes specific reference to a connection between Gen. 28.13 and Jn 1.51, there is nevertheless a feeling of kinship between Jacob's vision and Christ. Tertullian, in remarking on Jacob's exclamation, 'This is none other than the house of God; this is the gate of heaven!', says, 'For he (Jacob) had seen Christ the LORD, the temple of God, and also the gate by whom heaven is entered' ('Tertullian against Marcion', II, XXV in A. Roberts and J. Donaldson [eds.], *The Ante-Nicene Fathers*, III [Edinburgh: T. & T. Clark, 1872; repr. Grand Rapids: Eerdmans, 1986], p. 343).

35. In line with Bruce Schuchard's finding I take it that John is working mainly but not exclusively from the LXX or the Old Greek as Schuchard prefers to call it (see 3.6.4 n. 40).

36. Lindars, *John*, p. 604.

37. Hanson, *Prophetic*, p. 37.

mental bridge to Gen. 28.16b where similar words occur: ἐγὼ δὲ οὐκ ἤδειν. The weakness of this suggestion is that there is no objective pronoun in the Genesis reference. I therefore think it unlikely the reader would make the link from John the Baptist's utterance to Jacob's dream in Gen. 28. However, in spite of the weakness of this argument I believe the first three reasons mentioned present a strong case for seeing a reference to Gen. 28 in Jn 1.51.

Given then that there is a firm reference to Gen. 28.12 in 1.51, what is its significance?

5.4.2.2 *The Story of the Dream in Genesis 28.* First of all we need to look at the story of the dream in the Genesis text (28.10-19):

Καὶ ἐξῆλθεν Ἰακὼβ ἀπὸ τοῦ φρέατος τοῦ ὅρκου, καὶ ἐπορεύθη εἰς Χαρράν. καὶ ἀπήντησεν <u>τόπῳ</u> καὶ ἐκοιμήθη ἐκεῖ· ἔδυ γὰρ ὁ ἥλιος· καὶ ἔλαβεν ἀπὸ τῶν λίθων τοῦ <u>τόπου</u> καὶ ἐπέθηκεν πρὸς κεφαλῆς αὐτοῦ, καὶ ἐκοιμήθη ἐν τῷ <u>τόπῳ</u> ἐκείνῳ καὶ ἐνυπνιάσθη· καὶ ἰδοὺ κλίμαξ ἐστηριγμένη ἐν τῇ γῇ, ἧς ἡ κεφαλὴ ἀφικνεῖτο εἰς τὸν οὐρανόν, καὶ οἱ ἄγγελοι τοῦ θεοῦ ἀνέβαινον καὶ κατέβαινον ἐπ᾽ αὐτῆς.[38] ὁ δὲ Κύριος...καὶ εἶπεν ὅτι Ἔστιν Κύριος ἐν τῷ <u>τόπῳ</u> τούτῳ, ἐγὼ δὲ οὐκ ἤδειν. καὶ ἐφοβήθη, καὶ εἶπεν Ὡς φοβερὸς ὁ <u>τόπος</u> οὗτος· οὐκ ἔστιν

---

38. The Hebrew here is בו, which could refer either to Jacob or the ladder, which is masculine in Hebrew. The LXX had to make a decision because the word for ladder (κλίμαξ) is feminine. The LXX chose 'on the ladder' and translated בו by ἐπ᾽ αὐτῆς (as with עליו in v. 13). *Gen. R.* 68.12 has a discussion on this matter: 'R. Hiyya the Elder and R. Jannai disagreed. One maintained: They were *ascending and descending* the ladder; while the other said: they were *ascending and descending* on Jacob. The statement that they were ascending and descending the ladder presents no difficulty. The statement that they were ascending and descending on Jacob we must take to mean that some were exalting him and others degrading him, dancing, leaping, and maligning him. Thus it says, *Israel in whom I will be glorified* (Isa. XLIX, 3); it is thou, [said the angels], whose features are engraved on high; they ascended on high and saw his features and they descended below and found him sleeping.'

On the dating of the midrash, Jerome J. Neyrey, in 'The Jacob Allusions in John 1.51', *CBQ* 44 (1982), pp. 586-605 (604), says: '[T]he composition of these works is quite late, although many traditions contained in them may be dated much earlier, even to the first century.' But in the case of the Jacob midrashic materials I will be quoting, there is no evidence that any of the traditions mentioned in them existed in the first century. Neyrey offers an article by R. Bloch as a critical guide to the proper use of these works, especially in establishing the antiquity of traditions within the midrash: 'Note méthodologique pour l'étude de la littérature rabbinique', *RSR* 43 (1955), pp. 194-227.

τοῦτο ἀλλ' ἢ οἶκος θεοῦ...καὶ ἐκάλεσεν Ἰακὼβ τὸ ὄνομα τοῦ <u>τόπου</u> ἐκείνου Οἶκος θεοῦ·

'Place' (τόπος) occurs no less than six times. Evidently this is an important concept in the Genesis narrative. In fact the result of the dream is Jacob's exclamation that the place is awesome: 'This is none other than the house of God; this is the gate of heaven.' And he names the place Bethel (Οἶκος θεοῦ =אל בית = Bethel).

5.4.2.3 Rabbinic Readings

The idea of place became very important in later Jewish writings. In commenting on Gen. 28.11 ('He [Jacob] came to a certain place...'), R. Huna said in R. Ammi's name: 'Why do we give a changed name to the Holy One, blessed be He, and call him "the Place"? Because He is the Place of the world.'[39]

It is not hard to see with the emphasis on place and the presence of God in Gen. 28.12-18 how some later rabbinic interpreters understood the vision in Temple terms. Indeed *Genesis Rabbah* has on Gen. 28.12 a midrash that very clearly has the Temple in view:

> Bar Kappara taught: No dream is without its interpretation. *And behold a ladder* symbolizes the stairway; *set up on the earth*—the altar, as it says, *An altar of earth thou shalt make unto Me* (Ex. 20.21); *and the top of it reached to heaven*—the sacrifices, the odour of which ascended to heaven; *and behold the angels of God*—the High Priests; *ascending and descending on it*—ascending and descending on the stairway.[40]

---

39. *Gen. R.* 68.9. There is a footnote on 'Because he is the Place of the world', which says, 'The world is contained in Him, not He in the world.' This point is clarified in the subsequent midrash by R. Jose b. Halafta. Also Evans (*Word and Glory*, pp. 18-28) proposes a method for the use of rabbinic writings and targums in the exegesis of the New Testament. The method proposes careful use of later sources provided the following four criteria are met: (1) that there is antecedent (first century or earlier) documentation that reflects the traditions of the later source; (2) if there are signs that the later source has been influenced by the New Testament, then the use of the source is much more problematic, but not necessarily useless; (3) there must be some likelihood that the New Testament writer worked in a milieu where he would encounter the traditions of the later source; and (4) there should be a degree of coherence between the New Testament passage and proposed parallel—that is, a genuine and meaningful relationship of language and conceptuality.

40. *Gen. R.* 68.12. Augustine gave Jn 1.51 a Christian interpretation comparable to Bar Kappara's saying on Gen. 28.12: 'But what saw he (Jacob) then on the ladder? Ascending and descending angels. *So it is the Church*, brethren: *the angels of God are*

A footnote on the word 'stairway' makes the reference to the Temple quite explicit. It says: '(The stairway) was leading to the top of the altar *in the Temple.*'

But considering the late dating of this material can it have any relevance for interpreting Jn 1.51? In seeking an answer to this question I need to explore some pre-Christian Jewish writings in the Pseudepigrapha and Philo.

5.4.2.4 *Pre-Christian Links?* First, there is certainly a pre-New Testament link between Bethel and the priesthood in Jubilees. It is at Bethel that Levi has a similar experience to Jacob:

> And he abode that night at Bethel, and Levi dreamed that they had ordained and made him the priest of the Most High God, him and his sons for ever...and Levi discharged the priestly office at Bethel before Jacob his father in preference to his ten brothers, and he was a priest there...[41]

So there is a tradition in the Pseudepigrapha that Bethel and the priesthood are associated together, but I can find nothing there that specifically links Bethel with the Temple.

As for a pre-New Testament tradition on the idea of place Philo may have some relevance. Philo is discussing various meanings of 'place' and his springboard is Gen. 28.11 where we read 'he [Jacob] met a place':

> Now place has a threefold meaning, firstly that of a space filled by a material form, secondly that of the Divine Word, which God himself has completely filled throughout with incorporeal potencies; for 'they saw,' says Moses, 'the place where the God of Israel stood' (Exod. 24.10). Only in this place did he permit them to sacrifice, forbidding them to do so elsewhere: for they were expressly bidden to go up 'to the place which the LORD God shall choose' (Deut. 12.5), and there to sacrifice 'the whole burnt offerings and the peace offerings' (Exod. 20.24) and to offer the other pure sacrifices. And there is a third signification [and this is where Philo's remarks are possibly a precursor to what R. Huna said in R. Ammi's name], in keeping with which God Himself is called a place, by reason of His

good ministers, preaching Christ; this is the meaning of, "they ascend and descend upon the Son of Man"' (my emphasis). *Tractate VII On the Gospel of John*, in *The Nicene and Post-Nicene Fathers of the Christian Church: St Augustine*, VII (ed. P. Schaff; Edinburgh: T. & T. Clark; Grand Rapids: Eerdmans, 1986), p. 56.

41. Jub. 32.1, 9. The association of Levi's priesthood with Bethel is mentioned in *T. Levi* 8 and in ch. 9 Jacob also receives a vision at Bethel confirming Levi's priesthood: '[And when we came to Bethel], my father saw a vision concerning me, that I should be their priest unto God.'

containing all things, and being contained by nothing, whatever, and being
a place for all to flee into, and because He is Himself the space which holds
Him; for He is that which He Himself has occupied, and naught encloses
Him but Himself.[42]

Philo goes on to say that the meaning of the 'place' Jacob came to in Gen.
28.11 is in the second of the three senses he has proposed. I believe this
gives the best meaning for linking Gen. 28.11 with a place of worship
because Philo explains this second sense in terms of the place where
sacrificial offerings are made.

5.4.3 *'Place'*
5.4.3.1 *'Place' outside of John.* The word 'place' occurs six times in Gen.
28.10-19. This was taken by Philo to refer to the Temple. I will now
review the use of 'place' outside of John and then within John to see if
there are any further Temple connections.

There is the notion of holy place in Matthew and Acts, and this has
some affinity with what Philo has said above with regard to his second
sense of τόπος. H. Köster[43] draws attention to the fact that מקום in the
Old Testament is often used for holy places (e.g. Gen. 28.11 for Bethel),
but with Deuteronomy the term is reserved for the Jerusalem Temple. This
becomes clear with the oft-repeated formula that speaks of the Jerusalem
Temple as 'the holy place which YHWH your God shall choose...to cause
his name to dwell there' (see e.g. Deut. 12.5, 11; cf. 16.16; 17.8, 10; 18.6;
31.11). Other references to Jerusalem/Temple as a holy place include Ps.
24.3; Jer. 17.12; Ezra 9.8; Isa. 60.13. Especially interesting is Isa. 18.7,
which speaks about foreign peoples bringing gifts to Mount Zion, which is
then defined as 'the place of the Name of Yahweh Sabaoth'.

In the New Testament τόπος is used for 'Temple' only once in the
Synoptic Gospels, namely, Mt. 24.15 (ἐν τόπῳ ἁγίῳ). In Acts the
reference of τόπος to the Temple is in two passages, 6.13-14 and 21.28.
Here in the accusations against Stephen and Paul they are charged not only

---

42. Philo, *Somn.* 1.62-64 in *Philo in Eleven Volumes*, V (trans. F.H. Colson and
G.H. Whitaker; Cambridge, MA: Harvard University Press; London: Heinemann, 1988
[1934]), p. 329. Philo believes this third meaning of 'place' is the best meaning. Here
all the Old Testament elements of 'place' in terms of 'holy place' (later Temple) and
promised land, are abandoned in favour of a view of God as place absolutely in the
cosmic sense. As Köster says (see *TDNT*, VIII, p. 197 n. 39): '...the problem of the
Old Testament understanding of place is thus solved by spiritualising it...'
43. H. Köster, *TDNT*, VIII, p. 197.

with arguing against the law (Acts 16.13; 21.28) and the people (21.28) but also with attacking the Temple: Stephen speaks ῥήματα κατὰ τοῦ τόπου τοῦ ἁγίου [τούτου] (Acts 6.13) and has said of Jesus καταλύσει τὸν τόπον τοῦτον (6.14); Paul teaches κατὰ...τοῦ τόπου τούτου, and has brought Greeks into the Temple and so desecrated τὸν ἅγιον τόπον τοῦτον (21.28). The use of the words, holy place/place, very clearly has the Temple in mind in these passages.

5.4.3.2 *'Place' in John.* With this background in view I come to the Gospel of John. In 11.48 Caiaphas says that if they let Jesus go on 'οὕτως', then the Romans will come and 'ἀροῦσιν ἡμῶν καὶ τὸν τόπον καὶ τὸ ἔθνος'. Brown says that 'it is not impossible that the reference is to Jerusalem',[44] and he cites Chrysostom who has 'city' for τόπος, but Brown obviously favours Temple. He refers to 2 Macc. 5.19, which mentions nation and place (i.e. Temple) together: 'The LORD did not choose the nation because of the place, but he chose the place because of the nation.' Barrett also says that τόπος here 'means primarily the temple'.[45]

In Jn 4.20 the Samaritan woman says to Jesus, '...you (pl.) say that in Jerusalem is ὁ τόπος[46] ὅπου προσκυνεῖν δει.' The contention is over the place of worship and so τόπος must refer to the Temple in Jerusalem.[47]

The Temple figures prominently in the Gospel and there is a theological emphasis on Jesus himself being the replacement of the Temple in 2.21. On the other hand, Jerusalem receives no similar accent. I believe τόπος in 11.48 is referring to the Temple. I now turn to look finally at 'the Son of Man', after which I will weave the various strands of this chapter together to bring it to a conclusion.

5.5 *The Son of Man in John*

The title 'Son of Man' occurs 13 times in John: 1.51; 3.13, 14; 5.27; 6.27, 62, 53; 8.28; 9.35; 12.23, 34 (2x); 13.31-32. The literature on the Son of

44. Brown, *John*, I, p. 439.

45. Barrett, *St John*, p. 405, and cites Jer. 7.14 in support of his judgment.

46. It is true that Codex Sinaiticus omits τόπος, but there is such a strong textual attestation in favour of the τόπος that the editors of the fourth edition of the United Bible Societies' *The Greek New Testament* (1994) have not felt it necessary to mention the variant.

47. Athanasius calls Christ 'The Place'. I am indebted to Dr Alan Torrance, now Professor of Systematic Theology, St Andrews University, Scotland, for this information.

Man debate in general is immense[48] and discussion of the Son of Man in John is also very extensive and lacking in consensus.[49] Here I need not go into an extensive debate on the complex and many issues involved in interpreting the Son of Man sayings in the Fourth Gospel. Therefore, what I attempt in the following is a brief survey of the Johannine texts where the title 'Son of Man' occurs to see if a consistent meaning can be discerned, and if so, then read it back into 1.51 and see if it fits.[50]

5.5.1 Key 'Son of Man' Passage

The first occurrence of 'Son of Man' after 1.51 is in 3.13, and this verse may be set out as a three-part inverted chiasm that hinges on εἰ μή:

καὶ

A οὐδεὶς
  B ἀναβέβηκεν
    C εἰς τὸν οὐρανὸν

---

48. For a comprehensive bibliography of the earlier stages of the debate see, M.D. Hooker, *The Son of Man in Mark* (London: SPCK, 1967), pp. 201-12. For a survey of more recent discussion see D.R.A. Hare, *The Son of Man Tradition* (Philadelphia: Fortress Press, 1990).

49. F.J. Moloney, *The Johannine Son of Man* (Biblioteca di Scienze Religiose, 14; Rome: LAS, 2nd edn, 1978), advocates that 'Son of Man' refers to the earthly revelatory role of Jesus in ministry and in death. E.D. Freed ('The Son of Man in the Fourth Gospel', *JBL* 86 [1967], pp. 402-409) suggests that 'Son of Man' in John is simply a literary variation for 'Son of God'. Barrett (*St John*, p. 73) says, 'So much is in fact predicated of Jesus as the Son of man that it is doubtful whether the title as such has any distinctive significance.' Burkett, *Son of the Man*, argues that 'Son of Man' = 'Son of God' in John. Walker Jr, 'John 1.43-51', maintains that 'Son of Man' is a mediating title between two other titles, 'Son of Joseph' (Jn 1.45) and 'Son of God' (Jn 1.49). Barrett (*St John*, p. 73) tilts in a similar direction but without the appeal to 'Son of Joseph' as a title: 'The Son of man is the man who is also God...'

50. This is the procedure Loader, 'John 1.50-51', p. 263, follows. It is, however, contrary to J. Painter's suggested methodology in his 'The Enigmatic Johannine Son of Man', in F. van Segbroeck *et al.* (eds.), *The Four Gospels 1992: Festschrift Frans Neirynck*, III (Leuven: Leuven University Press; Peeters, 1992), p. 1872: 'Given that the Son of Man is introduced for the first time at the end of chapter one we might expect 1,51 to provide the key to the evangelist's use of this term.' However, the proleptic character of much of John means that the full significance of events and words is not discovered until later in the narrative. For example, the word 'hour' has a special significance that is not clear until the eve of the passion. We suggest that the significance of the title 'Son of Man' in 1.51 needs to be gathered cumulatively from a number of texts and applied to 1.51 and context.

εἰ μὴ

C' ὁ ἐκ τοῦ οὐρανοῦ
B' καταβάς
A' ὁ υἱὸς τοῦ ἀνθρώπου[51]

The meaning of this verse turns (as the chiastic structure suggests) on the two words εἰ μὴ. Most commentators take them in an exceptive sense. Thus, 'No one has ascended into heaven *except* (Jesus), the one who has come down from heaven, namely the Son of Man.' This places the emphasis on Jesus' ascension.

There are two problems with this. First of all 'has ascended' (ἀναβέβηκεν) is in the perfect, a past action with continuing implications for the present. This would mean that the verse is written from a post-Easter perspective, whereas the narrative context is pre-Easter. As Carson remarks, 'even in the immediate context, he [the narrator] goes on to treat the resurrection of Jesus as *future* to the stance at which he has placed Jesus.'[52] The second problem is that the emphasis on Jesus' ascension does not really connect with the previous verse as firmly as the accent on his descent from heaven does. Verse 12 has Jesus speaking to Nicodemus of heavenly things. He stumbles at earthly things, so how will he believe heavenly things? To my mind Jesus' descent from heaven will help Nicodemus more than his ascent. Jesus comes as a messenger from heaven and is therefore qualified to speak of heavenly things.

It is better, I believe, to argue with Carson that εἰ μὴ should be understood here as 'but'[53] and the οὐδεὶς ἀναβέβηκεν εἰς τὸν οὐρανὸν be

---

51. The alternative reading has the addition: ὁ ὢν ἐν τῷ οὐρανῷ. Metzger (*Textual Commentary*, p. 204) says that the minority of the Committee who favoured the reading, ἀνθρώπου ὁ ὢν ἐν τῷ οὐρανῷ, could see no discernible motive for a copyist adding these words. However, if the text was read so that the Son of Man is an exception to 'no-one has ascended to heaven', then clearly it is being read from a post-resurrection/ascension perspective, which means that the Son of Man is already in heaven. The textual addition could well have been made by a copyist who wished to offer a clue for such an interpretation. Loader ('John 1.50-51', p. 263) who favours this interpetation sees this textual addition as a support for his case. The majority of the Committee, however, favoured the shorter reading because of the strong external attestation.

52. Carson, *John*, p. 200 (the emphasis is Carson's).

53. Carson (*John*, p. 200) appeals to Rev. 21.27: 'Nothing impure will ever enter it, nor will anyone who does what is shameful or deceitful, but only [εἰ μὴ] those whose names are written in the Lamb's book of life.' Here the translation 'except' for εἰ μὴ

taken as a comprehensive negative, parallel in sense to 1.18a. Thus the first half of 3.13 functions as a rebuttal of any suggestion that such figures as Isaiah, Moses or Abraham have ascended to heaven and therefore mediate heavenly knowledge. No divine knowledge is to be found from these figures from the past, *but* there is one who has come down (καταβάς—an aorist verb signifying a single event in the past, the incarnation of the Word, cf. 1.14) from heaven, namely, the Son of Man, who manifests heavenly wisdom.

That this Son of Man did ascend to heaven is certainly true. Heaven, it seems is the home of the Son of Man—he came from heaven and he will return to heaven. But how does he ascend (return)? Verse 14b provides the answer. The Son of Man is lifted up. John consistently applies ὑψοῦν to the death of the Son of Man on the cross (cf. 8.28; 12.31-33),[54] but the verb is also associated with δοξαθῆναι (cf. 12.23, 31-32). The verb ὑψωθῆναι therefore has a double meaning in John. It speaks of the crucifixion of the Son of Man and also of his exaltation/glorification. Indeed one might say that the Son of Man is exalted/glorified via the crucifixion.[55]

So here we find the Son of Man title associated with revelation (v. 13) and exaltation/glorification via the cross (v. 14), with the suffering it involved.[56] The emphasis is on the glorified humanity of Jesus and his revelatory function. This is the Johannine Son of Man.

5.5.2 *The 'Murmuring' Passage*

The next passage I look at is 6.62. The disciples are murmuring about the difficulty of accepting the teaching that they must eat Jesus' flesh and

would be misleading to say the least. Bauer, Arndt and Gingrich (*Greek–English Lexicon*, p. 219, vi, 7b) also cite Gal. 1.7 for this usage of εἰ μή.

54. This last verse, 12.33, clinches it. Having mentioned that Jesus is to be lifted up from the earth, the narrator then makes it very clear that he was speaking of his crucifixion.

55. This double meaning is present in the Old Testament. In Gen. 40.20-22 Joseph tells two prisoners, the cupbearer and the baker, that in 'three days Pharoah will lift up (נשא from the verb נשא) your head'; one is raised to his former office, the other is decapitated.

56. Many scholars have seen in John elements of the Synoptic Son of Man sayings (e.g. A.J.B. Higgins, *Jesus and the Son of Man* [Philadelphia: Fortress Press, 1964], pp. 157-71), where the emphasis has been on the suffering of the Son of Man (e.g. Mk 10.33-34, and parallels) and allusions to Dan. 7.13 ([and Ps. 110.1] cf. Mk 14.62 and parallels) as the one who will come in glory. In John, with the accent on realized eschatology, the thorough-going emphasis is on the Son of Man who *has been glorified*. Even the cross becomes the instrument of that glorification.

drink his blood. Jesus is aware of this and says to them, 'Does this offend you? Then what if you were to see the Son of Man ascending to where he was before?'[57] Given 3.14, the ascent is via the cross, which would certainly be offensive to the disciples. How could the Messiah be crucified? But also the Son of Man's exaltation/glorification will bring offense to the unbelieving because of judgement, an implied element in the glorification of Jesus as we will see below.

5.5.3 *The 'I Am' Passage*

Like 3.14, 8.28 speaks of the lifting up of the Son of Man: 'When you have lifted up the Son of Man, then you shall know that I am [ἐγώ εἰμι], and that I do nothing of myself, but as the Father has taught me so I speak.' The exaltation/glorification of the Son of Man via the cross (which the Jews will precipitate, cf. 2.19, 20)[58] will become a revelation to the Jews of who he is—they shall know that he is 'I Am'[59]—an expression that identifies him closely with YHWH. Once again the title Son of Man is linked to revelation through crucifixion/exaltation and glorification.

57. Brown (*John*, I, p. 296) proposes three possible apodoses to this protasis: '(a) Those where the apodosis is connected with the scandal mentioned in verse 61.—"then your scandal really will be great" (Bultmann); or "then your scandal will be removed" (Bauer) [This suggestion implies that beholding the ascension of the Son of Man will lead to faith]; (b) those where the apodosis is related to what was said in vv. 48-50—"then you will understand the bread of life that has come down from heaven" (Thusing, p. 261); (c) those where the apodosis is related to vv. 51-58.—"then you will judge otherwise of my flesh."' I think the most natural reading is (a) and I will enlarge on this when I discuss this verse in my Chapter 7 (7.1.5.4) on the Passover Festival.

58. David Ball says ('*I Am' in John's Gospel: Literary Function, Background and Theological Implications* [JSNTSup, 124; Sheffield: Sheffield Academic Press, 1996], p. 86), 'Could it be that Jesus is actually saying that when the Jews lift him up in crucifixion they will actually be exalting him and achieving the opposite of what they intended?'

59. 'I am' used in this absolute sense has been linked to Deutero-Isaiah by Ball ('*I Am'*, pp. 188-94). He sees Jn 8.28 as being dependent on Isa. 43.10 and perhaps Isa. 52.6 where YHWH calls himself ἐγώ εἰμι/אֲנִי הוּא. The use of this expression by Jesus evoked a violent response from his opponents in Jn 8.58, 59 (they took up stones to stone him) and overwhelmed them in Jn 18.6 (they stepped back and fell to the ground). Obviously this expression on the lips of Jesus amounted to some claim to a special relationship with YHWH that in the eyes of his opponents in Jn 8.58, 59 amounted to blasphemy. See below 7.2.6 and especially 9.5.1-6 where this is discussed more fully.

5.5.4 *The 'Lifting up' Verses*

This association of the Son of Man with glorification/exaltation via the crucifixion is also present in John 12. In 12.16 (as already in 7.39) Jesus' glorification is mentioned and in 12.23 Jesus proclaims, 'The hour has come for the Son of Man to be glorified.' This is juxtaposed to the account of the coming of the Greeks who ask to see Jesus (12.20-22) and followed by the image of the dying seed that produces fruit (12.24). The death (and associated exaltation/glorification) of Jesus will be fruitful in mission. This is made more explicit a few verses later when Jesus says, 'And I, if I am lifted up from the earth, will draw all people to me' (12.23). The context makes clear that Jesus speaks of himself as the Son of Man to be lifted up (12.34). The lifting up via the cross will be the source of a harvest of men and women.[60] Verses 13.31-32 continue the theme of glorification through crucifixion: 'Now is the Son of Man glorified and God is glorified in him. If God is glorified in him God will also glorify him in himself and will glorify him immediately.'

So far the Son of Man texts have shown that this title is associated with revelation and Jesus' crucifixion and exaltation/glorification through his resurrection and ascension to the Father.

5.5.5 *Gifts that Flow from Glorification*

The texts that remain are 6.27, 53; 9.35 and 5.27. The first of these (6.27) says, 'Do not work for the food which perishes, but for the food that endures to eternal life, which the Son of Man will give you. For it is on him that the Father has set his seal.' This last sentence provides the clue for understanding the context in which the food that endures for eternal life is given. When does God the Father set his seal of approval (cf. 3.33) on the Son of Man?[61] I suggest that it is pre-eminently in his resurrection and ascension. The sense of the verse, it seems, is parallel to Jn 7.37-39 where the promise of the gift of the Spirit following Jesus' glorification is

---

60. Indeed there is a degree of doubt about the reading πάντας ἑλκύσω ('I will draw all people') (supported by ℵ^c A B K L W X Θ Π Ψ); the alternative is πάντα ἑλκύσω ('I will draw all things') (supported by ℵ* p^{66}).

61. The aorist tense does not preclude a future reference in John. There is a certain timelessness in the way in which verbs are sometimes used. The aorist emphasizes that the seal of approval was given to the Son of Man in a particular time, I believe, in his resurrection and ascension. On the linkage between sealing Jesus and the idea of the Son of Man, see Brown (*John*, II, p. 713) where he comments on Jn 16.10 saying, '...by glorifying Jesus (xvii 5), the Father has certified him.'

given. Likewise the gift of the 'food that endures for ever' flows out of the glorification/exaltation of Jesus (via the crucifixion) as the Son of Man.

Jn 6.53 is: 'Very truly, I tell you, unless you eat the flesh of the Son of Man and drink his blood, you have no life in you. Those who eat my flesh and drink my blood have eternal life…' This is similar to 3.14, 15, and particularly to 6.27, which I have just considered. In both cases the accent is on eternal life. The food that endures to eternal life (6.27) is here in 6.53 defined as the flesh and blood of the Son of Man. The former reference speaks of gaining eternal life through believing on the the Son of Man. In both cases it is the crucified, glorified and exalted Jesus who is in view, namely, the Son of Man. It is his flesh and blood that the disciples are enjoined to eat and drink in 6.53.

5.5.6 *A New Centre of Trust and Worship*
But what of 9.35 where the man-born-blind who has received his sight is invited to believe on the Son of Man? Once he believes he worships Jesus.[62] Mention of worship in 9.38 reminds the reader (who rereads John) of the climatic scene in Jn 20.28 when Thomas cries, 'My LORD and my God!' as he comes to put his trust in the risen, glorified Jesus, the Son of Man. But the one who is to be worshipped is also the one who will judge those who do not believe (9.39-40). It seems in the light of the above that the title 'Son of Man' here has links with the one who is the eschatological bringer of salvation and judgment. This is not one who comes on the clouds of heaven but one who is present (cf. 1.14) and already dispensing salvation and judgment.

5.5.7 *Qualified to Judge*
This leads to the final Son of Man text before I return to 1.51, namely, 5.27: '…and he has given him authority to execute judgement,[63] because he is the Son of Man.'[64] The context of this verse (vv. 26-30) is the

---

62. In worshipping Jesus, the Son of Man, he does what the Pharisees asked him to do in v. 24: 'Give glory to God!'

63. The judgement in view in 5.27 seems to be the final judgment associated with the resurrection. Brown (*John*, I, p. 345) has a summary on Jesus the judge. On the one hand, Jesus did not come for judgment but salvation (3.17; 12.47); on the other hand, Jesus' presence as the light of the world brings judgment (see 9.39, 5.22; 3.19; 12.48), a judgment that will have eternal consequences when Jesus acts in judgment at the resurrection of the dead (5.26-30).

64. Higgins (*Jesus*, p. 165) remarks: '[T]his saying about the Son of Man differs

judgment at the resurrection of the dead when, as the Son of Man, Jesus exercises that judgment which the Father has turned over to him. Jesus is qualified to act as judge because he is the exalted/glorified Son of Man.[65] Even though future judgment is in view in this passage, it seems that present judgment is also a feature of John (3.18b) just as with salvation.

5.5.8 *Son of Man in John 1.51*

I now return to 1.51. The foregoing exegetical analysis although brief and sketchy reveals that the title Son of Man is invariably associated with the exaltation/glorification of Jesus, but there are also frequent overtones of revelation. In a number of cases the exaltation is specifically mentioned as via the cross (3.13, 14; 8.28; 12.23; 12.34; 13.31); in others we are pointed towards the various functions that the exalted, glorified Jesus is able to carry out because he is the Son of Man; namely, to give eternal life (6.27; 3.14; 6.53); to bring judgment (6.62; 5.27; 5.39-40); to draw all to himself (12.34); and to care for those who trust him and be worshipped by them (9.38). I suggest that this is the sort of underlying significance the Son of Man has in 1.51. But the mention of the opened heaven and the emphasis on seeing indicate that the Son of Man is a revealer as well as a mediator of eternal life and the associated gifts.

The disciples have given Jesus various titles (see above 5.3.6 n. 22), but now he gives one to himself—Son of Man. He tells his disciples that they will see the angels[66] ascending and descending upon the Son of Man. This is never literally fulfilled in the Gospel, but in terms of exaltation-glorification via the crucifixion I believe it is fulfilled in the passion–resurrection

---

from all the others in this gospel in having an anarthrous form of the Greek for Son of Man—υἱὸς ἀνθρώπου, but given the context it is doubtful that it should simply be translated "man" (thus: "...to pass judgment on what man is") as some have suggested.'

65. Perhaps here more than with other Son of Man references, the tradition behind the Synoptic Son of Man sayings shines through. In the Synoptic picture of the final judgment and the separation of the good from the evil, the Son of Man has an important part to play (Mk 12.26; Mt. 13.41; 25.31; Lk. 21.36).

66. As I mentioned above, there are only two references to angels in John, here in 1.51 and at the empty tomb in 20.12. In conversation with Stephen Noll at Tyndale House, Cambridge, he made the point that in all of the Gospels the ministry of Jesus is framed by reference to angels. The distinctive note in John's reference is that the first reference is a promise that the disciples will see the angels ascending and descending sometime in the future. This is not literally fulfilled. The nearest fulfilment is the *seated* angels in the empty tomb. Could this signal the supreme moment of glorification to which 1.51 looks forward?

narrative (Jn. 18–20) and we see proleptic traces of the Son of Man's glory in the signs/works that he does.[67] They are, in fact, signs of his glory.[68] Moreover we find that the post resurrection gifts of fruitfulness in mission (12.32 being proleptically fulfilled in Samaria in 4.39-42) and new life (11.44), for example, are realized in the pre-Easter period. It is a case of receiving tomorrow's bread today![69]

5.6 *Findings*

A number of commentators have drawn attention to the fact that the allusion to Jacob's dream in Gen. 28.12-18 is made only by reference to the angels ascending and descending upon the Son of Man. There is no mention of the ladder, the stone, or the place, Bethel. It would therefore be unwise to press the details of Jacob's dream. However, a few conclusions may be drawn from the foregoing analyses.

First, since John is probably working from the LXX, then the angels will be ascending and descending on the ladder as in the account of the dream in Gen. 28 (see above), but in 1.51 he has substituted the Son of Man for the ladder. This suggests that Jesus as Son of Man is a mediator between heaven and earth.

The open heaven enables the disciples to see into heaven and to see the Son of Man in his glory. This 'seeing' is not physical sight but spiritual as the conclusion of John 9 makes clear.

67.   1. 2.1-11   The wine miracle at Cana when he manifested his glory (2.11).
      2. 4.46-54   The healing of the official's son.
      3. 5.1-15   The healing at Bethesda.
      4. 6.1-15   The feeding of the five thousand.
      5. 6.16-21   The miraculous crossing of the sea.
      6. 9.1-41   The healing of the man born blind.
      7. 11.1-44   The raising of Lazarus.

It may be that the answer to Jesus' prayer, 'Father, glorify your name' (12.28)—'I have glorified (complexive aorist) it and will glorify it'—refers to the glorification of the Father's name through the signs that have taken place and the glorification of the Father's name through the death, resurrection and ascension of Jesus. What is significant for my purpose is the emphasis on glorification. The Father is glorified in the Son and the Son in the Father (cf. 13.31-32; 17.1, 4, 5).

68.   The Book of Signs is also a Book of Glory (cf. Brown, *John*, I, p. cxxxviii).

69.   See again Jeremias's (*New Testament Theology*, p. 199) eschatological rendering of the petition in the LORD's Prayer: 'Tomorrow's bread, give us today!' We ask for the blessings of the age to come to be given now. Cf. my previous note to the same effect (3.3.3 n. 10).

The 'greater things' is polyvalent. In the immediate context it no doubt refers to seeing greater things than the insight the disciples have seen in relation to Nathanael. It could also refer to the confessional insights of John 1. The disciples will see greater things or 'insights' than those they have seen so far—they will see nothing less than the heavenly exaltation and glorification of Jesus, the Son of Man. In the third place, bearing in mind the density of allusions to Jacob and the fact that it was Jacob who saw the vision of Gen. 28.12-18, the disciples will see something greater than Jacob saw, they will see Jesus, the Son of Man, exalted and glorified. Pre-eminently they will see this through his crucifixion, resurrection and ascension, but they will also see signs of his glory through his earthly ministry (cf. 2.11).[70] Finally, bearing in mind, that the expression can be translated, 'You will see greater people than you have seen...,' Jesus may well be saying to the disciples, 'You will see One greater than Abraham (8.53) and Jacob (4.12), namely the glorified, exalted Son of Man who is to be worshipped and trusted.'

The purpose of this chapter has been to examine Jn 1.51 to see if there is a contrast drawn there between the holy place of Jacob's vision (the House of God) and the person of Jesus.[71] McKelvey also finds Temple allusions in 1.51 when he writes, 'What John would appear to be saying...is that the bond joining heaven and earth is no longer the temple of Jerusalem, where the glory or presence of God is in the holy of holies, but Christ, in whom the divine glory is made visible.'[72] Hanson is of a similar opinion: 'So the point of the passage in the Gospel is that the humanity of Christ is the habitation of God among men and the new Temple.'[73]

However, as I mentioned above, I can find in 1.51 no elements of Jacob's dream apart from the angels ascending and descending. There is no reference to ladder, stone and, most important, Bethel. Even if one were to con-

---

70. There is also the possibility that what the disciples see is greater than what Moses (5.46), the patriarchs (Jacob and Abraham [8.59]) and the prophets (12.41) saw.

71. W.D. Davies, *The Gospel and the Land*, pp. 296-97. Davies continues this theme in n. 13 on p. 297. He draws on what he calls 'an illuminating article by A. Jaubert, "Le Symbolique Des Douze" in *Hommages à Andre Dupont-Sommer*, Paris, 1971, pp. 453ff, who points out in Jewish tradition the stone at Bethel represented the unity of all the twelve tribes of Israel... Since the place where Jacob had slept was the house of God, it was possible to connect the stone at Bethel with the Temple, and with the *eben shettiyyâh*. The transition from John 1.51 to the cleansing of the Temple in 2.12ff is not so abrupt as it first appears.'

72. McKelvey, *The New Temple*, p. 77.

73. Hanson, *Prophetic*, p. 38.

cede that some of these elements were present in 1.51 by virtue of being part of the dream that 1.51 undoubtedly evokes, that would still not necessarily make a link with the Temple. I have found no pre-Christian evidence that Bethel is equivalent to the Temple. Certainly *Genesis Rabbah* 68 makes a direct link between Genesis 28 and the Temple, but while there are hints in earlier writings, especially on the growing significance of the word τόπος/מקום in Judaism, there is not sufficient evidence to see a Temple allusion in 1.51. After all the word τόπος is not present in 1.51, even though it dominates the LXX of Gen. 28.12-17. Therefore, I cannot agree with Davies, Hanson and McKelvey, who see the Temple in 1.51.

However, I do agree with Davies when he says 'the verse is kaleido-scopic'.[74] It is also enigmatic. Neither of these judgments, however, justi-fies reading into it whatever meaning we might like to see there. The sober conclusion of D. Moody Smith is a fitting finding for this chapter:

> Three inferences or conclusions about how John should be read may be drawn from John 1.51 and its Old Testament background. First, the con-tinuing importance of this verse for the understanding of the Fourth Gospel is underscored. The revelation in Jesus Christ harks back to and recapitulates the revelation of God to Israel. Second, revelation, that is, God's making himself known, is precisely the theme of this Gospel... Third, the enigmatic and symbolic nature of this statement must not be lost on us. That is, John does not paint a photographic picture of what the disciples, or Jesus' opponents, would have seen or heard. Rather, his language is deliberately, consciously, symbolic or suggestive, evoking both the Genesis scene and the coming ministry of Jesus.[75]

---

74. Davies, *The Gospel and the Land*, p. 296.

75. D. Moody Smith, *The Theology of the Gospel of John* (New Testament Theology Series; Cambridge: Cambridge University Press, 1995), pp. 24, 25.

Chapter 6

A New Centre of Worship: John 4.16-24

The third chapter focused on Jn 2.13-22 and traced how Jesus' activity in the Temple led to a reflection on how he himself would become the Temple that would be destroyed and raised again within three days. In this respect Jesus replaces the Temple.

However, there were also clear signs, especially in the light of the re-membered text from Ps. 69.9 in Jn 2.17, that Jesus himself would become that Passover Lamb and would be consumed as a sacrifice. There are intimations, therefore, that Jesus through his death on the cross, fulfils and replaces the Passover Lamb. It is not only the Temple Jesus replaces, but also the rituals associated with the Temple.

Justification for these observations emerged in the fourth chapter on the Prologue. There it seems John is laying down a hermeneutic for a radical revision of Judaism. With the coming of Jesus Christ, the Word made flesh, a new era has come. Moses and the law, including the Temple and associated rituals and festivals, are not ends in themselves, but signposts pointing towards Jesus Christ. The *raison d'être* of Judaism is Jesus. And one of the aspects of Judaism that must be changed under this 'new hermeneutic' is the place of worship. Worship will no longer be centred in a place, but in Spirit and truth. I turn now to the fourth chapter of the Gospel of John where this theme is developed.

6.1 *Chapter Plan*

One of the central purposes of the Temple is worship. The word 'worship' (προσκύνειν) is not especially prominent in John. There is, however, one passage where there is a dense cluster of references to worship and that is in Jesus' discourse with the Samaritan woman in Jn 4.16-26. Indeed 'worship' is used only in this discourse in John and in 9.38. Clearly the pericope of 4.16-26 has in some sense to do with worship. It is for that reason that I focus on this passage.

In the course of this chapter I will consider the verses of 4.16-26 carefully to see if they advance my thesis that, with the coming of Jesus, a new era has dawned in which the Temple has been replaced by Jesus himself—that he now becomes the 'place' of worship—the new house of God (see below 8.5.2 and 8.9).

This is the worship that Jesus describes as worship 'in Spirit and truth'. I will examine this phrase to see what it means in the context of the Gospel as a whole.

Towards the end of the chapter I will consider three possible examples of worship in John to indicate what worship 'in Spirit and truth' might mean in practice.

6.2 *Introducing the Dialogue with the Samaritan Woman*

6.2.1 *Structural Context of the Dialogue*

John 4.16-26 occurs in the wider context of Jesus' encounter with a Samaritan woman at Jacob's well in Sychar, and this in turn is set in the still wider context of the Gospel of John as a whole. How does this Samaritan episode fit in with the narrative flow in John?

George Mlakuzhyil's structural analysis[1] offers some illumination of this pericope in terms of its parallel with 2.13-22. He divides John up more or less along the lines Brown suggested[2] some decades ago, but with the useful innovation of a comprehensive use of bridge passages. For example, in Mlakuzhyil's scheme, 2.1-11 can function as part of the Gospel introduction belonging to 1.1-1.51 *and* as the beginning of the first part of the Book of Signs (2.1–4.54). His analysis of the part of John where 4.16-26 occurs is as follows:

A (2.1-12) The beginning of the signs in Cana in Galilee: the changing of water into wine.

    B (2.13-25+) The Cleansing of the Jerusalem-Temple and dialogue with the Jews on the new Temple.

        C (2.23-3.21) Dialogue with Nicodemus on the new birth from above and discourse on having eternal life.

---

1.   Mlakuzhyil, *Fourth Gospel*, p. 199.

2.   Brown, *John*, I, pp. cxl, cxli. Brown says that 2.1-11 both closes the previous section and opens the next one. However Mlakuzhyil exploits the notion of bridge passages more systematically and comprehensively than Brown.

C' (3.22-4.3+)[3] Dialogue of the Baptist with his disciples on the groom
from above and discourse on eternal life.[4]

B' (4.1-42) Dialogue with the Samaritan woman on living water and true
(Temple) worship.

A' (4.43-54) The second sign at Cana in Galilee: the healing of the royal
official's son.

The advantage of this analysis is that it balances the theme of the new
Temple in B (2.13-25) with the theme of the new worship in B' (4.1-42),
so that these two passages reinforce each other. However, there is a lot
more going on in 4.1-42 than new worship—there is also the theme of the
spiritual water (4.10-15) and spiritual food (4.34) from the spiritual
harvest (4.35-42). What perhaps unites all these aspects of 4.1-42 is the
Spirit. The living water, new worship and the food that comes from the
harvest are all contingent on the ministry of the Holy Spirit. There is no
hint of the Holy Spirit in 2.13-22, but the Holy Spirit is prominent in the
dialogue with Nicodemus (C).

So, as indicated in the chapter 'The New Beginning', there is a development in the Gospel of John, and what is lacking in an earlier parallel
pericope can be present in a later one. As already hinted, something of this
development from 2.13-22 is present in 3.1-21, which partly stands in
antithetic parallelism to 4.1-42, especially in relation to the characterization of Nicodemus as over against that of the Samaritan woman.[5]

Samaritan Woman/Men	Nicodemus
No name	Name
Woman	Man
Samaritan	Jew
No status	The teacher in Israel
Jesus makes a request of her	Nicodemus makes a request of Jesus
Context is country	Context is Jerusalem city
Noon—broad daylight	Night
Immoral history	Socially respectable
Comes to faith	Misunderstands

3. The '+' indicates that the pericope functions as a bridge passage; it both closes
the previous passage and introduces the next one.

4. The weakness of this structure is the parallel of C with C'. There is in fact a
better parallel with C and B' as I point out.

5. Stibbe (*John*, p. 62) offers some suggestions about this contrast and I have built
on them. Mary Margaret Pazdan, 'Nicodemus and the Samaritan Woman: Contrasting
Models of Discipleship', *BTB* 17 (1987), pp. 145-48, also suggests some differences
between the two characters.

Witnesses to village	Eventually falteringly witnesses
Sees Jesus as world's Saviour	Doesn't see Jesus as Israel's Saviour
Spiritual water	Spiritual birth
Spiritual worship	Spiritual teaching
Harvest	No harvest

But once again within the parallelism of character (antithetical in this case) there is development. Verses 3.1-21 mention the Spirit and water (3.5) as being indispensable for the birth from above. This is taken up in ch. 4 through the image of living water and the teaching of worshipping the Father in Spirit and truth.

6.2.2 *Thematic Context of the Dialogue*
6.2.2.1 *Water and Weddings.* As for links with the immediately preceding section (3.22-36) there is mention of the abundant supply of water at Aenon near Salim (3.23), which was the reason why John the Baptist was baptizing there. The theme of water, as noted above, is developed in 4.7-15. Further there is mention of the Spirit again, this time in 3.34 where the text reads οὐ γὰρ ἐκ μέτρου δίδωσιν τὸ πνεῦμα. It is not clear whether the subject here is God or Jesus. Brown thinks it is not crucial to decide between the Father or Jesus: '[I]n the present context the Spirit that begets and the Spirit that is communicated through baptism comes from above or from the Father, but only through Jesus.'[6] However, the activity of the Spirit has already been mentioned (in 3.3, 5) by the time we reach the reference to the Spirit in 4.23, 24 and the possible underlying allusions to the presence of the Spirit in the gift of living water and the eschatological harvest of believing Samaritans.[7]

There is perhaps a further link between 3.22-36 and 4.1-42. In 3.23-30 we discover that the Baptist is the bridegroom's friend, and that Jesus is the bridegroom. There has already been an intimation of the eschatological marriage between YHWH and his people in 2.1-11 and now we are given more detail. Jesus is the messianic bridegroom to whom John the Baptist, the eschatological best man, points. Who, then, is the bride? Mark Stibbe

---

6.   Brown (*John*, I, pp. 161-62). Brown points out that in John it is sometimes the Father who gives the Spirit (14.26) and sometimes it is Jesus (15.26).

7.   Does the harvest of 4.35-38 match the eschatological vintage of the Cana wedding? Cf. Amos 9.13. If this is so, then we could say that many similarly based motifs are coming together in ch. 4, and so this would tend to confirm the presence of a betrothal scene in the same chapter. See below where I introduce the possibility of a betrothal scene.

suggests that the Samaritan woman is the bride.[8] She is, presumably, the new representative of the people of YHWH. This is a striking suggestion that needs support.

6.2.2.2 *Meeting the Bride.* First of all there is reference in 4.6, 12 to Jacob's well where Jesus meets the Samaritan woman and engages her in conversation by asking her for a drink. This mention of Jacob's well and his cattle (τὰ θρέμματα αὐτοῦ) reminds the reader of the betrothal scene in Gen. 29.1-20 (cf. also Gen. 24.1-61; Exod. 2.15b-21), where Jacob journeys to the eastern peoples, meets Rachel at a well and becomes betrothed to her.

Secondly, the fundamental plot ingredients of the betrothal-type scene have been identified as:

(a) The bridegroom journeys to a foreign land.
(b) He meets a girl (or girls) at a well.
(c) Someone draws water from the well.
(d) This leads to the girl running home to announce the stranger.
(e) The man and the woman are betrothed generally in the context of a meal.[9]

Some of these elements are missing or not quite according to the type: it is not clear that anyone draws water from the well; the woman does not announce Jesus to her family, particularly the father, but to the men of the village; and there is no mention of a meal. However, by way of response I note: (a) Jesus invites the woman to accept the invitation to draw from his 'well of living water', which she eventually does; (b) while the announcement is not to her immediate family, it is to her ethnic family—her fellow villagers; (c) and the 'meal' of which Jesus partakes is 'doing the will of him who sent me and completing his work' in token of which is the Samaritan harvest; (d) the 'spiritualizing' of the food and water may also parallel the 'spiritualizing' of marriage. John 1.13 points out that relationships in the kingdom are 'spiritual'—that is of the Holy Spirit, of God.

Stibbe (*John*, pp. 68-69) also points out that if the woman has had five

---

8.   Stibbe (*John*, pp. 68, 69). Duke (*Irony in the Fourth Gospel*, pp. 101-103) argues that there is a betrothal scene, but v. 18 introduces an ironical tone to it. Whereas in the betrothal scenes in the Old Testament the potential bridegroom speaks with a virgin, in v. 18 it is revealed that Jesus is not talking to a virgin but with 'a five-time loser'. Calum C. Carmichael ('Marriage and the Samaritan Woman', *NTS* 26 [1980], pp. 322-46) argues on theological rather than literary grounds that the narrative of 4.4-42 presents Jesus and the Samaritan woman as husband and wife.

9.   Stibbe, *John*, p. 68.

husbands and is living *de facto* with a sixth, then Jesus is the seventh man in her life: 'Since seven is the perfect number in Judaism, the implicit commentary must be that Jesus is the man which she has been waiting for, the man in whose presence she will find wholeness (σωτηρία).' The surprise is that the bride is a Samaritan and not a Jew. Jesus, the bridegroom, is the Saviour of the world (4.42) not just of the Jewish people.

6.3 *Narrative Framework of John 4.1-42*

6.3.1 *The Whole Story*
So much then for the placement of 4.1-42 in the first part of the Book of Signs (2.1-4.54) (which could be entitled 'From Cana to Cana') and the various connections between it and preceeding pericopae. I will come back to some of these themes later in the chapter and also explore them throughout the Gospel as whole in order to elucidate key expressions in 4.16-26

This brings me to situating 4.16-26 in the narrative framework of 4.1-42. With Gail O'Day[10] my concern is with the narrative as it stands in the text. I am aware that vv. 8 and 27 are seen by some scholars as seams stitching together separate stories to make a whole narrative. Robert Fortna contends that, when secondary additions to the original story are removed (vv. 10-15, 20-24, 31-38), 'a coherent story, with only slight Johannine retouching, remains'.[11] However, as O'Day rightly points out, 'while the story postulated by such source theories may be coherent, it is not the story that the Fourth Gospel finally presents to us'.[12] I do not deny that the author used sources in the composition of this chapter, but, whatever the composition history of this chapter may be, it is apparent that the intention was to create a unified, coherent literary unity, and I believe that for the purposes of this study I am justified in reading it as such.

How shall we structurally analyse 4.1-42? It seems clear enough that vv. 4-6 provide an introductory setting for the conversation with the Samaritan woman that occupies vv. 7-26. But what of vv. 1-3? Are they not also introductory? Verses 1-2 provide the reasons for Jesus' journey and give the wider picture—Jesus is on his way from Judea to Galilee, and then v. 4 says 'but he had to go through Samaria'. So the stage is set.

However, Gail O'Day argues against this by pointing out that the

10. O'Day, *Revelation*, p. 50.
11. R. Fortna, *The Gospel of Signs: A Reconstruction of the Narrative Source Underlying the Fourth Gospel* (Cambridge: Cambridge University Press, 1979), p. 190.
12. O'Day, *Revelation*, p. 49.

Samaritan sojourn was really an interruption, albeit a pivotal one, to the Judea-to-Galilee journey.[13] Having spent two days in Samaria, Jesus resumed his original journey and went on to Galilee (v. 43). In the second place, 4.1-3 really functions better as a conclusion to the preceding section (particularly 3.22-30) with its final testimony to John the Baptist. John 4.1-3 brings to completion the role of John the Baptist by focusing on the successful disciple-making and baptismal activity of Jesus' disciples. John had said in 3.30 that Jesus must increase and he must decrease. Verses 1-3 of ch. 4 illustrate and underline that trend: 'Jesus is making and baptizing more disciples than John.'[14]

On the other hand, a case can be made for including v. 4 with vv. 5 and 6. This verse ('Jesus had [ἔδει][15] to travel through Samaria') clearly introduces the Samaria narrative and, together with the following two verses, sets the location and stage for Jesus' encounter.

6.3.2 *Where to Begin?*

Jn 4.7 marks the beginning of Jesus' dialogue with the woman. Jesus speaks first and says, Δός μοι πεῖν. This is followed by a narrator aside in v. 8—'The disciples had gone to the city to buy food.' In commenting on this verse Gail O'Day says:

---

13. O'Day, *Revelation*, p. 52.

14. Commentators often puzzle over the awkward syntax of vv. 1-3. It may be that John wanted to make it clear that the contrast was being drawn between John the Baptist and Jesus in the interests of illustrating 3.30 (that Jesus was indeed on the increase), but also wanted to extend the contrast to Jesus' disciples, who perform the baptism of new disciples.

15. Brown (*John*, I, p. 169) notes that Jesus' journey through Samaria was not a geographical necessity—if he had started from the Jordan valley (3.22) he could have gone up it and so come to Galilee. However, Carson (*John*, p. 216) cites Josephus (*Ant.* 20.118; *War* 2.232; *Life* 269), who says that despite antipathy between Jews and Samaritans the route through Samaria for Jews from Jerusalem was shorter and more popular. The most likely explanation of the ἔδει, and the one that fits in with what Jesus later says to his disciples, is that he was directed by God to pass this way so he could accomplish the Father's will (cf. 3.14; 4.34). Coloe ('The Dwelling of God', p. 163) specifies this will more precisely when she says, 'Jesus' journey through Samaria is an expression of his missionary task from the Father who is seeking true worshippers (4.23).' What is attractive about Coloe's suggestion is that it ties in with the Temple theme under discussion. The further suggestion that Jesus took this shorter route because he was in a hurry to get away from the Pharisees, who had heard that he was baptizing more disciples than John (cf. v. 1), does not apply because I believe v. 4 relates to the subsequent verses, not to those that precede it.

[A]t this juncture the narrated arrival of one character is balanced by the narrated departure of the other. The relationship between vv. 7 and 8 reflects the relationship between the two larger dialogues as a whole, although only one dialogue at a time occupies centre stage—the off-stage area is never just empty space. John has carefully positioned pointers in the narrative—of which v. 8 is just one example—that enable the reader to move from one stage to another, from one set of characters to another.[16]

The Samaritan woman's response to Jesus comes in v. 9 and Jesus' dialogue with her continues through to v. 26. This dialogue can be subdivided into two sections, each of which begins with a request or command of Jesus—first in v. 7 Δός μοι πεῖν and secondly in v. 16 Ὕπαγε φώνησον τὸν ἄνδρα σου. Verses 25 and 26 close off the dialogue and then in v. 27 the disciples are (as it were) brought on stage again and the woman departs, but as readers we follow her and hear her off-stage, giving testimony to her fellow townsfolk and read of their response. These verses seem to function as a sort of narrative hinge.

The ἐν τῷ μεταξὺ of v. 31 marks the setting of the dialogue of Jesus with the disciples which they begin with the characteristic request Ῥαββί φάγε.

6.4 *Narrative Analysis of the Dialogue*

6.4.1 *A Possible Narrative Framework*
In the light of this analysis of the narrative framework, Gail O'Day has suggested[17] the following outline of Jn 4.4-42. She uses the imperatives in

---

16. O'Day, *Revelation*, p. 53. O'Day also makes the point (p. 128 n. 9) that the deliberate narration of characters' movements isolates Jesus as the one character who does not move and thus makes him the focal point of the narrative.

17. O'Day, *Revelation*, p. 54. Stibbe (*John*, p. 63) suggests a chiastic structure that gives pride of place to vv. 16-26:

A   4-9 The Samaritan woman comes to Jesus
   B   10-15 Jesus speaks of spiritual water
      C   16-30 Jesus teaches about spiritual worship
   B'   31-38 Jesus speaks of spiritual food
A'   39-42 The Samaritan men come to Jesus

However, the subject matter of vv. 4-9 is scarcely the Samaritan woman coming to Jesus—if anything Jesus comes to her with his request for a drink. And should those Samaritans who come to Jesus from the village be confined to men? It is attractive to have Jesus' teaching on spiritual worship as the focus of a chiastic structure, but the structure itself is suspect. I think Gail O'Day's suggested outline is sounder.

the requests/commands as markers of the commencement of separate dialogues and phase changes within a dialogue.

I.	vv. 4-6	Introduction: setting of the narrative.
II.	vv. 7-26	First dialogue: Jesus and the woman.
	A. vv. 7-15	'Give me a drink.'
	B. vv. 16-26	'Go, call your husband.'
III.	vv. 27-30	Narrative hinge.
IV.	vv. 31-38	Second dialogue: Jesus and the disciples.
V.	vv. 39-42	Conclusion: Jesus and the Samaritans.

This brings us to the passage that I wish to consider in detail—the second half of Jesus' dialogue with the woman of Samaria, vv. 16-26.

6.4.2 *Transition from v. 15 to v. 16*

Jesus' command Ὕπαγε φώνησον τὸν ἄνδρα σου seems to come from nowhere. It marks a seemingly abrupt transition from v. 15 to v. 16. Commentators have offered various reasons for the change of subject.[18] However, if it is granted that the form is indeed a betrothal scene, then mention of a husband would not be a surprise at all. It would be quite in keeping with the context. What would be surprising, of course, would be the implication that the 'bride' already has a husband and therefore would not

---

18. Beasley-Murray (*John*, p. 61) says, 'Jesus' request for her to bring her husband leads to a revelation of her immoral life'; Brown (*John*, I, p. 177) says, 'Jesus takes the initative in leading the woman to recognize who he is by referring to her personal life'; Barrett (*St John*, p. 235) suggests that, because the woman continues to misunderstand, Jesus is obliged to try a new approach—hence the command to go and fetch her husband; Carson (*John*, p. 220) says, 'Jesus is indicating that she has misunderstood the true dimensions of her own need, the real nature of her self-confessed thirst'; Bernard (*St John*, I, p. 143) has a couple of suggestions and then adds: '[W]e cannot in any case assume more than a fragment of the conversation has been preserved, and much that was said is, no doubt, omitted in the narrative of John'; and Lindars (*John*, p. 185) offers the following: '[T]he woman has asked for Jesus' special water, without realizing what it really is; Jesus can begin to open her understanding by telling her that it applies just as much to her husband as it does to her, which would hardly be the case if he were talking about physical water, which it was her domestic duty to fetch.' Another suggestion is that Jesus' command for her to call her husband is to introduce an allegorical message based on 2 Kgs 17.24-31. The five husbands stand for the gods of the five nations mentioned in 2 Kgs, and the discussion that follows in Jn 4 is a reflection on the illegitmate forms of Samaritan worship (cf. Birger Olsson, *Structure and Meaning in the Fourth Gospel: A Text-Linguistic Analysis of John 2.1-11 and 4.1-42* [ConBNT, 6; Lund: C.W.K. Gleerup, 1974], p. 186).

be in a position to be betrothed to anyone else. But, as the narrative reveals, the Samaritan woman's man is not really her husband, so that leaves the door open for the entry of a further man into her life, namely, Jesus.[19]

Moreover, the surprise of the command is lessened and the narrative continuity is preserved through the use of the word ἐνθάδε. The woman earlier (v. 11) had asked Jesus from where (πόθεν) he could get the living water. She was obviously thinking of a place because her request mentions the technical equipment needed to haul the water out of the well. But as I pointed out in Chapter 5,[20] the use of πόθεν in John contains an element of irony. The woman is thinking of a well, a place, but the reader knows that the living water comes not from an earthly well but from Jesus himself. Verse 15 marks a distinct advance on verse 11. Here the woman asks Jesus for the living water ἵνα μὴ διψῶ μηδὲ διέρχωμαι ἐνθάδε ἀντλεῖν. As Gail O'Day rightly remarks, 'the comprehending reader knows the woman is making the correct request in spite of herself'.[21] She is asking Jesus for the living water and to this extent (in a fumbling sort of way) has shifted her focus from place to person. She wants to have the living water so that she does not have to come back to *this* place. However, Jesus' next word is to bring her back to this place! He tells her to go and call her husband

19. Jesus becomes her LORD and goes to her village (4.29, 39, 40).

20. See 5.3.1.

21. O'Day, *Revelation*, p. 65. J.E. Botha (*Jesus and the Samaritan Woman: A Speech Act Reading of John 4.1-42* [NovTSup, 65; Leiden: E.J. Brill, 1991], p. 139) says: 'To my mind, O'Day's explanation does not hold water, so to speak! It does not explain the sudden change of topic, and more significantly, it is definitely not clear that the woman has identified the gift of water with a place. Furthermore, there is no clear-cut evidence that she does not understand that the gift is dependent on the giver and not on any well. On the contrary, the woman does indeed understand that the water is not dependent on any place, that is why she wants the water, so that she does not need to return to any specific place. Moreover, it is not true that she does not understand that the giver is the important agent and not a well—how else can one explain her request for water from the person Jesus? She asks him, and does not request knowledge of any other source where water can be obtained. One must conclude that O'Day's explanation is not adequate.' In defence of O'Day it is sufficient to point out that she has taken account of the shift from v. 11 to v. 15. She says the focus has shifted from place (which is clearly implied in v. 11) to the person of Jesus. But Jesus brings place back into the narrative when in v. 16 he tells her to go and call her husband and ἐλθὲ ἐνθάδε. Botha does not take account of this. His explanation for the abrupt change from v. 15 to 16 depends on a speech act reading of the narrative (Botha, *Speech Act*, pp. 140-41).

and ἐλθὲ ἐνθάδε. 'Place' (τόπος) is going to play an important part in the ensuing dialogue, and it seems fitting that Jesus should advance the theme with a play on the word ἐνθάδε, which provides the continuity between this section and the previous section of the dialogue, which revolved around the place of the living water. (Does it indeed come from Jacob ['our father's'] well or does it come from a different source? The answer of course, seen in the light of the replacement of Israel's [and now Samaria's] institutions, is that the living water comes from Jesus himself.) But now with Jesus' command for the woman to call her husband and return to this place, the reader is beginning to be prepared for the shift from the place of the living water[22] to the place of worship.

The woman's reply to Jesus' command seems straightforward enough. She says simply, 'I have no husband.' At the most immediate level the reader will think, 'Jesus has made a mistake. The woman cannot do as he commands. She has no husband to bring to this place.' However, both the woman and Jesus know there is more to this answer than 'meets the eye'.

Jesus' answer in vv. 17b and 18 can be set out as follows:

1. Καλῶς εἶπας ὅτι
2. Ἄνδρα οὐκ ἔχω·
3. πέντε γὰρ ἄνδρας ἔσχες
4. καὶ νῦν ὅν ἔχεις οὐκ ἔστιν σου ἀνήρ·
5. τοῦτο ἀληθὲς εἴρηκας.

What strikes the reader is that the simple seemingly straightforward answer of the woman is an ironic understatement of her marital circumstances. Given that all the woman has provided in her answer is but the very 'tip of an iceberg', Jesus' double reference to the correctness of her answer (καλῶς, ἀληθές) has to be interpreted as irony. In effect what Jesus says is, 'You have told the truth, but it is only a miniscule portion of the truth.'

In each of lines 2, 3 and 4 (as I have written it) the word 'husband(s)' or 'man/men' (ἀνήρ) occurs. It is strongly emphasized. Further, given Jesus' revelation of what Carson calls the woman's 'morally messy past',[23] one can understand her calling Jesus 'a prophet' (v. 19). He has evidently a

---

22. As we shall see in a consideration of 7.37-39 (see below 7.2.4.7 and 7.2.5.1), the flow of the living water from Jesus is actually a fulfilment of the flow of water from the Temple (see Ezek. 47.1-12).

23. Carson, *John*, p. 220.

more-than-human insight into her life, and one can surmise from the other use of this term in 9.17 that she is on the way to faith.[24]

6.4.3 *Transition from v. 19 to v. 20*

The transition to the next stage in the dialogue is perplexing. From calling Jesus a prophet the woman then moves onto asking Jesus about the place of worship. What is the connection? Again the answers vary. Bernard says:

> [T]he woman diverts the conversation to another subject, and proceeds to raise a theological difficulty, either to evade the personal issue, or because she was honestly anxious to learn what a prophet with such wonderful insight would say about the standing controversy between Jews and Samaritans.

He then has it both ways and says that 'probably both motives affected her'.[25] Carson discounts the first motive and opts for the second and suggests that she wants to 'demonstrate her religious awareness'.[26] Carson is perhaps influenced in his opinion by F.F. Bruce, whom he quotes: 'There are some people who cannot engage in a religious conversation with a person of a different persuasion without bringing up the points on which they differ.'[27] Gail O'Day rightly criticizes those scholars who 'psychologize' the text based on a 'caricatured view of the "personality" and function of the woman'. She then goes on to say:

> [A]s she [the Samaritan woman] stands at or near a Samaritan holy place with someone she assumes to be a Jewish prophet, she puts before him a central issue of both Samaritan and Jewish worship. Her words about worship are therefore both textually and semantically linked to her acknowledgement of Jesus as a prophet.[28]

Certainly there is a textual link in the sense that the question about the place of worship immediately follows on from the woman's admission that Jesus is a prophet. But that is really to beg the question. Why does one

---

24. A number of the commentaries have some discussion as to whether the woman calls Jesus the prophet of Deut. 18.15-18 (cf. Jn 1.21). Lindars (*John*, p. 187) tends to favour this view, but Carson (*John*, p. 221) believes that 4.25 counts against it.

25. Bernard, *St John*, I, p. 145.

26. Carson, *John*, p. 222.

27. Bruce, *John*, p. 108.

28. O'Day, *Revelation*, pp. 67, 68.

follow from the other? And where is the semantic link Gail O'Day mentions? It is not clear. I find her explanation less than convincing.

6.4.3.1 *A Possible Allegorical Answer.* There is another explanation that has been put forward by scholars that would ease the transition from v. 19 to v. 20.[29] They[30] suggest these verses (4.17, 18) be interpreted allegorically of the idolatry of the Samaritans. 2 Kgs 17.29-34 tells us that the Assyrians repopulated the cities of Samaria with people of five different nations, who brought their own forms of worship. However, in 2 Kgs 17.30-31 we are given the names of seven gods. Josephus (*Ant.* 9.288) manages to reduce these to five. Since the Hebrew word for husband (בעל) is the same word used for a god, the woman representing Samaria has five בעלים (the five gods previously worshipped) and the בעל (יהוה) is not really her בעל because as Jn 4.22 indicates the Yahwism of the Samaritans was impure or, at best, confused.[31]

There have been those who have argued against this allegorical interpretation, but their arguments are not decisive.

Brown says, for example, that John gives no evidence of it. However, there may be something of a clue in the unusual emphasis on the 'husbands' in v. 18 mentioned above.

Lindars, on the other hand, says the details do not fit. He presumes the woman did not have her five husbands concurrently, as the suggestion of religious syncretism would naturally imply. But this is to interpret the allegory too literally. The five husbands stand for the five gods and it does not mean the woman literally had five husbands. And even though the Samaritans may have been monotheistic at the time of Jesus, it does not mean they knew which god they worshipped, as v. 22 indicates.

Schnackenberg argues against the allegorical interpretation mainly on the grounds that in 4. 29, 39 and 42 the woman is treated as an individual and not a representative of the Samaritan people. However, John has shown with Nathanael and Nicodemus that characters can function some-

29. In conversation with John Proctor, he suggested that v. 19 be considered as a bridge. Having recognized Jesus' prophetic power, the woman explores the relationship of that power to her situation in v. 20. She wants to know how Jesus, a Jew, who is also a prophet, relates to her, a Samaritan, when there is this religious gulf between the two peoples. What are Jesus' credentials as a 'Samaritan prophet'?

30. The following scholars discuss this view without necessarily agreeing with it: Hoskyns, *The Fourth Gospel*, pp. 242-43; Lindars, *John*, p. 185-87; Olsson, *Structure and Meaning*, pp. 186, 199, 203; Marsh, *Saint John*, pp. 208-10, 216.

31. See Brown, *John*, I, p. 171.

times as individuals and sometimes as representatives. Further, even in their individuality they can be representative.[32]

Consequently I do not find the arguments against the allegorical inter-pretation compelling. Apart from the arguments that the evidence for it is slight (just the unusual emphasis on ἀνήρ in v. 18 and the note in 2 Kgs 17.29-34) and that John does not allegorize, I think that the other points I have mentioned can all be answered.

While I do not find the evidence for the allegorical interpretation strong enough to subscribe to it at this stage, at least it does have the merit of easing the transition from v. 19 to v. 20. Given that Jesus has exposed the religious life, past and present, of the Samaritans (v. 18), it would be understandable for the focal place of their religious life to come up for discussion (v. 20).

6.4.3.2 *Jacob's Well and the Torah.* To establish the above more firmly I need to consider carefully the possible significance of 'Jacob's well'.

There is some evidence to link the Torah with a well in Qumran writings:

> And God remembered the covenant of the Patriarchs
> and raised out of Aaron men of understanding
> and out of Israel sages,
> and he caused them to hear (His voice) and they dug the well:
> The well which the princes dug,
> Which the nobles of the people delved with a rod.
> *The well is the law,*
> and those who dug it are the converts of Israel
> who went out from the land of Judah
> and were exiled in the land of Damascus.[33]

Also significant is the use of באר in relation to the Torah when in Deut. 1.5 Moses is said to 'expound this law' (באר את־התורה הזאת). Driver says that 'in post-biblical Hebrew, באר is common in the sense of "explain", ביאור being an "exposition" or "commentary"'.[34] Christensen repeats

32. Brown, *John*, I, p. 171; Lindars, *John*, pp. 186-87; Schnackenburg, *St John*, I, p. 433.

33. Damascus Document 6.2-5 (emphasis mine for הבאר היא התורה). Jerome H. Neyrey, 'Jacob Tradition and the Interpretation of John 4.10-26', *CBQ* 41 (1979), pp. 419-437, has an extensive discussion on possible allusions to rabbinic and targumic traditions in our passage and discusses the use of 'well' imagery to represent the Torah.

34. S.R. Driver, *A Critical and Exegetical Commentary on Deuteronomy* (Edinburgh: T. & T. Clark, 1902), p. 8 n. 5.

what Driver says.[35] William L. Holladay says the piel verb means 'make plain' in Deut. 1.5 and 'record carefully' in Deut. 27.8 and Hab. 2.2.[36] These scholars offer no encouragement to see a link between the Torah and a well. באר is understood in the sense of 'explain' or 'expound'.

However Jean-Georges Heintz allows for the possibility of a link with 'well' when he says that באר in Deut. 1.5 means that a 'well is a symbol of wisdom as a place of deepening thoughts (cf. Dt. 1.5)'.[37] It is possible that the other two texts mentioned by Holladay retain links with a well too. Deut. 27.8 has, 'You shall write upon the stones all the words of this law [באר היטב].' In the NRSV the Hebrew words are translated as 'very clearly' but they could mean 'making a good "well"', signifying that the chiselled depressions in stone are wells of wisdom. Similarly in Hab. 2.2 'And the LORD answered me and said, "Write a vision; make it plain [or, taking account of the verb, באר here, 'make depressions (wells)'] upon tablets, so that a runner may read it.' My argument is that the concrete associations with 'well' and 'digging wells' may have come before the more abstract ideas of 'explain' or 'write clearly' and that these associations lie behind later usage. What is clear from the Qumran Damascus Document, quoted above, is that the authors saw the law as a well and it is possible that this linkage is present here in John 4.[38]

The Samaritan woman clearly regards Jacob as the forefather of her people. She refers to him as πατρὸς ἡμῶν Ἰακωβ (4.12). If this point is taken in conjunction with the linkage of the well to the Torah, then we have in Jacob's well a symbol of the Samaritan Pentateuch—the source of Samaritan religious life. If this is granted then Jesus' offer of living water generates a contrast between not just physical water and 'living water', but between Samaritan religious life with all its institutions (including worshipping on Mt Gerizim) and the life that Jesus offers. This would parallel the narrative of the first miracle where the water in the jars of purification, representing Jewish Torah, is turned into the wine of the eschatological wedding feast that Jesus inaugurates. However, there is no organic link

---

35. D.L. Christensen (*Deuteronomy 1–11* [WBC, 6A; Dallas: Word Books, 1991], p. 8) adds: 'Tsumara has argued for parallels in Akkadian *burru*, the D-stem of *baru*, p. 8 meaning "to establish the true legal situation…by a legal proceedure involving ordeal, oath or testimony" (*ZAW* 94 [1982], pp. 294-95).'

36. Holladay, *Concise Hebrew and Aramaic Lexicon*, p. 32.

37. J.-G. Heintz, 'באר', *TDOT*, I, p. 466.

38. The symbolism of water is used to describe: God's revelatory word (Isa. 55.1, 10, 11); wisdom (Prov. 18.4; Prov. 16.22); and the wisdom of the Torah (Sir. 24.23-24).

between the water from Jacob's well in Samaria and the living water that Jesus offers, but there is an organic link between the water of purification and the wine. Could this be because 'salvation is from the Jews', not the Samaritans (4.22)?

If we allow that the religious life of Samaria has already been introduced by reference to Jacob's well, then it would be fitting to have some allusion to Samaria's past and present religious life in v. 18.

The other point that would help the transition from v. 19 to v. 20 is the previous emphasis on place. I pointed out above that the woman is interested in the place of the living water. She asks Jesus, 'From where [πόθεν] do you get that living water.' Later she speaks dismissively of Jacob's well when she asks for the living water so that she no longer needs to come to the well to draw. However, Jesus calls her to come back to the place of Jacob's well with her husband. She must begin there.

If the context of the religious life of Samaria is *already* under discussion in the dialogue and this is coupled with the previous references to *place*, then the transition from calling Jesus a prophet to asking him about place of worship poses no great difficulty. We have already been prepared for it in the dialogue.

6.4.3.3 *Samaria–Israel Bipolarity.* What the woman says is, 'Our fathers[39] worshipped on this mountain,[40] but you say that in Jerusalem is the place[41] where people must worship.' The use of the plural οἱ πατέρες and ὑμεῖς (see also vv. 12, 20, 22) suggests that the discussion has moved beyond two individuals having a conversation at a well. An opposition has been set up between Jews and Samaritans and the woman is championing the Samaritan cause, and there is a hint (as I mentioned above) that she has acquired something like representative status. At any rate there is a

---

39. The reference to οἱ πατέρες and ὁ πατήρ ἡμῶν Ἰακωβ (v. 12) prepares us for the reference to ὁ πατήρ in vv. 21-23 with the implication that this Father is greater than all other fathers.

40. In the Samaritan Pentateuch in Deut. 27.4, Joshua is instructed to set up a shrine on Gerizim, the sacred mountain of the Samaritans. Brown says: '[T]his reading is probably correct, for reading "Ebal" in MT may well be an anti-Samaritan correction' (*John*, I, pp. 172-73). Obviously the Samaritans believed strongly in the rightness of their worship place because it was made part of their decalogue. Their descendants still go to the top of Mt Gerizim each year to celebrate the Passover. See also the full and lucid discussion in Carson (*John*, p. 222).

41. The 'place' here refers to the Temple (see 11.48 and the extended discussion above in Chapter 5, that is, 5.4.3.2).

polarity between Jew and Samaritan at work in the dialogue and Jesus picks up on this in v. 21 and says, 'Believe me, woman,[42] the hour is coming when you will worship the Father neither on this mountain nor in Jerusalem.' The woman presented the issue of worship in terms of the past (προσεκύνησαν) and present (ἐστὶν ὁ τόπος ὅπου προσκυνεῖν δεῖ); Jesus begins to answer her in terms of the future (προσκυνήσετε).

The second point to note is that the woman did not specify the object of worship. Perhaps this is to underline what Jesus says in v. 22a: 'ὑμεῖς προσκυνεῖτε ὃ οὐκ οἴδατε.' However, in his answer Jesus introduces the object of worship by supplying 'the Father'. I have mentioned above the previous references to father/fathers (see above 6.4.3.3 n. 39), but, as Gail O'Day observes, 'all these referents for father are dramatically undercut, however, by the one expression of Jesus: you will worship *the Father*. By repetition and juxtaposition John has ironically shown that the Samaritan woman has no idea who the Father is.'[43]

When Jesus contrasts Samaritan and Jewish worship in v. 22[44] he is no doubt wanting to underline the belief that God's revelatory activity has been through the Jews rather than through the Samaritans. The Jews therefore 'know' whom they worship; the Samaritans do not know. As I mentioned previously, this is also the literary thrust of the dialogue. The woman does not specify the object of worship because she does not know; it is Jesus who specifies that it is the Father who is to be worshipped. And this introduces a *new* element that, as John emphasizes throughout the

---

42. This probably means the same thing as the more customary 'Truly, truly, I say to you'. Jesus has something important to say and he want the woman to pay close attention. See Bernard, *St John*, I, p. 146; Lindars, *John*, p. 188.

43. O'Day, *Revelation*, p. 69.

44. 'We know what we worship…' It is almost certain that the 'we' of this phrase refers to the Jews because of the words that immediately follow 'for salvation is of the Jews'. What is interesting is that Jesus identifies himself squarely with the Jews. He himself is a Jew. As Barrett (*St John*, p. 237) says: '[I]t is true that "his own" rejected Jesus, but John never doubts that it was to them that he came, or that they were his own.' Coloe ('The Dwelling of God', p. 151), however, argues that in the 'narrative time of the Gospel' the Jews never know correctly (cf. 6.42; 7.27; 8.14, 19, 52; 9.31) and that a second level of understanding of who is meant by 'we' in the phrase 'we worship what we know' is demanded. She says, 'True worship of the Father, known in the revealing activity of Jesus, lies in the future, in the time of the believing community (4.21). The "we" must therefore refer to the future Christian community.' However, within the immediate narrative the emphasis falls on the bipolarity of Samaritan and Jewish worship, not Christian and Jewish/Samaritan worship.

Gospel, even many of the Jews do not know either. It is this newness that I will take up in a moment after a digression on v. 22.

6.5 *Digression on John 4.22*

6.5.1 *The Significance of* 'ἐκ' *in v. 22*

Verse 22 deserves more attention. The issue is whether it should be regarded as an editorial gloss.[45] Jesus has just said that the hour is coming when people will not worship in Jerusalem and then he goes on in v. 24 to describe a worship that transcends national bounds. How then can he say something that is so nationalistic as 'salvation is of the Jews'?

Bultmann says:

> v. 22 is completely or partially an editorial gloss. The ὅτι ἡ σωτηρία ἐκ τ. Ἰουδ. ἐστίν is impossible in Jn., and that not only because of 8.41ff.; for 1.11 already made it clear that the Evangelist does not regard the Jews as God's chosen and saved people... And in spite of 4.9 it is hard to see how the Johannine Jesus, who constantly disassociates himself from the Jews (8.17; 10.34; 13.33...) could have made such a statement.[46]

Several remarks may be made against Bultmann's case for rejecting v. 22b: (a) Verse 4.9, should not be so lightly dismissed. Bultmann himself says, 'Jesus is a Ἰουδαῖος, even though he is a Galilean, because he belongs to the Jewish national and cultic community.'[47] (b) The disassociation implied in 8.17 and 10.34 is a disassociation not from the Jews, but from the Jewish law. And as I suggested in the chapter on the Prologue (Chapter 4), what Jesus distances himself from is not so much the law itself as the Jewish interpretation of the law. In so far as the law is interpreted as refering to Jesus John is positive (cf. 1.45; 5.45-47; 7.19). (c) Verse 13.33 puts the Jews and the disciples on the same footing. It does not call into question that salvation is from the Jews. (d) Bultmann interprets the οἱ ἴδιοι of 1.11 as referring to those whom Jesus, the Word, has created (cf. 1.10) and will not allow any possibility that οἱ ἴδιοι could refer to the Jews.[48] This fails to take into account what transpires in the Gospel narrative. Brown makes the point that 1.11 and 12 are short summaries of the

---

45. For a history of the exegesis of this verse see I. de la Potterie, '"Nous adorons, nous, ce que nous connaissons, car le salut vient des Juifs." Histoire de l'exegese et interpretation de Jean 4, 22', *Bib* 64 (1983), pp. 77-85.

46. Bultmann, *John*, p. 189 n. 6.

47. Bultmann, *John*, p. 178 n. 7.

48. Bultmann, *John*, p. 56 n. 1.

two parts of the Gospel: the Book of Signs where the Jews (οἱ ἴδιοι) do not accept Jesus,[49] and the Book of Glory where his disciples accept him. Indeed, *they* become οἱ ἴδιοι (cf. 13.2): '...in place of the Jewish people who had been his own (i.11), he has formed around himself a new "his own", the Christian believers (i.12).'[50] (e) The seemingly most compelling text in favour of Bultmann's case for dismissing 4.22 is 8.41-47 where Jesus says to his accusers, 'You are from your father the devil, and you choose to do your father's desires. He was a murderer from the beginning and does not stand in the truth.' This deserves a more comprehensive answer than the earlier points so I will take it up in a separate section.

6.5.2 *Is the Gospel of John Anti-Jewish?*
Bultmann quotes Merx (without agreeing) as supposing John to be extremely anti-Jewish. The basis of this verdict is the verses from Jn 8 that I have quoted above. They say that those with whom Jesus is debating are spawn of the Devil (esp. 8.44). Is John anti-Jewish?

(a) Who are the Jews of 8.44? This is a complex question to explore in depth. I believe Motyer is right when he says, '"The Jews" with whom Jesus clashes are a *party within Judaism*, the supremely religious, those whom Bornhauser calls the "Torafanatiker", Blank "die Jerusalmer Kult-gemeinde" and Morton Smith the "Yahweh-alone party"...'[51] This means that the term does not refer to Jews in general but a particular group of Jews. (b) Motyer has argued persuasively[52] that the charge ὑμεῖς ἐκ τοῦ πατρὸς τοῦ διαπόλου ἐστέ, and its negative counterpart ἐκ τοῦ θεοῦ οὐκ ἐστέ have an ethical and not an ontological force. In support of this contention he cites examples of ethical dualism in contemporary texts, the

---

49. This is the powerful message towards the end of the Book of Signs where the Jews do not believe in him (12.36b-40). Then follows a final challenge in terms of light and darkness, salvation and judgment. The outcome depends on whether they accept Jesus and his words or reject him and his words (12.44-50).

50. Brown, *John*, I, p. 29.

51. Motyer, 'Persuasion', p. 69. Motyer discerns four senses in which Ἰουδαῖοι is used in John: (1) The primary reference to those who adhere to the religion of Judaea, whether living in Judaea or not. (2) A derived sense designating adherents of the particularly strict, Torah-and Temple-centred religion. (3) A derived metaphorical sense in which 'the Jews' stand for 'the world'. Cf. 'the world' paralleling οἱ ἴδιοι in 1.10, 11. (4) The word acquires a pejorative connotation that becomes particularly clear in the passion narrative. Nevertheless, this connotation never supplants the word's basic reference—it never comes to mean 'unbelievers'.

52. Motyer, 'Persuasion', pp. 215-27.

ethical kinship with Abraham whom the Jews claim as their father[53] and the role of the law as it emerges in the context of Jn 8.44. The case for an ethical force is overwhelming. It is significant to compare what is said about Judas in 13.2. There he is in the same state as 'the Jews' of 8.44, with an idea in his mind. But with the actual entry of Satan into him, his destiny is set and he becomes ὁ υἱὸς τῆς ἀπωλείας (17.12). The Jews are not portrayed in such fixed terms in 8.44. (c) Motyer makes the point that John is written (at least in part) to persuade people to believe that Jesus is the Christ, the Son of God (20.31) and that this rhetorical element is present in Jn 8.44. Some Jews may therefore very well listen sympathetically, and the rhetoric of 8.44 could well pose the question sharply: Is it possible that 'the Jews' were acting under the direction of the Devil when they killed Jesus? Is it possible that Jesus was 'from God' after all? So it is possible that the polemic of John 8 serves not merely to denounce but to warn, to persuade, and to prompt its own non-fulfilment. It 'intensifies the alternative in order to provoke a decision.'[54] (d) Finally, 'the Jews' are not viewed uniformly negatively in John. They are treated warmly in the story of Lazarus (11.19, 31); Jesus raises no objection to being identified as a Jew by the Samaritan woman (4.9, 20); Nicodemus who comes to Jesus shows that his 'deeds have been done in God (3.21)'[55] and (if 4.22b is allowed to stand) 'salvation is from the Jews'.

The purpose of the foregoing discussion is to demonstrate that (contra Bultmann) the expression 'salvation is from the Jews' is entirely compatible with the Johannine Jesus. There is nothing discordant in it as far as the overall thrust of the Gospel is concerned. There is, however, a positive argument in favour of retaining 4.22b as integral to the thought and structure of the narrative. Verse 22 deals with the present and sits between vv. 21 and 23, both of which speak of the eschatological hour. If v. 23 followed on immediately from v. 21, then there would be no need for it to begin with ἀλλά. Γάρ would be sufficient since v. 23 would simply be

---

53. The Johannine Jesus places the emphasis not on the actual Abrahamic paternity of the Jews, but on their ethical kinship: 'If you were Abraham's children, you would be doing what Abraham did' (8.39). This is not to deny actual Abrahamic paternity, but rather places the context of the discussion in an ethos of ethical rather than ontological paternity.

54. Motyer, 'Persuasion', pp. 229-31, 246. The quotation is from Dunn, *Partings*, p. 159.

55. It is worth noting that 3.21 forms an inclusio with the beginning of the dialogue in 3.2 underlining the point that Nicodemus is still in the picture.

advancing the thought of v. 21. However, given that v. 22 does belong to the narrative, then it is appropriate for v. 23 to begin with ἀλλά since v. 23 is about to contrast the state of affairs in the present with what will happen in the eschatological moment.[56]

But not only is this verse necessary for the narrative of John 4, it also *fits* this Gospel as a whole, as the excursus above on the exoneration of anti-Semitism in John implies. Verse 22b says that salvation is from (ἐκ) the Jews. This is certainly true to the thrust of John. For example, it is the Jewish scriptures that testify to Jesus, whom the Samaritans correctly proclaim as 'the Saviour of the world'. It is perhaps no exaggeration to say that all the institutions and the great figures of Judaism (feasts, Temple, scriptures/law, Moses, Abraham, Jacob and Isaiah) find their fulfilment in Jesus, who comes as the source of salvation not just for Jews, but for all people. This does not mean that the Jews accepted the salvation that was the fulfilment of their religion. Jesus came to his own home (τὰ ἴδια)[57] but his own people (οἱ ἴδιοι) did not welcome him (1.11). John is not anti-Jewish, but the antagonism between Jesus and the Jews arises because they do not accept him. For John Judaism is meant to lead to Christ. The true Jew is a Christian. Salvation is from the Jews and finds its fulfilment in Jesus.[58]

---

56. Of course it is possible that ἀλλά is a gloss too, added so that v. 22b fits the narrative.

57. Walker (*Jesus and the Holy City*, p. 164) suggests this could refer to the Temple. 'In entering the Temple Jesus was coming in a vivid sense to "his own"'. 'The Temple belongs to Jesus in a special way' (Moloney, 'Reading John 2.13-22', p. 442).

58. We see this fulfilment exemplified in the introductory formulae of the citations from the scriptures from 12.38 onwards:

12.38 ἵνα ὁ λόγος Ἡσαίου τοῦ προφήτου πληρωθῇ ὃν εἶπεν,
12.39 ὅτι πάλιν εἶπεν Ἡσαίας,
13.18 ἀλλ᾽ ἵνα ἡ γραφὴ πληρωθῇ
15.25 ἀλλ᾽ ἵνα πληρωθῇ ὁ λόγος ὁ ἐν τῷ νόμῳ αὐτῶν γεγραμμένος ὅτι
17.12 ἵνα ἡ γραφὴ πληρωθῇ
19.24 ἵνα ἡ γραφὴ πληρωθῇ [ἡ λέγουσα]
19.28 ἵνα τελειωθῇ ἡ γραφη
19.36 ἵνα ἡ γραφὴ πληρωθῇ
19.37 καὶ πάλιν ἑτέρα γραφὴ λέγει

From 12.38 onwards all the introductory formulae (except 19.28) use the expression ἵνα πληρωθῇ or associate with it through the use of πάλιν (as in 12.39-40; 19.37). It is well known that the latter part of Jn 12 marks the commencement of Jesus' passion (e.g. 12.20-33 has Jesus predicting his death) and it seems that John wishes to

6.6 *In Spirit and Truth*

6.6.1 *The Time Has Come!*

I now return to the newness that Jesus has introduced in v. 21. Jesus says, 'Neither on this mountain nor in Jersusalem you will worship the Father.' As Dorothy Lee says: '[W]orship in the ancient world was generally associated with sacred sites...and for the Johannine Jesus to locate worship apart from sacred site means, at face value, to do away with the notion of worship altogether.'[59] However, the mention of the Father in v. 21 heralds the way in which Jesus will resolve this problem. This he develops in v. 23:

> But the hour is coming and now is here, when the true worshippers will worship the Father in Spirit and in Truth, for the Father seeks such to worship him. God is Spirit, and those who worship him must worship in Spirit and Truth.

This verse is an advance on v. 21. There we were told the hour was coming. Now in v. 23 it is not only coming but has arrived. This is the eschatological hour that is inaugurated with the death, resurrection and ascension of Jesus (cf. 13.1; 17.1; 12.27, 28). In this sense it is still coming, but when the words καὶ νῦν ἐστιν are added it means that the gifts and power of the eschatological era are unleashed already, as it were, proleptically in relation to the narrative (cf. 5.25). This new worship, then, has come already. It consists of a new relationship with God as Father in Spirit and Truth.

The expression ἐν πνεύματι καὶ ἀληθείᾳ has occasioned much

---

emphasize the fulfilment character of Jesus' rejection and death at the hands of the Jews in relation to Scripture and he does this through the almost uniform use of ἵνα πληρωθῇ. However, there is the exception in 19.28 where ἵνα τελειωθῇ is used. Moo suggests (rightly, I believe) that 'in conjunction with the use of τελειόω and Jn. 19.30, the cry represents a climactic fulfilment, "... not the isolated fulfilling of a particular trait in the scriptural picture, but the perfect completion of the whole prophetic image"' (D. Moo, *The Old Testament in the Gospel Passion Narratives* [Sheffield: Almond Press, 1983], pp. 278-79). The quotation is from Westcott (*St John*, II, p. 315).

59. Dorothy A. Lee, *The Symbolic Narratives of the Fourth Gospel: The Interplay of Form and Meaning* (JSNTSup, 95; Sheffield: Sheffield Academic Press, 1994), p. 80. Lee mentions that an exception to this rule is Stoicism, which she calls a philosophical rather than religious system. The pantheistic view of the universe and the ubiquity of the divine presence made it difficult to locate it within spatial or geographical constraints (n. 1).

discussion. Brown has suggested[60] that because both nouns are anarthous and there is only one preposition, the phrase is a hendiadys that could be translated as 'Spirit of truth'. The attractiveness of this is that later John uses just this expression in 14.17, 15.26 and 16.13 (τὸ πνεῦμα τῆς ἀληθείας). However, if John wished to say 'Spirit of truth' he could readily have done so. While the phrase in 4.23, 24 is very similar to 'Spirit of truth', it is not exactly the same and in spite of what Brown says about the foolishness of separating the Spirit from the truth,[61] I believe that John has given a chink of separation so as to make an emphasis that is not so obviously present in the term 'Spirit of truth'.

6.6.2 'Gift of God' and 'Living Water'

But I must address the question: Given that πνεῦμα and ἀληθεία may be separated what do they mean? To answer this I believe with de la Potterie it is necessary to backtrack in the narrative and endeavour to identify the 'living water'.[62] Since the narrative is a unit, my investigation of the significance of the 'living water' may well provide clues for unravelling the significance of ἐν πνεύματι καὶ ἀληθείᾳ.

Verse 4.10 can be set out as a chiastic pattern:

A Εἰ ᾔδεις τὴν <u>δωρεὰν</u> τοῦ θεοῦ
  B καὶ <u>τίς</u> ἐστιν ὁ λέγων <u>σοι</u>, Δός μοι πεῖν,
  B' <u>σὺ</u> ἄν ᾔτησας <u>αὐτὸν</u>
A' καὶ <u>ἔδωκεν</u> ἄν σοι ὕδωρ ζῶν.

In (A-A') the operative word is δωρεὰν/ἔδωκεν. The gift of God and the gift of Jesus are parallel. The gift of Jesus is specified as the 'living water'. Is this also the 'gift of God' as the parallelism seems to suggest?

In relation to the 'living water' de la Potterie quotes Num. 21.16-18:

> From there they continued to Beer (= well) of which the LORD said to Moses, 'Gather the people together and I will give them water.' Then Israel sang this song: 'Spring up, O well!—Sing to it!—the well that the leaders sank, that the nobles of the people dug, with the sceptre, with the staff.' From the desert (they went) to Mattanah...

He then goes on to say:

---

60. Brown, *John*, I, pp. 172, 180.
61. Brown, *John*, I, pp. 180-81.
62. This is similar to my earlier investigation of the 'well of Jacob' (cf. 6.4.3.2) when I suggested a possible link with the religious life of the Samaritans. This present investigation, however, concentrates on the 'living water' that Jesus offers.

> The haggadah here makes two remarkable identifications: on the one hand, the well, the source of *living water*, is identified as the Law; on the other one speaks readily in this respect of the well being a divine *gift* (= the gift of the Law), especially in reference to *Mattana* (מתנה), interpreted in the sense of 'gift'. The Targum of Onkelos on this passage in Numbers is particularly interesting: 'From there the well was *given* to them. This is the well about which the Lord told Moses, "Gather the people together and I will *give* them water"…and it was *given* to them since the wilderness. And after it was *given* to them it went with them right down to the rivers and it went up with them from the rivers to the high country.'[63]

One clear message from this text, the haggadah and Targum comment, conveniently highlighted by de la Potterie, is that the living water is a gift of God. In the haggadah the source of the living water is identified as the law, which I have shown above (see 6.4.3.2 and n. 33) is associated with the idea of a well.

There does, then, seem to be a possible equivalence between 'the gift of God' and 'the living water' of 4.10.

The law is regularly regarded in Jewish sources as a gift of God to Israel.[64] The Prologue of John reflects this in 1.17, which states that the law was given by the mediation of Moses. But John immediately adds 'grace and truth came by Jesus Christ'. In my Chapter 4 on the Prologue I argued that the function of the law changes with the coming of Jesus Christ. Instead of the law being a way of life, it (especially the scriptures) now becomes a witness to Jesus (5.39). The gift of God is now Jesus (3.16) and the grace and truth that come through him, the incarnate Word (1.14).

In Jer. 2.13 and 17.13 God himself is called the source of the living waters. Other texts speak of living water that flows and gushes as a symbol of messianic blessings (Zech. 14.8; Ezek. 47.1; Joel 3.18). Later[65] I will

---

63. 'La haggadah fait ici deux identifications remarquables: d'une part, le puits, la source d'*eau vive*, est identifié à la Loi; d'autre part, on parle volontiers à ce propos du *don* divin de ce puits (= le don de la Loi), surtout en référence à *Mattana* (מתנה), interprété au sens de "don". Le Targum d' Onqelos sur ce passage des Nombres est particulièrment intéressant: 'De là leur fut *donné* le puits. C'est le puits dont le Seigner dit à Moïse: "Rassemble le peuple et je leur *donnerai* de l'eau"…et depuis le desert le puits leur fut *donné*. Et après qu'il leur fut *donné*, il descendait avec eux jusqu' aux rivières et il montait des rivières avex eux sur la hauteur.' I. de la Potterie, *La vérité dans Saint Jean*, II (AnBib, 24; Rome: Biblical Institute Press, 1977), pp. 685-86 (author's emphasis).

64. Sifre Deut. 305; Josephus, *Ant.* 4.318.

65. See 7.2.4.7. Cf. 7.2.8.

propose that Zech. 14.8 and Ezek. 47.1-12 are possible sources for the enigmatic scripture allusion in Jn 7.37b, 38 where Jesus says, 'If someone thirsts, let him come to me. And let him who believes in me, drink. Just as the scripture says, rivers of living water will flow from his belly.' What are the 'rivers of living water'? Verse 39 gives the answer: 'Now he (Jesus) said this about the Spirit, which believers in him were to receive; for as yet there was no Spirit, because Jesus was not yet glorified.' The 'rivers of living water' is the gift of the Spirit.[66]

By way of summary: Jn 4.10 speaks of 'the gift of God' and 'living waters'. Within John (1.17; 3.16) 'the gift of God' is the grace and truth in Jesus Christ; the 'living waters' is the gift of the Spirit (7.37-39). However, these two go together as the parallelism of 4.10 and Jewish exegesis of Num. 21.16-18 testify.[67]

Whether or not the reader of John would be able to work this out is an open question, but I think it would be fair to say that there would be enough clues in the Gospel up to this point for the reader to realize that Jesus himself would be the giver of the living water—a gift of God—and it could well have something to do with the Spirit and a new Torah ('the gift of God' [4.10] was a commonplace term for the Torah) accompanying the new age that had dawned with the coming of Jesus. After all Jesus has so far turned the water of Jewish purification into the eschatological wine of the new age (2.1-11) and has spoken of a new birth by water and the Spirit (3.1-21). Furthermore, the episode in the Temple (2.14-16) followed by the exchange with the Jews (2.18-20), together with the editorial comment (2.17, 21, 22), would herald the end of the Temple to the discerning reader. So Jesus' answer to the Samaritan woman's question about the right place of worship is perhaps not too surprising.[68]

---

66. The Old Testament provides examples where the outpouring of God's Spirit is imaged as a flow of water (Isa. 44.3; cf. 32.15; Joel 2.28; Ezek. 36.25-27).

67. Brown (*John*, I, p. 179) states there are sound reasons for seeing the living water as a symbol for both Jesus' revelation and the Holy Spirit: 'Johannine symbolism is often ambivalent, especially where two such closely related concepts as revelation and Spirit are involved. After all, the Spirit of truth is the agent who interprets Jesus' revelation or teaching to men (xiv 26, xvi.13).'

68. Coloe ('The Dwelling of God', pp. 139-142) has a further attractive argument for linking the Temple theme with the flow of living water. (a) She suggests Ezek. 47.1-12 is the primary background for the symbol of water. (b) She claims that behind Ezek. 47.1-12 'lies a Jewish tradition that the Temple rests upon the fissure above the great abyss which is the source of the creative waters in Genesis 2.8' (p. 139). (c) Jesus sits upon (ἐπί) not beside (παρά) the well. (d) She goes on to say: '...Jesus, the New

6.6.3 *The New Worship*

οὔτε ἐν τῷ ὄρει τούτῳ
οὔτε ἐν Ἱεροσολύμοις
ἀλλὰ ἐν πνεύματι καὶ ἀληθείᾳ

In keeping with the expectation aroused in 2.13-22, not only Gerizim, but Jerusalem, are finished as places of worship. The new 'place' of worship is ἐν πνεύματι καὶ ἀληθείᾳ. The earlier discussion of 'living water' and 'the gift of God' in 4.10 has prepared the reader for understanding what this new worship will entail. The 'spirit' will be the Holy Spirit. This is confirmed by 4.24a: πνεῦμα ὁ θεός.

6.6.4 *God Is Spirit*

Commentators generally agree that this statement is not a philosphical proposition but a message about God in his relation to people.[69] Two similar sentences about God in 1 John bear a similar sense: God is light (1.5) and God is love (4.8). It is also generally agreed that 'Spirit' here captures the Old Testament nuances of רוח as the life-giving creative power of God.[70] The decisive issue for John is summed up in the stated purpose of the Gospel: 'These things are written that you may come to believe that Jesus is the Messiah, the Son of God, and that through believing you might have *life* through his name' (20.31). The goal is life (ζωή), and it is God the Spirit who gives life (6.63). This life is traced back to being born of the πνεῦμα, the life-Giver (3.5). In some way this life is bound up with knowing—knowing the only true God and Jesus Christ whom he has sent (17.3)—that is, knowing the truth.

Given this statement—πνεῦμα ὁ θεός—we must interpret ἐν πνεύματι in the light of it. It cannot refer to any spirit, but only to the Spirit that is God.[71] While the primary emphasis of ἐν πνεύματι is on the life-giving

---

Temple sits upon the rock over the waters of Jacob's well. In this way the images of Temple and well, and their life giving waters, are juxtaposed' (p. 140).

While I believe Ezek. 47.1-12 lies behind Jn 7.37, 38 and 19.34 and possibly 21.11 and is therefore an evocative text for John, I do not believe Coloe has put forward sufficient evidence to make a persuasive case for Ezek. 47.1-12 being the primary background for the symbol of water in Jn 4.

69. For example, Brown, *John*, I, p. 172; E. Schweizer, Πνεῦμα, *TDNT*, VI, p. 439; Westcott, *St John*, I, p. 158.

70. See Schweizer, Πνεῦμα, *TDNT*, VI, pp. 439-40.

71. πνεῦμα in John almost always refers to the Holy Spirit, the Spirit of God. The exceptions are 3.8 where πνεῦμα probably means wind, but even here πνεῦμα could

and creative power of the worship, there is also a secondary significance intimated by 3.8 where πνεῦμα is the unconfined, uncontrolled and uncomprehended wind/Spirit[72] that blows where it wills. The presence of God who is πνεῦμα is not to be confined to Jerusalem or Gerizim. The true worshipper should therefore not be confined by spatial limitations.

On the other hand, for John the Spirit is the Spirit of Jesus. This emerges most clearly in the pronouncement about the Johannine Paraclete, who extends and communicates the presence of Jesus while Jesus is away. So in Jn 14.18 Jesus can say, 'I am coming to you,' and refer directly to the Spirit Paraclete in the previous verses (14.16, 17).[73] C.F.D. Moule succinctly comments on how Christology dominated pneumatology in early pneumatic experience, a comment that aptly sums up the entwinment of the Spirit and Jesus in John: 'The Spirit is Christified; Christ is Spiritualized.'[74] So given Johannine pneumatology it would be in order to

---

mean 'Holy Spirit' where John reflects on the tradition of Acts 2.2 in which the Spirit comes with the sound of a rushing violent wind; and the other is 19.30 where Jesus gave up his spirit when he died (i.e. breathed his last). But here again πνεῦμα could refer to the Holy Spirit with the understanding being that Jesus gave over his Spirit when he died.

72. On Jn 3.8 Barrett (*St John*, pp. 210-11) remarks, 'The allegory in this verse is… so close that it depends not upon a symbolical meaning attached to a word or group of words but upon different meanings properly belonging to one word. We may translate either: The wind blows where it will and you hear the sound of it, but you do not know whence it comes and whither it goes; or, The Spirit breathes where he will and you hear his voice, but you do not know, etc. Each of these translations taken by itself is wrong; the point of John's Greek is that it means both, and the double meaning cannot simply be reproduced in English. The Spirit, like the wind, is entirely beyond both the control and the comprehension of man. It breathes into this world from another.'

73. Cf., e.g., Brown (*John*, II, p. 1140), who gives proper weight to 14.26 where the Paraclete is said to be the Holy Spirit. Brown (*John*, II, pp. 1140-41) also concurs with the above when after his analysis he concludes that the Paraclete is *another Jesus*. He goes on to say: '[S]ince the Paraclete can only come when Jesus departs, the Paraclete is the presence of Jesus when Jesus is absent. Jesus' promises to dwell within his disciples are fulfilled in the Paraclete. It is no accident that the first passage containing Jesus' promise of the Paraclete (xiv 16-17) is immediately followed by the verse which says, "I am coming back to you."'

74. C.F.D. Moule, *Origins of Christology* (Cambridge: Cambridge University Press, 1978), p. 105. 'In both Acts and John the presence of the Spirit in a sense compensates for the absence (at least from sight) of the ascended Christ, and in both writers presence of the Spirit continues the work of Christ' (p. 104).

say that worshipping 'in Spirit' would be partially equivalent to worshipping 'in Jesus'.

6.6.5 *In Truth*

This brings us to worshipping 'in truth'. I have already mentioned how 'truth' in 1.17 has connotations of a new 'Torah' (revelation) that comes through Jesus Christ (see 4.5). This thought is reinforced in 8.31: 'If you continue [μείνητε] in my word you shall know the truth and the truth shall make you free.' There is also a striking passage in *2 Bar.*, which indicates the Jewish Torah could bring freedom:

> Zion has been taken away from us, and we have nothing now apart from the Mighty One and his Law. Therefore, if we direct and dispose of our hearts, we shall receive everything which we have lost again by many times… And these things which I have said earlier should be before your eyes always, since we are still in the spirit of the power of our liberty.

In spite of the destruction of Zion there is hope if Israel will hold onto the Law, for she is 'still in the spirit…of our liberty' (*2 Bar.* 85.3-4, 7).

This citation indicates that some looked for freedom in the Torah. However, Jesus says that if his disciples continue in *his word* then they shall know the truth and the truth shall make them free. Freedom is not found in the Jewish Torah, but in the truth of the word of Jesus. Jesus' word replaces the old Torah.

This links in with the earlier discussion of 'the gift of God' and 'living water' in 4.10 where it was quite possible for both of these terms to refer to the Torah, not the old Torah of Moses, but the new Torah, Jesus' word, which he will give. This new Torah is the truth.

Verse 17 of the prayer of Jesus (Jn 17) advances understanding of Johannine 'truth'. Jesus prays: 'Sanctify them (the disciples) in the truth; your word is truth.' The Father's word is truth. But what/who is the Father's Word? The Word-made-flesh, that is, Jesus himself (1.14). Jesus is the Truth (14.6). Everywhere in John the truth always comes back to Jesus, the one who is God's definitive revelation, the Father's Word, the new Torah, the one whose word brings cleansing (15.3) and whose words are Spirit and life (6.63b). Pilate asks, 'What is truth?' Duke comments, 'The dramatic irony of the question lies in our knowledge that the one to whom the question about truth is asked is himself the Truth (14.6).'[75]

---

75. Duke, *Irony in the Fourth Gospel*, p. 130.

6.6.6 *In Spirit and Truth*

Worship in Spirit and truth is pre-eminently worship centred on Jesus. The Spirit is the Spirit of Jesus, who testifies to Jesus and glorifies Jesus (15.26; 16.13-15). Jesus is the truth, the definitive revelation of God.

The question has been asked, If 'worship in Spirit and truth' is equivalent to 'worship in Jesus', why did John not write that? The answer I believe is that Jesus leaves his disciples and goes to the Father (16.28) and in his place he sends the Spirit/Paraclete (14.26; 15.26; 16.7). Further, although Jesus has departed, the truth he revealed has not. The witness to the truth has been written down by the true witness who knows that he tells the truth (19.35; 21.24). The testimony to the truth and the Spirit continues though Jesus has departed to the Father. Therefore Jesus says that the true worshippers must worship the Father ἐν πνεύματι καὶ ἀληθείᾳ.

It is also clear that the former places of worship are no longer the key to 'true worship'. The focus of true worship is now Jesus.[76] Jesus has supplanted[77] the holy places and all the rituals associated with them. This is especially true of the Temple in Jerusalem, but also of Mt Gerizim and the Samaritan worship associated with it.

Jesus is indeed the new locus for meeting with and worshipping the Father. That is the implication of 2.13-22. The body of Jesus is now the Temple (2.21), the Father's house.[78]

76. Hoskyns has said (*The Fourth Gospel*, p. 245): 'Inadequate worship is worship that rests purely upon the hope of some future action of God. True worship is directed towards the flesh and blood of Jesus because there ye shall see heaven open, and the angels of God ascending and descending upon the Son of Man (1.51).' This needs to be balanced by Jn 6.63: 'It is the Spirit that gives life; the flesh is useless.' The truth of the Word made flesh needs to be combined with the Spirit of truth.

77. Neyrey ('Jacob Allusions', pp. 421-25) suggests that as Jacob was the supplanter of Esau, so Jesus has now supplanted him as the supplanter of all Israel's institutions. Coloe ('The Dwelling of God') entitles her Chapter 5, which deals with Jn 4, 'The Supplanter'.

78. Gary Burge (*The Anointed Community: The Holy Spirit in the Johannine Community* [Grand Rapids: Eerdmans, 1987], pp. 195-96) reflects on the kind of worship we find in John (christocentric and generated by God's Spirit within believers themselves—although I question whether it is quite so individualistically orientated) and why there is this particular emphasis. Burge notes Stephen's revolutionary speech in Acts 7 'which spurned the cult of Judaism, rejected the sanctity of the temple, and aroused keen hostilities against the Hellenists'. He also notes that the resultant persecution and dispersion resulted in Philip's mission to Samaria. When the evidence of how John presents Jesus as the replacement of the Jewish Temple and its services is

6.7 *What the Woman Misses*

The true worship belongs to the eschatological/postresurrection perspective that informs so much of John. Jesus has said that the new era 'now is' and has told the Samaritan woman what the true worship is. However, while she understands that Jesus is speaking about the new age, she misses the critical 'and now is'. She says, 'I know that Messiah[79] is coming (he who is called Christ); *when he comes*, he will show us all things' (v. 25). She does not realize that the time has *already* come. She has not fully grasped what Jesus is saying and therein lies the irony of the situation. The reader knows who Jesus is (cf. 4.10 where the question of Jesus' identity is first posed to the woman), but the woman who is on the way to knowing has not quite reached the point of discovery. As Gail O'Day puts it:

> not only has the woman missed the significance of Jesus' words about the eschatological hour, she also does not realize that the person *of* whom she speaks is the person *with* whom she speaks. She does not recognize that the person who speaks with her has not only initiated the anticipated time of salvation but also represents it in his person.[80]

Jesus' answer to the woman is ἐγώ εἰμι, ὁ λαλῶν σοι. Brown says it is not impossible that ἐγώ εἰμι is used here in an absolute way for Jesus to speak of his divinity. Barrett is sure this is not the case. However, O'Day is confident[81] that Jesus is using these words to point towards his divine identity. She refers back to v. 10 where Jesus says to the Samaritan woman, 'If you knew who it is who is speaking to you...[ὁ λεγῶν σοι]' and finds in the words ἐγώ εἰμι, the answer. The one who speaks with her is none other than YHWH himself. With this declaration the ultimate revelation of the Samaria narrative has been made.

combined with what Jesus says in Jn 4.20-24 then, as Burge (p. 197) says, 'one far-reaching conclusion becomes evident: the Johannine community had combined a theology of worship much like Stephen's with mission in Samaria, and this combination of factors now forms the setting of our present passage'.

79. Barrett (*St John*, p. 239) remarks: 'The Samaritans seem to have expected the advent of a Messiah, though it does not appear that they used that word. The Coming One was called by them Taheb, He who returns, or, He who restores.'

80. O'Day, *Revelation*, p. 72.

81. O'Day, *Revelation*, p. 72. She goes on to demonstrate how this revelation of Jesus' identity has a powerful impact on the reader because of the way in which 'the ironic "double exposure" of Jesus' statements and the woman's responses, allow for reader participation in the revelatory process in a way that declarative statements could not'. See also Brown, *John*, I, p. 172, and Barrett, *St John*, p. 239.

It is this revelation that underlies the immediately preceding discourse about worship. In claiming to be ἐγώ εἰμι[82] Jesus says that he is worthy to be worshipped, something that actually happens in the Gospel of John in 9.38,[83] 20.28 and possibly 12.3.

I have suggested what the phrase 'worship in Spirit and truth' might mean in John. But are there any examples of worship in John where the worship is indeed 'in Spirit and truth'? I believe there are and I now turn to three possible examples: the worship of the man born blind in 9.38; the worship of Thomas in 20.28; and more tentatively the worship of Mary in 12.3.

6.8 *Worship in John*

6.8.1 *Worship in John 9*

Since J.L. Martyn's *History and Theology in the Fourth Gospel* in 1968 many commentators[84] have read John 9 in the light of his theory that the Gospel presents a 'two-level drama', in which events in the life of Jesus are in fact 'a witness to Jesus' powerful presence in actual events experienced by the Johannine church'.[85] Moyter summarizes the proposed representative figures in the Johannine community who are actors in this two-level drama:

> Jesus is a Jewish Christian preacher and healer, a leader in the Johannine Church; the Sanhedrin is the 'Gerousia', the local Jewish council in John's 'city'; the Pharisees are the 'Jamnia loyalists', keen to enforce the decrees emerging from the new rabbinic academy at (?nearby) Yavneh; 'the Jews' are the 'rank-and-file Jews' of the local synagogue; Nicodemus represents secret Jewish believers who have not separated themselves from the synagogue and joined the Johannine church; the lame man and the blind man are Jews who were healed by a Christian, using the power of Jesus— with different results in each case: one believed in Jesus, and was expelled from the synagogue, while the other turned traitor; and supremely the expulsion from the synagogue mentioned in 9.22; 12.42 and 16.2, actually

---

82. See below at 9.5.2-8 for a full discussion of this title. My conclusion there is that ἐγώ εἰμι is equivalent to YHWH and that this is the name given to Jesus by the Father (17.11, 12). If this is so then Jesus is worthy of worship.

83. Note, 9.37 echoes 4.26.

84. Motyer ('Persuasion', p. 19 n. 30) has a large list that includes Barrett, Brown, Schnackenburg, Pancaro, Painter, Ashton. Those of a contrary opinion include Carson, Woll, Hengel, Robinson.

85. Martyn, *History and Theology*, p. 30.

refers to the action taken against Jewish Christians by the Yavneh academy in the introduction of the *birkat ha-minim*, which Martyn dates early in the period between 85 and 115 CE.[86]

However, subsequent historical evidence has shown that the *birkat ha-minim* was not necessarily the decisive factor in the separation of Jews and Johannine Christians as Martyn suggests. The separation between Jews and Christians was complex, occurring differently and at different times in different places.[87] Further, as Motyer discerns, Martyn's allegorization lacks effective external controls and the treatment of the narratives as allegorizations lacks form-critical justification.

Motyer proposes[88] an alternative to Martyn's reading of John 9. He cites as a control allegory the vision of the bereaved woman, who turns out to be a symbolic representation of Jerusalem in *4 Ezra* 9.38–10.59. Thinking that she is just an ordinary woman grieving for her dead son, Ezra reprimands her: 'Zion, the mother of us all, is in deep grief and great humiliation... you are sorrowing for one son, but we, the whole world, for our mother' (10.7-8). He tries to encourage her: '[I]f you acknowledge the decree of God to be just, you will receive your son back in due time' (10.16). Zion's troubles are so much greater than her individual sorrow— and the LORD will comfort her (10.19-24). Then Ezra is staggered when the woman is suddenly transformed into a city—the future city Jerusalem yet to be built by God.

This allegory was composed in the face of the collapse of Jerusalem's Temple in 70 CE. Taking his cue from this allegory in *4 Ezra* Motyer suggests that there is an allegory in Jn 9 composed in response to the same catastrophe.[89] He maintains that the man born blind[90] represents Judaism in the wake of the catastrophes of 70 CE—the turmoil and recrimination reflected in the debate over sin (9.2; 9.34)—who sinned—this man or his parents that he was born blind? The Pharisees confirm the man in his sin and blindness—their answer is to pursue a harsh and false 'purity'. They exile him, make him ἀποσυνάγωγος.

---

86. Motyer, 'Persuasion', p. 20.

87. See above 1.4.1 n. 76, esp. Kimelman's comment where he says: '...the separation was the result of a long process dependent on local conditions...'

88. Motyer, 'Persuasion', p. 163.

89. Motyer, 'Persuasion', p. 164.

90. 'Blindness' is used as an image for Israel/Jerusalem in relation to the Babylonian exile: Isa. 42.16-20; 43.8; Lam. 4.13-14; 4.17; 5.17-18.

However, Jesus' answer is not to apportion blame, but to see God manifest his works in him, first by healing him, and then by restoring him to worship outside the synagogue. This is the answer Jesus offers to the catastrophe: as the light of the world he offers sight to those who are blind (8.12) and as the Good Shepherd restoration to those who have been cast out (exiled) (cf. Jn 10; Ezek. 34).

The worship[91] of Jn 9.38 is entirely outside and independent of any cultic centre. There is no mention of the Temple and the man (representing Judaism) is ἀποσυνάγωγος.[92] The focus of his worship is Jesus, the Son of Man (see 9.35-37 where Jesus reveals himself as the Son of Man). Jesus is the answer to the fall of the Temple. He himself has become the centre of worship. He is the new Temple and the healed, restored man worships him (9.38). This is indeed the worship of which Jn 4.23, 24 speaks, worship 'in Spirit and truth'. However, those

> who think they 'see' who have their own answers to the problem of Israel's fate—especially the Pharisees, the 'disciples of Moses' (9.28), who still judge sin by the halakah (9.16) and persecute the followers of Jesus (9.22b, 34)—must give up their 'sight', abandon their own answers and position, and listen to the voice of the Good Shepherd.[93]

If they do not, then they, not the man born blind, are mired in their sin (9.41). I find Motyer's reading helpful and relevant to my thesis because it addresses some of the issues of Judaism following the demise of the Temple in 70 CE. It also illustrates Jn 4.23, 24.

6.8.2 *Worship in John 20*
I come now to the appearances of the risen Jesus to the disciples in Jn 20.

91. Calvin L. Porter argues ('John 9.38, 39a: A Liturgical Addition to the Text', *NTS* 13 [1967], pp. 387-94) that the text under consideration is a liturgical addition. The relevant point for my case is that he views the text as liturgical—therefore worship is in view. He cites some textual evidence but the editors of *The Greek New Testament* (Aland *et al.*), tend to favour the retention of the text in spite of the fact that 'several witnesses lack the words ὁ δὲ ἔφη, Πιστεύω κύριε καὶ προσεκύνησεν αὐτῷ. καὶ εἶπεν ὁ Ἰησοῦς (p75, ℵ* W itb.(1) copach; Diatessaronv lacks verses 38 and 39 entirely).' Metzger (*Textural Commentary*, p. 229) argues in favour of the retention of the longer text because of 'the overwhelming preponderance of external attestation in favour of [it]'. I accept the text as it stands and see it having liturgical significance.

92. In 11.52 there is more than a hint that with the death of Jesus there will be a new kind of synagogue for those children of God who are scattered: καὶ τὰ τέκνα τοῦ θεοῦ τὰ διεσκορπισμένα <u>συναγάγῃ</u> εἰς ἕν.

93. Motyer, 'Persuasion', p. 163.

The first commences with 20.19: 'When it was evening on that day, the first day of the week [τῇ μιᾷ σαββάτων]...' and the timing of the second is a week later (καὶ μεθ ἡμέρας ὀκτώ). In both cases the day was Sunday, and, as in Rev. 1.10, this indicates this day was designated as the LORD's day.[94] Barrett[95] suggests therefore that these manifestations of the risen Jesus take place in the context of the worship of the community, since, in addition to the significance of the day, there are some liturgical pointers: a blessing is given (εἰρήνη ὑμῖν, vv. 21, 26); the Holy Spirit descends upon the worshippers and the word of absolution is pronounced (vv. 22, 23); Christ himself is present (19, 26), bearing the marks of his passion (vv. 20, 27); and he is confessed as LORD and God (v. 28). Lindars says much the same thing when he comments: '[T]he timing of the Thomas episode (v. 26) suggests the pattern of regular Sunday worship.' He concludes with the general comment on resurrection appearances in all four Gospels: '[T]hus the traditions of actual appearances are related to the Church's worshipping life, in which the meaning of the Resurrection is realized, and this connection has to some extent shaped the form of the traditions themselves.'[96] Brown, on the other hand, is more cautious. He says:

94. Brown (*John*, II, p. 1020) has a useful note on the Sunday. Referring approvingly to an article by H. Riesenfeld ('Sabbat et Jour du Seigneur', in A.J.B. Higgins [ed.], *New Testament Essays in Memory of T.W. Manson* [Manchester: Manchester University Press, 1959], pp. 210-17), he says: '[O]riginally, on Saturday evening after the close of the Sabbath (ca. 6 p.m.) and thus, by Jewish reckoning, on what was already Sunday, Jewish Christians who had observed the Sabbath now met at their homes to break the eucharistic bread (cf. Acts ii.46), as a prolongation of the Sabbath. Thus it would seem that the earliest Christian celebrations on "the first day of the week" were not on the day of Sunday but late in the evening on the vigil of Sunday.' But I suspect that, by the time John came to be written, the pattern of Rev. 1.10 had been established and the Sunday was in fact the LORD's day and the dawning of that day spoke of the dawn of the new age proclaimed by the empty tomb and the appearance of the risen LORD to Mary Magdalene. There is an allusion to the new dawn in the emphasis in 20.1 when we are told of Mary coming to the tomb 'early on the first day of the week, while it was still dark'. With Ignatius the connection of the dawning of the LORD's day with the resurrection is clear: 'If then they who walking in ancient customs came to a new hope, no longer living for the Sabbath, but for the Lord's Day, on which also our life sprang up through him and his death...' (*Ignatius to the Magnesians in The Apostolic Fathers*, I [trans. K. Lake; London: Heinemann; New York: Macmillan, 1912], p. 205).
　　95. Barrett, *St John*, p. 573.
　　96. Lindars, *John*, p. 509.

the fact that John mentions the first day of the week at the beginning of both scenes (vv. 1,19) in this chapter and that he places the appearance to Thomas a week later (v. 26) suggests that his presentation may have been influenced by the Christian custom of celebrating the Eucharist on 'the first day of the week' (Acts 20.7; cf. 1 Cor 16.2).[97]

Whether or not Jn 20 contains all the liturgical elements Barrett claims to be present, it seems reasonably clear that Thomas, with his climactic confession of faith is involved in an act of worship. His words are a clear ascription of divinity to Jesus: 'My LORD and my God.'[98] Like the previous act of worship there is no mention of a cultic space. In the first appearance to the disciples no name is given to the space. All we are told is that the doors where they were had been shut (καὶ τῶν θυρῶν κεκλεισμένων ὅπου ἦσαν). The location is vague. And we find the same a week later: 'Again his disciples were within and Thomas with them. And Jesus came and stood in their midst, the doors being shut...' (πάλιν ἦσαν ἔσω οἱ μαθηταὶ αὐτοῦ καὶ Θωμᾶς μετ' αὐτῶν. ἔρχεται ὁ Ἰησοῦς τῶν θυρῶν κεκλεισμένων καὶ ἔστη εἰς τὸν μέσον...). Why this vagueness? I believe John is making the point that the place of the gathering of the disciples is not important—it is the presence of the risen Jesus that is all important. In both cases the marks of Jesus' passion are apparent when he appears to his disciples. The focus is not on the place, but on Jesus, the truth. Furthermore we may assume that the Spirit, given in the first appearance (v. 22), has continued with the disciples and is present in the second appearance. Thomas' focus is on Jesus, the crucified and risen LORD—the truth; the Spirit is present to enable Thomas to see the truth of Jesus. His worship is indeed in Spirit and truth.

6.8.3 *Worship in John 12*

My third Johannine example of worship 'in Spirit and truth' is less clear. I believe that Mary's[99] action of anointing the feet of Jesus in 12.3 is an act of worship. On the surface the text does not seem to point in this direction because Jesus interprets Mary's action as an anointing for his burial

97. Brown, *John*, II, p. 1019.

98. There seems also to be a reference back to the words Jesus spoke to Mary Magdalene at the tomb that he asked her to convey to his 'brothers': 'I am ascending to my Father and your Father, to my God and your God.'

99. This Mary is the sister of Lazarus and Martha. She is no doubt to be distinguished from Μαρία ἡ Μαγδαληνή, who is mentioned in 19.25 and who is the first witness of the resurrection (20.1-2).

(12.7).[100] And the sentence at the end of v. 3: ἡ δὲ οἰκία ἐπληρώθη ἐκ τῆς ὀσμῆς τοῦ μύρου, is taken to mean that her action will be spoken of throughout the world (cf. Mt. 26.13, Mk 14.9) or it simply underlines the extravagance of her act.[101]

There is another possibility. Recent scholarship[102] has suggested that Isa. 6 lies behind most of Jn 12. The following table will highlight some points of correlation:

Isaiah 6	*John 12*
v. 1: King Uzziah died.	v. 33: King Jesus will die.
v. 1: The LORD is lifted up.[103]	v. 32: Jesus is lifted up.
v. 1: Isaiah sees God's glory.	v. 41: Isaiah sees Jesus' glory.
v. 3: The earth is full of God's glory.	v. 32: Jesus will draw all things (includeing the Greeks [v. 20]) to himself.
v. 5: Isaiah/people have unclean lips.	v. 5: Judas is a man of unclean lips.
v. 5: Isaiah sees the King	v. 13: Jesus is greeted as king of Israel.
v. 9, 10: Israel cannot see.	v. 40: Israel cannot see (approx. citation).
5.30: Light grows dark with clouds	vv. 35, 36: Walk in the light before darkness comes.

The remaining parallel that we wish to focus on is the Isaiah 6 parallel to verse Jn 12.3b:

v. 4: The house filled with smoke.	v. 3: The house was filled with the fragrance of the perfume.

If it is granted that Isaiah 6 is echoed in John 12 and that there is a parallel between Isa. 6.4 and Jn 12.3, then what does that parallel signify? The

---

100. There is much debate amongst the commentators about the phrase ἵνα εἰς τὴν ἡμέραν τοῦ ἐνταφιασμοῦ μου τηρήσῃ αὐτό. The best solution, I think, is Brown's (*John*, I, p. 449), where he takes ἵνα as purposive and translates: 'The purpose was that she might keep it for my embalming.' This does not mean that she actually used it to embalm Jesus' dead body; rather she used all of it in an unconsciously prophetic action of loving devotion while Jesus was still alive. That she anoints only the feet echoes Jesus' washing only the feet of the disciples in Jn 13.5-11.

101. Lindars, *John*, p. 417.

102. Hanson (*Prophetic*, p. 170) offers a few seed parallels. Also relevant is C.A. Evans, *To See and Not to Perceive: Isaiah 6.9-10 in Early Jewish and Christian Interpretation* (JSOTSup, 64; Sheffield: JSOT Press, 1989), pp. 129-136, and also Judith Lieu's article, 'Blindness in the Johannine Tradition', *NTS* 34 (1988), pp. 83-95 (84-86).

103. The verb in MT is נשא, and in the LXX the word is ὑψηλοῦ, a noun related to the verb ὑψόω that is used of Jesus in Jn 12.32.

'house' of Is 6.4 obviously refers to the Temple (cf. v. 1c where the hem of his robe filled the Temple). This could imply that the house in Jn 12.3 was functioning as a place of worship[104] (only because Jesus is there) where Mary's deed of devotion is not only a prophetic action for Jesus' burial but also an act of worship. The place where this act takes place is the home of friends. The place is not important because Mary is not concerned with the place but with the person of Jesus. She anoints his feet, soon to be pierced with nails.

This act of devotion is really worship. Mary's devotion is directed to Jesus. She may not know but Jesus is her LORD and her God (20.28). So this act focuses on the person and body of Jesus. There is no cultic place or practice in view, just the body of Mary's LORD. Jesus points out in 12.7 that her action anticipates his passion, death and burial.

Certainly Mary's worship is centred in Jesus, who is the truth, but what, of the Spirit? There is no specific mention of the Spirit in the story of the anointing, but the focus on Jesus is surely a sign of the Spirit (16.13-15). Indeed, Mary glorifies Jesus through her act of devotional worship. This, then, is possibly also worship in Spirit and truth.

6.9 *Summary and Conclusion*

How can one assess whether worship is in Spirit and truth? Certainly a special place is not necessary. The man born blind worships outside the synagogue; Thomas worships in an unspecified place; and Mary worships in a house in Bethany. What is essential is a focus on Jesus, who has made the Father known. He is the Word of the Father, the Truth. The Spirit is likewise necessary. Without the Spirit the believer cannot see who Jesus is and what God has done in him (3.5).[105]

In the eschatological era that Jesus has ushered in, he advocates worship of the Father in Spirit and truth. This is worship that focuses on Jesus himself. Jesus has revealed himself to the Samaritan woman as the gift of God (4.10), as a prophet (4.17-19) and finally as the presence of the self-revealing God of Israel (Exod. 3.14; Isa. 52.6; Jn 4.26). Such worship is no

---

104. Motyer ('Persuasion', p. 155) agrees. He says Jesus 'does not go to the Temple to "purify" himself like everyone else (11.55), but instead undergoes his own ceremony of consecration in the house at Bethany; the house at Bethany begins to look like a Temple' (12.3b).

105. I take this to be the meaning of 'cannot see the kingdom of God' in 3.5.—that is, cannot see who Jesus is and what God is doing/has done in him.

longer tied to a physical cultic site, such as Gerazim or Jerusalem.

We have seen that the image of the living water can be read as representing both the Spirit and the new Torah. The Spirit is the Spirit of Jesus who glorifies Jesus (16.14) and testifies on his behalf (15.26). The new Torah is the revelatory Word (1.1, 17) who has become flesh and dwelt among us (1.14). This Word is truth (17.17; 14.6). Worship in Spirit and truth is worship centred in Jesus. In this sense Jesus replaces the Temple. Cultic place is superfluous.

Chapter 7

THE TEMPLE FESTIVALS

Festivals have a prominent place in the Gospel of John and all these festivals centre on Jerusalem and the Temple in particular. Since this study is concerned with the Temple theme in John, it is important to examine the way these festivals function in the Gospel as rituals of the Temple. Therefore, in this chapter I will be look at the following Temple festivals: the Passover, Tabernacles, Dedication and the Sabbath. I am aware that the Sabbath may not normally be considered a Temple festival, but I will argue that it should be included. I will propose that Jesus fulfils and replaces each of these four festivals.

Especially prominent in John is the Passover, first mentioned in the middle of John 2, where it forms the context of the Temple incident in 2.13-22. The second mention is in 6.4 (ἦν δὲ ἐγγὺς τὸ πάσχα, ἡ ἑορτὴ τῶν Ἰουδαίων) when Jesus is in Galilee up the mountain with his disciples. It is from this setting that Jesus multiplies the five loaves and two fish to feed five thousand. Then follows Jesus' walking on the Sea of Tiberias followed in turn by his synagogue sermon (6.59) in which he speaks of offering his flesh and blood for the life of the world (6.51-57). The third occurrence of 'passover' is 11.55 and 12.1 when Jesus is in the home of Lazarus and Mary anoints his feet with 'a pound of costly perfume made of pure nard'. This was 'six days before the Passover'. Then in 13.1, just before we are told the story of Jesus' washing the disciples' feet, there is a further reference to the same Passover adumbrated in 12.1: 'Now before the festival of the Passover, Jesus knew that his hour had come...' This same Passover is again mentioned in 18.28: the Jews did not 'enter the praetorium, so as to avoid ritual defilement and to be able to eat the Passover'. There is a further reference to the Passover in 18.39, this time by Pilate when he invokes a Passover custom to release a prisoner and asks if the Jews want him to release for them 'the King of the Jews'. The final occurrence of this word is in 19.14 when Pilate condemns Jesus to death:

'Now it was the day of the Preparation for the Passover; and it was about noon.'

In John there are three Passover festivals (2.13; 6.3; 19.14), but the third is obviously the most important as the Passover theme moves towards a climax with the death of Jesus.

The second festival named in John is the Festival of Tabernacles, first mentioned in 7.2 as ἡ ἑορτὴ τῶν Ἰουδαίων ἡ σκηνοπηγία. This festival forms the background to John 7 and 8 and very likely John 9 and 10.1-21.

The third festival John names is the festival of Dedication (ἐγκαίνια) in 10.22. This festival provides the context for the debate between Jesus and the Jews in 10.24-38.

There remains only one other mention of a festival and this is in 5.1. It is simply called a festival of the Jews (ἑορτὴ τῶν Ἰουδαίων). No name is given. It is perhaps mentioned to explain why Jesus went up to Jerusalem.

Commentators have wondered what this unnamed feast was. Attention has been drawn to a variant reading where it is called '*the* feast of the Jews' (ἡ ἑορτὴ…), which suggests that it was a prominent feast like Passover or Tabernacles, but the support for the addition of the definite article is not strong and the editors of the Greek New Testament have given the anarthous reading an 'A' rating, making it fairly solid.[1]

Aileen Guilding[2] has opted for *Rosh ha-Shanah* (Feast of the New Year) otherwise known as the Feast of the Trumpets. Her case seems to involve these steps: (a) the sick lay in the open air under the shelter of porches (5.2, 3), so it must have been summer or early autumn (Tammuz—Tishri); (b) within those months the feast could either be Pentecost or Rosh ha-Shanah on the first of Tishri; (c) to fit everything in satisfactorily this feast must come after the second Passover mentioned in 6.4; therefore chs. 5 and 6 must be inverted; (d) post-New Testament sources allow Guilding to pinpoint the synagogue scripture readings for the second year of the Johannine Jesus' ministry; (e) she discovers that the readings for Tishri the first (festival of the New Year) for that particular year have as themes, resurrection, judgment and witness—the very themes which characterize Jn 5.

There are a number of weaknesses in this argument: (a) the assumption that the season of the year was a decisive factor in the presence of the sick

----

1. Aland *et al.*, *The Greek New Testament*, p. 337.

2. A. Guilding, *The Fourth Gospel and Jewish Worship: A Study of the Relation of St John's Gospel to the Ancient Jewish Lectionary System* (Oxford: Clarendon Press, 1960), pp. 70-92.

in the porch is unfounded—people can brave adverse weather conditions if they can see the possibility of being healed; (b) changing the order of chs. 5 and 6 is extreme surgery even though it has been suggested before in the interests of bringing chs. 5 and 7 closer together;[3] (c) the late sources for determining the Jewish lectionary means there is a question mark over whether these were current when John was written; she assumes the events took place in 30–33 CE, which is also dubious.

So Guilding establishes her link between the lectionary and ch. 5 at the cost of altering the narrative order in John and making a foundational assumption about the sort of weather sick people can tolerate.

Other suggestions about this unnamed feast depend, as Carson says, 'on too many speculative connections to be considered plausible'.[4] Consequently, I do not think it is possible to identify the unnamed feast with any reasonable degree of certainty. But the anonymity may itself be deliberate. John is usually specific in naming places, people and also festivals. In referring to no particular feast he may be referring to all feasts of the Jews.[5] I will return to this question when I make some concluding remarks on the Festivals.

7.1 *The Passover*

In my third chapter dealing with Jn 2.13-22 I noted how the Passover Festival is in view in the 2.17 allusion to Ps. 69.9, especially in the use of the word 'consume' (see 3.6.5). I also made reference to John the Baptist's title for Jesus in 1.29, 35, the Lamb of God. I now consider this in more detail.

---

3. Bultmann (*John*, p. 209) is a strong advocate for reversing the order of chs. 5 and 6 for a number of reasons, including bringing chs. 5 and 7 close together.

4. Carson, *John*, p. 240. Carson is speaking specifically against the proposal that the unnamed feast is Purim, but what he says applies to every suggestion that tries to tie it down to a particular feast.

5. W.W. Watty ('The Significance of Anonymity in the Fourth Gospel', *ExpTim* 90 [1979], pp. 209-12) draws attention to the precision in John and concludes that anonymity, where it occurs, is often deliberately serving the Johannine purpose. However, Margaret Pamment ('The Fourth Gospel's Beloved Disciple', *ExpTim* 94 [1983], pp. 363-67) suggests 'the unnamed groups and individuals serve a representative function'. This may also be true for unnamed festivals. See also David Beck, 'The Narrative Function of Anonymity in Fourth Gospel Characterization', *Semeia* 63 (1993), pp. 143-55.

7.1.1 *The Lamb of God*

The question arises as to what kind of lamb John the Baptist may be referring. I believe a good case can be made for John presenting Jesus as the Passover Lamb.

7.1.1.1 *Passover Pivotal and Pervasive.* The Passover Feast is evidently pivotal in the Gospel. As I noted, three Passover feasts are mentioned (2.13; 6.4; 13.1). The context of the first feast is the Temple episode where Jesus drives out the traders and sacrificial animals. The setting of the second is the feeding of the five thousand where Jesus speaks of offering his flesh and blood for the life of the world (6.53-58). And the situation of the third is the death of Jesus. John's narrative of the death of Jesus contains a number of allusions, which, in my view, provide a strong case that Jesus is the Passover Lamb. First, the Passover is in the minds of the disciples as Judas is released from fellowship (13.27, 28). They thought Jesus was telling him, 'Buy what we need for the festival.'[6] Secondly, the Passover custom is invoked by Pilate (18.39, 40). The people are offered Jesus as the Son of the Father or Barabbas (meaning 'son of the father'). They reject Jesus and take the bandit. Thirdly Jesus dies at Golgotha[7] on the day of Preparation for the Passover[8] (19.14) at the sixth hour, the very

---

6.   There is Johannine irony here. Far from making provision for the festal joy of the disciples Judas was going out to betray (sell!—if Johnnine readers may assume the Synoptic tradition) Jesus as the Passover Lamb for the festival.

7.   Jesus is crucified at Golgotha at the same time as the Passover Lambs are slaughtered in the Temple. Is this John's way of saying that the efficacy of the Temple is finished? Jesus the true Passover Lamb is not slaughtered in the Temple, but at the place called 'The Skull'.

8.   Carson (*John*, pp. 603, 604; cf. also B.D. Smith, 'The Chronology of the Last Supper', *WTJ* 53 [1991], pp. 29-45, who presents the same argument) argues that παρασκευὴ τοῦ πάσχα does not refer to the day before the Passover, but to the day of Preparation for the Sabbath, namely, the Friday. He believes παρασκευή used in a time context invariably refers to the Friday, the day of Preparation for the Sabbath. I deliberately capitalize the 'P' because Carson seems to invest the word with that sort of special significance, that is, παρασκευή = Friday. The NRSV also does this in 19.31, 42 where the context clearly indicates that παρασκευή refers to the Preparation of the Sabbath (cf. Josephus, *Ant.* 16.163; *Didache* 8.1; *Martyrdom of Polycarp* 7.1). Carson further argues that τοῦ πάσχα can refer to (a) the Passover meal; (b) the day of the Passover meal; and (c) the entire Passover week. He cites *Ant.* 14.21; 17.213; *War* 2.10; Lk. 22.1 by way of justification. He chooses the third meaning and concludes that 'παρασκευή τοῦ πάσχα probably means "Friday of Passover week" (i.e. Passover day plus the immediately ensuing Feast of Unleavened Bread)'. Carson criticizes

hour when the Paschal lambs began to be slaughtered in the Temple (19.14).[9] Fourthly, in 19.29 John mentions that Jesus was offered a sponge filled with sour wine placed on hyssop. Hyssop is closely associated with the Passover. In Exod. 12.22, Moses instructs the elders of Israel to take a bunch of hyssop, dip it in the blood of the slaughtered Paschal lamb and touch it to the lintel of the doorposts. Hyssop (19.29) was part of the annual Paschal liturgy and was used to carry the blood of the Paschal lamb. I believe that John's reference to hyssop is a deliberate signal to the reader—here is Jesus, the Passover Lamb![10] Finally there is the scripture

Barrett for not offering any evidence of a single instance where παρασκευή refers to the day before any feast day other than the Sabbath, but neither does he offer any instance where παρασκευή τοῦ πάσχα refers to the Friday of Passover week. Preparation (ἑτοιμάζειν) was involved for the Passover meal (Mt. 26.17; Mk 14.12; Lk. 22.8). Why should John not use παρασκευή to indicate the same sort of preparation suggested by the Synoptics? Perhaps he deliberately chose this word rather than ἑτοιμασία because he wanted to evoke the Sabbath Preparation Day (cf. 19.31). R.T. France ('Chronological Aspects of "Gospel Harmony"', *Vox Evangelica* 16 [1986], pp. 33-59) remarks, 'A glance at the majority of commentators on these verses [Jn 13.1; 18.28; 19.14] will soon show that these reinterpretations [of Carson and others], however cautiously presented, cannot claim to offer a natural understanding of the text, but are clearly motivated by the desire to harmonize.' Carson and others seem to take the 'synoptic chronology' as the standard and adjust the 'Johannine chronology' to fit. However France (p. 48) offers external evidence that favours a 'Johannine' rather than a 'synoptic' chronology.

9.   The discussion in Brown (*John*, II, pp. 882-83) is helpful and the concluding section worth quoting in full: 'The hour of noon on the Preparation Day for the Passover was the hour for beginning the slaughter of the Paschal lambs. The ancient law of Exod. xii 6 required that the Paschal lamb be kept alive until the 14th Nisan and then slaughtered in the evening (literally, "between the two evenings", a phrase sometimes interpreted as meaning between sunset and darkness). By Jesus' time the slaughtering was no longer done at home by the heads of families but in the temple precincts by the priests. A great number of lambs had to be slaughtered for the more than 100,000 Passover participants in Jerusalem, and so the slaughtering could no longer be done in the evening, in the technical sense of after sunset. By casuistry "evening" was interpreted to begin at noon when the sun began to decline, and thus the priests had the whole afternoon of the 14th to accomplish their task.'

10.   Schuchard (*Scripture within Scripture*, p. 137, n. 22) draws attention to the Johannine irony in reference to the hyssop that bears the 'bitter wine of death' (cf. mention of the cup in 18.11). Jesus takes the sour wine of death and suffering and gives us his blood, the 'good wine' of the eschaton (2.10). This eschatological wine of life comes from Jesus' side. Cf. 19.34 where the blood and the water come from Jesus' side—Jesus the new Temple. I will have more to say about this in 7.2.5.1.

citation in 19.36, 'These things occurred so that the scripture might be fulfilled, "None of his bones shall be broken."' The most likely source for this quotation is Exod. 12.10 or 12.46 or both,[11] where the requirements for the Passover Lamb are being established. No bones shall be broken.[12] Now why draw attention to this? Because John wants us to see that Jesus is the Passover Lamb.[13] There have also been other suggestions in support of Jesus being the Passover Lamb.[14]

7.1.1.2 *Passover Sacrifice.* However, scholars have argued that the slaughtering of the Paschal lambs had no sacrificial significance in the Old

11. Schuchard, *Scripture within Scripture*, p. 140. There is no reference to not breaking bones in Exod. 12.10 in the MT, but there is mention in the LXX, and with respect to Exod. 12.46 it is present in both MT and LXX. Why does John cite this Old Testament phrase? Schuchard's conclusion is to the point: 'John proposes with this citation to establish that Jesus died as the true Paschal Lamb in fulfilment of what was prophetically anticipated by the Old Testament.' Schuchard also allows a reference to Ps. 33.21 (LXX), but this is not germane to my argument.

12. Bruce Longenecker ('The Unbroken Messiah: A Johannine Feature and its Social Functions', *NTS* 41.3 [1995], pp. 428-41) suggests that lack of mention of Jesus' breaking the bread in the feeding miracle is significant. He suggests this ties in with the unbroken Messiah on the cross (the unbroken Paschal Lamb).

13. Something of the irony of the Jew's concern for Sabbath purity (19.31) is apparent in this remark by Brown: 'They fear that ritual impurity will prevent their eating the Passover Lamb, but unwittingly they are delivering up to death him who is the Lamb of God (1.29) and thus are making possible the true Passover' (Brown, *John*, II, p. 866). Duke (*Irony*, p. 135) highlights further irony arising out of a Passover context when he comments on the words in 19.15c: 'We [the Jews] have no king but Caesar.' He says: 'It is a sacrilege no Jew could utter without forfeit of faith. Israel has but one King (Judg. 8.3; 1 Sam. 8.7; Isa. 26.13). In the Passover Haggadah soon to be rehearsed, the concluding hymn of the Greater Hallel, the *Nišmah*, would read:

> "From everlasting to everlasting thou art God;
> Beside thee we have no king, redeemer, or saviour,
> No liberator, deliverer, provider.
> None who takes pity in every time of distress or trouble.
> We have no king but thee."'

Duke has also shown the Passover context is crucial because of its covenantal overtones. Passover is a celebration of God's faithfulness to his covenant with Israel. 'How terribly ironic that the chief priests will abandon Israel's faith at the very moment when they are to begin preparations for the celebration of God's faithfulness to them!' (Duke, *Irony*, p. 135).

14. For example, J.M. Ford, '"Mingled Blood" from the Side of Christ (John xix.34)', *NTS* 15 (1969), pp. 337-38.

Testament. This poses a problem because John the Baptist speaks of Jesus in 1.29 as 'the lamb of God that takes away the sin of the world'. This lamb that John is talking about evidently has sacrificial efficacy. Some scholars have therefore concluded that whatever John the Baptist means by 'lamb of God' he cannot mean the Passover Lamb.

This is not an insurmountable problem. Pancaro[15] makes several points in favour of the Passover having sacrificial significance and thus overcomes the objection apparently posed by the words 'that takes away the sin of the world'. First, he draws attention to Deut. 16.1-5 where both the killing and the eating of the Paschal lamb must take place at the sanctuary thus implying some sacrificial significance. Then he mentions how Exod. 13.11-16 considers the animal a substitution for the firstborn of Israel in the Passover event. The firstborn are not only redeemed by the slaughter of the lamb and the smearing of the blood over the lintel and posts of the door, but spared death by the angel of destruction, thus implying the lamb is sacrificial. Finally, he points out that the early Christian community had associated Jesus' death with the Paschal liturgy, especially in the celebration of the Eucharist (cf. 1 Cor. 5.7, 8 and see also 1 Pet. 1.18-19). So by the time the Gospel of John was written Paschal themes associated with the death of Jesus were possibly part of the liturgical currency of even the widely diverse early church communities.

This brief survey has highlighted the Passover theme in John. It is clearly pervasive and is also pivotal. Jesus, it seems, is deliberately presented as the Passover Lamb who takes away the sins of the world (1.29).

However, I believe Jn 6 has a dense thicket of Passover motifs and I now want to explore this chapter in relation to the Passover theme.

7.1.2 *Links with Jewish Passover Haggadah in John 6?*
Bertil Gärtner wrote a book entitled *John 6 and the Jewish Passover* in 1959[16] and suggested a number of parallels between Jn 6 and the Jewish

---

15. Pancaro, *Law*, p. 348. Cf. also J. Terence Forestell (*The Word of the Cross* [AnBib, 57; Rome: Biblical Institute Press, 1974], pp. 157-66), who sees Jn 1.29 as a brilliant synthesis of Old Testament imagery, including the imagery of the paschal lamb and the patient lamb of Isa. 53.7. J. D'Souza (*The Lamb of God in the Johannine Writings* [Allahabad: St Paul Publications, 1968], p. 172) has a similar conclusion, but adds a third possibility: 'So, in the mind of the Evangelist, the Lamb is the Messianic King of Israel, the Suffering Servant, and the Paschal Lamb.' My focus is on the Lamb of God as the Paschal Lamb.

16. Bertil Gärtner, *John 6 and the Jewish Passover* (ConNT, 17; Copenhagen:

Passover Haggadah. The Jewish Passover Haggadah (JPH) has a characteristic tripartite form: event–question–interpretation.[17] The parallel with John 6 may be noted:

JPH	John 6
Form and content of meal	The miraculous feeding (6.1-14)
Questions by four sons	Four questions by the Jews (6.26-52)
Interpretation by father	Interpretation by Jesus (6.26-52)

The questions by the four sons in the JPH are as follows:

(a) חכמה   questions concerning points of law;
(b) הגדה   questions concerning apparently contradictory passages in the scriptures;
(c) ברות   questions which seek to ridicule some interpretation;
(d) דרך ארץ   questions concerning a moral and successful life.

7.1.2.1 *Some Correspondences.* The Jews in John 6 ask Jesus four questions that roughly parallel those that the four sons ask in the Jewish Passover Haggadah:[18]

(1)   'What must we do, to be doing the work of God?' (6.28). This is the question in JPH that the wise (חכמה) son asks concerning guidance (תורה) for life. Given that תורה in its general sense can mean 'guidance', this question is a reasonable fit.

(2)   'What sign are you going to give us then, so that we may see it and believe you? What work are you performing? Our ancestors ate manna in the wilderness; as it is written, "He gave them bread from heaven to eat"' (6.30, 31). These are the הגדה questions concerning contradictory passages of scripture. The perceived contradiction the Jews are asking about is between the authority of Jesus and the authority of Moses, through whom the manna came to their fathers. By way of answer Jesus points away from Moses to 'my Father', who gave the bread from heaven(v. 32). This fits reasonably well, but the point of conflict is not over interpretations of texts but of people (Moses and Jesus).

Lund, 1959), pp. 26-29. Edward Kilmartin ('Liturgical Influence on John 6', *CBQ* 22 [1960], pp. 183-91) also outlines Gärtner's analysis.

17. Gärtner, *John 6*, p. 26. This is roughly what we find in Exod. 12. Verses 21-25 describe the event; v. 26 has the children asking the question; v. 27 has the interpretation.

18. Gärtner, *John 6*, pp. 26, 27.

(3)   'Is not this Jesus, the son of Joseph, whose father and mother we know? How can he now say, "I have come down from heaven?"' (6.42). This is the ברות question, which ridicules Jesus' claim to have come down from heaven (v. 38) by pointing to his earthly ancestry. This is probably the best fit of all four questions.

(4)   'How can this man give us his flesh to eat?' (6.52) This fourth question is the דרך ארץ question 'concerning a moral and successful life'. This question does not fit that category.

These four questions[19] in John 6 do not fit neatly into the JPH mould, but there are some correspondences.

7.1.2.2 *Ill-Fitting Correspondences*
Another point that the JPH and John 6 have in common is words of the father before the four questions were asked in the JPH. The father raised the seder dish and said, 'This is the bread of oppression, which our fathers ate in the land of Egypt. Everyone who hungers may come and eat; everyone who is needy may come and celebrate the Passover Feast...'[20] This bears some similarity to the words of Jesus in 6.35: 'I am the bread of life. Whoever comes to me shall not hunger, and whoever believes in me shall never thirst.' But again it is ill fitting—'bread of oppression' is hardly parallel to 'bread of life'. It could, however, qualify as antithetic parallelism.

Finally, the ἐγώ εἰμι is found in the JPH. In the description of Israel's deliverance from Egypt, it is used to emphasize the activity of God both in the events and signs described in Exod. 12:

> For I will pass through the land of Egypt, I and no angel; and I will smite all the firstborn, I and no seraph; and over all the gods of Egypt, I will execute judgement, I and no messenger; I, the LORD, I am and no other [אני יהוה אני הוא ולא אחר]...[21]

The ἐγώ εἰμι is found four times in Jn 6.26-58, however, never in an absolute form, always with a predicate.

What conclusions can be drawn from this survey of the possibility of finding a JPH form in Jn 6.26-58?

It is possible to see some parallels between JPH and John 6 but they are

---

19. There are two other questions in 6.25-52 that this schema does not accommodate, namely, 'Rabbi, when did you come here?' (v. 25) and 'Sir, give us this bread always' (v. 34), a request that functions like a question.

20. Gärtner, *John 6*, p. 28.

21. Gärtner, *John 6*, p. 29.

rather weak and certainly not firm enough[22] to make a conclusive case for direct dependence of John 6 on JPH. There are perhaps traces of the JPH in John 6, suggesting that there could have been some form of JPH in the background that has been worked over and moulded into the narrative dialogue of Jesus with the Jews. My conclusion is that there is a general allusion to JPH rather than specific correspondences. This conclusion suggests that there is Passover imagery in John 6, but it remains to be seen how this emerges in the text.

7.1.3 *Intertextuality with Exodus*

In addition to the vague JPH allusion mentioned above, I believe a case can be made for finding Passover motifs in John 6 through discovering Old Testament (particularly Exodus tradition) textual allusions in John 6 and using the work of Peder Borgen as well as a special focus on Jn 6.63.

The intertextual allusions between John 6 and the Exodus are as follows:

Exodus	*John 6*
Moses on Mt Sinai.	Jesus on the mountain (v. 3).
The Passover (Exod. 12).	The Passover (v. 4).
'Where can I get meat for all these people?' (Num. 11.13).	'Where shall we buy bread for these people to eat?' (v. 5).
'Would they have enough if all the fish in the sea were caught for them?' (Num. 11.22).	The two small fish (v. 9).
The crossing of the Sea of Reeds.	Jesus crosses the sea (v. 16).[23]
'Now the people grumbled about their hardships' (Num. 11.1).	The Jews (v. 43) and the disciples (v. 61) grumble.
'Give us flesh [בָשָׂר, κρέα] to eat' (Num. 11.13).	'This bread is my flesh' (v. 51).
'I am going to rain bread from heaven for you' (Exod. 16.4).[24]	As it is written, 'he gave them bread from heaven to eat' (v. 31).

22. In fact Brown (*John*, I, p. 267) says they are 'quite artificial and strained'.

23. Brown asks (*John*, I, p. 255), 'Is there also a Passover symbolism in the walking on the sea by way of a reference to the crossing of the Reed Sea at the time of the Exodus? (This would fit the miracle into the general context of ch. vi). The Passover *Haggadah*...as it is preserved for us from a slightly later period, closely associates the crossing of the sea and the gift of the manna.' Cf. 7.1.6 n. 49.

24. Brown (*John*, I, p. 255) thinks Jn 6.31 recalls Ps. 78.24, the first half of which is very close to Exod. 16.4. In the LXX Exod. 16.4 has ὕω ὑμῖν ἄρτους ἐκ τοῦ οὐρανοῦ, whereas Ps. 78.24 has ἔβρεξεν αὐτοῖς μάννα φαγεῖν, καὶ ἄρτον οὐρανοῦ ἔδωκεν αὐτοῖς. Both texts clearly state that God gave bread from heaven.

In the light of the above table there are a number of allusions to the Exodus traditions of Exodus and Numbers. In particular it seems that the Passover tradition is very much in view. There is mention of the Passover in 6.4 ('the Passover, the festival of the Jews, was near').

I have argued above (see 7.1.1.2 and n. 15) that Jesus is the Passover Lamb (cf. esp. 1.29, 36 and 19.14 and the other many paschal 'hints' in the narrative). It should not be surprising then to find the Passover present in John 6 with its many textual allusions back into the Exodus traditions in Numbers and Exodus.

7.1.4 *A Homiletic Pattern in John 6.31-58*
I now examine the text of John 6 to see how the Exodus allusions are made and in particular how the Passover comes to the fore.

Peder Borgen has given some helpful insights about the composition of the discourse that follows the episode of Jesus walking on water and I will use these as a way into the paschal significance of the discourse as a whole, namely 6.31-58. I will argue against those who maintain that 6.51-58 is an addition.

Borgen[25] has found a homiletic pattern in Philo and Palestinian midrashim and he has distilled some features of Jewish preaching in Jesus' time.

The pattern is to begin with a citation of Scripture (usually from the Pentateuch), which is sometimes paraphrased. A homily would then follow in which the text was scrutinized word for word. This would presuppose not only the cited/paraphrased verse, but also the verse in its immediate context. Often this comment would be accompanied by a subordinate quotation from the prophets, before the homily was concluded with the statement with which it began.

It is possible that Jesus follows this pattern in 6.31-58. The beginning of

---

25. Borgen Peder, *Bread from Heaven* (NovTSup, 10; Leiden: E.J. Brill, 1965), pp. 28-86. U. Schnelle (*Antidocetic*, p. 196 nn. 128, 129) opposes Borgen's hypothesis. On the other hand, Barrett (*St John*, p. 284), who follows Borgen says: 'The argument on the whole is convincing, but it must be stated in such a way as to make due allowance for other influences upon John's method.' Also Moloney (*Signs and Shadows*, p. 31), remarks, 'The epoch-making study of P. Borgen convinces me that the so-called discourse is a homiletic midrash on a text provided by Jesus' interlocutors in v. 31: "He gave them bread from heaven to eat."' Borgen has responded to criticisms of his hypothesis in his essay, 'John 6: Tradition, Interpretation and Composition', in M.C. de Boer (ed.), *From Jesus to John: Essays on Jesus and New Testament Christology in Honour of Marinus de Jonge* (JSNTSup, 84; Sheffield: JSOT Press, 1993), pp. 279-85.

the sermon follows an exchange between Jesus and the Jews in which they ask, 'What sign are you going to give us then, so that we may *see it and believe you*' (v. 30). The text of the homily follows.

7.1.4.1 *The Pentateuchal Text and its Interpretation.* The text is, 'He gave them bread from heaven to eat.' This may be from the Pentateuch,[26] Exod. 16.4 (paraphrased), although it has elements of Exod. 16.15. This would not be surprising because the passage is saturated with Exodus motifs as mentioned above.

The text is scrutinized: 'He' becomes 'my Father' and 'gave' becomes 'gives' and the 'bread' becomes 'real [ἀληθινόν] bread'. It sounds as though the Father is giving this real bread to the Jews at this very moment. Jesus then goes on to explain more about the real bread. It is that which/he who[27] comes down from heaven and gives life to the world. Then in v. 35 Jesus makes it quite clear that he is the bread of life. Verse 36 echoes v. 29 where the work of God is to believe in God's Envoy. But now Jesus underlines the fact that his listeners have *seen him and still do not believe* (cf. v. 30 where we learn Jesus himself is the sign/work). Believing in Jesus as God's Envoy is crucial to this discourse. It receives heavy emphasis throughout (vv. 29, 30, 36, 40, 47; cf. also vv. 64, 65). On the other hand, it is the Father's work (cf. v. 29 where faith is God's work)[28] to give believers to Jesus and Jesus' responsibility to give them life and keep them in life.

The Jews then begin to complain because they think they know Jesus' origin and he claims to have come from heaven. He reiterates what he has said before: 'No-one can come to me unless drawn by the Father who sent me; and I will raise that person up on the last day.'

7.1.4.2 *The Prophetic Text and its Interpretation.* Then, in v. 45, comes the supplementary quotation from the prophets, which Brown calls 'a free citation of Isa. liv. 13': וכל בניך למודי יהוה (All your sons shall be taught

---

26. Barrett (*St John*, p. 289): 'The source of this quotation is uncertain.' He suggests Neh. 9.15; Ps. 78.24; Exod. 16.15. He further says, 'John may well have combined all these passages.'

27. 'ὁ' could be impersonal (bread) or personal (Jesus). Possibly John intends both.

28. The Jews ask, 'What does God require us to do?' Jesus' answer is capable of double meaning: (1) God requires you to believe on his Envoy; (2) God's work is to generate faith in you towards his Envoy.

by the LORD).[29] This refers to the teaching of Jesus. The words of Jesus are the words of the Father. Jesus is the means by which the people are taught about God. No one has seen the Father except the Son (6.46), the Word of God (cf. 1.18)[30] who communicates the words of God to the children of God. And by hearing Jesus they are drawn to Jesus (v. 45).

In keeping with the midrashic pattern that Borgen has discerned, the last verses of this section of the homily (vv. 47-51b) repeat the message of the Pentateuchal text. Jesus reminds the Jews that their fathers who ate the manna in the wilderness are dead. The 'new' bread that comes down from heaven will give eternal life, so that those who eat of it will not die, but live forever. Jesus is this bread of life (v. 48) and people eat this bread by believing (the persistent theme of 6.31-58) on Jesus (v. 47).

The message of this homily is that the manna in the wilderness will not suffice. Those who ate of it in the wilderness are dead. Jesus is the living bread come down from heaven who will satisfy the hungry and thirsty forever. He will give eternal life.

7.1.4.3 *The Scandal Teaching: Is it Part of the Discourse?*
The end of v. 51 marks a new development. Jesus says: '[T]he bread that I will give for the life of the world is my flesh.' Brown and others insist that vv. 51c-59 is an interpolation.[31] His heading is 'Duplicate of the preceding discourse in which the Bread of Life is now the Eucharist'.[32] However, Borgen's conclusion after a thorough study is that 'these verses [51c-59] *continue the midrashic exposition of the quotation* and do not break off from the exegetical paraphrase' (italics mine).[33] Dunn is also of the

---

29. Brown, *John*, I, p. 271. The LXX has καὶ πάντας τοὺς υἱούς σου διδακτοὺς θεοῦ. Barrett (*St John*, p. 296) thinks John was probably dependent on the LXX.

30. Jesus brings the words of the Father, but he himself is the Word, ὁ λόγος. Borgen (*Bread from Heaven*, p. 150) makes the point that according to Exod. 33.20 Moses was not allowed to see God and live, but he and the people were taught by God. This is the case in Jn 6.45, 46: those who are taught by God have heard from God without actually seeing him.

31. In an extensive footnote Borgen (*Bread from Heaven*, p. 25 n. 1) lists those who hold the view that vv. 51c-59 do not fit the overall tenor of Jn 6 and believe they have been inserted. Borgen calls this view a 'strong, stereotyped exegetical tradition'. He believes it is 'not convincing'. Schnelle (*Antidocetic*, pp. 201-202) highlights five shifts in content and believes they 'compel us to posit a new literary layer in 6.51c-58'. Like Brown (see below 7.1.5.3 n. 41) he calls 6.51c-58 a 'eucharistic section'.

32. Brown, *John*, I, p. 281.

33. Borgen, *Bread from Heaven*, p. 26.

opinion that these verses are not an addition and makes much of the point that v. 63 must refer back to vv. 51-8. He points to the links of σάρξ and 'giving life' in v. 63 with vv. 51-58 and says: '[B]esides, v. 63 rings very oddly as a conclusion to a discourse which does not include vv. 51c-58.'[34] However, from my point of view it does not matter greatly whether vv. 6.51c-58 are an interpolation or not. My concern is to endeavour to make sense of the text as it stands, and I believe that can be done without deciding the issue in debate over literary layers.

It is true that the Johannine Jesus' words in vv. 51-58 must have been a shock to the Jews. For him to identify the 'bread' with his flesh and then to go on to say that his flesh was real food and his blood real drink would have been deeply offensive to Jewish people. The law of Moses (cf. Lev. 17.10-14) forbade the drinking of blood, and even the eating of meat with the blood still in it. Therefore no Jewish reader would be surprised at the reaction of some of Jesus' disciples (6.60, 66).

When the Johannine Jesus says: '[T]he bread that I will give for the life of the world is my flesh,' the reader[35] may recall Jn 1.14: 'And the Word became flesh and dwelt amongst us...' The sacrificial offering of the incarnate Word is therefore possibly in view. The Jews, however, are in a quandary: 'How can this man give us his flesh to eat?' By way of answer Jesus underlines the necessity of eating the flesh of the Son of Man and drinking his blood if they are to have any life (v. 53). I believe this brings the paschal theme back into focus.

7.1.5 *Theological Appropriation of the Paschal Theme*
7.1.5.1 *The Son of Man.* What is the significance of the title 'Son of Man' in this context? In my discussion of Jn 1.51 I argued that the title 'Son of Man' (see 5.5.1-8 but esp. 5.5.8) is invariably associated with the exaltation/glorification of Jesus. In a number of cases that exaltation is specifically mentioned as via the cross (3.13, 14; 8.28; 12.23; 12.34; 13.31); in others we are pointed towards the various functions that the exalted, glorified Jesus is able to carry out because he is the Son of Man, namely,

---

34. J.D.G. Dunn, 'John VI—A Eucharistic Discourse?', *NTS* 17 (1970), pp. 328-38 (332).

35. Other readers of course have immediately thought of the Eucharist where the body and blood of Jesus are consumed by the believer. However, John does not use the term σῶμα, but σάρχ. Everywhere else in the New Testament σῶμα is used when the Eucharist is clearly in view. Furthermore there is John's silence about the institution of the LORD's Supper. It is not certain that Jn 6 has the Eucharist as its *primary* focus.

to give eternal life (6.27; 3.14; 6.53); to bring judgment (6.62; 5.27; 5.39-40); to draw all to himself (12.34); and to care for those who trust him and be worshipped by them (9.35). Overarching all is the representative character of the Son of Man—in making God known to humankind and in offering himself on behalf of humankind.

This last point is to the fore in Jn 6.51 where Jesus as the Son of Man speaks of giving his flesh for the life of the world and in keeping with a number of Son of Man passages (namely, 3.13, 14; 8.28; 12.23; 12.34; 13.31), he does this through his death on the cross as the Paschal Lamb.

7.1.5.2 *The Paschal Theme.* The theme of the Passover underlies John 6, as I pointed out above.[36] And it is not only present in John 6 but through-out the Gospel. The reference to the three Passovers underlines the power-ful paschal motif that is present in John as a whole. So when there is mention of eating and drinking in John 6, John could very well want his readers to associate those actions with the Passover meal.

It is true that in the Jewish Passover the blood was poured out and only the flesh was eaten (Exod. 12.8, וְאָכְלוּ אֶת־הַבָּשָׂר; LXX καὶ φάγονται τὰ κρέα); here Jesus says that both his flesh must be eaten (τρώγω = gnawed or munched, in vv. 54, 56-58) and his blood drunk. This provides us with a clue to what Jesus is talking about. He is not urging his hearers to eat his flesh and blood as though he were the Passover Lamb to be consumed; rather he is pointing towards *his death as the Passover Lamb* in which his flesh and blood would be offered for the life of the world (6.33, 57). The ingesting is not by literal eating and drinking but by Spirit-worked faith (6.63, 47; 3.15, 16; 20.30, 31).

Jesus says that his flesh is true[37] food and his blood is true drink. This is

36. While discounting Gärtner's JPH schema as a detailed framework of Jn 6, I nevertheless believe there are traces of JPH in Jn 6 (see, e.g., 7.1.3, n. 23 where the crossing of the Reed Sea and the gift of manna are linked in a Passover liturgy [cf. n. 49]). Since JPH links the Exodus manna (very much the focus of 6.30-51) into the Passover liturgy, one should not assume the Passover theme has been lost sight of in the bread of life homily.

37. Brown (*John*, I, pp. 500, 501) says ἀληθής means 'true, despite appearances'. Jesus' flesh is truly food and his blood truly drink. Cf. the western tradition that reads ἀληθῶς, which in Brown's view catches the meaning of the verse. Barrett (*St John*, p. 299) has this comment: 'These passages show the meaning of ἀληθῶς here. My flesh and blood really are what food and drink should be, they fulfil the ideal, arche-typal function of food and drink, that is in giving eternal life to those who receive them.' But what does this mean? Does this mean that milk, bread and butter which

almost an explanation of v. 27: 'Do not work for the food that perishes, but for the food that endures to eternal life, which the Son of Man will give you.' And he will make that 'food' available through his sacrificial death. I therefore take v. 55 to mean that the food of Jesus' flesh and the drink of Jesus' blood (which the Son of Man will give you) will do for the one who eats and drinks what other food and drink will not do, that is, impart eternal life (cf. 6.35, 58). In particular the manna that was given in the wilderness could not impart eternal life (cf. v. 58)—neither could the Passover Lamb and the blood smeared over the doorposts and lintel of the house grant the kind of life that Jesus' flesh and blood (the new Passover Lamb) can give. The manna from heaven and the Passover Lamb[38] is the food that perishes and cannot provide eternal life. Jesus' flesh is true food and his blood is true drink and those who ingest[39] this food and drink will abide (μένει) in him and he in them. Jesus is the true manna and the true Passover Lamb.[40]

---

sustain life for a short time, would, if they were real food and drink, impart eternal life? I rather think ἀληθής contrasts Jesus' flesh and blood with the ephemeral character and effect of the food and drink used in Temple festivals (Passover and Tabernacles especially) where Jews participated in Exodus events. Cf. the use of ἀληθινή in 15.1 where Jesus says he is the true vine thereby replacing Israel as the vine (Isa. 5.7).

38. Although the context of Jn 6.27 no doubt equates 'food that perishes' with the loaves Jesus provided the multitude (6.26), in the wider Johannine context it is possible to read 'food that perishes' more broadly to include not only manna, but all food and drink involved in Temple festivals, including the Passover. This food and drink does perish and cannot provide the eternal life that Jesus offers through his death on the cross. The Temple festivals find their fulfilment not in themselves, but in the death and resurrection of Jesus.

39. The point has often been made that the 'eating and drinking' is a vivid metaphor for believing. I have already mentioned how Jn 6 strongly emphasizes the need for faith (cf. vv. 29, 30, 36, 40, 47, 64, 65). Believing in Jesus as God's Envoy is crucial. If the crowd want to do any work for God that work is to believe on God's Envoy (v. 29), although it is the Father who works that work in them. And throughout the whole of John there is a similar emphasis on the necessity of faith (cf. 3.16 and esp. 20.31). While it may be true that there is a reference here to eating and drinking of the Eucharistic elements, what John is saying is for that eating and drinking to do any good it must be mixed with Spirit-worked faith.

40. The gift of manna seems to dominate 6.31-51, but, given the close link of manna with the Passover in the JPH, no doubt the Passover theme undergirds the homily of 6.31-51. The Passover theme comes powerfully into the open when Jesus begins to speak of his flesh and blood from 6.51-58. The manna recedes into the background as John urges his hearers to believe on Jesus the Passover Lamb who gives

7.1.5.3 *The Eucharist?* There is a debate over whether Jesus is speaking here about the eucharist. A number of commentators tend to assume that the Eucharist is clearly in view, and there are others who do not think it is so prominent.[41] For example, James Dunn[42] ('John VI', p. 337) believes that in these verses John is combating (a) docetism, by emphasizing in the most graphic way the flesh and blood character of Jesus, and (b), more delicately, sacramentalism, by saying that the elements of the Eucharist of themselves are useless (cf. v. 63). Dunn, apparently assuming a Eucharistic setting to John 13, says:

> Nor can I believe it to be an accident that in John's account of Jesus' last meal with his disciples the only handling of the elements which John describes is Jesus giving (διδώσιν) of the bread to Judas; and far from the eating of the sop meaning a chewing of the Son of Man's 'living (= life-giving) flesh', for Judas it is immediately followed by *Satan*'s entry into him (xiii.27)—τὸ πνεῦμα ἐστιν τὸ ζωοποιοῦν, ἡ σάρξ οὐκ ὠφελεῖ οὐδέν.[43]

The thrust of Dunn's remarks is in the direction of vv. 63 and 64, which counter sacramentalist currents. It is not the flesh and blood of Jesus, as such, that does any good; it is the Spirit that gives life (v. 63).

Udo Schnelle[44] has written extensively on the antidocetic character of John's Christology, and there may well be some antidocetic polemic in the way John emphasizes so strongly eating the flesh of Jesus and drinking his blood. However, I do not think that is the primary thrust of what Jesus says, and neither do I accept that the eucharist is initially in view. I believe it makes more sense to see Jesus speaking of himself as the Passover Lamb whose sacrificial death alone can provide eternal life. The polemic is directed, I believe, towards those Jews who observe the Jewish Pass-

himself as a sacrificial offering for the life of the world (3.16; 6.33).

41. For example, Barrett (*St John*, p. 299) says of v. 53: '[T]his unmistakably points to the Eucharist.' With Lindars (*John*, p. 268) references to the Eucharist/Last Supper tend to slip into his discussion without justification. Carson (*John*, pp. 276-280), on the other hand, wrestles with this issue and allows some possible allusion to the Eucharist, but it is not primary.

42. J.D.G. Dunn, 'John VI', p. 337. While not labelling John as anti-sacramental, Dunn nevertheless believes he downplays the Eucharist so as to highlight the need for faith in Christ.

43. In support of Dunn's reference to Jn 13 I note that Borgen (*Bread from Heaven*, p. 93) has found a link between Jn 6.58 ὁ τρώγων τοῦτον τὸν ἄρτον and Jn 13.18 ὁ τρώγων μου τὸν ἄρτον (Ps. 41.10).

44. Schnelle, *Antidocetic*.

over. That Passover will not bring life. The Passover Lamb who will bring life is Jesus himself—his blood and his flesh.[45]

Verse 58 brings the homiletic midrashic debate to an end by referring back to the text (v. 31) and Jesus summarizes his whole message in very few words.[46] Verse 59 confirms the synagogue setting and lends credibility to Borgen's hypothesis.

The discussion that follows in vv. 60-71 is between Jesus and his disciples as distinct from the crowd (v. 22) and the Jews (vv. 41, 52).

7.1.5.4 *Exacerbating or Removing the Offence of John 6.61?* Verse 62 is a protasis without an apodosis: 'If therefore you were to see the Son of Man ascending to where he was before?' What follows?

First, on one level the offence will be increased. Jesus' ascension will mean his being lifted up on the cross (cf. 12.32), and the crucifixion of the Son of Man will be a scandal to the unbelieving Jews (cf. 1 Cor. 1.23). But his death will indeed be the fulfilment of himself as the Passover Lamb—his blood will flow and his flesh will be offered. Secondly, on another level Jesus' ascension will mean the gift of the Spirit. This is the consistent teaching throughout the Gospel. The Spirit will come only with the departure and glorification of Jesus. In 7.39 there was no Spirit because Jesus was not yet glorified, and in 16.7 the coming of the Paraclete (the Spirit)[47] is contingent on Jesus' departure. So the meaning of v. 62 in this case would be: 'If therefore you were to see the Son of Man lifted up, ascending to where he was before, then following such glorification the Spirit will be given and with the gift of the Spirit you will gain life from my words (anticipating vv. 63, 64) and you will no longer be offended.' Barrett suggests[48] that John has omitted the apodosis to allow for the double level possibility. I think that could well be the case. If so then the

---

45. The perspective I have adopted has, I believe, more in favour of it than those who argue for a Eucharistic setting. If it is accepted that one of the overall thrusts of the Gospel is that Jesus is the fulfilment and replacement of the Temple and its associated festivals, then the force of the arguments in favour of a *primary* Eucharistic setting for Jn 6.51-58 are diminished. In so far as the Passover has finished and is 'replaced' by the Eucharist, I think it is possible to read elements of the Eucharist into Jn 6.51-58. However, it makes better sense to see the primary reference to the Passover.

46. The comprehensive tenor of this verse points to the unity of 31-58, contrary to Brown and others who argue that 51c-58 is an interpolation.

47. The Paraclete is also the Spirit in John. Cf. 6.6.4 n. 73.

48. Barrett, *St John*, p. 303.

protasis forms a bridge between vv. 61 and 63. On the one hand, through the first possibility it refers back to the offence and its confirmation; on the other, the second interpretation looks forward to the Spirit and the dissolution of the offence.

7.1.6 *The Spirit as the Life-Maker*

This brings me to v. 63 which functions as an interpretative key for the preceding discourse. It is the Spirit that gives life (ζῳοποιοῦν). This is already the teaching of Jesus in John. He has spoken of the Spirit generating new life in 3.5 (γεννηθῇ ἐκ πνεύματος). The life-making character of the Spirit is contrasted with the flesh in the two references: τὸ γεγεννημένον ἐκ τῆς σαρκὸς σάρξ ἐστιν, καὶ τὸ γεγεννημένον ἐκ τοῦ πνεύματος πνεῦμά ἐστιν (3.6); τὸ πνεῦμά ἐστιν τὸ ζῳοποιοῦν, ἡ σὰρξ οὐκ ὠφελεῖ οὐδέν (6.63a).

The point that is being made in both references is that the flesh cannot give life; it is the Spirit that gives life.

How shall we understand this in the overall Johannine picture? First, we need to remind ourselves that the Passover is especially in view in John 6. By way of evidence I observe and, in some cases, reiterate the following: the specific mention of the Passover (6.4); the reference to 'much grass' (6.10), a sign of the Passover season; the focus is on the bread (6.13) and not the fish, because the bread will become a picture of the sacrificial provision of Jesus as the Paschal Lamb; the miraculous crossing of the sea evoking Exodus imagery (6.16-21) used in Passover liturgy;[49] Jesus is the sacrificial food given for the life of the world (6.33); the reference to manna (Exod. 16.4, 15; Jn 6.31) recalls the Exodus, which was launched with the Passover; the pronounced emphasis on eating and drinking (6.52-58) recalls the Passover feast; those who believingly participated in the

---

49. Gärtner, *John 6*, pp. 15, 16, quotes the *Haggadah*, which he dates back to the Maccabaean Ages, and in some cases to even before 167 BCE. The verses of the *Haggadah* that link the crossing of the Reed Sea with the manna in the Passover liturgy are as follows:

> Had he cleft us the sea,
> and not brought us through it dryshod
> It had sufficed us!...

> Had he satisfied our wants in the wilderness for forty years,
> And not fed us with the manna
> It had sufficed us!...

Passover were saved and now those who believingly participate in Jesus have eternal life (6.47).

Secondly, given the Passover context of this chapter, we recall that I have argued (see above 7.1.5.2 n. 38) that the words of v. 63 can apply to the 'flesh' of the Passover ritual. The 'flesh' of the Jewish Passover is powerless to bring life. Indeed, we could read v. 63 as: 'It is the Spirit that gives life; the "flesh" of the Passover is of no avail.' And significantly this has certain parallels with 4.22, 23: 'Neither on this mountain nor in Jerusalem will you worship the Father...but the hour is coming and now is here, when the true worshippers will worship the Father in Spirit and truth.' The 'flesh' of place is of no avail; it is the Spirit of truth that generates the authentic worshipper. So with the 'flesh' of Passover and manna traditions. They are of no avail. And even their replacement with the flesh and blood of Jesus is of no avail. It is the Spirit that gives life. And Jesus is the bearer of the Spirit (1.32) and the one to whom God gives the Spirit without measure (3.34). That is why Jesus can say that his words are Spirit and life. They are the product of the life-giving Spirit, and when received with faith (5.24) they generate life. As the true worshippers worship in Spirit and truth, so too will true disciples find life as they participate believingly in Christ the Incarnate Word (the truth, 14.6) through the Spirit.

It is possible that 6.63 could also apply to the Eucharist—the celebration of the fulfilment of the Jewish Passover festival. In that case the flesh and blood of Jesus of itself would be 'flesh' and would be powerless to give life; it is the Spirit that gives life.[50]

---

50. Against Brown (*John*, I, pp. 284-85), who is unwilling to consider that the flesh of Jesus (cf. 1.14) is in view here. Dunn's counter-argument ('John VI', p. 336) about the worthlessness of the flesh of Jesus is worth quoting in full: 'John is not trying to lessen the offensiveness of the incarnation, rather to stress it...σάρξ in John is always used to designate the sphere of humanity in its weakness and helplessness. The offence of the incarnation, which docetism sought to avoid, is that Jesus entered that sphere and became flesh and died (i.14; 1 Jn iv. 2; v. 6). The substitution of σάρξ for ἄρτος and of τρώγειν (to chew) for φάγειν (if the latter substitution is significant theologically) is best understood as a deliberate attempt to exclude docetism by heavily, if somewhat crudely, underscoring the reality of the incarnation in all its offensiveness. "To eat Jesus' flesh and drink his blood is none other than to accept his true humanity." (O.S. Brooks, 'The Johannine Eucharist: Another Interpretation', *JBL* 82 [1963], pp. 293-300 [297]). This does not mean, however, that John attempts to meet the challenge of docetism by...insisting that eternal life comes through the actual eating of the bread and drinking of the wine in the LORD's Supper on the part of those who believe (as Ignatius did some years later), for John's second point is that eternal life comes only through the Spirit given by the Son of Man in his exaltation (vv. 62-3).'

7.1.7 *Faith-Full and Unfaith-Full Participation in the Word*

The emphasis on a believing participation in Jesus, the Word, is developed among the disciples. Jesus tests the disciples to see who are born of the Spirit (have faith) and who are not (do not believe, cf. v. 64). Verse 65 underlines previous messages about the impossibility of faith being generated from a would-be disciple—faith comes from above, from being born of the Holy Spirit (see above the remarks on v. 29). Those who come to Jesus therefore do not come of themselves; it is granted to them by the Father. And Peter's representative response to Jesus (vv. 68-69) is a believing response. He accepts that Jesus has the words of eternal life (cf. v. 63b) and that Jesus is God's consecrated messenger (cf. 10.36 where consecration is linked with an emissary task). In this sense Jesus is the new Moses, who has inaugurated a new Passover in his own flesh and blood and a new Exodus with a manna that gives eternal life. Death was the end of those who ate the Passover and followed Moses. Jesus is different. He has the words of eternal life and those who 'feed' on him shall live and those who follow him shall 'have the light of life' (8.12).

The final verses (70, 71) describe the opposite of faith—unbelief. Despite Judas being one of the select 12 and outwardly sharing in the words of Jesus and eating and drinking with him, and perhaps even of him[51] (cf. Dunn's comments above on 13.26-30), nevertheless there was no faith in him. Chosen by Jesus (v. 70), Satan entered into him and he became the traitor. Election is no protection against the Devil.[52]

7.1.8 *Conclusion*

Given the pervasive and pivotal presence of the Passover Festival in John as a whole, I have argued for that same presence in John 6. While I have not followed Bertil Gärtner's contention that John 6 is based on the JPH, I have found that there are strong Exodus motifs in John 6. When I took up Peder Borgen's suggestion that much of the text in John 6, namely, vv. 30-59, follows a Jewish exegetical proceedure that applies scriptures to the present, we saw how Jesus represents himself as the bread from heaven. He says, 'I am the bread that came down from heaven' (6.35, 41, 51).

---

51. The question has been asked, Could one say this of the pre-crucifixion last supper? If we follow Dunn and allow a Eucharistic context for ch. 13, then there is a possibility of proleptically sharing in the flesh and blood of Jesus.

52. It is possible that John is offering some kind of theodicy for the catastrophes of the Jewish War (66–70 CE). Even though the Jewish nation was chosen of God, there was no guarantee the Devil could not infiltrate the nation and for her to become a traitor in the eyes of God.

Encouraged by this I endeavoured to interpret the latter part of the chapter (vv. 51-71) in terms of Jesus being the the present Passover Lamb in whom the disciples share by Spirit-generated faith. The Jewish Passover Festival is superseded by Jesus becoming the Passover Lamb. The 'flesh' of the Jewish Passover is of no avail; it is the spiritually ingested Jesus, the Passover Lamb, appropriated by faith, that brings life.

7.2 Tabernacles

7.2.1 Some Guidance

The purpose of this section is to consider the Tabernacles' Festival in John. Tabernacles provides the setting for Jn 7.1–10.22, although there is some debate whether the Tabernacles' Festival is still in view after 8.59 when Jesus leaves the Temple.

A central passage in relation to the Tabernacles' Water Ceremony is 7.37-39. The discussion of this passage begins with a consideration of the punctuation of the text and then moves on to identifying the Scripture quotation and trying to locate a source. To assist the location of the source the question of the referent of the much-disputed αὐτοῦ in 7.38b must be discussed. After arguing for the location of the source in two texts, I then discuss the significance of the passage in relation to furthering the theme of Jesus being the replacement of the Temple.

In tandem with Jn 7.37-39 is 8.12 where Jesus declares himself to be the light of the world during the Tabernacles' Festival. While I do not discuss this in detail, it is coordinated with the discussion of Jn 7.37-39.

7.2.2 Rituals in the Tabernacles' Festival

The Mishnah describes the rituals of Tabernacles but its post-Christian dating poses a problem. However, scholars assume that the Mishnah preserves older traditions predating the destruction of the Temple. In particular Yee states, 'There is no question that some of its legislation reflected a much earlier period when the temple was still in operation.'[53]

The feast began on the fifteenth day of Tishri, shortly after the Day of Atonement (the tenth of Tishri), and lasted for seven days, with the addition of a special eighth day of celebration (cf. Lev. 23.36). During these days

---

53. G.A. Yee, *Jewish Feasts and the Gospel of John* (Wilmington, DE: Michael Glazier, 1989), p. 74. Moloney (*Signs and Shadows*, p. 66) offers the *Mishnah* description but says that it is nevertheless speculative with respect to the Jewish liturgical procedures in the first century.

the participants lived in specially constructed booths originally made of myrtle, willow and palm branches (Neh. 8.13-18). This represented the tent experience of the Israelites in the desert, cared for by YHWH, with whom Israel now had a covenant. The feast came to be a memorial of God's protective care and presence during the wilderness time. In post-exilic times, the feast developed an eschatological motif, looking ahead to the Day of YHWH when all the nations would gather to worship at Jerusalem (Zech. 14.16-19; Isa. 2.2-4; 56.6-8). Later Zech. 14 was one of the *haphtarah* passages read on the day of the festival.[54]

Two aspects of Tabernacles' ritual seem to be reflected in the Johannine narrative, the water-pouring ceremony (7.37-39) and the illumination of the Court of the Women (8.12). Both of these are described in the Mishnah. Of the water-pouring ceremony the Mishnah says:

> They used to fill a golden flagon holding three *logs* with water from Siloam. When they reached the Water Gate they blew [on the *shofar*] a sustained, a quavering and another sustained blast. [The priest whose turn of duty it was] went up the [Altar-]Ramp and turned to the right where were two silver bowls...the bowl to the west was for water and that to the east was for wine...[55]

This ceremony was performed for seven days, and on each occasion the water and wine in the bowls would be poured out before the LORD.

As for the illumination of the Court of the Women, the Mishnah has the following description:

> At the close of the first Festival-day of the Feast they went down to the Court of the Women where they had made a great amendment. There were golden candlesticks there with four golden bowls on the top of them and four ladders[56] to each candlestick, and four youths of the priestly stock and in their hands jars of oil holding a hundred and twenty *logs* which they poured into all the bowls. They made wicks from the worn out drawers and girdles of the priests and with them they set the candlesticks alight, and there was not a courtyard in Jerusalem that did not reflect the light of the Beth ha She'ubah [House of the Water Drawing].[57]

This impressive aspect of the festival occurred each night.

54. Yee, *Jewish Feasts*, p. 73.
55. *Suk.* 4.9. References to the *Mishnah* are taken from H. Danby, *The Mishnah* (Oxford: Oxford University Press, 1933).
56. According to the Talmud the candlesticks were 75 feet high.
57. *Suk.* 5.2, 3. On Beth ha She'ubah Danby (*The Mishnah*, p. 179 n. 12) suggests 'the probable sense is "the place (or the act) of the Water-Drawing"'.

7.2.3 *Setting*

That the whole of Jn 7.1–10.21 can be placed under a Tabernacles' rubric is disputed,[58] but seems convincing. The term ἡ σκηνοπηγία is mentioned in 7.2 and forms the setting, certainly for John 7, with Jesus making a pronouncement on the last and great day of the feast in 7.37, and if we allow that 8.12 follows on from 7.52,[59] then the Tabernacles' setting continues. Jesus' declaration in 8.12 that he is the light of the world seems to echo the festival illuminations that, as I indicate above, were possibly part of the festival at this time, and the dialogue carries on until 8.59 when Jesus leaves the Temple. While John 9 does not mention the Tabernacles' Festival, the water and light themes are certainly apparent. The man born blind is instructed to wash in the pool of Siloam, the very pool from which the water is drawn for the water-pouring ceremony, and Jesus again declares himself to be the light of the world (9.5). Finally, there is the theme of the flock of God in 10.1-21 before the Feast of Dedication is noted in 10.22.

Chapters 7 and 8 and half of ch. 10 is a relatively large section of John to devote to themes in the Festival of Tabernacles. But of course the focus is not on Tabernacles as such, but on Jesus. The purpose of this emphasis is for John to persuade his readers that Jesus is the one who fulfils and

---

58. E.g. Schnackenburg, *St John*, II, p. 187.

59. 7.53-8.11 is the pericope of the adultress. Metzger comments on the textual inadmissibility of this pericope in his *Textual Commentary*: 'The evidence for the non-Johannine origin of the pericope of the adultress is overwhelming.' He then cites the evidence, draws attention to the non-Johannine style and vocabulary and that it interrupts the narrative sequence. He concludes: '[A]lthough the Committee was unanimous that the pericope was originally no part of the Fourth Gospel, in deference to the evident antiquity of the passage a majority decided to print it, enclosed within double square brackets, at its traditional place following 7.52' (*Textual Commentary*, pp. 219-21). Despite this textual judgment the place of this pericope in John is still a live issue. Gail O'Day ('John 7.53-8.11: A Study in Misreading', *JBL* 111 [1992], pp. 631-40) maintains that this pericope was marginalized by an androcentric interpretative community that was anxious and embarrassed by Jesus' failure to condemn the woman taken in adultery. J.P. Heil in 'The Story of Jesus and the Adultress Reconsidered', *Bib* 72.2 (1991), pp. 182-91, has argued that there are strong internal grounds for including the pericope, but Daniel Wallace ('Reconsidering "The Story of Jesus and the Adultress Reconsidered"', *NTS* 31 [1993], pp. 290-96) contends that Heil's linguistic and thematic arguments for retaining the pericope actually strengthen the case for excluding it. The current consensus is fairly reflected by Metzger. The placing of the pericope at a variety of other places in John and Luke suggests that it was textually suspect from a very early date.

replaces the Festival of Tabernacles. This is most clearly seen in Jn 7.37-39, where Jesus presents himself as the fulfilment of the water-pouring ceremony, and in 8.12, where he declares himself to be the light of the world, and it is to these passages I now turn.

7.2.4 *The Key Passage: John 7.37-39*
7.2.4.1 *Which Day Is the 'Last Day'?* In Jn 7.37-39 Jesus makes his pronouncement on the last day of the festival, the great day. Scholars are undecided whether this is the seventh day or the eighth. Lindars[60] makes the point that, although the eighth day was regarded as a Sabbath and there was worship, the water-pouring ceremony and the illumination of the Court of the Women were omitted. Thus the particular features that gave point to Jesus' words in 7.37, 38 and 8.12 were missing on the eighth day.

On the other hand, Bruce Grigsby cites rabbinic texts that answer the question, Why did God provide for us this additional eighth day? They were designed as a homiletic midrash on the Scripture lesson for the 'eighth day festival'. Grigsby finds that these texts provide valuable insights into the rabbinic understanding of the great feast and its central symbolic act, the water ceremony. He mentions that 'at least one rabbi (R. Judah), suggests that a water ceremony was celebrated on the eighth day (*t. Suk.* 3.16).[61] So Lindar's point is dubious. Jesus perhaps could have made his pronouncement on the eighth day.

A third possibility is that 'day' in Jn 7.37 has an eschatological tone, signifying that Jesus is pronouncing the end of the old Jewish Festival of Tabernacles and the inaugurating a new one in his person. Mary Coloe, who suggests this line of thought, remarks: '[T]he text of verses 37 and 38 supports this interpretation and its eschatological thrust, without becoming totally divorced from its meaning within the feast.'[62] She draws attention to other uses of 'the last day' (6.39, 40, 44, 54; 11.24; 12.48) that bear an eschatological reference to the resurrection of the believer. She goes on to say:

> The next time the reader hears of a 'great' day is the Passover-Sabbath day after the crucifixion (19.31). During this Sabbath, 'while it was still dark'

---

60. Lindars (*New Testament Apologetic* 297, 298) says we have evidence from Josephus (*Ant.* 3.247) that there was an eighth day for the feast. Bultmann and Brown assume the seventh day is meant. Hoskyns favours the eighth day.

61. Bruce H. Grigsby, ' "If Any Man Thirsts…": Observations on the Rabbinic Background of John 7, 37-39', *Bib* 67 (1986), pp. 101-108 (103).

62. Coloe, 'The Dwelling of God', p. 185.

and so according to Jewish reckoning, not yet over, Mary Magdalene discovers the empty tomb (20.1). The 'great' day in the Johannine Gospel is the day of Jesus' resurrection, with a promise that the believer will share this resurrection experience.[63]

If, as I have argued above, the context of the 'last day, the great day' has a distinctive Johannine eschatological perspective, then we should not be surprised to find that same perspective continuing from Jn 7.37 into vv. 38 and 39. And indeed we do find the thrust of these verses is eschatological. Verse 38 looks to the future when rivers of living water will flow; v. 39 refers to the future when the Spirit will be given after Jesus has been glorified.[64]

Within the narrative time of the feast, Coloe opts for the eighth day rather than the seventh. Her reason hinges on the likely absence of the water and light rituals (cf. *Suk.* 4.1) on the eighth day. She says:

> In the stark absence of water rituals and light Jesus announces that the water has not dried up and the light has not been extinguished. He is the source for the thirsty (v. 37) and light for those in darkness (8.12). In asserting the eighth day as most appropriate I point to a key Johannine theme that has been developing throughout the narrative—the paradox of presence in absence. For a Christian community living at the end of the first centry when the Temple has been destroyed and they no longer have access to synagogue worship, how can God be present to them? In the absence of a physical Temple, Jesus provides a new Temple where God may be encountered and worshipped (2.21; 4.21). In the absence of water rituals, and Temple candelabras, Jesus provides water and light.[65]

---

63. Coloe, 'The Dwelling of God', p. 185.

64. Coloe ('The Dwelling of God', p. 186) also draws attention to the strong eschatological overtones in Zech. 14, one of the *haphtarah* readings for the feast of Tabernacles. In n. 53 she says, 'A very thorough discussion on the rich historical and eschatological symbolism of Tabernacles can be found in Bienaimé, *Moïse et le don de l'eau*, pp. 200-29. In summary, see especially p. 229: "Dès une date ancienne, à la signification primitive de la fête des Tents liée au rythme des saisons s'étaient ajoutées la commémoration du don de l'eau au désert et l'attente des eaux eschatologiques jaillissant du Temple."'

65. Coloe, 'The Dwelling of God', p. 187. She draws attention to the significance of the eighth day in the post-Easter stories. On the eighth day (also the first day of the Jewish week) Jesus breathes the Spirit on to the disciples (20.19, 20) fulfilling 7.39 and thereby preparing them for his absence. The next eighth day Jesus announces a blessing to all who believe without seeing his presence. 'Within this Gospel the eighth day juxtaposes presence and absence and invites all to experience the eschatological blessings of the eighth day.'

My discussion of the eighth day has highlighted the possibility of an eschatological dimension to Jesus' utterance, and I keep this in mind as I turn to consider it in detail.

Hanson describes Jn 7.37, 38 and 39 as 'probably the most thoroughly discussed three verses in the entire Gospel'.[66] It will be helpful to discuss them under three headings—punctuation, source of the quotation and interpretation—even though these areas overlap, because it is not possible to discuss one issue without considering the others.

7.2.4.2 The Comma and the Full Stop. The fourth revised edition of the United Bible Societies' Greek New Testament places a full stop after πινέτω and a comma after εἰς ἐμέ.

Ἐάν τις διψᾷ ἐρχέσθω πρός με καὶ πινέτω.
ὁ πιστεύων εἰς ἐμέ, καθὼς εἶπεν ἡ γραφή, ποταμοὶ ἐκ τῆς κοιλίας
αὐτοῦ ῥεύσουσιν ὕδατος ζῶντος.

If anyone thirsts let him come to me and drink.
He who believes in me, as the scripture says,
rivers of living water will flow out of his belly.

The ὁ πιστεύων εἰς ἐμέ is then a *nominativus pendens* that is taken up by the αὐτοῦ after the intervening phrase, καθὼς εἶπεν ἡ γραφή. The effect of this punctation is to say that rivers of living water shall flow out of those who believe in Jesus, and it is to this that the scripture refers. I shall call this the traditional punctuation.

The alternative is to place a comma after πρός με and a full stop after εἰς ἐμέ, giving:

Ἐάν τις διψᾷ ἐρχέσθω πρός με,
καὶ πινέτω ὁ πιστεύων εἰς ἐμέ.
καθὼς εἶπεν ἡ γραφή,
ποταμοὶ ἐκ τῆς κοιλίας αὐτοῦ ῥεύσουσιν ὕδατος ζῶντος.

The translation would then be:

If anyone thirsts let him come to me;
and let him who believes in me drink.
As the scripture says:
'Out of his belly shall flow rivers of living water'.

This is ambiguous. Are the rivers of living water to flow out of Christ's belly or the believer's or both? The Scripture quotation is indicated by the

66. Hanson, *Prophetic*, p. 99.

quotation marks. Because this allows for the water to flow out of Christ's belly, we shall call it the christological punctuation.

This alternative forms a couplet where both lines centre on Jesus, but the parallelism is rather rough and not too much should be read into it. Barrett points out that the traditional punctuation has textual support from p66 (second century) and the majority of the Greek Fathers,[67] whereas the christological punctuation has support from some Western Fathers, the old Latin MSS. d and e, a Coptic MS., and a possible allusion in the Epistle of the Martyrs of Vienne.[68] Barrett also says that the traditional reading has a certain logic: '[A]s thirsty, a man is properly summoned to come and drink; as a believer, who has come and drunk, he can be the subject of a statement.'[69] Grammatically it is Johannine. Making the participle ὁ πιστεύων ('he who believes') the head of a new construction is a pattern found 41 times in John, whereas tacking it on to the previous conditional sentence is a practice seemingly not found in John. On the other hand, Kilpatrick[70] has shown that making the participle the anticipated subject of the Scripture citation has little support in Johannine style despite attempts to prove otherwise.[71] It seems that on the basis of

67. Origen is a principal supporter among the Eastern Fathers. Modern commentators who support it are Barrett, Behem, Bernard, Cortes, Lightfoot, Michaelis, Rengstorf, Schlatter, Schweizer, Zahn, Reim, Fee, Kohler, Allison, Hodges, Balagué, Miguens, Robert, Lindars, Carson. Those who support the christological interpretation or western interpretation are Hippolytus, Tertullian, Cyprian, Irenaeus, Aphraates, Ephraem and modern commentators like Boismard, Braun, Bultmann, Dodd, Hoskyns, Jeremias, Mollat, Stanley, Power, Schnackenburg, Grigsby, Brown.

68. Barrett, *St John*, p. 327. Quoting from Eusebius, *Hist. Eccl.* 5.1.22 says the martyr Sanctus was refreshed and strengthened in his sufferings ὑπὸ τῆς οὐρανίου πηγῆς τοῦ ὕδατος τῆς ζωῆς τοῦ ἐξίοντος ἐκ τῆς νηδύος τοῦ Χριστοῦ. Barrett realizes the allusion is so vague it could refer to 19.34 just as well as 7.38-39.

69. Barrett, *St John*, p. 327.

70. G.D. Kilpatrick, 'The Punctuation of John vii 37-38', *JTS* 11 (1960), pp. 340-42.

71. Brown, *John*, I, p. 321. Brown gives a third way to translate the Greek, one that gives no definite indication as to the identity of the source of the water and effectively makes the phrase ὁ πιστεύων εἰς ἐμέ a gloss: 'If anyone thirst, let him come to me and drink (i.e., he who believes in me). As the Scripture says, "From within him shall flow rivers of living water."' J. Blenkinsopp ('John vii 37-39: Another Note on a Notorious Crux', *NTS* 6 [1959–60], pp. 95-98) supports this on the basis that he believes the phrase 'he who believes in me' (v. 38) has been drawn from οἱ πιστεύσαντες εἰς αὐτόν in v. 39 and is therefore parenthetical. Brown notes that there is some versional evidence for dropping 'he who believes in me', but it is weak. I do not believe Brown's reading is justified.

grammar and style the arguments cancel each other out. Either way the expression is awkward.

7.2.4.3 *What about Verse 39?* Gordon Fee believes that these sorts of arguments lead to a stalemate. He says:

> Stylistically it can be shown that *nominativus pendens* is a recurring feature of Johannine style (see e.g., 1.12; 6.39; 15.2; 17.2); but it is also true that the chiastic parallelism of the second [christological] solution fits Johannine style (cf. 6.35) and that the καθὼς εἶπεν ἡ γραφή formula is ordinarily the first member of its clause in the Fourth Gospel.[72]

I think Fee is right—the argument on grammatical, textual[73] and stylistic grounds leads to a stalemate.

Fee's proposed solution, following a suggestion by Lindars,[74] focuses on v. 39. He argues (successfully, I believe) that the τοῦτο δὲ εἶπεν introducing v. 39 must refer back to v. 38 in its entirety, or, as Fee puts it, 'the author of verse 39 almost certainly intended the content of verse 38 to belong to the words of Jesus'. But I do not think that Fee goes far enough. The explanation of v. 39 refers to *all the words of Jesus* in vv. 37 and 38 and not just the Scripture citation of v. 38.

The crucial word in v. 39 is λαμβάνειν. What is in view is the reception of the Spirit. But how does one receive the Spirit? The obvious answer is by coming to (often equivalent to believing, cf. 6.35) Jesus and drinking.[75] This is what Jesus says in the first part of his utterance (v. 37c), irrespective of how the punctuation goes.

If, however, the reference in v. 39 is confined to what immediately precedes it, namely, the Scripture quotation: 'From within him shall flow rivers of living water,' then the question arises as to how this explicates the reception of the Spirit. Whether one prefers the traditional punctuation or the christological, on neither count is there a firm linkage with v. 39. If one takes the traditional punctuation, then the words, 'From within him [the believer] shall flow rivers of living water,' say nothing about the reception of the Spirit (they possibly say something about the *result* of the

72. G. Fee, 'Once More—John 7.37-39', *ExpTim* 89 (1977), pp. 116-18.

73. Fee, whose doctoral dissertation was on p[66] in relation to the Gospel of John, believes that the textual support of p[66] is not sufficient to tip the case in favour of the traditional interpretation.

74. Lindars, *John*, p. 301.

75. The notion of 'drinking the Spirit' is present in Paul—1 Cor. 12.13.

reception of the Spirit).[76] The immediate reference, however, must be back to the first words[77] Jesus utters, which speak directly about the reception of the Spirit.

On the other hand, if one takes the christological punctuation then the quotation becomes, 'From within him [possibly Jesus with this punctuation—it is ambiguous] shall flow rivers of living water.' The link with v. 39 becomes even more tenuous. This says nothing about the reception of the Spirit by believers. One could infer that it is to Jesus one could come for receiving the Spirit, but the words do not actually say that. The inference is made only because of the preceding words, which speak directly about the reception of the Spirit—one comes to (believes in) Jesus and drinks. Whatever punctuation we choose, v. 39 refers us back to the first words of Jesus: 'If anyone thirsts let him come to me...'

So what can be said of Fee's conclusion: 'For the author of verse 39 almost certainly intended the content of verse 38 to belong to the words of Jesus; therefore, the most natural meaning of the third personal pronoun αὐτοῦ is the believer, rather than the Messiah'?

In the light of the above discussion, I take issue with Fee's 'therefore'. It does not follow that the most natural meaning of αὐτοῦ is the believer. In fact the question is still wide open, because the natural reference of v. 39 is not back to the sentence with αὐτοῦ, but right back to the opening words of Jesus, and so consideration of v. 39 leaves the troubling reference of αὐτοῦ untouched.

Textual evidence, grammar, style and finally the relevance of v. 39 all prove to be inconclusive in the determination of the punctuation. It is now time to press on to other considerations and to see if there is any decisive argument for opting for one punctuation or the other.

---

76. Fee ('Once More—John 7.37-39', pp. 116, 117) makes a distinction between the believer's *reception* of the Spirit and the Messiah's *giving* of the Spirit. The implication of what he says is that the Messiah's giving of the Spirit is in view in v. 37b and the reception of the Spirit in v. 38. My contention is that *both* giving and receiving are in view in v. 37b, but v. 39 is about receiving, not giving.

77. Fee ('Once More—John 7.37-39', p. 117) maintains that if v. 39 refers back to v. 37b and thereby 'jumps over' v. 38, then John would have written εἰρήκει rather than εἶπεν as in 11.13 where there is a break between Jesus' words and the evangelist's further comment. The answer to this is that while the primary reference of v. 39 is back to v. 37b., v. 38 is also included as part of the total package. I believe v. 38 functions within the package as a confirmation of the invitation of Jesus to come and drink what he has to give to those who believe.

7.2.4.4 *Defining the Quotation*. Before I do that, however, I will endeavour to fix the limits of the Scriptural quotation. There is not too much diversity on this. According to Hanson, Da Silva[78] differs from the majority opinion by proposing the following:

> 'If anyone thirsts, let him come to me
> and drink, he who believes in me,
> as the Scripture says.'

Here the phrase 'as the Scripture says' refers to what has gone before and not what comes after. Hanson points out[79] that this has the merit of solving the problem of the source of the Scripture quotation. There are clear links with Isa. 55.1-3. The difficulty with it is what to make of the following phrase: 'Rivers of living water will flow from within him.' It seems to be left hanging. Further, we are in doubt as to who is speaking— Jesus or the narrator. If it is the narrator, then v. 39 has an awkward intro- duction, because the τοῦτο δὲ εἶπον looks as though the narrator's com- ment is beginning at this point and not back at ποταμοὶ. Καθὼς formulae follow quotations or allusions in 18 cases in John and precede in 13, so there is nothing unusual in Da Silva's suggestion that the quotation pre- cedes the formula. However, on the grounds of the havoc it creates for the interpretation of the subsequent phrases, I think it should be set aside.

The strong consensus of opinion is that the scriptural quotation follows the introductory formula, even by some who have decided in favour of the traditional punctuation. For example, Glenn Balfour says: '[W]e prefer not to regard ὁ πιστεύων εἰς ἐμέ as part of the quotation since nowhere else does John place the introductory formula in the middle of the quotation.'[80]

7.2.4.5 *The Pivotal Pronoun*. Before going on to look at the source list for the quotation, I will attempt to determine the reference to the αὐτοῦ, now part of the Scripture quotation in v. 38. Does it refer to Jesus or to the believer? The evidence I am about to offer is more circumstantial than direct. I will argue that, since Jesus is central in the context and throughout the Gospel, the christological punctuation is the most appropriate.

---

78. Hanson, *Prophetic*, p. 103, quoting A.P. da Silva's article 'Giovanni 7, 37-9', *Salesianum* 45.3 (1983), pp. 575-92.

79. Hanson, *Prophetic*, p. 103.

80. G. Balfour, 'Is John's Gospel Anti-semitic? With Special Reference to its Use of the Old Testament' (unpublished PhD thesis, University of Nottingham, 1995), p. 107 n. 92.

The following points support the view that αὐτοῦ refers to Jesus and hence that he is the source of the rivers of living water. My reasons:

(a)   The focus of the narrative of John 7 has been on Jesus. Jesus is the eschatological prophet of Deut. 18 (v. 40); he is the one who brings wholeness on the Sabbath (v. 23); he is the one who is sent by God (v. 29); his teaching is from God (v. 16); and the Jews surmise that Jesus (not his disciples)[81] may go to the Dispersion among the Greeks and teach them (7.35). In keeping with the tenor of this chapter, then, it is appropriate that Jesus continues to be the focus, in v. 37b as well as in the scriptural quotation in v. 38.

(b)   Jesus gives the Spirit (20.20). The water of the Spirit flows out from him to those who believe in him. Jesus is the source of the Spirit. Therefore it would be fitting if the scriptural allusion 'Out of his innermost being rivers of living water shall flow' applied to Jesus.

(c)   The 'I am' saying of 6.35 parallels the thought of this passage when it is christologically punctuated. The Johannine Jesus says in 6.35, 'I am the bread of life; whoever comes to me shall never hunger and whoever believes on me shall never thirst.' There is an equivalence of meaning between believing and coming. Similarly, in 7.37, 38 believing, coming and drinking[82] all converge towards the same meaning expressed in different metaphors. The Spirit is in view (cf. 7.39) and Jesus calls believers to come and 'drink' the Spirit that flows out from him in abundance, as the Scripture says. As Jesus is central in 6.35, so in 7.38.

(d)   In connection with 7.37, 38 mention is often made of Jesus giving water in 4.14: '...but those who drink of the water that I will give them will never be thirsty. The water that I will give will become in them a spring of water gushing up to eternal life' (...πηγὴ ὕδατος ἁλλομένου εἰς ζωὴν αἰώνιον). Jesus is certainly the source of this water (as I argue in 7.37, 38), and the

81. Lindars (*John*, p. 301) takes 7.35 to be a hint of the Gentile Mission of the Church and therefore an appropriate prelude to such words as 'rivers of living water shall flow out of his (the believer's) heart'. However, the words of the Jews speak of Jesus going to the Greeks, not the disciples—although no doubt they would have gone in the name of Jesus (cf. 20.21).

82. See above (7.1.5.2; 7.1.7) where the eating and drinking of 6.53 is a metaphor for believing.

water in the believers (those who drink) becomes a spring of water bubbling up into eternal life. Glenn Balfour implies this text in 4.14 signifies 'the believer as indwelt by the Spirit'.[83] While there is plenty of activity going on within the believer in 4.14, the emphasis seems to be on the benefits to the believer. However, in 7.38 the emphasis is not on movement within the confines of the believer's life; rather it is on what flows out (of Jesus or the believer) and presumably becomes of benefit to others—'rivers of living water shall flow'. Rivers suggest outward movement, an outflowing. So there is a subtle difference between 4.14b and 7.38b. They are not to be equated. Even on the traditional punctuation of 7.38, 4.14b has the benefits of the believer in mind, whereas 7.38b has the believer offering those benefits to others. That is, even on the basis of the traditional punctuation, it is not valid to appeal to 4.14b as a precisely equivalent text.[84]

My conclusion is that αὐτοῦ refers to Jesus, and if it refers to Jesus then the christological punctuation follows. Given the christological punctuation, therefore, the meaning of the scriptural quotation is that rivers of living water flow out from Jesus. This conclusion is in keeping with the strong christological emphasis throughout the Gospel and that it is Jesus who is the source of the Spirit for others, which is the overall thrust of Jn 7.37-39.

7.2.4.6 *Where Does* 'κοιλία' *Come From?* I now come to the question, What is the source of the quotation ποταμοὶ ἐκ τῆς κοιλίας αὐτοῦ ῥεύσουσιν ὕδατος ζῶντος? Freed[85] has a string of possibilities laid out at the beginning of his discussion of Jn 7.37, 38 in both MT and LXX versions where appropriate, and he also includes six possibilities from the Qumran texts. With such a plethora of possibilities it would be helpful to limit my discussion at this stage to a consideration of ἐκ τῆς κοιλίας. None of the texts listed by Freed has this expression. He has a lengthy

83. Balfour, 'Is John's Gospel Anti-semitic?', p. 110 n. 106. He is arguing for the equivalence of the expressions in 4.14b and 7.38b—they both, he implies, refer to the believer being indwelt by the Spirit. However, I do not think this does justice to the difference in wording.

84. Even with the christological punctuation 4.14 and 7.38 are quite close in implication. The living water in both cases comes from Jesus.

85. Freed, *Old Testament Quotations*, pp. 21, 22.

discussion on it[86] and, because the LXX is inconsistent in translating בטן,
נפש מעים, לב, and קרב and its use of κοιλία, he says 'it is impossible to
tell what Hebrew word John had in mind when he used κοιλία'.
Nevertheless he goes on to cite a large number of Old Testament texts so
as 'to understand somewhat the general background which may have
partly motivated John to use the quotation'.[87] But in fact he is no further
ahead. Hanson alights on the suggestion that Ps. 40.9-11 is a possibility
('Your law is within my inward parts [מעי בתוך, ἐν μέσῳ τῆς καρδίας
(κοιλίας, אAT) μου]... I have not hid your righteousness within my heart
[בתוך לבי, ἐν τῇ καρδία μου].') Hanson says: 'Instead of the Torah in his
heart, Jesus has God's will, and the Spirit is the motive of his action rather
than the Torah.'[88] While it is true that the Torah is a dominant theme in
John 7,[89] this passage in Psalm 40 has nothing about living waters flowing
like a river. Furthermore important though the manuscripts אAT are, the
linkage with κοιλία is only through them.

M.-E. Boismard[90] has suggested that ἐκ κοιλίας αὐτοῦ is a literal
translation from the Aramaic or Hebrew of a targumic version actually
spoken by Jesus. Thus κοιλία represents the Aramaic גוה (interior, belly),
which simply means 'out of' when prefixed by מן. This is accepted by
Grelot[91] and Power.[92]

I believe there is merit in Boismard's theory. Κοιλία may very well
simply mean nothing more than 'from within', but perhaps John has chosen
to retain a bodily reference to reinforce that the Spirit is a gift from the

86. Freed, *Old Testament Quotations*, pp. 24-29.

87. Freed, *Old Testament Quotations*, p. 25.

88. Hanson, *Prophetic*, pp. 111, 112.

89. George Brooke ('Christ and the Law in John 7-10', in B. Lindars [ed.], *Law
and Religion: Essays on the Place of the Law in Israel and Early Christianity* [Cam-
bridge: James Clarke, 1988], pp. 102-12, 180-84) has discovered significant references
to the decalogue in Jn 7-10: first commandment, 10.30; second, 10.33; third, 10.25
(that is, the 'Dedication' passage is marked by allusion to the commandments concerning God) and nos. 4-10 in the Tabernacles passage, 7.1–10.21: Sabbath 7.23 (cf.
5.18); honouring father 8.49 (cf. 5.23); murdering 7.19; 8.40, 44 (cf. 5.18); committing
adultery 8.41; stealing 10.1, 8, 10; bearing false witness 8.14, 44; coveting 8.44 (only
occurrence of ἐπιθυμία in John).

90. M.-E. Boismard, '"De son ventre couleront des fleuves d'eau" (Jo vii, 37)', *RB*
65 (1958), pp. 523-46 (542-44).

91. P. Grelot, '"De son ventre couleront des fleuves d'eau"', *RB* 66 (1959),
pp. 369-74 (369).

92. F. Power, '"Living Waters"', *Review of Religion* 19.1 (1960), pp. 5-11 (8).

incarnate Word. I think too, that Hoskyn's suggestion that the water flow-ing from the side (τὴν πλευρὰν) of the crucified Jesus (19.34) may be in view is not so far-fetched as Freed maintains.[93] At least, subsequent scholars have not thought so.[94] Could John have retained this bodily reference of κοιλία (albeit a slightly different part of the body from πλευρά, a term retained perhaps in the interests of preserving the passion tradition) so as to make a link with 19.34? I think it is possible.

7.2.4.7 *Could* Κοιλία *Mean Navel?* There has also been the suggestion that κοιλία (the source of the living water) may refer to Jerusalem or the Temple. Zech. 14.8[95] has 'On that day living waters shall flow out from Jerusalem...' Ezek. 47.1 speaks of water flowing out from the Temple. Even prior to the rabbinic period Jerusalem was regarded as the navel[96] of the earth. Jub. 8.19 calls Mt Zion the centre of the navel of the earth and Ezek. 38.12 uses the expression 'navel of the earth' but its reference is less clear.[97] This would be a very fragile connection if it were not for the fact that both Zech. 14.8 and Ezek. 47.1-12 are strong contenders as sources of the quotation of 7.38.[98] If it is granted that κοιλία could refer to Jerusalem

---

93. Freed, *Old Testament Quotation*, p. 26. I have more about this below at 7.2.5.

94. Schnackenburg gives a list (*John*, II, p. 478 n. 81). Brown (*John*, I, p. 323) says, 'Most authors agree on the connection between vii 38 and xix 34.' Beasley-Murray (*John*, p. 116) advises that we should dissociate the record of 19.31-37 from the logion of 7.37-38, but he does not offer any convincing explanation of why John uses κοιλία in 7.38.

95. Grigsby, Barrett and Brown all give strong support for Zech. 14.8 being the source.

96. It is not clear what the import of the term 'navel' is. Does it refer to the centre that nourishes the earth? Or is this the point where we are connected to the source of life?

97. MT has טבור and LXX has ὀμφαλός. H. St J. Thackeray (*The Septuagint and Jewish Worship* [Schweich Lectures, 1920; London: British Academy, 1920], p. 67) links 'navel' firmly with the Holy City, Jerusalem.

98. There are many other contenders. Feuillet, Grigsby and Grelot favour Num. 20.11 where we are told Moses struck the rock and 'water came forth abundantly'. Commentators Schlatter and Brown also believe the riven rock is in the background. John is fond of Exodus themes (see, e.g., Glasson, *Moses in the Fourth Gospel*, esp. pp. 48-59) so the rock in the desert could have been an intended reference from the quotation. If one believes αὐτοῦ refers to the believer rather than Christ, then Wisdom passages would be relevant (e.g. Prov. 18.4, Isa. 58.11 and Sir. 24.30-34 also contain the idea of Wisdom as a fountain or river within a person). 1QH 8.16-17 also gives a slight parallel in the course of a poem that is built up on this theme. Some see Jn 4.13, 14

in Zech. 14.8, then the only element of the quotation missing is ποταμοί and that could be implied from living waters that flow. Also in favour of Zech. 14.8 is the prominent reference to the Tabernacles' Festival later in the chapter (Zech. 14.16-19) and the reference to continuous light in the previous verse (Zech. 14.7), perhaps a rationale for the constant illumination of the Court of the Women during the Festival of Tabernacles. With Zech. 14.8 embedded in a network of Tabernacles' allusions, it would not have been unlikely to invoke the words of Zech. 14.8 at the festival in Jerusalem, especially if Zech. 14 was the *haphtarah* reading during the festival. What was unique was the application of these words to Jesus himself.

In commenting on the Tabernacles' *haphtarah* reading of Zech. 14. H. St J. Thackeray draws attention to 14.6-8, which speaks of an unfailing water supply and perpetual daylight and remarks:

> an unfailing water-supply and perpetual daylight inevitably recall the Water-drawing and the Illumination. Nor can we fail to note with reverence that it is just these two ideas—Water and Light—which the greatest Visitor to the feast, fastens on and applies to Himself.[99]

Thackeray then quotes Jn 7.37-38[100] and 8.12.

Given that the Jews had lost the Temple cultus with the fall of the Temple in 70 CE, what the Johannine Jesus offers here on the great day of the festival is not the answer *to* Judaism, but the answer *for* a Judaism that

---

as the source, especially with its strong reference to the living water gushing up into eternal life within the believer. Then there are a group of texts from Isaiah that have been claimed as influential: Isa. 48.21-22, accepted by Boismard; Isa. 44.3 and 55.1-2, this latter being acknowledged by Hanson but favoured by Da Silva. Carson (*John*, p. 326) locates the source in 'the entire matrix of thought' found in Neh. 9.15, 19-20. In this passage Spirit, manna and water all come together in connection with the Feast of Tabernacles. Freed (*Old Testament Quotations*, p. 37) notes this reference but makes nothing of it.

99. Thackeray, *The Septuagint and Jewish Worship*, pp. 64-67. Hoskyns (*The Fourth Gospel*, p. 365) insists that the words of Jesus in 7.37, 38 were not occasioned by any liturgy at the Feast of Tabernacles. Barrett (*St John*, p. 327) remarks: '[T]here is no reason to doubt that [this ceremony] was carried out before the destruction of the Temple'—*m. Suk* 4.9 and Josephus, *Ant.* 13.372 suggest that it may go back to Alexander Jannaeus.

100. Israel Abrahams (*Studies in Pharisaism and the Gospels*, I [Cambridge: Cambridge University Press, 1917], p. 11) makes the point that Jn 7.37-38 was drawing on the Zechariah lesson.

is in disarray.[101] As I argued in my second chapter, the catastrophic fall of the Temple had thrown Judaism into a turmoil of self-questioning and a search for answers as to why this had happened. What John offers, therefore, is not in opposition to Judaism, but an answer to the trauma that had overtaken it with the destruction of the Temple. Jesus is the eschatological Temple of Ezek. 47.1-11 (cf. 2.21 where the Temple is specifically identified with Jesus' body), and it is from this Temple that the rivers of living waters shall flow. He is the fulfilment of Zech. 14.8 and Ezek. 47.1-11. I do not deny that there are a host of possible allusions,[102] but I believe the words of Jesus focus especially on Zech. 14.8 and Ezek. 47.1-11. With the former's strong connections with the Tabernacles' Festival and the latter's Temple reference I suggest the two of them together provide the primary source for Jesus' quotation.[103]

7.2.5 *The Connection with John 19.34*

I believe it is difficult in this context to escape the connection of Jn 7.38, 39 with 19.34, where, from the pierced side of the body of Jesus (the eschatological Temple!), water and blood flow. One of the main factors that counts against a connection is that not only water, but also blood flows from Jesus' wound. There is no mention of blood, only water in 7.37-39. However, if we allow the possibility that John is bringing not one, but two motifs together in this climactic moment on the cross, then the difficulty may be solved. What I suggest and argue for below is that the blood flowing from Jesus' side evokes the image of the Passover Lamb. Jesus' blood is shed as the Lamb of God (cf. 1.29, 34). On the other

101. Glenn Balfour makes this distinction.

102. In addition to texts already listed that have water associations, there are Isa. 49.10; Ps. 42.3; Prov. 10.11; 13.14; 16.22. In *1 En.* 48.1 and 49.1 water is associated with Wisdom. Balfour ('Is John's Gospel Anti-semitic?', p. 113) mentions these metaphors are found at Qumran: 1QH 8.16 speaks of a fountain of living water; in CD 3.16-17; 6.4-11 we learn the well is Torah; in 19.34 water is equated with Torah; and in 1QS 4.20 water refers to the Holy Spirit. This gives some indication of the pervasiveness of this imagery within Jewish circles.

103. This is also Grigsby's conclusion ('"If Any Man Thirsts"', pp. 101-108) after looking at the Rabbinic evidence from *Pes. R.* 52, 4.6 and *Tosefta, Suk.* 3.3-12. Joel Marcus makes a reasonable case for Isa. 12.3 being one of the scriptures in view: 'With joy you shall draw water from the wells of salvation.' In his article 'Rivers of Living Water from Jesus' Belly (John 7.38)', *JBL* 117.2 (1998), pp. 328-30 (330 n. 13), Marcus concedes that in Isa. 12.3 there is no mention of 'rivers of living water' and suggests that Zech. 14.8 may also have had some influence on Jn 7.37, 38.

hand, I believe the water gathers up the previous Johannine references to the Spirit (cf. esp. 7.37-39) and in the moment of death Jesus gives over the Spirit to his disciples.[104]

7.2.5.1 *The Flow from the Temple of Jesus' Body.* I turn now to discuss in more detail the significance of the blood and water in Jn 19.34. Irenaeus (*Adv. Haer.* 3.22.2) understood this text as an antidocetic apologetic because of the emphasis that Jesus was truly a man and truly dead. However, the mention of water coming out of his body undermines his suggestion. Real people do not 'bleed' water. Another suggestion is that the mention of blood and water is an allusion to the sacraments of the Eucharist and baptism.[105] The water may possibly refer to baptism, but it would be a secondary reference. Blood certainly refers to Jesus' death (1 Jn 5.6-8; cf. 1 Jn 1.7) but it is difficult to prove a reference to the Eucharist.[106] Another approach is to look for parallels in Old Testament concepts concerning sacrificial victims. For instance, the Mishnah requires that the blood of the victim not be congealed so that it may be sprinkled.[107]

---

104. There is some evidence of water and blood being found in combination. Glasson cites the Midrash Rabbah on Exodus where, in an interpretation of Ps. 78.20 we read, 'Moses struck the rock twice, and first it gushed out blood and then water' (Glasson, *Moses in the Fourth Gospel*, p. 54; see further L. Ginzberg, *The Legends of the Jews* [7 vols.; Philadelphia: Jewish Publication Society of America, 1909–66], V, p. 421 n. 132). Similarly, the Palestinian Targum on Num. 20.11 has 'and Moses lifted up his hand, and with his rod struck the rock twice: at the first time it dropped blood, but at the second time there came forth a multitude of waters'. This tradition is developed in the later Aggadah legends of the midrash *Petirat Aharon*. There the blood is explained through the violence of Moses striking it. Cf. Ginzberg, *Legends*, III, p. 320; see also Glasson, *Moses in the Fourth Gospel*, p. 55.

105. For example, Bultmann, Hoskyns, Cullmann. Carson (*John*, p. 624) totally rules out any sacramental reference. Coloe ('The Dwelling of God', pp. 283, 284) suggests that because of the emphatic testimony of a witness (19.35) the blood and water must have special significance to the readers. She says, 'The first person testimony indicates that the blood and water is the link between the events narrated and the community of believers of [a] later generation. Here we glimpse the sacramental life of the Johannine community. When Jesus is no longer a physical presence with them, the community can still be drawn into Sonship and participate in the sacrificial gift of his life in their Sacraments of Baptism and Eucharist.' This interpretation seems to depend on a later developed theology of the sacraments.

106. So Brown, *John*, II, pp. 951-52.

107. *Pes.* 5.3, 5. Danby (*The Mishnah*, p. 468 n. 15) comments: 'At least three modes of applying the blood to the Altar are distinguished: "pouring" it out at the base

J.M. Ford has applied these ideas to the Jewish Passover tradition: hyssop, unbroken bones and mingled blood were all part of that rite.[108]

However, I think it is best to look within John for the meaning of this flow of blood and water from Jesus' side. I have already given a detailed discussion in 7.1 of how Jesus is presented in John as the fulfilment of the Passover Lamb. At the same time that the Passover Lambs are being handed over to the priests for the Passover sacrifice in the Temple, Pilate is handing over Jesus to the Jews who are demanding his death. I have also noted that within the narrative of the crucifixion there is a dense cluster of allusions to the Passover. I believe this serves to indicate to the reader that Jesus' death is the death of God's new Passover Lamb. The blood that flows from his side is a sign of his death as the Passover Lamb who liberates his people from the bondage to sin (1.29; 8.34-36).[109]

The flow of water ties in with the Feast of Tabernacles and here requires more extended discussion than the flow of blood. Jn 7.37-38 anticipates a future time when rivers of water will flow from Jesus' body that is specifically linked to the Temple in 2.21. Jn 7.39 explicitly refers to Jesus' glorification. As I have noted elsewhere, this glorification includes the cross. There is no doubt that the moment of the Johannine Jesus' death is a triumph. His cry is τετέλεσται (it is finished). This is the announcement of victory (cf. 4.34; 17.4); there is no defeat. Even death does not overtake him. Jesus lays down his own life. He continues to be the subject of active verbs (κλίνας, παρέδωκεν). It is as he said in 10.18: 'No one takes [my life] from me, but I lay it down of my own accord.' The moment of Jesus' lifting up on the cross to die is the beginning of the moment of his glorification and we are told in 7.39 that the Spirit, represented as the flow of living waters from Jesus' body, will be given when he is glorified.[110]

---

of the Altar, "tossing" it out of the bowl against the side of the Altar, and "sprinkling" it (or daubing it) with the fingers.'

108. Ford, '"Mingled Blood"', pp. 337-38. See also 7.1.1.1.

109. Coloe ('The Dwelling of God', pp. 274-77) argues that Jesus' death as Passover Lamb liberates from sin. This fits nicely with the original significance of the Passover in the Exodus. But to insist, as she does, that the death of Jesus has no expiatory significance goes too far. While the expiatory sacrifice of Jesus may not be explicitly mentioned in the Gospel (as it is in 1 Jn 2.2; 4.10), I see no reason to exclude it.

110. Coloe ('The Dwelling of God', p. 278) sees in the cry τετέλεσται as an echo of Gen 2.1 when God finished the work of creation. She comments: 'Throughout the Gospel Jesus had claimed that God in fact was still working (5.17), that the creative work of God had not yet been completed, and that he has been sent to complete (τελέω) this work (4.34; 5.36; 17.4). In the hour, as the sixth day comes to an end,

7.2.5.2 *Convergence of Motifs*

Several motifs come together in Jn 19.28-34. First, Jesus says, 'I thirst' (διψῶ). No doubt in the first instance this refers to the sufferings of Jesus on the cross. This is the cup the Father has given him (18.11). But there is also irony echoing 4.13 and 7.37. The source of the living water now thirsts! Yet at this moment of thirsting he will indeed become the source of the living water, the Spirit. Secondly, in relation to the phrase παρέδωμεν τὸ πνεῦμα (19.30b),[111] Gary Burge says: 'Nowhere in Greek literature is παραδίδωμι τὸ πνεῦμα used as a description of death.'[112] He concludes from this that John is wanting to say more than that Jesus died. Dodd says that παραδοῦναι is often used of 'handing on' a piece of property (or a piece of information, or the like) to a successor. In this case Jesus would be 'handing over' the Spirit to those who were his followers. On the other hand, παραδοῦναι can quite properly mean 'surrender', in which case Jesus was simply surrendering his spirit (life force) to God, who gave it. Dodd does not feel able to decide between these two.[113] However, there is little notion of surrender in the death of Jesus. There is an unremitting note of triumph as I pointed out above. Even the cry διψῶ is not so much a cry of surrender to bodily weakness (though that may be present) but a cry to fulfil Scripture so that the work of the Father may be completed (19.28). It seems more likely that, rather than surrendering his life force to God, Jesus, who is in complete control of everything up to the moment of death, should finally 'hand over' the Spirit. This would be in keeping with 7.39. The glorification/death of Jesus would release the Spirit. This would also explain why the flow of blood precedes the flow of water. Blood, signifying death, must come before the water that signifies the Spirit (cf. 7.37-39).

It is important to note that the Spirit is not *actually* given. The giving of the Spirit does not happen until the risen Jesus breathes on his disciples and says, 'Receive the Holy Spirit' (20.22). But at the point of the 'shift-

---

Jesus announces the completion of God's creative work so the Sabbath can truly begin (19.31). As one creative act draws to its end, the new eschatological age is ushered in and its first gift is the Spirit.'

111. τὸ πνεῦμα could refer to Jesus' 'life force' or the Holy Spirit. I believe it refers to both.

112. Burge, *Anointed*, p. 134 n. 75. The note supplies ample references to justify his statement.

113. Dodd, *Interpretation*, p. 428 including n. 3.

ing of eras when the moment of sacrifice comes',[114] the Spirit is 'given' symbolically and proleptically.[115] By way of summary Brown says: 'The symbolism here is proleptic and serves to clarify that, while only the risen Jesus gives the Spirit, that gift flows from the whole process of glorification in "the hour" of the passion, death, resurrection, and ascension.'[116]

In a remarkable way John has brought together the prophecy of the waters flowing from the eschatological Temple (Ezek. 47.1-11) and the proclamation of Jesus at the Festival of Tabernacles (7.37, 38) in the climactic moment on the cross. Here Jesus' body, soon to become the new Temple (2.21), becomes the source of living waters—the Spirit.

McHugh's remarks summarize this discussion of 7.37-39:

> So, in public, in Jerusalem, Jesus offers to all who hear him rivers of life-giving water, flowing from the Temple, divinely promised for the end-time, the Day of the LORD. The words of Psalm 36.9-10 come to mind.[117]

And those words gather up not only Jesus' fulfilment of the Water Ceremony, but also the illumination of the Court of the Women:

> For with you is the fountain of life; in your light we see light. O continue your steadfast love to those who know you, and your salvation to the upright of heart!

From Jesus come the rivers of living water and he is the light of the world. Jesus fulfils the Feast of Tabernacles and thereby replaces it.

7.2.6 *Jesus as the Light*

McHugh's reference to Ps. 36.9-10, with its mention not only of water but also light, is a reminder that as well as the water ceremony the Festival of the Tabernacles also has the great lights burning in the Court of Women each night. It was said that these lights illuminated the whole of Jerusalem, but in Jn 8.12 Jesus claims to be a guiding light not only for Jerusalem but

---

114. Burge, *Anointed*, p. 135.

115. The significance of the flow of blood and water is strongly highlighted by 19.35: 'He who saw this has testified so that you also may believe. His testimony is true, and he knows he tells the truth.' The outflow of blood and water is something that is not to be missed. It is obviously very important and perhaps Burge's phrase 'shifting of eras' is the appropriate way to describe this moment.

116. Brown, *John*, II, p. 951.

117. J. McHugh. ' "In Him Was Life": John's Gospel and the Parting of the Ways', in J.D.G. Dunn (ed.), *Jews and Christians: The Parting of the Ways A.D. 70-135* (WUNT, 66; Tübingen: J.C.B. Mohr [Paul Siebeck], 1992), pp. 123-58 [141].

for the entire world: 'I am the light of the world. Whoever follows me will never walk in darkness but will have the light of life.' This is, in part, a reiteration of what has already been stated in the Prologue: 'What came into being in him [the *logos*] was life, and the life was the light of all people' (1.4). But whereas the light in the Court of Women was most likely extinguished after the seventh day of the feast, the light of the Word is inextinguishable: 'The light shines in the darkness and the darkness did not overcome [κατέλαβεν] it' (1.5). Bauer, Arndt and Gingrich[118] suggest that κατέλαβεν has a double meaning here. It could mean 'grasp' (in the sense of comprehend) or 'put out' (so E.J. Goodspeed). Barrett (*St John*, p. 158) catches the double sense well: 'The darkness neither understood nor quenched the light.' Both of these senses are in evidence throughout the Gospel. Jesus the light is constantly misunderstood,[119] and there is every effort on the part of the Jews to destroy Jesus and thereby extinguish the light.

This is especially the case in the debate between Jesus and the Pharisees in Jn 8.12-59. Misunderstandings occur in 8.21, 22, 27 and Jesus gives the reason for the Jews' failure to understand in 8.43-47:

> Why do you not understand what I say? It is because you cannot accept my word. You are from your father the devil, and you choose to do your father's desires. He was a murderer from the beginning and does not stand in the truth, because there is no truth in him. When he lies, he speaks according to his own nature, for he is a liar and the father of lies. But because I tell you the truth, you do not believe me... Whoever is from God hears the words of God. The reason you do not hear them is that you are not from God.

This quotation also highlights the Jews' desire to kill Jesus, that is, to extinguish the light. Because the Jews are from their father the devil, who was a murderer from the beginning, they choose to do their father's desires, which is to kill Jesus (cf. vv. 37, 40).

The theme of misunderstanding and extinguishing the light reaches a climax at the end of John 8 when Jesus says to the Jews, 'Your ancestor Abraham rejoiced[120] that he would see my day; he saw it and was glad.'

118. Bauer, Arndt and Gingrich, *Greek–English Lexicon*, pp. 413-14.

119. Cf. D.A. Carson, 'Understanding Misunderstandings in the Fourth Gospel', *TB* 33 (1982), pp. 59-89.

120. Coloe ('The Dwelling of God', pp. 198-99) has a helpful discussion of this verse: 'The book of Jubilees, written in Hebrew prior to 100 BCE, names Abraham as the first to celebrate Tabernacles, "*And he first observed the feast of booths on the*

Then the Jews said to him, 'You are not fifty years old and have you seen Abraham?'

Jesus' 'day', as I mentioned in earlier chapters,[121] is the eschatological day, the day of YHWH. This, as suggested above, is the theological thrust of 'day' in 7.37 when 'on the *last day of the festival, the great day*, while Jesus was standing there, he cried out'. And Jesus announces some of the blessings of the eschatological day of YHWH that are heralded in Zech. 14.8 and Ezek. 47.1-12. This is the day of Jesus that Abraham rejoiced to see.

But the Jews do not understand. They think Jesus is talking about calendrical time and is claiming contemporaneity with Abraham, and so they ask how he can have seen Abraham.[122] But Jesus is talking about the day of YHWH and so he confirms this. He says, 'Before Abraham was, I am' (8.58).

The use here of the absolute ἐγώ εἰμι has been much discussed. I give more space to it later (see 9.5.2-6) but, anticipating the results of that discussion now, I can say that ἐγώ εἰμι recalls the self-revelation of YHWH in Dt. Isa. (cf. esp. 43.10-12). Jesus then claims to be the revelation of YHWH, and with that revelation comes the day of YHWH inaugurated by Jesus in his ministry, but supremely in the drama of his hour, his lifting up (crucifixion), resurrection and departure (ascension).

Mary Coloe comments, 'The fivefold repetition of the phrase ἐγώ εἰμι (8.12, 18, 24, 28, 58) in the Temple, within the feast affirming worship of Israel's one God, gives the phrase the character of a theophany.'[123] Jesus' claim to be the light of the world (8.12) is entirely in keeping with this.

However, the desire of the Jews to extinguish the light spills over into

---

earth"' (Jub. 16.21). Abraham's joy in this feast is striking. The text of Jubilees mentions joy many times.' Here she quotes Jub. 16.20, 25, 27 and then continues: 'The cause of Abraham's joy and blessing lies in the future he is permitted to see. "*...for he knew and perceived that from him there would be a righteous planting for eternal generations and a holy seed from him...*" (Jub. 16.26). Abraham's perception enables Jesus to say "Your Father Abraham rejoiced that he was to see my day; he saw it and was glad" (Jn 8.56).'

121. See, e.g., section 3.3.

122. Metzger (*Textual Commentary*, pp. 226-27) comments on the alternative reading (ἑώρακές σε, Has Abraham seen you?) and says, 'The reading chosen for the text, besides having much stronger manuscript attestation...is more fitting on the part of the Jews, who, assuming the superiority of Abraham (ver. 53) would naturally represent Jesus as seeing Abraham rather than Abraham as seeing Jesus.'

123. Coloe, 'The Dwelling of God', p. 203.

action when Jesus declares that he is ἐγώ εἰμι, the presence of YHWH. 'They picked up stones to throw at him (8.59).'

7.2.7 *The Significance of John 8.59b*
I have mentioned above how the Feast of Tabernacles seems to be in view from 7.1 to 10.22.[124] However, the last verse of ch. 8 marks the end of Jesus' debate with the Jews and the beginning of ch. 9, the commencement of the story of the healing of the man born blind. W.D. Davies takes Jesus' leaving the temple in 8.59 as a decisive leaving that amounts to a deliberate rejection of the Holy Place:

> For John, 'I am' has departed from the Temple, that 'holy space' is no longer the abode of the Divine Presence. The Shekinah is no longer *there*, but is now found wherever Christ is, because later (10:36 makes this probably, if not unmistakably clear) Christ himself is the Sanctified One, the altar and Temple, the locus of the Shekinah.[125]

There is much truth in this. That the Johannine Jesus replaces the Temple, becoming the 'locus of the Shekinah', is a recurring theme indicated by more than just 10.36. Stephen Motyer makes a further point:

> [I]t may be that some readers would hear overtones of Ezekiel's vision of the departure of the *Merkabah* from Jerusalem, which heralded the destruction of the city in 587 BC (Ezek. 10)—especially since an equivalent departure before the final destruction in 70 AD had become a matter of popular legend, even finding its way into the Roman historian Tacitus.[126]

---

124. The Tabernacle links with Jn 10.1-21 may come via the Hallel, which was evidently sung during the festival (Danby, *The Mishnah, Suk.* 3.9, 4.8). In this case the reference ('I am the door/gate' Jn 10.9) could possibly be to Ps. 118.19-20, 'the door of righteousness, the door of Yahweh', by which alone the Israelite enters into the true Temple and dwelling place of God on earth (cf. Jn 1.14; 14.6). Some supporting connections are possibly present in 10.1, which has κλέπτης καὶ λῃστής. Here the λῃτής may recall Mk 11.17 where Jesus calls the Jewish Temple a σπήλαιον λῃστῶν, which in turn seems to be dependent on Jer. 7.11: Μὴ σπήλαιον λῃστῶν ὁ οἶκός μου, οὗ ἐπικέκληται τὸ ὄνομά μου ἐπ᾽ αὐτῷ ἐκεῖ, ἐνώπιον ὑμῶν. Further, κλέπτης may harmonize with the reason Jesus gives for driving out the money changers and animals in Jn 2.13: 'Stop making my Father's house a market place!' Whether the commercial activity was irregular or not it is possible that any commercial activity in the Father's house was tantamount to theft. If these connections with 10.1-21 are valid then it is possible that the Temple theme is present here too.

125. W.D. Davies, *The Gospel and the Land*, p. 295 (his emphasis). The discussion occupies pp. 290-96.

126. Motyer, 'Persuasion', p. 238. The reference to Tacitus in his n. 151 is *Histories*

However, to describe Jesus' departure as a 'definitive rejection of Judaism and its "holy place"' [127] goes too far. Jesus goes secretly ('Jesus hid himself and went out of the Temple' [8.59b]), just as he came (7.14). There is no public act of rejection; and he *returns* to the Temple in 10.22. [128]

It is true that 8.59 marks the Jews' rejection of Jesus, but he is still ready to shine in their world and indeed in 9.5 he renews his claim to be the light of the world, and seeks out a Jew who is already alienated from the cult and from the Jews who have rejected him. Such a man would not normally be found in the Temple. [129] So it is possible that Jesus' action in leaving the Temple is just the necessary step he must take in order to meet and help the man born blind.

On the other hand, there may perhaps be an element of judgment in 8.59. Jesus' departure from the Temple looks like a forced exit from his Father's house. In fact the Johannine Jesus is never forced to do anything. He is always sovereignly in control (cf. 18.6-8). He comes and goes always of his own volition. If the action of 8.59 is not an escape, then his hiding and departure begin to look like a symbolic pronouncement of judgment against the Jews and the Temple.

7.2.8 Conclusion

Jesus distances himself somewhat from the Festival of Tabernacles. He has his own καιρός (7.6), which, within the context of the festival is to proclaim its fulfilment in himself. But that fulfilment is contingent on the events of Jesus' 'hour' of glorification (7.39). On the last day of the festival, the great day (possibly the eighth day), Jesus cites Scripture to proclaim

5.13; and he compares this with Josephus, *War* 6.297-300 (the vision of chariots departing and the voice in the Temple); cf. also *2 Bar.* 8.1-5; *War* 5.412.

127. Davies, *The Gospel and the Land*, p. 291.

128. Davies (*The Gospel and the Land*, p. 292) strenuously endeavours to minimize this return and say it is not really a return, but he is not convincing.

129. Motyer ('Persuasion', p. 239 n. 154) notes that in *m. Ḥag* 1.1 ' "a lame man [cf. Jn 5.1] and blind man" are included in the list of those with various physical disabilities who are exempted from the three pilgimage festivals. Since some of the disabilities did not affect mobility, and since women and slaves are also listed, it seems likely that such people were actually discouraged from attending, at any rate, by some teachers. The strict rule given to the priesthood in Lev. 21.16-23 could well have been more widely applied by those whose guiding principle was the extension of Temple purity to the community generally. This was certainly the case at Qumran: "No blind man, or maimed, or lame, or deaf man…shall enter into the Community, for the Angels of Holiness are with them" (CD 15, Vermes, p. 109)'.

himself (taking the christological punctuation) as the source of living waters. The two most likely Scripture texts behind Jesus' utterance (7.38) are Zech. 14.8 and Ezek. 47.1-12. The first (Zech. 14.8) is embedded in a prophetic announcement of the eschatological day of YHWH presented in terms of the Tabernacles' festival; the second is an eschatological vision of rivers of water flowing from the Temple threshold. Both texts are appropriate for the context of what Jesus says in 7.37, 38. Jesus makes this announcement within the Festival of Tabernacles itself, and, since Jesus' body has been explicitly identified as the Temple (2.21), Ezek. 47.1-12 is a fitting text, especially when 7.37-39 is read in conjunction with 19.34 where both blood and water flow from the side of the crucified body (the new Temple) of Jesus.

The illumination of the Court of Women, which lit up the whole of Jerusalem during seven nights of the Tabernacles' festival, finds fulfilment in Jesus' declaration that he is the light not only of Jerusalem and hence Israel, but of the world (8.12). Throughout the remainder of John 8 the Jews continue to misunderstand Jesus and the chapter ends with them endeavouring to extinguish Jesus the light of the world. In this they are unsuccessful. But with the departure of Jesus from the Temple there is a hint that the old institutions of the Temple are under judgment.

7.3 *Dedication*

7.3.1 *Introduction*

For the third part of this chapter I make some brief observations on the Festival of the Dedication and the way in which it provides a setting for the debate in Jn 10.22-39 and also informs the subsequent chapter (John 11) in which the oppressor death is defeated. As with Passover and Tabernacles I note that Jesus is also the fulfilment of this festival.

The Festival of the Dedication (τὰ ἐγκαίνια)[130] is announced in Jn

---

130. Stefan Reif's article on חנך and חנכה ('Dedicated to חנך', *VT* 22 [1972], pp. 495-501) builds a strong case that חנך should be translated as 'start, begin, initiate'. The discussion of Deut. 20.5 in the light of the subsequent parallels (Deut. 20.6,7) is quite convincing. Prov. 22.6 poses a problem for those who wish to translate the imperative חנך as 'dedicate'. Whybray (*Proverbs*, p. 320) says the verb is attested in other Semitic languages in the sense of instruction or direction, but offers no evidence for this. It seems better to stay with the meaning Reif (and before him O.S. Rankin) has advocated and translate the verse, 'Start a boy at the beginning of the (right) road and he will not be turned aside from it when he is old.'

In discussing the significance of this for the festival of Hanukkah Jacob Milgrom

10.22. This took place in Jerusalem in winter. The festival may possibly be in view from 10.22 to 11.53,[131] since the connections with 1 Macc. appear to span all of these verses, as I will illustrate from the table below.[132]

The institution of this festival is described in 1 Macc. 4.59.[133] Antiochus Epiphanes had desecrated the Temple in Jerusalem by setting up his own pagan altar and offering sacrifice on 25 Kislev, 167 BCE. Exactly three years later, after some remarkable military victories over the armies of Antiochus by Judas Maccabees, the desolated Temple was cleansed and refurbished and sacrifice was offered 'as the Law commands' on the newly built altar of burnt offering:

> And Judas and his brethren and the whole congregation of Israel ordained, that the days of the dedication of the altar be kept (ἵνα ἄγωνται αἱ ἡμέραι ἐγκαινισμοῦ θυσιαστηρίου) in their seasons from year to year for eight

---

(*Leviticus 1–16* [AB, 3; Garden City, NY: Doubleday, 1991], pp. 592-95) quotes 1 Macc. 4.56: 'They celebrated the dedication of the altar for eight days, joyfully bringing burnt offerings and sacrificing well-being offerings and thank offerings.' He goes on to say, 'But the altar was "dedicated" through its use.' He then draws attention to the fact that Josephus has studiously (it appears) refrained from using the Greek word ἐγκαινίζω in describing what happened at the altar. He uses Greek words connoting resumption or restoration or renewal, but never consecration. But a puzzle remains: if, as Milgrom argues, ἐγκαινίζω is an inappropriate translation of חנך, why does it appear so often in the LXX as a rendering? I therefore hesitate to endorse Reif's and Milgrom's proposal completely.

131. However, there appears to be a closure in the narrative in 10.40-42 with Jesus' permanent departure from the Temple. Stibbe (*John*, p. 117) draws attentions to an *inclusio* in the architectural description of the colonnades of Solomon (10.23) and the colonnades (στοὰ) near the Bethesda pool (5.2) where John began his section on the feasts of the Jews.

132. There may be other links with the Temple in Jn 11. For example, the loosing of Lazarus, may echo Ps. 116 where in v. 3 'the snares of death encompassing' are later loosened by God (116.16, 'you have loosed my bonds'). Ps. 116 is part of the Great Hallel that, as I mentioned above (7.2.7 n. 124) was sung at the Festival of the Tabernacles. Ps. 118 as part of the Hallel would also be sung and in v. 22 are the well-known words: 'The stone which the builders rejected has become the chief cornerstone.' The rejecting of the 'stone' now takes place in Jn 11.45-53. The irony is that the rejection of the 'stone' (Jesus) will mean the rejection/destruction of 'our place', that is, the Temple. Jesus' prayer before Lazarus's grave, Πάτερ, εὐχαριστῶ σοι ὅτι ἤκουσάς μου (v. 41) may possibly allude to Ps. 118.21. The weakness of this suggestion is that Ps. 118.21 (LXX) does not have εὐχαριστῶ but ἐξομολογήσομαί. I suspect the connection is rather fragile.

133. See also 2 Macc. 10.1-8; Josephus, *Ant.* 12.316-25.

days, from the twenty-fifth (day) of the month of Kislev, with gladness and
with joy (1 Macc. 4.59).

There are a number of parallels and some crucial differences between the
origins of the festival and the narrative in John 10 and 11.

7.3.2 Parallels

Maccabaean Origins of the Feast	*John 10 and 11*
1. A man makes himself God (i.e. blasphemy) (θεός on Antiochus' coins).[134]	A man is accused of making himself God[135] (i.e. blasphemy) (Jn 10.33).
2. Maccabaeans fear the loss of their Holy Place (1 Macc. 3.43).	Jews fear the loss of their Holy Place (Jn 11.48-50).
3. Some considered Antiochus a madman (μαινόμενος).[136]	Jesus is accused of being mad (10.20, μαίνεται).
4. Antiochus profanes the Temple (1 Macc. 1.54, 55; 2.12).	The Jews take up stones against Jesus, the new Temple (Jn 10.31).

134. James C. VanderKam ('John 10 and the Feast of the Dedication', in H.W. Attridge, J.J. Collins and T.H. Tobin [eds.], *Of Scribes and Scrolls: Studies on the Hebrew Bible, Intertestamental Judaism, and Christian Origins, Presented to John Strugnell on the Occasion of his Sixtieth Birthday* [Lanham, MD: University Press of America, 1990], pp. 203-14 [211, 212]): 'The extant coins that were minted during Antiochus IV's reign prove that he, like a number of hellenistic monarchs, advertised himself as a god.'

135. VanderKam ('John 10', p. 213) draws attention to Antiochus's deathbed speech (no doubt a fanciful report that became part of the Jewish literary heritage about Antiochus) in 2 Macc. 9.12 where he exclaims, 'It is right to be subject to God, and no mortal should think that he is equal to God' (δίκαιον ὑποτάσσεσθαι τῷ θεῷ, καὶ μὴ θνητὸν ὄντα ἰσόθεα φρονεῖν). These reported words of Antiochus have some affinity with the response of Jesus' interrogators to his claim of being one with the Father (10.30; cf. 5.18c) in 10.33c (σὺ ἄνθρωπος ὢν ποιεῖς σεαυτὸν θεόν). Further, Jesus does not make himself God. Brown (*John*, I, p. 408) notes, 'For John, Jesus never makes himself anything; everything that he is stems from the Father. He is not a man who makes himself God; he is the Word of God who has become man. That is why vs. 36 really answers the Jewish charge [of blasphemy implied in vs. 31 where the Jews take up stones to stone him]; it was the Father who consecrated Jesus.'

136. W.R. Paton's translation of *Polybius: The Histories in Six Volumes* (ed. T.E. Page *et al.*; trans. W.R. Paton; LCL; London: Heinemann; New York: G.P. Putnam's Sons, 1922–54, 1926), V, p. 483 (26.1, 7) has 'all respectable men were entirely puzzled about him [Antiochus IV], some looking on him as a plain simple man and others as a madman (μαινόμενον)'. Polybius quipped that he was not ἐπιφανής, but ἐπιμανής (p. 481) (26.1.1).

Differences

5. The Temple of stone is sanctified (1 Macc. 4.54).	The Temple of Jesus is sanctified (Jn 10.36).
6. Stones are raised into an altar (1 Macc. 4.48).	Stones are lifted to destroy Jesus (Jn 10.31).
7. Antiochus IV is a false manifestation of God (1 Macc. 1.10).	Jesus is a true manifestation of God (Jn 10.30).[137]
8. One flock with Antiochus as shepherd (1 Macc. 1.41-53).	One flock with Jesus as the Good Shepherd (Jn 10.16b).
9. The Maccabaeans fight against the oppressor Antiochus.	Jesus fights against the oppressor death[138] (Jn 11 but esp. vv. 51-52).

7.3.3 *Complex of Literary Echoes*

The purpose of these parallels and differences is to draw attention to a complex of literary echoes that the reader may have been able to hear in John 10 and 11, but especially in 10.22-36. The figure of the Johannine Jesus is polyvalent: sometimes he is like Antiochus IV (1, 3, 8); sometimes in direct contrast (7); and sometimes like the Maccabaean Jews (9). The contemporary Jews are like their Maccabaean ancestors (2) and unlike them (6). There is no direct one-line correspondence, but rather there are polyphonic echoes weaving through the narrative. The reader knows that Jesus is the true Temple (2.21), and John wants him/her to see that the Festival of Dedication finds its fulfilment in the *consecration* of Jesus by the Father (10.36). The Jews, on the contrary, show themselves to be followers of Antiochus because they are ready to *desecrate* the true Temple of God (2.21) by taking up stones, not to build an altar as the Maccabean Jews did, but to stone Jesus (10.31). Even though they walk in the porch of Solomon, the first of the Temple builders in Israel's history and the first to dedicate the Temple,[139] the king whose name means

137. VanderKam ('John 10', p. 214 n. 30) offers the suggestion of his colleague, Professor William Adler, that in the Jewish demand to have Jesus reveal himself 'plainly' 10.24 (παρρησία) readers might see some parallel with the Jewish rejection of Antiochus's claim to be god 'made manifest'.

138. This is especially prominent in Jn 11 where Lazarus is loosed (11.44) from bondage to death.

139. VanderKam ('John 10', p. 205) says, 'As is well known, the verb that is used for his [Solomon's] dedicating the temple in 1 Kgs 8.63; 2 Chr 7.5, 9 (ויחנכו) is the one to which the noun *hanukkah* is related. Moreover, Josephus implies that the portico of Solomon was a structure from the first Temple that had somehow escaped destruction and had become part of the second sanctuary. In *War* 5.185 he relates that Solomon, "having walled up the eastern side, a single portico was reared on this built-up ground" (cf. also *Ant.* 15.401).'

'peace', they have no peace in their hearts towards Jesus.

There was no security from the wolf (10.12) in the old Temple of Jerusalem. Antiochus the pre-eminent wolf (in this context of the Feast of Dedication) entered the holy place and desecrated it and even though the Maccabaean Fathers dedicated the refurbished Temple anew, it now offers no security for the sheep of Jesus. It has been destroyed (2.19) and the sheep have been scattered (10.12; cf. Mt. 26.31; Zech. 13.7). The new 'place' of security and safety is in the hands of Jesus and the Father (10.28, 29). Jesus will gather into one the 'other sheep' (10.16) and 'the dispersed children of God' (11.52). This new 'place' of safety is characterized by a personal relationship between the sheep and Jesus the good shepherd (10.3-5, 27).[140]

This new 'place' is in fact Jesus the new Temple where the Father is present. This presence is contingent on Jesus' union with the Father, which is forcefully expressed in 10.30: 'I and the Father are one.'[141] A new 'Temple Dedication' is announced in 10.36. Jesus is the one whom the Father has sanctified (ὅν ὁ πατὴρ ἡγίασεν). Brown has the heading in this point in his commentary: 'Jesus is consecrated in place of the Temple altar.'[142] Parallel statements in 17.9, where Jesus tells the Father that he

---

140. Verse 3b finds a specific fulfilment in 20.16 when the risen Jesus calls Mary by name.

141. Jn 10.29 indicates that the unity of Father and Son is not an undifferentiated unity. The Father is 'greater than all else' and acts in relation to the Son, who is distinct from the Father. E. Pollard ('The Father–Son and God–Believer Relationships According to St John: A Brief Study of John's Use of Prepositions', in M. de Jonge [ed.], *L'Évangile de Jean: Sources, rédaction, théologie* [BETL, 44; Gembloux: Ducolot, 1977], pp. 363-69 [367]) clarifies the Son's union with the Father when he says, 'Everywhere in John from the first verse of the prologue the unity of the Father and Son is never the undifferentiated unity of identity. It is a unity which permits distinctions. Always the relation between the Father and the Son is the paradoxical relation of distinction-in-unity.' As far as Jn 1.1 (καὶ θεὸς ἦ ὁ λόγος) is concerned, D.A. Fennema ('John 1.18: "God the Only Son"', *NTS* 31 [1985], pp. 124-35 [131]) speaks of the *logos sharing* in the divinity of God. J. Painter ('Tradition, History and Interpretation in John 10', in J. Beutler and R. Fortna [eds.], *The Shepherd Discourse of John 10 and its Context* [Cambridge: Cambridge University Press, 1991], pp. 53-74 [69]) speaks of ontological equality and functional subordination.

142. Brown, *John*, I, p. 401. Coloe ('The Dwelling of God', p. 216) comments, 'In the restoration program following the victory of the Maccabees, the same verb ἁγιάζω is used to describe the consecration of the Temple courts—καὶ τὰς αὐλὰς ἡγίασαν (1 Macc. 4.48, similarly 3 Macc. 2.9, 16). The word central to the celebration of this Feast of Dedication is now applied to Jesus.'

has consecrated himself, and in 6.69, where Peter describes Jesus as 'God's Holy One', indicate that Jesus is the 'Dedicated One'—dedicated by the Father (by means of his willing obedience) to be not only the 'place' of sacrifice, but also the sacrificial Lamb. In this way Jesus not only replaces the Feast of Dedication but also fulfils it by becoming both the locus of God's presence and the sacrificial victim.

Later (in 17.17-19) the words of 10.36, ἁγιάζω and ἀποστέλλω, are applied to the disciples. Jesus prays that they may be consecrated in truth and sent into the world. Coloe remarks:

> There will come a time when Jesus is no longer present in the world, but the disciples, who remain in the world (cf. 17.11, 15), will continue to be a consecrated presence of the Father and Son in the world (17.17).[143]

7.3.4 *Conclusion*

I believe the consecration of Jesus described in Jn 10.36 echoes the consecration of the Temple courts celebrated in the Feast of Dedication. The many allusions to this feast in Jn 10 and 11 confirm my judgment that Jesus is here presented as the fulfilment and replacement of this Jewish festival.

7.4 *The Sabbath*

In this chapter I have been arguing that Temple festivals have been fulfilled and replaced by Jesus. So far I have endeavoured to demonstrate how the Johannine Jesus has fulfilled and replaced the Temple festivals of Passover, Tabernacles and Dedication. Now in this section we turn to the Sabbath.

7.4.1 *The Sabbath as a Temple Festival*

First, can the Sabbath be classed as a festival?[144] According to Lev. 23.2 it can: 'These are the appointed festivals of the LORD [מוֹעֲדֵי יהוה] that you shall proclaim as holy convocations, my appointed festivals. Six days shall work be done; but the seventh day is a Sabbath of complete rest, a holy convocation…'[145] This Sabbath is to be a day of joy and refreshment (Exod. 23.12; Isa. 58.13; Hos. 2.11).

---

143. Coloe, 'The Dwelling of God', p. 218.

144. Brown (*John*, I, p. 404) brings Passover, Tabernacles, Dedication and Sabbath together and classes them all as festivals that Jesus has fulfilled and replaced.

145. The word מוֹעֵד means 'appointed time, set time' and is used of the 'Tent of Meeting' (אֹהֶל מוֹעֵד). Gen. 1.14 supports the view that the sun, the moon and the stars have been created by God for, among other things, מוֹעֲדִים. The Sabbath is one of the

The Sabbath was also a time for worship. This is implied by the fact that in Lev. 23.3 the Sabbath is:

> מִקְרָא קֹדֶשׁ, a time in which the community lays aside all usual work in order to assemble in worship of God and in celebration of the joys of life. These days are קֹדוּשׁ, 'holy, sacred', for the worship of Yahweh is their singular focus.[146]

In relation to the phrase at the end of Lev. 23.3, 'in all your settlements' (בְּכֹל מוֹשְׁבֹתֵיכֶם) means 'in all your homes, not just at the sanctuary'.[147] This presupposes that there was a sanctuary celebration as well as observance in all Israelite homes. What is clear is that the story of Jesus' healing of the man who had been ill for 38 years is set in Jerusalem (5.1), and Jesus' later meeting with the healed man is in the Temple (ἐν τῷ ἱερῷ, 5.14), and it appears that his discussion with the Jews is also in the Temple. No commentary I have consulted makes anything of this Temple reference except Morris whose suggestion is, I believe, untenable.[148] However, when this healing is compared to the healing of the man born blind (Jn 9; see below for a table setting out similarities and differences), then the significance of the Temple reference begins to emerge. Jesus found the man born blind outside the synagogue, a place of worship. He was ready to believe, and when he discovered who Jesus was he worshipped him. In contrast the healed man of John 5 is found in the Jewish place of worship, the Temple. Far from worshipping Jesus he informs on

מוֹעֲדִים. In his commentary on Leviticus Martin Noth (*Leviticus: A Commentary* [OTL; London: SCM Press, 1962], p. 168) thinks that vv. 1-3 of Lev. 23 were added later as a kind of superscription of the festival list. J.E. Hartley (*Leviticus* [WBC, 4; Dallas, TX: Word Books, 1992], pp. 375-76) thinks the opposite—that v. 4 is a repetition of v. 2b. However, the text as we now have it and as it possibly would have been when John was writing the Gospel is that the Sabbath was included in the list of Levitical Festivals.

146. Hartley, *Leviticus*, p. 375.
147. Hartley, *Leviticus*, p. 376.
148. L. Morris, *The Gospel According to John* (NICNT; Grand Rapids: Eerdmans, 1971), p. 307: 'We may not unfairly conjecture that the man had gone there to offer thanks to God (cf. Mark 1.44; Luke 17.14).' This is unlikely. He showed no gratitude to Jesus. On the contrary he informed on him. Why should he show gratitude to God? Bultmann (*John*, p. 243 n. 5): 'The temple is probably mentioned as a place where one could expect to find plenty of people.' Then he actually refers to Jn 9 when he remarks, 'Εὑρίσκει clearly refers to a chance meeting, as in…9.35,' but he makes nothing of it. Lindars, Barrett, Schnackenburg, Brown, Carson, Beasley-Murray offer no comment on 'temple'.

him and the Temple becomes, not a place of grateful worship, but murder-seeking debate (5.18).

7.4.2 *Two Sabbath Healings Compared and Contrasted*

The healing of the 38-year-old man was simple: Jesus said to him, 'Stand up, take your mat and walk.' And the man was made well at once, and he took up his mat and began to walk. But it got Jesus into strife with the Jews. He had told the man to carry his mat on the Sabbath, and carrying loads on the Sabbath was disallowed.[149] The Jews picked up on *this* and were blind to the wonderful healing Jesus had performed. Unlike the man born blind (Jn 9), the healed man was not at all grateful and was ready to tell the Jews it was Jesus who had made him well (5.15). There are many similarities between the healing stories in John 5 and 9, but also some important differences:

Similarities

John 5	John 9
Jesus heals a man who has been ill for a long time (38 years) (v. 5).	Jesus heals a man born blind (v. 1).
The setting is Jerusalem (v. 1).	The setting is Jerusalem (v. 7).
It is the Sabbath (v. 9).	It is the Sabbath (v. 14).
Jesus is accused of breaking the Sabbath (v. 16).	Jesus is accused of breaking the Sabbath (v. 16).
Water is mentioned (v. 7).	Water is mentioned (v. 7).
The Jews question the healed man (vv. 11-12.	The Pharisees question the healed man (vv. 15-17, 24-34).
The Jews dialogue with Jesus (vv. 17-47).	The Jews dialogue with Jesus (vv. 40-41).
Jesus meets the healed man later (v. 14).	Jesus meets the healed man later (vv. 35-38).
The Son does the Father's works (v. 19).	Jesus does the works of him who sent him (v. 4).
The man has to do something to be healed (vv. 8, 9).	The man has to do something to be healed (v. 7).

149. Carrying things from one domain to another is the last of 39 works forbidden in Mishnah tractate *Šab.* 7.2 (Danby, *The Mishnah*, p. 106). Carrying empty beds is implicitly forbidden in *Šab.* 10.5 (Danby, *The Mishnah*, p. 109). Jesus, however, does not carry any burden; it is the healed man who carries his mat. However, the man is quick to tell the Jews that he is only doing what Jesus has commanded; he is not culpable, but Jesus is by virtue of his instruction.

Differences

John 5	*John 9*
Sin is a factor in the illness[150] (v. 14).	Sin is not a factor[151] (v. 3).
Jesus meets the healed man in the Temple[152] (v. 14).	Jesus meets the healed man outside the synagogue (ἀποσυνάγωγος) (v. 35).
When the healed man discovers who Jesus is he reports to the Jews (v. 15).	When the healed man discovers who Jesus is he worships him (v. 38).
The Jews persecute Jesus (vv. 16-18).	The Pharisees persecute the healed man (v. 34).

The above comparison shows that despite significant differences the two narratives are parallel in that Jesus does his work on the Sabbath and in both instances he is challenged about this Sabbath activity. Nevertheless the narrative of John 9 demonstrates a shift of focus away from Jesus (present in Jn 5) to the disciple of Jesus, namely, the healed man of John 9. Finally the comparison underlines the obvious importance the Sabbath has for John and therefore intimates justification for a separate treatment in this chapter.

7.4.3 *Jesus' Defence*

Jesus' defence of this activity is different from his defence in the Synoptic Gospels. In Mk 3.1-6 Jesus defends his healing of the man with the withered hand by appealing to the Sabbath as a day to do good and to save life, and in the previous pericope (Mk 2.23-28) he defends his disciples' action of plucking grain on the Sabbath by citing the occasion when David and his men ate the bread of the Presence in the Temple and points out that 'the Sabbath was made for humankind, and not humankind for the Sabbath; so the Son of Man is lord even of the Sabbath'. However, Jesus' defence of his Sabbath activity in John is explicitly tied to his relationship with his Father. In 5.17 Jesus gives his answer to the Jews: 'My Father is at work even until now, and so I am at work too' (Ὁ πατήρ μου ἕως ἄρτι ἐργάζεται κἀγὼ ἐργάζομαι).

---

150. Just how sin is a factor is not clear. Barrett (*St John*, p. 255) mentions that J.L. Martyn thinks that the 'worse thing' that may befall that man is that he will be judged for being an informer. However, as Barrett says, the man has already started down that track (v. 11) when Jesus speaks to him and later, when he completes the sin of being an informer, no 'worse thing' happens to him.

151. At least Jesus refuses to apportion blame in the matter of sin (cf. 9.3).

152. This contrast is striking. In Jn 5 the man healed in the Temple displays his loyalty to the Jews; in Jn 9 the healed man thrown out of the place of worship (the synagogue) displays his loyalty to Jesus.

7.4.4 *God's Sabbath Work*

It was widely asserted in rabbinic literature that God worked on the Sabbath. People are born on the Sabbath and die on the Sabbath, so God is active in giving life and judging (*Gen R.* 11.10; cf. *b. Ta'an.* 2a).[153] It was also accepted that Temple work was permitted on the Sabbath, which allowed God to work because the universe is God's Temple (*Mek. Shabbata* 2). On the specific matter of bearing burdens on the Sabbath, Tinneus Rufus asked R. Aqiba:

> 'If it is true, as you say, that the Holy One, blessed be he, honours the Sabbath day, then he should not raise up winds on that day or bring down rain.' R. Aqiba said to him, 'Woe to that man [you]! It is in the same category [for God to do these things] as for a human being to carry four cubits [which is permitted]. [God owns the whole world and is carrying in his own, private domain.] (*Gen R.* 11.5).[154]

What kind of work is Jesus referring to when he says, 'My Father is still working…'? Samuele Bacchiocchi has a discussion on this.[155] He rejects the view that Jesus is speaking about 'cura continua' or 'creatio continua' and accepts that 'acta salutis' are in view.[156] However, it is perhaps unhelpful to enquire into what God does or does not do on the Sabbath. As Hoskyns has pointed out, the emphasis here in John is not on the continuous and unbroken invisible work of God whether it be described as 'cura continua' or 'creatio continua', but rather on the visible work of Jesus Christ, the Son of the Father.[157]

This dovetails with what we understand by the much discussed words, ἕως ἄρτι in Jn 5.17. Bacchiocchi[158] has an extended discussion of these words and concludes that 'the adverbial phrase "until now" must be taken as a reference to the culmination of God's activity—the time when God

153. While these rabbinic references postdate the New Testament, it is generally felt that they reflect traditions that were current in the New Testament era.

154. Cited from Jacob Neusner's *Genesis Rabbah: The Judaic Commentary to the Book of Genesis: A New American Translation*. I. *Parashiyyot One through Thirty-Three on Genesis 1.1 to 8.14* (BJS, 104; Atlanta: Scholars Press, 1985), p. 115.

155. S. Bacchiocchi, 'John 5.17: Negation or Clarification of the Sabbath?', *AUSS* 19 (1981), pp. 3-19.

156. I explore these 'acta salutis' below in my discussion of 5.19-29 where I focus on salvation and judgment.

157. Hoskyns, *The Fourth Gospel*, p. 296.

158. Bacchiocchi, 'John 5.17', pp. 11-13.

will no longer work, at least not in the same way'. Others[159] take it to refer to the constancy of God's working on the Sabbath from the creation to the present. However, in the light of the present debate between the Jews and Jesus over the healing of the lame man, while not denying the constancy of God's working, I believe the emphasis falls on the present working of God, the 'now', as it comes to expression in the works that Jesus is doing and that the Jews have witnessed in the healing of the lame man in particular.

7.4.5 *The Son's Works are the Father's Works*
The works of Jesus are the Father's works. And the fact that these works take place on the Sabbath has implications that I will explore in a moment, but first we must see how Jesus defends his claim of v. 17 in the ensuing verses. In 5.19 Jesus says, 'Very truly, the Son can do nothing on his own, but only what he sees the Father doing; for whatever the Father does, the Son does likewise.' That is, the Son's works are the Father's works.

In 5.21-29 we see these works are works of salvation (raising the dead—note the echo between v. 21 and v. 8 through the use of the verb ἐγείρω) and judgment, both in the present and in the future. Broadly 5.19-25 represents realized eschatology and 5.26-30 future eschatology,

---

159. Barrett (*St John*, p. 255): 'ἕως ἄρτι means "up to the present", with no implication that the time has now come, or soon will come, for work to stop.' Lindars (*John*, p. 218) 'without intermission'; Brown (*John*, I, p. 212) 'even until now'; Bultmann (*John*, p. 245) stresses constancy but suggests in a footnote (p. 245 n. 5) that 'ἕως ἄρτι…in the first instance indicates the terminus ad quem'. I do not believe that this expression *of itself* signals the termination of the Sabbath as some have said. For example, Hoskyns (*The Fourth Gospel*, p. 296) says, 'The significance of the words *even until now* does not therefore consist in the fact that His work cannot cease with the Sabbath, but, as in ix.4 (cf. 1 John ii.9), that the hour of his death is not yet. In the work of Jesus the Jews are confronted by the work of God (iv. 34, xvii.4, xix.30). This work involves, not the violation of the law of the Sabbath, but its complete overthrow and fulfilment; for its vacuum is filled with the creative, life-giving love of God.'

'O. Cullmann has it both ways in *Sabbat und Sontag nach dem Johannesevangelium: Vorträge und Aufsätze* (Tübingen: Mohr, 1966), pp. 187-91, where he says that ἕως ἄρτι refers both to Jesus' resurrection (on the first day of the week) and to the rest of the new creation "at the End" and on this basis concludes that the text is "an indirect theological reflection" that connects the Old Testament God-ordained *Ruhetag* ("day of rest") with the primitive Christian *Auferstehungstag* ("Resurrection day").' (Cited from D. Carson, 'Jesus and the Sabbath in the Four Gospels', in *From Sabbath to Lord's Day* [Grand Rapids: Zondervan, 1982], p. 96 n. 148). I think this is correct for John as a whole, but to see this in the ἕως ἄρτι of 5.17 is stretching the text too far.

although it is difficult to make a precise separation in these verses because elements of realized and future eschatology tend to intermingle. What is clear, however, is that the Son has been given works of salvation and judgment by the Father. Jesus defends this claim by calling on four witnesses: John the Baptist (vv. 33-35); the works themselves (v. 36); the Father himself (vv. 37-38); and the Scriptures (vv. 39-40). In the concluding verses of ch. 5 (vv. 41-47) Jesus passes judgment on the Jews by (ironically) bringing them to the bar of Moses' words (v. 46).

The works of Jesus, as Jn 5.19-30 testifies, are eschatological works. In 5.33-47 Jesus marshals witnesses to verify that they are also God's works. In particular, one of these works (the healing of the lame man) is accomplished on the Sabbath. Could it be that Jesus is saying to his opponents, 'The works I do are God's works—works of salvation and judgment. The day of YHWH has come. The eschatological Sabbath has arrived'?

7.4.6 *The Work of Salvation*
7.4.6.1 *Making People Whole.* In Jn 7.21[160] Jesus advances the argument of Jn 5.17-47. In John 7 he points more explicitly to the eschatological significance of his healing work.

The nature of the specific Sabbath work of Jesus in healing the lame man is developed in 7.22-24:

> Moses gave you circumcision (it is of course, not from Moses, but from the patriarchs),[161] and you circumcise a man on the Sabbath. If a man receives circumcision on the Sabbath in order that the law of Moses may not be broken (λυθῇ), are you angry with me because I healed a man's whole body (ὅλον ἄνθρωπον ὑγιῆ ἐποίησα) on the Sabbath? Do not judge by appearances, but judge with right judgement.

160. Some commentators say that the 'one work' Jesus refers to is probably the work of healing in Jn 5.2-9. Bultmann (*John*, p. 10) says '7.15-24 harks back directly to the sabbath healing that lies far off in chapter 5' and so has rearranged the text of the Gospel so that 7.15-24 follows on from 5.41-47 (pp. 268-78).

161. Rabbi Judah (c. 165–200), says, 'Great is circumcision, for despite all the religious duties Abraham our father fulfilled, he was not called "perfect" until he was circumcised, as it is written, Walk before me and be thou perfect [םימת means "whole"] (Gen.17.1).' This offers a rabbinic source (albeit late) for the idea of circumcision in some way signifying wholeness. Rudolf Meyer ('Περιτέμνω', *TDNT*, VI, pp. 72-84 [75-76]) says that circumcision has two functions, 'being on the one side a sacrifice of redemption [the wholeness aspect] and on the other a tribal or covenantal sign. Both play a part in the Old Testament, though the covenantal aspect comes to predominate.' See also J. Duncan Derrett, 'Circumcison and Perfection: A Johannine Equation (John 7.22-23)', *EvQ* 63 (1991), pp. 211-24.

Circumcision, which pointed to the restoration of the whole man, was permitted on the Sabbath, so why object to Jesus performing the comprehensive work of healing on the Sabbath, which is the redemptive purpose of circumcision?[162] The relevance of this for our theme of Jesus fulfilling the Sabbath will become clearer below.

7.4.6.2 *Not Superficial, but Penetrating Judgment*

It is v. 24 of John 7 that alerts us to how we should understand Jesus' Sabbath work. He says, 'Do not judge by appearances, but judge with right judgement.'[163] Presumably it is the Jews who are judging superficially. They only see Jesus infringing the Sabbath (5.10; 9.16); they do not see the wonder of a man made whole (5.9), of a man who has received his sight (9.30). They judge that Jesus is a sinner because he is a Sabbath breaker (5.16; 9.16, 24). In particular they do not see that Jesus is the one who, under his Father's instruction, has inaugurated the eschatological Sabbath[164] with works of salvation and judgment. The Sabbath festival has been transformed with the coming of Jesus.

This is also the emphasis of 9.4, 5 as Jesus prepares to heal the man born blind: 'We[165] must work the works of him who sent me while it is

---

162. Pancaro (*Law*, p. 165) comments, 'The Jewish rite of initiation, which made man a member of God's people, was unable to give man what Jesus came to bring. Jesus alone gives men the power to become children of God and to have life in abundance, and this is what was prefigured by circumcision.' What Pancaro says is doubtless true about the covenantal aspect of circumcision. Membership of God's family is not by circumcision but by the Spirit and receiving Jesus (1.12, 13). However, what is in view in Jn 7.22, 23 is not the covenantal, but the redemptive aspect of circumcision. This aspect prefigures the wholeness that Jesus has come to bring to humankind. The wholeness is summed up in the word salvation. Thus the healing of the lame man in Jn 5 is an act of salvation.

163. The 'right judgment' in Jn 7 is concerned the the law as a whole; here we are concerned specifically with the Sabbath.

164. It may be possible to link this to the seven-day schema in Jn 1–2 (see 3.3.2). The problem is that we do not know which day is which. Nevertheless it seems probable that the wedding is on the seventh day, the eschatological sabbath—the day of wholeness and joy. The seventh day is often seen as the climax of the week. In the discussion of 2.13-22 I argued that the miracle of turning water to wine signified the eschatological day of the LORD (cf. 2.11). Jesus turns from the eschatological joy of 2.1-11 to the eschatological judgment of 2.13-22.

165. Most commentators favour the more difficult reading of ἡμᾶς...με. This reading corresponds to other readings, such as 3.11, where Jesus associates himself with his disciples whom he has gathered around him. 'As the Father has sent him, so he sends

day; night is coming when no one can work. As long as I am in the world, I am the light of the world.' So Jesus provides a licence for treating the time as 'daytime' (cf. 12.35-36). It is his presence that makes it daytime— eschatological daytime! What Jesus does in the ensuing narrative is to bring physical sight and understanding faith to the man born blind. For him it is salvation. However, the Jews, who think they see, become blind; they are condemned by Jesus' light (3.19). This healing work of Jesus was done on the Sabbath[166]—the eschatological Sabbath. It is perhaps going too far to say that the eschatological Sabbath replaces the Jewish Sabbath. It is better to see the Jewish Sabbath as having come to fulfilment, that is, having been transformed.

7.4.7 *The Night is Coming*

H. Weiss's comments in his article 'The Sabbath in the Fourth Gospel' are illuminating:

> What the Fourth Gospel affirms is that both the Father and the Son work on the Sabbath, during the day. In other words, the Sabbath is not being compared to the night, when no work may be done, but to the day, when the eschatological work needs to be done. While Jesus is on earth it is daytime because he is the light of the world. It is also Sabbath.[167]

However, Jesus makes clear in 9.4 that the day will come to an end and the night will come when no one can work. When does this night come? John tells us in 13.30. The disciples are at the supper together and

> Jesus was troubled in spirit and declared, 'Very truly, I tell you one of you will betray me.'

The disciples wondered who he was talking about and Simon Peter asked the Beloved Disciple to ask Jesus:

---

them (20.21), and therefore upon them, as upon him, there rests the obligation to do the work of God while opportunity lasts' (Barrett, *St John*, p. 357).

166. The breaches of the Sabbath *Halakah* for the healing of the man born blind are listed by Carson ('Jesus and the Sabbath in the Four Gospels', p. 82): mixing (*Šab.* 24.3); kneading (*Šab.* 7.2); and smearing mud on the eyes might come under prohibited anointing (*Šab.* 14.4).

167. H. Weiss ('The Sabbath in the Fourth Gospel', *JBL* 110 [1991], pp. 311-21 [318]) argues that Jesus' constant Sabbath work is the eschatological work of the One sent down from heaven and this work is climaxed in John by the cross (19.28-31), which introduces the Sabbath of eternal rest.

> Jesus answered, 'It is the one to whom I give this piece of bread when I
> have dipped it in the dish.' So when he had dipped the piece of bread, he
> gave it to Judas Son of Simon Iscariot. After he received the piece of bread,
> Satan entered into him. Jesus said to him, 'Do quickly what you are going
> to do.'... So, after receiving the piece of bread, he immediately went out.
> *And it was night.*

There is night in Judas's heart and there is night for Jesus and his
disciples. It was night when they came to arrest Jesus in the garden (18.1-
3), and throughout that night the darkness is lit by the shadowy flames of
torches and the charcoal fire (18.3,18). This is John's way of saying that
the night had come. The time for working had come to an end. And the
end of Jesus' work is pronounced from the cross when he says, 'It is
finished [τετέλεσται].' I take this to refer to the work that the Father had
given him to do on earth. It was an hour of darkness when evil seemingly
had triumphed and Jesus was dying, but also it was an hour of victory—
Jesus' assignment was completed.

This hour of darkness seems to extend to Jesus' burial. We are told that
because it was a great Sabbath (19.31) (γὰρ μεγάλη ἡ ἡμέρα ἐκείνου τοῦ
σαββάτου) the Jews asked Pilate to hasten the death of the three crucified
men so their bodies could be removed. There is perhaps a shadow cast
over the discipleship of the two men who bury Jesus. Joseph of Arimathea
is a secret disciple for fear of the Jews and Nicodemus is still the disciple
who came to Jesus by night.[168] It seems John is making an ironical
comment on the Jews' scrupulous care to keep this great Sabbath by
making sure the body of Jesus, the light of the world, is out of sight. This

---

168. Weiss ('Sabbath', p. 320) unfairly calls Nicodemus 'a creature of the dark'. It
is certainly true that he came to Jesus 'by night' (3.2), but it seems that he made progress in the dialogue with 'the light of the world' (cf. 3.21). Further, in 7.50 Nicodemus is not characterized as the one who 'came to Jesus by night' and he speaks up in
favour of 'right judgement' in 7.51 (cf. 7.24). Finally, in coming to bury Jesus, Nicodemus is making a commitment even though it seems from his point of view it is too late.
I think progress for Nicodemus is intimated in the way he is described in 19.39—ὁ
ἐλθὼν πρὸς αὐτὸν νυκτὸς τὸ πρῶτον. The emphasized words are τὸ πρῶτον.
When he first came to Jesus he came by night. The implication is that he has developed
in discipleship since then. Weiss allows for no movement in Nicodemus's character,
but I believe movement is present in the narrative. Still, there is the reminder that he
did first come to Jesus 'by night', perhaps indicating that he has not fully come into the
light of Jesus. No matter how abundant the spices and how splendid and new the tomb,
there is no hope in the burial—the hope is in the risen Jesus of the new day.

great Sabbath is to become the last of all Sabbaths as the darkness of the first day of the week gives way to the dawn of a new age (20.1, 19).[169]

7.4.8 *The Birth of the Eschatological Sabbath*

Some would argue that John is not interested in a special day of worship,[170] but the threefold reference to the first day of the week (20.1, 19, 26) suggests that this day was special to the author as marking the day when Jesus rose from the dead. Acts 20.7 tells us that Christians met on the first day of the week to break bread, so already this day had become a special day of worship for believers. That the Johannine community may have sat lightly to worshipping on Sunday is possible, and what Weiss says, parodying 4.21, 23, 'neither on this day nor on the Sabbath will you worship the Father; the true worshippers will worship the Father in spirit and truth'—may well be true.[171] Nevertheless there is at least the suggestion in 20.1, 19 and 26 that the first day of the week, being the day of Jesus' resurrection, was special.

On the other hand, there is the theme of the consummation of the Sabbath running through the Gospel. The words of A. Corell[172] succinctly summarize the theme:

> …it was by an appeal to the nature of his works that Jesus refuted the Jews when they accused him of breaking the Sabbath—'My Father worketh until now and I work' (5.17). Thus he pointed out that while the Law of Moses forbade that man should do their own work on the Sabbath, it could in no wise forbid or prevent the accomplishment of God's work on that day. He, himself, had come to do the works of God…which, being of an eschatological significance, belonged to the Sabbath in a very special way… Indeed, his very doing of these things was a sure sign that the real Sabbath of fulfilment had come. Since, moreover, the risen and ascended Christ lives and works within the Church, her life is one continuous Sabbath—a pledge and foretaste of the great Sabbath of eternity.

Out of the darkness of the great Sabbath of 19.31 a greater Sabbath is born (20.1).

---

169. Indeed, as I pointed out earlier (7.2.4.1), the closing moments of the great Sabbath of 19.31 may include the moment of the resurrection, since Mary Magdalene comes to the tomb (20.1) while it was still dark, that is, in the closing moments of the great Sabbath.

170. Weiss, 'Sabbath', p. 321.

171. Weiss, 'Sabbath', p. 320.

172. A. Corell, *Consummatum Est* (London: SPCK, 1958), p. 63.

7.4.9 *Conclusion: A Transformed Sabbath*

It is not clear in John that Jesus replaces the Jewish Sabbath with the Sunday as the celebration day of his resurrection, as some have claimed.[173] It is also not clear that John equates the new eschatological Sabbath rest with the present eternal life the disciples enjoy, as Weiss does.[174] However, as the foregoing analysis shows, John has indicated how the Jewish Sabbath has been overtaken by the day of the Father's works through the Son and the Son's works through the disciples. In this sense the eschatological Sabbath has come and the disciples of Jesus live in it. But this does not rule out the possibility of a future dimension for a Sabbath rest. While John tends to major on realized eschatology, he is not averse to future eschatology. 'The first day of the week' is mentioned twice in John 20. It was obviously special, but how special? Certainly it did not become a new Sabbath. Perhaps its link with the Sabbath was that it marked the real beginning of the eschatological Sabbath of which the works of Jesus were intimations of what was to come. Now the disciples are charged in this new era to do the works of Jesus and in fact do greater works in the power of the Spirit (14.12).

7.4.10 *Conclusion to Festivals*

This chapter on the Jewish festivals takes up a wide sweep of the Gospel, namely chs. 5–10.42, with considerable interaction with references to the Passover in chs. 13,18 and 19. There is of course a great deal going on in these chapters, but it is fair to say that the context for much of the content is the festivals of the Passover, Tabernacles, Dedication and Sabbath.

It is worth noting that Jesus seemed to have little respect for the festivals. He scarcely attended them, and when he did go to the Tabernacles' Festival he hijacked it for his own purposes (7.14); and for the purification for the Passover in Jerusalem he undergoes his own consecration in the house at Bethany (11.55; 12.3). He 'worked' on the Sabbath (5.9; 9.14). There seems to be an underlying critique of the festivals running through

---

173. For example, Oscar Cullmann, cf. above n. 159.

174. Weiss, 'Sabbath', p. 319: '…the Johannine community has come to understand that its whole life is being lived on the Sabbath. As far as they are concerned, they have eternal life (John 3.15, 16, 36; 5.24; 6.40, 47, 54; 20.31). They are enjoying the Sabbath rest. As they see things, Jesus did not abolish the Sabbath but established the eschatological Sabbath among them.' But it seems to be going beyond the bounds of the Johannine evidence to say that the Johannine community 'eschatologized the Sabbath into its own vision of eternal life and felt free to ridicule those who were concerned with weekly observances' (p. 321).

chs. 5–11 of the Gospel. They are not an end in themselves. This may perhaps be the significance of 5.1. If indeed the unnamed festival represents all festivals (cf. p. 206 and n. 5), then John may be pointing in the subsequent verses to a picture of Judaism (including the festivals) in its weakness and impotence. It cannot bring the salvation the lame man longs for. Jesus alone is the one who can do this.

In my analysis I have suggested how the Johannine Jesus is presented as the focus and fulfilment of at least three of these festivals. Not only does he fulfil them, he replaces them with his own person. Through his death on the cross he becomes the Passover Lamb; he is the true Tabernacle (1.14), the Giver of the living water of the Holy Spirit, and he is the light not only of Jerusalem, but of the world; and Jesus is the true Temple (2.21) consecrated by the Father (10.36) for the sake of the world. The issue of the Sabbath is not so clear. But the Sabbath is certainly transformed. Jesus has ushered in the eschatological Sabbath with works of salvation and judgment, supremely and definitively with his death and resurrection.

Chapter 8

THE FATHER'S HOUSE:
POSSIBLE TEMPLE CONNECTIONS IN JOHN 13 AND 14

8.1 *Introduction*

So far this study has concentrated on establishing that the Johannine Jesus is the fulfilment and replacement of the Temple and its associated cultus. As Glenn Balfour has argued (see 7.2.4.7 and n. 101) this is not an answer so much *to* a Judaism that continues to flourish, but an answer *for* a Judaism that has suffered the profound loss of the Temple and those festivals that centred on the Temple. In the various Johannine texts I have examined we have discovered that the body of Jesus is now the Temple (2.21) not just for Jews, but for all people (4.42); Jesus is the Passover Lamb who has been sacrificed for the world (1.29); Jesus inaugurates the eschatological Sabbath and does the works of God (9.3-5; 5.17) that bring life and wholeness (11.43, 44; 7.23) to the dead and afflicted; Jesus is the light of the world who gives the light of life (8.12); Jesus is the Giver of the living water that will quench the thirst of all who come to him (4.13, 14; 7.37-39); and Jesus is the centre of a new worship, a worship of the Father in Spirit and truth (4.20-24).

Thus Jesus has come and brought the Temple and its associated ritual to a grand fulfilment, but the question surely remains, What does that mean when the Fulfiller himself disappears? What happens when the 'answer' for Judaism departs to the Father? Are those who put their hope in Jesus abandoned? Has the Spirit brought them to birth (3.5) and now left them as orphans (cf. 14.18)?

The answer to these anxious questions is contained in John 13–17, commonly known as the Farewell Discourses,[1] and it is to the first of these

---

1. Most scholars separate out Jn 13-17 as a distinctive pericope in John and assign it some such title as 'The Farewell Discourse(s)'. For an extensive survey of views on the macro-structure of John see Mlakuzhyil (*Fourth Gospel*, pp. 137-68). J.C. Thomas

that I turn in this chapter. I begin by considering the genre of Farewell Discourse and then focus on structural matters so that some insight might be gained into the text of 14.2-3, on which I wish to focus. I believe these verses contain an allusion to the Temple, and therefore it will be valuable to see what further light they can shed on the Temple theme in John, especially in relation to the basic thrust of John 13–17, which is apparently to reassure the disciples that they will not be orphans when Jesus departs. To provide credence for a Temple allusion in John 14.2-3, I appeal to John's presentation of the Temple theme throughout John 1–12, which has been set out in the previous chapters of this study. But in addition I explore the possibility of Temple/cultic themes in John 13. To my knowledge this has never been done in a systematic way so considerable space is devoted to investigating John 13 as a foundation to the discussion on 14.2-3. Examination of the key text (14.2-3) involves looking at the various phrases in the verses: 'my Father's house'; 'many rooms'; 'I am going to prepare a place for you'; and 'I will come again'. The chapter concludes with a summary statement.

8.2 *Farewell Genre*

Recent research has shown that there is a genre of farewell speech in pre-Christian Hellenistic and Jewish literature that can be applied to these chapters. While the genre is somewhat elastic, the most defining characteristic is clear enough, namely, a discourse given in anticipation of imminent death.[2]

(*Footwashing in John 13 and the Johannine Community* [JSNTSup, 61; Sheffield: Sheffield Academic Press, 1991], pp. 63, 64) discusses the arguments in favour of ch. 13 marking the beginning of a new section. Staley (*The Print's First Kiss*, pp. 58-66) offers an alternative division. He defines the literary structure of John by means of the four ministry tours (1.19–3.36; 4.1–6.71; 7.1–10.42; 11.1–21.25), but acknowledges that ch. 13 is pivotal: 'The first major division in the second half of the gospel (11.1–21.25) occurs at chapter 13. The section is universally recognised as the place in the story where Jesus turns toward his disciples and starts to reveal himself to them more openly through extended private discourses' (p. 107).

2.   See S. Fernando, *The Farewell of the Word: The Johannine Call to Abide* (Philadelphia: Fortress Press, 1991), pp. 7, 8. The elements of farewell discourses are variously listed in Thomas (*Footwashing*, p. 65) and Stibbe (*John*, p. 143). But the distinctiveness of the Johannine Farewell Discourse is well delineated by Brown (*John*, II, p. 582): '...it [the Last Discourse] is not like other last testaments, which are the recorded words of men who are dead and can speak no more...[these words have] been

This certainly fits chs. 13-17. Jesus is about to depart. Indeed the narrator tells us in the first verse of this section of John that 'his hour had come to depart from this world and go to the Father' (13.1), and this departure is emphasised throughout these chapters. Jesus does this in unmistakable terms when he tells his disciples that where he goes they cannot follow him (13.33). He had told the Jews this (7.34b), but now he tells his disciples (his own τεκνία). The disciples are to be severed from the One who is the 'answer' to all their hopes. 'Where I am going, you cannot come' (13.33), must have come as a bewildering and shattering word. And this departure is underlined several times in the subsequent chapters (14.12c, 28; 16.5; 28), but not so strongly as in 13.33. Moreover the disciples know that this departure is by way of death (11.16; 13.37). Their hearts are troubled (14.1, 27b) and heavy with sorrow (16.20).

8.3 *Provisional Structural Analysis*

It is to this sort of situation that John 13–17 is addressed. How shall we grasp the overall message of these chapters? I believe it is helpful to begin by attempting a provisional structural analysis. However, there is no consensus concerning the literary structure or even the literary unity as it stands. Fernando Segovia said in 1982 that 'nowadays hardly any exegete would vigorously maintain that Jn 13.31–18.1 constitutes a literary unity as it stands',[3] but in 1992 he wrote:

> in terms of its overall thematic flow, the farewell speech that leads up to the climactic prayer of John 17 can indeed be regarded as a self contained artistic whole that is highly unified and carefully developed from beginning to end. Its overall structure reveals a chiastic arrangement following an ABBA pattern.[4]

This latter quotation indicates a greater willingness to consider the literary unity of Johannine pericopae than some years ago.

---

transformed in the light of the resurrection through the coming of the Paraclete into a living discourse delivered, not by a dead man, but by one who has life (vi 57), to all readers of the Gospel.' See also Ernst Bammel ('The Farewell Discourse of the Evangelist John and its Jewish Heritage', *TB* 44 [1993], pp. 103-16), who discusses in detail the distinctiveness of the Johannine Farewell Discourses.

3.   F. Segovia, *Love Relationships in the Johannine Tradition* (Chico, CA: Scholars Press, 1982), p. 82.

4.   S. Segovia, *The Farewell of the Word: The Johannine Call to Abide* (Philadelphia: Fortress Press), pp. 288-89.

Nevertheless the obstacles to treating 13–17 as a literary unit are indeed formidable, the most notable being the aporia in 14.31, where Jesus says, 'Rise, let us be on our way', but then immediately continues on to speak of the true vine and the branches (15.1). It seems reasonable to conclude that 14.31 should immediately lead onto 18.1.[5] One wonders why a redactor would have left it in its present position.[6] Nevertheless, despite the difficulties, scholars have found signs of literary coherence in these chapters,[7] and such signs are evidence that the composition of these chapters was not without design and reflection. Therefore it seems legitimate to attempt a structural analysis of the chapters as they now stand.

What I offer here is an adaptation of Thomas's structural suggestions in his book *Footwashing in the Johannine Community*:[8]

A 13.1-30 Preparation through Cleansing and Prediction of Betrayal
    B 13.31–14.31 Jesus' Departure and Encouragement of Disciples
        C 15.1–17 The True Vine
        C' 15.18–16.4a The World's Hatred
    B' 16.4b-33 Jesus' Departure and the Work of the Spirit
A' 17.1-26 Preparation through Jesus' Prayer

The first section (A 13.1-30) is preparatory. First, the footwashing prepares the disciples for entering into membership with Jesus (v. 8). I will discuss below (see 8.6.5) how this functions as a cleansing. Secondly, the identifi-

---

5.   Segovia (*Farewell*) has an account of traditional resolutions of compositional difficulties (pp. 25-35) and most recent resolutions (pp. 35-47).

6.   Attempts at relocation create difficulties that would result in further disruption of the given text to 'improve' the narrative flow. Bultmann's efforts (*John*, pp. 459-60) are a good example of the domino effect of shifting 14.31c so that it immediately precedes 18.1. This means that chs. 15–17 have to be relocated. Possibly the redactor thought it better to leave the end of ch. 14 intact. P. Walker (*Jesus and the Holy City*, p. 173 n. 45) has an interesting note on the perplexing aporion. He suggests that Jesus and the disciples do leave wherever the footwashing took place and chs. 15–17 are given 'on the move'. He points out that in 18.1 Jesus and his disciples 'went out' (ἐξῆλθεν), which may refer to leaving not the room, but rather the city walls. John uses the same verb in 19.17 and 20.3 without specifying what it was that was 'left'; but in 19.17 it is clearly the city that is 'left' (see 19.20, which indicates that the crucifixion took place outside the city). Interestingly, Bammel ('Farewell Discourse', p. 107) speaks of a *peripatos* after the meal of ch. 13. He locates the *peripatos* in the beginning of Jn 18, but why should it not be after 14.31?

7.   See, for example, Yves Simoens (*La gloire d'aimer: Structures stylistiques et interprètatives dans le Discours de la Cène (Jn 13–17)* (AnBib, 90; Rome: Biblical Insitute Press, 1981) and Segovia, *Farewell*, esp. pp. 288-89.

8.   Thomas, *Footwashing*, pp. 68-70.

cation and exit of the traitor prepares the way for the discourse on Jesus' departure.

The second section (B 13.31–14.31) marks the beginning of the Farewell Discourse proper. Given that 14.31 ends with the command, 'Rise, let us be on our way,' it is very likely that B is the first of two farewell discourses with the other being 15.1–16.33. Section B involves four dialogues: (1) Jesus and Peter (13.36-38); (2) Jesus and Thomas (14. 5-7); (3) Jesus and Philip (14. 8-21); and (4) Jesus and Judas (14.22-26). Apart from the dialogue with Peter the tenor of B is consolation and promise, especially the promise of the Paraclete, the Holy Spirit, whom the Father will send in Jesus' name (14.26).[9]

Section C introduces the second of the two Farewell Discourses with an exhortation for the Johannine community to maintain its unity with Jesus by remaining in him and keeping his commands, especially the command to love one another. On the other hand, section C' is about those outside the Johannine community (the world) hating them. This is in contrast to section C: instead of being disciples they are of the world, and instead of loving they are hating. C and C' are in antithetic parallelism.

Section B', like section B, has elements of dialogue (16.17-24, 29-33) and also the sense of being forsaken by the disciples (16.32; cf. 13.38, where Peter's denial is foretold). The work of the Spirit (14.26), the Paraclete, is more fully developed (16.8-15).[10]

Section A' is the prayer. Whereas Jesus prepared the disciples in section A (13.1-30) by turning to the disciples and washing their feet and seeing them 'cleansed' of Judas (cf. 17.12), in section A' he now prepares them by turning to the Father and praying for them. In A he communes with his disciples; in A' he communes with the Father.

There are some parallels (synthetic and antithetic) between the sections of this structure, but, given the lack of consensus on structural proposals, we advance the above proposal tentatively as an aid to grasp the overall thrust of John 13–17.

An alternative structure proposed by Yves Simeons[11] and adapted slightly focuses on the theme of love:

---

9. As well as this possible ABCC'B'A' structure there is also both a parallelism between 13.31–14.31 and 15–16, and a progression. As elsewhere in John, one single analysis cannot pick up everything.

10. Brown (*John*, II, pp. 589-91, Chart I) lists a large number of parallels between B and B'.

11. Simeons, *La gloire de'aimer*, p. 79.

A 13.1-38 Themes of glorification and love
  B 14.1-31 Jesus' departure and the encouragement of the disciples
    C 15.1-11 The themes of abiding and joy
      D 15.12-17 Mutual agape
    C' 15.18-16.3 The themes of hatred and exclusion
  B' 16.4-33 Jesus' departure and the encouragement of the disciples
A' 17.1-26 Themes of glorification and love

The weakness of this structural suggestion is that it lumps all of ch. 13 together. A good case can be made for ending the first sub-section at v. 30 and taking 13.31-38 with 14.1-33. The main argument in favour of a split is that at the end of 13.30 Judas the traitor has gone and immediately afterwards Jesus announces his glorification and departure, a theme that continues through to the end of ch. 14. Verse 31 of ch. 13 therefore is the beginning of the Farewell Discourse proper, whereas 13.1-30 is prepara-tory to the discourse involving cleansing—symbolic (footwashing) and communal (the exit of Judas). On the other hand, F.J. Moloney[12] has argued for the integrity of 13.1-38 by seeing the double ἀμὴν formulae (13.16; 20.21, 38) as structural markers indicating the beginning and end-ing of units. However, the double ἀμὴν formula does not seem to function consistently as a structural marker in John. The other weakness in Simeon's proposal is that there is no mention of the work of the Holy Spirit. This work involves the encouragement of the disciples through the Holy Spirit testifying of Jesus, teaching and reminding.[13]

8.4 *The First Farewell Discourse*

I wish at this stage to focus on the First Farewell Discourse (13.31–14.31) and a tentative structure[14] for this is as follows:

---

12. F.J. Moloney, 'The Structure and Message of John 15.1–16.3', *ABR* (1987), pp. 35-49.

13. See D. Bruce Woll, *Johannine Christianity in Conflict: Authority, Rank, and Succession in the First Farewell Discourse* (SBLDS, 60; Chico, CA: Scholars Press, 1981), pp. 97-108.

14. As well as this suggested structure there is also a progression in the four dia-logues, in that each one explores an obscurity in the answer to the previous one. (a) (13.36-38) Peter: 'LORD, where are you going?' Jesus: 'You will follow afterward.' (b) (14.5-7) Thomas: 'How can we know the way?' Jesus: 'I am the way…no-one can come to the Father except through me.' (c) (14.8-21) Philip: 'Show us the Father.' Jesus: 'Those who have seen me have seen the Father.' (d) (14.21-24) Judas: 'How can you show yourself to us and not to the world?' Jesus: 'Those who love me will keep

13.31-35   The hour has come for Glorification—love one another!

13.36-38   Dialogue with Peter: prediction of threefold denial.

14.1-4   'Let not your hearts be troubled.'

14.5-7   Dialogue with Thomas: the disciple comes to the Father through the Son.

14.8-21   Dialogue with Philip:

        vv. 9-14 'The Father is in me and I am in the Father.'

        vv. 15-22 'I am in the Father and you are in me, and I am in you.'

14.22-26   Dialogue with Judas: The Father and the Son come to the disciple.

14.27-29   'Let not your hearts be troubled.'

14.30-31   The ruler of this world is coming—love for the Father.[15]

For my purposes the key passage of this pericope is 14.2-3, and it is interesting to note the parallels with 14.27-29 signalled by the repetition of the words, 'Let not your hearts be troubled...'

Parallels between 14.1-4 and 14.27-29

Let not your hearts be troubled (v. 1)	Let not your hearts be troubled (v. 27)
Believe (v. 1)	Believe (v. 29)
I go to prepare a place for you (v. 2)	I am going to the Father (v. 28)
I will come again (v. 3)	I am coming to you (v. 28)

Here we see a reinforcement of the themes of a call to faith and reassurance in the face of Jesus' departure. In both passages Jesus emphasizes that it is good (cf. 16.7) for him to depart: in 14.2-3 his departure means preparing a place for the disciples and in 14.28 his departure signifies the completion of the work the Father has given him to do, a work that will be for the benefit of the disciples.[16] Moreover, in both 14.1-4 and 14.27-29 there is the promise of Jesus' return.

---

my word, and my Father will love them, and we will come to them and make our home with them.'

15. This analysis draws on Stibbe (*John*, p. 155), but since he does not allow for the inclusion of 13.31-38 in the pericope, I have adapted his structural proposal. Mlakuzhyil (*Christocentric*, p. 226) seems to see 13.31-38 functioning as a bridge passage, so it could belong to 13.1-30 or 14.1-31.

16. See Brown (*John*, II, p. 655) who accepts Peder Borgen's suggestion ('God's Agent in the Fourth Gospel', in J. Neusner [ed.], *Religions in Antiquity: Essays in Memory of Erwin Ramsdell Goodenough* [Leiden: E.J. Brill, 1968], pp. 137-148 [140; not p. 153 as in Brown]) that the significance of 'my Father is greater than I' is to be found in the notion that the Sender (the Father) is greater than the one who is sent (Jesus). Hence the mission of Jesus is in view. So Brown argues that the meaning of 14.28b is 'probably the same as in xvii 4-5: Jesus is on the way to the Father who will glorify him. During his mission on earth he is less than the One who sent him, but his

8.5 *John 14.2-3*

8.5.1 *The Text Itself*

Given this thematic background suggested by the structural analysis, I am now ready to look at the passage of 14.2-3 itself:

ἐν τῇ οἰκίᾳ τοῦ πατρος μου μοναὶ πολλαί εἰσιν·[17]
εἰ δὲ μή εἶπον ἂν[18] ὑμῖν
ὅτι[19] πορεύομαι ἑτοιμάσαι τόπον ὑμῖν
καὶ ἐὰν[20] πορευθῶ καὶ ἑτοιμάσω τόπον ὑμῖν,
πάλιν ἔρχομαι[21] καὶ παραλήμψομαι[22] ὑμᾶς πρὸς ἐμαυτόν,
ἵνα ὅπου εἰμὶ ἐγὼ καὶ ὑμεῖς ἦτε.[23]

departure signifies that the work that the Father has given him to do is completed. Now he will be glorified with that glory that he had with the Father before the world existed. This is a cause of rejoicing to the disciples because when Jesus is glorified he will glorify his disciples as well as granting them eternal life (xvii 2).'

17. There is a variant reading for this first line: πολλαὶ μοναὶ παρὰ τῷ πατρί. There is patristic but no manuscript evidence for this. It may provide a literary link with Jn 14.23, but can scarcely be a serious contender for the text since it lacks manuscript support.

18. M. Zerwick and M. Grosvenor (*A Grammatical Analysis of the Greek New Testament* [Rome: Biblical Institute Press, 1981], p. 330) describe εἶπον ἂν as an apodosis that has not been realized because the protasis, εἰ δὲ μή, represents an unrealized state of affairs (Cf. M. Zerwick, *Biblical Greek* [Scripta Pontificii Instituti Biblici, 114; Rome: Editrice Pontificio Instituo Biblico, 1963], § 313B; Bauer, Arndt and Gingrich, *Greek–English Lexicon*, pp. 47-48 1bβ) . There are many dwelling places in the Father's house—the contrary is not the case. However, if the contrary were the case, then, says Jesus, 'I would have told you.'

19. Some witnesses omit ὅτι, wrongly, in Barrett's opinion (*St John*, p. 457). Metzger (*Textual Commentary*, p. 243) agrees with Barrett and suggests that copyists took the ὅτι as recitative, which is often omitted as superfluous. Bultmann (*John*, p. 601 n. 4) has a discussion of the various ways of translating ὅτι, namely, with εἶπον or as I have translated it above or as explicative (i.e. 'Otherwise I would have told you...'—this assumes the places are already prepared) or as a question ('Would I not otherwise have said that I am going ...?'; cf. 12.26; 17.24).

20. Zerwick and Grosvenor (*Grammatical Analysis*, p. 330) remark that the text has 'ἐάν where one would expect ὅταν'. Bauer, Ardnt and Gingrich (*Greek–English Lexicon*, ἐάν [210-11, 1 d.]) provide other references where ἐάν has a similar meaning: for example, Jn 12.32; Heb. 3.7; 1 Jn 2.28. In this last reference NRSV translates ἐάν as 'when'.

21. F. Blass and A. Debrunner (*A Greek Grammar of the New Testament and Other Early Christian Literature* [trans. and ed. R.W. Funk; Chicago: University of Chicago

My translation:

> In my Father's house there are many dwelling places;
> (and if it had not been so I would have told you),
> for I am going to prepare a place for you
> and when I do go and prepare a place for you,
> I am [certainly] coming back and I will take you to myself,
> so that where I am you also may be.

This translation retains the ὅτι as weakly causal and puts εἰ δὲ μὴ εἶπον ἀν ὑμῖν in parenthesis. The effect is that the parenthetical phrase εἰ δὲ μὴ εἶπον ἀν ὑμῖν emphasizes the certainty of Jesus' promise of many dwelling places.

8.5.2 *The Father's House*

Jesus tells the disciples that in his Father's house there are many μοναί. What is meant by 'my Father's house'? Commentators tend to leap to the conclusion that 'my Father's house' is heaven.[24] Certainly the Johannine

---

Press, 1961], §323) says, 'In confident assertions regarding the future, a vivid, realistic present may be used for the future.' This is the case with ἔρχομαι in 14.3.

22. παραλήμψομαι is a future of παραλαμβάνομαι, middle voice, indicating a reflexive significance (Blass and Debrunner, *Greek Grammar*, §§310, 316 [3]), hence 'I will receive you to myself'. Although the reflexion is already present in the middle verb, it is actually stated, πρὸς ἐμαυτόν, thereby making it emphatic.

23. The pronouns ἐγὼ and ὑμεῖς are both stated, indicating emphasis.

24. So Carson (*John*, p. 489): 'The simplest explanation is best: *my Father's house* refers to heaven...' Barrett (*St John*, p. 456) mentions Lk. 2.49 and Jn 2.16 and says 'both of these passages refer to the Temple' and draws attention to Jn 8.35. These are relevant texts, but Barrett makes nothing of them. Immediately he goes on to say: '[T]he thought of heaven is of course very widespread in most religions...' However, he does have a cautionary word about identifying 'the Father's house' with heaven. He says, '...to speak of "heaven" may, if the term is not carefully understood, misinterpret the "Father's house". Communion with God is a permanent and universal possibility.' Lindars (*John*, p. 470) has a similar remark: 'Just as the Temple was regularly called the house of God (cf. 2.16), so heaven was pictured as a palace by many ancient peoples.' Morris (*John*, p. 638) says without any supporting evidence that '"my Father's house" clearly refers to heaven'. Schnackenburg (*St John*, III, pp. 60, 61) quotes from Jewish and non-Jewish (particularly Gnostic) texts many references to 'heavenly dwellings'. The closest reference to heaven being 'my Father's house' seems to be Philo's remarks about the soul's return to the paternal house (οἶκός) after being alienated in the world. However, this thought is foreign to John where the emphasis is on the 'enfleshment' of the Word (cf. 1.14) and on the resurrection of the body (not the soul, cf. John 11.25).

Jesus speaks of coming down from heaven on a number of occasions (3.13; 3.31; 6.33; 6.38) and when he addresses the Father he lifts his eyes to heaven (17.1), but this is no justification for making an immediate and unsubstantiated equation between 'heaven' and 'my Father's house'.

This phrase, 'my Father's house', occurs only one other time in John (in 2.16) and there it unambiguously refers to the Temple. Jn 2.13-22 is also unique in John for the frequency and variety of its Temple vocabulary.[25] Moreover it is centred entirely on the Temple itself as the Jewish place of worship, and unfolds within the precincts of the Temple. The editorial comment in 2.21 explicitly refers the words of 2.19 about the Jerusalem Temple to the body of Jesus. There is doubtless an unremitting emphasis on the Temple in 2.13-22.

In addition to the verbal link between 14.2-3 and 2.13-22 ('my Father's house') there is also an identical chronological setting of an immediate future Passover in both pericopae. Jn 2.13 speaks of ἐγγὺς ἦν τὸ πάσχα and 13.1 has πρὸ... τοῦ πάσχα (cf. 11.55; 12.1). Also the general framework of a pilgrimage to the Jerusalem Temple is common to both passages (ἀνέβη εἰς Ἱεροσόλυμα, 2.13; ἀνέβησαν πολλοὶ εἰς Ἱεροσόλυμα, 11.55-56; 12.20). The scene of the Temple episode (2.13-22) and the Footwashing/Farewell Discourses/Prayer (chs. 13–17) both unfold after a pilgrimage to the Jerusalem Temple and in the perspective of an immediate future Passover. Thus 2.13-22 and 14.2-3 have similar settings and have a significant verbal link in the words 'my Father's house'.

As I have noted, it is clear enough that in 2.16 'my Father's house' refers to the Temple, and the surrounding verses abound in Temple reference, as is evident from the vocabulary survey above. But do these carry over into 14.2-3? I have already detailed other connections between these two passages beyond the bare verbal link, so it would not be exceptional to read some kind of Temple theme into Jn 14.2-3. Is there any other supporting evidence that confirms this view? There are two kinds of confirmatory evidence: the first is the way in which a large portion of the Gospel has been concerned to present Jesus as the fulfilment and replacement of the Temple and its associated festivals; the second is an interpretation of ch. 13.1-30 that points towards preparation for entry into the 'Temple'.

---

25. All the Johannine equivalents for the Temple occur here more than once, except the term τόπος (cf. Jn 4.20; 11.48); and two of them, οἶκος and ναός, occur nowhere else with reference to the Temple: (a) ἱερόν (Jn 2.14, 15); (b) ὄκος (Jn 2.16, 17); and (c) ναός (Jn 2.19, 21).

As regards the first line of evidence, I rest my case on the previous chapters of this study. I have argued at length that Jesus is indeed the fulfilment and replacement of the Temple and its cultus. He is the One who could fill the great void that had opened up in national Jewish life with the destruction of the Temple. Jesus *is* now the new Temple, not only for Jews, but for all people (4.42). But how does this occur? If the Temple is the body of Jesus (2.21), how could he be 'the Father's house'? How could he provide his disciples with 'many dwelling places'? In the course of this chapter I will suggest that Jn 14.2-3, and indeed the whole of ch. 14, addresses those questions, and they are explored more completely in the discussion on John 17 in my Chapter 9. Given the Johannine pre-occupation with the Temple theme, as well as much else in chs. 1–12, it is not surprising that it should resurface in the Farewell Discourses and the Great Prayer. However, I now want to look at John 13 and see how the footwashing can be understood as a preparation for entry into the new 'Temple'—the many-roomed house of the Father.

8.6 *Temple Concerns in John 13*

8.6.1 *Survey of Temple Washing Rituals in the Old Testament*
The second line of evidence has been suggested to me by Thomas's survey of foot washing in the Old Testament and Early Judaism.[26] Evidence from the Old Testament indicates that some kind of washing was necessary for entry to the Temple or holy presence of God. Washings of various kinds were enjoined upon those who approached the holy place of the Taber-nacle to offer sacrifice upon the altar. Exod. 30.17-21 depicts Moses as receiving these commands:

> Then the LORD said to Moses, 'Make a bronze basin, with its bronze stand, for washing. Place it between the Tent of Meeting and the altar, and put water in it. Aaron and his sons are to wash their hands and feet with water from it. Whenever they enter the Tent of Meeting, they shall wash with water so that they will not die. Also, when they approach the altar to minister by presenting an offering made to the LORD by fire, they shall wash their hands and feet so that they will not die. This is to be a lasting ordinance for Aaron and his descendants for the generations to come.'

Exod. 40.30-32 describes the carrying out of these instructions:

> He placed the basin between the Tent of Meeting and the altar and put water in it for washing, and Moses and Aaron and his sons used it to wash

26. Thomas, *Footwashing*, pp. 26-31.

their hands and feet. They washed whenever they entered the Tent of Meeting or approached the altar, as the LORD commanded Moses.

Similar, although more elaborate, provisions for this washing are made in the Solomonic Temple. Both 1 Kgs 7.38 and 2 Chron. 4.6 mention ten lavers as well as 'the sea' in which the priests were to wash. Josephus (*Ant.* 8.87) confirms that a sea was available for the priests:

> Now he appointed the sea to be for washing the hands and feet of the priests when they entered the temple and were about to go up to the altar...

Similar washing were enjoined on Isaac as he approached the altar:

> And at all of the (appointed) times be pure in your body and wash yourself with water[27] before you go to make an offering upon the altar. And wash your hands and feet before you approach the altar. And when you have completed making the offering, wash your hands and feet again (Jub. 21.16).

While the washings in the references above generally indicate the washing of the extremities of the body (hands and feet) only, Lev. 16.4 seems to advocate a more comprehensive wash: 'He [Aaron] shall bathe his body in water' (cf. Exod. 29.4). Milgrom is convinced that this is complete immersion. He says:

> Ibn Ezra is certainly wrong in claiming that the priests' washing was limited to their hands and feet. The latter act, as pointed out by Mizrahi, would have been expressed by רחץ מים, without the preposition ב (e.g. Exod. 30.20). The prefixed במים, implies full immersion (Sipra, Rashi), as evidenced by 16.4.[28]

---

27. It is possible that the washing for this initial approach may have been a complete comprehensive washing of the whole body, but it is unclear.

28. J. Milgrom, *Leviticus 1–16* (AB, 3; Garden City, NY: Doubleday), p. 501. Thomas points out (*Footwashing*, p. 28 n. 2) that the LXX has ἔλουσεν to translate the MT, which suggests 'bath' rather than washing parts of the body. Thomas (*Footwashing*, p. 28 n. 3) also quotes *P. Oxy.* 840 to buttress the notion that a purificatory rite involved complete immersion. In this quote a Pharisaic chief priest confronts Jesus and his disciples, who have entered the outer court of the Temple. In defence of his own purity, the Pharisaic chief priest responds, 'I am clean. For I have bathed [ἐλουσάμην] in the pool of David and have gone down by one stair and come up by the other and have put on white and clean clothes and only then have I come hither and viewed the holy utensils' (dated c. 400 CE).

This bath seems to have been an initiatory wash.[29] The context of Exod. 29.4 (cf. Lev. 8.6) clearly has initiatory consecration of the priests in view. Following the washing, Moses clothes them with the priestly robes, he anoints the Tabernacle with oil, consecrates the altar with the blood of a bull, offers the first of two rams as a burnt offering and uses the blood of the second to ordain Aaron and his sons. Finally he sprinkles Aaron and his sons and their vestments with some of the anointing oil and some of the blood from the altar.

It seems then that the priests were consecrated with a complete bath in water, but thereafter the washing of hands and feet denote repeated acts of purification to prepare the priests for a variety of sacred activities.

In the light of this survey one could say that, for the priests at least, entry to and service within the Temple was conditional upon washing, at least parts of the body, if not all of it.

What of those who were not priests? We know that ritual purity was necessary for everyone to enter the Temple/Tabernacle (Lev. 15.31), but whether by water or other means is not clear.[30] Nor is it clear whether the complete bodily immersion in water for the priests was once in a lifetime or once every period of Temple service. What is clear is that some kind of washing was involved in approaching the presence of God in the Temple for some people, and to this extent the footwashing could point in this direction.

8.6.2 *Establishing the Text of 13.10 in Favour of the Longer Reading*

It is now time to turn to the text of John 13 and endeavour to see what the footwashing signifies and if there are any Temple connections. Since 13.10 is a crucial text for determining the significance of the footwashing, I will now seek to establish that text before passing on to related matters. The two main contenders for the controversial section of text in 13.10 are: (a) ὁ λελουμένος οὐκ ἔχει χρείαν εἰ μὴ τοὺς πόδας νίψασθαι, commonly known as the longer reading; and (b) ὁ λελουμένος οὐκ ἔχει

---

29. There is some evidence that the complete bath was repeatable. *Tam.* 1.1, 2 clearly speaks of the priests immersing themselves in the Chamber of Immersion when they came on duty.

30. Sanders (*Practice and Belief*, pp. 217-30) has an extensive discussion of purificatory rites and the underlying assumption is that the Temple was holy and those who entered the Temple needed to be pure. Water was essential to purification, and the discovery of numerous immersion pools (p. 223) suggests that complete immersion was a widespread and common means of purification.

χρείαν νίψασθαι. In establishing this text I am indebted to Thomas whose reasons for adopting the longer reading I now summarize and evaluate. (a) External textual considerations as set out by Thomas favour the longer reading.[31] (b) The longer reading distinguishes between a washing of the whole body (a large wash) and the washing of parts of the body (in this case the feet, amounting to a small wash), whereas the shorter reading makes no such distinction. This distinction is attested in the ancient literature. Seneca makes a distinction between the regular washing of arms and legs and the less frequent weekly bathing of the whole body.[32] (c) The philological evidence points to λούω and νίπτω generally referring to two different kinds of washings, λούω to the complete washing of the body (Exod. 29.4; Lev. 8.6)[33] and νίπτω to the partial washings (Exod. 30.17-21; 40.30-32; 1 Kgs 7.38; 2 Chron. 4.6).[34] If one accepts the general, but not universal use of λούω to describe the complete large washing and νίπτω to describe the small washing, then we see how the two verbs function in the longer reading. (d) If we are to accept the longer reading how can the origin of the shorter reading be explained? Thomas suggests two possibilities: (1) the omission of εἰ μὴ τοὺς πόδας may be the result

---

31. 'The great preponderance of witnesses favour inclusion of εἰ μὴ τοὺς πόδας. This reading has the support of the Proto-Alexandrian p[66] (second/third century), B (fourth century) and cop[sa] (third century). Alexandrian witnesses include: C*,[3] (fifth century), W (fifth century), and cop[bo] (fourth century). The Western support is strong and early as well. The witnesses range from D (sixth century) to the versions syr[s] (second/third century), it[a] (fourth century), it[b,c,d,e] (fifth century). The Byzantine family is represented by A (fifth century) and E* (sixth century). The Caesarean tradition includes: arm (fourth/fifth century), geo (fifth century), Origen (third century), along with some later witnesses. Thus the support for the inclusion of εἰ μὴ τοὺς πόδας is strong, early, well-distributed and includes a number of different kinds of witnesses. If a decision were to be made on the basis of external evidence alone, a verdict would have to be rendered in favour of the longer reading' (Thomas, *Footwashing*, p. 23).

32. Seneca, *Seneca ad Lucilium Epistulae Morales* (ed. T.E. Page; trans R.M. Gummere; LCL; 3 vols.; London: Heinemann; New York: G.P. Putnam's Sons, 1920–30), 86.12: 'Friend, if you were wiser, you would know that Scipio did not bathe every day. It is stated by those who have reported to us the old-time ways of Rome that the Romans washed only their arms and legs daily—because they were the members which gathered dirt in the daily toil—and bathed all over only once a week.'

33. Bauer, Arndt and Gingrich (*Greek–English Lexicon*, pp. 481-82) remarks that λούω is, as a rule, used of the whole body and so has the sense of 'bathe'. However, the whole body may not be in view in Acts 16.33 where wounds are washed and λούω is used.

34. But cf. *P.Oxy* 34-35, where νίπτω is used of bathing in a pool.

of the difficulty of reconciling those words with the words ἀλλ' ἔστιν καθαρὸς ὅλος that follow; (2) the omission may have been a mistake, possibly by homoioteleuton. Metzger offers both these possibilities (1) and (2) in his *Textual Commentary*.[35] (e) In terms of internal coherence of the passage the longer reading makes better sense. Robinson says:

> If τοὺς πόδας alone were missing, it would make sense to say that 'he who has had a bath only needs to wash', but to say that 'he has no need to wash' cannot be squared with Jesus' insistence on the absolute necessity of the washing (v. 8).[36]

That is, the bath is not the footwashing, but many commentators assume they are one and the same. I therefore conclude that the longer reading is preferable.

8.6.3 *The Sacrificial Character of Footwashing in 13.1-4*
Having established the text of 13.10, it is necessary to enquire about the character of the footwashing. I will argue that it has a sacrificial, cleansing, essential, paradigmatic character.

Mention of the Passover (13.1) in John brings the death of Jesus into view and ties what follows to it. Jesus knew that his hour of departure—a departure by death—had come. Jesus is said to love his own (ἰδίους) in the world to the end (εἰς τέλος),[37] which brings the cross into view. Jesus laid aside his clothes; the verb τίθημι often signifies in Johannine literature the laying down of one's life (see 10.11, 15, 17, 18; 13.37, 38; 15.13; 1 Jn 3.6).[38] Jesus washes his disciples' feet, the task of a slave. And in all

---

35. Metzger, *Textual Commentary*, p. 240.

36. J.A.T. Robinson, 'The Significance of the Foot-Washing', in A.N. Wilder *et al.* (eds.), *Neotestamentica et Patristica* (Leiden: E.J. Brill, 1962), pp. 144-47 (146 n. 3).

37. This τέλος is an adumbration of the word Jesus utters from the cross (19.30)— Τετέλεσται. So his love for his own led him to finishing the work that the Father had given him to do. R.M. Ball ('S. John and the Institution of the Eucharist', *JSNT* 23 [1985], pp. 59-68) points out the difficulty of referring the aorist ἠγάπησεν to the passion because at the stage of 13.1 it has not happened. Ball maintains that εἰς τέλος ἠγάπησεν αὐτοὺς must refer to something else, namely, it 'is intended primarily to mean "he instituted the eucharist"' (p. 61). What counts decisively against this is that there is no evidence in the text for it. Ball himself recognizes this and says, 'Indeed, we expect to find it related at just this point [i.e. immediately after 13.1], though our expectation is disappointed' (p. 61).

38. Cf. Barrett (*St John*, p. 439), Brown (*John*, II, 551), J. Dunn, 'The Washing of the Disciples' Feet in John 13.1-20', *ZNW* 61 (1970), pp. 247-52 (248).

likelihood, though John does not present a Eucharist, the readers of John would understand the meal to be the Last Supper[39] with the death of Jesus (the Passover Lamb in John) very much in the picture. All these elements combine to present a vivid proleptic portrayal of Jesus the Suffering Servant,[40] the Lamb of God (1.29) going to the cross and dying so that the sins of the world might be forgiven. The theme of servanthood comes through powerfully in 13.13-17, not merely servanthood in itself, but sacrificial, suffering servanthood exemplified in the Suffering Servant passages of Deutero-Isaiah (42.1-4, 5-9; 49.1-6, 7-13; 50.4-9, 10-11; 52.13–53.12).[41]

8.6.4 *The Essential Character of the Footwashing in 13.8b*

Verses 6-11 are a dialogue between Jesus and Peter and provide some further clues as to the significance of the footwashing. I note the following points:

(a) The words οὐκ ἔχεις μέρος μετ' ἐμοῦ underline the necessity of Jesus' action. The footwashing is not optional, but it is essential if Peter is to have a share in Jesus. Brown[42] mentions that μέρος is used to translate Heb. חלק in the LXX, the word that describes the God-

---

39. Knowledge of the institution of the Eucharist was basic and widespread by the last part of the first century (1 Cor. 11.23-26; Mk 14.22-25; Mt. 26.26-30; Lk. 22.15-20; Did. 9; 10; 14).

40. Following the exit of Judas, Jesus says in 13.31, Νῦν ἐδοξάσθη ὁ υἱὸς τοῦ ἀνθρώπου, καὶ ὁ θεὸς ἐδοξάσθη ἐν αὐτῷ. This is similar to Isa. 49.3 where YHWH says to Israel, Δοῦλός μου εἶ σύ, Ισραηλ, καὶ ἐν σοὶ δοξασθήσομαι. Other links with Isa. 49.1-6 are κύριος (Jn 13.13, 16; Isa. 49.4, 5); δοῦλος (Jn 13.16; Isa. 49.5). Jn 13.8 has μέρος (very likely reflecting חלק), which may link with Isa. 53.12a, which has the verb חלק twice: לכן אחלק לו ברבים ואת עצומים יחלק שלל. D. Ball (*'I Am'*, pp. 198, 199) finds the background of the ἐγώ εἰμι in Jn 13.19 in v. 10 of Isa. 43, which, although not numbered in the Servant Songs, is closely related. Further evidence that the passion and resurrection is in view in Jn 13 may be offered by the quotation in v. 18: Ὁ τρώγων μου τὸν ἄρτον ἐπῆρεν ἐπ' ἐμὲ τὴν πτέρναν αὐτοῦ. This seems to be a clear reflection of Ps. 41.9: Ὁ ἐσθίων ἄρτους μου ἐμεγάλυνεν ἐπ' ἐμὲ πτερνισμόν. But following this verse there is a strong emphasis on YHWH raising (καὶ ἀνάστησόν με) up the psalmist and establishing him (41.10, 11, 12). If this wider context is in view through the Jn 13.19 allusion, then more than the betrayal is being referred to; there is a subtle reference to the passion and beyond to the resurrection.

41. So C. Westermann, *Isaiah 40–66: A Commentary* (OTL; London: SCM Press, 1969), p. 92.

42. *John*, II, pp. 565-66.

given heritage of Israel. Be that as it may, it is clear that what Jesus is saying to Peter is that belonging to him is contingent upon Jesus washing his feet. Thomas puts it this way: '[I]t appears that μέρος here denotes continued fellowship[43] with Jesus, and a place in his community which ultimately results in uninterrupted residence in the Father's house (14.1-14).'[44] Whatever the footwashing signifies[45] Jesus regards it as essential.

(b) The footwashing (for which the verb νίπτειν is used) may be distinguished from a bathing (λούειν). Despite Thomas's insistence that these two words are sharply and always distinguished, I am not convinced, especially when Bauer, Arndt and Gingrich cite possible exceptions to λούω meaning 'a bath of the whole body'. Λούω is used of washing before eating in Tob. 2.5. Presumably this does not mean taking a bath of the whole body, although it could. However, Thomas himself[46] points out that *P. Oxy.* 840 is often appealed to as evidence that λούω and νίπτω can be used synomynously, and after a careful examination Thomas concludes that the evidence is ambiguous, that is, the text may be interpreted with λούω and νίπτω as synomyns, but not necessarily so. However, I believe the words do not have exclusive semantic fields and that there could be overlap in meaning here in Jn 13.10 (cf. above, 8.6.2 and nn. 33 and 34).

8.6.5 *The Cleansing Character of Footwashing in 13.10b, 11*

The use of καθαρός (13.10b) and καθαροί in 13.10c and 13.11 indicates

---

43. Fernando Segovia, 'John 13.1-20, The Footwashing in the Johannine Tradition', *ZNW* 73 (1982), pp. 31-51 (43): '...an acceptance of that which the washing symbolizes grants the disciples continued union with Jesus.' The context of the Book of Glory (13–20; cf. Brown) suggests that the footwashing does not initiate fellowship, but continues it.

44. Thomas, *Footwashing*, p. 94. The significant point here is the way in which Thomas has linked his interpretation of μέρος with dwelling in the Father's house (14.2-3).

45. It is often thought that the ὑπόδειγμα significance of the footwashing and the soteriological significance (as, for example, the forgiveness of sins) reflect two different literary strands in Jn 13, namely, 13.1-11 (the soteriological motif) and 13.12-20 (the exemplary motif). This is well summarized in Arland J. Hultgren's article, 'The Johannine Footwashing (13.1-11) as a Symbol of Eschatological Hospitality', *NTS* 28 (1982), pp. 539-46 (540). Carson (*John*, pp. 458-60) also has a lucid discussion of the issues.

46. Thomas, *Footwashing*, pp. 97-99.

that some kind of cleansing is involved. It seems that those who have bathed (λελουμένος) are wholly clean and have no need of any further wash except for the feet. But clearly what Jesus is talking about is not the mere sluicing off of dirt from the flesh because he immediately goes on to speak of Judas, who is not καθαρός. No doubt he had his feet washed along with the disciples, but that did not make him clean. The Devil had already put it into his heart to betray Jesus (13.2). Did he have the 'bath' that Jesus speaks of? If it is baptism from John the Baptist, he may have. On the other hand, the 'bath' may be metaphorical for being 'washed' clean from one's sins through the death of Jesus. Whatever outward rites Judas had received, Jesus is emphatic that he was not clean and the implication is that the fellowship at the meal was contaminated.

8.6.6 *The Paradigmatic Character of the Footwashing in 13.12-17*
In 13.15 Jesus describes his action as a ὑπόδειγμα.[47] As Jesus has washed his disciples' feet so they ought to wash one another's feet.

8.7 *Footwashing: Some Possible Meanings*
Having isolated the sacrificial, essential, cleansing and paradigmatic character of the footwashing, the challenge is to find a meaning that does justice to these elements. I offer three possibilities: footwashing as eschatological hospitality; footwashing as the forgiveness of post-baptismal sins; and footwashing as sacrificial service that is open to martyrdom.

8.7.1 *Footwashing as Eschatological Hospitality*
I have mentioned a cleansing significance to the footwashing. Arland Hultgren, however, contests this. He says:

> It is clear that in the present text of the Fourth Gospel the footwashing has a soteriological significance (13.8b), and that being 'clean' (13.10-11) is a prerequisite for salvation. But it would be incorrect to conclude that the footwashing represents a form of cultic washing of purification.[48]

---

47. Thomas (*Footwashing*, p. 110) advances strong reasons why 13.15 should be interpreted as an injunction for the disciples to wash one another's feet and not to lessen its particularity by widening it to signify offering humble service in general (cf. J. Calvin, *The Gospel According to St John 11–12 and the First Epistle of John* [trans. T.H.L. Parker; Calvin's Commentaries; Edinburgh: Oliver & Boyd, 1961], p. 60).
48. A.J. Hultgren, 'The Johannine Footwashing (13.1-11) as a Symbol of Eschatological Hospitality', *NTS* 28 (1982), pp. 539-46 (542-43).

On the contrary Hultgren believes the footwashing is an expression of eschatological hospitality whereby Jesus, on behalf of the Father, welcomes the disciples into the Father's house (14.2). That is why, according to Hultgren, the footwashing has 'soteriological significance'.

His argument is as follows: he accepts the shorter reading of 13.10 and interprets 13.9-10 as Jesus' rejection of a cultic washing. He maintains that Peter's request for a washing of his hands and head as well as his feet

> has overtones of a ritual form of cleansing, which Jesus in 13.10 rejects. 'He who has bathed' (ὁ λελουμένους) in 13.10a applies to Peter and the rest, who are beneficiaries of the footwashing as eschatological hospitality, and they are 'clean' (13.10b).[49]

They therefore have no need to have a ritual purificatory wash (νίψασθαι).

Hultgren's evidence for viewing Peter's request for a wash as a desire for a ritual cleansing is not exegetically convincing. He says it 'has overtones of a ritual form of cleansing' and cites a number of texts where various parts of the body are washed in a cultic setting. This does not prove that Peter is asking for a cultic wash. He may simply be asking for more of the same kind of wash Jesus gives in the footwashing, which Hultgren calls eschatological hospitality.

While it is true that the verbs λούω and νίπτω overlap (see above, 8.6.2 and nn. 33 and 34), the former is generally used of bathing while the other is used of a smaller wash. It would be surprising, therefore, to reverse the general usage and have λούω to describe the footwashing and νίπτω to describe the larger bathing that Peter requests. In the examples Hultgren cites of footwashing in antiquity[50] some form of the verb νίπτω is almost invariably used, but no form of the verb λούω is ever used.

In the third place καθαροί is used. Hultgren offers the unconvincing explanation that the cleanness of the disciples is based 'upon Jesus granting them a share in his own destiny (13.8b)'. But how does that effect the disciples' cleansing? Hultgren offers no explanation. It seems to me better to take καθαροί as signifying cultic cleansing whether effected by water (13.5) or the word of Jesus (15.3).

Finally Hultgren fails to clarify convincingly why Jesus regards submission to this act as essential if the disciples are to have a share in him (13.8b). Hultgren says that this act of eschatological hospitality does have 'soteriological significance' (see quotation above), but it is not clear what

---

49. Hultgren, 'Johannine Footwashing', p. 543.
50. Hultgren, 'Johannine Footwashing', pp. 541-42.

he means. The strong and urgent appeal to Peter (13.8b) suggests more than the need to submit to an act of hospitality, even eschatological hospitality.

I conclude therefore that the footwashing is probably not an act of eschatological hospitality.

8.7.2 *Footwashing as the Forgiveness of Post-Baptismal Sins*

Thomas contends that λελουμένος indicates a bath that does not need to be repeated—a bath that presumably cleanses. He believes that this very likely refers to baptism.[51] But in 13.10 he notes the emphasis falls not on baptism, but on the need for the washing the feet, the little washing, the continuing regular requirement for cleansing. Thomas suggests that what may lie behind this emphasis is the need for the forgiveness of post-baptismal sins. That there was such a need is powerfully underlined in the first of the Johannine Epistles:

> If we say we have no sin, we deceive ourselves, and the truth is not in us…
> If we say we have not sinned, we make him a liar, and his word is not in us.
> My little children, I am writing these things to you so that you may not sin.
> But if anyone does sin, we have an advocate with the Father, Jesus Christ
> the righteous; and he is the atoning sacrifice for our sins, and not for ours
> only but also for the sins of the whole world (1 Jn 1.8, 10; 2.1-2).

Post-baptismal (cf. 1 Jn 5.13) sin was not only a possibility in the Johannine community (1 Jn 2.1), but also a reality not to be denied (1 Jn 1.8, 10). But forgiveness was possible through the atoning sacrifice of Jesus.

Taking this suggestion of Thomas further one can ask, What meaning then can we attribute to Jesus' injunction for the disciples to wash *one another's* feet (13.14)? If the washing of feet denotes the forgiveness of sins, one can understand how Jesus is in the position to forgive sins, but what of the disciples when they wash one another's feet?[52] I believe this could point to the mutual forgiveness of sins (as, e.g., Eph. 4.31-32). What the Johannine Jesus says is, 'Do for one another what I have done for

---

51. So Thomas, *Footwashing*, p. 100.

52. By looking for a significance in the footwashing I do not thereby wish to discount Thomas's advocacy (8.6.6 n. 47) that when Jesus told the disciples to wash one another's feet, he meant what he said in its particularity—they were actually to bend down and pour water over the feet and wash them. But granted the particular, definite act it is still legitimate (and important) to ask, What does it mean?

you.' This suggested denotation is confirmed by the injunction to love one another (13.34, 35). The mutual forgiveness of sins does not exhaust the significance of this commandment (cf. 15.13), but it would certainly be included in it.

Further, in the context of this emphasis on cleansing in Jn 13 it is worth noting that Judas leaves the body of disciples and goes out into the night where he belongs (13.30; 17.12). Though presumably having bathed in water and had his feet washed, he is not clean (13.10c) and is thereby excluded from the fellowship. On the other hand, Peter, who sins through his threefold denial of Jesus, nevertheless is proleptically cleansed through the washing of his feet (signifying ongoing forgiveness of sins) and able to continue in the fellowship of Jesus and the disciples.

Finally, one may note the importance the forgiveness of sins had for John in 20.22-23. Immediately on the reception of the Holy Spirit, the Johannine Jesus commissions his disciples with respect to the remission and retention of sins: 'If you forgive the sins of any they are forgiven them; if you retain the sins of any, they are retained.' Here the disciples are viewed as agents of Jesus in the world (20.21) and their authority has to do with the remission and retention of sins. This ministry is parallel to the ministry of Jesus and is an outworking of what is declared in the words of the Baptist: 'Behold the Lamb of God who takes away the sin of the world' (1.29).

There are, however, a number of weaknesses with this suggested meaning for the footwashing. First, there is no real evidence that λελουμένος does refer to baptism. Thomas offers none. All that we have to go on is that baptism elsewhere in the New Testament is seen as a cleansing rite (e.g. Heb. 10.22), and Jesus says with respect to the ὁ λελουμένος that they are wholly clean. Secondly, if there is a sacrificial character to the footwashing, can that also be involved in the disciples forgiving one another's sins? Certainly there can be no sense of dying for another and atoning for their sins. It is the blood of Jesus Christ that cleanses from sins (1 Jn 1.7), not the blood of the disciples.

8.7.3 *Footwashing as Cleansing Contingent on the Death of Jesus*
In an insightful essay J.A.T. Robinson[53] has drawn attention to some interesting parallels between John 13 and Mk 10.32-45:

---

53. Robinson, 'Foot-Washing', pp. 144-47.

Mark 10.32-45	*John 13.1-20*
Jesus is going up to Jerusalem ahead of the disciples (v. 32).	Jesus is departing from the world to go to the Father (v. 1).
The Son of Man will be handed over (παραδοθήσεται) to the chief priests (v. 33).	Judas will betray (παραδώσει) Jesus (vv. 2, 21).
The disciples will share in drinking the cup that Jesus drinks (v. 38).	Jesus and the disciples share a meal together (v. 28). Peter offers to drink Jesus' cup (v. 37) but he will drink it later (vv. 21, 18, 19) and (like Jesus) glorify God through his death.
The disciples will share in the baptism of Jesus (v. 39).	The disciples must share in the footwashing/bathing otherwise they will not share in Jesus (v. 8).
'For the Son of Man came not to be served but to serve and give his life a ransom for many' (v. 45).	Jesus takes off his outer robe (symbolic of laying down his life) and washes the disciples' feet and wipes them with the towel (v. 4).
'Whoever wishes to be great among you must be your servant, and whoever wishes to be first among you must be the slave of all.'	'I have set you an example, that you should do as I have done to you. Very truly, I tell you, servants are not greater than their master, nor are messengers greater than the the the one who sent them' (vv. 15, 16).

The purpose of this comparative table is not to argue that John was dependent on Mark, but simply through the juxtaposition of the two passages to see if we can obtain any clues about the significance of the bathing/footwashing in John 13. What is highlighted, I think, is that baptism for Jesus in Mk 10 signifies his passion and death. It is also called his 'cup'. And the disciples share in both cup and baptism, that is, they share in Jesus' passion and death.

I have already noted in the brief investigation of Jn 13.1-4 that the passion and death of Jesus are to the fore, and I have suggested that the footwashing/bathing is directed towards that. The theme of the Suffering Servant is entwined with this emphasis.[54]

---

54. Indeed the humiliation involved in the footwashing coupled with intimations of Jesus' death puts one in mind of Phil. 2.6-8 where Jesus is referred to as one ὅς ἐν μορφῇ θεοῦ ὑπάρχων οὐχ ἁρπαγὸν ἡγήσατο τὸ εἶναι ἴσα θεῷ, ἀλλὰ ἑαυτὸν ἐκένωσεν μορφὴν <u>δούλου</u> λαβών...καὶ σχήματι εὑρεθεὶς ὡς ἄνθρωπος

8.8 *A Twofold Significance of Footwashing*

Given these observations, what does the bathing/footwashing signify? I believe it has a twofold significance.

8.8.1 *The Footwashing as a Cleansing Preparation*

On the one hand, it speaks of the cleansing that comes from the death of Jesus. In the light of the specific mention of cleansing in 13.10b, 11 and 1 Jn 1.7–2.1 I think this dimension is inescapable.[55] H. Weiss has uncovered three intriguing passages in Philo and one in *P. Oxy.* 840, which speak of footwashing, and link it to access to the Temple and/or the presence of God. They are as follows:

(a) *Quaest. in Gen.* 4.5 (*Philo*, I, pp. 277-77) where Philo comments on Gen. 18.4: 'Let water be taken and let them wash [νυψάτωσαν] your feet…' Philo allegorizes this and then says, 'Men are sanctified when washed with water, while the water itself (is sanctified) by the divine foot.' The emphasis on sanctification perhaps suggests people are fitted for the presence of God.[56]

(b) *Quaest. in Exod.* 1.2 (*Philo*, II, p. 7). Here Philo comments on Exod. 30.19, which mentions the washing of hands and feet before the priests

---

ἐταπείνωσεν ἑαυτὸν γενόμενος ὑπήκοος μέχρι θανάτου, θανάτου δὲ σταυροῦ.

55. H. Weiss ('Foot Washing in the Johannine Community', *NT* 21.4 [1979], pp. 298-325) maintains that in John 'there is a polemic against cleansing'. He believes this is clearly expressed in the story of the transformation of water into wine. He points out that the water used to make the wine had been destined to serve in Jewish ceremonial cleansing (2.6). But the point of the story is not polemic against cleansing per se, but rather that Jesus had come to transform Jewish cleansing rites by offering himself as the Lamb of God that takes away the sins of the world. Weiss argues from 15.3 that 'to be clean' is equivalent to 'to bear fruit', but this is surely placing too much weight on the vine metaphor. It may be that cultic cleansing rites are minimized in John, but cleansing from sin was important for him (1.29; 20.23; cf. 1 Jn 1.7-2.1) and should not be swept aside when considering the significance of the footwashing.

56. Philo's reasoning is based on Gen. 1.2: 'The spirit (breath/air) of God was borne upon the waters.' 'The foot is the last and lowest (part) of the body, while to the air is allotted the last portion of divine things, for it animates the congregated things that have been created [mentioned in Gen. 1.10].' Therefore the spiritualizing of the human foot into the divine 'foot' (= air/spirit of God) and the intermingling of that with the water, sanctifies the water. When humans are washed in such water, they, in turn, are sanctified.

offer sacrifice.[57] He says a proper preparation of the soul and body before sacrifice is necessary 'in order that it (the soul) might be released, even though not altogether, from the passions that disturbed it, for according to the saying, *one should not enter with unwashed feet on the pavement of the Temple of God*' (emphasis mine).

(c)   *Spec. Leg.* 1.206-207 (*Philo*, VII, p. 217). Here Philo comments on a different type of footwashing. The levitical law established that in the case of a whole burnt offering the belly and feet of the animal were to be washed. Philo says:

> the direction to wash…the feet is highly symbolical… By the washing of the feet is meant that his steps should no longer be on earth but tread the upper air. For the soul of the lover of God does in truth leap from earth to heaven and wing its way on high, eager to take its place in the ranks and share the ordered march of sun and moon and the all-holy, all-harmonious host of other stars, marshalled and led by the God Whose Kingship none can dispute or usurp, the kingship by which everything is justly governed.

Here the washing of the feet symbolizes entry into heaven and a sharing in the all-holy and all-harmonious rule established by God.

So the three Philonic references view the washing of the feet as a preparation for entry into some manifestation or other of the presence of God. For Philo in passage (b) at least, this is explicitly symbolized as the Temple, 'for according to the saying, one should not enter with unwashed feet on the pavement of the Temple of God'.

(d)   *P. Oxy.* 840. Although this document is dated in the fourth century, it is in agreement with Philo. In the section of interest to us, Jesus visits the Temple and a Pharisaic priest called Levi challenges his right to walk on the Temple pavement and to look on the sacred vessels 'without having bathed yourself and your disciples not having washed their feet'.

Cleansing, therefore, signified by footwashing, seems to be a prerequisite for priests to enter the Temple, according to Philo. And according to *P. Oxy.* 840 Temple entry for Jesus' disciples was also conditional upon footwashing. Could something similar also be the case in John 13? By washing the disciples' feet, is Jesus preparing them for entry into the

---

57.   *Vit. Mos.* 2.138 (*Philo*, VI, p. 517) has a similar passage: '…the laver…to serve for lustration to priests who should enter the temple (εἰς τὸν νεὼν) to perform the appointed rites, especially for washing the hands and feet.'

new Temple he is going to establish through his death, resurrection and ascension?

8.8.2 *Footwashing as Participation*

On the other hand, the bathing/footwashing also seems to involve some kind of incorporation into the sufferings and death of Jesus as the Suffering Servant. This seems to be especially implied by the word μέρος in v. 8, which is variously translated as 'share', 'belong to', 'part', 'portion' (reflecting Heb. חלק, 'inheritance/land'). It seems the case that becoming 'part' of Jesus through footwashing means disciples will also suffer and may well die in his service. This is true for Peter, who, in feeding Jesus' sheep (21.15-17), is called to be like the Good Shepherd and lay down his life (21.18-19). Jn 15.12-16.4a sets out the general call for disciples to share in suffering and to love one another to the extent of dying for one another (15.13) as Jesus did for them. I stop short, however, of saying as H. Weiss does, that washing one another's feet is a preparation for martyrdom paralleled by the anointing of Jesus' feet in preparation of his burial (12.1-3).[58]

8.8.3 *Conclusion*

Can these two understandings of the footwashing (preparatory cleansing and participation) be brought together? Earlier in this chapter it was intimated that 'the Father's house' of Jn 14.2 has Temple connotations, and if taken together with 2.21 (where Jesus spoke of his body as the Temple), then it is quite possible (and I will argue that it is the case) that the Father's house of 14.2 is Jesus himself. Through his passion, death and resurrection he has prepared a new place, a new Temple for his disciples, that is nothing less than himself representing the presence of the Father. So, if the footwashing signifies preparation for 'entry to this Temple', entry of itself means participation in all the 'Temple' represents, namely, the passion, death and resurrection of Jesus. However, this is looking ahead and will need to be argued in subsequent pages.

---

58. Weiss ('Foot Washing', pp. 312-14) argues that the anointing of Jesus' feet for his burial and the washing of the disciples' feet are parallel acts. Both the anointing and the washing mean the same thing. What counts against this is that different words are used: Jesus' feet were anointed; the disciples' feet were washed. The parts of the body are the same but the actions are different and signify different things. Jesus' feet were anointed for burial; the disciples' feet were washed so they could be prepared to share in Jesus.

8.9 *Returning to the 'Father's House'*

Having made the point that the footwashing in John 13 signifies a puri-ficatory preparation with possible Temple associations, I now return to Jn 14.2-3. Jesus speaks of 'my Father's house'. I have already noted that this phrase occurs in 2.16 and has unmistakable reference there to the Jeru-salem Temple. However, it is not likely the Johannine Jesus is talking of the Jerusalem Temple in 14.2. What then is Jesus speaking of when in Jn 14.2 he says 'my Father's house'?

8.9.1 *Father's House as Jesus*
The editorial comment in Jn 2.21 connects the Temple with the body of Jesus. We have already seen how significant this is in interpreting a pass-age like Jn 7.37-39 where Jesus speaks at the Festival of Tabernacles of rivers of living water flowing out from his κοιλία. There the links with Ezek. 47.1-11 and Zech. 14.8 were apparent. Jesus is the eschatological Temple who is the source of the rivers of living water. The symbolism of this is underscored in the emphatic witness of the piercing of the side of Jesus' body:

> One of the soldiers pierced his side with a spear, and at once blood and water came out. (He who saw this has testified so that you also may believe. His testimony is true, and he knows that he tells the truth.)

The flow of blood from the Passover Lamb issues in the flow of water— new life in the Spirit (7.39).[59] But now in 14.2 Jesus speaks of 'many dwelling places' being in 'my Father's house'. It is not possible to make a simplistic equation 'Father's house' = Temple = Jesus' body on the basis of Jn 2.21. To suggest that 'many abiding places' for the disciples were in Jesus' *literal* body would be bizarre. But to identify 'my Father's house' with Jesus in some sense would be possible. Brown concurs with this when he says 'his [Jesus'] body is his Father's house; and wherever the glorified Jesus is, there is the Father'.[60] And this tends to be confirmed by what Jesus says in 14.3: 'I am coming back to take you *to myself*.'[61] So I

---

59. The gift of the Holy Spirit is always contingent on the departure (glorification) of Jesus (16.7).

60. Brown (*John*, II, p. 627).

61. As noted above (8.5.1 n. 22) the 'to myself' is emphatic. A. Lewis Humphries ('A Note on πρὸς ἐμαυτόν [John 14.3] and εἰς τὰ ἴδια [John 1.11]', *ExpTim* 53 [1941–42], p. 356) suggests that πρὸς ἐμαυτόν is equivalent to Jesus' home. But see below for more on this when I come to discuss μοναί.

suggest that 'my Father's house' has Temple connotations and refers in some sense to Jesus himself.

8.9.2 *Father's House as Family*
8.9.2.1 *House is Not Spatial.* I have made the point previously (6.4.3.3; 6.6; 6.8.3) about the inappropriateness in John of tying the new Temple (Jesus) to any particular place. The Samaritan woman is told 'neither on this mountain nor in Jerusalem you will worship the Father' (4.23). The geographical origin of Jesus is presented as a mystery (7.27, 40-44; 9.29).[62] The worship of the disciples in John 20 on the first day of the week is at an unspecified place. As I indicated earlier (6.8.2), in 20.19 the word 'house' is not even mentioned in the Greek text. All we are told is that the doors were shut for fear of the Jews. And likewise in 20.26 there is no mention of 'house'. The disciples are simply said to be within (ἔσω). I believe this relativizing of space with respect to the Johannine Jesus is deliberate. The new Temple of YHWH is not to be found in any special place, but in the presence of Jesus, who is the Spirit of truth (cf. 4.24). So the understanding of 'my Father's house' in Jn 14.2 should not be in spatial terms even though the metaphors (οἶκος, μοναὶ, τόπος) are spatial.

8.9.2.2 *The Nathan Oracle.* The Nathan oracle contains a play on the term 'house' (2 Sam. 7.5-17; 1 Chron. 17.4-15). The prophecy is built around a contrast: David is to build a house (meaning Temple) for God (2 Sam. 7.5; 2 Chron. 17.4), but God is to build a house (meaning dynasty/family) for him (2 Sam. 7.11; 1 Chron. 17.10). The substance of the prophecy is the perpetuity of the Davidic dynasty (2 Sam. 7.12-16). David himself understood it in this way (2 Sam. 7.19, 25 , 27, 29; 23.5) and it was also understood elsewhere in the Old Testament (Ps. 89.29-37; 132.11-12) where it becomes the first in a series relating to the Davidic Messiah (cf. Isa. 7.14; Mic. 2.2-5a).

There are significant modifications in the parallel accounts of this oracle not in the LXX but in the MT.

2 Samuel 7.12	*1 Chronicles 17.11*
LXX	
Καὶ ἀναστήσω	καὶ ἀναστήσω
τὸ σπέρμα σου μετὰ σέ,	τὸ σπέρμα σου μετὰ σέ,

---

62. Cf. Lk. 2 where the earthly origin of Jesus is clearly located in Bethlehem. John actually locates the origin of Jesus εἰς τὸν κόλπον τοῦ πατρος (1.18) and 'in' the Father (10.38).

ὅς ἔσται ἐκ τῆς κοιλίας σου...   ὅς ἔσται ἐκ τῆς κοιλίας σου...

MT

והקימתי   והקימתי

את זרעך אחריך   את זרעך אחריך

אשר יצא ממעיך   אשר יהיה מבניך

The MT of 2 Sam. 7.12 has offspring from David's body, but in 1 Chron. 17.11 the offspring shall be raised up from one of his sons.

2 Samuel 7.16	*1 Chronicles 17.14*
LXX	
καὶ πιστωθήσεται	καὶ πιστώσω αὐτὸν
ὁ οἶκος αὐτοῦ	ἐν οἴκῳ μου
καὶ ἡ βασιλεία αὐτοῦ	καὶ ἐν βασιλείᾳ αὐτοῦ
ἕως αἰῶνος ἐνώπιον ἐμοῦ...	ἕως αἰῶνος...
MT	
ונאמן ביתך	והעמדתיהו בביתי
וממלכתך עד עולם [63]לפניך	ובמלכותי עד העולם

In 1 Chron. 17.14 the son who will build a house for God (1 Chron. 17.12) will abide permanently 'in my house' (ἐν οἴκῳ μου/בביתי). In the MT 'my house' is paralleled with 'my kingdom', but in the LXX the possessive pronoun switches from 'my' to 'his'. The oracle in 2 Sam. 7 is therefore interpreted in the Hebrew of 1 Chronicles 17 as David's descendants being established in YHWH's house and kingdom, not his own. The LXX tries to retain the link with David by keeping the line καὶ ἐν βασιλείᾳ αὐτοῦ. However, it follows the switch of emphasis to YHWH's house by faithfully translating the Hebrew בביתי as ἐν οἴκῳ μου. Once this expression found its way into the text, then it is not surprising that later interpreters saw here a reference to the Temple.

So the thought of dwelling permanently 'in my house' receives emphasis and amplification in the Targum on 1 Chron. 17.14: 'And I shall establish him as a faithful one among my people in my sanctuary house [בבית מקדשי] and in my kingdom forever, and the throne of his kingdom will be established forever.'[64] The phrase בבית מקדשי almost certainly refers to the Temple.[65]

Finally I note the well-known father/son relationship between David's

---

63. The editor suggests לפני following the LXX, but the fact that the overall thrust of the Hebrew is on the second person singular may favour the retention of the MT.

64. J. Stanley McIvor (trans.), *The Targum of Chronicles* (ed. K. Cathcart *et al.*; Aramaic Bible, 19; Collegeville, MN: Liturgical Press, 1994), p. 106.

65. McCaffrey, *The House with Many Rooms*, p. 52 and n. 23.

son and YHWH: 'I will be his father [εἰς πατέρα] and he will be my son' (εἰς υἱόν, 2 Sam. 7.14/1 Chron. 17.13). There are no textual variations on this verse either in LXX or MT, but the author of the Targum is careful to demonstrate the purely figurative character of the father/son imagery scrupulously guarding against any suggestion that YHWH actually fathers the son: 'I shall love him as a father (loves) his son, and he will be cherished before me as a son is cherished by his father.'[66] Thus there is an expectation in Jewish tradition that a son of David who is to have some kind of father/son relationship with YHWH will remain permanently *in his people* and in the Temple.

Although the Johannine Jesus is never presented as a son of David, he certainly is portrayed as a Son of the Father. In fact, that is presented as the fundamental relationship Jesus has with God. This emerges powerfully in John 17 when Jesus prays to God with the address of 'Father' (17.1, 5, 11, 21, 24, 25) and usually[67] refers to himself as 'Son' (17.1 [2x]). So the Johannine Jesus is presented as one who has a father/son relationship with YHWH and may thereby qualify to 'remain permanently in his people and in the Temple'.

8.9.3 *Precedents for Seeing Temple as Community*

In my Chapter 2 I have looked at some Qumran texts and have seen that the Qumran Council 'is the *foundation*[68] on which the Community is built as a Temple with the cultic function of offering up "sweet fragrance" which…is the deeds of the law' (2.7.1). I now draw attention to a further text that reinforces this conclusion.

In the *Manual of Discipline*, we see that the community functions as God's house:

> At this moment the men of the Community shall set themselves apart (like) a holy house (בית קודש) for Aaron, in order to enter the holy of holies and (like) a house of the Community for Israel (להוחד קודשים ובית יחד לישראל) (for) those who walk in perfection (1QS 9.5-6).[69]

---

66. McIvor, *The Targum of Chronicles*, p. 106; cf. D. Juel, *Messiah and Temple: The Trial of Jesus in the Gospel of Mark* (SBLDS, 31; Missoula, MT: Scholars Press, 1977), p. 186.

67. In Jn 17.3 Jesus refers to himself as 'Jesus Christ'.

68. For my conclusion that the Council of Qumran is the *foundation* of the Temple for the whole Qumran Community, see 2.7.1 and n. 64.

69. García Martínez, *The Dead Sea Scrolls*, p. 13. The translator's parentheses ('like' [2x] and 'for') tend to mute the Temple imagery for the Community. He offers

It seems then that the Qumran community, having separated itself from what it understood as the ungodly leadership of Temple Judaism (cf. CD 4.2) now saw itself in terms of Temple imagery.[70]

In addition to the Qumran texts there is a significant passage in Ben Sirach 49.12:

οὕτως Ἰησοῦς υἱὸς Ἰωσεδεκ,
οἱ ἐν ἡμέραις αὐτῶν ᾠκοδόμησαν οἶκον
καὶ ἀνύψωσαν ναὸν ἅγιον κυρίῳ
ἡτοιμασμένον εἰς δόξαν αἰῶνος.

There is nothing exceptional in the text as it stands: 'So Jesus son of Josedek built a house in their time and lifted up a holy Temple to the LORD which was prepared for everlasting glory.' However, there is a variant on ναὸν, namely, λαὸν.[71] Mary Coloe comments:

> This means that it was possible in late second Temple Judaism to speak of setting up both a holy Temple and a holy people. A community perceiving themselves as the new Temple, prepared by the lifting up of Jesus in death, could well look back to this text and its many association with Johannine terms Ἰησοῦς, οἶκον, ἀνύψωσαν, ἡτοιμασμένον, δόξαν.[72]

There are also precededents for Temple-as-Community language in the Pauline literature: 1 Cor. 3.16-17; 1 Cor. 6.19; 2 Cor. 6.16; Eph. 2.21.

With these precedents in mind I now return to the Gospel of John and

---

no evidence to justify this interpretation. It is just as possible to translate 'the men of the community shall set themselves apart *as* a holy house for Aaron' where the community would function as a replacement (albeit temporary) of the בית קודש, an expression that very likely derives from the Jerusalem Temple. Further, the translation of להוחד (a niphal infin. cs. of יחד) as 'to enter' seems unwarranted. Rather I would translate as 'to be united as a holy of holies, namely (explanatory *waw*) a united house for Israel' or 'a house of the Community for Israel'.

70. Temple imagery is used to describe the community elsewhere, for example, CD 3.18–4.10 and 1QpHab 12.3-4. Chris Marshall (*Faith as a Theme in Mark's Narrative* [SNTSMS, 64; Cambridge: Cambridge University Press, 1989], pp. 159-72) provides a confirmatory interpretation from a Synoptic Gospel that Temple refers to 'community'. In commenting on Mk 11.20-25, Marshall equates the community of Jesus, the praying community, as *the Temple not made with hands*. The 'house of prayer for all nations' has supplanted the 'den of robbers'. The praying disciples have become the new Temple (pp. 162-63).

71. See J. Ziegler (ed.), *Sapientia Iesu Filii Sirach XII, 2, Septuaginta Vetus Testamentum Graecum* (Göttingen: Vandenhoeck & Ruprecht, 2nd edn, 1980), p. 356. Λαον is attested by B-S V 336 Syh Sa Aeth.

72. Coloe, 'The Dwelling of God', p. 238.

see if I can further unravel the family associations in the phrase 'in my Father's house'.

8.9.4 *House in John 8*

A clue to assist our understanding of the Johannine text in 14.2 is offered in the usage of οἰκία in the Gospel of John,[73] especially 8.35 (ὁ δὲ δοῦλος οὐ μένει ἐν τῇ οἰκίᾳ εἰς τὸν αἰῶνα, ὁ υἱὸς μένει εἰς τὸν αἰῶνα). McCaffrey has pointed out that there are significant links between these two passages and their contexts.

8.35	*14.2-3*
ἐν τῇ οἰκίᾳ	ἐν τῇ οἰκίᾳ
μένω (2x)	μοναί (a noun from μένω)
ἐν denotes relationship of indwelling	ἐν denotes relationship of indwelling
Filial relationship (ὁ υἱός)	Filial relationship (τοῦ πατρός μου)
Discipleship theme (8.31)	Discipleship theme (13.35)
Faith theme (8.30-31)	Faith theme (14.1)

There are therefore striking connections between these two passages and McCaffrey has shown that as οἰκία refers to family in 8.35[74] so there is a strong possibility that it refers to the same entity in 14.2-3; hence we could read 'in my Father's house' as 'in my Father's family'. This is a crucial step forward in understanding John's treatment of the Temple theme in the Gospel. In 2.21 there has been a shift from the Temple of Jerusalem ('my Father's house') to the Temple as the body of Jesus; and now in Jn 14.2-3 there is this further shift to incorporate not only Jesus, but also the disciples as 'my Father's family'.[75] Thus the Father's house includes Jesus,

---

73. McCaffrey (*The House with Many Rooms*) has surveyed the usage of οἰκία and οἶκος in John and concluded that while οἰκία may refer to 'family' or 'household' it is not confined to that usage and may also refer to a building as in 11.31 and 12.3; on the other hand, he believes οἶκος *always* refers to a building.

74. Brown (*John*, I, p. 627) comments, 'This special house or household where the son has a permanent dwelling place suggests a union with the Father reserved for Jesus the Son and for all those who are begotten as God's children by the Spirit that Jesus gives.'

75. This makes S. Aalen's suggestion ('"Reign" and "House" in the Kingdom of God in the Gospels', *NTS* 8 [1961–62], pp. 215-40 [238]) not unlikely. He takes 'my Father's house' to mean the people of God in the manner of Heb. 3.2-6 and thinks that 14.2-3 is dependent on the Targum of 1 Chron. 17.9: 'And I will make (or, appoint) *for my people a prepared place, and they shall dwell in their places,* and they shall *not tremble any more.*' (The italics indicate the close resemblances between the Targum and John 14.1-3.) The Cambridge and Vatican manuscripts have singular ('place') for

but also includes those who have become 'children of God' (cf. 1.12-13) through faith in Jesus. Indeed only a few verses prior to 14.2-3 Jesus has called his disciples τεκνία (13.33), showing his love for them as members of the family. And of course the same word is frequently used in 1 John.

This opening up, as it were, of the 'Father's house' does seem to indicate a widening of the communion between Father and Son to include those whom the Father has given to the Son and this possibly extends particularly to the Greeks and Jews in the Diaspora (cf. 10.16; 12.20; 17.20). Perhaps this is why Jesus says, 'In my Father's house there are *many* rooms.'

8.10 *Many Rooms*

8.10.1 *Old Testament and Extra-Biblical Occurrences of* μονή
The term μονή occurs only once in the LXX (1 Macc. 7.38):

Ποίησον ἐκδίκησιν ἐν τῷ ἀνθρώπῳ τούτῳ καὶ ἐν τῇ παρεμβολῇ αὐτοῦ,
καὶ πεσέτωσαν ἐν ῥομφαίᾳ.
μνήσθητι τῶν δυφημιῶν αὐτῶν,
καὶ μὴ δῷς αὐτοῖς μονήν.

The two lines in bold type are parallel; the meaning of one parallels the other. The first line is positive: 'Take vengeance on this man and on his army, *and may they perish by the sword*.' The second line is negative: 'Remember their blasphemies, *and may you not give them* μονήν.'

The parallelism suggests that the meaning of μονή is 'continued existence' or 'permanent dwelling'.

The word μονή occurs twice in Josephus. In *Ant.* 13.2.1: 'So Jonathon took up his residence in Jerusalem [τὴν μονὴν ἐποιεῖτο], making various repairs in the city and arranging everything according to his liking.' Jerusalem became then his 'dwelling place', a 'place of permanent dwelling'.

The other reference in *Ant.* 8.13.7 is less clear: 'And he (Elijah) found in it (Mt Horeb) a certain hollow cave, which he entered, and there made his abode for some time [καὶ διετέλει ποιούμενος ἐν αὐτῷ τὴν μονήν].' At first sight μονή seems to mean 'resting place' or 'station' for refreshment on a journey, but the use of the words 'some time' indicates rather 'dwelling place'.

'in their places' while the editions of Lagarde and Sperber have the plural. The singular is probably preferable.

8.10.2 *Rooms in the Temple*

The word μονή is never used to designate rooms in the Temple, but there is ample evidence to show the Jerusalem Temple had several 'rooms' or apartments:

> David gave his son Solomon the plans for the Temple and the building, the treasuries, the upper rooms, the inner apartments... He also gave him the plans which he had in mind for the courts of the Temple of the Lord, all the surrounding apartments, the treasuries of the house of the Lord, and treasuries of dedicated gifts (1 Chron. 28.11-12; cf. 1 Kgs 6.5-6; 2 Chron. 31.11; Ezra 8.29; Neh. 12.44; 13.4-9; Jer. 35.2, 4; 36.10).

So, too, the eschatological Temple of Ezekiel's vision has many rooms:

> Then he brought me into the outer court (εἰς τὴν αὐλὴν τὴν ἐσωτέραν) and behold, there were two chambers (παστοφόρια) and a pavement, round about the court; there were thirty rooms on the pavement (τριάκοντα παστοφόρια) (Ezek. 40.17; cf. Ezek. 41.6).

8.10.3 Μονή *in John*

The word for 'rooms' in 14.2-3 is μοναί, most likely a derivative from μένειν, which is strikingly prominent in John. In my translation (dwelling places), I have endeavoured to retain the link with μένειν. Most commentators make the point that the μοναί refers to permanent dwellings and not lodging places or stations.[76] This would be true, too, for 14.23 where the word 'home'[77] seems a good translation for μονή.

---

76. Lindars (*John*, pp. 470-71): 'It does not refer to lodging places along the way or to different departments in heaven on arrival'; Brown (*John*, II, p. 619) goes into some detail about the Aramaic cognate, Patristic usage, Latin and English translations and concludes, 'It would be much more in harmony with Johannine thought to relate μονή to the cognate μένειν, frequently used in John in reference to staying, remaining, or abiding with Jesus and with the Father'; Morris (*John*, p. 638), 'In the present chapter...it is the sense of permanence that is required'; Schnackenburg (*St John*, III, pp. 60-61) opts for 'permanent abodes' and remarks, 'There is no suggestion here of any grading according to status or merit...' However, Westcott (*St John*, II, p. 167) has a contrary opinion based, it seems, on the Latin Vulgate rendering of 'mansiones', 'which were resting places, and especially the "stations" on a great road where travellers found refreshment. This appears to be the true meaning of the word here [i.e. in Jn 14.2]; so that the contrasted notions of repose and progress are combined in this vision of the future.' This is a valiant attempt to combine the notions of movement and rest. But the Vulgate rendering has been a red herring and does not do justice to the significance of μονή at all.

77. So NRSV. Humphries ('Note on πρὸς ἐμαυτόν', p. 356) also wants to bring the notion of 'home' into 14.2-3, but not through the translation of μονή but πρός

Is there a Temple link with μοναί in Jn 14.2? As noted above, there is evidence in the Jewish tradition for a division of the Jerusalem Temple and the eschatological Temple into 'rooms' and 'compartments'. However, the term μοναί is never used in connection with the Temple. But given other Temple links discussed previously, it could well apply to the Temple.

What meaning might μοναί bear in Jn 14.2? In Jn 1.38-39 there is the narrative where two disciples of John the Baptist follow Jesus:

στραφεὶς δὲ ὁ Ἰησοῦς καὶ θεασάμενος αὐτοὺς ἀκολουθοῦντας λέγει αὐτοῖς, Τί ζητεῖτε; οἱ δὲ εἶπαν αὐτῷ, Ῥαββί, ὃ λέγεται μεθερμηνευόμενον Διδάσκαλε, ποῦ <u>μένεις</u>; λέγει αὐτοῖς, Ἔρχεσθε καὶ ὄψεσθε. ἦλθαν οὖν καὶ εἶδαν ποῦ <u>μένει</u> καὶ παρ᾽ αὐτῷ <u>ἔμειναν</u> τὴν ἡμέραν ἐκείνην·

The verb μένειν occurs three times here and some commentators[78] concede that there is a link with later parts of the Gospel and mention especially John 15 where the disciples abide in the vine. G.B. Caird[79] sees a link with ch. 14 and suggests that the most profound answer to the question of the two disciples, 'Master, where do you live?' is to be found in that chapter where Jesus reveals that he lives with the Father, and that the words 'Come and see' are an invitation not only to the two disciples, but all disciples, and especially those who read the Gospel. They are invited to come and see where Jesus' home is and to stay with him.

Robert Gundry favours this understanding of μοναί and uses the singular μονή in 14.23 to interpret the plural in 14.2. He comments:

> The two occurrences of μονή in John 14 demonstrate a reciprocal relationship: as believers have abiding places in Christ, so Jesus and the Father have an abiding place in each believer. The plural form in verse 2 emphasizes the individuality of the places which all believers have in Christ. Inversely, the singular μονήν in verse 23 emphasizes that the Father and Jesus dwell in each disciple individually.[80]

ἐμαυτόν. He is convinced that in that phrase we have an occasional and special use of the reflexive pronoun in New Testament Greek that designates one's home. He also thinks that παραλαμβάνω should be translated as 'to take along with one's self, in one's company'. Thus his translation of 14.3: 'I will come again and take you with me to my home.' This is an interesting suggestion and would support the translation of μονή as 'home' in 14.23, but it is doubtful whether Humphries is correct.

78. Carson, Barrett (tentatively), but Lindars (*John*, p. 113) says a connection with later parts of the Gospel (e.g. ch. 15) is reading too much into the text.

79. This was a remark by G.B. Caird in a lecture at the University of Otago, Dunedin, in 1982.

80. Robert H. Gundry. '"In my Father's House There Are Many Μοναί" (John

8.10.4 Πολλαί

One of the central ideas of Jewish eschatology is the reunion of Israel at the divine dwelling place (2 Macc. 1.27-29; cf. 2.7-8, 17-18). The extension of this concept to include the Gentiles marks an important development (Isa. 2.2-4//Mic. 4.1-3; Isa. 54.2; 56.6-7; 60.1-13; 66.18-21; Zech. 8.20-23; 14.16-21; Tob. 14.4-7; cf. 13.10-14).

Thus the Jerusalem Temple is seen as the goal of the complete and universal salvation of the eschatological age, the centre of unity, not only for Israel, but for the whole world.

Further, we find this universalism also associated with the heavenly Temple in *1 Enoch*. The old Temple is torn down and in its place a magnificent new one is erected (*1 En.* 90.28-29). The advent of the new Temple marks great changes. The hostility between Jews and Gentiles comes to an end, and the Gentiles worship in the Temple (*1 En.* 90.33). As a token of their reconciliation the sword that had been given to the Jews to destroy their enemies is put away in the Temple (*1 En.* 90.34-35). The author concludes, 'And I saw that that house was large and broad and very full' (*1 En.* 90.36).

With this sort of background in mind it is possible that πολλαί is meant to convey that in this new Temple there will be 'space' for all to be accommodated. Marsh[81] speaks of space enough for the Gentiles as well as the Jews and other exegetes speak of the universal love of God. This latter suggestion is in keeping with Johannine expressions of God's purposes, such as 1.29; 3.16; 4.42; 10.16; 11.52; 12.32; 17.20 and perhaps 21.11.[82]

14.2)', *ZNW* 53 (1967), pp. 68-72 (69-70). Gundry goes on to say that μοναί in 14.2 signifies 'not mansions in the sky, but spiritual positions in Christ, much as in Pauline theology.' I am unsure about the theological comparison with Paul. I think there is a stronger familial emphasis in the Gospel of John than Paul and rather than use the term 'spiritual positions in Christ' I would say that what we are given in Christ are family relationships generated by the Holy Spirit (cf. 1.12, 13; 3.5). Interestingly, McCaffrey (*The House with Many Rooms*, p. 247), in writing of the meaning of μονή, says: '[I]t indicates a spiritual "abiding-space" or "dwelling-space" in the eternal temple... Moreover, all believers will dwell there spiritually, or have their *spiritual positions* there, when Jesus returns to take them there' (my emphasis).

81. Marsh (*Saint John*, p. 501), Lindars (*John*, p. 470), 'accommodation for everyone'; Barrett (*St John*, p. 457), 'communion with God is a permanent and universal possibility'; Brown (*John*, II, p. 625), 'the "many" simply means that there are enough for all'.

82. Bultmann (*John*, p. 709) says the number 153 must have an allegorical meaning because it is not a round number. He says that the 'multitude of fish represents the

The expression μοναί πολλαί, then, may well have rich Temple connotations, signifying secure, permanent dwelling places, not only for the disciples who have seen him, but also for all who have not seen him and believe (20.29).

8.11 Τόπος

Jesus says to the disciples that he is going to prepare a τόπος for them. I have mentioned in the chapter on Jn 1.51 that τόπος in John can be used for the Temple (cf. 11.48; 4.20). However, behind John's usage of τόπος to designate the Temple lies a strong Jewish tradition. The word is found repeatedly in the Deuteronomic formula 'the place [τόπος] where YHWH has chosen to establish/place his name' (Deut. 12.5; cf. Deut. 12.11).[83]

I begin by looking at Exod. 15.17, which seems to be the original source of the Jewish Temple tradition:

multitude of believers who are won through the apostolic preaching'. But though he surveys suggested meanings of the number 153 (p. 709 n.2) he comes to no conclusions. If the 153 fish netted is meant to represent a full harvest on the part of the Church, then this may be an indication of the fullness of God's purposes for the mission of the Church. J.A. Emerton ('The Hundred and Fifty Three Fish', *JTS* 9 [1958], pp. 86-89) links 153 with Ezek. 47.10 where the water flows out from the Temple and becomes a great river and men come to fish in it from En-gedi (עֵין גֶּדִי) to En-eglaim (עֵין עֶגְלַיִם). So גֶדִי = 3 + 4 + 10 = 17 (the significance of 17 is that the sum of the first 17 natural numbers is 153) and עֶגְלַיִם = 40 + 10 + 30 + 3 + 70 = 153. Brown (*John*, II, p. 1075) points out that what gives some credence to this suggestion is that in very early Christian art Peter and John are portrayed next to a stream of water flowing from the Temple, which in turn may be connected with the rock of Jesus' sepulchre. In addition to this I draw attention to the important significance Ezek. 47.1-12 has for this Gospel (see 7.2.4.7). Other suggestions are: (a) Brown (*John*, II, p. 1076) tentatively suggests that 153 may be what the eyewitness saw. (b) Hoskyns (*The Fourth Gospel*, pp. 553-54) notes that 153 is a triangular number but that in itself is not especially illuminating. (c) Barrett (*St John*, p. 581) fastens on to the fact that 17 = 10 + 7 (both numbers indicative of completeness and perfection) and 7 can be discovered in 21.2 where 7 'apostles' are mentioned—so 17 could be construed as representing the fullness of the Church. (d) Carson (*John*, p. 673) concludes, 'If the Evangelist had some symbolism in mind connected with the number 153, he has hidden it well.'

83. There are two variations of this formula: (1) 'to establish his name there' (לְשַׁכֵּן) (Deut. 12.11; 14.23; 16.2, 6, 11; 26.2; Neh. 1.9); (2) 'to place his name there' (לָשׂוּם) (Deut. 12.5, 21; 14.24). Both variations mean the same thing. The 'place' is Jerusalem and the Temple where Josiah centralized the nation's worship.

εἰσαγαγὼν καταφύτευσον αὐτοὺς εἰς ὄρος κληρονομίας σου, εἰς ἕτοιμον κατοικητήριον σου, ὅ κατηρτίσω, κύριε, ἁγίασμα, κύριε, ὅ ἡτοίμασαν αἱ χεῖρες σου.

Also of importance is the Nathan oracle where YHWH says to David:

> I will appoint a place [θήσομαι τόπον] for my people Israel and will plant them, that they may dwell in their own place [καθ' ἑαυτὸν] and never be disturbed again; and violent men shall afflict them no more (2 Sam. 7.10/1Chron. 17.9).

Since the issue in question here is David building a house for YHWH, it is very likely that the future building of the Temple is in view and τόπος here refers to the Jerusalem Temple. However, the Qumran midrash (4Q174.1-3) offers a different interpretation of 2 Sam. 7.10:

> *2 Sam. 7.10* ["And] an enemy [will trouble him no mo]re, [nor will] the son of iniquity [afflict him again] as at the beginning. From the day on which [I established judges] over my people, Israel". This (refers to) the house which [they will establish] for [him] in the last days, as is written in the book of [Moses: *Exod. 15.17-18* "A temple of the LORD] will you establish with your hands. YHWH shall reign for ever and ever".[84]

It appears then, that the interpreter, by appeal to Exod. 15.17, has related the 'τόπος' in 2 Sam. 7.10a not to the Jerusalem Temple that Solomon builds, but to the eschatological Temple that God will build.

There also seems to be some ambiguity about the referent of τόπος in the Temple address in Jeremiah 7. The meaning of 'land' seems to be present at first:

> I will cause you to dwell in this place [ἐν τῷ τόπῳ τούτῳ, Jer. 7.3], that is, I will cause you to dwell in this place, in the land [ἐν τῷ τόπῳ τούτῳ ἐν γῇ, Jer. 7.7].

But as the passage continues we read:

> But go you now to my (holy) place [εἰς τὸν τόπον μου] which was in Shiloh, where I caused my name to tabernacle at first (Jer. 7.12).

And then finally:

> Therefore I will do to this house [τῷ οἴκῳ τούτῳ] over which my name is named and in which you trust, and the place [τῷ τόπῳ] which I gave to you and to your father as I have done to Shiloh (Jer. 7.14).

84. García Martínez, *The Dead Sea Scrolls*, p. 136.

However, the ambiguity is only apparent. Temple and land belonged together. The Temple was considered to be the source of all fertility and blessing for the land (Ezek. 47.1-12; Ps. 36.9, 10; 46.5; Joel 3.18; Zech. 14.8). To dwell (worship) in YHWH's house carried with it the privilege of dwelling (living) in his land (cf. the significant juxtaposition of land and holy place in Ps. 24.1, 3).[85]

However, there is no reference to land in the Maccabaean literature's use of τόπος. There the theological understanding of τόπος is fully directed towards the Temple as the holy place. 2 Macc. 1.27-29 firmly identifies τόπος with the eschatological Temple through a clear allusion to Exod. 15.17 in the last line:

> Gather together [ἐπισυνάγαγε] our scattered people [τὴν διασπορὰν ἡμῶν], set free those who are slaves among the Gentiles, look upon those who are rejected and despised, and let the Gentiles [ἔθνη] know that you are God. Afflict those who oppress us and affront us by their insolence. Plant your people in your Holy Place, as Moses said [καταφύτευσον τὸν λαόν σου εἰς τὸν τόπον τὸν ἅγιόν σου].[86]

A further example of the gathering of the people of God to the Temple (where τόπος is equivalent to Temple) is in the letter sent by the Jews of Jerusalem to their fellow Jews in Egypt:

> ...to conclude... God who has saved his whole people, conferring on all the heritage, kingdom, priesthood and sanctification, as he promised through the law, will surely, as our hope is in him, be swift to show mercy and gather us together [ἐπισυνάξει] from everywhere under heaven to the Holy Place [εἰς τὸν ἅγιον τόπον] since he has rescued us from great evils and has purified the Temple [τὸν τόπον] (2 Macc. 2.17-18).

The above texts demonstrate that within Jewish tradition there was a tendency to designate land/sanctuary/Temple by the word τόπος. It is not always clear whether it is the Jerusalem Temple or the eschatological Temple that is in view. However, in the Deuteronomic texts (cited above) τόπος was identified in the Deuteronomistic history as the Jerusalem Temple (1 Kgs 8.29; 11.36; 14.21; 2 Kgs 21.4, 7) and in some texts (e.g. Exod. 15.17 in the light of 4Q174 and 2 Macc. 1.29) τόπος referred to the eschatological Temple.

Τόπος therefore has a rich history in Jewish tradition of being asso-

---

85. See R.E. Clements, 'Temple and Land: A Significant Aspect of Israel's Worship', *TGUOS* 19 (1963), pp. 16-28.

86. There seem also to be strong echoes in Jn 11.52 to this passage in 2 Macc.

ciated with the Temple, either the Jerusalem Temple or the eschatological Temple. In Jn 14.2-3 it is unlikely to refer to the Jerusalem Temple, but there is a real possibility it may refer to the eschatological Temple of Exod. 15.17.

Further, the use of the word ἑτοιμάσαι in relation to τόπος in Jn 14.2-3 strengthens the possibility that the eschatological Temple is in view. This is the very word used in Exod. 15.17 for the preparation of the eschatological Temple (the ἁγίασμα) for the Exodus people. Again I suggest there is in Jn 14.2-3 an echo of the fountain text of Jewish Temple tradition, which we have seen has been interpreted to refer to the eschatological Temple.

The survey above gives some force to the proposition that τόπος signalled the locus of the meeting between God and people particularly by way of the Temple (Jerusalem or eschatological). Jesus tells his disciples that he is going to prepare a place (τόπος) for them. To do this he must go to Golgotha, 'The Place (Τόπος) of the Skull' (19.17). This place is the antithesis of the place Jesus is going to prepare for his disciples. 'The Place of the Skull' is a place of death and darkness; the place he goes to get ready for his disciples is a 'place' of life (14.18; cf. 10.10; 20.30-31). It is in line with such preparation that Athanasius later called Jesus Christ 'The Place'.[87] Jesus himself is, in a sense, 'the Father's house' in whom the disciples may dwell and have communion with the Father and the Father with them (14.23; 17.21).

8.12 *The Preparation*

In what sense is Jesus preparing a place for his disciples? Brown (*John*, II, p. 627) comments:

> If by his death, resurrection and ascension Jesus is to make possible a union of the disciples with his Father, he must prepare his disciples for the union by making them understand how it is to be achieved. Augustine (in *Jo* LXVII 2; PL 35.1814) expresses this cleverly: 'He prepares the dwelling places by preparing those who are to dwell in them.'[88]

---

87. See above in 5.4.3.2 n. 47. Cf. also Marsh (*Saint John*, p. 501) who says, 'Jesus Christ is "the place..."' Woll (*Conflict*, p. 45) says in relation to the preparation of a place for the disciples, 'Jesus functions as the sacred centre, the place where heavenly reality—light, life, the bread of heaven, etc.—is made available to the disciple.' The disciples' 'place', as with other divine realities, is mediated through Jesus.

88. Lindars (*John*, p. 470), however, takes the phrase as simply a word-picture of

On the other hand, Jesus actively prepares 'a place' for his disciples by dying, rising again and ascending to the Father. The preparation is by way of his passion.

But what place? Here McCaffrey's survey of texts has produced a cluster of references that speak of preparation of the Temple:

(a) I have already mentioned Exod. 15.17, but I set it out again for completeness:

> The place you have made your dwelling, Yahweh [ἕτοιμον κατοικητήριον] the sanctuary, Yahweh, prepared by your own hands [ὃ ἡτοίμασαν αἱ χεῖρες σου].

(b) Sir. 47.13 concerns the building of the first Temple:

> Solomon reigned in the days of peace and God gave him rest on every side, that he might build a house for his name and prepare a sanctuary to stand forever [ἐτοιμάσῃ ἁγίασμα εἰς τὸν αἰῶνα].

(c) Sir. 49.12 is with reference to Zerubbabel and Joshua building the second Temple:

> Who in their days built the Temple [ᾠκοδόμησαν οἶκον] and raised to the LORD a holy Temple [καὶ ἀνύψωσαν ναὸν ἅγιον κυρίῳ] ready for everlasting glory [ἡτοιμασμένον εἰς δόξαν αἰῶνος].

(d) In 2 Chron. 8.16 the whole work of building, or construction of the Temple from beginning to end is designated as a process of preparation:

> Thus was prepared all the work of Solomon [καὶ ἡτοιμάσθη πᾶσα ἡ ἐργασία] from the day the foundation of the LORD's house [τὸν οἶκον κυρίου] was laid until it was finished (cf. Zech. 5.11).

(e) Finally we observe that the parallel texts of Mic. 4.1 and Isa. 2.2 represent the eschatological Temple as the goal of the pilgrimage of the nations and that it is explicitly described as a place 'prepared'. There are some differences that I will highlight by setting the texts in parallel:

---

an earthly domestic situation: '[S]omeone goes on ahead to the hotel, books rooms for all the party, and returns to fetch them when all is ready.' But if it is a word-picture, what is it a picture of? Lindars is not clear with his answer. Others see in the word 'prepare' some allusion to preparation for the Passover (cf. Hoskyns' link with Mk 14.12-16). Given that the Gospel of John is saturated with Passover imagery and that Jesus dies on the Day of Preparation (19.14), this is perhaps not altogether unlikely.

Isaiah 2.2	*Micah 4.1*
῞Οτι ἔσται ἐν ταῖς ἐσχάταις ἡμέραις	Καὶ ἔσται ἐπ᾽ ἐσχάτων τῶν ἡμερῶν
ἐμφανὲς τὸ ὄρος τοῦ Κυρίου.	ἐμφανὲς τὸ ὄρος τοῦ Κυρίου,
<u>καὶ ὁ οἶκος τοῦ θεοῦ</u>	<u>ἕτοιμον ἐπὶ τὰς κορυφὰς τῶν</u>
ἐπ᾽ ἄκρου τῶν ὀρέων καὶ <u>ὑψωθήσεται</u>	ὀρέων, καὶ <u>μετεωρισθήσεται</u>
ὑπεράνω τῶν βουνῶν	ὑπεράνω τῶν βουνῶν

The use of the verb ἑτοιμάζω in Jn 14.3 with reference to the direct object 'place' may, in the light of the constellation of references above, be interpreted of preparing a Temple, possibly the eschatological Temple that is to the fore in Isa. 2.2/Mic. 4.1. There is certainly a very strong precedent for using this verb in relation to the Temple, both the Jerusalem Temple and the eschatological Temple, but as far as Jn 14.2-3 is concerned, if a choice is to be made between the two possible referents, then the Johannine context favours the eschatological Temple.

8.13 *The Departure and Return of Jesus*

Barrett (*John*, p. 457) says 'the journeying away of Jesus means (a) his death, and (b) his going to the Father's house, or more simply, to the Father (17.11)'. Certainly, Jesus' departure from his disciples is through his death as the Gospel indicates frequently, but the Gospel never states that Jesus is journeying to his 'Father's house'. That expression, I think, should be reserved for the manner in which Jesus speaks of it in 2.16 and here in 14.2. But Barrett is certainly right to say that Jesus is going to the Father.

There is also disagreement about the return of Jesus. Jesus says he is coming back, but when does he come back? Jesus says, 'A little while, and you will no longer see me, and again in a little while, and you will see me' (16.16).[89] The disciples were perplexed. They said, 'What does he mean by "a little while"? We do not know what he means' (16.18). And scholars have been as perplexed as the disciples and asked the same question. One can see this perplexity in Brown's (*John*, II, pp. 626-27) discussion of 14.2-3. He thinks that initially 14.2-3 referred to the return of Jesus at the end of the age (the parousia), but he goes on to say:

89. The disciples 'seeing' Jesus makes one think initially of the post-resurrection appearances (Jn 20), but in the overall context of Johannine thought (particularly the permanence of their joy [16.22]), Brown (*John*, II, p. 730) concedes that the 'seeing' of Jesus is in relation to the presence of the Paraclete/Spirit.

some scholars think that xiv 2-3 refer to Jesus' coming to his disciples at the hour of their death to take them to heaven.[90] We would see this as a possible reinterpretation of the parousia theme when it was realized that the parousia had not occurred soon after the death of Jesus and when the disciples began to die.

But Brown goes further than this because he detects the theme of an *earthly* divine indwelling of the disciples later in John 14. So he says: '…could the phraseology [of 14.2-3] have been secondarily reinterpreted to make it harmonious with the indwelling theme of the rest of the chapter?'[91] This is an extraordinarily complicated exegesis—reinterpretation of reinterpretation.[92] Is there a simpler solution?

90. Bultmann (*John*, p. 602 n. 1) holds this view: 'The eschatology that lies at the basis of this promise is not that of the Jewish-Christian hope but is the individualistic eschatology of the Gnostic myth…' This is unlikely since the promise has a collective force indicated by the plural pronouns and the death in view is Jesus' death, not the death of the disciples. Further, the ethos of the imagery is Jewish as I have endeavoured to demonstrate in the foregoing pages.

91. Dodd (*Interpretation*, pp. 404-405) had expounded this suggestion prior to Brown, although according to Beasley-Murray (*John*, p. 251), W. Heitmüller (*Das Evangelium des Johannes: Die Schriften des New Testament*, II [Göttingen: Vandenhoeck & Ruprecht, 1908], p. 824) succinctly stated it earlier. Dodd (p. 405) proposes that Jn 14.3 represents traditional Christian eschatology similar to 1 Thess. 4.13-18. John reinterprets this in subsequent verses of Jn 14 and Dodd (p. 405) concludes: 'By now it is surely clear that the return of Christ is to be understood in a sense different from that of popular Christian eschatology. It means that after the death of Jesus, and because of it, His followers will enter into union with Him as their living LORD, and through Him with the Father, and so enter into eternal life.' Beasley-Murray (*John*, p. 251) thinks this reinterpretation is 'highly improbable': '[I]t is a strange proceedure that makes vv. 2-3 the decisive ground of consolation and then drastically corrects it…'

92. Brown is trying to trace, of course, what he sees as the adjustment from a futurist eschatology to a realized eschatology. There are expressions of futurist eschatology in 5.28-29, 6.39-40, 44, 54 and 12.48 that are not later additions (contra R. Bultmann, *Theology of the New Testament*, II [London: SCM Press], pp. 37-39; E. Käsemann, *The Testament of Jesus According to John 17* [Philadelphia: Fortress Press, 1968], pp. 14, 72-73), but traditional themes retained by John. Interestingly, Burge (in addition to Brown) thinks John 14.1-3 also reflects the parousia hope (*Anointed*, p. 144). Burge finds indicators that 14.1-3 is dealing with the second advent: (a) 'My Father's house', which, as parallels show, points to heaven (Burge refers to Philo, *Somn.* 1.256; cf. Eccl. 5.1 [Heb.], but no other parallels). (b) More important for Burge is the room that awaits the believer in the other world. In common usage this word had a local sense of a position in heaven (1 Macc. 7.38; cf. 1 *En.* 39.4; 2 *En.* 61.2) that the believer obtained either in death or in the final day of the LORD. (c) The verbs used of

One way out of the conundrum is to affirm that vv. 2-3 includes *all forms of the coming of Jesus*[93]—the appearances of the risen Jesus to the disciples,[94] the coming of Jesus at the moment of the death of individual disciples[95] and the Parousia.[96] This is a convenient solution, but I do not believe it is tenable.

The appearances of the risen Jesus in themselves are not enough to meet the requirement of permanency indicated by the word 'dwelling places' (μοναί) and the phrase 'that where I am there you may be also'. Those appearances of the risen Jesus, profoundly significant though they were, nevertheless were spasmodic and temporary and would not have fulfilled the promise of Jesus.

The coming of Jesus at the death of individual disciples is contrary to the thrust of the passage. The promise is addressed to the disciples collectively, not individually and nothing is said about the death of disciples generally.

The Parousia does not really fulfil the imminent expectancy that is present in John 14. For example, Jesus says to his disciples, 'I will not leave you orphaned; I am coming to you. In a little while the world will no longer see me, but you will see me; because I live, you also shall live' (14.18-19). This coming of Jesus sounds imminent. The disciples will see Jesus in 'a little while'. If his coming had been delayed until the coming in the Parousia (which had not happened at the time of the writing of the Gospel), then the disciples would have been effectively orphaned. It sounds as though 14.18-19 have the resurrection of Jesus in view, but, as I mentioned above, not even those momentous appearances of the risen Jesus would suffice to fulfil the promise of 14.3.

How then should we understand the promised return of Jesus in 14.3?

Jesus' coming point to the future. Πάλιν ἔρχομαι occurs only here, and the use of the future παραλήμψομαι suggests that the future should be read for ἔρχομαι also. These points need not, of course, indicate a futurist eschatology. I do not believe with Burge (*Anointed*, p. 145) that it is 'certain that the original intention of Jn 14.1-3 pointed to the parousia'. A fair interpretation can be made of the text as it stands without indulging in textual archaeology.

93. Proposed clearly by Westcott (*St John*, II, p. 168), but affirmed with variations by Hoskyns (*The Fourth Gospel*, p. 454); Strachan (*Fourth Gospel*, p. 280); Barrett (*St John*, p. 457); and McCaffrey (*House*, p. 249).

94. Lindars, *John*, p. 471.

95. Bultmann, *John*, p. 602 n. 1.

96. Beasley-Murray (*John*, p. 250) calls this the 'common view' and lists numerous scholars who have endorsed it.

The answer, I believe, lies in the solution of another problem, namely, the relationship of the promised Paraclete to the Son. The problem is highlighted by comparing 14.12-17 with 14.18-24. In the first Jesus says that he is going to the Father and he will ask the Father and he will give the disciples another Paraclete to be with them forever. This is the Spirit of truth who will abide with the disciples and be in them. Then, in the latter verses (vv. 18-24), Jesus says that he himself, together with the Father, will come and dwell with the disciples (v. 23). In reflecting on this Bruce Woll says, 'Jesus becomes his own successor!' He has an extended discussion on this problem, examining at length the proposals of Wellhausen, Windisch and Bornkamm. He concludes, 'We cannot escape Windisch's conclusion: "an organic structure [of the text of Jn 14] is possible only if one identifies the sending of the Spirit with the promised return of Jesus."'[97]

Later Woll says:

> Jesus returns to the disciples in the same way that the Spirit comes to them. He returns as Spirit. The parallelism [between 14.12-17 and 14.18-24] suggests the identification between Jesus and the Spirit, and this identification is supported by the commissioning scene [20.21-22]…where the Spirit is conferred by Jesus' breath! Jesus returns to the disciples in the form of the Spirit.[98]

97. Woll, *Conflict*, p. 80.

98. Woll (*Conflict*, p. 88) suggests the Johannine Jesus speaks in this way because of the concern to establish an authentic succession. Woll envisages a situation in what he calls 'the charismatic Johannine community' where a number of leaders were claiming to be the authentic successors to Jesus with similar direct access to the Father. Indeed Woll postulates that 'it is even possible that they [some disciples in the community] were understood to be claiming to be Jesus himself'. So John writes to answer this urgent question: Who is Jesus' successor? The answer is the One whom Jesus asked the Father to send—the Spirit of Truth, who testifies to Jesus and glorifies him (15.26; 16.8-15) and will teach the disciples and remind them of all that Jesus has said to them (14.26). This is the authentic successor and the disciples are to listen to the Spirit of Truth. But Jesus is the Truth (14.6), so there is an identity between Jesus and the Spirit. Plausible as this appears it is not clear that Woll's 'situation' of a charismatic Johannine community looking for an authoritative successor to Jesus is correct. The concerns of Jn 14-16 are pastoral, not political. There seems to be little sign of a search for authority; rather the search is for Jesus' presence and the life that he brings. The only time John mentions ἐξουσία (apart from 19.10.11) is in relation to becoming 'children of God' (τέκνα θεοῦ, 1.12) and I argue later (see 9.9.2) that ἐξουσία there carries notions of 'privilege' and 'honour' and perhaps even 'glory', but not the political power Woll seems to envisage within the Johannine community.

While I agree that Woll is correct to see the fulfilment of the promise in the presence of Jesus in the Spirit, I do not think one can wholly identify Jesus with the Spirit. The Paraclete/Spirit and Jesus are to be distinguished. Jesus speaks of giving 'another Paraclete', that is, one who is other than himself (14.16). Moreover, this new Paraclete glorifies Jesus, implying that Jesus is separate from the Paraclete. Never in John is there self-glorification—one glorifies another (16.14).

It is better to see the Paraclete as a functional parallel to Jesus. The Paraclete serves as the presence of Jesus while Jesus is away. To have the Spirit is to have Jesus (and the Father) dwelling within (14.23; cf. 1 Jn 4.12-16).[99] There is a closeness between Jesus and the Paraclete. While it is not sufficient to maintain an identity between the two, it is enough to maintain the presence of Jesus in the life of the disciples and so fulfil the promise of 14.3. The return of one is the coming of the other.

The return of Jesus, then, brings the presence that he has promised: πάλιν ἔρχομαι καὶ παραλήμψομαι ὑμᾶς πρὸς ἐμαυτόν, ἵνα ὅπου εἰμὶ ἐγὼ καὶ ὑμεῖς ἦτε. The abundant Temple imagery explored earlier suggests that Jesus' return and dwelling with the disciples should be understood in terms of the Temple.[100]

8.14 *Conclusion*

In the context of a farewell meal, Jesus gathers his own and prepares them for his departure. He washes their feet, not only as a paradigmatic pattern (13.15), but also that they might have a share in him (13.8) and be cleansed (13.10) in preparation for entry into a new Temple. I have suggested that this new Temple is centred in Jesus himself and that entry means participation in the Temple.

This suggestion received confirmation and elaboration when I went on

99. Brown (*John*, II, p. 1141) speaks of the Spirit as 'another Jesus'. 'This binitarianism is only apparent. The unity and distinction of Jesus and the Spirit is paralleled by the same close relationship between Jesus and the Father. There is oneness (10.30; 14.18, 23) and at the same time there is separation (14.28; 16.7)' (Burge, *Anointed*, pp. 144-47).

100. Woll makes a direct connection between 14.23 and the Temple when he remarks, 'As the place where the Father, with the Son, comes to make his μονή, or dwelling place (14.23), *the disciple assumes the role of the Temple.*' Woll, however, sees the Temple role of the disciples not in terms so much of representing the presence of God to the world (20.21), but as having the power to grant or deny access to that presence through the forgiving or retention of sins (20.23).

to consider Jn 14.2-3. I found the abundance of Temple imagery in 14.2-3 pointed to Jesus establishing the new eschatological Temple, where he is 'the Father's house' and his disciples are incorporated into it as members of the new family (1.12). This new house ('house' as a family, cf. 8.35; 20.17) has many dwelling places, indicating, I believe, that there are 'places' for all who believe in Jesus (17.20), including the 'other sheep' of 10.16.[101] The departure of Jesus makes possible the gift of the Spirit (16.7; cf. 7.37-39), who is the continuing presence of Jesus (14.3) accessible to those who have not seen Jesus and yet have come to believe (20.29).

---

101. Coloe ('The Dwelling of God', p. 231) has the attractive suggestion that 'the phrase ἐν τῇ οἰκίᾳ τοῦ πατρός μου μοναὶ πολλάι ἐσιν is best understood, within the context of this Gospel, to mean a series of interpersonal relationships made possible because of the indwelling of the Father, Jesus and the Paraclete with the believer.' While I am drawn to this suggestion I believe more research needs to be done on the semantic field of μένω and its cognate μονή to see if there are any precedents for what Coloe proposes.

Chapter 9

POSSIBLE HIGH PRIESTLY AND TEMPLE ALLUSIONS IN JOHN 17

9.1 Introduction

In this chapter I investigate the prayer of John 17 to see what the possibilities are for high priestly and Temple allusions. The results of this preliminary and fragmentary research are offered here as a basis for further investigation and analysis.

There are echoes of Temple imagery in Jesus' prayer in Jn 17 that have been noted by commentators, but not much has been made of them. For example, in commenting on 17.6 'I have made your name known...', Brown cites:

> the significant...Deuteronomic custom of speaking of the central site of Israel's worship (where the Tabernacle or Temple was) as the place where God has put his name (Deut xii 5,21, etc.). For John, Jesus replaces the Tabernacle and the Temple, and so is now the place where God has put His name.[1]

Walker sees a cluster of 'Temple themes'[2] in John 17: glory (vv. 1, 4, 5, 10, 22, 24), holiness and consecration (vv. 11, 19, 25), the revelation of God's name (noted by Brown above) (vv. 6, 11, 26), divine indwelling (vv. 21-23). He goes on to say:

> There is also an implicit contrast drawn with the Jerusalem Temple in one important respect: whereas that Temple had excluded Gentiles, now Jesus prays that all those who believe will be 'one even as we are one' (vv. 20-23). Moreover, in contrast to the popular Jewish expectation that there would be an ingathering of exiles to Jerusalem, Jesus asks that his followers might be gathered to him to be 'with me where I am, to see my glory' (v. 24).[3]

---

1. Brown, *John*, II, p. 754.
2. Walker, *Jesus and the Holy City*, p. 173.
3. Cf. my discussion (see 8.3 n. 6) of Walker's suggestion for resolving the aporia

My purpose then in this chapter is to explore some of John 17 in order to tease out a few of the Temple themes that are hinted at in the prayer.

9.2 *Jesus as High Priest*

9.2.1 *Preliminary Matters*
In my introductory chapter I discovered that there is a reasonable possibility that the author of John had high priestly connections (see 1.3.2). Therefore it would not be unlikely that the author would have a special interest in the Temple, and especially the possibility that Jesus is the new Temple and the new high priest. I believe this could be true of John 17.

Older commentators have seen the Jesus of John 17 as high priest. There is explicit mention of it in Cyril of Alexandria[4] and the term, 'High-Priestly Prayer' (*Precatio Summi Sacerdotis*) to describe John 17 seems to go back to D. Chytraeus (1531–1600). Schnackenburg has a list of twentieth-century scholars who have taken up this question, some of whom endorse Jesus as high priest and others who do not.[5]

Scholars have remarked on the paucity of evidence of the high priestly character of Jesus in John as a whole.[6] Certainly there is no explicit reference to Jesus being high priest, but there may possibly be some oblique allusion to it.

9.2.2 *Jesus' Encounter with the High Priesthood*
In 18.13-24 Jesus is brought before the high priesthood.[7] First he is brought before Annas, who is described as 'the father-in-law of Caiaphas,

---

of 14.31. He proposes that the disciples do leave the place of the footwashing and are on the move during the teaching of Jn 15-16 and at the Temple for the prayer of Jn 17 (Walker, *Jesus and the Holy City*, p. 173 n. 45). This may have relevance for Temple themes in Jn 17. Just as Westcott wondered whether the imagery of the vine was inspired by reflection on the vine over the Temple doorways, so Walker wonders if the predominance of Temple themes in Jn 17 was in some way influenced by increasing proximity to the area of the Temple.

4. 'Since he is the High Priest of our souls…he most fittingly makes prayer on our behalf… Then also, since he is a High Priest, insomuch as he is man, and, at the same time, brought himself a blameless sacrifice to God the Father…he moulds the prayer for blessing towards us, as mediator and high priest' (Hoskyns, *The Fourth Gospel*, p. 494).

5. Schnackenburg, *St John*, III, p. 433 n. 2.

6. E.g. Carson (*John*, p. 614) comments that 'unlike the Epistle to the Hebrews, the Fourth Gospel does not dwell on Jesus' high priestly ministry'.

7. There are eight references to the high priest in Jn 18.13-27 (vv. 13, 15 [2x], 16, 19, 22, 24, 25).

the high priest that year'. By way of editorial comment John reminds us that it was Caiaphas who advised the Jews that it was better to have one person die for the people (11.51).

What follows in vv. 15-18 seems to be an intervention. It is the first part of Peter's denial, but the thread of continuity is the theme of the high priesthood. Peter gains access to the courtyard through the 'other disciple who was known [γνωστός] to the high priest'. This disciple is characterized twice in this way within the space of two verses.

Why this emphasis? Is it only as Bultmann says: 'But does he [the other disciple known to the high priest] owe his existence solely to the necessity of providing a reason for Peter's being able to enter the αὐλή of the High Priest?'[8] Or is it possible that there is some ambiguity in the reference to the 'high priest'—that this disciple is known not only to the Jewish high priest, but also to Jesus the high priest? If this 'other disciple' can be identified as the 'Beloved Disciple',[9] then it would certainly be the case that he was γνωστός to Jesus, indeed he was loved by him!

Jn 18.15-18 contains echoes with John 13. There the denial is foretold (13.36-38). But also there Peter and the Beloved Disciple are together (13.23-25) at the table with Jesus. Given the recollection of this scene in John 18, it is possible they are together once more—only this time in the αὐλή of the Jewish high priest. Peter denies his discipleship (18.17); the other, Beloved Disciple presumably remains faithful.[10] So one followed (18.15a) faithfully; the other did not.

I have suggested above that there is some ambiguity over the high priest. Caiaphas is introduced as 'the high priest that year' (18.13). Annas is said to be the 'the father-in-law of Caiaphas' (v. 13). Jesus is first taken to Annas. Then in v. 19 we read 'the high priest questioned Jesus about his disciples'. The reader would be entitled to assume that in the interim Caiaphas, the high priest, has come on the scene and is interrogating Jesus.

8.   Bultmann, *John*, p. 645.

9.   Carson (*John*, p. 582), drawing on the work of Frans Neirynck (*Evangelica: Gospel Studies—Etudes d'Evangile. Collected Essays* [ed. F. van Segbroeck; Leuven: Leuven University Press, 1982], pp. 335-364), 'concludes, rather tentatively, that the "other disciple" is the Beloved Disciple'. For a contrary opinion see Bultmann (*John*, p. 645 n. 4). But see my discussion where I conclude the 'other disciple' is the Beloved Disciple (see 1.3.1.3).

10.   Commentators (e.g. Lindars, *John*, p. 34, but see 1.3.1.2 and n. 44) have often maintained that the Beloved Disciple is the model disciple. If it is accepted that the Beloved Disciple did not deny his discipleship in a place of dark hostility, then that would be an encouragement to other disciples.

But this is not the case. Verse 24 reveals that Annas has been conducting this interrogation all along. 'Then Annas sent him bound to Caiaphas the high priest.' Who, then, is the high priest? Caiaphas is introduced as the high priest, but Annas is also called the high priest (v. 19).

Various attempts have been made to solve this puzzle. One has been to change the order of the verses. In syr[s] v. 24 is placed after v. 13 so as to make the examination of vv. 19-23 take place before Caiaphas. But if this is the original order, then what is the purpose and content of the appearance before Annas?

I suggest that rather than tinkering with the text by transposing verses and excising uncongenial passages,[11] it is better to leave the text intact and accept that there is indeed ambiguity with reference to the high priest. Even a casual reader could detect this. Certainly it would be obvious to the author(s). Why not accept it as deliberate?

But if it is accepted as deliberate, what would be the point of it? I suggest that it would raise the question in the minds of readers, Who is the *real* high priest?[12] At the very least such a question indicates that the Jewish high priesthood is in disarray. It is not clear who their high priest is. But could it also be just possible that in casting about for an answer Jesus too becomes a candidate for high priesthood?

There is something similar in Jn 19.9-11 where Jesus is interrogated for the second time by Pilate. Jesus' answer to Pilate in v. 11—Οὐκ εἶχες ἐξουσίαν κατ' ἐμοῦ οὐδεμίαν εἰ μὴ ἦν δεδομένον σοι ἄνωθεν. διὰ τοῦτο ὁ παραδούς μέ σοι μείζονα ἁμαρτίαν ἔχει—raises the question, Who is the *real* judge? It seems that Jesus is the real judge. He is pointing to the limitation of Pilate's power and pronounces judgment on those who sit in judgment on him.[13] So in this encounter also questions are raised as

11. Bultmann (*John*, p. 644 nn. 1, 2, 3) has a concise summary of the ways various scholars have proposed to solve the ambiguity.

12. Lindars (*John*, p. 550) uses the term '*real* High Priest' with reference to Annas in an attempt to resolve the ambiguity. However, I think it better to retain the ambiguity as deliberate. Coloe ('The Dwelling of God', p. 286) also reads the text (18.12-24) as I have suggested: 'The confusion about the identity of the high priest raises the question—who is the real High Priest?'

13. This is also Schnackenburg's finding: 'With these words [of v. 11], Pilate, who subjects Jesus to his supposed power, becomes the one subjected, and Jesus, the seemingly powerless one, shows himself to be the one who is free and possesses power. With the freedom of the one who holds firm to God alone, and judges everything as God does, Jesus immediately pronounces his judgement also, concerning those who sit in judgement on him' (*St John*, III, p. 261).

to who is who. Here it is the question, Who is the *real* judge? I suggest in the encounter with the Jewish high priest it is: who is the *real* high priest?

Finally, in my discussion of 18.12-24 it is worth examining the exchange between Jesus and the high priest in vv. 19-21: 'Then the high priest questioned Jesus περὶ τῶν μαθατῶν αὐτοῦ καὶ περὶ τῆς διδαχῆς αὐτοῦ.' Jesus' answer does not make a distinction between his disciples and his teaching. His disciples are included in what he has to say about his teaching. He says, Ἐγὼ παρρησίᾳ λελάληκα τῷ κόσμῳ, ἐγὼ πάντοτε ἐδίδαξα ἐν συναγωγῇ καὶ ἐν τῷ ἱερῷ, ὅπου πάντες οἱ Ἰουδαῖοι συνέρχονται, καὶ ἐν κρυπτῷ ἐλάλησα οὐδέν. τί με ἐρωτᾷς; ἐρώτησον τοὺς ἀκηκοότας τί ἐλάλησα αὐτοῖς ἴδε οὗτοι οἴδασιν ἃ εἶπον ἐγώ.

The emphasis on ἐν παρρησίᾳ in v. 20 recalls 7.4 and 10.24. Jesus has had a public ministry and it concluded with his words at the end of 12.36a: 'After Jesus had said this, he departed and hid [ἐκρύβη] from them' (12.36b). This was a ministry to the world (τῷ κόσμῳ) that included the Jews (οἱ Ἰουδαῖοι). The world is characterized by unbelief. Bultmann[14] capitalizes on this in his comment:

> any desire that Jesus should make his claim credible by demonstrative publicity or unambiguous plain speech, so that the hearer is relieved of the necessity of decision, rests on unbelief. He has spoken publicly and openly, and it is only for unbelief that his word has been spoken ἐν κυπτῷ. In the present situation the statement of Jesus no longer signifies an indirect appeal for decision or for faith; rather it affirms, 'You have already decided!' It is too late for discussion; the confrontation with Judaism is at an end. Insofar as Judaism represents the 'world'—and that this is the case is shown by the λελάληκα τῷ κόσμῳ (rather than ὑμῖν or the like)—it says: In the moment when the world imagines that it can drag Jesus before its forum and make him answerable to it, then the verdict 'Too late' must be pronounced. In this way Jesus refuses to give an account of himself to it.

Jesus in effect says, 'My time for testimony is over. Ask those who heard what I said.'[15] The door seems to have been closed on Judaism. He has testified within the institutions of Judaism where Jews gathered—the synagogues and the Temple—but now that era is over.

It is striking that Jesus speaks the way he does. He himself is a Jew and he is speaking to leaders of the Jews, and yet he puts himself at some distance from the Jews when he says of the synagogues and the Temple

---

14. Bultmann, *John*, pp. 646-67.

15. If this is a formal trial, then Jesus could well be insisting on the right for witnesses to be produced to support the charges rather than be judged on self-testimony.

that these are the places where the Jews come together. Why does he distance himself from the Temple and the synagogues? I believe it is because he sees them as having fulfilled their purpose. He has come and become the new Temple (2.19), and soon he will gather into one all the dispersed children of God (τὰ τέκνα τοῦ Θεοῦ τὰ διεσκορπισμένα συναγάγη εἰς ἕν, 11.52) and become the new synagogue. So the Jews may continue to gather at the synagogues and the Temple, but that is not where the children of God gather—they gather in Jesus.

If Jesus speaks of Judaism in this way, what can we say of the high priesthood? It too must be finished. Some hint of this is contained in the irony of v. 24: 'Then Annas sent him [Jesus] bound [δεδεμένον] to Caiaphas the high priest.' But who is bound? Those who reject the word of Jesus, which includes Annas and Caiaphas, because, as Bultmann suggests, they have already decided (cf. 19.7) that Jesus is a liar. The way to freedom (being unbound) is not to dismiss Jesus as a liar but to receive his word as truth. As Jesus has said in his public ministry, 'If you continue in my word, you are truly my disciples; and you will know the truth, and the truth will make you free' (8.31-32). So if Caiaphas and Annas are paralysed by unbelief, who then is the high priest? Our answer is that Jesus is high priest.

9.2.3 *The Tunic at the Cross*
The tunic for which the soldiers cast lots in Jn 19.23 has often been taken as a sign of Jesus' high priestliness. The fact that it is described as ὁ χιτὼν ἄραφος, ἐκ τῶν ἄνωθεν ὑφαντὸς δι' ὅλου, has encouraged some commentators to see a parallel with the tunic worn by the priest on the Day of Atonement. This, along with other holy vestments, is described in Lev. 16.4. However, the only link between Jn 19.23 and Lev. 16.4 is the one word χιτὼν. This is a very slender connection.

It may be more promising not to identify the robe so closely with the white linen tunic worn by the high priest on the Day of Atonement. Could the seamless tunic of Jesus be evocative of the ephod of the high priest?[16] In this case the relevant text would seem to be Exod. 28.32 (cf. Exod. 39.23).[17] But here the emphasis is not on the seamlessness of the ephod, but the strengthening of the edge of the neck so that it may not be torn.

---

16. I. de la Potterie, 'La tunique sans couture, symbole du Christ grand prêtre?', *Bib* 60 (1979), pp. 255-69 (260).

17. Coloe ('The Dwelling of God', p. 287) states that the ephod of Exod. 28.32 is seamlessly woven but offers no evidence.

The only idea (not the words) Exod. 28.32 has in common with Jn 19.23 is that the garment be not torn.

However, a quotation from Josephus has offered further encouragement. In *Ant.* 3.161 he describes a priestly garment (not the ephod that Josephus describes in 3.162) in these words: ἔστι δ᾽ ὁ χιτὼν οὗτος οὐκ ἐκ δυοῖν περιτμημάτων, ὥστε ῥαπτὸς ἐπὶ τῶν ὠμῶν εἶναι καὶ τῶν παρὰ πλευράν, φάρσος δ᾽ ἓν ἐπίμηκες ὑφασμένον (Now this tunic was not composed of two pieces nor was it sewed together upon the shoulders and the sides, but it was one long garment so woven as to have an aperture for the neck).

The links here are slightly more promising. This time the χιτὼν is described as not ῥαπτὸς (not sewn), which may indicate that it is ἄραφος (seamless). Josephus is describing a priestly garment, but it is not the garment described in Lev. 16.4. Josephus's tunic is blue (or violet), embroidered with flowers and a mixture of gold interwoven, with fringes hanging from the bottom with golden bells and pomegranates (cf. *Ant.* 3.159-60). This is a far cry from the simple white linen tunic used by the high priest on the Day of Atonement.[18]

Where does that leave us? Jn 19.23 speaks of Jesus wearing a seamless garment described as ὁ χιτὼν. Josephus writes of ὁ χιτὼν, a high priestly garment, not sewn. This is not the garment mentioned in Lev. 16.4 and is not the ephod. Josephus therefore provides us with no bridging link between any text in the Old Testament and Jn 19.23. Contrary to the opinions of some commentators,[19] I find no evidence of an allusion to Jesus' high priestly character in Jn 19.23 beyond Josephus, *Ant.* 3.161, which I believe is too fragile a base on which to reach any conclusion.[20]

This brings to an end the survey of evidence for a high priestly character of Jesus outside of John 17.[21] I have noted that Jesus' encounter with the

18. Cf. C.T.R. Hayward (*The Jewish Temple*, p. 50), who, besides Lev. 16.4, gives rabbinic references: *m. Yom.* 3.6; *Lev. R.* 16.3; *PJ* of Lev. 16.4.

19. Notably, Brown (*John*, II, p. 921), who remarks that 'the priestly symbolism of the tunic is plausible'. Cf. also J.P. Heil, 'Jesus as the Unique High Priest in the Gospel of John', *CBQ* 57 (1995), pp. 729-45.

20. If the seamless coat did indeed point to Jesus' high priestly character, then it is difficult to see what the disposal of the coat by lot might mean. Bultmann (*John*, p. 671 n. 2) comments, 'The disposal by lot could of course symbolise in a derisive manner the finish of the Jewish high priesthood; but this cannot be represented as the χιτὼν of Jesus!'

21. Philo makes a connection between the Logos (Jn 1.1) and the high priest in *Somn.* 1.215: δύο γάρ...ἱερὰ θεοῦ, ἓν μὲν ὅδε ὁ κόσμος, ἐν ᾧ καὶ ἀρχιερεὺς ὁ

Jewish high priesthood in Jn 18.12-24 offers some hope of high priestly allusion, especially when tied in with Jesus being the fulfilment of the Temple and the synagogue.[22]

I now turn to the prayer itself to see if there are any pointers there to Jesus as high priest.

9.3 *A Prayer for the People of God*

While it is true that Jesus prays for himself in Jn 17.1-8, he does so only to pray for those whom the Father has given to him. The focus is prayer for his immediate disciples rather than the world: ἐγὼ περὶ αὐτῶν ἐρωτῶ, οὐ περὶ τοῦ κόσμου ἐρωτῶ ἀλλὰ περὶ ὧν δέδωκάς μοι, ὅτι σοί εἰσιν (v. 9). And then the prayer is extended to all those who will become disciples through the word of the original disciples: Οὐ περὶ τούτων δὲ ἐρωτῶ μόνον, ἀλλὰ καὶ περὶ τῶν πιστευόντων διὰ τοῦ λόγου αὐτῶν εἰς ἐμέ (v. 20). Jesus' prayer is a prayer offered on behalf of those who belong to the Father and to him (vv. 9-10). These are the children of God (1.12; 11.52; 20.17), the people of God.

This is intercession, but is it priestly intercession? What is the function of the priest/high priest in intercession for the people of God within the Temple? Sanders has some discussion of this question and remarks that in the context of the Temple and the offering of sacrifices (especially those offered on the Day of Atonement) 'the priests blessed the people and asked God for forgiveness'.[23] Philo comments on the universality of Jewish high priestly prayer in the Temple:

> Among the other nations the priests are accustomed to offer prayers and sacrifices for their kinsmen and friends and fellow-countrymen only, but the high priest of the Jews makes prayers and gives thanks not only on behalf

πρωτόγονος αὐτοῦ θεῖος λόγος…(For there are…two temples of God: one of them this universe, in which there is also as High Priest, his first-born, the divine Word…). See also *Somn.* 2.183.

22. Can Jesus be both Temple and high priest? I see no difficulty in this. John clearly views Jesus as the Passover Lamb and in 2.21 he says Jesus is the Temple. The point of this study is to demonstrate how the Johannine Jesus fulfils the complex of Temple life—festivals, high priesthood and sacrificial service, place of encounter with God, place of revelation of God, the locus of the glory of God, etc. Within this perspective Jesus can be high priest, sacrificial lamb, the bread of life, light of the world, the water of life, etc.

23. E.P. Sanders, *Judaism: Practice and Belief 63 BCE–66 CE* (London: SCM Press, 1992), p. 203.

of the whole human race but also for the parts of nature, earth, water, air, fire. For he holds the world to be, as in very truth it is, his country, and in its behalf he is wont to propitiate the Ruler with supplication and intercession, beseeching Him to make His creature a partaker of His own kindly and merciful nature (*Spec. Leg.* 1.97; cf. 1.168).

Ben Sira (c. 200 BCE) certainly associated the sacrifices offered by Simon the high priest in the Temple service with prayer and blessing (Sir. 50.11-26; cf. Jdt. 9.1):

> And the people besought [ἐδεήθη] the LORD, the most High, by prayer before him that is merciful, till the solemnity of the LORD [κόσμος Κυρίου] was ended, and they had finished his service (50.19).

Then Simon, the high priest came down and blessed the people.

Philo makes the point that sacrifices themselves constitute thanksgiving ans prayer. In *Spec. Leg.* 1.169 he mentions the daily sacrifice of two lambs: 'One at the dawn of the day, and the other in the evening; each one of them being a sacrifice of thanksgiving...' He also suggests that the sacrifice he calls θυσίας σωτηρίου (after the LXX Lev. 7.1; cf. MT 7.11, זבח השלמים), the 'welfare' or 'preservation' sacrifice, constitutes a petition for 'the safe preserving and bettering of human affairs' (ἐπὶ σωτηρίᾳ καὶ βελτιώσει τῶν ἀνθρωπίνων πραγμάτων) (*Spec. Leg.* 1.197).

Josephus also wrote that at the sacrifices prayers were offered for the welfare (σωτηρίᾳ) of the community (*Apion* 2.196) and that at the festivals people prayed 'for future mercies' (*Ant.* 4.203).

Ben Sira, Philo and Josephus all testify that prayer was associated with the Temple and intimately connected with the sacrifices offered by the priests and, in particular, by the high priest. Priestly prayer was made on behalf of the people and priestly blessing was placed on the people. John 17 is a prayer prayed by Jesus on the eve of his sacrificial death. The focus of his prayer, as with the high priest in the Temple, is not for himself, but for his people, his disciples. Jesus' prayer in John 17, then, displays some consistency with the high priestly prayers of the past in Israel.

9.4 *Outline of Remainder of the Chapter*

Given that there is some evidence of a high priestly and Temple motif elsewhere in John, I turn now to John 17 itself, remembering that it is indeed a prayer for Jesus' disciples.

I will limit my consideration to two retrospects and three petitions, namely:

(a) The retrospect:[24] 'I have made your *name* known...' (vv. 6, 26).
(b) The petition for preservation in the *name* the Father has given Jesus (vv. 11, 13).
(c) The petition for unity (vv. 21-23).
(d) The retrospect: 'The glory which you have given to me I have given them' (v. 22).
(e) The petition for sanctification (vv. 17, 19).

In (a) and (b) the word 'name' is used and I have emphasised it. Before I embark on an exegesis of the retrospects and petitions I will endeavour to demonstrate that the name the Father has given to Jesus, and which Jesus has made known to his disciples, is ἐγὼ εἰμι, which, I believe, is equivalent to Yʜwʜ.

9.5 *God's Name is Given to Jesus*

9.5.1 *Text and Meaning*
G. Franklin Shirbroun has made an in-depth study of the giving of the name of God to Jesus in Jn 17.11-12. One of his first tasks was to establish the text of Jn 17.11-12. He has devoted a rigorous analysis of the merits of the various readings for vv. 11-12 found in the Greek manuscripts, and his conclusion is that the most likely reading of the text is, Πάτερ ἅγιε, τήρησον αὐτοὺς ἐν τῷ ὀνόματί σου ᾧ[25] δέδωκάς μοι, ἵνα ὦσιν ἕν καθὼς ἡμεῖς. ὅτε ἤμην μετ᾽ αὐτῶν ἐγὼ ἐτήρουν αὐτοὺς ἐν τῷ ὀνόματί σου ᾧ δέδωκάς μοι...

Given the text then, the question I wish to pursue is, What is the name

---

24. This term arises in Appold's structural proposal for the prayer in Jn 17 as six alternations between petition and retrospect. The retrospect is a rehearsal of what God has done. Retrospects are especially frequent in the psalms. For example, in Ps. 80.8-11 there is a retrospect in which the psalmist reflects on the exodus of Israel under the image of the vine (M. Appold, *The Oneness Motif in the Fourth Gospel: Motif Analysis and Exegetical Probe into the Theology of John* [WUNT, 2.1; Tübingen: J.C.B. Mohr (Paul Siebeck), 1976], p. 204).

25. ᾧ: this is a dative pronoun so formed because it is attracted to the case of the antecedent. This is the crux of the textual problems. Some scribes have thought the referent of the relative pronoun to be not the name (ὀνόμα), but the disciples (αὐτοῖ) and so the variants, namely, the acc. ὅ (D* X 2148 it[d]) or the plural acc. οὕς (D[b] 892[vid] 1009 it[aur,f,q] vg goth eth geo[2] cop[sa mss] Diatessaron[1] Ath[ed.2] etc.) have arisen. The latter correction could have been prompted by 17.6 or 18.9. G. Franklin Shirbroun ('The Giving of the Name of God to Jesus in John 17:11,12' [PhD dissertation, Princeton Theological Seminary, 1985]) has an extensive and thorough discussion of this textual problem (pp. 9-49) and it would be superfluous to rehearse it here.

given to Jesus? Commentators are divided.[26] Shirbroun comes to no conclusion but he evidently favours ἐγώ εἰμι. In questions for further research he says:

> It is possible that 'I AM' is the name of God given to Jesus. There is evidence that 'I AM' was understood as a divine name in Deutero-Isaiah (sometimes in contexts which are heavily laden with instances of the *shem/onoma* of God) and in pre-Christian Judaism. As a name for Jesus, 'I AM' is nonrestrictive and therefore may be used to comprehend the meaning of the *onoma* of God [as it occurs in Jn 17.11, 12].[27]

He also quotes Wayne Meeks with approval:

> 'It can scarcely be doubted that this reference to a special revelation of God's name [Jn 17.6, 26] is derived from the tradition of the revelation of the ineffable name YHWH to Moses described in Exod. 3.13-14 and 6.2-3, and vastly elaborated in post-biblical tradition'.[28]

Subsequent to Shirbroun's research David Ball has carried out detailed investigations into the use of ἐγώ εἰμι in John's Gospel.[29] He identified predicated 'I am' sayings (6.35; 8.12; 10.9; 10.11; 11.25; 15.1; 14.6) and unpredicated 'I am' sayings (4.26; 6.20; 8.18; 8.24; 8.28; 8.58; 13.19; 9.9; 18.5-7). The latter, he says, concern Jesus' identity; the former concern his identity as it is worked out in his role among humanity.[30] I will focus on two (8.58; 18.5-7) of those unpredicated 'I am' sayings concerned with the identity of Jesus to provide some appreciation of the way in which this expression functions in the Gospel of John.

---

26. Zerwick and Grosvenor (*Grammatical Analysis*, p. 336) suggest it denotes 'the whole revelation of God in Christ'; Brown thinks of ἐγώ εἰμι (*John*, II, pp. 755-56); Bultmann (*John*, p. 380) posits the disclosure of God; Lindars (*John*, p. 521) speaks of 'the character of the Father'; Barrett (*St John*, p. 505) appeals to Exod. 3.15 and especially Isa. 52.6, 'My people shall know my name,' but concludes, 'We are not to think of the revelation of a particular name.... The language is both biblical and gnostic.' Dodd (*Interpretation*, p. 417) suggests אני הוא or אני והוא. Schnackenburg (*St John*, III, p. 175 and n. 24) is sceptical about finding a particular name. He says, 'The combination of words in vv. 11,12 and 26, however, call for an interpretation that goes further than this [i.e. 'simply pointing to the name of the Father']. The name stands for God's being and nature, his holiness, "justice" and love, which are certainly expressed in the address to the Father and the attributes connected with the name.'

27. Shirbroun, 'Name of God', p. 291.

28. Shirbroun, 'Name of God', p. 232; Meeks, *The Prophet-King*, pp. 290-91.

29. Ball, *'I Am'*.

30. Ball, *'I Am'*, p. 258.

9.5.2 'Very truly, I tell you, before Abraham was, I am' (John 8.58)
An 'I am' inclusio defines the pericope (8.12-59). Verse 12 is a predicated
'I am' saying where Jesus says he is the light of the world; v. 58 is an
unpredicated 'I am' saying. We are partly prepared for the powerful and
provocative statement of 8.58 by the unpredicated 'I am' sayings in 8.24,
28 which raise questions in the reader's mind.

(a) 8.24: ἐὰν γὰρ μὴ πιστεύσητε ὅτι ἐγώ εἰμι, ἀποθανεῖσθε ἐν ταῖς
ἁμαρτίαις ὑμῶν. What can this mean? It is obviously very important, because believing that Jesus is ἐγώ εἰμι is the way to avoid
dying in one's sins. There is no explanation, but the reader of John,
puzzled though he or she is, must see that whatever ἐγώ εἰμι means
it is crucial. Believing or not believing is a matter of life or death.

(b) 8.28: ῞Οταν ὑψώσητε τὸν υἱὸν τοῦ ἀνθρώπου, τότε γνώσεσθε
ὅτι ἐγώ εἰμι... Again this is perplexing. It is evidently referring to
the crucifixion, where the Jews are instrumental in lifting Jesus up.
Bultmann thinks[31] that when Jesus is lifted up, then they will realize
that he is the Son of Man, but this is not clear from the text. If such
had been intended why did Jesus not say, 'When you have lifted me
up, then you will know that I am the Son of Man'? So this ἐγώ εἰμι
is something that should be believed and will be known by the Jews
when the Son of Man is lifted up.

(c) 8.58: πρὶν Ἀβραὰμ γενέσθαι ἐγώ εἰμι. David Ball[32] draws attention
to the startlingly vivid contrast between the two Greek verbs. γενέσθαι
is the aorist infinitive of γίνομαι, which expresses the coming into
existence of Abraham, maybe even his birth.[33] The aorist expresses
an event usually in the past—a point on the time scale.[34] ἐγώ εἰμι is
in stark contrast. There is a tense change to the present. The construction of Jesus' statement itself shows that his claim is not simply to
pre-existence; for that Jesus could have claimed that he was (ἤμην,
imperfect of εἰμι, cf. 1.1), or even came into existence (ἐγενόμην)
before Abraham. But he does not do that—he says πρὶν Ἀβραὰμ
γενέσθαι ἐγώ εἰμι. So they picked up stones to throw at him! That
is, they judged that he had committed the capital crime of blasphemy.

---

31. Bultmann (*John*, p. 349). Bultmann's point that the statement does not arouse
anger (as expected, cf. 8.58) but more questions, is valid. However the ἐγώ εἰμι may
not have been sufficiently clear to the Jews. It is not clear to modern exegetes!

32. Ball, '*I Am*', p. 92.

33. Barrett, *St John*, p. 352; Morris, *John*, p. 473.

34. See Blass and Debrunner, *Greek Grammar*, §318 (1).

The ἐγώ εἰμι seems to have constituted a claim to be one with YHWH (cf. Jn 10.30-31). Subsequent discussion of a possible background for ἐγώ εἰμι will strengthen the suggestion that it is equivalent to YHWH. But before I come to that I want to discuss one further use of ἐγώ εἰμι in John.

9.5.3 *John 18.4-8a*

> Then Jesus, knowing all that was to happen to him, came forward and asked them, 'Whom are you looking for?' They answered, 'Jesus of Nazareth'. Jesus replied, 'I am'. Judas who betrayed him, was standing with them. When Jesus said to them, 'I am', they stepped back and fell to the ground. Again he asked them, 'Whom are you looking for?' And they said, 'Jesus of Nazareth'. Jesus answered, 'I told you that I am'.

Without going into the structure of the Passion Story as a whole it is enough to note that 18.1-14 is concerned with the arrest of Jesus and can be considered as a unit. The structure of the earlier part of this unit is as follows:

v. 1   Jesus leads the disciples to the garden.
vv. 2-3   Judas leads the soldiers to the garden.
vv. 4-5a   Jesus confronts his captors and identifies himself: ἐγώ εἰμι.
v. 5b   Judas is in their midst.
v. 6   The reaction to Jesus' self identification: ἐγώ εἰμι.
vv. 7-8   Jesus again confronts his captors and identifies himself: ἐγώ εἰμι.
v. 9   Jesus' word is fulfilled.

This structural analysis emphasizes how Jesus' arrest is dominated by his confrontation with Judas and the authorities. Judas takes the lead in bringing the authorities to arrest Jesus. Judas knows where Jesus is, and the little phrase 'Judas is in their midst' (v. 5b) is deliberate, heightening the confrontation between Jesus, who is the light of the world, and Judas, who is a devil (6.70). Judas comes with a show of power and light, but the lanterns and torches bespeak an inner darkness in Judas' heart (13.30), and he and his company are powerless before this sovereign Jesus of Nazareth. They fall to the ground at the pronouncement of ἐγώ εἰμι. Jesus is supremely sovereign.

The use of the words 'I am' in Jn 18.5-6 and 8 clearly show that, while ἐγώ εἰμι is used as a simple identification formula,[35] the two words may

---

35. Bultmann in an extended footnote (*John*, p. 225 n. 30), attempted to define the 'I am' sayings in John according to their function in the text rather than their form: (a) *Presentation formula* answering the question, 'Who are you?' Cf. Gen. 17.1, 'The

simultaneously have a deeper meaning. The reason that the soldiers fall down when Jesus utters the words ἐγώ εἰμι is not stated. It is assumed that the reader will know. While accepting the fact that Jesus identifies himself to the soldiers with these words, the reader must look for something that would explain their strange reaction. Bultmann posits a miracle to account for the reaction[36] and there may be some truth in that, but more needs to be said. I believe Ball is right to see the words here acting as a trigger to point to the other occurrences of the term in the Gospel to explain Jesus' words.[37] The threefold repetition of ἐγώ εἰμι in 18.5, 6, 8 emphasizes the importance of the expression. That this saying occurs at the moment of betrayal particularly points back to 13.19, where the fulfilment of Scripture and Jesus' own words were linked to the betrayal in order that the disciples might believe 'that I am'. Thus a simple recognition formula in which Jesus states that he is the person whom the soldiers

---

LORD appeared to Abraham and said to him, "I am El Shaddai. . ."' (b) *Qualificatory formula* answering, 'What are you?' Cf. Isa. 44.6, 'I am the first and the last, and apart from me there is no God' or 44.24, 'I am the LORD, who made all things.' (c) *Identification formula* in which the speaker identifies himself with another person or object. (d) The *recognition formula* where ἐγώ is predicate. Surprisingly, Bultmann assigns the predicated 'I am' sayings: 6.35, 41, 48, 51; 8.12; 10.7, 9, 11, 14; 15.1, 5 to the *recognition formula* category. His reason for this is that 'in the context of the Gospel the ἐγώ is strongly stressed and always contrasted with false or pretended revelation (cf. 6.49-51; 10.10, 11-13; cf. also 5.43). On the other hand 11.25, and perhaps 14.6, are probably *identification formulae*.' Such comments highlight how fluid Bultmann's categories are and raise questions about their usefulness. Brown (*John*, I, p. 534) provides a more balanced and useful perspective when he says, 'The stress in all these "I am" statements is not exclusively on the "I", for Jesus wishes to give emphasis to the predicate which tells something of his role. The predicate is not an essential definition or description of Jesus in himself; it is more a description of what he is in relation to man.' J. Ashton, (*Understanding the Fourth Gospel* [Oxford: Clarendon Press], p. 184 n. 50) remarks, 'By classing most of the "I am" sayings as "recognition formulae"…he [Bultmann] empties them of any real content.' Jn 8.58 poses a problem for Bultmann (*John*, p. 327, nn. 4 and 5). He seems to imply that it is an *identification formula*, identifying Jesus with God (p. 327), but he appears to reject this (p. 327 n. 5), so he is left with a saying that does not fit his categories of function. Jn 18.5-6, 8 are dismissed because they are profane uses of the term. But if that is so, how does Bultmann account for the astonishing reaction of Judas and the authorities? How can a profane utterance provoke such a response? 'It is a miracle,' says Bultmann (*John*, p. 639).

36. Bultmann, *John*, p. 639.
37. Ball, *'I Am'*, pp. 144, 145.

seek is given a double meaning by the reaction of those same soldiers to his words as well as by the previous use of ἐγώ εἰμι in the Gospel. Although it is correct to talk of Jesus' identity in terms of Jesus of Nazareth on one level, on another there is something that cannot be explained without probing the possible background and powerful impact of the words ἐγώ εἰμι. John can take simple words and, by the way they are formulated (8.24, 28; 13.19) as well as by the reactions to them (8.58; 18.5, 6, 8), indicate that something profound is signified in relation to Jesus' identity. It is to the significance of ἐγώ εἰμι in the LXX (especially of Deutero-Isaiah) that I turn now, and, having looked at the significance of the expression, I will then assess Deutero-Isaiah as a possible background for the unpredicated 'I am' sayings in John. The goal of this investigation is to endeavour to demonstrate that the name the Father has given to Jesus is the holy name of YHWH, the name borne on the turban of the high priest and the name in which Jesus 'keeps' his disciples.

9.5.4 *The Significance of* ἐγώ εἰμι *in the LXX*

Here I wish to focus on two texts in the Old Testament where ἐγώ εἰμι seems to be linked closely to the name YHWH. I will look at Exod. 3.14 briefly and Isa. 40–55 at greater length.

In the Exod. 3 theophany on Mt Sinai, Moses asks God for his name (3.13), and God replies by saying, אהיה אשר אהיה, which is rendered in the LXX as ἐγώ εἰμι ὁ ὤν. Various translations of this name can be offered,[38] but what is probable is that in some way the phrase אהיה אשר אהיה constitutes the name of God. However, the LXX makes it difficult to make a firm link between the name of God and ἐγώ εἰμι because ὁ ὤν is formally just as valid a candidate.[39]

So now I turn to Deutero-Isaiah. In particular the MT of Isa. 45.18c and the LXX version provide a remarkably clear link between the name of God—יהוה—and ἐγώ εἰμι:

MT אני יהוה ואין עוד   LXX ἐγώ εἰμι, καὶ οὐκ ἔστιν ἔτι

The LXX translators evidently understood that the Hebrew אני יהוה could be translated as ἐγώ εἰμι. ἐγώ εἰμι, therefore, is here considered to

---

38. For example the NRSV suggests in the text 'I AM WHO I AM' and in the footnotes 'I AM WHAT I AM' and 'I WILL BE WHAT I WILL BE'. Presumably 'I WILL BE WHO I WILL BE' and 'I WILL BE THAT I WILL BE' would also be acceptable.

39. Ball agrees: 'In light of the fact that LXX translates the Hebrew as ἐγώ εἰμι ὁ ὤν and not as ἐγώ εἰμι ἐγώ εἰμι (Exod. 3.14), it must be questioned how closely the phrase ἐγώ εἰμι should be connected with the name of God in Exodus' (*'I Am'*, p. 42).

be virtually equivalent to the convenant name of God—יהוה.[40] But ἐγώ
εἰμι also translates אני הוא (Isa. 43.10, 13, 25; 52.6)[41] and it seems that
from the parallelism between 43.10b and 11a, that אני הוא corresponds to
אני יהוה.[42]

Harner makes a further point about אני הוא:

> Second Isaiah is always attributed to Yahweh. It is a solemn statement or
> assertion that only he can properly make. If anyone else spoke these words,
> it would be a sign of presumptuous pride, an attempt to claim equality with
> Yahweh or displace him. This is very nearly the case in Is 47.8, 10, in
> which Babylon makes the presumptuous statement, 'I am, and there is no
> one besides me'. In these verses it is interesting that Second Isaiah uses the
> single word 'I' (אני) to express the idea 'I am'. He is evidently contrasting
> Babylon's claims with the אני הו of Yahweh. Yet even here he refrains
> from attributing the phrase to anyone other than Yahweh.[43]

It seems then that ἐγώ εἰμι is very closely associated with the name
YHWH. It is so close that we can virtually say the two expressions are
equivalent.

---

40. Variant readings in the critical edition of the Septuagint of Isaiah (J. Ziegler
(ed.), *Septuaginta Vetus Testamentum Graecum*, XIV [Göttingen: Vandenhoeck &
Ruprecht, 3rd edn], p. 294) reflect an unease with the accepted LXX translation (אני
יהוה = ἐγώ εἰμι). A few versions and manuscripts add κύριος, presumably to translate
יהוה. On the other hand, the LXX for Isa. 45.19c [MT has אני יהוה] has ἐγώ εἰμι ἐγώ
εἰμι κύριος but Codex Alexandrinus omits the κύριος, suggesting that for these
translators ἐγώ εἰμι is sufficient to translate יהוה.

41. Dodd (*Interpretation*, p. 94) lists a number of other examples: (a) Isa. 48.12,
אני הוא אני ראשון אף אני אחרון, LXX ἐγώ εἰμι πρῶτος, καὶ ἐγώ εἰμι εἰς τὸν αἰῶνα.
(b) Isa. 43.25, אנכי אנכי הוא מחה פשעיך, LXX ἐγώ εἰμι ἐγώ εἰμι ὁ ἐξαλείφων τὰς
ἀνομίας σου, which Dodd translates as 'I am, "I AM", who blots out your iniquities.'
(c) Isa. 45.19c, אני יהוה דבר צדק, LXX ἐγώ εἰμι ἐγώ εἰμι Κύριος ὁ λαλῶν
δικαιοσύνην, 'I am, "I AM", the LORD, who speaks righteousness' (Dodd's translation).
The curious point here, noted by Dodd, is that יהוה seems to be rendered twice by the
LXX, once by ἐγώ εἰμι and once by Κύριος. Dodd's contention (which I support) is
that ἐγώ εἰμι, אני הוא and יהוה all basically represent the Divine Name.

42. Westermann (*Isaiah 40–66*, p. 123) says, 'The first clause [of 43.11a], "I, I,
Yahweh" corresponds to the words of v. 10b just discussed "that I am he".' P.B.
Harner (*The 'I Am' of the Fourth Gospel* [Facet Books: Philadelphia: Fortress Press,
1970], p. 14) similarly maintains that 'Second Isaiah regarded the phrase "I am he" as
an abbreviated form of other expressions, especially "I am Yahweh", summing up in
concise terms everything represented by the longer terms.'

43. Harner, *'I Am'*, p. 7.

9.5.5 *Probable Background to* ἐγώ εἰμι *sayings in John*

But is Deutero-Isaiah a candidate for background to these ἐγώ εἰμι sayings in John? There is a growing consensus that this is the case. Ball quotes a number of scholars who argue that Deutero-Isaiah lies behind the 'I am' sayings of John,[44] and he himself presents a strong argument. For example, he argues that Isa. 43.10 lies behind the absolute ἐγώ εἰμι in Jn 8.58.

He begins by observing verbal links between the LXX of Isa. 43.10 and Jn 8.18, 24 and 28. The LXX of Isa. 43.10 is as follows:

Γένεσθέ μοι μάρτυρες, καὶ ἐγὼ μάρτυς, λέγει Κύριος ὁ Θεός, καὶ ὁ παῖς μου ὃν ἐξελεξάμην, ἵνα γνῶτε καὶ πιστεύσητε, καὶ συνῆτε ὅτι ἐγὼ εἰμι (אני הוא). ἔμπροσθέν μου οὐκ ἐγένετο ἄλλος Θεός, καὶ μετ' ἐμὲ οὐκ ἔσται.

This links with the ἐγὼ εἰμι of 8.18: ἐγὼ εἰμι ὁ μαρτυρῶν περὶ ἐμαυτοῦ καὶ μαρτυρεῖ περὶ ἐμοῦ ὁ πέμψας με πατήρ. Jesus seems to identify himself as the servant of the LORD, and the LXX indicates that the LORD also witnesses (καὶ ἐγὼ μάρτυς, λέγει Κύριος ὁ θεός). There are also links with 8.24 and 28 through the verbs πιστεύσητε (8.24) and γνώσεσθε (8.28), and of course the expression ἐγὼ εἰμι. Further, perhaps 8.24 may link with Isa. 43.25 where a double ἐγὼ εἰμι prefaces a promise of forgiveness of sins.[45]

Given possible links already in earlier ἐγὼ εἰμι verses in John 8, it should not be surprising to find that 8.58 also has links with Isa. 43.10. There are the following verbal parallels:

Isaiah 43.10	John 8.58
ἐγὼ εἰμι	ἐγὼ εἰμι
ἔμπροσθέν	πρὶν
ἐγένετο	γενέσθαι

Not only do both passages show a contrast between the verb 'to be' (εἰμι) and the verb 'to come to be' (γίνομαι), even the contrast in tenses between the aorist and the present occurs in both. Just as God's very nature is

---

44. See Ball (*'I Am'*, pp. 33-34) who cites J. Richter, H. Zimmermann, A. Feuillet, R. Brown, J. Coetzee and P. Harner as scholars who focus on Deutero-Isaiah for an understanding of the 'I am' sayings of John. To this must be added Dodd (*Interpretation*, pp. 93-94), who has a succinct and pertinent discussion.

45. In relation to Jn 8.28 Dodd (*Interpretation*, p. 95) says, 'It is difficult not to see here an allusion to the divine name אני הוא. The implication would seem to be that God has given His own Name to Christ; and this is actually stated in xvii.11.'

contrasted with the temporal existence of the gods of the nations, so Jesus' nature is contrasted with that of Abraham. A further parallel to Jn 8.58 occurs in the *Targum of Isaiah* 43. What is striking is the reference to Abraham, who is nowhere mentioned in the text of Isaiah 43 itself:

> *I am he that was from the beginning, even the everlasting ages are mine,* and there *is* no God *besides me*. I, I am the LORD, and besides me there is no saviour. I declared *to Abraham your father what was about to come,* I saved *you from Egypt*…also from *eternity* I am He; there is none who can deliver from my hand (Targum of 43.10-13). [46]

It seems, then, that there is a reasonable likelihood that Isa. 43.10 lies behind ἐγώ εἰμι verses in John 8 and not only Isa. 43.10, but also its larger context.

9.5.6 *Preliminary Conclusion*

If it is accepted that Deutero-Isaiah forms a major part of the background of ἐγώ εἰμι in John, then the fact that Jesus takes to himself a phrase that is reserved for YHWH alone means that he intimately identifies himself with God. This is what we find in the opening words of the Gospel when Jesus is identified with the Logos (1.2-3, 14), who in turn is identified with God, and from Thomas's confession towards the close of the Gospel (20.28). It also helps to explain the hostile reaction of the Jews in 8.59 and the prostration of the arresting party in 18.6. In the former case the Jews heard Jesus' claim to be one with YHWH, which for them constituted blasphemy (cf. 10.30-31), and in the latter the use of the name functioned like a theophany—a manifestation of YHWH—before which people fell to the ground (cf. Dan. 10.9; Rev. 1.17).

In the foregoing discussion we have seen that ἐγώ εἰμι is a pervasive name for Jesus in the Gospel of John. It occurs with a predicate and without a predicate. We have seen in Exod. 3.14, and more especially in Deutero-Isaiah that ἐγώ εἰμι is closely associated with the name יהוה, and in some Deutero-Isaiah passages is directly equivalent to יהוה. I suggest

---

46. Bruce D. Chilton, *The Isaiah Targum: Introduction, Translation, Apparatus and Notes* (ed. K. Cathcart *et al.*; Aramaic Bible, 11; Edinburgh: T. & T. Clark, 1987), p. 85. This targumic evidence cannot be pressed because it postdates John. Chilton (*The Isaiah Targum*, pp. xxvi-xxviii) contends that the Synoptic Jesus had a knowledge of the traditions contained in the Isaiah Targum, but more work is necessary on the relationship of the Johannine Jesus and the Targums before the above evidence can be properly evaluated.

therefore that the name given by the Father to the Son in Jn 17.11-12 is the name, ἐγώ εἰμι, so powerfully evocative of the name יהוה.[47]

9.5.7 *The High Priest Bears the Name* יהוה

Shirbroun emphasizes that the Father's giving of his name to the Son is unique. The name is not given to the disciples, but manifested (17.6) or made known (17.26) to them:

> This means that the pattern observed in the Fourth Gospel, whereby the Son gives his followers the things that have been given to him by the Father (e.g. λογος, ῥήματα, ἐντολή), is broken in the case of ὄνομα. This pattern is also broken in the case of judgement (κρίσις, 5.22, 27), all things (πάντα, 15.15)[48] and life in himself (ζωή ἐν ἑαυτῷ, 5.26). One may conclude that there are some gifts and prerogatives given to Jesus, which may be shared more or less fully with others; but there are others which cannot be given to Jesus' followers. These unique gifts witness to the unique relationship of oneness between the Father and the Son and define his person in a fundamental way that distinguishes him from his disciples.[49]

In the Old Testament God's name was especially resident in the Temple.[50] This is repeatedly emphasized in Deuteronomy as the people were urged

---

47. C.H Dodd (*Interpretation*, p. 95) has an interesting argument that revolves around the association of the glory of God with the Name of God. Isa. 42.8, a strong monotheistic statement has in the MT אני יהוה הוא שמי וכבודי לאחר לא אתן, and in the LXX ἐγώ κύριος ὁ θεός, τοῦτο μου ἐστὶ τὸ ὄνομα, καὶ τὴν δόξαν μου ἑτέρῳ οὐ δώσω. 'Now in John xii.23 we have the statement, ἐλήλυθεν ἡ ὥρα ἵνα δοξασθῇ ὁ υἱὸς τοῦ ἀνθρώπου, and this is followed by the prayer, πάτερ, δόξασόν σου τὸ ὄνομα (xii.28). Later, in xvii.5, Christ prays, δόξασόν με σύ, πάτερ, παρὰ σεαυτῷ τῇ δόξῃ ᾗ εἶχον πρὸ τοῦ τὸν κόσμον εἶναι παρὰ σοί. Thus the eternal glory of God is given to Christ, and in the same act the Name of God is glorified. This would seem to be the presupposition of the use by Christ of the divine name ἐγώ εἰμι = אני הוא.'

48. Shirbroun is in error here. Jesus says that he *has* made known all things (πάντα) that he has heard from his Father (Jn 15.15). Despite this Shirbroun's point holds good: there are some things he has received from the Father that he has not passed on to his disciples, including the name the Father has given him.

49. Shirbroun, 'Name of God', p. 231.

50. This is repeatedly emphasized in Solomon's dedicatory prayer in 1 Kgs 8 where the idea of a house for YHWH's name occurs four times (vv. 18, 19, 20, 29). The last reference ties the dwelling of YHWH's name to prayer: 'O LORD my God, heeding the cry and the prayer that your servant prays to you today; that your eyes may be open night and day toward this house, the place of which you said, "My name shall be there", that you may heed the prayer that your servant prays toward this place. Hear the plea of your servant and of your people Israel when they pray towards this place...'

to reject all places of worship except 'the place that the LORD your God will choose out of all your tribes as his habitation to put his name there' (12.5). There is one significant difference between the MT and LXX of Deut. 12.5 I want to highlight.

The MT has the rather neutral לָשׂוּם אֶת־שְׁמוֹ שָׁם, whereas the LXX has the stronger ἐπονομάσαι τὸ ὄνομα αὐτοῦ ἐκεῖ.[51] The expression conveys the idea that YHWH is staking out this place as his own by naming it with his name. On the other hand, the gift of the Father's name to the Son that we find in Jn 17.11-12 has personal dimensions of giving and receiving that cannot be present in YHWH naming his name on a place. Nevertheless there are elements of similarity. I suggest that YHWH gives his name to the place of worship in much the same way as he gives his name to his Son. I suggest further that it is the name יהוה that is given in both cases.

Within the Temple the name יהוה is specifically found on the turban of the high priest. In Exodus 28, where instructions are given concerning the vestments of the high priest, Moses is told to 'make a rosette of pure gold, and engrave on it, like the engraving on a signet, 'Holy to Yahweh (קֹדֶשׁ לַיהוה)].[52] You shall fasten it on the turban with a blue cord; it shall be on the front of the turban' (Exod. 28.36-37). Thus the high priest who bears the divine name on his golden headdress on his forehead, recalls the angel who went before Israel in the days of the desert wanderings after the Exodus, of whom God said, 'My name is in the midst of him (MT שְׁמִי בְּקִרְבּוֹ, Exod. 23.21).[53] Certainly in later writings the word in the

---

51. A further difference to note in passing is that the MT has the idea of residency of the name conveyed by the verb שָׁכַן, whereas the emphasis in the LXX is on the invocation of the name conveyed by the verbal form ἐπικληθῆναι. This difference in emphasis is consistently present in Deut. 12.11; 14.23, 24; 16.2, 11; 26.2. Cf. also Jub. 1.10, which speaks of 'My sanctuary, which I (Yahweh) have hallowed for myself... that I should set my name upon it...' Other passages in Jubilees speak of God's name dwelling in the sanctuary (32.10; 49.21; cf. 49.19-20), and God's name is so bound up with the sanctuary that a defilement of the Temple can be spoken of in the same breath as profanation of God's holy name (30.15; cf. 23.21). And that name is regarded by Jubilees as the author of the whole creation: 'And now I make you swear a great oath—for there is no oath which is greater than it by the name glorious and honoured and great and splendid and wonderful and mighty, which created the heavens and the earth and all things together—that you will fear him and worship him' (36.7).

52. The LXX has Ἁγίασμα Κυρίου. The Hebrew 'לְ' has been understood by the LXX translators as genitive.

53. The LXX has ἐπ᾽ αὐτῷ, which is more reminiscent of the name being upon (not 'in' as with MT) the high priest.

inscription that was singled out was the name יהוה. For example, Aristeas, in describing the headdress of the high priest, mentions only the name of God:

> And on his head he had what is called the 'tiara', and upon this the inimitable 'mitre', the hallowed diadem having in relief on the front in the middle in holy letters on a golden leaf the name of God, ineffable in glory (98).

Similarly with Philo:

> Above the turban is the golden plate on which the graven shape of four letters, indicating, as we are told (φασὶ φηνύεσθαι), the name of the Self-Existent (ὄνομα τοῦ ὄντος)[54] are impressed, meaning that it is impossible for anything that is to subsist without the invocation of Him (*Vit. Mos.* 2.132).

Although ben Sira's grandson[55] does not specifically mention the name יהוה engraved on the gold leaf fastened to the high priest's turban, he does indicate that the crown and engraving was the glory of the high priest's attire:

> A golden crown upon the mitre,
> An engraving of a seal of holiness;
> The glory of honour, work of might,
> The desires of the eyes, beautiful ornaments (45.12).

In commenting on the words 'glory of honour' C.T.R. Hayward says:

> these words represent the Hebrew *hwd kbwd*, 'majesty of glory'. From this text we may deduce that a principal element in Simon's [the high priest's] 'majesty' (*hôd*), which features so prominently in performing the Tamid, consists in his wearing the Divine Name above his forehead.[56]

Finally, the Divine Name, which the high priest himself bears on his forehead, may in a sense put that Name on the people of Israel through the priestly utterance of the Aaronic blessing of Num. 6.26:

יברכך יהוה וישמרך
יאר יהוה פניו אליך ויחנך
ישא יהוה פניו אליך וישם לך שלום

---

54. Philo's interpretation of the Divine Name has some kinship with the ἐγὼ εἰμι in Jn 8.58, and his use of φασὶ suggests he is passing on a tradition, a tradition that might have its origins with Exod. 3.14, but I have no evidence that this is the case.

55. The Hebrew version of 45.12 of the Wisdom of ben Sira is too fragmentary to work from and so I have to rely on the Greek version written by the grandson.

56. Hayward, *The Jewish Temple*, p. 83.

As a result of this blessing pronounced by Aaron and his sons, the Divine Name is placed upon the people (v. 27) as a gift:

ושמו את־שמי על־בני ישראל ואני אברכם

Thus the priests mediate the name יהוה, a name of blessing, to the people.

I therefore conclude from the foregoing that the name יהוה was engraved in gold and tied to the turban of the high priest; that this was the highlight of the high priest's attire; that the name was associated with holiness; and that the name could be mediated as a gift to the people by way of the priestly blessing.

9.5.8 *Final Conclusion: the Divine Name Given to Jesus*
Jn 17.11-12 speaks of the Father's name, which he has given to the Son. The previous discussion has demonstrated that the most likely name is ἐγὼ εἰμι. This name pervades the Gospel of John both in its predicative and absolute forms. It has further been argued that this name is intimately associated with the Hebrew name יהוה, and once that linkage is allowed then one can see how ἐγὼ εἰμι undergirds the Johannine Christology, which is climatically summarized in Thomas's confessional statement before the risen Jesus: Ὁ κύριός μου καὶ ὁ θεός μου (20.28). Jesus is one with YHWH. Jesus has effectively been given the name יהוה by the Father.

This is also the name the Jewish high priests carried on their foreheads, engraved in gold. For Jesus it is not engraved in gold; it is given not ἐπ᾽ αὐτῷ, but rather ἐν αὐτῷ or בקרבו as the MT describes the giving of the name of God to the angel of YHWH (Exod. 23.21) (discussed above, 9.5.7). For the high priests there was a sense in which the name יהוה was external—they wore it as part of their priestly attire—whereas for Jesus the name was part and parcel of who he was. It is because of this that Shirbroun is right when he says that the name the Father gives the Son cannot be given to the disciples. It belongs to Jesus by virtue of who he is—it cannot be passed on to his disciples in the same sense in which he has been given it.

Nevertheless he does have the name יהוה, and in having it, not just upon him, but within him as it were, he is the fulfilment of the high priest.

Having established a link with the high priesthood and the Johannine Jesus, it now remains to explore how Jesus' prayer of John 17 functions as a prayer of *the* high priest. I will do this not by a systematic exegesis of the prayer, but by considering the two retrospects and three petitions mentioned earlier.

9.6 *'I Have Manifested your Name'*

9.6.1 *Exegesis*

This expression occurs in 17.6 (Ἐφανέρωσά σου τὸ ὄνομα τοῖς ἀνθρώποις οὓς ἔδωκάς μοι ἐκ τοῦ κόσμου) and with the replacement of ἐφανέρωσά with ἐγνώρισα and a future dimension (γνωρίσω) in 17.26 (καὶ ἐγνώρισα αὐτοῖς τὸ ὄνομά σου καὶ γνωρίσω). Both verses mean much the same even though there are some small differences.[57]

Looking first at 17.6, it is interesting to note that φανεροῦν occurs nine times in John: four times in reference to Jesus (21.1(2x); 21.14; 1.31); once in the manifestation of his δόξα (2.11); twice in reference to τὰ ἔργα (3.21; 9.3); and finally in the manifestion of the name of the Father (17.6).

The manifestation of the name of יהוה comes in times of salvation in the history of Israel. In the Exodus from Egypt there is a manifestation of the name יהוה to Moses at the burning bush (Exod. 3.14, see earlier discussion) and in the second Exodus from the exile in Babylon (Duetero-Isaiah) there is also a pronounced emphasis on the revelation of the name of אני הוא/יהוה. For example, Isa. 52.6:

MT

לכן ידע עמי שמי לכן ביום ההוא כי אני הוא המדבר הנני

LXX

Διὰ τοῦτο γνώσεται ὁ λαός μου τὸ ὄνομά μου ἐν τῇ ἡμέρᾳ ἐκείνῃ, ὅτι ἐγὼ εἰμι αὐτὸς ὁ λαλῶν, πάραειμι...

---

57. The different verbs in 17.26 (ἐγνώρισα, γνωρίσω) are possibly due to a play on words in vv. 25 and 26 (ἔγνω, ἔγνων, ἔγνωσαν, ἐγνώρισα, γνωρίσω). The making known of the name is founded on Jesus' own unitive knowledge of the Father (v. 25c), a point not made in the earlier part of the prayer (v. 6). Furthermore, the purpose of making known the name of God is this time made explicit, namely, ἵνα ἡ ἀγάπη ἣν ἠγάπησάς με ἐν αὐτοῖς ᾖ κἀγὼ ἐν αὐτοῖς. The parallel in 15.15 also has love as the goal, but it is expressed there in terms of the commandment Jesus gives the disciples rather than as it is here in terms of the indwelling of God's love. Finally the repetition of γνωρίζειν in the future has given rise to diverse interpretations. My view is that Jesus makes known God's name to all believers at all times through the disciples (17.10, 20) (without ruling out the Holy Spirit given to the disciples in 20.22). Shirbroun (p. 236 n. 109) suggests, with the help of G. Knight and then R. Hayward, 'The aorist and future of γνωρίζειν in 17.26 may reflect the use of "I am" in Exod. 3.14 and the explanations of the doubling which appear in later Judaism.' The notion of a continuing revelation intimated in the Targum on Exod. 3.14 : 'Why does אהיה occur twice?' And the answer given is that the first refers to the past; the second to the future: God will be there.

'Therefore my people shall know my name in that day because [it is] "I am"
who speaks: "Here am I!"…'[58]

The manifestation of God's name by Jesus also signals a day of salvation—indeed earlier discussion in relation to the exegesis of Jn 2.13-22
(see above my 3.3-4) indicates that with the coming of the Johannine Jesus
the day of YHWH has arrived. The eschatological day has dawned. And
within this day Jesus has manifested the Father's name to his disciples.
How has the Johannine Jesus done this?[59] I have looked at how the unpredicated name of ἐγώ εἰμι functions in John to highlight Jesus' identity,
but now in regard to the manifestation of the name of God I will look at
how that name (ἐγώ εἰμι) functions in revealing God's 'grace and truth'
(Jn 1. 14, 17) towards humanity. That is, I will look at the predicated ἐγώ
εἰμι sayings, in the belief that they will reveal the significance of the name
of God (YHWH) for all who follow Jesus.

9.6.2 *YHWH is the Bread of Life*

The first of the predicated 'I am' sayings is Jn 6.35, where Jesus says, ἐγώ
εἰμι ὁ ἄρτος τῆς ζωῆς· ὁ ἐρχόμενος πρὸς ἐμὲ οὐ μὴ πεινάσῃ, καὶ ὁ
πιστεύων εἰς ἐμὲ οὐ μὴ διψήσει πώποτε.

If we take ἐγώ εἰμι as the name of God, יהוה, then the saying effectively becomes 'YHWH is the bread of life'.[60] This was so in the Exodus

---

58. The editors of *BHS* suggest the second לכן should be deleted so I have not
included it in my translation. The 'it is' in square brackets has been inserted to capture
the emphatic sense conveyed by αὐτός/הוא and to preserve the notion of a proper
name of God, namely, ἐγώ εἰμι/יהוה/הוא אני. Other Dt-Isa. texts that involve the name
of God in some way or another include 56.5, 43.7 and 62.2. Shirbroun, 'Name of God',
p. 228 n. 92) draws attention to the fact that on some occasions the LXX uses ὄνομα for
a Hebrew word of an entirely different meaning (e.g. in Isa. 42.4 the LXX has ὄνομα
for MT תורה).

59. If we keep in mind that the name that has been manifested is ἐγώ εἰμι /יהוה,
then it is worth recalling that this name is a covenant name—a name that expresses
God's willingness to be one with his people and come to them with salvation. G.A.F.
Knight (*From Moses to Paul: A Christological Study in the Light of our Hebraic Heritage* [London: Lutterworth Press, 1949], p. 104) translates the name of God in Exod.
3.14 as 'I will be that I will be', meaning that God is there for his people. In the preface
to the Ten Commandments God identifies himself in terms of the Exodus, of his saving
grace: 'I am the Yahweh your God, who brought you out of the land of Egypt, out of
the house of slavery' (Exod. 20.2; Deut. 5.6).

60. Can the 'equation' be put this way around? I think there is some parallel with 1
Jn 4.8, which has 'God is love'. It is right to say this, but not right to reverse the order

when Yʜᴡʜ provided food and drink for his people in the wilderness, but now Jesus has demonstrated the provision of Yʜᴡʜ in the multiplication of bread and fish for the multitude (6.1-13). Climatically there is full and comprehensive provision through Jesus offering himself as the Passover Lamb. Those who participate in this provision will be completely satisfied. They will have eternal life (6.54).[61]

9.6.3 *Yʜᴡʜ is the Light of the World*

The second Johannine 'I am' saying flows out of the Tabernacles' Festival that forms the context of John 7. If I omit 7.53–8.11 as recommended by the editors of the United Bible Societies Greek New Testament,[62] then the 'I am' saying follows immediately after the chief priests and Pharisees have challenged Nicodemus to find any prophet in Galilee. Then follows 8.12, where Jesus says, Ἐγὼ εἰμι τὸ φῶς τοῦ κόσμου· ὁ ἀκολουθῶν ἐμοὶ οὐ μὴ περιπατήσῃ ἐν τῇ σκοτίᾳ, ἀλλ᾽ ἕξει τὸ φῶς τῆς ζωῆς.

We believe the connection with Galilee is deliberate. The chief priests and Pharisees effectively ask Nicodemus, 'Is any light to arise in Galilee?' And of course the answer is 'Yes'. Speaking of Galilee of the Gentiles (Γαλιλαία τῶν ἐθνῶν), Isaiah, the prophet declares, 'The people who walked in darkness [ὁ λαὸς ὁ πορευόμενος ἐν σκότει] have seen a great light; those who lived in a land of deep darkness—on them light has shined' (Isa. 9.2).[63] There are connections between Isa. 9.2 and Jn 8.12; τῶν ἐθνῶν connects with κόσμου;[64] ὁ πορευόμενος ἐν σκότει contrasts with οὐ μὴ περιπατήσῃ ἐν τῇ σκοτίᾳ; and of course the emphasis on light in both verses.[65] The light in Isa. 9.1-2 is the light of יהוה as he acts for his people to bring deliverance and peace (Isa. 9.2-7). Jesus similarly

---

and have 'Love is God'. So I suggest that it is legitimate to say 'Yʜᴡʜ is the bread of life' but not 'The bread of life is Yʜᴡʜ'.

61. This Passover focus of Jn 6 has been argued at length in 7.1 and 7.1.3.

62. See 7.2.3 n. 59 for a discussion of the merits of including 7.53–8.11 in the Johannine text.

63. This may be John's way of making a traditional connection between Jesus and this text. Matthew (4.15-16) quotes Isa. 9.1-2 directly with reference to the commencement of Jesus' ministry.

64. John's preference for τοῦ κόσμου rather than τῶν ἐθνῶν could be explained by the fact that he has already developed the theme of light coming into the world (3.19; 1.9) and wishes to link passages where Jesus has already been referred to as the light with those that refer to the world (cf. 1.9,10; 3.16-19; 7.5).

65. Ball ('*I Am*', pp. 215-24), with some justification, believes Isa. 42.6; 49.6; 51.4 also provide a background to Jn 8.12. However, he discusses no other background apart from Isa. 9.1-2.

acts as the light of the world (Jn 9.5) to bring deliverance to the man born blind in John 9 and so manifest the name of God for all who are prepared to see (Jn 9.40-41; 12.46).

The context of the Festival of Tabernacles is also relevant. I mentioned in my discussion of the Tabernacles Festival (see 7.2.6) the nightly illumination of the Temple Court of the Women. This was perhaps to commemorate the provision of the flaming light of YHWH's glory leading his people through the darkness of the night (Exod. 13.21) to the promised land. I suggested that the implied setting of Jn 8.12, is the Temple and the illumination of the Court of the Women by the four golden candlesticks (see 7.2.3). All Jerusalem was reflected in that light and in the Gospel scene Jesus stands in this same court and proclaims that he is the light not only of Jerusalem, but of the world;[66] those who follow him will not journey in the darkness, but will have the light of life. As the light of the glory of YHWH led his people through the darkness in the desert to the promised land, so Jesus who is ἐγώ εἰμι (= יהוה) will lead his disciples to life.

Finally it is worth noting that it seems this utterance took place in the Temple (cf. 8.59), where perpetual[67] light burned (Exod. 27.21; Lev. 24.2-4). This light so impressed Hecataeus of Abdera that he wrote of the 'inextinguishable [ἀναπόσβεστος] light' that burned on the altar and lampstand 'both night and day'.[68] While the emphasis in Jn 8.12 is not on the perpetual character of the light, but rather its life-giving power, it is significant that despite the 'perpetual' light having been extinguished with the destruction of the Temple, the light of YHWH still shines in Jesus the new Temple.[69]

9.6.4 *YHWH is the Door*
Jesus says in Jn 10.9, ἐγώ εἰμι ἡ θύρα· δι᾽ ἐμοῦ ἐάν τις εἰσέλθῃ σωθήσεται καὶ εἰσελεύσεται καὶ ἐξελεύσεται καὶ νομὴν εὑρήσει.

---

66. For evidence regarding the ceremonies of Tabernacles as they had developed by Jesus' time see the brief discussion in 7.2.2 and n. 53.

67. LXX has διαπαντός and MT תמיד both of which mean perpetual or continual. The NRSV has 'regular', which is misleading.

68. *Apion* 1.199.

69. In an Old Testament passage where there is a remarkable emphasis on the Festival of Tabernacles (Zech. 14.16, 18, 19) there is a reference to continuous day: 'And there shall be continuous day (it is known to the LORD), not day and not night, for at evening time there shall be light' (Zech. 14.7). Interestingly, the following v. 8 speaks of the living waters flowing out from Jerusalem, thus bringing together the themes of light and water that are highlighted in ceremonies of the Tabernacles' Festival.

John 10 is a parable about the sheepfold, the sheep, the shepherd and thieves and robbers. Tabernacle links with Jn 10.1-21 may come via the Hallel, which was evidently sung during the festival.[70] In this case the reference ('I am the door/gate', Jn 10.9) could possibly be to Ps. 118.19-20, 'the door of righteousness, the door of YHWH', by which alone the Israelite enters into the true Temple and dwelling place of God on earth (cf. Jn 1.14; 14.6). A supporting connection is possibly present in 10.1, which has κλέπτης καὶ λῃστής . Here the λῃστής may recall Mk 11.17, where Jesus calls the Jewish Temple a σπήλαιον λῃστῶν, which in turn seems to be dependent on Jer. 7.11, μὴ σπήλαιον λῃστῶν ὁ οἶκός μου, οὗ ἐπικέκληται τὸ ὄνομά μου ἐπ᾽ αὐτῷ ἐκεῖ, ἐνώπιον ὑμῶν.

There are also parallels in vocabulary (with the LXX of Ps. 118) and concepts. The Psalmist asks to enter through the gate/door (Ps. 118.19), just as in John the sheep enter by Jesus (εἰσέλθῃ, Jn 10.9). Likewise the sheep are to go in (εἰσελεύσεται, Jn 10.9) and come out and find pasture. In Ps. 118.21, for those who go through the gate/door YHWH becomes their salvation. In John 10 anyone who enters by Jesus, the ἐγώ εἰμι (יהוה), will also experience salvation. Here too Jesus manifests the name of אני הוא by being the door of salvation.

9.6.5 *YHWH is the Good Shepherd*
In Jn. 10.11 Jesus says ἐγώ εἰμι ὁ ποιμὴν ὁ καλός· ὁ ποιμὴν ὁ καλὸς τὴν ψυχὴν αὐτοῦ τίθησιν ὑπὲρ τῶν προβάτων·

Perhaps the main Old Testament allusion in John 10 is to the prophecy of Ezekiel 34 where Ezekiel is told to prophesy against the 'shepherds of Israel'—the leaders of God's people. No doubt this would include priests as well as princes. The similarities between Ezekiel 34 and John 10 are well summarized by C.H. Dodd,[71] but there is one striking point he fails to mention, namely, Ezek. 34.15:

MT

אני ארעה צאני...נאם אדני יהוה

'I myself will shepherd my sheep...says the LORD YHWH'.
However, the LXX has a significant addition:

ἐγὼ βοσκήσω τὰ πρόβατα μου...καὶ γνώσονται ὅτι ἐγώ εἰμι Κύριος· τάδε λέγει Κύριος Κύριος.

---

70. Danby, *The Mishnah, Suk.* 3.9, 4.8.
71. Dodd, *Interpretation*, pp. 358-59.

The inclusion of ἐγώ εἰμι here is arresting. One could speculate as to why the LXX translators inserted it here, but in Jn 10.11 Jesus, the ἐγώ εἰμι, not only proclaims *himself* as the good shepherd, but goes further even than YHWH in Ezek. 34.15-16. Jesus says he is going to lay down his life for the sheep! So Jesus makes known the name of YHWH, who provides for his sheep even to the extent of being ready to give his life for them. The use of ὑπέρ is a sign that sacrifical language is being employed, language evocative of the Temple altar.

9.6.6 YHWH *is the Resurrection and the Life*

When Jesus assures Martha that her brother will rise again, she replies, 'I know that he will rise again in the resurrection at the last day' (Jn 11.24). It is in response to this declaration in a final resurrection that Jesus says, Ἐγώ εἰμι ἡ ἀνάστασις καὶ ἡ ζωή· ὁ πιστεύων εἰς ἐμὲ κἂν ἀποθάνῃ ζήσεται. That is, Jesus transforms Martha's future hope into a present reality that is fulfilled in himself.

References to resurrection are sparse in the Old Testament. Dan. 12.1-2 speaks of a resurrection in terms of judgment:

> But at that time your people shall be delivered, everyone who is found written in the book. Many of those who sleep in the dust of the earth shall awake, some to everlasting life, and some to shame and everlasting contempt.

Something similar is expressed in 2 Macc. 7.9 where the tortured second Maccabaean brother speaks:

> And when he was at his last breath he said, 'You accursed wretch, you dismiss us from this present life, but the King of the universe will raise us up to an everlasting renewal of life, because we have died for his laws'.

Likewise the third brother expressed his hope in a bodily resurrection when he would receive back the limbs he lost in persecution (2 Macc. 7.9-11). However, the emphasis in this hope of resurrection is not so much for future life, but rather for vindication of the oppressed and tortured righteous. The hope was that YHWH would bring deliverance and vindication, if not in this life, then in the next, through a bodily resurrection.

The background to this torture of the Maccabaean brothers was the rebellion against Antiochus Epiphanes, who desecrated the Temple. The Temple was eventually restored and the altar dedicated. The Dedication Festival mentioned in Jn 10.22 recalls this history.

Now the reader has moved on to the story of raising Lazarus in John 11, and the Daniel and Maccabaean traditions may be the background to Jesus' claim to be the resurrection and the life. In the Maccabaean period the oppressed and tortured looked to YHWH for a future vindication in a resurrection body; with the coming of Jesus this hope is brought into the present for those oppressed by death. Jesus thus manifests the name of God as the resurrection and the life.

9.6.7 *YHWH is the Way, the Truth and the Life*
In John 14 Jesus speaks to his disciples of his departure, and he says in v. 4, 'And you know the way to the place where I am going.' In reponse Thomas says, 'LORD, we do not know where you are going. How can we know the way?' And Jesus answers with an 'I am' saying, Ἐγώ εἰμι ἡ ὁδὸς καὶ ἡ ἀλήθεια καὶ ἡ ζωή· οὐδεὶς ἔρχεται πρὸς τὸν πατέρα εἰ μὴ δι᾽ ἐμοῦ.

It is clear from the context indicated above that the emphasis is on 'the way' and not on 'the truth and the life'. Those words, ἀλήθεια and ζωή, simply serve to make clear in what sense Jesus is ἡ ὁδός.

The only other occurrence of ἡ ὁδός in John is in 1.23, where John the Baptist quotes Isa. 40.3 to point away from himself to Jesus. As David Ball says, 'The manner in which John the Baptist makes "straight the way of the LORD" (Jn 1.23) is in his witness to Jesus as the voice calling in the wilderness.'[72]

In Isa. 40 the result of making straight the way of YHWH in the wilderness is that 'the glory of YHWH shall be revealed, and all people shall see it together' (Isa. 40.5). The emphasis of the revelation of glory is readily apparent in the ministry of Jesus (Jn 1.14; 2.11). In Jn 13.31 there is a declaration of mutual glorification of the Son of Man and of God. This verse is quite close to the beginning of John 14, and possibly this theme persists into that chapter. J. Proctor is one who finds links with Jn 13.31 and Jn 14.6 through the intermediary passage of Isa. 49.3. Scholars have discerned a connection between Jn 13.31 and Isa. 49.3[73] and Proctor tentatively concurs with these. Isa. 49.3 says, 'You are my servant, Israel, in whom I will be glorified.' Proctor goes on to comment:

> Strikingly as we read through the following chapter of Isaiah we find, successively, proclamation of a way of redemption from exile (49.8-13), affirmation of the covenant faithfulness of God to Israel (vv. 14-18), and the emergence of new life out of barrenness and death within the covenant

72. Ball, *'I Am'*, p. 233.
73. Carson, *John*, p. 482; Barrett, *St John*, p. 450.

community (vv. 19-23). On that basis 'all flesh shall know that I am Yahweh your Saviour' (v. 26). Way, truth and life, given by Yahweh to Israel, make Yahweh known in the world, as God majestic and unrivalled. We should at least consider the possibility that some influence from this chapter in Isaiah has emerged in the Johannine saying.[74]

It is difficult to be sure that the terms 'truth and life' derive from Isa. 49 since there are no verbal, but rather only conceptual, parallels. However, there is a stronger connection with the term ὁδός because YHWH declares that the mountains shall be made a ὁδός for the people (v. 11).[75]

In a time of exile YHWH comes to his people to prepare a ὁδός to lead them back home. Similarly Jesus comes and declares that he is the ὁδός— the glorious highway—that will lead his disciples home (μονή, 14.23) to the Father's house where there are many rooms (14.2-3). Finally we note that 'the Father's house' is how Jesus describes the Temple (Jn 2.16).

9.6.8 *YHWH is the True Vine*

The final example of Jesus manifesting God's name through an 'I am' saying is in Jn 15.1, where he says, ἐγώ εἰμι ἡ ἄμπελος ἡ ἀληθινή, καὶ ὁ πατήρ μου ὁ γεωργός ἐστιν.

David Ball has an extensive discussion on the background of this saying,[76] and he considers a number of Old Testament passages, Ps. 80; Isa. 5.1-7; Jer. 2.21, and makes mention of Jer. 12.10; Ezek. 15.1-8; 17.3-10; 19.10-14 and Hos. 10.1-2. However, he is reluctant to settle on any paticular text as the background and concludes:

> While many of the individual concepts of the vine discourse are present in the Old Testament, it is not these small allusions that are important in Jesus' claim (though they may add support for the fact that John's language is steeped in Old Testament imagery). John does not simply use the Old Testament imagery as a sort of 'reservoir for individual concepts in the imagery'. Instead he takes the essence of what is implied by that imagery, 'the picture of Israel as the vine of Yahweh', and applies the 'entire impression' to the person of Jesus.[77]

74. J. Proctor, 'The Way, the Truth and the Life: Interfaith Dialogue and the Fourth Gospel' (unpublished paper, 1991), p. 19 n. 25.

75. Ball ('*I Am*', pp. 235-36) finds other texts in Isaiah that may have links with Jn 14.6 through the word ὁδός, namely, Isa. 42.16; 43.19; 48.17; 59.8; 57.14; 62.10.

76. Ball, '*I Am*', pp. 241-48.

77. Ball, '*I Am*', p. 248. The quotations in Ball's conclusion are from R. Borig (*Der Wahre Weinstock: Studien zum Alten und Neuen Testament* [Münich: Kösel, 1967], p. 94).

Despite a thorough consideration of Old Testament texts with vine allusions, Ball has neglected one critical dimension that emerges in a first-century Jewish writing. I refer to the linkage between the Temple and the vine. This is especially prominent in Pseudo-Philo, particularly in Moses' prayer for God's mercy on Israel:

> And then Moses went up into the mountain and prayed to the LORD, saying, 'Behold now, you O God, who have planted this vine and set its roots into the abyss and stretched out its shoots to your most high seat, look upon it in this time, because that vine has lost its fruit and has not recognized its cultivator. And now, if you are angry at your vine and you uproot it from the abyss and dry up its shoots from your most high and eternal seat, the abyss will come no more to nourish it, nor will your throne come to cool that vine of yours that you have burned up. For you are he who is all light; and you have adorned your house with precious stones and gold; and have sprinkled your house with spices and balsam wood and cinnamon and roots of myrrh and costum; and you have filled it with various foods and the sweetness of various drinks. Therefore if you do not have mercy on your vine, all things, LORD, have been done in vain, and you will not have anyone to glorify you'.[78]

The vine undoubtedly refers to Israel, God's planting, but

> this imagery is [also] bound up with the sanctuary, since God has planted Israel on his mountain, the sanctuary which his hands have made according to Exod. 15.17, the very verse which the Rabbis took to mean that the earthly and heavenly dwelling places of God correspond to one another... The vine-symbol belongs firmly in the realm of beliefs about the Temple... The earthly sanctuary, which Moses was shown in a pattern, is inextricably bound up with Israel as vine, holding together the component parts of the universe. For God to forsake this vine is tantamount to his forsaking creation; by showing mercy to the vine He ensures that His work has not been in vain.[79]

---

78. Pseudo-Philo 12.8, 9 (*OTP*, II, p. 320). D.J. Harrington (n. h) suggests that 'house' refers possibly to paradise, but more likely to the universe. However, the sanctuary (tabernacle/Temple) is to be preferred above both these suggestions for the following reasons: (a) the earthly sanctuary with its incense, food of animal sacrifices and wine of drink offerings is mentioned elsewhere in Pseudo-Philo (11.15; 13.1); (b) a description of the precious stones and the light is given in 26.13 and the stones are put in the ark of the covenant that will eventually be placed in the Temple built by Jahel who 'should be Solomon' (*OTP*, II, p. 338 n.e).

79. Hayward, *The Jewish Temple*, pp. 160-61. See further C.T.R. Hayward, 'The Vine and its Products as Theological Symbols in First Century Palestinian Judaism', *Durham University Journal* 82 (1990), pp. 9-18. No doubt Pseudo-Philo would have been aware of the golden vine that decorated the entrance to the sanctuary (Josephus,

However, the Temple was destroyed in 70 CE. Judgment fell on the 'pleasant planting' (Isa. 5.7) of YHWH. In the midst of the distress and confusion that followed the voice of the Johannine Jesus manifests the name of God when he says, ἐγώ εἰμι ἡ ἄμπελος ἡ αληθινὴ, καὶ ὁ πατήρ μου ὁ γεωργός ἐστιν. The name of God is no longer resident in the Jewish Temple, but in Jesus, who replaces and fulfils the Temple, imaged, as we have seen, by the vine. Pseudo-Philo's fear that with the destruction of the vine, everything would be in vain and God would have no one to glorify him, is answered with what Jesus says: 'My Father is glorified by this, that you bear much fruit and become my disciples' (Jn 15.8).

9.6.9 *Summary*
The foregoing discussion has demonstrated the appropriateness of understanding Jesus' manifestation of the name of God in terms of the name YHWH, which the LXX renders as ἐγώ εἰμι. Jesus declares that he is YHWH, the God who is there for his people.[80] This presence is a saving presence and represented by images from the history of Israel—bread, light, door, shepherd, resurrection, way and vine. Each of these images has links either directly with the Temple or with associated festivals. So in manifesting the name of God which has been given to him, the Johannine Jesus reflects the Temple ethos of the Gospel.

I turn now to the three petitions and the retrospects mentioned earlier. The first is the petition for the preservation of the disciples in the name the Father has given Jesus. I will suggest that the Old Testament background to the preservation of God's people was understood in terms of the Temple and high priestly intercession and something of this background is functioning in this petition of Jesus.

9.7 *'Holy Father, Keep Them in Your Name'*

9.7.1 *The Petition in John 17*
This petition concerning the Father's keeping (Jn 17.11) and the retrospect concerning the Son's keeping (v. 12) are obviously closely related and

---

War 5.210-11; *Ant.* 15.395). The close juxtaposition of Israel and Temple suggests that for Pseudo-Philo the destiny of one was tied up with the destiny of the other. It seems that the image of the vine embraced both Israel and Temple.

80. This sounds colloquial, but the final words of the Hebrew text of Ezekiel (48.35) provide some precedent for the expression שמה יהוה מיום העיר ושם ('And the name of the city from that day shall be The LORD is There'). Interestingly the LXX does not specify the name.

cannot be interpreted in isolation from each other. Nevertheless, v. 11 is clearly the focus of attention because it contains the actual petition that forms part of the main intercession introduced in v. 9 and developed in vv. 15 and 17. Thus I will concentrate on v. 11 and treat the retrospect as the discussion unfolds.

Jesus' address to the Father, Πάτερ ἅγιε, is in keeping with the tenor of Jesus' prayer for his disciples. In v. 15 he prays that they may be kept from the evil one and in v. 17 that they may be sanctified (ἁγίασον αὐτούς) in the Father's word of truth. This separation, being made holy, is so they can carry out their mission to the world (vv. 18-19).

The opening address, Πάτερ ἅγιε, is followed by the imperative τήρησον, which carries the main idea of the petition.[81] Almost parallel ideas are found in 1 Jn 5.18: οἴδαμεν ὅτι πᾶς ὁ γεγεννημένος ἐκ τοῦ θεοῦ οὐχ ἁμαρτάνει, ἀλλ᾽ ὁ γεννηθεὶς ἐκ θεοῦ τηρεῖ αὐτὸν καὶ ὁ πονηρὸς οὐχ ἅπτεται αὐτου, that is, 'We know that anyone born of God does not sin, but he who was born of God keeps him, and the evil one does not touch him.'[82] The understanding here is that γεννηθεὶς ἐκ θεοῦ refers to Jesus. He keeps the disciple from ὁ πονηρὸς (cf. Jn 17.15). The goal of the keeping is the disciple's freedom from the evil one and therefore from sin, that is, preservation from being lost (ἀπόλλυναι). Thus, 1 Jn 5.18 continues the emphasis on Christ's protection of his own that is found in the Johannine corpus. We may infer from a consideration of the context of 1 Jn 5.18 that the disciple is kept in a sphere of safety. In 1 Jn 5.19-20 we read, 'We know that we are of God [ἐκ τοῦ θεοῦ], and the whole world is in the power of the evil one [ἐν τῷ πονηρῷ]…we are in the true one [ἐν τῷ ἀληθινῷ], in his Son [ἐν τῶ υἱῶ αὐτοῦ] Jesus Christ.' The use of the preposition ἐν (and also ἐκ) suggests differing spheres, the sphere of danger in the evil one and the sphere of safety in God and the Son.

---

81. τηρεῖν is used relatively frequently in John—a little over a quarter of all the occurrences in the New Testament can be found in John. The most common usage is τηρεῖν in the sense 'observe' or 'fulfil' the word(s) or commandment(s) of God or Jesus (e.g. 17.6b; 14.21, 23). But τηρεῖν is also used in the sense 'hold', 'reserve' or 'preserve' something or someone. This usage is found in 17.11, 12 with a personal direct object. There is a similar usage in 1 Jn 5.18.

82. Metzger makes the point that 'elsewhere John always uses ὁ γεγεννημένος, never ὁ γεννηθεὶς, of the believer' (*Textual Commentary*, p. 719). This tilts the textual variation in favour of αὐτὸν rather than ἑαυτόν. For other options for translation see R.E. Brown (*The Epistles of John* [AB, 30; Garden City, NY: Doubleday, 1982], pp. 620-22).

The context in John 17 is that Jesus is departing from the disciples and they are staying in the world. The subject of τηρεῖν in v. 11 is the Father and in v. 12 the Son. This twofold subject emphasizes the continuity of the keeping of the disciples and reminds us of the mutual working of Father and Son in the preservation of disciples in Jn 10.28-29. There, no one (not even ὁ πονηρός!) is able to snatch them out of the hands of the Father and the Son. The oneness of Father and Son (10.30) is a guarantee of double security. But the goal of that oneness of Father and Son that issues in a twofold keeping in 17.11-12 is the oneness of the disciples.

What is the force of the ἐν in the ἐν τῷ ὀνοματί following τηρεῖν? Shirbroun has considered this question and, while an instrumental force for ἐν would make good sense in this context, believes (on the basis of usage of τηρεῖν ἐν elsewhere in the New Testament, and especially in John) that 'it seems best…to understand ἐν in 17.11-12 in a locative sense with the result that the ὄνομα of God means the area or sphere in which the disciples are kept'.[83]

The locative sense also holds good for the preposition ἐκ in Jn 17.15-16: οὐκ ἐρωτῶ ἵνα ἄρῃς αὐτοὺς ἐκ τοῦ κόσμου, ἀλλ᾿ ἵνα τηρήσῃς αὐτοὺς ἐκ τοῦ πονηροῦ. ἐκ τοῦ κόσμου οὐκ εἰσὶν καθὼς ἐγὼ οὐκ εἰμὶ ἐκ τοῦ κόσμου. The petition is parallel to vv. 11-12. The reason is the same: Jesus is departing and the disciples are remaining in the world. The subject of the keeping is again the Father. The goal of the keeping is the protection of the disciples from the evil one. This is related to the goal of the petition in vv. 11-12. Jesus cannot pray that the disciples be taken out (αἱρεῖν) of the world because they have a mission in and to the world (vv. 18, 20). This mission is carried out partly through the witness of their one-ness, which is the goal of τηρεῖν in v. 11. Their oneness, and, therefore, their mission, is in danger from the evil one from whom they must be protected. In order to protect them it is not necessary to take them ἐκ τοῦ κόσμου, but rather within the world, that is, within the sphere of operation of the evil one, to keep them ἐκ τοῦ πονηροῦ. Shirbroun concludes:

> [B]oth the parallel between vv. 15-16 and vv. 11-12 and the contrast between ἐν (vv. 11, 12) and ἐκ (vv. 15, 16) suggest two spheres in which people may live in the world: the sphere of the ὄνομα of the Father given to Jesus or the sphere of the evil one.[84]

83. Shirbroun, 'Name of God', pp. 259-60. He has a footnote (n. 12) in which he points out that the Johannine verbs, μενεῖν and εἶναι, are also followed by a locative ἐν (cf. 6.56; 15.4; 8.31).

84. Shirbroun, 'Name of God', pp. 260-61.

9.7.2 *Possible Significance of the Petition in the Light of the Old Testament*

What does it mean for the disciples to be kept in the sphere of the name of God given to Jesus? Earlier discussion revealed that the name of God given to Jesus is ἐγώ εἰμι (= יהוה), possibly the name revealed in the burning bush (Exod. 3.14) as a prelude to the first Exodus but more likely the name subsequently and repeatedly proclaimed in Deutero-Isaiah in the period of the second Exodus. There is some hint of what it might mean to be kept in the name of יהוה in Prov. 18.10: 'The name of the LORD is a strong tower; the righteous run into it and are safe.'

MT
מגדל עז שם יהוה בו ירוץ צדיק ונשגב
LXX
Ἐκ μεγαλωσύνης ἰσχύος ὄνομα Κυρίου, αὐτῷ δὲ προσδραμόντες δίκαιοι ὑψοῦνται.

Comparison of the two versions reveals that the LXX has made an abstraction out of מגדל (μεγαλωσύνης ἰσχύος = majestic strength) and thereby lost some of the point of the image. The picture is specifically 'concrete'—people having run into a strong tower have gained height over their enemies with resultant dominance and a greater degree of safety (נשגב/ὑψοῦνται). The tower (that is, the name of יהוה) is a place of protection and safety for the righteous. This picture vividly captures the locative force of the ἐν in the ἐν τῷ ὀνόματί σου of Jn 17.11-12. However it is unlikely that this particular verse lies behind the words of Jesus' prayer in Jn 17.11-12, 15,16. What is more probable is that Jesus is echoing the widespread longing of God's people for protection and safety. We find this cry, for example, in the Psalms.[85] Words evoking defence and protection are prolific throughout the Psalms. For example, Ps. 18.3 (MT), which is especially dense in such words:

יהוה סלעי ומצודתי ומפלטי אלי צורי אחסה בו מגני וקרן ישעי משגבי

---

85. E.g. Ps. 12.5, 7: '"Because the poor are despoiled, because the needy groan, I will now rise up," says the LORD; "I will place them in the safety for which they long."… You, O LORD, will protect [φυλάξεις] us; you will guard [διατηρήσεις] us from this generation forever.' Cf. also Ps. 20.1, 2: 'The LORD answer you in the day of trouble! The name of the God of Jacob protect you [ישגבך = make you high, the same verb used in Prov 18.20]! May he send you help from the sanctuary, and give you support from Zion' (NRSV). Significantly, the help/protection is envisaged as coming from the sanctuary [i.e. the Temple]! Furthermore the 'name of God' is repeated three times in this psalm.

'YHWH is my rock, my fortress, and my deliverer, my God, my rock in whom
I take refuge, my shield, and the horn of my salvation, my stronghold.'

YHWH is all these to the psalmist. Furthermore the concept of YHWH keeping his people is frequently expressed in the Psalms. Ps. 121 is a psalm for
protection as pilgrims make their way to the Temple.[86] The psalm opens
with 'I lift my eyes to the hills—from where will my help come?' Dahood
suggests, 'I lift my eyes to the Mountain, whence will my help come to
me?' He takes הרים as a plural of majesty (cf. Ps. 61.2b) and says 'the
Mountain probably designates both YHWH's celestial abode and YHWH
himself'.[87] For support of identifying the mountain with YHWH he cites
Albright,[88] who translates Ps. 18.32b, 'And who is a Mountain, except our
God?'

This is attractive, but if the psalmist lifts his eyes to YHWH (the
Mountain), why ask where his help comes from? The psalmist knows very
well help comes from YHWH who made heaven and earth (v. 2). It seems
better to take the traditional view and think of the pilgrim approaching
Zion, and who, seeing the mountains, is then anxious and asks, 'From
where will my help come?' The answer is first in standard form: 'My help
comes from YHWH, who made heaven and earth.' Thereafter follows a
beautiful affirmation of YHWH's protecting care for his festal pilgrims:

---

86.   The heading for Ps. 121 is שיר למעלות, 'A Song for the Ascents', a title that
with a slight variation is found in all of Pss. 120–34. The meaning of the title is disputed. Some scholars say it is a technical term where 'ascents' refer to the 'step-like'
repetition of certain words or phrases in successive verses (e.g. in 121.1-2, 3-4, 4-5).
However, this pattern is not confined to this group of psalms. Another suggestion is to
link the 15 'Songs of Ascent' to the 15 steps leading from the court of the women to
the court of Israel (cf. *Mishnah, Mid.* 2.5). S. Mowinckel (*The Psalms in Israel's
Worship*, II [Oxford: Basil Blackwell, 1967], p. 82) says this happened at the Feast of
Tabernacles (Tosefta, *Suk.* 4, 7-9). A more recent view regards the 'Songs of Ascents'
as a collection of psalms chanted by pilgrims on their way to Jerusalem. What reinforces this is that עלה was often used as a term for going on a pilgrimage (cf. 24.3;
122.4) or for the processional ascent to the sanctuary. It is enough for my purpose to
note that these psalms were associated with the Temple, very likely with festal occasions of joy (cf. A.A. Anderson, *The Book of Psalms*, II [NCB; London: Oliphants,
1972], pp. 847-48).

87.   Dahood, *Psalms III: 101-150* (AB, 17 A; Garden City, NY: Doubleday, 1970),
p. 200.

88.   Dahood, *Psalms III*. W.F. Albright, *Yahweh and the Gods of Canaan: A Historical Analysis of Two Contrasting Faiths* (Garden City, NY: Doubleday, 1968),
p. 25.

אל יתן למוט רגלך אל ינום שמרך
הנה לא ינום ולא יישן שומר ישראל
יהוה שמרך יהוה צלך על יד ימינך
יומם השמש לא יככה וירח בלילה
(121.3-8) יהוה ישמר צאתך ובואך מעתה ועד עולם

Six times שמר[89] occurs in this psalm and the subject is invariably יהוה, who protects his people Israel: 'Listen! He who keeps Israel [שומר ישראל] neither slumbers nor sleeps' (cf. 1 Kgs 18.28).

This same YHWH who has come in the person of Jesus has also kept his disciples (Jn 17.12), but now that he is leaving he asks his Father to keep them (17.11).

In the Psalms YHWH's protection of his people is sometimes likened to the strong and impregnable Mt Zion. For example, Ps. 125.1-2:

הבטחים ביהוה כהר ציון לא ימוט לעולם ישב
ירושלם הרים סביב לה ויהוה סביב לעמו מעתה ועד עולם

> 'Those who trust in YHWH are like Mount Zion which is not shaken and re-mains forever.[90] As the mountains surround Jerusalem, so YHWH surrounds his people, from now and for ever.'

Dahood comments, 'The girdle of mountains about Jerusalem reminds the psalmist of Yahweh's enfolding protection of his people.'[91]

In the psalms, Jerusalem, Mt Zion and the Temple tend to coalesce and become synonymous. Hans-Joachim Kraus remarks:

> From his Temple Yahweh shows his power over Jerusalem (Ps. 68.29). In other words, the city of Jerusalem lies within the sphere of the glory and might of the sanctuary. Thus 'Jerusalem' can be used as a synonym for 'Zion' (Ps. 102.21; 135.21) and also as a designation for the place where Yahweh dwells (Ps. 135.21).[92]

Thus the psalmist envisages the protective sphere of the Temple to extend to the city of Jerusalem itself.

In keeping with a general expectation about temples being places of asylum in the ancient world, there is evidence that the Jerusalem Temple

---

89. The LXX uses not τηρεῖν but φυλασσεῖν. However both words occur in the keeping theme of Jn 17. In v. 12 Jesus says: καὶ ἐφύλαξα.

90. The LXX takes Jerusalem into the first colon and so has οἱ πεποιθότες ἐπὶ Κύριον ὡς ὄρος Σιών, οὐ σαλευθήσεται εἰς αἰῶνα ὁ κατοικῶν Ἰερουσαλήμ.

91. Dahood, *Psalms III*, p. 215.

92. Hans-Joachim Kraus, *Theology of the Psalms* (trans. Keith Crim; Minneapolis: Augsburg–Fortress, 1986), p. 73.

functioned in this way too. Adonijah, fearing Solomon, fled to the sanctuary and grasped the horns of the altar (1 Kgs 1.50) and likewise Joab, when he saw his life was in danger (1 Kgs 2.28). But it seems that not even the sanctuary could protect him from 'Yahweh bringing back his bloody deeds on his own head' (1 Kgs 2.32), and so Benaiah killed him at the altar. But there was certainly the expectation that the altar was a sphere of protection.

It is significant that in the high priestly blessing of Num. 6.24-27, the name יהוה and the keeping of the Israelites come together. The priest says, 'YHWH bless you and keep you…[93]' (יברכך יהוה וישמרך) And then the comment in v. 27 is, 'So shall they put my name on the Israelites, and I will bless them' (ושמו את־שמי על־בני ישראל ואני אברכם). The blessing amounts to placing the name of YHWH upon the children of Israel—possibly it is envisaged that they were enveloped within the sphere of the name of YHWH. But the pertinent point here is that the blessing involved protection (שמר) and that protection came by way of having the name of YHWH placed upon them by the utterance of Aaron and his sons. The blessing and the name obviously go together. This is close to the petition of Jesus in Jn 17.11 when he prays for his disciples, the new children of God (Jn 1.12): Πάτερ ἅγιε, τήρησον αὐτοὺς ἐν τῷ ὀνόματί σου ᾧ δέδωκάς μοι…[94]

93. The LXX has φυλάξαι σε. This is consistent with the translation of שמר that I noted in the Psalms.

94. What follows in Jesus' prayer is an admission that not all 12 disciples have been kept. One has been lost, namely, ὁ υἱὸς τῆς ἀπωλείας, ἵνα ἡ γραφὴ πληρωθῇ. This is undoubtedly Judas and the scripture fulfilled is most likely Ps. 41.9 (NRSV) quoted in Jn 13.18. This is against Wendy Sproston ('"The Scripture" in John 17.12', in Barry P. Thompson [ed.], *Scripture: Meaning and Method* [FS A.T. Hanson; Hull: Hull University Press, 1987], pp. 24-36), who argues that 'the Scripture' refers to Jesus' comment on Judas in 6.70. The mention of the Twelve in Jn 6.67, 70 (the only occasion in the Gospel) recalls the 12 stones representing the 12 tribes of Israel on the high priest's breast. The names of the 12 tribes engraved on precious stones and set in the high priest's breastplate effect a memorial for Israel (Exod. 28.12, 21). Ben Sira 45.11 (Heb.) has, 'Precious stones were upon the breastplate engraved as a seal in set[tings]: Every precious stone as a memorial in engraved writing according to the number of the tr[ibes of Is]rael' (trans. Hayward, *The Jewish Temple*, pp. 63-64). The word for 'engraved' (חרות) is found only once in the Bible and that is in Exod. 32.16 where it describes the Ten Commandments engraved (חרות) on two stone tablets, writing that was the 'the work of God' and 'the writing of God'. By the use of this rare word Ben Sira infers that the engraving of the names of the 12 tribes on the breastplate was also the work of God (cf. Hayward, *The Jewish Temple*, p. 69). Similarly in John with the 12 disciples; their election was not their own doing, but God's (Jn 6.37, 70; 15.16; 17.9, 10).

In the famous theophany passage (Exod. 34.5-7), when YHWH passes before Moses proclaiming the name יהוה and what the name means:

ויעבר יהוה על פניו ויקרא יהוה יהוה[95]

אל רחום וחנון ארך אפים ורב חסד ואמת׃

נצר חסד לאלפים...

The only noun that occurs twice is 'steadfast love' (חסד) and in both cases the impression is of lavish abundance. YHWH is the God characterized above all by steadfast love. So when Jesus prays to the Father to keep his disciples in the name that has been given to him, the name of יהוה, he means, 'Keep them in all that the name means—keep them in truth [אמת] and above all, steadfast love [חסד].' This connects with the emphasis in Jesus' prayer on truth (17.17) and love (17.23, 26).

9.7.3 *Summary*

Jesus prays that his disciples will be kept in the name of God that the Father has given him. Examination of 1 Jn 5.18, a passage parallel to Jn 17.11-12, hinted that the prepositions ἐν and ἐκ were locative. It seemed therefore appropriate to follow that lead, and I suggested that the force of ἐν in ἐν τῷ ὀνόματί σου is locative. Recalling earlier discussion in which it was proposed that the name given to Jesus by the Father was YHWH, I then turned to Old Testament texts where the protective, keeping work of YHWH is evident. I looked at Prov. 18.10 where the name of YHWH is called a strong tower—a place into which the righteous can run and be safe. The locative force of the reference was readily apparent. I observed further that the protective care of YHWH for his people was abundantly evident in such psalms as 18 and 121. I noted in Pss. 125.2-3 that YHWH's keeping of his people could be compared to the protection the surrounding mountains offered those who dwelt in Jerusalem and even the Temple. Indeed two examples were cited to illustrate the expectation that the Temple altar itself afforded a safe place for those in flight. The Aaronic blessing, part of which included a prayer for protection, seems to have resulted in those blessed living within the sphere of the name of YHWH. Finally, the meaning of the name of YHWH, proclaimed in the theophany to Moses (Exod. 34.5-7) included a strong emphasis on steadfast love (חסד), which is doubtless an important element in Jesus' petition for his

---

95. It may be that the repetition of the name is an echo of Exod. 3.14 where the verb אהיה is repeated.

disciples in John 17.11-12, especially when compared with Judas' failure in חסד (cf. Jn 17.12b).

The foregoing survey of what YHWH's keeping of Israel meant in the past has revealed a Jewish background with Zion/Temple, the high priest's blessing of the children of Israel and the special significance of the name of YHWH in terms of protective care for his people. All this helps to flesh out the meaning of Jesus' petition in John 17 and highlight the possible Temple background in the prayer.

This favours the conclusion of the work done in the study, namely, that Jesus is the fulfilment and replacement of the Temple, its festivals and priestly service.

This is confirmed by an aspect of the preservation of the disciples that has been neglected so far in Jn 10.27-30:

> τὰ πρόβατα τὰ ἐμὰ τῆς φωνῆς μου ἀκούουσιν, κἀγὼ γινώσκω αὐτὰ καὶ ἀκολουθοῦσίν μοι, κἀγὼ δίδωμι αὐτοῖς ζωὴν αἰώνιον καὶ οὐ μὴ ἀπόλωνται εἰς τὸν αἰῶνα καὶ οὐχ ἁρπάσει τις αὐτὰ ἐκ τῆς χειρός μου. ὁ πατήρ μου ὃ δέδωκέν μοι πάντων μεῖζόν ἐστιν, καὶ οὐδεὶς δύναται ἁρπάζειν ἐκ τῆς χειρὸς τοῦ πατρός. ἐγὼ καὶ ὁ πατὴρ ἕν ἐσμεν.

From the disciples' side security is found in Jesus, whose voice they know and heed. Jesus knows them and they follow him. He is the good shepherd who gives his sheep eternal life and who is ready to lay down his life for the sheep (10.11). No one is able to snatch them out of his hand because his Father has given him the sheep, and the Father is greater than all else and because of that unsurpassed power no one is able to snatch them from the Father's hand. Jesus and the Father are one in purpose and function. The Father is in Jesus and Jesus is in the Father. God is present in Jesus.

Since this is said in the context of the Feast of the Dedication, it has Temple implications that are well expressed by Moloney:

> As Israel celebrated God's presence at the feast of the Dedication, Jesus is telling 'the Jews' that there is another way God is present to them, there is another way they can be sure they are in the Father's hand: belief in the word of Jesus. Within the context of the feast of the Dedication 'the Jews' pride themselves in their reconsecrated Temple, the physical evidence of their belonging to God and, in some way, of God's belonging to them. But Jesus insists that faith in his word ties the believer not only to Jesus but to God, the Father of Jesus. The affirmation of 10.30 confirms what the reader already knows: 'I and the Father are one'. There is no longer any need to look to the physical building on the Temple Mount to know of God's

presence to his people. Jesus, who stands before 'the Jews' in the portico of Solomon in the Temple, points to himself and claims that he is the visible presence of God among them. The argument over Jesus' messianic claims comes to a conclusion. No Messiah in the Jewish expectation would claim to replace the Temple itself, but that is what Jesus does in 10.30... The setting of these words of Jesus within the feast of the Dedication determines the reader's understanding that the union between God and the Temple which was seen as God's presence to his people, is perfected in Jesus because of his oneness with the Father.[96]

It is evident from this text (10.27-30), then, that the security of believers is undergirded by the oneness between Jesus and the Father,[97] and it is to the subject of that oneness in the prayer of Jn 17 that I now turn.

9.8 *'So That They May Be One, As We Are One'*

9.8.1 *Exegesis in John 17*

It is appropriate to consider this because a common understanding of the Temple was that God was especially present there. If Jesus is one with the Father, then the presence of God the Father is especially present in him, and if the disciples share in that oneness, then they too share in the presence of God. Together, Father, Son and disciples constitute a new kind of Temple. I believe this theme is present in John 17, where Jesus (the new high priest) seeks the unity of his people in the new Temple.

The petition for unity arises first in Jesus' prayer for the original disciples in conjunction with the prayer for their keeping (17.11): Πάτερ ἅγιε, τήρησον αὐτοὺς ἐν τῷ ὀνόματί σου ᾧ δέδωκάς μοι, ἵνα ὦσιν ἓν καθὼς ἡμεῖς. But it also occurs with more elaboration in the prayer for the disciples who will believe because of the word of the original disciples (17.21-23a):

> ἵνα πάντες ἓν ὦσιν, καθὼς σύ, πάτερ, ἐν ἐμοὶ κἀγὼ ἐν σοί, ἵνα καὶ αὐτοὶ ἐν ἡμῖν ὦσιν, ἵνα ὁ κόσμος πιστεύῃ ὅτι σύ με ἀπέστειλας. κἀγὼ τὴν δόξαν ἣν δέδωκάς μοι δέδωκα αὐτοῖς, ἵνα ὦσιν ἓν καθὼς ἡμεῖς ἕν· ἐγὼ ἐν αὐτοῖς καὶ σὺ ἐν ἐμοί, ἵνα ὦσιν τετελειωμένοι εἰς ἕν...

Lindars (*John*, p. 525) suggests that ἵνα ὦσιν ἓν καθὼς ἡμεῖς in 17.11 should be omitted because the thought seems to intrude on the main theme of protecting the disciples 'as guardians of the revelation'. Further, he

---

96. Moloney, *Signs and Shadows*, pp. 147-48.

97. Brown, *John*, I, p. 408: 'This unity which is communicated to believers is what prevents anyone from snatching them from either Father or Son.'

questions whether a petition for the unity of the disciples is necessary. He says, 'John never elsewhere questions the unity of the disciples, whereas we have the precedent of 10.16 for the theme of the unity of the Church' (p. 525).

I believe, on the contrary, that there is no dislocation of the theme of protection with the introduction of a petition for unity. The context is Jesus' departure from the world and leaving his disciples in the world: καὶ οὐκέτι εἰμὶ ἐν τῷ κόσμῳ, καὶ αὐτοὶ ἐν τῷ κόσμῳ εἰσίν...

Being left in the world the disciples are under threat of apostasy and disunity. The unity of the Twelve has already been shattered with the departure of Judas from the supper (13.27-30). And the apostasy of Judas is highlighted in the next few words of Jesus' prayer (17.12). Further, the scattering of the disciples is clearly in view in 16.32 and recalls Matthew's allusion to Zech. 13.7 in Matt. 26.31: Πατάξω τὸν ποιμένα, καὶ διασκορπισθήσονται τὰ πρόβατα τῆς ποίμνης. On the eve of the passion with its treachery and violence, it would seem entirely appropriate for Jesus to pray for the protection and unity of his disciples. What is especially significant for our purpose is that the context of this brief prayer for unity (17.11) makes connection with texts that have to do with the shepherd and the sheep. This is not surprising since the two previous Johannine verses dealing with unity of God's flock/children (10.16; 11.52) also have pastoral connotations.

The petition for unity in 17.21-23 for the wider community of disciples is more substantial and complex, and I will come to that in due course.

In the meantime we recall that the reference to Jesus' oneness with the Father in Jn 10.30 (in the context of the Feast of the Dedication) sent a message to the Jews that God's union with the Temple had now been replaced by Jesus' union with God the Father.[98] God's presence was no longer in the Jewish Temple in Jerusalem but was now in the person of Jesus. Jesus is the new Temple (2.21). While the context of Jn 17.21-23 is Jesus' prayer for his disciples as they engage in mission in the world, the oneness proclamation of Jn 10.30 should be recalled.

9.8.2 *Oneness and Temple in the Old Testament, Especially Psalm 133*

God's oneness with his people had been centred in the Temple. Mention has already been made (see 8.11) of Exod. 15.17 and how it was applied to the Temple:

---

98. See Moloney's relevant comment above at 9.7.3. See also 9.8.1.

> You brought them [your people] in and planted
> them on the mountain of your own possession,
> the place, O LORD, that you made your abode,
> the sanctuary, O LORD, that your hands have established.

YHWH's presence was in the Temple; it was his dwelling place (Ps. 84.1-2; 26.8). One met with YHWH in the Temple. This oneness of YHWH with the Temple and its worship drew the people together into one. As an example Psalm 133[99] celebrates this unity of the people of Israel through the ordination of the high priest who mediated between YHWH and the people at Zion, the place of YHWH's presence. I now consider this psalm to see how the theme of oneness is related to the person of the high priest and the place of Zion.

MT
שִׁיר הַמַּעֲלוֹת לְדָוִד
הִנֵּה מַה טּוֹב וּמַה נָּעִים שֶׁבֶת אַחִים גַּם יַחַד
כַּשֶּׁמֶן הַטּוֹב עַל הָרֹאשׁ יֹרֵד עַל הַזָּקָן
זְקַן אַהֲרֹן שֶׁיֹּרֵד עַל פִּי מִדּוֹתָיו
כְּטַל חֶרְמוֹן שֶׁיֹּרֵד עַל הַרְרֵי צִיּוֹן
כִּי שָׁם צִוָּה יהוה אֶת הַבְּרָכָה חַיִּים עַד הָעוֹלָם

Kraus eliminates זְקַן אַהֲרֹן שֶׁיֹּרֵד עַל פִּי מִדּוֹתָיו on the grounds that it interrupts the parallelism of the two comparisons in the third and fifth lines with what he calls a 'digressive statement'. He quotes H. Schmidt: 'It is completely absurd for the whole meaning of this little poem to think of a particular beard, and on top of it all the beard of a historical person.'[100] In defence of the psalmist one needs to remember that Aaron was a unique 'historical person'. He was the original high priest and the father of the Aaronic priesthood. The oil flowing down was very likely the anointing oil of ordination (Exod. 29.7; Lev. 8.12). This could be why it is described as שֶׁמֶן הַטּוֹב. Anointing oil is טוֹב by virture of its special and symbolic use and also by its fragrance (Exod. 30.23-25, 30).

Kraus also emends צִיּוֹן to צִיָּה (dry place) because '"to the hills of Zion" is topographically impossible and also absurd in a highly fanciful poetic style'.[101]

---

99. I choose Ps. 133 as my example because it highlights the theme of the oneness of the people of God through the high priest in the sanctuary. I believe this same theme is present in Jn 17 where Jesus (the new high Priest) seeks the unity of his people in the new Temple.

100. H.-J. Kraus, *Psalms 60–150 A Commentary* (trans. H.C. Oswald; Minneapolis: Augsburg–Fortress, 1989), p. 484.

101. Kraus, *Psalms 60–150*, p. 484. The unlikely transference of dew from Mt

The overall effect of the elimination of the line and the emendation is to make the psalm 'secular' so that 'Psalm 133 points to a profane, everyday connection' of brothers living harmoniously together on 'the undivided inheritance'. The oil 'is a soothing cosmetic that brings refreshment' and the dew 'refreshes and moistens the land'. 'Curious in both pictures is the verb ירד, which…probably alludes to the role of the oldest brother, who is not to insist on his rights but is to show himself kind and friendly to the younger ones.'[102]

Kraus's 'secular' interpretation has its difficulties. There is no mention of an 'undivided inheritance' in the text, although it is probably a fair assumption. It is not clear how the oil becomes a 'soothing cosmetic that brings refreshment'. Neither is it apparent how the oil and dew relate to brothers living harmoniously together. And how the verb ירד 'probably alludes to the role of the oldest brother' is nowhere evident. Significantly Kraus has completely ignored the first two words of the psalm's superscription—שיר המעלות.

It may be that originally the psalm was a wisdom statement in the style of the משל with illustrative comparisons, commending married brothers living together in the family homestead (cf. Deut. 25.5).[103] However, that is not the thrust of Psalm 133 as we have received it in the book of Psalms. It belongs to a collection called 'Songs of Ascent', which can best be understood as 'Pilgrim Songs'.[104] Consequently, cultic allusions will not be unexpected. Allen draws attention to the overlapping in terminology with Psalms 132 and 134.[105] 'Zion' clearly functions as a prominent motif in 132.13 and 134.3. שם (there) (133.3b) features emphatically in 132.17 and the concept of blessing (133.3b) is found in 132.15 and 134.2. Both Psalms 132 and 134 are obviously cultic, so it should not be surprising in view of the terminological links with them and the title of Psalm 133

Hermon to Mt Zion has also prompted other emendations, such as עיון ('Ijon', which is at the foot of Mt Hermon (cf. 1 Kgs 15.20; 2 Kgs 15.29).

102. All quotations are from Kraus, *Psalms 60–150*, p. 486.

103. Leslie C. Allen (*Psalms 101–150* [WBC, 21; Waco, TX: Word Books, 1983], p. 214) concludes: 'In form, then, the psalm is probably to be regarded as a Song of Zion influenced by wisdom characteristics.'

104. Kraus himself calls each one, including Ps. 133, 'A Pilgrimage Song'. Cf. also Allen, *Psalms 101–150*, p. 146: 'Pss 120-134 form a collection of cultic songs of diverse origins, probably sung by pilgrims in festival processions.' Later, in commenting on the collection as a whole he says: '…there is no total coherence apart from the nearly unbroken thread of Zion' (p. 221).

105. Allen, *Psalms 101-150*, p. 215.

('A Pilgrim Song') to discover references to the Temple and to the high priesthood.

The psalm celebrates the people of God (Israel, אָחִים) coming together to worship (שֶׁבֶת)[106] at festival time. They are not merely a collection of individuals, but rather a single community (גַם יַחַד).[107] This יַחַד[108] is likened to two things: the anointing oil of Aaron that runs down his beard and over the collar of his robes; and the dew of Hermon that flows down upon the mountains of Zion.[109] The first picture is the anointing of Aaron as high priest at the sanctuary. The high priest, resplendent in his robes and bearing the names of the sons of Israel in the breastpiece on his heart (Exod. 28.12, 19, 29), functions as a symbol of unity as he goes into the holy place. All the people come before YHWH through him and he mediates the blessing upon the family of God who gather at the sanctuary/Temple. The second picture is, as Kraus says, 'topographically impossible'. Mt Hermon is far north of Zion, situated in Syria, and perhaps notable for the heavy dew that fell on it. But the claims of Zion eclipse those of Hermon. The mountains of Zion inherit this precious and refreshing moisture, and it flows down their sides bringing fertility and growth. If Aaron is the one person through whom the whole community (יַחַד) is blessed, then Zion is the one place of blessing. This is emphasized in the final line:

---

106. יָשַׁב is used in relation to worship at the Temple in Pss 27.4 and 140.13.

107. The Qumran Community used this word to describe itself. Schnackenburg (*St John*, III, p. 439 n. 82) notes that יַחַד was a theological concept that was concerned with the communal life of the community, with strong cultic and ritual connections. Brown (*John*, II, p. 777) believes that the Johannine image of unity had a great deal in common with the יַחַד of Qumran, and A.T. Hanson ('Hodayot XV and John 17: A Comparison of Content and Form', *Hermathena* 18 [1974], pp. 45-58) compares the whole of the prayer of Jn 17 with this Qumran hymn. However, I think Ps. 133 has more in common with Jn 17 than with Qumran texts. As Schnackenburg points out (*St John*, III, p. 193) Qumran saw itself as a 'holy remnant' of Israel and aimed at community with God through angels. Neither of these points is true of the festal pilgrims of Ps. 133 or the Johannine community.

108. I take the point of comparison to be the יַחַד not the 'pleasure' as Kraus does.

109. Intriguingly a Jewish commentator, Rabbi David Kimhi (*The Commentary of Rabbi David Kimhi on Psalms CXX–CL* [ed. and trans. J. Baker and E.W. Nicholson; Cambridge: Cambridge University Press, 1973], pp. 57, 59), who sees Ps. 133 as post-exilic, understands 'Aaron' to correspond to Joshua son of Jehozadak, the high priest (Zech. 6.11), and the 'dew' to refer to the Messianic King (Zech. 6.12; cf. also Prov. 19.12; Mic. 5.6), Zerubbabel. He therefore understands that the opening of the Psalm refers to these two living together as brothers.

כי שם צוה יהוה את הברכה חיים עד העולם. This is possibly the blessing of Num. 6.23-27, the so-called Aaronic blessing.

This psalm, then, celebrates the family of God (Israel) coming together as a single community, united before YHWH in the high priest and in the holy place, ready to receive the blessing YHWH has commanded, which comes down like the precious anointing oil and the heavy dew. It provides a window through which we can glimpse something of the way in which the Temple and the high priest drew the family of YHWH together and united them. But these institutions drew their cohesive power from YHWH's choice of place (Deut. 12.5) and person (Exod. 28.1) to meet with his people.

Something of this thought lies behind Jesus' petition for his disciples. I have suggested above that in John Jesus is both the new high priest (see my 9.2.2) and the new Temple (2.21). God 'has become' united to Jesus. Those who seek God must come to Jesus (14.6). Jesus and the Father are one (10.30).[110]

Jesus' prayer is that both his present (Jn 17.11c) and future (Jn 17.21-23a) disciples will share in this oneness. I now turn to look at the second of these texts in greater detail.

9.8.3 *The Second and Longer Prayer for Oneness (17.21-23)*
The parallels, as well as the developments, in thought between v. 21 and vv. 22-23 can be seen more clearly when set out as follows:[111]

v. 21	*vv. 22-23*
ἵνα πάντες ἓν ὦσιν,	ἵνα ὦσιν ἓν
καθὼς σύ, πάτερ, ἐν ἐμοὶ	καθὼς ἡμεῖς ἕν·
κἀγὼ ἐν σοί,	ἐγὼ ἐν αὐτοῖς
	καὶ σὺ ἐν ἐμοί,

110. This echoes Zech. 14.9: MT ביום ההוא יהיה יהוה אחד ושמו אחד; LXX ἐν τῇ ἡμέρᾳ ἐκείνῃ ἔσται Κύριος εἷς, καὶ τὸ ὄνομα αὐτοῦ ἕν. We have seen how the Father has given his name to Jesus the Son (17.11, 12), so effectively both Jesus and the Father are of one name—יהוה. And in Jn 10.30 Jesus claims oneness with the Father.

111. The phrase that is at the beginning of v. 22 (κἀγὼ τὴν δόξαν ἣν δέδωκάς μοι δέδωκα αὐτοῖς) does not find a place in the table since it is dealing with the theme of glory rather than oneness. However, it is significant that the phrase is present in a passage expounding the oneness motif. I will consider this issue below. Cf. also the similarity of the table with v. 11: ἵνα ὦσιν ἓν καθὼς ἡμεῖς. Clearly vv. 21-23 are an elaboration on v. 11 with the addition of the goal of the world believing/knowing that the Father has sent the Son (and has loved the disciples as the Father has loved the Son).

ἵνα καὶ αὐτοὶ ἐν ἡμῖν ὦσιν,   ἵνα ὦσιν τετελειωμένοι εἰς ἕν,
ἵνα ὁ κόσμος πιστεύῃ   ἵνα γινώσκῃ ὁ κόσμος
ὅτι σύ με ἀπέστειλας.   ὅτι σύ με ἀπέστειλας
                                   καὶ ἠγάπησας αὐτοὺς
                                   καθὼς ἐμὲ ἠγάπησας.

Verse 21 sets out the goal of Jesus' new intercession, namely, the one-ness of the first and second generations of disciples. This request not only continues Jesus' earlier petition for the oneness of his disciples (v. 11), but also extends it in two ways: first, the oneness now includes believers other than the original disciples (cf. 10.16); and, second, the oneness of the disciples is not an end in itself, but a means to convince the world that Jesus is the sent one from the Father.[112] The fact that the oneness of the disciples is based in the oneness of the Son and the Father, is repeated in v. 21 (cf. v. 11), but this is developed in terms of the mutual indwelling of the Father and the Son (cf. v. 23; 14.10-11, 20).

With vv. 22-23 the prayer returns to a retrospect that suggests how Jesus has effected the oneness between the disciples, the Son and the Father. According to v. 22 it is τὴν δόξαν that the Father has given the Son and the Son has given the disciples that is the medium of the oneness shared by the Father, the Son and the disciples. The goal of the gift of glory from Father to Son, and Son to disciples, is their oneness, just as the goal of the τηρεῖν of the Father and the Son was also oneness (cf. vv. 11, 12). As in v. 11, the oneness mentioned here is based on the oneness of the Father and the Son. Verse 23 continues and develops the theme of oneness (cf. vv. 11-12, 21) through the concept of indwelling, which repeats with variations the theme of mutual indwelling found in v. 21.

Schnackenburg's comments are pertinent:

112. In both v. 21 and vv. 22-23 there are three ἵνα clauses. Most commentators (e.g. Bernard, Bultmann, Brown, Morris, Schnackenburg) take the first two in each set of verses as parallel final clauses dependent on the leading verb (ἐρωτῶ, v. 20; δέδωκα, v. 22) and the third ἵνα clause as a final clause dependent on the first two, that is, the unity of the disciples convinces the world. Given that the first two clauses in both cases concern the unity of the disciples, it seems best to take them together as the precondition for the world to believe that the Father sent the Son. However, E.C. Earwaker ('John xvii.21', *ExpTim* 75 [1964], pp. 316-17) proposed that all three clauses in each series be taken as independent final clauses. This would remove the dependence of the request for the world to believe on the unity of the disciples. This is unlikely. Jesus does not pray directly for the world (cf. 17.9) but through the testimony (the manifestation of unity) of the disciples the world is not bereft of hope.

By Jesus being in the disciples and the Father being in Jesus, the community of disciples is entirely filled with God's being and in this way joined and kept together themselves. It becomes a perfect unity (εἰς ἕν) and is at the same time called to make the mystery of divine unity visible in brotherly love. It is this that will enable the world to know that Jesus, who makes the Christian community the visible manifestation of the divine being, is the one sent by God. The community's unity and expression of love is ultimately a mystery of divine love.[113]

9.8.4 *Conclusion*

The unity for which Jesus prays has its genesis in his oneness with the Father. Four times he refers to his disciples becoming one and each time he defines that unity in terms of his relationship with the Father (vv. 11, 21, 22, 23). As I showed in my consideration of Psalm 133, Israel's unity was defined in terms of a special place (the Temple) and special person (the high priest) both of which brought them into the presence of YHWH. But now Jesus has replaced the Temple and high priest. He is the one who now brings his disciples into the presence of YHWH, indeed he is the one through whom oneness with the Father is effected (14.6). Whereas in the past the unity was achieved through the institutions of the Temple, now it is accomplished through believing in Jesus through the word of the original disciples (v. 20).

9.9 *'The Glory Which You Have Given to Me I Have Given Them'*

9.9.1 *Exposition of the Retrospect within the Gospel of John*

This retrospect (v. 22) has to do with the unity discussed in the last section. Indeed the intended effect of Jesus giving the Father's gift of glory to his disciples is ἵνα ὦσιν ἕν καθὼς ἡμεῖς ἕν. How this happens is a matter I will discuss later. For now I will focus on the δόξα/δοξάζειν motif that occurs throughout this prayer[114] and see how it impinges on the theme of Jesus as the fulfilment of the Temple complex.

---

113. Schnackenburg, *St John*, III, p. 193.

114. (a) The petition for mutual glorification of the Father and the Son (v. 1). (b) A retrospect in which Jesus says to the Father, 'I have glorified you on earth by finishing the work you gave me to do' (v. 4). (c) A further petition in which Jesus asks the Father to glorify him with the glory he had in his presence before the world existed (v. 5). (d) A retrospect in which Jesus says he has been glorified in the disciples the Father has given him (v. 10). (e) A retrospect in which Jesus says he has passed on the glory the Father has given him to the disciples so that they may be one (v. 22). (f) Jesus

In my discussion of the Prologue, and especially 1.14 (see 4.4.4), I noted that there were Exodus allusions in these passages. I pointed to Exod. 25.8 where YHWH commands Moses: (MT) ועשׂו לי מקדשׁ ושׁכנתי בתוכם; that is, 'And make me a sanctuary, so that I may dwell among them.' For this the LXX has Καὶ ποιήσεις μοι ἁγίασμα, καὶ ὀφθήσομαι ἐν ὑμῖν; namely, 'And you shall make a sanctuary for me and I shall be seen among you.' In the next verse (v. 9) this sanctuary is called a מִשְׁכָּן (LXX σκηνῆς, which is related to the verb σκηνόω used in Jn 1.14 to describe the Word becoming flesh and tenting among us). This Old Testament sanctuary (מִשְׁכָּן) was filled with the glory of YHWH (Exod. 40.34-35, וכבוד יהוה מלא את המשׁכן). It seems that neither Moses nor the people actually saw the glory of YHWH. What Moses saw was the back of YHWH's goodness (equivalent to glory; Exod. 33.17-22) and the people saw the 'reflection' of that vision of YHWH's 'muted' glory in Moses' face (34.29-35), but even that had to be veiled. In contrast the disciples of Jesus beheld the glory of the Word made flesh, the glory of the Father's only Son (Καὶ ὁ λόγος σὰρξ ἐγένετο καὶ ἐσκήνωσεν ἐν ἡμῖν, καὶ ἐθεασάμεθα τὴν δόξαν αὐτοῦ, δόξαν ὡς μονογενοῦς παρὰ πατρός...) without impediment.[115] It seems then that Jesus, the Word made flesh, is the new sanctuary/Temple[116] who has 'tented amongst us' and his disciples saw his glory. As Jn 1.14 hints this glory has been given to him by the Father (17.22), and if the analogy with the Old Testament sanctuary holds firm, then it is the glory of YHWH that has been given to Jesus.[117]

How did the disciples see the glory of Jesus? Following the miracle at

---

prays that the disciples the Father has given him may be with him to see his glory, which the Father has given him because he loved him before the foundation of the world (cf. [c]) (v. 24).

115. Dodd (*Interpretation*, p. 207 n. 1): 'Christ as Logos, as the Son of the Father, is invested with the nature, character, and power of the Eternal, from eternity (πρὸ καταβολῆς κόσμου); the manifestation of this nature, character, and power, in time, takes place in the words and works of the incarnate Logos, in which accordingly, the כבוד, δόξα, is "manifested" and "seen" by those who have faith.'

116. Ps. 26.8 is a clear statement about the Temple being a dwelling place for YHWH's glory: יהוה אהבתי מעון ביתך ומקום משׁכן כבודך (LXX: Κύριε, ἠγάπησα εὐπρέπειαν οἴκου σου, καὶ τόπον σκηνώματος δόξης σου). Whether it is a dwelling for YHWH as the NRSV suggests is not so clear. מעון perhaps could signify a dwelling or habitation for God when taken in conjunction with Deut. 26.15, but the LXX distances itself from such a suggestion by translating מעון as εὐπρέπειαν (beauty).

117. See above at 9.5 for the extensive argument to to show that Jesus identifies as ἐγώ εἰμι and that expression, in turn, is equivalent to יהוה.

the wedding in Cana of Galilee we read, ἐφανέρωσεν τὴν δόξαν αὐτοῦ, καὶ ἐπίστευσαν εἰς αὐτὸν οἱ μαθηταὶ αὐτου (2.11). Prior to raising Lazarus from the dead Jesus says to Martha, Οὐκ εἶπόν σοι ὅτι ἐὰν πιστεύσῃς ὄψῃ τὴν δόξαν τοῦ θεοῦ... (11.40). Brown[118] suggests that these two verses form an inclusion between the first and the last of the signs that Jesus performed publicly, thus implying that all the signs manifested the glory of Jesus.[119]

9.9.2 *An Intriguing Text*

However, what does it mean that the Father has given his glory to Jesus (17.22)? Shirbroun has discovered an intriguing text[120] where glory is used to describe the ordination of Joshua at the hands of Moses, namely, Num. 27.18-23, whose text is as follows:

MT	ונתתה מהודך עליו למען ישמעו כל עדת בני ישראל
LXX	Καὶ δώσεις τῆς δόξης σου ἐπ᾽ αὐτόν, ὅπως ἂν εἰσακούσωσιν αὐτοῦ οἱ υἱοὶ Ἰσραήλ
NRSV	You shall give him some of your authority, so that all the congregation of the Israelites may obey him.

The fact that the LXX has translated הוד as δόξα indicates that for the translators of the LXX, הוד and כבוד are related. In fact G. Warmuth notes that הוד and כבוד are found in synonymous parallelism in Ps. 21.6(5) and argues that 'it is best to translate הוד here [Num. 27.20] by "glory, majesty, authority"'.[121]

The context of Num. 27.20 makes clear that the giving of the הוד/δόξα is the commissioning of Joshua to carry on the task of leadership that had originally been given to Moses. What authorizes Joshua's leadership in the future is his share in the הוד/δόξα of Moses. But that leadership/authority is viewed in the semantic context of הוד/δόξα. It may be that something of this thought lies behind the use of ἐξουσία in Jn 1.12: ἔδωκεν αὐτοῖς ἐξουσίαν τέκνα θεοῦ γενέσθαι. Commentators have drawn attention to

118. Brown (*John*, I, p. 436). Cf. also Schnackenburg (*St John*, II, p. 338) who misses the inclusion but makes the same point.

119. Shirbroun ('Name of God', pp. 161-63) sees these signs of Jesus as deeds of salvation and a fulfilment of Isaiah's and Deutero-Isaiah's eschatological vision of the glory of Yhwh (closely related to salvation) being revealed throughout the whole world (cf. Isa. 6.3; 40.5; 59.19; 60.1-2; 66.18-19).

120. Shirbroun ('Name of God', pp. 167-68) has extensive evidence to prove that 'glory' is a valid translation for הוד and I will not repeat it here.

121. G. Warmuth, *TDOT*, III, pp. 353-55.

ἐξουσία being a surprising word to use, especially when becoming a child of God is the work of God (v. 13).[122] No doubt ἐξουσία should be translated as 'authority', but with the understanding that the the the word lies within the semantic field of הוד/δόξα. Within that field it acquires notions of 'privilege' and 'honour' and perhaps even 'glory'. That is, belonging to the family of God is to share in the 'family' of God (Father and Son) (cf. 20.19), which, according to Jn 1.12, is a privilege/honour.

This perspective allows us to gain some insight into what Jesus means when in 17.22 he says that passing on the gift of the Father's glory to the disciples will effect their unity. What is the glory of the Father? That he should be a true Father to the Son; and the glory of the Son is that he should be a true Son to the Father. This is implied in the mutual indwelling language that is used of the Father and Jesus: 'As you, Father, are in me, and I am in you' (17.21). This mutuality in the Father/Son relationship is the Father's glory, which has been given to the Son. Giving this glory to the disciples means they share in the family of God, that is, the Father and the Son. And since the disciples share in this family, they must also reflect the oneness between Father and Son in their corporate life.

The word group of הוד/δόξα raises another possibility that is more useful for my purpose of discerning Temple and high priestly connections in John 17. Earlier I discussed Ben Sira 45.12 (see 9.5.7). This text describes the mitre with the golden plate on which the divine name was inscribed as a καύχημα τιμῆς (a 'pride' of honour).[123] Even though the Hebrew of 45.12 is fragmentary, it is clear enough that the Greek words, καύχημα τιμῆς, represent the Hebrew הוד כבוד, 'majesty of glory'. Hayward's comment on 45.12 is worth repeating: 'From this text we may now deduce that a principal element in Simon's 'majesty' (הוד), which features so prominently in his performing the Tamid, consists in his wearing the Divine Name above his forehead.'[124]

---

122. Brown (*John*, I, p. 11) comments: '[T]o make of this [ἐξουσία] a semi-judicial pronouncement whereby the Word gave men the right to become God's sons is to introduce an element strange to Johannine thought: sonship is based on divine begetting, not on any claim on man's part.' Bultmann (*John*, pp. 57-58 n. 5) thinks ἐξουσία is an awkward attempt to translate נתן, 'he gave them to become'. He goes on to say, 'There is no semitic equivalent to ἐξουσία in the sense of "authority".' Lindars (*John*, p. 91) remarks that 'the expression is open to misunderstanding'.

123. The English translation of the LXX (Brenton) has 'an ornament of honour', which fails to capture the thrust of the Greek.

124. Hayward, *The Jewish Temple*, p. 83.

In discussion above I suggested that Jesus was given the name יהוה, a name which marks Jesus out as a high priest (see 9.5.7). Now we learn from Ben Sira that this name carries honour and glory. This, in part, may be the glory referred to in 17.22—the Father's gift to the Son—his name. What would it mean, then, for Jesus to give this glory to his disciples? It could mean doing the task of the high priest, namely, placing that name upon the disciples, the new Israel, in blessing.[125] This would be a fitting task for Jesus, who comes to fulfil the work of the high priest.

I suggest that it is through the honour and glory of sharing in the name of Y~H~WH, through Jesus, that the disciples are drawn together as one. Jesus is the focus of the corporate life of the disciples—the Jesus who is both high priest and Temple.

9.9.3 *Summary*

The theme of glory pervades John. It is introduced in 1.14 where Exodus echoes indicate that Jesus, the Word made flesh, not the Jewish sanctuary, now tabernacles the glory of God. This glory is made manifest in the signs Jesus performs in his public ministry.

In an attempt to discover the meaning of the Father giving Jesus his glory, I follow Shirbroun's lead and consider Num. 27.20, where Moses gives some of his authority/glory to Joshua. This lead is taken up with respect to the ἐξουσία given to those who received Jesus to become the children of God (Jn 1.12). Consideration of the context tilted the meaning of ἐξουσία towards honour and glory rather than in a judicial direction. Conscious of the honour and glory associated with belonging to the family of God I looked at Jn 17.22 and concluded that the glory gifted to the Son and passed onto the disciples could well be the glory and honour of being children of God, participating in the oneness of the family of Father and Son.

Another possibility I explored was the glory of the name (יהוה) engraved on the high priest's turban. Previous discussion had raised the likelihood that the Father had given this name to Jesus and that as high priest he had placed this name upon his disciples, the new Israel. By sharing in this name through Jesus, who is the replacement of the high priest and the holy place of the Temple, the disciples are drawn into the oneness Jesus enjoys with the Father.

---

125. Cf. Num. 6.23-27 and the discussion above at 9.5.7.

9.10 'For Their Sakes I Sanctify Myself'

This petition occurs in a context where the theme of sanctification dominates: ἁγίασον αὐτοὺς ἐν τῇ ἀληθείᾳ· ὁ λόγος ὁ σὸς ἀλήθειά ἐστιν. καθὼς ἐμὲ ἀπέστειλας εἰς τὸν κόσμον, κἀγὼ ἀπέστειλα αὐτοὺς εἰς τὸν κόσμον· καὶ ὑπὲρ αὐτῶν ἐγὼ ἁγιάζω ἐμαυτόν, ἵνα ὦσιν καὶ αὐτοὶ ἡγιασμένοι ἐν ἀληθείᾳ (vv. 17-19).

The only previous occurrence of the verb ἁγιάζειν in John is 10.36, where Jesus is defending himself against the Jews' charge of blasphemy in Solomon's porch of the Temple during the Festival of the Dedication. Jesus says that the Father has sanctified him and sent him into the world. Moloney points out that most scholars pay little attention to the context of the Feast of Dedication[126] and argue that the expression has no sacral significance, and that it simply means 'to set apart'. However, he goes on to say:

> But Dedication remembered the consecration of the altar of holocausts that replaced 'the desolating sacrilege' of Antiochus IV. Jesus' presence to the world as the one sent by the Father, and the visible presence of God in the world, brings to perfection what was only a sign and a shadow in Judas's act of consecration in 164 B.C. God is no longer present in the consecrated stone altar, but in the flesh and blood of the consecrated and sent Son.[127]

In Jn 17.17-19 there are two occurrences of the verb ἁγιάζειν: the first (v. 17) when Jesus asks the Father to sanctify the disciples and the second when Jesus sanctifies himself for the sake of his disciples (v. 19). These two uses of the verb are dissimilar in the sense that the purpose of the sanctification is different in each case. In the case of the disciples they are sanctified to be sent into the world; in the case of Jesus he sanctifies himself 'for their sakes' (ὑπὲρ αὐτῶν).

The sanctification of the disciples in v. 17 is partly parallel to the Father's sanctification of Jesus in 10.36. In both instances those sanctified are sanctified to be sent into the world. In Jesus' case, as Moloney pointed out (see above, 9.10 and n. 138), he is sanctified as the flesh and blood presence of God in the world. The disciples are also sanctified to be God's 'sent ones' in the world, but their sanctification is evidently dependent on Jesus' self-sanctification.

---

126. See, however, my discussion of the Feast of Dedication at 7.3.1-4.
127. Moloney, *Signs and Shadows*, pp. 149-50. Brown (*John*, I, p. 411) entitles his study of 10.22-39, 'Jesus is consecrated in place of the temple altar'.

The means by which the disciples' sanctification is accomplished is the truth of the word of the Father (ἁγίασον αὐτοὺς ἐν τῇ ἀληθείᾳ· ὁ λόγος ὁ σὸς ἀλήθειά ἐστιν). Earlier discussion of the preposition in the phrase ἐν τῷ ὀνόματί σου (vv. 11-12), concluded that the ἐν was not instrumental but locative. Schnackenburg[128] believes the same applies with regard to the phrase ἐν τῇ ἀληθείᾳ (v. 17), which he says 'corresponds to' ἐν τῷ ὀνόματί σου. If this is the case, then Jesus is asking the Father in v. 17 to sanctify his disciples in the sphere of truth. The truth is not only the teaching (ῥήματα) Jesus has passed on to the disciples, but also himself, ὁ Λόγος (1.14), the truth (17.17). As the disciples are drawn to Jesus (12.32) and united to him (cf. the subsequent requests for unity, vv. 21-23) and live in the sphere of his teaching, then they are sanctified and become those sent of God into the world.

Mention of Jn 12.32 leads on to the retrospect of 17.19: καὶ ὑπὲρ αὐτῶν ἐγὼ ἁγιάζω ἐμαυτόν, ἵνα ὦσιν καὶ αὐτοὶ ἡγιασμένοι ἐν ἀληθείᾳ. As mentioned above Jesus' self-sanctification provides the basis for the sanctification of the disciples. Indeed there is a sense in which their sanctification comes about by living in the sphere of Jesus' sanctification because his sanctification is ὑπὲρ αὐτῶν.

In agreement with many others Lindars says:

> the use of the preposition ὑπὲρ unmistakably introduces a sacrificial con-notation. John has used it in the context of laying down one's life in the Shepherd allegory (10.11, 15-18), in the unwitting prophecy of Caiaphas (11.51f.), and in the Vine allegory (15.13).[129]

Whether Jesus is also sanctifying himself as priest in 17.19 (cf. Exod. 28.41) as well as sacrifice (Exod. 13.2; Deut. 15.19) is not clear. Bultmann (*John*, p. 510 n. 5) argues against the double sanctification by saying that he would be therefore 'depicted as both priest and sacrifice'. But this is not

---

128. Schnackenburg, *St John*, III, p. 185; Lindars (*John*, p. 528) makes the link with v. 11 too.

129. Lindars, *John*, pp. 528-29. Hoskyns (*The Fourth Gospel*, pp. 502-503), especially, has an extensive discussion on the sacrificial character of Jesus' sanctification and entitles his treatment of v. 19 'Jesus dedicates himself as an effective sacrifice'. Lindars also mentions 6.51 as an allusion to the eucharistic words of Jesus. However, as I have argued in dealing with the Passover Festival, I believe that Jesus is speaking of himself in 6.51 primarily as the Passover Lamb. See 7.1.5.2. This is against Hoskyns (*The Fourth Gospel*, p. 506) and Bultmann (*John*, p. 511), who believe the Eucharist and the words of institution (Mk 14.22-25) are in view.

an insuperable problem. Jesus elsewhere is represented as both priest and
victim (Heb. 9.11-14), and John is not averse to seeing Jesus fulfilling
multiple aspects of Temple life. Against Bultmann I favour the double
aspect of Jesus' sanctification. However, Bultmann is correct when he says,
'Jesus' self-sacrifice takes the place of priestly sacrifice' (*John*, p. 510
n. 5).

My conclusion is that Jesus' sanctification of himself is a consecration
to sacrifice for the sake of his disciples. The sacrificial language clearly
evokes Temple echoes that have been simmering throughout my discussion of this prayer.

9.11 *Summary and Overall Conclusion*

In my introductory first chapter I argued that in the light of internal considerations of the Gospel of John and a brief statement from Polycrates
where 'John' is described as ὁ ἐγενήθη ἱερεὺς τὸ πέταλον πεφορεκώς,
the author, the Beloved Disciple, had priestly connections (see 1.3.2). I
believe this provides some justification for searching for high priestly and
Temple allusions in Jesus' prayer of John 17. Some preliminary investigation of Jesus' encounter with the Jewish high priesthood in Jn 18.12-24
revealed a subtle critique of the priesthood and a hint that it had been
superseded by Jesus himself. Encouraged by this I then turned to John 17
and analysed a number of petitions that seem to indicate that in his prayer
Jesus was functioning as a high priest.

I examined 17.11c where Jesus speaks of the name that the Father has
given him. I concluded this name was ἐγὼ εἰμι, which is closely related,
if not equivalent, to YHWH, the name worn on the head of the high priest
when he goes to offer sacrifice (and prayers) on behalf of the people. I
discovered that in the manifestation of the name of YHWH (17.6, 24) by
means of the predicated 'I ams' there were links with the Temple itself and
the Temple festivals, perhaps with the exception of Jn 14.6. I found 'the
bread of life' evokes the Festival of the Passover; 'the light of the world',
the Festival of Tabernacles; 'the door' has links with the door of the Temple; 'the good shepherd who lays down his life for [ὑπὲρ] the sheep',
points to sacrifice on the Temple altar; 'the resurrection and the life',
echoes the Festival of Dedication; the 'way, the truth and the life', has
strong Exodus allusions; and we saw how 'the true vine', through Pseudo-
Philo, points to Jesus as the true Temple. Therefore the retrospect on the

manifestation of the name of Jn 17.6, 24, as I have interpreted it within the Gospel, has links with the Temple and the Temple festivals.

The petition for the preservation of the disciples (17.11-12) echoes the powerful petition of God's people for protection and safety, especially as it comes to expression in the psalms. We found that the sphere of safety was often perceived to be the Temple (Zion) (e.g. Ps. 125.2-3; 1 Kgs 1.50; 2.28) and the name of YHWH (Num. 6.24-27; Prov. 18.10). The oneness of Jesus and the Father (Jn 10.30) strengthens the preservation of the disciples (10.28-29).

I illustrated the prayer for the unity of the disciples (17.11, 21-23a) by an exegesis of Psalm 133 where we saw that YHWH's choice of place (the Temple) and person (the high priest) brought the people together as a community. I believe that this reflects something of the Johannine Jesus. He has become the new Temple and the new high priest and thereby brings his disciples together into a new community, a new Temple.

In relation to the petition that the glory gifted to the Son be given to the disciples (17.22), we saw this may refer to the glory and honour of being the children of God (cf. 1.12; 20.17b), and thereby participating in the oneness of the family of Father and Son. We also observed that the Divine Name of YHWH, worn by the high priest, is associated with glory and honour and that this name was placed upon the people of God by the high priest in blessing (Num. 6.23-27). Now Jesus as the new high priest blesses his disciples and places the name of YHWH upon them. By sharing in this name through Jesus they share in the honour and glory associated with the name.

The final petition I considered was Jesus' petition: 'For their sakes I sanctify myself' (17.17-19; cf. 10.36). This is sacrificial language. The Father has already sanctified Jesus (10.36). However, in *his* prayer Jesus *sanctifies himself* (17.19) for the sake (ὑπὲρ) of his disciples. So this is a further sanctifying of Jesus, a self-sanctification. I believe this latter sanctification indicates that Jesus is a sacrificial victim. Such a victim would traditionally have been sacrificed on the Jerusalem Temple altar by a priest. But Jesus is not to be sacrificed in the Jerusalem Temple by the high priest. He will go to Golgotha and lay down his life of himself (10.18). He is both high priest and victim, so he must offer himself.[130]

On the basis of his self-consecration Jesus prays for the sanctification of

---

130. Cf. 19.17 where Jesus carries 'the cross by himself', whereas in Lk. 23.26 Simon of Cyrene is made to carry it.

his disciples. This undergirds the prayer as a whole, especially the petitions I have highlighted: the prayer for the preservation of the disciples, their one-ness and their glory. Each of these aspects of the disciples' communal life derives its significance from the Temple imagery that I have discussed.[131]

131. I believe that the language of mutual indwelling, especially in 17.21, 23 and perhaps 26c, could provide a bridge between the Temple imagery and the nature of the oneness for which Jesus prays in this prayer. Mutual indwelling language is also found in Jn 10.38; 14.17, 20; 15.1-9. Does this language come from the Temple? Certainly some of the psalmists longed to dwell permanently in the Temple to be close to YHWH (e.g. Pss. 23.6b; 27.4). And there are indications that the Temple was a dwelling place for YHWH and his glory (Ps. 26.8). Is this a possible background for the mutual indwelling language of John? This could be a topic for further research, and should it be discovered that this sort of language can be traced to Temple life in Israel, then it would certainly strengthen the case for finding Temple allusions in Jesus' prayer for the oneness of his disciples. Pascal-Marie Jerumanis has made an in-depth study of 'demeurer' in John (*Réaliser La Communion avec Dieu: Croire, vivre et demeurer dans l'évangile selon S. Jean* [Ebib, NS 32; Paris: Librarie Lecoffre J. Gabalda et Marie Curie, 1996]). However, his investigation lacks a focus on Temple imagery.

Chapter 10

Summary and Conclusions

The goal of this study has been to explore the Temple theme in the Gospel of John. In the introductory chapter I noted that, until Mary Coloe's recent research, this has not been done systematically and extensively. But in the commentaries and a number of publications there have been references to the Temple and Jesus' relationship to it. These encouraged me to search for a Temple theme in John.

I began by considering briefly the authorship, dating and intended readership of John. My purpose in this was to see if any of the conclusions would favour the possibility of a Temple theme in John. On authorship I concluded from external and internal evidence that the author possibly had priestly connections, which may have prompted an interest in the Temple and its institutions. With regard to the intended readership, I believe that both Jews and Gentiles, both Christians and non-Christians, could well have been among John's intended readership. I believe further that this intended readership would be people who were concerned, along with other matters, about Jewish questions with respect to the relevance of the festivals and the place of worship. With regard to dating I decided the evidence favoured a post-70 CE date for John, possibly around 85 CE. This means that John would be writing into a situation where the Temple and its associated rituals would be gone. For those concerned with Jewish matters the urgent question would be, What now?

This question set the stage for my next chapter, 'Outside the Johannine Text'. Given that the evidence demonstrates that the Jerusalem Temple was a foundational institution in the history and life of first-century Judaism and was well supported by both Palestinian and Diaspora Jews,[1] it was not surprising that contemporary writings reflected much grief and

---

1. It seems that the importance of the Temple was also acknowledged by the Romans. Their very determination to destroy it highlighted their belief that it was a strategic rallying point for Jewish loyalties.

soul-searching over the demise of the Temple in 70 CE. Various explanations for this demise were offered, the most popular among the writers I looked at being the plan and will of God. While the authors reflect the struggle of accepting this explanation, it does at least leave the way open for new possibilities in the wake of the fall of the Temple. I traced a number of responses, one of the most important being the replacement of the Temple cult with a renewed emphasis on the Torah. I noted that those involved in this response advocated deeds of lovingkindness (obedience to the Torah) as an effective sacrifice and saw their community in terms of Temple imagery. A second response, not exclusive of the first, was the emergence of *merkabah* mysticism and apocalypticism. With the elimination of the Temple, the meeting place with God, it is not surprising that individuals sought God through mysticism and visions of a heavenly Temple. In the third and fourth responses I considered two opposite stances on the question of re-establishing a physical Temple in Jerusalem. Both of these have political implications. On the one hand, those who supported a quietist eschatology (*2 Baruch* and Yohanan ben Zakkai) left all in God's hands and did not advocate any military agenda. On the other hand, those who endorsed an activist eschatology were willing to fight. The fact that there was a war in 135 CE testifies that this was a sufficiently popular view to spark a rebellion.

Given that the Temple had fallen in 70 CE and that it had generated a number of responses, it is not unexpected that the Christians also offered a response. Indeed, Neusner in his article lists four responses to the demise of the Temple, the second being the response of the Christian community.[2] My special concern in this study was to look at the Johannine Christian response. Consequently the subsequent chapters of the study were concerned with the exegesis and discussion of selected passages of John.

I looked first at Jn 2.13-22 where the Temple theme is obviously present. Jesus enters the Temple, drives out the sacrificial animals and possibly also the sellers, overturns the tables of the moneychangers pouring the coins onto the ground, and says, 'Stop making my Father's house a house of trade.' I noted that this passage stands in an eschatological context within John and, further encouraged by possible allusion to Zech 14.21 (also eschatological in context), I suggested that the episode should be interpreted as a two-sided sign heralding the day of YHWH, with attendant judgment and salvation. The judgment involves the destruction of the

---

2.   J. Neusner, 'Judaism in a Time of Crisis: Four Responses to the Destruction of the Second Temple', *Judaism* 21 (1972), pp. 313-27.

Temple, and, at a deeper level, the body of Jesus will be sacrificially consumed. But hope is intimated when Jesus announces that he will raise up the Temple in three days. The editorial comment in 2.21 makes it clear that he is talking of his body as a Temple, and therefore the resurrection is in view. I underlined the importance of 2.21 and suggested that this could be used as a kind of lens through which to see other Johannine references to the Temple that might not otherwise be detected. I suggested that this verse then provides a rationale for turning to other texts in John and exploring them for Temple allusions with respect to Jesus.

I then turned to the Prologue and observed that John presents the reader with a new beginning with the incarnation of the Word. This is in harmony with the eschatological thrust of 2.13-22 that I argued for in my exegesis of that passage. With the coming of Jesus Christ there is a fresh beginning.

In the Prologue John also offers a new hermeneutic of the Torah. The Torah becomes a signpost pointing towards Jesus. Jesus is the fulfilment of the Torah. And this is true of every aspect of Judaism, including the Temple and its associated ritual and festivals. There is some intimation of how this works out in my consideration of ἐσκήνωσεν in 1.14. Jesus 'tabernacles amongst us' in his flesh and so becomes a new Tent of Meeting with God. I noted that through Sinai imagery John presents the incarnation of the Word as a theophany (cf. Exod. 33.17–34.8) 'full of grace and truth'.

In the third place the proposed chiastic focus of the Prologue presents a new way of becoming members of God's family. Membership does not come through the old institutions of Israel, but now it is 'to those who receive him [the incarnate Word], who believe in his name, he gave power to become the children of God' (1.12).

Encouraged by these findings I turned to the programmatic vision of Jn 1.51. Despite the optimism of Davies, Hanson and McKelvey I found no pre-Christian evidence that Jacob's dream (undoubtedly alluded to in 1.51) had been connected to the Jerusalem Temple. Consequently I concluded that a Temple reference in 1.51 was unlikely. However, I noted the strong emphasis on the revelation of God through the Son of Man. Certainly the christological focus is maintained. Yet the conclusions of my exploratory probe into 1.51 indicate that the Temple theme is not necessarily found everywhere in John and that one needs to proceed with caution.

Next I turned to John 4. In the eschatological era Jesus has inaugurated through his crucifixion and resurrection, he advocates (proleptically) the worship of the Father in Spirit and in truth (4.24). The image of the living water (4.10, 14) can be read as representing the Spirit of Jesus who glorifies Jesus (16.14) and testifies on his behalf (15.26). Indeed it is possible that the Johannine Spirit functions as another Jesus. The living water can also be understood as representing the new Torah, the revelatory Word (1.1, 17) who has become flesh and dwelt among us (1.14). This Word is truth (17.17; 14.6). So worship in Spirit and truth is worship centred in Jesus. In this sense Jesus replaces the Temple.

Jesus replaces the Temple in John 4, but what of the Temple festivals in John 5–10? How does Jesus relate to the Festivals of Passover, Tabernacles, Dedication and the Sabbath?

It seems that Jesus has his own agenda when it comes to the Festivals. When the Passover of the Jews was near (2.13) Jesus drives out the sacrificial animals from the Temple; Jesus has his own καιρὸς (7.6) when it comes to the Festival of Tabernacles; at the time of the Festival of Dedication Jesus speaks of his own consecration by the Father (10.36); and he does the Father's works on the Sabbath (5.17; 9.3, 14).

I pointed to the pervasive and pivotal presence of the Passover Festival in John as a whole and I argued for that same presence in John 6 and interpreted the latter part of the chapter (6.51-71) in terms of Jesus being the present Passover Lamb in whom the disciples share by Spirit-generated faith. I concluded that the 'flesh' of the Jewish Passover is of no avail; it is the spiritually ingested Jesus, the Passover Lamb, appropriated by faith, that brings life (cf. 6.63). Jesus therefore fulfils the Jewish Passover by becoming the Passover Lamb himself.

In consideration of the Festival of Tabernacles I suggested that Jn 7.37-39 very likely has connections with the water that flows from the Temple in Ezek. 37.1-12. When these texts are read in conjunction with Jn 19.34 it seems that Jesus' crucified and pierced body is the new Temple from which the water, representing the Spirit, flows.

Also at the Festival of Tabernacles the illumination of the Court of Women finds fulfilment in Jesus' declaration that he is the light of the world (8.12).

At the Festival of Dedication I noted that the Jews repeat the profanations of Antiochus IV by taking up stones against Jesus (10.31), who is consecrated as the new Temple (10.36), the presence of God in their midst (10.30). In this sense Jesus brings the Festival of Dedication to fulfilment.

As for the Jewish Sabbath in John, it is overtaken by the day of the Father's works of salvation and judgment through the Son and the Son's works through the disciples. In this sense the eschatological Sabbath has come and the disciples of Jesus live in it. I do not believe there is sufficient evidence to say the Jewish Sabbath has been replaced by Sunday as a new Sabbath, but I do believe that the Sabbath has been transformed supremely and definitively through the death and resurrection of Jesus. 'Out of the darkness of the great Sabbath of 19.31 a greater Sabbath is born (20.1)' (see 7.4.8).

In Chapter 8 I explored John 13 and 14 and saw that, in the context of a farewell meal, Jesus gathers his own and prepares them for his departure. He washes their feet so they might have a share in him (13.8) and be cleansed (13.10) in preparation for entry into a new Temple, which is centred in Jesus himself.

This Temple is described more fully in Jn 14.2-3, where Jesus is 'the Father's house' in which his disciples share (cf. 13.8). There are many dwelling places, indicating, I believe, that there are places for all who believe in Jesus (17.20), including the 'other sheep' of 10.16. The departure of Jesus makes possible the gift of the Spirit, who is the continuing presence of Jesus (14.3) accessible to those who have not seen Jesus and yet come to believe (20.29).

In John 14 the primary focus is on Jesus as the new Temple, 'the Father's house', and it is in a secondary and derivatory sense that we can say the community of Jesus and his disciples are the new Temple.

In Chapter 9 I explored the prayer of John 17 for possible high priestly and Temple allusions. I argued that the name the Father gave to Jesus (17.11, 12) is ἐγώ εἰμι, a prominent name in the Gospel. Using Dt. Isa. I found a close association and evidence for equivalence of this name with YHWH, the name on the turban of the high priest when he went into the Temple to offer sacrifice and prayers on behalf of the people. This provided a high priestly link with Jesus as he, the fulfilment of the Temple, offered prayers for his people and consecrated himself (17.19) as a sacrificial offering for the sake of his people. I investigated the petitions for the safety of the disciples, their oneness and glory, and found they reflected Temple connections and high priestly allusions.

Encouraged by my conclusions on the authorship of John and some of the contemporary responses to the fall of the Jerusalem Temple, I entered the text of John where the Temple was especially and obviously prominent, namely at 2.13-22. Using 2.21 as a lens I focused on the Prologue, 4.16-26, and found the Temple theme further developed. I looked at the Temple Festivals of Passover, Tabernacles, Dedication and

Sabbath and discovered that in the first three Jesus fulfils them and in the case of the Sabbath, he transforms it. There are Temple themes in John 13 and 14 and also the great prayer of John 17. John 1.51 seemed to offer some development of the Temple theme, but when I assessed the evidence I concluded that I would be straining the text to find clear Temple allusions there.

I do not believe this study has by any means exhausted this rich Temple theme in John. I am confident there are still further passages which should be investigated from this perspective. For example, Judith Lieu has drawn attention to Jn 18.20 where Jesus testifies to the high priest that he has 'always taught in synagogues and in the Temple'.[3] While Lieu's analysis results in conclusions different from mine, I believe it is fruitful to explore all of John to see if further seams of Temple reference can be detected. Finally Mark Kinzer has suggested that the Temple theme in John can be linked with Wisdom Christology through careful consideration of Sir. 24.8-12.[4] However, despite a very tentative probe in this direction in my Appendix in Chapter 4.8, the detailed exploration of such a linkage has yet to be carried out.

3.   Lieu, 'Temple and Synagogue in John', *NTS* 45 (1999), pp. 51-69 (51).
4.   Kinzer, *Temple Christology*, pp. 451-52.

BIBLIOGRAPHY

Reference Works and Sources

Aland, B. *et al.* (eds.), *The Greek New Testament* (Stuttgart: United Bible Societies, 4th edn, 1994).

Bauer, W., W. Arndt and F.W. Gingrich, *A Greek–English Lexicon of the New Testament and Other Early Christian Literature* (Chicago: University of Chicago Press, 1957).

Blass, F., and A. Debrunner, *A Greek Grammar of the New Testament and Other Early Christian Literature* (Chicago: Chicago University Press, 1961).

Botterweck, G.J., and H. Ringren (eds.), *Theological Dictionary of the Old Testament* (trans. J.T. Willis, G.W. Bromiley and D.E. Green; 8 vols.; Grand Rapids: Eerdmans, 1974–1996).

Brenton, L., *The Septuagint with Apocrypha: Greek and English* (Peabody, MA: Hendrickson 1986 [1851]).

Brown, F., S.R. Driver and C.A. Briggs, *Hebrew and English Lexicon of the Old Testament with an Appendix Containing the Biblical Aramaic* (Peabody, MA: Hendrickson, 1979 [1906]).

Charlesworth, J. (ed.), *The Old Testament Pseudepigrapha. I. Apocalyptic Literature and Testaments* (Garden City, NY: Doubleday, 1985).

—*The Old Testament Pseudepigrapha. II. Expansions of the 'Old Testament' and Legends, Wisdom and Philosophical Literature, Prayers, Psalms and Odes, Fragments of Lost Judeo-Hellenistic Works* (Garden City, NY: Doubleday, 1985).

Chilton, B., *The Isaiah Targum* (ed. K. Cathcart *et al.*; Aramaic Bible, 11; Edinburgh: T. & T. Clark, 1987).

Cicero, 'Pro Flacco', in *Cicero in Twenty-Eight Volumes* (ed. G.P. Goold; trans. C. MacDonald; LCL, 10; Cambridge, MA: Harvard University Press; London: Heinemann, 1977), pp. 434-574.

Danby, H., *The Mishnah* (Oxford: Oxford University Press, 1933).

Elliger, K., and K. Rudolph, *Biblia Hebraica Stuttgartensia* (Stuttgart: Deutsche Bibelgesellschaft, 1983).

Freedman, H., and M. Simon (eds.), *Midrash Rabbah* (5 vols.; Hindhead, Surrey: Soncino, 2nd edn, 1977).

Funk, R. (trans. and ed.), *A Greek Grammar of the New Testament and Other Early Christian Literature: A Revision of F. Blass and A. Debrunner 'Grammatik des neutestamentlichen Greichisch,' Incorporating Supplementary Notes by A. Debrunner* (Chicago: University of Chicago Press, 1961).

García Martínez, Florentino, *The Dead Sea Scrolls Translated: The Qumran Texts in English* (trans. W.G.E. Watson; Leiden: E.J. Brill, 1994).

Ginzberg, L., *The Legends of the Jews* (7 vols.; Philadelphia: Jewish Publication Society of America, 1909–66).

Goldin, J. (trans.), *The Fathers According to Rabbi Nathan* (Yale Judaica Series, 10; New Haven: Yale University Press, 1995).

Harrington, D.J., and A.J. Saldarini, *Targum Jonathan of the Former Prophets* (ed. K. Cathcart *et al.*; Aramaic Bible, 10; Wilmington, DE: Michael Glazier, 1987).

Hatch, E., and H. Redpath, *A Concordance to the Septuagint and Other Greek Versions of the Old Testament* (Oxford: Clarendon Press, 1897).

Holladay, W.L., *A Concise Hebrew and Aramaic Lexicon of the the Old Testament* (Leiden: E.J. Brill, 1971).

Ignatius of Antioch, *Magnesians*, in *The Apostolic Fathers*, I (trans. K. Lake; London: Heinemann; New York: Macmillan, 1912).

Josephus, *Ten Volumes* (trans. H. St J. Thackeray, vols. 1–4; H. St J. Thackeray and R. Marcus, vol. 5; R. Marcus, vols. 6 and 7; R. Marcus completed and edited by A. Wikgren, vol. 8; L.H. Feldman, vols. 9 and 10; ed. T.E. Page *et al.*; LCL; London: William Heinemann, 1956–63).

Kittel, G., and G. Friedrich (eds.), *Theological Dictionary of the New Testament* (trans. G. Bromiley *et al.*; 10 vols.; Grand Rapids: Eerdmans, 1964–76).

Liddell, H.R., and R. Scott, *A Greek—English Lexicon: A New Edition Revised and Augmented throughout by H.S. Jones with the Assistance of R. McKenzie* (Oxford: Clarendon Press, 1925–40).

McIvor, J. Stanley (trans.), *The Targum of Chronicles* (ed. K. Cathcart *et al.*; Aramaic Bible, 19; Collegeville, MN: Liturgical Press, 1994).

McNamara, M., and M. Maher, *Targum Neofiti 1: Exodus; Targum Pseudo-Jonathan: Exodus* (ed. K. Cathcart *et al*; Aramaic Bible, 2; Edinburgh: T. & T. Clark, 1994).

Metzger, B., *A Textual Commentary on the Greek New Testament* (London: United Bible Societies, 1971).

Mills, W.E., *The Gospel of John: Bibliographies for Biblical Research* (NTS, 4; Lewiston, NY: Edward Mellen Press, 1995).

Neusner, J. (trans. and ed.), *The Tosefta: Quodoshim* (New York: Ktav, 1979).

Philo, *Philo in Eleven Volumes* (trans. F.H. Colson and G.H. Whitaker, vols. 1–5; and F.H. Colson, vols. 6-9; and R. Marcus, Suppl. I and II; ed. T.E. Page *et al.*; LCL; London: William Heinemann, 1929–53).

Polybius, *Polybius: The Histories in Six Volumes* (trans. W.R. Paton; ed. T.E. Page *et al.*; LCL; London: Heinemann; New York: G.P. Putman's Sons, 1922–54).

Rahlfs, A. (ed.), *Septuaginta id est Vetus Testamentum Graece iuxta LXX Interpretes* (2 vols.; Stuttgart: Privilegierte Württembergische Bibelanstalt, 1935).

Roberts, A., and J. Donaldson (eds.) *The Ante-Nicene Fathers*, I (Edinburgh: T. & T. Clark, 1872; repr. Grand Rapids: Eerdmans, 1981).

—*The Ante-Nicene Fathers*, III (Edinburgh: T. & T. Clark, 1872; repr Grand Rapids: Eerdmans, 1986).

Schaff, P. (ed.), *The Nicene and Post-Nicene Fathers of the Christian Church: St Augustine* VII (Grand Rapids: Eerdmans 1986 [1888]).

Schechter, S. (ed.), *Aboth de Rabbi Nathan* (Hildesheim: Georg Olms, 1979).

Seneca, *Seneca ad Lucilium Epistulae Morales* (trans. R.M. Gummere; ed. T.E. Page; LCL; London: Heinemann; New York: G.P. Putnam's Sons, 1920–30).

Tacitus, C., *The Histories IV–V: Annals I–III* (trans. C.H. Moore and J. Jackson; ed. T.E. Page *et al.*; LCL; London: Heinemann; New York: G.P. Putman's Sons, 1931).

Van Belle, G., *Johannine Bibliography, 1966-1985* (Leuven: Leuven University Press, 1988).

Vermes, G., *The Dead Sea Scrolls in English* (Sheffield: JSOT Press, 3rd edn, 1987 [1975]).

Wagner, G. (ed.), *An Exegetical Bibliography of the New Testament: John and 1, 2, 3 John*, III (Macon, GA: Mercer University Press, 1987).

Young, R. *Analytical Concordance to the Holy Bible* (London: Lutterworth Press, 8th rev. edn, 1939 [1879]).

Zerwick, M. *Biblical Greek* (Scripta Pontificii Instituti Biblici, 114; Rome: Editrice Pontificio Istituto Biblico 1985 [1963]).

Zerwick, M., and M. Grosvenor, *A Grammatical Analysis of the Greek New Testament* (Rome: Biblical Institute Press, 1981).

Ziegler, J. (ed.), *Septuaginta Vetus Testamentum Graecum*, XIV (Göttingen: Vandenhoeck & Ruprecht, 3rd edn, 1983).

—*Sapientia Iesu Filii Sirach XII, 2, Septuaginta Vetus Testamentum Graecum* (Göttingen: Vandenhoeck & Ruprecht, 2nd edn, 1980).

Commentaries on the Gospel of John

Barrett, C.K., *The Gospel According to St John* (London: SPCK, 2nd edn, 1978).

Beasley-Murray, G.R., *John* (WBC, 36; Waco, TX: Word Books, 1987).

Bernard, J.H., *The Gospel According to St John* (ICC; Edinburgh: T. & T. Clark, 1928).

Brown, R.E. *The Gospel According to John* (AB, 29–29a; 2 vols.; Garden City, NY: Doubleday, 1966, 1970).

Bruce, F.F., *The Gospel of John* (Basingstoke: Pickering & Inglis, 1983).

Bultmann, R., *The Gospel of John: A Commentary* (trans. G.R. Beasley-Murray *et al.*; Oxford: Basil Blackwell, 1971).

Calvin, J., *The Gospel According to St John 1–10* (trans. T.H.C. Parker; Calvin's Commentaries; Edinburgh: Oliver & Boyd, 1959).

—*The Gospel According to St John 11–12 and the First Epistle of John* (trans. T.H.L. Parker; Calvin's Commentaries; Edinburgh: Oliver & Boyd, 1961).

Carson, D.A., *The Gospel According to John* (Grand Rapids: Eerdmans, 1991).

Dodd, C.H., *The Interpretation of the Fourth Gospel* (Cambridge: Cambridge University Press, 1953).

Ellis, P.F., *The Genius of John: A Composition-Critical Commentary on the Fourth Gospel* (Collegeville, MN: Liturgical Press, 1984).

Haenchen, E., *A Commentary on the Gospel of John* (Hermeneia Commentary; 2 vols.; Philadelphia: Fortress Press, 1984).

Hoskyns, E.C., *The Fourth Gospel* (ed. F.N. Davey; London: Faber & Faber, 1947).

Léon-Dufour, X., *Lecture de l'évangile selon Jean*, I (Paris: Seuil, 1988).

Lindars, B., *The Gospel of John* (NCB; London: Oliphants, 1972).

Marsh, J., *Saint John* (Pelican New Testament Commentaries; Harmondsworth: Penguin Books, 1979).

Moloney, F.J., *Belief in the Word: Reading John 1–4* (Philadelphia: Fortress Press, 1993).

—*Signs and Shadows: Reading John 5–12* (Philadelphia: Fortress Press, 1996).

Morris, L., *The Gospel According to John* (NICNT; Grand Rapids: Eerdmans, 1971).

Schnackenburg, R., *The Gospel According to St John*, I (trans. K. Smyth *et al.*; HTCNT; London: Burns & Oates, 1968).

—*The Gospel According to St John*, II (trans. C. Hastings *et al.*; HTCNT; London: Burns & Oates, 1980).

—*The Gospel According to St John*, III (trans. D. Smith and G.A. Kon; HTCNT; New York: Crossroad, 1982).

Stibbe, M., *John: Readings: A New Bible Commentary* (Sheffield: JSOT Press, 1993).

Strachan, R.H., *The Fourth Gospel: Its Significance and Environment* (London: SCM Press, 3rd edn, 1941).

Westcott, B.F., *The Gospel According to St John: The Greek Text with Introduction and Notes* (2 vols.; London: John Murray, 1908 [1880]).

General References

Aalen, S., '"Reign" and "House" in the Kingdom of God in the Gospels', *NTS* 8 (1961–62), pp. 215-40.

Abrahams, I., *Studies in Pharisaism and the Gospels* (Cambridge: Cambridge University Press, 1917).

Albright, W.F., *Yahweh and the Gods of Canaan: A Historical Analysis of Two Contrasting Faiths* (Garden City, NY: Doubleday, 1968).

Allen, L.C., *Psalms 101–150* (WBC, 21; Waco, TX: Word Books, 1983).

Alon, G., 'The Burning of the Temple', in *Jews, Judaism and the Classical World: Studies in Jewish History in the Times of the Second Temple and Talmud* (trans. I. Abrahams; Jerusalem: Magnes Press, 1977), pp. 252-68.

Anderson, A.A., *The Book of Psalms*, II (NCB; London: Oliphants, 1972).

Anderson, H., *Old Testament Pseudepigrapha*, II (ed. J.H. Charlesworth; Garden City, NY: Doubleday, 1985).

Appold, M., *The Oneness Motif in the Fourth Gospel: Motif Analysis and Exegetical Probe into the Theology of John* (WUNT, 2.1; Tübingen: J.C.B. Mohr [Paul Siebeck], 1976).

Ashton, J., 'The Transformation of Wisdom: A Study of the Prologue of John's Gospel', *NTS* 32 (1986), pp. 161-86.

—*Understanding the Fourth Gospel* (Oxford: Clarendon Press, 1991).

Attridge, H., 'Historiography', in M.E. Stone (ed.), *Jewish Writings in the Second Temple Period* (Assen: Van Gorcum; Philadelphia: Fortress Press, 1984), pp. 157-84.

Bacchiocchi, S., 'John 5.17: Negation or Clarification of the Sabbath?', *AUSS* 19 (1981), pp. 3-19.

Balfour, G., 'Is John's Gospel Anti-semitic? With Special Reference to its Use of the Old Testament' (unpublished PhD thesis, University of Nottingham, 1995).

Ball, D., 'S. John and the Institution of the Eucharist', *JSNT* 23 (1985), pp. 59-68.

—*'I Am' in John's Gospel: Literary Function, Background and Theological Implications* (JSNTSS, 124; Sheffield: Sheffield Academic Press, 1996).

Bammel, E., 'The Farewell Discourse of the Evangelist John and its Jewish Heritage', *TB* 44 (1993), pp. 103-16.

Barker, M., *The Gate of Heaven: The History and Symbolism of the Temple in Jerusalem* (London: SPCK, 1991).

Barrett, C.K., *New Testament Essays* (London: SPCK, 1971).

Bauckham, R., 'Jesus' Demonstration in the Temple', in B. Lindars (ed.), *Law and Religion: Essays on the Place of the Law in Israel and Early Christianity* (Cambridge: James Clarke & Co., 1988), pp. 72-89.

—'The Beloved Disciple as Ideal Disciple', *JSNT* 49 (1993), pp. 21-44.

—'Papias and Polycrates on the Origin of the Fourth Gospel', *JTS* 44 (1993), pp. 24-68.

—'For Whom Were the Gospels Written?', in Bauckham (ed.), *The Gospels for All Christians*, pp. 9-48.

—'John for Readers of Mark', in Bauckham (ed.), *The Gospels for All Christians*, pp. 147-71.

—'Response to Philip Esler', *SJT* 51 (1998), pp. 249-53.

Bauckham, R. (ed.), *The Gospels for All Christians: Rethinking the Gospel Audiences* (Grand Rapids: Eerdmans, 1998).

Beck, D., 'The Narrative Function of Anonymity in Fourth Gospel Characterization', *Semeia* 63 (1993), pp. 143-55.

Blenkinsopp, J., 'John vii 37-39: Another Note on a Notorious Crux', *NTS* 6 (1959–60), pp. 95-98.

Bloch, R., 'Note méthodologique pour l'étude de la littérature rabbinique', *RSR* 43 (1955), pp. 194-227.

Boismard, M.-E., *St John's Prologue* (trans. Carisbrooke Dominicans; London: Blackfriars Publications, 1957).

—'"De son ventre couleront des fleuves d'eau" (Jo vii, 37)', *RB* 65 (1958), pp. 523-46.

—'Le titre de "fils de Dieu" dans les évangiles', *Bib* 72 (1991), pp. 442-50.

Borgen, P., *Bread from Heaven* (NovTSup, 10; Leiden: E.J. Brill, 1965).

—'God's Agent in the Fourth Gospel', in J. Neusner (ed.), *Religions in Antiquity: Essays in Memory of Erwin Ramsdell Goodenough* (Leiden: E.J. Brill, 1968), pp. 137-48.

—'John 6: Tradition, Interpretation and Composition', in M.C. de Boer (ed.), *From Jesus to John: Essays on Jesus and New Testament Christology in Honour of Marinus de Jonge* (JSNTSup, 84; Sheffield: JSOT Press, 1993), pp. 268-91.

Borig, R., *Der Wahre Weinstock: Studien zum Alten und Neuen Testament* (Munich: Kösel, 1967).

Botha, J.E., *Jesus and the Samaritan Woman: A Speech Act Reading of John 4:1-42* (NovTSup, 65; Leiden: E.J. Brill, 1991).

Brooke, G., 'Christ and the Law in John 7-10', in B. Lindars (ed.), *Law and Religion: Essays on the Place of the Law in Israel and Early Christianity* (Cambridge: James Clarke, 1988), pp. 102-12 and 180-84 for notes.

Brooks, O.S., 'The Johannine Eucharist: Another Interpretation', *JBL* 82 (1963), pp. 293-300.

Brown, R.E., *The Epistles of John* (AB, 30; Garden City, NY: Doubleday, 1982).

Bultmann, R., 'Der religionsgeschichtliche Hintergrund des Prologs zum Johannes-Evangelium', in *Eucharisterion*, II (FS H. Gunkel; Göttingen: Vandenhoeck & Ruprecht, 1923), pp. 3-26.

—*Theology of the New Testament* (trans. K. Grobel; 2 vols.; London: SCM Press, 1955).

Burge, G.H., *The Anointed Community: The Holy Spirit in the Johannine Community* (Grand Rapids: Eerdmans, 1987).

Burkett, D., *The Son of the Man in the Gospel of John* (JSNTSup, 56; Sheffield: JSOT Press, 1991).

Burney, C.F., *The Aramaic Origin of the Fourth Gospel* (Oxford: Clarendon Press, 1922).

Carmichael, C., 'Marriage and the Samaritan Woman', *NTS* 26 (1980), pp. 322-46.

Carson, D.A., 'Jesus and the Sabbath in the Four Gospels', in D.A. Carson (ed.), *From Sabbath to Lord's Day* (Grand Rapids: Zondervan, 1982), pp. 58-97.

—'Understanding Misunderstandings in the Fourth Gospel', *TB* 33 (1982), pp. 59-89.

—'The Purpose of the Fourth Gospel: John 20.30-31 Reconsidered', *JBL* 106.4 (1987), pp. 639-51.

Charlesworth, J.H., *The Beloved Disciple: Whose Witness Validates the Gospel of John?* (Valley Forge, PA: Trinity Press International, 1995).

Charlesworth, J.H., and R.A. Culpepper, 'The Odes of Solomon and the Gospel of John', *CBQ* 35 (1973), pp. 298-322.

Chilton, B.D., *The Glory of Israel: The Theology and Proveniance of the Isaiah Targum* (JSOTSup, 23; Sheffield: JSOT Press, 1983).

—'[ὡς] φραγέλλιον ἐκ σχοινίων (John 2.15)', in W. Horbury (ed.), *Templum Amicitiae: Essays on the Second Temple presented to Ernst Bammel* (JSNTSup, 48; Sheffield: JSOT Press, 1991), pp. 330-44.

Christensen, D.L., *Deuteronomy 1–11* (WBC, 6A; Dallas, TX: Word Books, 1991).

Clark, D.J., 'Criteria for Identifying Chiasm', *Linguistica Biblica* 5 (1975), pp. 63-72.

Clements, R.E., 'Temple and Land: A Significant Aspect of Israel's Worship', *TGUOS* 19 (1963), pp. 16-28.

—*God and Temple* (Philadelphia: Fortress Press, 1965).

Cohee, P., 'John 1.3-4', *NTS* 41 (1995), pp. 470-77.

Cohen, S.J.D., *Yahvneh Revisited. Pharisees, Rabbis, and the End of Jewish Sectarianism* (SBLASP; Chico, CA: Scholars Press, 1982), pp. 45-61.

Cohn, H., *The Trial and Death of Jesus* (New York: Harper, 1971).

Coloe, M., 'The Dwelling of God among Us: The Symbolic Function of the Temple in the Fourth Gospel' (unpublished Dr Theol. thesis, Melbourne College of Divinity, Australia, 1998).

Collins, R.F., 'From John to the Beloved Disciple: An Essay in Johannine Characters', *Int* 49 (1995), pp. 359-69.

Congar, Y., *The Mystery of the Temple: The Manner of God's Presence to his Creatures from Genesis to the Apocalypse* (trans. R. Trevett; London: Burns & Oates, 1962).

Corell, A., *Consummatum Est* (London: SPCK, 1958).

Cross, F.M., *Canaanite Myth and Hebrew Epic: Essays in the History of the Religion of Israel* (Cambridge, MA: Harvard University Press, 1973).

Culpepper, A., 'The Pivot of John's Prologue', *NTS* 27 (1981), pp. 1-31.

Dahood, M., *Psalms III: 101–150* (AB, 17A; Garden City, NY: Doubleday, 1970).

Dahl, N., 'The Johannine Church and History', in W. Klassen and G.F. Snyder (eds.), *Current Issues in N.T. Interpretation: Essays in Honour of O.A. Piper* (New York: Harper, 1962), pp. 124-42.

Daniélou, J., *The Presence of God* (trans. W. Roberts; London: Mowbray, 1958).

Davies, W. D., *The Gospel and the Land: Early Christianity and Jewish Territorial Doctrine* (Berkeley: University of California Press, 1994).

de la Potterie, I., *La vérité dans Saint Jean* (AnBib, 24; 2 vols.; Rome: Biblical Institute Press, 1977).

—'La tunique sans couture, symbole du Christ grand prêtre?', *Bib* 60 (1979), pp. 255-69.

—'"Nous adorons, nous, ce que nous connaissons, car le salut vient des Juifs", Histoire de l'exegese et interpretation de Jean 4,22', *Bib* 64 (1983), pp. 77-85.

Delling, G., 'Πλήρωμα', *TDNT*, VI (1968), pp. 298-306.

Derrett, J.D., 'Circumcision and Perfection: A Johannine Equation (John 7.22-23)', *EvQ* 63 (1991), pp. 211-24.

Dodd, C.H., *Historical Tradition in the Fourth Gospel* (Cambridge: Cambridge University Press, 1963).

Driver, S.R., *A Critical and Exegetical Commentary on Deuteronomy* (ICC; Edinburgh: T. & T. Clark, 1902).

D'Souza, J., *The Lamb of God in the Johannine Writings* (Allahabad: St Paul Publications, 1968).

Duke, P., *Irony in the Fourth Gospel* (Atlanta: John Knox Press, 1993).

Dunn, J., 'The Washing of the Disciples' Feet in John 13.1-20', *ZNW* 61 (1970), pp. 247-53.

Dunn, J.D.G., 'John VI—A Eucharistic Discourse?', *NTS* 17 (1970), pp. 328-38.

—'Let John Be John: A Gospel for its Time', in P. Stuhlmacher (ed.), *Das Evangelium und die Evangelien: Vortäge vom Tübinger Symposium* (Tübingen: J.C.B. Mohr, 1983), pp. 293-322.

—*Romans 1–8* (WBC, 38A; Dallas, TX: Word Books, 1988).

—*The Partings of the Ways between Christianity and Judaism and their Significance for the Character of Christianity* (London: SCM Press, 1991).

Earwaker, E.C., 'John xvii.21', *ExpTim* 75 (1964), pp. 316-17.

Edwards, R., *'XARIN ANTI XAPITOΣ* (John 1.16): Grace and Law in the Johannine Prologue', *JSNT* 32 (1988), pp. 3-15.

Emerton, J.A., 'The Hundred and Fifty-Three Fishes in John 21:11', *JTS* 9 (1958), pp. 86-89.

Esler, P., 'Community and Gospel in Early Christianity: A Response to Richard Bauckham's *Gospels for All Christians*', *SJT* 51 (1998), pp. 235-48.

Evans, C.A., 'Obduracy and the Lord's Servant: Some Observations on the Use of the Old Testament in the Fourth Gospel', in C.A. Evans and W.F. Stinespring (eds.), *Early Jewish and Christian Exegesis: Studies in Memory of William Hugh Brownlee* (Atlanta: Scholars Press, 1987), pp. 221-36.

—'Jesus' Action in the Temple: Cleansing or Portent of Destruction?', *CBQ* 51 (1989), pp. 237-70.

—*To See and Not to Perceive: Isaiah 6.9-10 in Early Jewish and Christian Interpretation* (JSOTSup, 64; Sheffield: JSOT Press, 1989).

—*Jesus' Action in the Temple and Evidence of Corruption in the First-Century Temple* (ed. D.J. Lull; SBLSP, 28; Atlanta: Scholars Press, 1989), pp. 522-39.

—*Word and Glory: On the Exegetical and Theological Background of John's Prologue* (JSNTSup, 89; Sheffield: JSOT Press, 1993).

Fee, G., 'Once More—John 7.37-39', *ExpTim* 89 (1977), pp. 116-18.

Fennema, D.A., 'John 1.18: "God the Only Son"', *NTS* 31 (1985), pp. 124-35.

Fernando, S., *The Farewell of the Word: The Johannine Call to Abide* (Philadelphia: Fortress Press, 1991).

Feuillet, A., *Le Prologue de Quatrième Evangile* (Paris: Desclée de Brouwer, 1968).

Ford, J.M., '"Mingled Blood" from the Side of Christ (John xix.34)', *NTS* 15 (1969), pp. 337-38.

Forestell, J.T., *The Word of the Cross* (AnBib, 57; Rome: Biblical Institute Press, 1974).

Fortna, R.T., *The Gospel of Signs: A Reconstruction of the Narrative Source Underlying the Fourth Gospel* (Cambridge: Cambridge University Press, 1979).

—*The Fourth Gospel and its Predecessor: From Narrative Source to Present Gospel* (Edinburgh: T. & T. Clark, 1989).

France, R.T., 'Chronological Aspects of "Gospel Harmony"', *Vox Evangelica* 16 (1986), pp. 33-59.

Freed, E.D., *Old Testament Quotations in the Gospel of John* (Leiden: E.J. Brill, 1965).

—'The Son of Man in the Fourth Gospel', *JBL* 86 (1967), pp. 402-409.

Gärtner, B., *John 6 and the Jewish Passover* (ConNT, 17; Copenhagen: Lund, 1959).

—*The Temple and Community in Qumran and the New Testament* (SNTSMS, 1; Cambridge: Cambridge University Press, 1965).

Giblin, C.H., 'Two Complementary Literary Structures in John 1:1-18', *JBL* 104 (1985), pp. 87-103.

Glasson, T.F., *Moses in the Fourth Gospel* (SBT, 40; London: SCM Press, 1963).

Grabbe, L.L., *Judaism from Cyrus to Hadrian* (London: SCM Press, 1994).

Greimas, A.J., *Semantique structurale* (Paris: Larousse, 1966).

—*Du sens* (Paris: Seuil, 1970).

Grelot, P., '*Problèmes Critiques du IVe Évangile*', *RB* 94 (1987), pp. 519-73.

—'"De son ventre couleront des fleuves d'eau"', *RB* 66 (1959), pp. 369-74.

Grigsby, B.H., '"If Any Man Thirsts…": Observations on the Rabbinic Background of John 7, 37-39', *Bib* 67 (1986), pp. 101-108.

Guilding, A., *The Fourth Gospel and Jewish Worship: A Study of the Relation of St John's Gospel to the Ancient Jewish Lectionary System* (Oxford: Clarendon Press, 1960).

Gundry, R.H., '"In My Father's House There Are Many Μοναί" (John 14.2)', *ZNW* 53 (1967), pp. 68-72.

Hanson, A.T., 'Hodayot XV and John 17: A Comparison of Content and Form', *Hermathena* 18 (1974), pp. 45-58.

—'Jn 1,14-18 and Exodus 34', *NTS* 23 (1976), pp. 90-101.

—*The New Testament Interpretation of Scripture* (London: SPCK, 1980).

—*The Prophetic Gospel* (Edinburgh: T. & T. Clark, 1991).

Hare, D.R.A., *The Son of Man Tradition* (Philadelphia: Fortress Press, 1990).

Harner, P.B., *The 'I Am' of the Fourth Gospel* (Facet Books; Philadelphia: Fortress Press, 1970).

Harris, E., *Prologue and Gospel: The Theology of the Fourth Evangelist* (JSNTSup, 107; Sheffield: JSOT Press, 1994).

Harris, J.R., *The Origin of the Prologue to St John's Gospel* (Cambridge: Cambridge University Press, 1917).

Hayward, C.T.R., 'The Vine and its Products as Theological Symbols in First Century Palestinian Judaism', *Durham University Journal* 82 (1990), pp. 9-18.

—*The Jewish Temple: A Non-Biblical Sourcebook* (London: Routledge, 1996).

Hartley, J.E., *Leviticus* (WBC, 4; Dallas, TX: Word Books, 1992).

Heil, J.P., 'The Story of Jesus and the Adultress Reconsidered', *Bib* 72.2 (1991), pp. 182-91.

—'Jesus as the Unique High Priest in the Gospel of John', *CBQ* 57 (1995), pp. 729-45.

Heintz, J-G., 'בֵּאר', *TDOT*, I (1974), pp. 463-66.

Heitmüller, W., *Das Evangelium des Johannes: Die Schriften des New Testament*, II (Göttingen: Vandenhoeck & Ruprecht, 1908).

Hengel, M., *The Johannine Question* (trans. John Bowden; London: SCM Press, 1989).

Higgins, A.J.B., *Jesus and the Son of Man* (Philadelphia: Fortress Press, 1964).

Hooker, M.D., *The Son of Man in Mark* (London: SPCK, 1967).

—'John the Baptist and the Johannine Prologue', *NTS* 16 (1969–70), pp. 354-58.

—'The Johannine Prologue and the Messianic Secret', *NTS* 21 (1975), pp. 40-58.

Horbury, W., 'The Benediction of the Minum and Early Jewish–Christian Controversy', *JTS* 33 (1982), pp. 19-61.

Horsley, R.A., *Jesus and the Spiral of Violence* (San Francisco: Harper, 1987).

—*Sociology and the Jesus Movement* (New York: Crossroad, 1989).

Howton, J., 'The Son of God in the Fourth Gospel', *NTS* 10 (1963–64), pp. 227-37.

Hultgren, A.J., 'The Johannine Footwashing (13.1-11) as a Symbol of Eschatological Hospitality', *NTS* 28 (1982), pp. 539-46.

Humphries, A.L., 'A Note on πρὸς ἐμαυτόν (John 14.3) and εἰς τὰ ἴδια (John 1.11)', *ExpTim* 53 (1941–42), p. 356.

Jeremias, J., *Jesus' Promise to the Nations* (trans. S.H. Hooke; SBT, 24; London: SCM Press, 1958).

—*Jerusalem in the Time of Jesus: An Investigation into Economic and Social Conditions during the New Testament Period* (trans. F.H. and C.H. Cave; London: SCM Press, 1969).

—*New Testament Theology: Part I. The Proclamation of Jesus* (trans. John Bowden; London: SCM Press, 1971).

Jerumanis, P.-M., *Réaliser La Communion avec Dieu: Croire, vivre et demeurer dans l'évangile selon S. Jean* (Ebib, NS 32; Paris: Librarie Lecoffre J. Gabalda et Marie Curie, 1996).

Joubert, S.J., 'A Bone of Contention in Recent Scholarship: The "Birkat Ha-Minim" and the Separation of Church and Synagogue in the First Century AD', *Neot* 27 (1993), pp. 351-63.

Juel, D., *Messiah and Temple: The Trial of Jesus in the Gospel of Mark* (SBLDS, 31; Missoula, MT: Scholars Press, 1977).

Käsemann, E., *The Testament of Jesus According to John 17* (Philadelphia: Fortress Press, 1968).

Kieffer, R., 'L'espace et le temps dans l'evangile de Jean', *NTS* 31 (1985), pp. 393-409.

Kilmartin, E., 'Liturgical Influence on John 6', *CBQ* 22 (1960), pp. 183-91.

Kilpatrick, G.D., 'The Punctuation of John vii 37-38', *JTS* 11 (1960), pp. 340-42.

Kimelman, R., 'Birkat ha-minim and the Lack of Evidence for an Anti-Christian Prayer in Late Antiquity', in E.P. Sanders *et al.* (eds.), *Jewish and Christian Self-Definition*. II. *Aspects of Judaism in the Graeco-Roman World* (London: SCM Press, 1981), pp. 226-44.

Kimhi, D., *The Commentary of Rabbi David Kimhi on Psalms CXX–CL* (ed. and trans. J. Baker and E.W. Nicholson; Cambridge: Cambridge University Press, 1973).

Kinzer, M., *Temple Christology in the Gospel of John* (SBLSP, 37; Atlanta: Scholars Press, 1998), pp. 447-64.

Knight, G.A.F., *From Moses to Paul: A Christological Study in the Light of our Hebraic Heritage* (London: Lutterworth, 1949).

Koester, C.R., *The Dwelling of God: The Tabernacle in the Old Testament, Intertestamental Jewish Literature, and the New Testament* (CBQMS, 22; Washington: Catholic Biblical Association of America, 1989).

—'Messianic Exegesis and the Call of Nathanael (John 1.45-51)', *JSNT* 39 (1990), pp. 23-34.

Kossen, H.B., 'Who Were the Greeks of John XII 20?', in A. Geyser *et al.* (eds.), *Studies in John Presented to Professor Dr J.N. Sevenster on the Occasion of his Seventieth Birthday* (NovTSup, 24; Leiden: E.J. Brill, 1970), pp. 97-110.

Köster, H., 'Τόπος', *TDNT*, VIII (1972), pp. 187-208.

Kraus, H-J., *Theology of the Psalms* (trans. K. Crim; Minneapolis: Augsburg–Fortress, 1986).

—*Psalms 60–150: A Commentary* (trans. H.C. Oswald; Minneapolis: Augsburg–Fortress, 1989).

Kümmel, W.G., *Introduction to the New Testament* (trans. A.J. Mattill, Jr; London: SCM Press, 1966).

Lamarche, P., 'Le prologue de Jean', *RSR* 52 (1964), pp. 529-32.

Lee, D.A., *The Symbolic Narratives of the Fourth Gospel: The Interplay of Form and Meaning* (JSNTSup, 95; Sheffield: Sheffield Academic Press, 1994).

Léon-Dufour, X., 'Le Signe du Temple selon saint Jean', *RSR* 39 (1951), pp. 155-75.

Lieu, J., 'Blindness in the Johannine Tradition', *NTS* 34 (1988), pp. 83-95.

—'Temple and Synagogue in John', *NTS* 45 (1999), pp. 51-69.

Lightfoot, R.H., *The Gospel Message of Mark* (Oxford: Oxford University Press, 1950).

Lindars, B., *New Testament Apologetic: The Doctrinal Significance of the Old Testament Quotations* (Philadelphia: Westminster, 1961).

Loader, W.R.G., 'John 1:50-51 and the "Greater Things" of Johannine Christology', in C. Brey-tenbach and H. Paulsen (eds.), *Sonderdruck aus Anfänge der Christologie für Feredinand Hahn zum 65. Geburtstag* (Göttingen: Vandenhoeck & Ruprecht, 1991), pp. 255-74.

Longenecker, B.W., *Eschatology and the Covenant: A Comparison of 4 Ezra and Romans 1– 11* (JSNTSup, 57; Sheffield: JSOT Press, 1991).

—*2 Esdras* (Sheffield: Sheffield Academic Press, 1995).

—'The Unbroken Messiah: A Johannine Feature and its Social Functions', *NTS* 41 (1995), pp. 428-41.

Lund, N., 'The Influence of the Chiasmus upon the Structure of the Gospels', *ATR* 13 (1931), pp. 42-46.

Lundquist, J.M., 'What Is a Temple? A Preliminary Typology', in H.B. Huffmon *et al.* (eds.), *The Quest for the Kingdom of God: Studies in Honor of George E. Mendenhall* (Winona Lake, IN: Eisenbrauns, 1983), pp. 205-19.

Macdonald, W.G., 'Christology and "The Angel of the Lord"', in G.F. Hawthorne (ed.), *Current Issues in Biblical and Patristic Interpretation* (Grand Rapids: Eerdmans, 1975), pp. 324-35.

Manson, T.W., *Only to the House of Israel?: Jesus and the Non-Jews* (Philadelphia: Fortress, 1964 [1955]).

Marcus, J., 'Rivers of Living Water from Jesus' Belly (John 7:38)', *JBL* 117 (1998), pp. 328-30.

Marshall, C., *Faith as a Theme in Mark's Narrative* (SNTSMS, 64; Cambridge: Cambridge University Press, 1989).

Martyn, J.L., *History and Theology in the Fourth Gospel* (Nashville: Abingdon, 2nd edn, 1979).

Matson, M.A., *The Contribution to the Temple Cleansing by the Fourth Gospel* (ed. E.H. Lovering; SBLSS; Atlanta: Scholars Press, 1992).

McCaffrey, J., *The House with Many Rooms: The Temple Theme of Jn 14, 2-3* (Rome: Biblical Institute Press, 1988).

McHugh, J., '"In Him Was Life": John's Gospel and the Parting of the Ways', in J.D.G. Dunn (ed.), *Jews and Christians: The Parting of the Ways A.D. 70–135* (WUNT, 66; Tübingen: J.C.B. Mohr [Paul Siebeck], 1992), pp. 123-58.

McKelvey, J., *The New Temple: The Church in the New Testament* (Oxford Theological Monographs; Oxford: Oxford University Press, 1969).

Meeks, W.A., *The Prophet-King: Moses Traditions and the Johannine Christology* (NovTSup, 14; Leiden: E.J. Brill, 1967).

Merrill, E.H., *An Exegetical Commentary: Haggai, Zechariah, Malachi* (Chicago: Moody Press, 1994).

Meyer, R., 'Περιτέμνω', *TDNT*, VI (1968), pp. 72-84.

Meyers, C.M., and E.M. Meyers, *Zechariah 9–14* (AB, 25C; Garden City, NY: Doubleday, 1993).

Michaelis, W., 'Joh. 1.51, Gen. 28.12 und das Menschensohn-Problem', *TLZ* 85 (1960), pp. 561-78.

Michaels, J.R., 'Nathanael under the Fig Tree', *ExpTim* 78 (1966–67), pp. 182-83.

Milgrom, J., *Leviticus 1–16* (AB, 3; Garden City, NY: Doubleday, 1991).

Miller, E.L., *Salvation History in the Prologue of John: The Significance of John 1:3/4* (NovTSup, 40; Leiden: E. J. Brill, 1989).

Minear, P.S., 'The Original Functions of John 21', *JBL* 102 (1983), pp. 85-98.

Mlakuzhyil, G., *The Christocentric Literary Structure of the Fourth Gospel* (AnBib, 117; Rome: Pontifical Biblical Institute, 1987).

Moloney, F.J., *The Johannine Son of Man* (Biblioteca di Scienze Religiose, 14; Rome: LAS, 2nd edn, 1978).

—'The Structure and Message of John 15.1-16.3', *ABR* 35 (1987), pp. 35-49.

—'Reading John 2.13-22: The Purification of the Temple', *RB* 97 (1990), pp. 443-44.

Moo, D., *The Old Testament in the Gospel Passion Narratives* (Sheffield: Almond Press, 1983).

Moody Smith, D., *John among the Gospels: The Relationship in Twentieth-Century Research* (Philadelphia: Fortress Press, 1992).

—*The Theology of the Gospel of John* (New Testament Theology Series; Cambridge: Cambridge University Press, 1995).

Morgen, M., '*La Promesse* de Jésus à Nathanaël (Jn 1.51) Eclairée par la Hagaddah de Jacob-Israël', *RSR* 67 (1993), pp. 3-21.

Motyer, S., 'John 8:31-59 and the Rhetoric of Persuasion in the Fourth Gospel' (unpublished PhD thesis, Kings College, University of London, 1993).

Moule, C.F.D., *Origins of Christology* (Cambridge: Cambridge University Press, 1978).

Mowinckel, S., *The Psalms in Israel's Worship* (2 vols.; Oxford: Basil Blackwell, 1967).

Mowvley, H., 'John 1:14-18 in the Light of Exodus 33:7-34:35', *ExpTim* 95 (1984), pp. 135-37.

Murphy, F., 'The Temple in the Syriac *Apocalypse of Baruch*', *JBL* 106 (1987), pp. 671-83.

Neirynck, F., 'The "Other Disciple" in Jn 18,15-16', *Ephemerides Theologicae Lovaniensis* 51 (1975), pp. 113-41.

—*Evangelica: Gospel Studies—Etudes Evangile. Collected Essays* (ed. F. van Segbroeck; Leuven: Leuven University Press, 1982).

Nereparampil, L., *Destroy This Temple: An Exegetico-Theological Study on the Meaning of Jesus' Temple-Logion in Jn 2:19* (Bangalore: Dharmaram College, 1978).

Neusner, J., *A Life of Rabban Yohanan ben Zakkai Ca. 1–80 C.E.* (Leiden: E.J. Brill, 1962).

—'Emergent Rabbinic Judaism in a Time of Crisis: Four Responses to the Destruction of the Second Temple', *Judaism* 21 (1972), pp. 313-27.

—Judaism in a Time of Crisis: Four Responses to the Destruction of the Second Temple', *Judaism* 21 (1972), pp. 313-27.

—'The Formation of Rabbinic Judaism. Methodological Issues and Substantive Theses', in *idem*, *Formative Judaism: Religious, Historical and Literary Studies, Third Series: Torah, Pharisees, and Rabbis* (BJS, 46; Chico: Scholars Press, 1983), pp. 99-144.

—'Judaism after the Destruction of the Temple: An Overview', in *idem*, *Formative Judaism: Religious, Historical and Literary Studies, Third Series: Torah, Pharisees, and Rabbis* (BJS, 46; Chico: Scholars Press, 1983), pp. 83-98.

Neyrey, J., 'Jacob Tradition and the Interpretation of John 4.10-26', *CBQ* 41 (1979), pp. 419-37.

—'The Jacob Allusions in John 1.51', *CBQ* 44 (1982), pp. 586-605.

Noth, M., *Leviticus: A Commentary* (trans. J.E. Anderson; OTL, 6; London: SCM Press, 1965).

O'Day, G., *Revelation in the Fourth Gospel* (Philadelphia: Fortress Press, 1986).

—'"I Have Overcome the World" (John 16.33): Narrative Time in John 13–17', *Semeia* 53 (1991), pp. 153-66.

—'John 7.53-8.11: A Study in Misreading', *JBL* 111 (1992), pp. 631-40.

Okure, T., *The Johannine Approach to Mission: A Contextual Study of John 4:1-42* (Tübingen: J.B.C. Mohr [Paul Siebeck], 1988).

Olsson, B., *Structure and Meaning in the Fourth Gospel: A Text-Linguistic Analysis of John 2.1-11 and 4.1-42* (ConBNT, 6; Lund: Gleerup, 1974).

Painter, J., 'Tradition, History and Interpretation in John 10', in J. Beutler and R. Fortna (eds.), *The Shepherd Discourse of John 10 and its Context* (SNTSMS, 67; Cambridge: Cambridge University Press, 1991), pp. 53-74.

—'The Enigmatic Johannine Son of Man', in F. van Segbroeck *et al.* (eds.), *The Four Gospels 1992*, III (Leuven: Leuven University Press; Peeters, 1992), pp. 1869-88.

—*The Quest for the Messiah: The History, Literature and Theology of the Johannine Community* (Edinburgh: T. & T. Clark, 2nd edn, 1993).

Pamment, M., 'The Fourth Gospel's Beloved Disciple', *ExpTim* 94 (1983), pp. 363-67.

—'The Son of Man in the Fourth Gospel', *JTS* 36 (1985), pp. 56-66.

Pancaro, S., *The Law in the Fourth Gospel: The Torah and the Gospel, Moses and Jesus, Judaism and Christianity According to John* (NovTSup, 42; Leiden: E.J. Brill, 1975).

Pazdan, M.M., 'Nicodemus and the Samaritan Woman: Contrasting Models of Discipleship', *BTB* 17 (1987), pp. 145-48.

Peder, B., *Bread from Heaven* (NovTSup, 10; Leiden: E.J. Brill, 1965).

Pollard, E., 'The Father–Son and God–Believer Relationships According to St John: A Brief Study of John's Use of Prepositions', in M. de Jonge (ed.), *L'Evangile de Jean: Sources, rédaction, théologie* (BETL, 44; Gembloux: Ducolot, 1977), pp. 363-69.

Porter, C.L., 'John 9.38,39a: A Liturgical Addition to the Text', *NTS* 13 (1967), pp. 387-94.

Power, F., '"Living Waters"', *Review of Religion* 19 (1960), pp. 5-11.

Quast, K., *Peter and the Beloved Disciple: Figures for a Community in Crisis* (JSNTSup, 32; Sheffield: JSOT Press, 1989).

Richardson, P., *Why Turn the Tables? Jesus' Protest in the Temple Precincts* (ed. E.H. Lovering; SBLSP; Atlanta: Scholars Press, 1992), pp. 507-23.

Reif, S., 'Dedicated to חנך', *VT* 22 (1972), pp. 495-501.

Riesenfeld, H., 'Sabbat et Jour du Seigneur', in A.J.B. Higgins (ed.), *New Testament Essays in Memory of T.W. Manson* (Manchester: Manchester University Press, 1959), pp. 210-17.

Rissi, M., 'Die Hochzeit in Kana Joh 2.1-11', in F. Christ (ed.), *Oikonomia: Heilsgeschichte als Thema der Theologie. Oscar Cullmann zum 65. Geburtstag gewidmet* (Hamburg: H. Reich, 1967), pp. 76-92.

—'Jn 1.1-18 (The Eternal Word)', *Int* 31 (1977), pp. 395-401.

Robinson, J.A.T., 'The Destination and Purpose of St John's Gospel', in *idem, Twelve New Testament Studies* (SBT, 34; London: SCM Press, 1962), pp. 107-25.

—'The Significance of the Foot-Washing', in A.N. Wilder *et al.* (eds), *Neotestamentica et Patristica* (Leiden: E.J. Brill, 1962), pp. 144-47.

—*Twelve New Testament Studies* (London: SCM Press, 1962).

—*Redating the New Testament* (London: SCM Press, 1976).

—*The Priority of John* (ed. J.F. Coakley; London: SCM Press, 1985).

Roth, C., 'The Cleansing of the Temple and Zechariah 14.21', *NT* 4 (1960), pp. 174-81.

Rowland, C.C., 'John 1.51. Jewish Apocalyptic and Targumic Tradition', *NTS* 30 (1984), pp. 498-507.

Sanders, E.P. *Jesus and Judaism* (London: SCM Press, 1985).

—*Jewish Law from Jesus to Mishnah: Five Studies* (London: SCM Press; Valley Forge, PA: Trinity Press International, 1990).

—*Judaism: Practice and Belief 63 BCE–66 CE* (London: SCM Press; Valley Forge, PA: Trinity Press International, 1992).

Saxby, H., 'The Time-Scheme in the Gospel of John', *ExpTim* 104 (1992), pp. 9-13.

Schneiders, S.M., '"Because of the Woman's Testimony…": Reexamining the Issue of Authorship in the Fourth Gospel', *NTS* 44 (1998), pp. 513-35.

Schnelle, U., *Antidocetic Christology in the Gospel of John: An Investigation of the Fourth Gospel in the Johannine School* (trans. L.M. Maloney; Philadelphia: Fortress Press, 1992).

Schrage, W., 'Ἀποσυνάγωγος', *TDNT*, VII (1971), pp. 848-52.

Schuchard, B.G. *Scripture within Scripture: The Interrelationship of Form and Function in the Explicit Old Testament Citations in the Gospel of John* (SBLDS, 133; Atlanta: Scholars Press, 1992).

Schweizer, E., 'Πνεῦμα', *TDNT*, VI (1968), pp. 389-455.

Segovia, F., 'John 13.1-20: The Footwashing in the Johannine Tradition', *ZNW* 73 (1982), pp. 31-51.

—*Love Relationships in the Johannine Tradition* (Chico, CA: Scholars Press, 1982).

—*The Farewell of the Word: The Johannine Call to Abide* (Philadelphia: Fortress Press, 1991).

Shirbroun, G.F., 'The Giving of the Name of God to Jesus in John 17:11,12' (unpublished PhD dissertation, Princeton Theological Seminary, 1985).

Simoens, Y., *La gloire d'aimer: Structures stylistiques et interpretatives dans le Discours de la Cene (Jn 13–17)* (AnBib, 90; Rome: Biblical Institute Press, 1981).

Skehan, P.W., and A.A. Di Lella, *The Wisdom of Ben Sira* (AB, 39; Garden City, NY: Doubleday, 1987).

Smalley, S.S., 'The Sign in John XXI', *NTS* 20 (1974), pp. 275-88.

Smith, B.D., 'The Chronology of the Last Supper', *WTJ* 53 (1991), pp. 29-45.

Smith, J.Z., *Map Is Not Territory: Studies in the History of Religions* (Leiden: E.J. Brill, 1978).

Sproston, W., '"The Scripture" in John 17.12', in B.P. Thompson (ed.), *Scripture: Meaning and Method: Essays Presented to Anthony Tyrell Hanson for his Seventieth Birthday* (Hull: Hull University Press, 1987), pp. 24-36.

Staley, J.L., *The Print's First Kiss: A Rhetorical Investigation of the Implied Reader in the Fourth Gospel* (SBLDS, 82; Atlanta: Scholars Press, 1988).

Stibbe, M., *John as Storyteller: Narrative Criticism and the Fourth Gospel* (SNTSMS, 73; Cambridge: Cambridge University Press, 1992).

Taylor, V., *The Gospel According to St Mark* (London: Macmillan, 1952).

—*The Names of Jesus* (London: Macmillan, 1953).

Thackeray, H. St J., *The Septuagint and Jewish Worship* (London: British Academy, 1920).

Thomas, J.C., *Footwashing in John 13 and the Johannine Community* (JSNTSup, 61; Sheffield: Sheffield Academic Press, 1991).

Trebilco, P., *Jewish Communities in Asia Minor* (SNTSMS, 69; Cambridge: Cambridge University Press, 1991).

van der Horst, P., 'The Birkat ha-minim in Recent Research', *ExpTim* 105 (1994), pp. 363-68.

VanderKam, J.C., 'John 10 and the Feast of the Dedication', in H.W. Attridge, J.J. Collins and T.H. Tobin (eds.), *Of Scribes and Scrolls: Studies on the Hebrew Bible, Intertestamental Judaism, and Christian Origins, Presented to John Strugnell on the Occasion of his*

Sixtieth Birthday (College Theology Society Resources in Religion, 5; Lanham, MD: University Press of America, 1990), pp. 203-14.

—*The Dead Sea Scrolls Today* (Grand Rapids: Eerdmans, 1994).

Walker, P., *Jesus and the Holy City: New Testament Perspectives on Jerusalem* (Grand Rapids: Eerdmans, 1996).

Walker, W.O., Jr, 'John 1.43-51 and "The Son of Man" in the Fourth Gospel', *JSNT* 56 (1994), pp. 31-42.

Wallace, D.B., 'John 5,2 and the Date of the Fourth Gospel', *Bib* 71 (1990), pp. 177-205.

—'Reconsidering "The Story of Jesus and the Adultress Reconsidered"', *NTS* 31 (1993), pp. 290-96.

Warmuth, G., 'הוד', *TDOT*, III (1978), pp. 352-56.

Watty, W.W., 'The Significance of Anonymity in the Fourth Gospel', *ExpTim* 90 (1979), pp. 209-12.

Weiss, H., 'Foot Washing in the Johannine Community', *NovT* 21 (1979), pp. 298-325.

—'The Sabbath in the Fourth Gospel', *JBL* 110 (1991), pp. 311-21.

Westermann, C., *Isaiah 40–66: A Commentary* (trans. D.M.G. Stalker; OTL, 19; London: SCM Press, 1969).

Whybray, R.N., *Proverbs: New Century Bible Commentary* (London: Marshall Pickering; Grand Rapids: Eerdmans, 1994).

Woll, D.B., *Johannine Christianity in Conflict: Authority, Rank, and Succession in the First Farewell Discourse* (SBLDS, 60; Chico, CA: Scholars Press, 1981).

Wright, N.T., 'Jerusalem in the New Testament', in P.W.L.Walker (ed.), *Jerusalem Past and Present in the Purposes of God* (Cambridge: Cambridge University Press, 1992), pp. 53-77.

—*The New Testament and the People of God* (London: SPCK, 1992).

Yee, G.A., *Jewish Feasts and the Gospel of John* (Wilmington: Michael Glazier, 1989).

INDEXES

INDEX OF REFERENCES

OLD TESTAMENT

PSEUDEPIGRAPHA

OTHER ANCIENT REFERENCES

JOURNAL FOR THE STUDY OF THE NEW TESTAMENT
SUPPLEMENT SERIES